INSTRUCTOR'S MANUAL

THE STRATEGY PROCESS:
Concepts, Contexts, Cases

INSTRUCTOR'S MANUAL

Penny C. Paquette
Dartmouth College

John Voyer
University of Southern Maine

THE STRATEGY PROCESS:
Concepts, Contexts, Cases

Henry Mintzberg
James Brian Quinn

 Prentice Hall, Upper Saddle River, New Jersey 07458

Project Editor: *Evyan Jengo*
Acquisitions Editor: *David Shafer*
Editorial Assistant : *Brett Moreland*
Manufacturing Buyer: *Vinny Scelta*

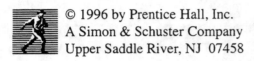
Printed in the United States of America

10 9 8 7 6 5 4 3

ISBN 0-13-234048-8

Prentice-Hall International (UK) Limited, *London*
Prentice-Hall of Australia Pty. Limited, *Sydney*
Prentice-Hall Canada Inc., *Toronto*
Prentice-Hall Hispanoamericana, S.A., *Mexico*
Prentice-Hall of India Private Limited, *New Delhi*
Prentice-Hall of Japan, Inc., *Tokyo*
Simon & Schuster Asia Pte. Ltd., *Singapore*
Editora Prentice-Hall do Brasil, Ltda., *Rio de Janiero*

Table of Contents

Page Number

Introduction   viii

Section I   1

Chapter 1
1-1 Strategies for Change   3
1-2 Five Ps for Strategy   5

Chapter 2
2-1 The Manager's Job   10
2-2 Good Managers Don't Make Policy Decisions   15
2-3 Strategic Intent   21

Chapter 3
3-1 The Concept of Corporate Strategy   26
3-2 Evaluating Business Strategy   30
3-3 Core Competencies and Strategic Outsourcing   36

Chapter 4
4-1 How Competitive Forces Shape Strategy   43
4-2 Generic Business Strategies   47

Chapter 5
5-1 Logical Incrementalism: Managing Strategy   51
5-2 Crafting Strategy   61
5-3 The Honda Effect   66

Teaching Notes for Section I Cases   69

I-1 Edward Marshall Boehm, Inc.   71
I-2 Genentech, Inc.   76
I-3 MacArthur and the Philippines   89
I-4 New Steel Corporation   96
I-5 Intel Corporation   105
I-6 Apple Computer, Inc. (A)   121
I-7 Apple Computer 1992   132
I-8 Microsoft Corporation (A)   143
I-9 E & J Gallo Winery   148
I-10 The IBM 360 Decision   159
I-11 The Transformation of AT&T   174
I-12 Nintendo Co., Ltd.   182
I-13 Magnetic Levitation Train   188
I-14 Ford: Team Taurus   195
I-15 Argyle Diamonds   212

		Page Number
Section II		225
Chapter 6		
6-1	Strategy and Organization Planning	227
6-2	The Structuring of Organizations	230
6-3	New Forms of Organizing	237
6-4	Collaborating to Compete	247
Chapter 7		
7-1	Ideology and the Missionary Organization	251
7-2	Building Structure in Managers' Minds	254
7-3	Politics and Political Organization	259
7-4	Competitive Maneuvering	262
7-5	Who Should Control the Corporation	266
Chapter 8		
8-1	Artists, Craftsmen, and Technocrats	272
8-2	The Leader's New Work	274
8-3	Middle Managers to "Do Things Right"	282
Teaching Notes for Section II Cases		287
II-1	The New York Times Company	289
II-2	Matsushita Electric Industrial Company 1994	314
II-3	The Hewlett Packard Company	323
II-4	TCG, Ltd./Thermo Electron Corporation	346
II-5	Microsoft Corporation (B)	352
II-6	NovaCare, Inc.	359
II-7	Orbital Engine Company	372
II-8	Andersen Consulting (Europe)	384
II-9	Polaroid Corporation	396
II-10	Exxon Corporation 1994	411
II-11	Sony Corporation: Innovation System	431
Section III		443
Chapter 9		
9-1	The Entrepreneurial Organization	445
9-2	Competitive Strategy in Emerging Industries	449
9-3	How Entrepreneurs Craft Strategies that Work	452
Chapter 10		
10-1	The Machine Organization	458
10-2	Cost Dynamics	467
Chapter 11		
11-1	The Professional Organization	472
11-2	Balancing the Professional Service Firm	479

Chapter 12
    12-1 The Innovative Organization   484
    12-2 Managing Innovation: Controlled Chaos   492

Chapter 13
    13-1 The Diversified Organization   500
    13-2 Generic Corporate Strategies   505
    13-3 Managing Large Groups in the East and West   507
    13-4 From Competitive Advantage to Corporate Strategy   511

Chapter 14
    14-1 Global Strategy . . . In a World of Nations?   518
    14-2 Managing Across Borders   522

Chapter 15
    15-1 Beyond Configuration   527
    15-2 Convergence and Upheaval   536
    15-3 The Crescendo Model of Rejuventation   543

Teaching Notes for Section III Cases   549

    III-1   Sony Entertainment   551
    III-2   The Vanguard Group, Inc. (A)   558
    III-3   The Battle for Paramount Communications, Inc.   564
    III-4   Honda Motor Company 1994   599
    III-5   The Pillsbury Company   614
    III-6   Cadbury Schweppes, P.L.C.   624
    III-7   SAS and the European Airline Industry   627
    III-8   Peet, Russ, Anderson & Detroit   642
    III-9   Nintendo of America   652
    III-10 Mountbatten and India   658

The Strategy Process, Third Edition represents a significant synthesis of prevailing ideas about Business Policy or Strategic Management courses. While trying to honor the best that each traditional framework brings to these subjects we have tried to integrate them in a different and more useful fashion. Consequently, while our text starts with a more or less traditional focus on strategy, the strategist, strategic analysis, and strategy formulation, it quickly moves into the more complex subjects of strategy formation, emergent strategies, incremental strategies, and managing the strategy process and the power relationships related to it. We then go on to a series of contexts in which strategy occurs, notably the entrepreneurial, mature, diversified, innovative and professional contexts. We believe this organization is most constructive and useful.

In the text itself are several sections which you should read carefully before designing your own course. The introduction provides the authors' perspective on the text and the teaching of business policy or strategic management. The individual chapter introductions offer insights into the choice of readings and suggest ways to reconcile the sometimes contradictory theories they put forth.

Because our approach is different, we have tried, in this *Instructor's Manual,* to provide you with as much guidance and information as possible on how you might use and relate the concepts and cases in your own course. For an overview of the relationship between the chapter contents and the cases, refer to the matrix which follows. In this matrix, the numbers 1 and 2 following the case names indicate primary or secondary focus on the subjects covered in the chapter heading at the top of that column.

Included here are two model syllabi, one for semester length courses and one for quarter (term) length courses. They contain a reasonably even mix of concepts and cases. Since the approaches discussed in this book are divided into prescriptive and descriptive categories, the syllabi suggest a course framework organized around that major distinction.

We have also provided suggestions for written assignments (both on individual readings in the chapters and cases) and for devices to integrate the concepts and cases. We have also suggested some video tapes from the video library maintained by Prentice Hall which complement certain of the cases and are available to any professor who adopts this text.

The bulk of the *Instructor's Manual* is organized around the three sections in the text. For each reading in the chapters, Professor Voyer has written a summary of the material and a set of discussion questions covering that material. In addition he has provided extensive comments on how each discussion might be developed. These discussion questions are designed to stimulate provocative discussion about the concepts and theories presented and to prompt students to relate these to issues and topics from earlier readings. As such, they should not only ensure an in-depth consideration of theories and concepts presented in a particular reading but help integrate students' insights into the strategy process itself.

For each case we include a detailed teaching note. The teaching note for most of the cases begins with an overview describing: (1) the kinds of issues raised by the case, (2) the general concepts the case touches on, and (3) other information useful in positioning the case in a course sequence. Following this is a detailed discussion plan and analysis for the case to give you maximum assistance in teaching it. This main body of the note was purposely written with key points and session flow underlined or listed in outline fashion to allow the instructor to scan the note rapidly for planning purposes. Since the cases are predominantly from real institutions, we feel sure each of you will be able to add many lively insights for the students. However, again to help you, we have included a short section, "Summary of Outcomes," stating what actually did happen at the end of the case. When appropriate, we have updated the information contained in this section to point out the major events over the past several years since the teaching notes were first written. We are sure that different professors will find a wide variety of successful ways to

Matrix 1

Case	Strategy and Its Formation					Organization & Structure			Context						
	1 — The Strategy Concept	2 — The Strategist	3 — Formulating Strategy	4 — Strategy Analysis	5 — Strategy Formation	6 — Structure & Systems	7 — Culture and Power	8 — Managerial Styles	9 — Entrepreneurial Context	10 — Mature Context	11 — Professional Context	12 — Innovation Context	13 — Diversified Context	14 — International Context	15 — Managing Change
Andersen Consulting	2		1	2	1	1	1		1		1			2	1
Apple Computer (A)		2	1	1				2							1
Apple Computer 1992	2	2	1	1	2	1	2		1	2			2		2
Argyle Diamonds		2	1	1		2	1	1		2			2		1
Transformation of AT&T	2	2	1	1	2	2	1	2	1	2			1	1	
Cadbury Schweppes			1		1	1				1					2
E.M. Boehm	2	2	1	2				2				2	2	1	2
E&J Gallo	1	2	1	2		2	1		2	1		1	2	1	1
Exxon 1994			1		1	1	1		1	2			1		1
Ford: Team Taurus					1		2	1			2	2			
Genentech, Inc.			2	2	1	2	2		2	2		1	2	2	2
Hewlett Packard	1	1	2	2	1	2	2	1	1			1	2		
Honda Motor 1994	1	1	2	1		1	1			1				1	
IBM 360 Decision			1	2	2	1	2		2			2		2	2
Intel Corp.	1	1	1	1	1	2	1	1	1	2		1	2	1	1
MacArthur and the Philipp.		2		1	2				2						2
Matsushita 1994				1	2	1	2		1	1			2	1	1
Maglev Train	2	2	1	2	1	1	2		1		1	2	1	2	2
Microsoft (A)	1						1	2	2						2
Microsoft (B)		1		1											
Mountbatten and India			1	1	1	2	1	1	1			1	1	1	
New Steel		2	1	2		2	1	2	1	2				2	
New York Times			1	1		1		1			2		2	2	2
Nintendo Corp., Ltd.	2	2	2	1		1	2		1	1				1	2
Nintendo of America	1		2	1	1	1	2	2		1		1	1	2	
NovaCare, Inc.	1	2	1	1	2	2	1		1	1					1
Orbital Engine Co.	1	2	1	2	2	1	1	2				1	2	2	
Battle for Paramount		1		1		2	1	1	2				1	1	1
PRA&D	1	1	2	1	2		2		1		1				2
Pillsbury	1	2	1	1	1	1	1	1		1		1	1		1
Polaroid	1	1	1	2	2	2	2		2	2		1	1		
SAS and European Airline Ind.		1	1	2	2	2	2	2		1			2	2	1
Sony Innovation			1	1		2	1		1	1		1		2	2
Sony Entertainment		1	1	2	2	2	2		1			1	1		1
TCG/Thermo Electron		1	1	2	1	1	1			1		1	1		
Vanguard Group	1		1	2		2	1			2	2	2	1		2

use the cases. However, we have tried to provide very thorough teaching notes for them as opposed to presenting abbreviated teaching notes along with sample written case analyses done by students.

In the section which follows, Professor Quinn presents further details about the cases themselves and their arrangement by section. He also comments on case preparation by students and the goals of case discussions in general. Let us know if we can help you in any other way.

NOTES ON CASES

Business cases are the most convenient way to introduce practice into the classroom, to tap a wide variety of experiences, and to involve students actively in analysis and decision making. However, we must reiterate that our cases are not intended as *examples* of either weak or exceptionally good management practices. Nor do they provide *examples* of particular concepts. They are discussion vehicles for probing the benefits and limitations of various approaches. They are analytical vehicles for applying and testing concepts and tools developed throughout the curriculum and from one's personal experience.

Virtually every case in our text has its marketing, operations, accounting and financial, organizational behavior, planning and controls, external environmental, ethical, political, and quantitative dimensions. Each dimension should be addressed in preparations and classroom discussions, although some aspects may inevitably emerge as more important in one situation than another. The cases are consciously constructed to recognize that no realistic strategy situation is *just* an organizational problem or *just* a financial or economic-analytical one. Both types of data should be analyzed, and an integrated solution developed.

Despite their complexity, we have tried to keep the cases as short as possible. And we have tried to write them in a lively style that captures some of the flavor of the real organizations. We have tried to mix product and services cases, technological and "non-tech" cases, entrepreneurial, small company, and large enterprise situations. The new cases in this edition emphasize situations involving the service industries, international aspects, entrepreneurial efforts, technology-driven strategies, and the use of new organizational structures. In the cross-section of cases, we have tried to capture some of the most important and exciting issues, concepts, and products of our times. We have tried to convey some of the fun and importance of management in the current society.

From time to time, you will find a series of questions at intermediate "decision points" in a case. Discussion can occur on the materials up to that point just as if it were a short case. The case materials immediately following such decision points consciously leave out much detail on what actually happened so that students can arrive at their own specific solutions, but later see these in the context of a longer time horizon—much like a mystery story that unfolds in phases. They should analyze the specific situations, consider alternatives, and arrive at explicit conclusions—understanding that later events might have looked a bit different if their solution had been implemented. As in any good mystery story, the case provides many clues—never quite all those actually present—but, surprisingly, often more than most executives would have had time to absorb in the real situation.

The matrix which follows characterizes the cases by industry type, company size, and emphasis on organization, technology, and international aspects of management. This along with the first matrix, should help you select cases to meet your specific needs.

Believing that no "canned" approach is viable for all strategic situations, we have selected cases which cut across a variety of issues and theoretical constructs. We have clustered them around the three major sections of the book for convenience to students and professors. Within each section, the cases are arranged in the general order in which they are likely to be taught. Smaller companies and simpler situations precede larger companies or more complex situations.

Matrix 2

CASE	INDUSTRY TYPE	COMPANY SIZE	ORGANI-ZATION EMPHASIS	TECH-NOLOGY EMPHASIS	INTERNA-TIONAL EMPHASIS
Andersen Consulting	service	large	yes		yes
Apple Computer (A)	product	small	yes	yes	
Apple Computer 1992	mixed	large		yes	
Argyle Diamonds	product	small	yes		yes
Transformation of AT&T	service	large	yes	yes	yes
Cadbury Schweppes	product	large	yes		yes
Edward Marshall Boehm	product	small			
E&J Gallo Winery	product	medium	yes		
Exxon Corporation 1994	product	large	yes		yes
Ford: Team Taurus	product	large	yes	yes	yes
Genentech, Inc.	mixed	small	yes	yes	
Hewlett Packard Company	product	large	yes	yes	
Honda Motor Company 1994	product	varies	yes		yes
IBM 360 Decision	product	large	yes	yes	yes
Intel Corporation	product	varies	yes	yes	yes
MacArthur and the Philip.	other				
Matsushita Elect. Ind. Co.	product	large	yes		yes
Maglev Train	mixed	large	yes	yes	yes
Microsoft Corporation (A)	service	medium	yes	yes	yes
Microsoft Corporation (B)	service	large	yes	yes	yes
Mountbatten and India	other				
New Steel Co.	product	small		yes	yes
New York Times Co.	mixed	large	yes	yes	
Nintendo Corp., Ltd.	mixed	varies		yes	yes
Nintendo of America	mixed	varies	yes	yes	yes
NovaCare, Inc.	service	medium	yes	yes	
Orbital Engine Co.	product	small	yes	yes	yes
Battle for Paramount	service	large	yes		yes
PRA&D	service	large	yes	yes	yes
The Pillsbury Company	mixed	large	yes		
Polaroid Corporation	product	medium	yes	yes	yes
SAS & European Airline Ind.	service	large	yes		yes
Sony Corp.: Innovation	product	varies	yes	yes	yes
Sony Entertainment	service	large	yes		yes
TCG/Thermo Electron	mixed	small	yes	yes	yes
Vanguard Group	service	medium	yes		

They major focus of early cases tends to match the focus of early text material in each section. Techniques needed for later case analyses appear earlier in each section' case sequence. And so on. Almost any of the cases is so complex that it can be positioned at a number of different spots in a good strategy course. Consequently, the cases could equally well be taught in a variety of sequences.

We suggest that you use extra cases—available from earlier editions of the text or other sources for three purposes: (1) as possible examination cases which students do not already have access to, (2) as extra cases to increase emphasis selectively on one or another section of the course or to expand the conceptual material, and (3) as extra cases to create industry groupings of cases.

Professors who adopt the third edition of The Strategy Process: Concepts, Contexts, Cases, have permission to reproduce the Edward Marshall Boehm, Inc. and New Steel Corporation cases for use in a first session class. Similarly, those who adopt the book may reproduce the cases for earlier editions of the book, but not included in this edition, for use in direction connection with the courses for which the third edition was adopted. Otherwise, these cases are copyrighted and special permission must be obtained from the copyright holders for their reproduction. Letters should be addressed to copyright holder or:

Professor James Brian Quinn
20 Low Road
Hanover, NH 03755

Student Preparation and Class Discussions

We have posed a few questions at the end of most of the cases. These are designed to help students see relevant issues, but not limit or channel their thinking. Students generally find such questions helpful in organizing their thinking about the case. However, you are free to substitute your own set of questions designed to achieve your own specific objections. Whatever the questions, students should also be expected to do the following in preparation for class discussion: understand the facts (by underlining them or whatever), identify the main issues presented by the case and cluster the facts around those issues, lay out feasible alternatives for action, evaluate those alternatives, choose the "best" one, and consider issues of implementation relative to that course of action.

Students who have followed this process should be able to handle any questions you pose in the class itself. We believe that the class discussion should build on their preparations and carry them into further depth rather than require students to recite the results of those preparations. Professor Quinn's teaching notes are organized to facilitate this level of discussion. They provide a thorough outline of how the case can be taught, key questions, concepts, and analytical data needed. Because the cases are complex, the teaching notes are purposely quite thorough. A skilled professor should have little difficulty in teaching these cases for the first time.

There is no "correct" answer to any case. There may be several "good" answers and many poor ones. The purpose of strategy discussions should be to help the student to understand the nature of "better" answers, what to look for, how to analyze alternatives, and how to see through the complexities of arriving at and implementing solutions in real organizations. The total number of variables in a real strategy situation is typically beyond the capacities of any one person or group to control them all. Hence, the students should be warned that they cannot rely on what a company actually did to be a thorough guide to action. The company may have succeeded or failed—not because of its specific decisions—but because of luck, an outstanding personality, the bizarre actions of an opponent, international events over which it had no control, and so on. One of the products of a successful strategy discussion should be to bring out the full dimensions of these "unknowables."

xii

Some professors may choose to limit the students to using only the materials contained in the case. This keeps the students from "second guessing" the top management's decisions. On the other hand, other professors may find it useful to allow the students to do whatever library research they wish. This allows the cases to remain vital and living, up through today's headlines. Very often, issues developed in the case will show up in *The Wall Street Journal, Business Week, Fortune,* or other business media during the week in which the case is taught.

Written assignments can easily be developed using Professor Voyer's discussion questions and the teaching notes for each case. In addition, the devices described below can be used to integrate concepts presented in the chapter text with the case material.

SUGGESTIONS FOR WRITTEN ASSIGNMENTS

Written assignments can easily be developed using Professor Voyer's discussion questions and the teaching notes for each case. In addition, the devices described below can be used to integrate concepts presented in the chapter text with the case material.

The McGill "Position Outline"

At McGill University, to stimulate class discussion and closer reading of the material, policy instructors use a device called the "Position Outline." Here is the description of the Position Outline from the course syllabus:

> For each class session where a case is to be discussed, students will hand in a position outline three hours before class. This may be printed neatly or typed and should consist of one side of one page, double spaced. The PO should present your main idea(s) linking the reading(s) and the case. Don't summarize (we have read the material); give us what you think is important about the material, synthesizing the concepts in the case. *Please underline or highlight in some other way in the PO, in a few words, the single most significant contribution you wish to bring to the class discussion.* These POs are designed to focus your reading and to stimulate your thoughts for class. We have found that people read much better and retain what they read when they comment on it in writing. The POs will be used by us to get a sense of your reaction to the readings and the cases and to select people to call on in class. We shall read the POs each week and assign an overall grade for them at the end of the year. We shall give you feedback on the early ones to assure you that you are on track.

SWOT Analyses

The following cases are probably the most appropriate for written (or in class) analyses of strengths, weaknesses, opportunities and threats (SWOT). Students can be asked to define each element of the SWOT analysis in relation to concepts developed in the text. Please refer to the individual case teaching notes for more information.

Apple Computer , Inc. (A)	E&J Gallo Winery
Apple Computer 1992	Genentech, Inc.
Argyle Diamonds	Honda Motor 1994
Edward Marshall Boehm, Inc.	Intel Corporation
Matsushita Electric Industrial Co. 1994	The New York Times Company
Magnetic Levitation Train	Nintendo Co., Ltd.
Microsoft Corporation(A)	Nintendo of America
New Steel Corporation	Polaroid Corporation

Competitive Analyses

The following cases are very useful for written assignments on competitive analysis. Please refer to the individual case teaching notes for more information.

Apple Computer 1992
Argyle Diamonds
Cadbury Schweppes, P.L.C.
Nintendo Co., Ltd.
NovaCare, Inc.
Orbital Engine

Intel Corporation
Microsoft Corporation (A)
New Steel Corporation
The Battle for Paramount Commun., Inc.
Polaroid Corporation
Sony Entertainment

Other Ideas

The following cases can be used as relatively specific examples of certain concepts developed in the text. Students can be asked to prepare written analyses of the cases relating them to the appropriate concepts. Please refer to the individual case teaching notes for more information.

Case	Concepts
Andersen Consulting	network organization
Apple Computer, Inc. (A)	core competency and outsourcing strategies
Exxon Corporation 1994	international politics
E&J Gallo Winery	industry analysis, Porter's five forces
Hewlett Packard Company	culture, missionary organization
Honda Motor Company 1994	entrepreneurial context
The IBM 360 Decision	logical incrementalism
MacArthur and the Philippines	strategy formation, strategy concept
Matsushita Electric Industrial Co. 1994	configuration, culture
Mountbatten and India	transition, managing incrementalism
The New York Times Company	competitive and competitor analysis
NovaCare, Inc.	new forms of organizing
Peet, Russ, Anderson & Detroit	professional service firms, prof. context
The Pillsbury Company	power, diversified context
Polaroid Corporation	organizational structure
TCG, Ltd. /Thermo Electron Corp.	new forms of organizing
Sony Corp.: Innovation System	innovation context

STRATEGY SIMULATION GAME

In teaching the Strategy course, we have found large-scale simulations to be extremely valuable. Professor Quinn designed several such games including *STRAT, Tycoon*, and contributed heavily to *Super Tycoon,* described below. The last stage in the evolutionary process, *Super Tycoon*, includes the better features of previous games, while adding levels of sophistication and flexibility that only modern software can provide. *Super Tycoon* is a superb vehicle for tracking the practical dynamics of strategy formulation and implementation. It forces students to integrate their concepts from all functional fields. It offers a break in the regular routine of case classes. It fosters the integration of social dynamics with strategy dynamics. And it can involve faculty members in an inter-disciplinary school activity.

The simulations tend to be extremely involving for student teams. The Tuck School normally shuts down its entire class activities for several days to allow all students in one class to participate fully in the simulation. Invariably, students comment that the simulation is one of the greatest learning experiences of their academic careers. They remember their participation in the simulation long after they leave the institution.

Super Tycoon™ Description

Super Tycoon is the most realistic and sophisticated global strategy simulation available for MBA education. *Super Tycoon* provides firsthand opportunities for participants to:

- Demonstrate acquired functional skills
- Work in teams, and resolve conflicts
- Develop and use analytic tools

- Implement strategy paradigms
- Explore a globalized industry
- Make decisions under uncertainty

In *Super Tycoon*, participants form management teams and assume functional roles, submit bids for each of the companies in the consumer electronics industry, and operate their newly purchased company through several years of operations in a highly stimulating, competitive, and somewhat uncertain environment.

Regional business environments have distinct characteristics—operating a business in South America requires a different set of assumptions than in the U.S., which is different than either Europe or Japan. This feature is unique, and it arises from ENSAR's experience running the simulation in Japanese MBA programs over the past six years. This feature has also generated interest from business schools overseas, who distrust those simulations that only reinforce U.S. business biases as unrealistic or narrow.

The software design is very flexible, and can easily be customized at very reasonable rates for specific regional interests, paradigms, or teaching objectives. Most of ENSAR's clients choose some level of customization, either to reinforce a particular paradigm being taught in a course, or to make the simulation appear to be a locally sponsored product.

Super Tycoon software is commercially available for a license fee. ENSAR Group, Ltd. was formed to help businesses and educational institutions implement the game. Many universities have adopted it, both in the United States and abroad. For further information, please contact the ENSAR Group, Post Office Box 341; Hanover, New Hampshire 03755; Voice/fax (800) 45-ENSAR; E-mail ensar@dartmouth.edu; Internet www.ensar.com.

Other Instructional Resources Available Through Simon & Schuster

Your Prentice Hall/Simon & Schuster representative can also supply both *ABC News* and *Wall Street Journal Report* videos for use in teaching several of the cases. See the list below for details.

For the Ford: Team Taurus case:

World News Tonight   "Ford's Global Automobile Strategy," September 15, 1994

For the IBM or Microsoft cases:

WSJ Report   "Big Blue Bytes Back," January 29, 1994   #592-1

WSJ Report   "Power Play: IBM/Lotus," June 10, 1995   #663-1

For the Intel Corporation case:

WSJ Report   "Chip War," March 13, 1994   #598-1

For The Battle for Paramount Communications, Inc. case:

WSJ Report   "It's a Warp, or is it?" September 18, 1993   #573-2

WSJ Report   "Media Marriage—Viacom," February 19, 1994   #595-1

For The Transformation of AT&T case

WSJ Report   "Reaching Out," August 22, 1993 #569-2

WSJ Report   "Robert Allen of AT&T," April 29, 1995   #657-3

MODEL SYLLABUS #1

This syllabus is for a fourteen-week semester. Weeks are divided into Session 1 and Session 2. This is to show how the material can be organized into two sessions per week (as in many daytime programs) or one double session per week (as in many evening programs). The first column indicates what text material could be covered and the second lists possible case material.

	Text Material	Cases (Select Balance Desired[1])
Week 1 Session 1	Chapter 1 Mintzberg	Edward Marshall Boehm, Inc.
Session 2	Chapter 1 Quinn	Genentech, Inc. New Steel Corporation
Week 2 Session 1	Chapter 2 Mintzberg Wrapp	MacArthur and the Philippines The Pillsbury Company
Session 2	Chapter 2 Hamel and Prahalad	E & J Gallo Winery Intel Corporation
Week 3 Session 1	Chapter 3 Andrews	Argyle Diamonds Intel Corporation
Session 2	Chapter 3 Rumelt Quinn & Hilmer	Microsoft Corporation (A) Magnetic Levitation Train
Week 4 Session 1	Chapter 4 Porter	Apple Computer 1992 Nintendo Co., Ltd.
Session 2	Chapter 4 Mintzberg	Apple Computer, Inc. (A) The New York Times Co.
Week 5 Session 1	Chapter 5 Quinn & Voyer	The IBM 360 Decision The Pillsbury Company
Session 2	Chapter 5 Mintzberg Pascale	The Transformation of AT&T Honda Motor Company 1994
Week 6 Session 1	Chapter 6 Galbraith Mintzberg	Hewlett Packard Company Ford: Team Taurus
Session 2	Chapter 6 Quinn, Anderson & Finkelstein Bleeke & Ernst	NovaCare, Inc. TCG, Ltd./Thermo Electron Corp.
Week 7 Session 1	Chapter 7 Mintzberg, "Ideology" Bartlett & Ghoshal	Sony Corp.: Innovation System
Session 2	Chapter 7 Mintzberg, "Politics" Henderson Mintzberg, "Who Should Control?"	Matsushita Electric Industrial Co. 1994 Exxon Corporation 1994
Week 8 Session 1	Chapter 8 Senge	Polaroid Corporation or The New York Times Co.

Session 2	Chapter 8 Pitcher Sayles	SAS and The European Airline Industry
Week 9 Session 1	Chapter 9 Mintzberg	Orbital Engine Co.
Session 2	Chapter 9 Porter Bhide	TCG, Ltd./Thermo Electron Corp. The Vanguard Group, Inc. (A)
Week 10 Session 1	Chapter 10 Mintzberg	Ford: Team Taurus Honda Motor Company 1994 Nintendo of America
Session 2	Chapter 10 Abell & Hammond	The New York Times Co. The Pillsbury Company
Week 11 Session 1	Chapter 11 Mintzberg	Andersen Consulting The Vanguard Group, Inc. (A)
Session 2	Chapter 11 Maister	Peet, Russ, Anderson & Detroit
Week 12 Session 1	Chapter 12 Mintzberg	Sony Corp.: Innovation System
Session 2	Chapter 12 Quinn	Microsoft Corporation(B)
Week 13 Session 1	Chapter 13 Mintzberg, "Diversified" Mintzberg, "Generic Corporate"	The Battle for Paramount Communications, Inc.
Session 2	Chapter 13 Porter Lassere	The Pillsbury Company Sony Entertainment
Week 14 Session 1	Chapter 14 Yip	Cadbury Schweppes, P.L.C.
Session 2	Chapter 14 Bartlett & Ghoshal	TCG, Ltd./Thermo Electron Corp.
Week 15 Session 1	Chapter 15 Mintzberg	Mountbatten and India
Session 2	Chapter 15 Tushman, Newman & Romanelli Baden-Fuller & Stopford	SAS and The European Airline Industry

A professor may choose not to use a case each session. The list of cases presented is illustrative only. Please refer to the matrix following the Notes on Cases for other possibilities. The professor should balance text and cases depending on her or his style, desired length of assignments, etc.

MODEL SYLLABUS #2

This syllabus is for a ten-week quarter.

	Text Material	Cases (Select Balance Desired[1])
Week 1 Session 1	Chapter 1 Mintzberg	Edward Marshall Boehm, Inc.
Session 2	Chapter 1 Quinn	Genentech, Inc. New Steel Corporation
Week 2 Session 1	Chapter 2 Mintzberg Wrapp	MacArthur and the Philippines The Pillsbury Company
Session 2	Chapter 3 Andrews Rumelt	Argyle Diamonds Intel Corporation or Magnetic Levitation Train
Week 3 Session 1	Chapter 4 Porter	Apple Computer 1992 Nintendo Co., Ltd.
Session 2	Chapter 4 Mintzberg	Apple Computer Corp. (A) The New York Times Co.
Week 4 Session 1	Chapter 5 Quinn & Voyer	The IBM 360 Decision The Pillsbury Company
Session 2	Chapter 5 Mintzberg Pascale	The Transformation of AT&T Honda Motor Company 1994
Week 5 Session 1	Chapter 6 Mintzberg Quinn, Anderson & Finkelstein	Hewlett Packard Company Ford: Team Taurus
Session 2	Chapter 7 Mintzberg, "Ideology" Mintzberg, "Politics"	Sony Corp. : Innovation System Matsushita Electric Industrial Co. 1994 Exxon Corporation 1994
Week 6 Session 1	Chapter 8 Senge Sails	Polaroid Corporation or The New York Times Co.
Session 2	Chapter 9 Mintzberg Bhide	Orbital Engine Co. TCG, Ltd./Thermo Electric Corp. The Vanguard Group, Inc. (A)
Week 7 Session 1	Chapter 10 Mintzberg Abell & Hammond	Ford: Team Taurus Honda Motor Co. 1994 Nintendo of America
Session 2	Chapter 11 Mintzberg Maister	Andersen Consulting The Vanguard Group, Inc. (A) Peet, Russ, Anderson & Detroit
Week 8 Session 1	Chapter 12 Mintzberg Quinn	Sony Corp. : Innovation System Microsoft Corporation (B)

Session 2	Chapter 13 Mintzberg, "Diversified" Mintzberg, "Generic Corporate"	The Pillsbury Company The Battle for Paramount Communications, Inc.
Week 9 Session 1	Chapter 13 Porter Lassere	Sony Entertainment
Session 2	Chapter 14 Yip Bartlett & Ghoshal	Cadbury Schweppes, P.L.C. TCG Ltd./Thermo Electron Corp.
Week 10 Session 1	Chapter 15 Mintzberg	SAS and The European Airline Industry
Session 2	Chapter 15 Tushman, Newman & Romanelli Baden-Fuller & Stopford	Mountbatten and India

[1]A professor may choose not to use a case each session. The list of cases presented is illustrative only. Please refer to the matrix following the Notes on Cases for other possibilities. The professor should balance text and cases depending on her or his style, desired length of assignments, etc.

SECTION I: STRATEGY

Quinn, "Strategies for Change"

<u>Summary of Reading</u>

Some useful definitions

This section of the reading sets forth some definitions and some discussion of the concept of strategy:

Strategy: the pattern or plan that integrates an organization's major goals, policies, and action sequences into a cohesive whole.

Helps to marshal and allocate an organization's resources into a unique and viable posture based on its relative internal competencies and shortcomings, anticipated changes in the environment, and contingent moves by intelligent opponents.

Goals: state what is to be achieved by when.

Policies: rules or guidelines that express the limits within which action should occur.

Programs: the step-by-step sequence of actions necessary to achieve major objectives.

Strategic decisions: determine the overall direction of an enterprise and its ultimate viability in light of the predictable, the unpredictable, and the unknowable changes that may occur in its most important surrounding environments.

Tactics: short-duration, adaptive, action-interaction realignments used to accomplish limited goals. Strategy defines a continuing basis for ordering these adaptations toward more broadly conceived purposes.

The classical approach [to strategy]

This section of the reading contains an extended example of military strategy, namely, Philip and Alexander's actions at Chaeronea (338 B.C.). This is followed by a section which expands on this theme by drawing from other military thinkers, e.g., Von Clausewitz, Von Bulow, Liddell-Hart.

Dimensions of strategy

This section pulls together four "lessons" from the preceding military discussion:

1. Effective formal strategies have three essential elements:

    a. goals
    b. policies
    c. programs

2. Effective strategies develop around a few key concepts and thrusts, which give them cohesion, balance, and focus.

3. Strategy deals not just with the unpredictable but also with the unknowable. Consequently, the essence of strategy is to build a posture that is so strong (and potentially flexible) in selective ways that the organization can achieve its goals despite these conditions.

4. Just as military organizations have multiple echelons of grand, theater, area, battle, infantry, and artillery strategies, so should other complex organizations have a number of hierarchically related and mutually supporting strategies.

The reading concludes with a discussion of seven criteria for effective strategy:

1. Clear, decisive objectives

2. Maintaining the initiative

3. Concentration (pinpoint aiming of superior power in a decisive way)

4. Flexibility

5. Coordinated and committed leadership

6. Surprise

7. Security (protecting resources, having a good intelligence system)

Discussion Questions

1. What is the distinction between strategic formulation and simpler programmatic planning?

Programmatic planning is short-range. It simply aims resources at the accomplishment of the limited objectives that flow from a broader strategic plan. In other words, one cannot even have an intelligent operating or tactical plan without first having a broader strategy.

A "true strategy," as Quinn puts it, goes well beyond mere coordinative plans and programs. It is a whole new set of concepts, aimed at ensuring the effectiveness of the organization. These new concepts are based on organizational strengths and weaknesses, changes in the environment, and the moves of intelligent competitors. This kind of analysis is much more far-reaching than any programmatic plan's.

2. Why should analysts study patterns rather than formal strategic documents?

First of all, Quinn points out that one would often be hard-pressed to find complete formal statements of corporate strategy that are actually followed. Secondly, objective observers may be able to deduce the existence of a strategy, even if it is not apparent to the executives making critical decisions. Lastly, Quinn implies that formal strategic documents may not reflect what the firm is actually doing. As he puts it, "One . . . must look at the actual emerging pattern of the enterprise's operant goals, policies, and major programs to see what its true strategy is."

3. Quinn says that there is good analogy from military strategy to business strategy. What is your opinion?

This question is intended to stimulate discussion. It does not have a right or wrong answer. Some students will argue that the analogy from military to business strategy is a good one. They will point to the many arguments made by Quinn in the reading. Others may not be so sure. They may feel that war is so different from business that the analogy breaks down quickly. There have even been some academicians who question the analogy, saying that much of the literature trying to make this link overemphasizes battle tactics and de-emphasizes "true" military strategic thinking.

4. Quinn says that strategy deals with the unknowable. What is your opinion? What are the implications of your position?

This question is intended to stimulate discussion. It does not have a right or wrong answer. Some students will disagree with Quinn's contention. They will argue that it is possible, through better environmental scanning, forecasting, etc., to know well enough what is going to happen. They will say that strategy will therefore be the drafting of more precise plans, and especially will be the development of elaborate contingency plans.

Other students will agree with Quinn. They will argue that it is impossible to know everything that is going to happen. As Quinn puts it, "No analyst could predict the precise ways in which all impinging forces could interact with each other, be distorted by nature or human emotions, or be modified by the imaginations and purposeful counteractions of intelligent opponents." Under these assumptions, strategy will be the creation of a strong and flexible organization that is able to respond intelligently regardless of what happens.

5. How important is surprise in the context of business strategy?

This question is intended to stimulate discussion. It does not have a right or wrong answer. Some students will argue that surprise is crucially important to successful business strategy. They will say that effective strategy must use speed, secrecy, and intelligence to attack exposed or unprepared opponents. Other students will argue that even if surprise is an important concept for tactical reasons (e.g., getting a new product out before a rival company does, using aggressive price cuts when other companies don't expect it), it is not as important for strategic purposes. The latter deal more with the creation of new concepts, new directions for the business, all based on strengths, weaknesses, and environmental contingencies. In other words, these students will argue, surprise may be important in a particular battle, but not as important to winning the whole war.

Mintzberg, "Five Ps for Strategy"

Summary of Reading

Strategy has been defined in one way, but used implicitly in different ways.

Most people define strategy as a *plan*—a consciously intended course of action. Plans are made in advance of the actions to which they apply, and they are developed consciously and purposefully.

Strategy can also be a *ploy*—a "maneuver" intended to outwit an opponent or competitor.

But defining strategy as a plan is not sufficient; we need a definition that encompasses the resulting behavior. Strategy may be a *pattern in a stream of action*. By this definition, strategy is consistency in behavior, whether or not intended. Even though few people would define strategy this way, many seem at one time or another to so use it.

Plans and patterns may be independent; plans may go unrealized, patterns may appear without preconception. Where previous intentions are realized, we have deliberate strategies. Where patterns developed in the absence of intentions, we have emergent strategies. Purely deliberate or purely emergent strategies are probably rare. Most strategies probably sit on a continuum between the two (from most deliberate to most emergent):

planned: centrally-formulated intentions are precisely stated, and implemented using formal controls; environment is benign or controllable

entrepreneurial: intentions are the personal, unarticulated vision of a single leader, who personally controls the organization, which is in a protected environmental niche

ideological: intentions are the collective vision of the organization's members, controlled through shared norms; the organization is active vis-à-vis the environment

umbrella: organization's members must act within boundaries defined by leadership; strategies are partly deliberate and partly emergent, or "deliberately emergent"

process: leadership controls process of strategy (e.g., recruitment, structure), leaves strategy content to others; strategies are partly deliberate, partly emergent, or "deliberately emergent"

disconnected: patterns in their own actions are developed by loosely coupled members or subunits, whether or not central intentions exist

consensus: members converge, using mutual adjustment, on patterns that pervade the organization even though central or common intentions don't exist

imposed: the external environment dictates patterns in actions, either through direct imposition or by bounding choice

People often label important things "strategy" and the details "tactics." But it is often wrong to do so, because details are important. It may be better to talk about shades of "strategic."

The fourth definition is that strategy is a *position*, i.e., a means of locating an organization in what organization theorists like to call an "environment." This definition is compatible with all the others—a position may be preselected and sought through a plan, or it may be reached or found through a pattern of behavior. Even though most positional definitions are based on the idea of competition, this view may be based on the achievement of any viable position, whether or not directly competitive. Strategy as position has recently been extended to "collective" strategy, i.e., cooperation between organizations.

The fifth definition of strategy looks inside the organization, indeed inside the heads of the collective strategists. Strategy is a *perspective*, its content consisting not just of a chosen position, but of an ingrained way of perceiving the world. In this view, strategy is to the organization what personality is to the individual. It suggests that strategy is a concept, that all strategies are abstractions which exist only in the minds of interested parties. What is of key importance here is that the perspective is shared.

Strategy as position and perspective can be combined with strategy as plan and pattern. Perspective may be a plan, or it may give rise to plans. Or patterns may be recognized and give rise to formal plans, perhaps within an overall perspective. Perspectives probably arise from long-standing patterns. Change in perspective is difficult, but change within a perspective is relatively easy.

No single definition takes precedence over the others. They compete, but they also complement. Each adds important elements to our understanding of strategy:

1. **Plan**: deals with how leaders set direction; also deals with how intentions form in the human brain.

2. **Ploy**: takes us into the realm of direct competition, the use of threats and feints to gain advantage.

3. **Pattern**: the focus here is on action, but also on the achievement of consistency in that action; encourages us to consider the notion that strategies can emerge as well as be deliberate.

4. **Position**: encourages us to look at organizations in their competitive environments, enabling us to think of organizations in ecological terms (i.e., organisms seeking protected niches).

Strategy is not just a notion of of how to deal with an enemy or a set of competitors or a market. It draws us into some fundamental issues about organizations as instruments for collective perception and action. The use of various definitions enriches our ability to understand and manage the processes by which strategies form.

Discussion Questions

1. Is it truly possible for a firm to have a strategy in the absence of intention?

This question is intended to stimulate discussion. It does not have a clearly right or wrong answer. For some firms, it would not be likely that strategies would exist in the absence of intention. The best examples would probably be utilities. To a great extent, the absence of intention would be unlikely for most machine organizations and divisionalized firms. These kinds of organizations are large, and standardization is an integral part of their functioning. Also, they typically face stable environments. These factors make planning (i.e., the formation of intentions prior to action) more feasible, and sometimes even necessary.

Other types of organizations, notably innovative one, also known as adhocracies, often plunge right into action, without the prior development of intentions. Any kind of firm that faces an uncertain and dynamic environment is a good candidate for strategy forming out of a pattern of action without preconceived intentions. In larger, complex organizations, there are often subunits that act without any explicit set of intentions from upper management. Patterns emerge from their activities; these subunit strategies may later be adopted by the parent organization. Hence, even in large organizations it is possible for strategies to form in the absence of intention.

2. Are plans and patterns independent, at least in theory? What about in practice?

In theory, plans and patterns may be independent. For example, a new organization developing a plan may not have any previous pattern on which to draw. The plan is indeed being done from scratch. This would also be true for ad hoc plans drawn up by organizational committees. Patterns certainly may develop without any prior intention-developing, i.e., planning. Many embryonic companies would start "working" without fully planning their actions.

But in many practical circumstances, plans and patterns would be linked. Many organizations that decide to do strategic planning bring a lot of historical "baggage" with them; in other words, they have formed patterns which influence the way they approach the planning task. One could argue that part of the internal analysis which is usually done in strategic planning is a form of identifying patterns, some of which have worked, some of which have not. And it is certainly possible, though not as common as is thought, that plans ultimately shape patterns of action.

3. What is the difference between umbrella strategy and process strategy?

These two types of strategies are similar in that they both are "deliberately emergent," i.e., the details of strategies are allowed to emerge within particular boundaries. They differ in the way in which these boundaries are set. For umbrella strategies, the boundaries are articulated by the leadership, and these boundaries are widely publicized and known within the organization. One of the best examples is 3M Corporation's requirement that 25% of sales must come from products developed within the past five years. For process strategies, the boundaries may not be widely circulated by the leadership. Instead, organizational processes (recruitment, promotion, structure) are manipulated in such a way that strategic activity stays within bounds.

4. What is the difference between ideological strategy and "strategy as perspective?"

They are very similar. Strategy as perspective could be the worldview of an individual, but it is more likely the ingrained way of viewing the world for a collective of people. Ideological strategy is the *active seeking* of that collective worldview. It tries to achieve a collective vision by means of strong shared norms, which Mintzberg calls ideology.

In other words, the pursuit of an ideological strategy, using shared norms, is designed to create a strategic perspective among the members of large organizations. But a strategic perspective may arise out of experiences that are not so dependent on ideology.

5. Mintzberg says that the distinction between strategy and tactics is dangerous. What is your opinion on this?

This question is designed to stimulate discussion. Some students may disagree, saying that strategy is definitely more important than tactics. They may say that the "big picture" is what top management should stress, and that details should be worked out by others. Excessive attention to details is what causes top managers to fritter away their time while the whole organization drifts away.

Other students may agree with Mintzberg. They will argue that top managers who neglect details do not have any raw experiences upon which to draw when they are trying to come up with strategic ideas. In other words, they have nothing upon which to build a perspective. They don't even have a good knowledge base upon which to plan. They simply don't have an intimate knowledge of the business.

6. The author says that it pays to manage the details and let the strategies emerge. What is your opinion?

This question is designed to stimulate discussion. Many students will disagree with this statement. They will argue that strategy is too important to just let it emerge. These will be the students who strongly believe in planning. They will want to see a more active, formulative approach undertaken by top management.

Other students will agree with the author. They will argue that in many, perhaps most, industries, it is simply not possible for top management to know what will need to be done. They will also argue that innovation is becoming increasingly important. Both of these factors make centralized planning less attractive and less effective. Adaptation and innovation are facilitated through the use of umbrella, process, and consensus strategies, which are the forms of strategy where strategy content details are allowed to emerge.

7. The author quotes Rumelt as saying that strategy means seeking an advantageous position, whether or not directly competitive. What do you think of this?

This question is designed to stimulate discussion. Most students think of head-to-head action when they hear the word competition. The discussion in this part of the article implies that strategy may involve less of that and much more of an *avoidance* of competition. A great deal of strategy theory talks about the creation of strong positions that deter competition, e.g., Miles's and Snow's *Defender* strategy, or Porter's *Cost Leadership* strategy. Another area of heavy discussion in the literature is the seeking out of protected niches, e.g., Miles's and Snow's *Prospector* strategy, or Porter's *Focus* strategy. The question is aimed at getting students to realize that, even though competitive forces are constantly being trained on the organization, strategists often try to position the organization to dodge, and not confront, these threats.

8. If strategy as perspective must be based on shared perspective, in what kinds of organizations might it be useful?

Shared perspective requires, almost by definition, that there be many people in the organization, so that there are people to do the sharing. This implies that strategy as perspective is likelier in medium and large organizations. There are many well-known examples: Hewlett Packard, IBM, Sony, Apple Computer. These organizations spend a lot of energy and resources getting their people indoctrinated in the proper norms.

This is not to say that strategy as perspective can't have a role in smaller organizations. Perspective doesn't come only from indoctrination. Shared experiences can also be the root of shared perspective. One kind of strategy that encourages shared experience is consensus strategy, where strategic content emerges over time through mutual adjustment. The small organizations that are likely to use consensus strategy could therefore develop a shared perspective.

Of course, the experiences of an individual will shape her or his individual worldview. In simple structures, or entrepreneurial organizations, strategy is the vision of the leader. This vision will certainly be influenced by her or his worldview. So strategy as perspective is a concept also applicable to the smallest of organizations.

9. In what ways are the five Ps of strategy related? Does the author's answer to this make sense? Are there other ways that they fit together?

The second and third sub-questions are designed to stimulate discussion. As for the first part, Mintzberg offers the following:

The conventional hierarchy of the strategy definitions is that perspective gives rise to plans, which position the organization and allow them to create patterns in their actions. Another scenario has the pattern or position leading to plans, i.e., the formalization of emergent strategy; this all happens within a given perspective. A third combination has the pattern or position producing a particular perspective. The last possibility mentioned by the author is perspective constraining changes in position, i.e., the organization repositions itself from Point A to Point B, which are both within its worldview, when it *should* move from Point A to Point X, the latter being *outside* the organization's worldview. (The author gives the example of the Egg McMuffin—position changed, but it was still well within McDonald's fast-food worldview.)

CHAPTER 2: THE STRATEGIST

Mintzberg, "The Manager's Job"

Summary of Reading

Major thinkers about management work seem to emphasize one aspect of the job to the exclusion of others. Peters emphasizes doing, while Porter stresses thinking. Zaleznik and Bennis say that the essence of management is leadership, but the classical writers Fayol and Urwick stressed controlling as the key part of the job..

Some folklore and fact

Folklore: The manager is a reflective, systematic planner.

Fact: Study after study has shown that managers work at an unrelenting pace, that their activities are characterized by brevity, variety, and discontinuity, and that they are strongly oriented to action and dislike reflective activities.

Folklore: The effective manager has no regular duties to perform.

Fact: In addition to handing exceptions, managerial work involves performing a number of regular duties, including ritual and ceremony, negotiations, and processing of soft information that links the organization with its environment.

Folklore: The senior manager needs aggregated information, which a formal management information system best provides.

Fact: Managers strongly favor oral media—namely, telephone calls and meetings.

Folklore: Management is, or at least is quickly becoming, a science and a profession.

Fact: The managers' programs—to schedule time, process information, make decisions, and so on—remain locked deep inside their brains.

The manager's job is characterized by brevity, fragmentation, and oral communication.

Toward a basic description of managerial work

Definition of manager: that person in charge of an organization or one of its units. This can be vice presidents, head nurses, hockey coaches and prime ministers. These diverse roles do have something in common if we build the image of the job from the inside out.

The person in the job

People come to management jobs with five things:

- values
- experience
- competencies
- knowledge
- mental models

The frame of the job

At the core of the management job is its frame, which is strategy, vision, purpose, perspective and positions. Frame gives rise to a first role in the management model—*conceiving*, which means thinking through the purpose, perspective, and positions of a particular unit to be managed over a period of time.

The agenda of the work

The agenda comes with an associated role—*scheduling*. The frame is manifested as a set of *issues*. If the frame is loose, there may be many (perhaps too many) issues. If the frame is very tight, there may only be one "magnificent obsession." The frame and the issues are manifested in a schedule, with its associated priorities.

The core in context

The core of the manager's job is the frame manifested by an agenda. This core may be placed in a context, which is split into three areas:

- *inside*: the unit being managed.
- *within*: the rest of the organization.
- *outside*: the rest of the context that is not part of the organization.

" . . . Much of managerial work is clearly directed either to the unit itself, for which the manager has official responsibility, or at its various boundary contexts, through which the manager must act without that responsibility."

Managing on three levels

From the outside in, managers can manage *action* directly, they can manage *people* to take action, or they can manage *information* to influence the people.

Managing by information

"Managers' own activities focus . . . on information as an indirect way to make things happen . . . . *Communicating* refers to the collection and dissemination of information." Managers scan, monitor, share and disseminate. They are nerve centers. Specialists may know more, but the manager has the broadest knowledge.

In a more *controlling* role, managers try to use information to evoke action somewhat more directly. They can do this in three ways:

- Developing systems
- Designing structures
- Issuing directives

The manager as a controller is less an actor and more a reviewer. The controlling role is what people have in mind when they refer to the "administrative" aspect of managerial work.

Managing through people

The controlling role that dominated early management thought gave way to a greater emphasis on people. Much of this emphasis was on insiders, often called "subordinates." But outsiders take up almost as much of a manager's time.

The internal aspect of managing through people is the *leader* role. Managers play this role in three ways. They can lead *individuals*. They can lead *groups*. And they can lead *units*, especially with regard to the creation and maintenance of culture.

The external aspect of managing through people is the *linking* role. With the proliferation of joint ventures, strategic alliances, and other networks, this role is performed more and more. Both the leader and linking roles result in managers trying to influence people but also having people trying to influence managers.

Managing action

" . . . [Managers] also manage actively and instrumentally by their own direct involvement in action." The attention paid to controlling and leading has obscured this. Leonard Sayles has insisted that managers must be the focal point of action in and by their units. "Their direct involvement must, in his view, take precedence over the pulling force of leadership and the pushing force of controllership."

This is the *doing* role, but managers hardly ever "do" anything. They talk, listen, watch and feel. So "doing" really means getting closer to the action. "A 'doer' is really someone who gets it done." *Doing inside* involves problems and projects, but sometimes it means doing "regular" work just to keep informed. *Doing outside* takes place when negotiations and deals are going on.

A well-rounded job of managing

Too much doing can lead to centrifugal explosion—the job flies off out of control. Too much thinking can produce centripetal implosion—the job closes in on itself and loses connection to actions. The two must be balanced. Too much leading leads to lack of content, but too much linking detaches the job from its roots. Only communicating or only conceiving means almost total lack of action. And too much controlling is an all-too-familiar trap.

The manager must practice a well-rounded job. Its elements may be conceptually separated, but cannot be behaviorally separated. Some of the most interesting aspects of the job fall on the edges between the component parts.

Managers who do outside but not inside will get into trouble. Conceiving without leading and doing is what has gotten strategic planning into disfavor. Doing without conceiving is equally nonsensical. There are, however, legitimate styles of management that emphasize various roles:

- *Conceptual*: focuses on development of the frame
- *Administrative*: focuses on controlling
- *Interpersonal*: concerned with leading and linking
- *Action*: a style oriented toward tangible doing.

There are also styles based on interrelationships among the components of managerial work. A *deductive* approach proceeds from the core out, as the conceived frame is implemented through scheduling and information. This is a cerebral, deliberate style. An *inductive* approach goes from the outer surface to the inner core and is much more emergent and insightful.

Discussion Questions

1. The author says that the four concepts of planning, organizing, coordinating, and controlling tell us little about what managers actually do. What do you think of this assertion?

This question is intended to stimulate discussion. Most students will have a hard time agreeing with Mintzberg on this. Almost all the introductory textbooks on management rely on this familiar four-part classification. But Mintzberg was not interested in perpetuating Fayol's conceptual scheme. He wanted to examine what managers actually do, and to develop a descriptive classification. The resulting framework is what this reading is all about. Looking at it, it is difficult to classify what managers actually do neatly into Fayol's four categories. In that sense, Mintzberg's statement is correct; some students may agree with it.

2. Perhaps, as the author says, managers aren't reflective, systematic planners. The question then is, "Should they be?" What is your answer to this question?

12

This question is designed to stimulate discussion. Some students will argue forcefully that managers should be more systematic, and should plan. Others will counter that the nature of managerial work is such that it is futile to push managers to be reflective, systematic planners.

There is a germ of truth to each position. Even Mintzberg recognizes that managers must often act rationally and systematically. But it is equally true that many times they cannot, and should not. The key may lie in what Peters and Waterman asserted in *In Search of Excellence*—like the organizations they manage, managers must be simultaneously loose and tight.

3. In what way, if at all, is it surprising that the manager does have regular duties to perform?

It is only surprising when juxtaposed with the typical view of managers, whether that view comes from textbooks or from popular ideas about management. The typical view holds that managers should delegate everything, and never do anything themselves. Mintzberg's empirical model proves that there are some things that the manager simply can't delegate. They must lead, they must link to the outside, they must allocate resources, and so on.

4. The author says that managers don't, and shouldn't, make much use of MIS systems. What is your opinion on this?

This question is intended to stimulate discussion. Mintzberg clearly believes that managers are better off using oral communication than written communication, especially computer printouts. Some students will agree with this. Others will disagree, saying that managers would do a better job if they systematically used aggregated data from an MIS.

Each side of this argument has some merit. Oral media are clearly richer than written media. Research has shown that upper-level managers need large quantities of rich data. Top managers may not benefit from the somewhat lean information provided by an MIS. On the other hand, lower-level managers may be able to use aggregated data very effectively. They often need large quantities of lean information, the provision of which is a strength of management information systems.

5. Do you agree that a firm's strategic data bank is in the minds of its managers? If so, should it be?

Many students will disagree with this statement. They will assert that large, complex organizations will have their strategic databases in some codified form, either a strategic plan, a formal planning unit, or something along those lines. This position is valid for a small percentage of firms, mostly large bureaucracies. Since most of them are large firms, this view tends to dominate. Although most students will not think of this, it is also true that firms with a strong culture have their strategic data banks in their culture. Of course, the argument could be made that culture, being a non-tangible thing, resides in the minds of the organization's members.

Others will agree with the assertion in the question. They will argue that since most organizations don't bother to state their plans formally, the information that makes up their strategic concepts is held inside the minds of the top managers. This position is largely correct. Managers in small firms tend not to state their strategic intentions explicitly. Yet these managers often have a clear vision of what they want to accomplish. Similarly, even the managers of large firms often rely less on formal systems, and more on their own interpretations, to define strategies. This is particularly true during periods of crisis.

6. Do you think that management is a profession? If yes, why? If no, can it ever become one?

This question is intended to stimulate discussion. Many students, especially those who are very vested in their programs of study, will argue vehemently that management is a profession, one for which they are studying. They will point to the many skills in finance, marketing, production, and so on, that they are learning in their programs. They may refer to the often-heard phrase "professional manager."

But for the most part it is difficult to characterize managerial work as professional. The term "professional" can usually be properly applied only to work which is complex yet standardizable. Managerial work is certainly complex, but it is not standardized. Yes, we do teach financial skills that help in the allocation of resources, but research has shown that political skills are just as important in determining "who gets what." The parts of management education that come closest to professional deal with the application of quantitative skills to the solution of structured problems. But those kinds of problems make up only a fraction of the problems faced by managers. Most of the tasks that need to be done—leading, figure-heading, communicating, disturbance handling, entrepreneuring, negotiating, resource allocating—are not structured tasks. Being a manager is not like being a doctor or a lawyer or a public accountant, where one can turn to the recognized references in physiology or constitutional law or financial accounting standards.

7. How do the figurehead role and spokesperson role differ?

The figurehead role is non-verbal. Managers simply have to "be there" in order to fulfill that role. They show up a weddings, funerals, lunches, dinners, and other kinds of ceremonies. Even if they are called upon to speak, their utterances are usually pro-forma, and not as important as their mere presence. The spokesperson role requires verbal communication, either oral or written. Top managers make speeches to stakeholder groups, they write letters to relevant publications, they address stockholders, they testify at legislatures, they write the letter to stockholders in the annual report. Lower level managers attend staff meetings, they report to their superiors (orally and in writing), they fill out reports that must be sent to staff people elsewhere in the organization.

8. What are the implications of the way the author describes the entrepreneur?

Mintzberg's description of the entrepreneur has two components, having to do with the projects he/she develops. The first is that the development projects "emerge as a series of small decisions and actions sequenced over time." The second is that entrepreneurs sponsor many (up to 50 in one instance) projects, at various stages of development, at one time.

The implications of this, which will be explored in greater depth in the reading by Wrapp and various readings by Quinn, are that effective managers shouldn't be looking for "home runs." Strategies for the organization will develop over time as the product of many small, seemingly unrelated, efforts by its members. The manager is in the unique position of being able to appreciate all these streams of action, of being able to integrate them. Another implication is related to innovation. Research on innovation has highlighted its "probabilistic" nature, i.e., it takes many attempts to get a few winners. Mintzberg's description of the entrepreneur role jibes with this; effective managers will juggle many projects at once, in the hopes that a small number of them will succeed.

9. Which description of the manager-as-symphony-conductor do you think is more accurate— Drucker's or Sayles's? Which should be the more accurate one?

This question is intended to stimulate discussion. Many students will want to identify with Drucker's description. It fits nicely with the "Commander Model" of management that is fed by the standard textbooks. In this description, the manager is fully in control, able to coordinate the efforts of disparate organizational members. Not only this, but the manager is the creative force, composer as well as conductor.

Sayles's view is more prosaic. True, the manager is still in charge, but in his metaphor, has descended from Olympus. This manager must handle many disturbances and demands from stakeholders. Employees may be unmotivated, equipment may malfunction, customers may become unruly, the board of directors may insist on irrational changes in strategy, the economic environment may become hostile, etc. The manager is not in control nearly as much in this analogy. That is why this one is probably a little closer to the truth.

Wrapp, "Good Managers Don't Make Policy Decisions"

Summary of Reading

The author has identified five skills or talents which seem especially significant in distinguishing effective executives.

Keeping well informed

Successful executives have a special talent for keeping well informed about a wide range of operating decisions being made at different levels in the company. Superficially, they seem to fall into the trap of being lost in operating detail and making too many decisions. But they know that keeping well informed is the only way of avoiding the sterility (and excessive abstraction) caused by isolation. Boulding is quoted about how hierarchy is an information filter "with little wastebaskets all along the way."

Focusing time and energy

Effective executives know how to save their energy and hours for those few particular issues, decisions, or problems to which they have to give their particular attention. Recognizing that they can bring their special talents to bear on only a limited number of matters, they choose those which will have the greatest long-term effect. "Under ordinary circumstances he will limit himself to three or four major objectives during any single period of sustained activity."

Playing the power game

"The . . . notion that the 'prime mover' continually creates and forces through new programs, like a powerful majority leader in a liberal Congress, is in my opinion very misleading." Successful executives recognize the firm's power structure. Any proposal will elicit responses ranging from great support to outright opposition. In the middle of the response range there will be several aspects of the proposal to which most people are indifferent. These are corridors of comparative indifference. "He seldom challenges when a corridor is blocked, preferring to pause until it has opened up."

Effective executives also rely on trial balloons, floated by others. They gauge the reaction to these balloons, allowing them "to make a better assessment of how to limit the emasculation of the various proposals." There are few proposals that meet with support from everywhere. "The emergence of strong support in certain quarters is almost sure to evoke strong opposition in others."

A sense of timing is crucial for effective executives. Goals at a given point in time are hazy. The timetable, also hazy, suggests that some goals may be accomplished earlier than others. How to reach these goals is haziest of all. The power blocks within the firm make decisions along the way, allowing executives to plot the corridors of comparative indifference. They take action accordingly.

15

The art of imprecision

Successful executives know how to satisfy their organizations that they have a sense of direction without ever publicly committing to any specific objectives. The main reason for this is that they find it "impossible to set down specific objectives which will be relevant for any reasonable period into the future." Greater specificity makes it more difficult to shift when needed.

It is impossible to state objectives clearly enough so that they are understood by everyone. "Objectives get communicated only over time by a consistency or pattern in operating decisions. Such decisions are more meaningful than words." Subordinates are actually better off with less precise objectives, since precision narrows their scope of operation.

The effective executive wants to avoid policy straitjackets. More time may be spent arbitrating policy disputes than moving the company forward. Good policies "evolve over time from an indescribable mix of operating decisions." MBO is good for lower levels, but unworkable at higher levels.

Detailed objectives must be communicated to the organization in small doses. But too detailed a spelling out of objectives may only complicate the task of reaching them, by allowing the opposition an opportunity to organize its defenses.

Muddling with a purpose

It is futile to try to push total packages through the organization. It is better to get partial programs and modest progress toward goals. Effective executives piece together parts of various proposals into programs that move part of the way toward their objectives. This process requires wide ranging interests and the ability to see how things interrelate, not intellectual brilliance.

If the organization is solid, "it will be difficult for the manager to come up with an idea which no one in the company has ever thought of before. His most significant contribution may be that he can see relationships which no one else has seen."

Contrasting pictures

The typical metaphor used for executives pictures them as great thinkers who sit at their desks drafting master blueprints for their companies. Wrapp has a different metaphor. His manager sits in a stream; operating problems float by. The manager quickly examines each one. He/she keeps the good ones in his/her pocket. After he/she's collected a few, he/she begins to see ways in which they interrelate, how they might move the organization toward its objectives, and how they might be perceived by the power structure in the organization.

Conclusion

1. Keep open many pipelines of information.

2. Concentrate on a limited number of significant issues.

3. Identify the corridors of comparative indifference.

4. Give the organization a sense of direction with open-ended objectives.

5. Spot opportunities and relationships in the stream of operating problems and decisions.

<u>Discussion Questions</u>

1. The author says that it is a mistake for top managers to avoid involvement with operating problems. What is your opinion on this?

This question is intended to stimulate discussion. Some students will disagree with Wrapp on this point. They will side with the mainstream view that says that top managers should be concerned with the "big picture," and should never be involved with operating details and decisions. They may even cite the many examples of owners of small companies who were unable to delegate decision making, and got bogged down in minor decisions, allowing their companies to decline.

Other students will agree with Wrapp. Top managers are like anybody else—they need concrete experiences from which to build their mental models. Finding the right balance of "big picture" thinking and involvement in operating detail will facilitate this process. This idea is similar to what Peters and Waterman mention in *In Search of Excellence*, which is that excellent firms are characterized by "hands on" management.

2. *What do you think of Boulding's comment that "the purpose of a hierarchy is to prevent information from reaching higher layers?"*

This question is designed to stimulate discussion. Clearly, hierarchy has its place. Many efficient and effective large firms have many layers of hierarchy. But there can be no doubt that information is filtered out as it moves up the hierarchy. This is virtually inevitable. That's why it's so important that effective managers maintain networks of information that circumvent the official hierarchy. This same idea is what is driving the movement toward flatter structures.

3. *Can a manager limit him/herself to three or four major objectives during any single period of sustained activity? Should he/she?*

Of course there is no definitive answer to the first part of this question. Many pressures impinge upon managers. Most would probably find it difficult to be limited to three or four major objectives. But there seems to be some evidence that it pays to try to do this. Part of the reason is that managers don't dissipate their energy. A more significant reason is that the rest of the organization will have an easier time focusing on what is needed to achieve the objectives.

Bear in mind that Wrapp is not advocating that organizations and managers do *only* three or four things. They have to do *many* things, but these things should be directed toward the achievement of a limited number (3 or 4) of objectives.

4. *Why should a manager want to transmit his know-how "short of giving orders?"*

This concept has been well substantiated in the literature on the exercise of power. Since power is a reciprocal relationship (you have only as much power as others are willing to concede to you), it is almost always better to exercise that power discretely. Naked use of power seems to result in a subtle (and sometimes not-so-subtle) loss of it. Another reason why Wrapp's suggestion is sensible is that allowing your power to be exercised for you by others empowers them, which is usually a good thing. When many people in the organization feel that they have control, research has shown an increase in organizational effectiveness.

5. *What are "corridors of comparative indifference?"*

Students often have a difficult time grasping this idiosyncratic concept of Wrapp's, but it is a useful idea. He argues that for any given proposal, it is possible, for an executive who is sensitive to the power structure, to plot the sentiments of the various "interest groups." Some parts of the proposal will be repugnant to some groups, other parts will be objectionable to other groups. But some aspects (however narrow) of the proposal will be neutral for all the groups. Compared to the parts they don't like, the interest groups will be indifferent to these neutral elements.

These are "corridors" in the mental plot drawn by the executive, corridors of comparative indifference. If you can think of the "territory" bounded by the proposal as a minefield, riddled with objections, the corridor of indifference is a lane where the interest groups have forgotten to bury mines. The executive can walk through this part of the minefield in comparative safety. Executives can use these neutral parts, along with the neutral parts from other proposals, to gradually craft a program that moves the organization toward its objectives.

6. Why is it good for managers to have only "hazy" notions of their objectives, timetables, and available means?

Some students will take exception to the very question. They will argue that it is *not* good for managers to be so hazy about these things. Managers should be clear about objectives, at the very least. And since timetables are such an important part of objectives, those should be clear, too. Lastly, strategic managers should make it their business to know what means are available to the organization for implementation.

Wrapp's assertion is reflective of the reality that exists in most firms. Most effective executives have a good *general* idea of what they want the firm to accomplish, but would rather not be too specific about it—too many things can change. It's best to be generally clear about overall desires and a little less specific, until the time is right, about detailed objectives. Also, the executive doesn't know when that time will be right, so a detailed timetable may simply not be possible. Lastly, it takes time for the executive to assess all the key individuals and groups in the organization. Better to wait until the corridors of comparative indifference become clearly delineated; otherwise, good ideas may be blocked or stalled.

7. Why is it a good idea for a manager to avoid public commitment to a specific set of objectives?

Some students will respond that it is a bad idea for managers to avoid public commitment. Political leaders are often criticized for this. And there certainly *are* times when it is appropriate for managers to publicly commit to objectives. This may be particularly true during times of crisis, when the organization needs firm direction. It may also be true for large bureaucracies in stable environments.

But Wrapp list several reasons for his assertion:

a. it is impossible to set down specific objectives that will be relevant for any reasonable period into the future

b. there are many threats facing the firm, making precise direction difficult to ascertain

c. it is impossible to state objectives clearly enough so that they will be understood by everyone

d. objectives are better if they are communicated over time in the pattern of operating decisions

e. precise objectives limit the range of actions available to the people subject to them.

8. Why should managers find it "impossible" to set down specific objectives which will be relevant for any reasonable period into the future?

This assertion by Wrapp is probably a little too strong. Some managers of some firms may find it possible to specify objectives into a reasonable period into the future. This would be true for firms facing stable environments. But for firms operating in dynamic environments, the assertion

18

may well be true. Things change so quickly that what once seemed reasonable now seems not so reasonable. The setting of overly specific objectives is what often gets such firms in trouble. Rather than adapting to the changing conditions, firms sometimes become wedded to their plans, which are now irrelevant. It would be far better under such circumstances to be less precise and more adaptable.

9. Why is it that "objectives get communicated only over time by a consistency or pattern in operating decisions?"

This is because, as Wrapp puts it, "such decisions are more meaningful than words." It's one thing to say that you're going to do something, it's quite another to actually do it. What the firm *actually does* communicates a great deal to its members. Actual decisions and actions indicate those things to which the organization is truly committed. Members are usually skilled at interpreting the meaning of these actions and decisions. So, over time, they become aware of what the firm's true objectives are.

10. What do you think of the author's contention that well-defined policies are not typical of well-managed companies?

This question is meant to provoke controversy and discussion. Some students will be skeptical of this assertion. They will insist that policies must be clear and well-defined. They will be sure that this clarity is true for all well-managed companies.

But Wrapp offers some interesting reasons for why his assertion might be true. First, detailed policies often give rise to time-consuming arbitration of disputes which distract the company from moving forward. Second, detailed statements of policy are often a sign of atrophy. Lastly, the policies of well-managed companies "are those which evolve over time from an indescribable mix of operating decisions. From any single operating decision might have come a very minor dimension of the policy as the organization understands it; from a series of decisions comes a pattern of guidelines for various levels of the organization."

11. Does the notion that policies "evolve over time from an indescribable mix of operating decisions" relate to any previous readings?

This relates directly to Mintzberg's reading in Chapter 1, "Five Ps for Strategy." There, Mintzberg proposed that strategy could be defined as a pattern in a stream of action over time. These two notions are very similar. In each case, the things to which the firm is truly committed emerge. Observers, including most organizational members, need not rely on statements of intention or professed desire. They can see for themselves where the firm has placed its resources, which markets it has sought, which policies it has found are truly needed.

12. Why might management by objectives be unworkable at top levels of organizations?

MBO can be a very useful tool for motivating lower-level employees, since the deadlines can prod people toward useful behaviors. The specificity of the stated objectives also helps these people, and their supervisors, tell if the goals have been achieved. These two characteristics have a negative effect at higher levels of the organization.

Top managers need flexibility in timing when they will state their objectives. Some objectives need to be stated only at the exactly proper time. MBO reduces, sometimes even removes, this flexibility, because it forces managers either to state all their objectives up front, or to have to explain why particular objectives, not mentioned earlier, are not being sought. The precise statement of objectives required by MBO also places the manager in all the straitjackets mentioned by Wrapp in the reading.

13. What do you think of the author's contention that top management should not be a comprehensive, systematic, logical, well-programmed science?

Some students will dislike this assertion. They would like to think that management could, and should, be a science. At the very least, they would like it to be logical. The problem is, as the literature has shown quite well, that only a small percentage of management decisions are well-structured. Well-structured problems <u>do</u> lend themselves to programmed decision making. But the great majority of management decisions are unstructured, and require political and incremental processes.

Wrapp's assertion is to some extent an echo of what Mintzberg says in his reading in this chapter: management is not, and likely never will be, a science or a profession. But Wrapp's point goes beyond that. He is saying that it is futile to try to push entire programs through the organization, as if they were new production schedules. Executives must be willing to accept a large number of partial solutions, achieving modest success with each one, thereby piecing together a comprehensive program. In other words, most executive decisions call for incrementalism, not programming.

14. What do you think of the author's contention that top management does not require intellectual brilliance or unusual creativity?

Intellectual brilliance and unusual creativity are inborn traits. One cannot learn to be brilliant. One can perhaps learn to increase one's creativity, but one is not likely to learn to be "unusually creative." If management required these traits, the vast majority of the population, and certainly a large percentage of typical students, would be discouraged about becoming managers. And there would be little point to teaching management, except to the gifted. The implications of Wrapp's assertion is that anyone can become a good manager. The five skills he mentions in the reading are all "learnable." The fifth one, muddling with a purpose, is enhanced by having wide ranging interests and by constantly looking for ways to combine seemingly disparate proposals. These are things that any reasonably intelligent person can learn how to do.

15. What are the implications of a top manager's being "skilled as an analyst, but even more talented as a conceptualizer?"

Management education tends to emphasize the analytical. This is mostly because analytical skills, which involve breaking down the whole into its parts, are easy to teach. The problem is that Wrapp and others are saying that management is not primarily an analytical activity. It is mostly the *piecing together of parts* into a coherent whole, or what Wrapp calls conceptualizing. If that is true, and indications are that it is, then we are teaching the wrong things, or, at least, not enough of the right things.

16. Which view of management should hold: "drafting master blueprints" or "spotting opportunities and relationships in the stream of operating problems and decisions?"

This question is intended to stimulate discussion. Some people will advocate the "blueprint" metaphor, for two reasons. First, it fits well with the "Commander Model" idea of strategic management. Second, it fits well with the idea that management is mostly analysis and planning.

Other people will buy into the "stream" metaphor. It fits better with the notion that strategic management is a synthesis-oriented activity, the putting together of pieces into a whole. It is also consistent with the idea that a primary responsibility of top management is to guide the overall organizational and political process in a subtle, incremental, way, and not by the handing down of full-blown (and probably overly-specific) plans from above.

Prahalad and Hamel, "Strategic Intent"

Summary of Reading

Regaining competitiveness means rethinking basic strategic concepts. Western perspective is fundamentally different from that of the new global competitors. They started with excessive ambition and then fostered, and sustained, an obsession with winning global leadership. "We term this obsession 'strategic intent.'"

Strategic intent envisions a desired leadership position, complete with criteria for charting progress. It also encompasses an active management process that includes focusing on winning, motivating by communicating the value of the target, encouraging team and individual contributions, sustaining enthusiasm, and using strategic intent to guide resource allocation.

Strategic intent captures the essence of winning. It is stable over time, lengthening the organization's attention span but ensuring short term consistency. It sets a target that deserves personal effort and commitment. American managers talk in term of shareholder wealth. Firms guided by strategic intent talk in terms of global market leadership. The latter—to beat or stay the best—is more motivational.

Global leadership will emerge neither from planning nor by accident. Nor will it come from "Silicon Valley" type innovation using tools like skunkworks. A management that waits for entrepreneurial successes from below adds little value.

By contrast, strategic intent is clear about ends but creative about means. Creativity is unbridled but not uncorraled. Top management provides the criterion for testing actions, and middle management must keep their departments heading in the direction specified by the strategic intent.

Strategic intent implies sizable stretch. Traditional strategic prescribes a fit between capabilities and opportunities. Strategic intent implies an "extreme misfit." Top management challenges the organization to close the gap by systematically building new advantages.

"Strategic intent is like a marathon run in 400 meter sprints." No one knows the terrain at mile 26, so management focuses the organization on the terrain in the next 400 meters. This might be done with a series of corporate challenges as a way to create focal points for employees' attention in the near to medium term. Again, management is specific about ends but less prescriptive about means.

Challenges succeed only when people in the organization understand them and see their implications for their own jobs. Some of the things top management can do:

Create a sense of urgency

Develop a competitor focus at every level through widespread use of competitive intelligence

Provide employees with the skills they need to work effectively

Give the organization time to digest one challenge before launching another

Establish clear milestones and review mechanisms to track progress and ensure motivation

Managers should practice "reciprocal responsibility," sharing pain and gain with their employees. This is crucial because competitiveness ultimately depends on the pace at which the firm embeds new advantages deep within itself. Less important is the stock of advantages at any given moment. The scorecard must be expanded beyond the usual of low costs and price premiums.

Few competitive advantages are long lasting, and the first organization to develop one gains a greater advantage. "The essence of strategy lies in creating tomorrow's competitive advantages faster than competitors mimic the ones you possess today . . . . An organization's capacity to improve existing skills and learn new ones is the most defensible competitive advantage of all."

To win against better-resourced competitors, managers must fundamentally change the game in ways that disadvantage stronger rivals. The goal is competitive innovation, not imitation. Four approaches to competitive innovation have been popular:

Building layers of advantage

Searching for loose bricks

Changing the terms of engagement

Competing through collaboration

A wider portfolio of advantages leads to less risk. Global brands are more defensible advantages than are lower costs.

Several Western practices lead to lower advantage levels. "Fast-tracking" of managers creates over-reliance on numbers for management, since managers rarely develop deep business knowledge and must therefore rely on "numbers." Short-term assignments lead either to goals that fail to get commitment or to unrealistically short time frames. "Aiming to be number one in a business is the essence of strategic intent; but imposing a three- to four-year horizon on that effort simply invites disaster." The familiar dichotomy between strategy formulation and implementation "undermines competitiveness by fostering an elitist view of management that tends to disenfranchise most of the organization."

Two other reasons for elitist management are (1) successful managers want to perpetuate myths about themselves and (2) top managers don't want to admit that they don't have all the answers when a crisis looms. The latter—a widely perceived threat that no one talks about— creates more anxiety than a clearly defined threat that becomes the focal point for organizational problem-solving. "That is one reason honesty and humility on the part of top management may be the first prerequisite of revitalization. Another reason is the need to make participation more than a buzzword."

Administrative innovations require more than new structures. They require genuine two-way communication. "Japanese companies win . . . because they have developed ways to harness the 'wisdom of the anthill.'" Astronauts get the glory, but the real intelligence behind the mission is firmly on the ground.

"Developing faith in the organization's ability to deliver on tough goals, motivating it to do so, focusing its attention long enough to internalize new capabilities—this is the real challenge for top management. Only by rising to this challenge will senior managers gain the courage they need to commit themselves and their companies to global leadership."

Discussion Questions

1. *What is your reaction to the authors' definition of strategic intent?*

Students may be positively impressed by the apparent simplicity of strategic intent— excessive ambition and an obsession with winning global leadership. Strategic intent envisions a desired leadership position, complete with criteria for charting progress. This simplicity and vision base are some of the reasons this concept is so appealing. However, its simplicity does not imply that strategic intent is easy. It also encompasses an active management process that includes focusing on winning, motivating by communicating the value of the target, encouraging team and individual contributions, sustaining enthusiasm, and using strategic intent to guide resource allocation. It is vital to get students to realize the great difficulty (and hence the great value) of strategic intent.

2. What is the significance of strategic intent's being "stable over time?"

As Mintzberg will point out in later readings, strategy is a force for stability—it *implies* stability. Strategy is a "pattern in a stream of action over time." The coherence needed to create a pattern is provided by some stability. Strategic intent provides long-term stability (and hence patterning) through its overall vision and obsession with global dominance. It provides short-term stability by helping to guide actions, like resource allocations, "in the moment."

3. What is your reaction to the authors' criticism of the "Silicon Valley" approach to innovation?

Students may have a hard time with the authors on this one. Theirs is a stinging criticism. The authors say that most of the cherished tools of American management—pay-for-performance schemes, quality circles, and especially skunkworks and intrapreneurship—are bankrupt. They assert that managers who wait for entrepreneurial successes from below are "non value adding." These are probably valid criticisms, but it should be interesting to see how students react to them. If their faith in some of what they have been taught in other courses is shaken, that is probably a good (albeit upsetting) thing.

4. What is the significance of strategic intent's being "unbridled but not uncorraled?"

The authors are, in essence, arguing for "umbrella strategy," to use Mintzberg's term from Chapter 1—set up a motivating and challenging target and let the details of the strategy emerge. The target is the corral, and letting the details emerge is the unbridled aspect.

5. The authors say that strategy should be an "extreme misfit" between resources and opportunities. What do you think?

One of the most common complaints in organizations is the lack of resources. So it seems odd that Prahalad and Hamel should be arguing *in favor* of resource constraints. Some students may pick up on the reason—the resource shortage is designed to be a spur to creativity. Firms that have lots of resources typically let their creativity atrophy. There is no motivation to change anything. So rival firms pass them by. Strategic intent gets around this problem, in theory, by setting up a brass ring that is always out of reach of the company. In striving to grasp it anyway, its members are *forced* to be creative.

6. What is your reaction to the metaphor of strategic intent being like a "marathon run in 400 meter sprints?"

Even students who are not into sports should recognize the value of this metaphor. Marathons are sufficiently long races that they *are* analogous to the "never ending journey" of business. But the authors make some changes to adjust for the inevitable breakdown of the analogy. For example, in most marathons, the runners have scouted the course and know the terrain. But in business, no one knows what the future will bring. So cutting the race up into smaller pieces where people *can* know what to expect is a good idea. Another breakdown: most marathon runners pace themselves for the course. But in business, a company that "coasts" will lose enough in the short distances to end up losing the whole race. So the "runners" must sprint each of the increments.

7. What do you think of the list of things top management can do to engage the entire organization?

The list—(1) create a sense of urgency; (2) develop a competitor focus at every level through widespread use of competitive intelligence; (3) provide employees with the skills they need to work effectively; (4) give the organization time to digest one challenge before launching another; and (5) establish clear milestones and review mechanisms to track progress and ensure motivation—is a good one. The overall impression is one of *focused action*—keep moving forward with the needed skills and capacity. The only exception is number four, giving the organization time to digest challenges. People who are sprinting through a marathon need to catch their breath a little bit.

8. The authors think that "reciprocal responsibility" is crucial to competitiveness. Why do they say that, and what is your reaction to their argument?

The rank-and-file members of an organization must feel that they are being fairly treated, otherwise they will not be sufficiently motivated. If they are not motivated, they will not do the one thing that is a sustainable advantage—keeping up the pace of adding advantages to their operations. Since most students are unlikely to see themselves in the position of CEO anytime soon, they are likely to understand and agree with the authors here. There may be a few who see management as a ticket to personal fortune, as opposed to organizational achievement, and those may not like the idea of reciprocal responsibility.

9. What do the authors say is the "essence of strategy?" What are the implications of their point?

Few competitive advantages are long lasting, and the first organization to develop one gains a greater advantage. "The essence of strategy lies in creating tomorrow's competitive advantages faster than competitors mimic the ones you possess today . . . . An organization's capacity to improve existing skills and learn new ones is the most defensible competitive advantage of all." The implications are clear—the organization's members must constantly be learning new things and new ways of doing things. Whatever you are currently doing can ultimately be copied, so you have to "stay ahead of the curve" by creating new things that force your rivals to copy you even more, and so on. This is difficult and requires a lot of effort by everyone, which is another aspect of the "reciprocal responsibility" mentioned in the previous question.

10. What do the authors say is necessary for winning against stronger competitors? What is your reaction to their argument?

To win against better-resourced competitors, managers must fundamentally change the game in ways that disadvantage stronger rivals. The goal is competitive *innovation*, not imitation. Four approaches to competitive innovation have been popular: building layers of advantage; searching for loose bricks (finding "weak spots" in rivals' strategies); changing the terms of engagement (inventing "new rules" for the competitive dynamics of the industry); and competing through collaboration (forming strategic alliances, both for gaining short-term advantage and long-term learning). Students are likely to be confused by this whole line of thinking by Prahalad and Hamel. They can easily understand the idea of playing a game, but may not realize that "industry games" don't have independent rule-makers. The organizations involved may change the "rules" whenever they wish. The problem is that only the global leaders actually *do* change the rules.

11. What are the many points of the authors' critique of Western management practices? What do you think of their critique?

Several Western practices lead to lower advantage levels. "Fast-tracking" of managers creates over-reliance on numbers for management, since managers rarely develop deep business knowledge and must therefore rely on "numbers." Short-term assignments lead either to goals that fail to get commitment or to unrealistically short time frames. The familiar dichotomy between strategy formulation and implementation undermines competitiveness by fostering an elitist view of management. Managerial elitism is also fostered by the perpetuation of myths about managers and unwillingness to admit not having all the answers.

Students who have been socialized in a business program may have a hard time with these ideas. They want to believe that managers can "manage by the numbers." They may believe that short-term assignments are how one should get ahead. They may believe in the action orientation of short time frames. They may also aspire to being powerful managers who want to share in the mythology. They may not even believe that most managers *don't* have all the answers. Yet most experienced people would agree that the picture painted by the authors is in sharp focus.

12. What are the implications of "tapping the wisdom of the ant hill?" What do you think of this metaphor?

Most students will not like this metaphor very much, but it is actually a pretty good one. Much research on ants (as well as termites and honeybees) has shown that relatively "dumb" individuals, working together in a "hive mentality;" will be able to accomplish remarkable things. Since people are much more intelligent than insects, the potential for "human hives" (or ant colonies) is enormous. In other words, if many "dumb" individuals acting together can do so much, how much more could many *intelligent* creatures do?

Andrews, "The Concept of Corporate Strategy"

Summary of Reading

I. THE STRATEGY CONCEPT

What strategy is

Pattern of decisions:

> *determines and reveals* objectives, purposes, goals

> *produces* the principal policies and plans for goal achievement

> *defines* the range of business the company is to pursue, the kind of economic or human organization it is or intends to be, and the nature of the economic and noneconomic contribution it intends to make to its shareholders, employees, customers, and communities.

Strategic decisions cover long periods of time and commit large amounts of resources. The pattern defines the central character of the company, its image, and its position in its industry and markets. The pattern will allow the specification of action plans and resource allocations.

Parts of the pattern will rarely change, parts will change a lot. Company character is likely to persist. A strategy must be set of integrated goals and policies "that crystallizes from the formless reality of a company's environment a set of problems an organization can seize upon and solve."

Summary statement of strategy

What is contained in a summary statement of strategy:

> product line or services, offered or planned

> markets and segments served, present and planned

> distribution channels

> financing methods

> profit objectives

> statement of the relative emphasis on safety versus return
> policy in central functions

>> marketing
>> manufacturing
>> procurement
>> R&D
>> labor relations
>> personnel

> statements about organizational size, form, and climate

26

Formulation of strategy

Corporate strategy is an organizational process that may be analytically divided into formulation and implementation.

Formulation has several subactivities. First is what the firm *might* do, i.e., identifying the threats and opportunities in the environment. Second is what the firm *can* do, i.e., appraising the firm's strengths and weaknesses. Third is what the firm *wants* to do, i.e., considering the personal values of the top management. Lastly, there is what the firm *should* do, i.e., the ethical aspects of strategizing.

Implementation of strategy

Implementation subactivities are primarily administrative. The first is the design of an appropriate organizational structure. The second is the directing of organizational processes and systems, e.g., performance measurement, motivation, control, recruitment, and development. Lastly, there is the role of personal leadership.

II. RELATING OPPORTUNITIES TO RESOURCES

The nature of a company's environment

Technology: the fastest-changing and most far-reaching element

Ecology: trends in the protection of the physical environment have become much more important

Economics: generally one of the better-monitored areas

Industry: risks are often blurred by familiarity and uncritical acceptance of the status quo

Society: demographic trends, cultural trends, changes in attitudes

Politics: East-West relations, North-South relations, and business/government relations

Identifying corporate competence and resources

To carry out a strategy, organizations must know their strengths and weaknesses. This is actually more difficult than environmental analysis, because of subjectivity, lack of confidence, and unwillingness to face reality.
Sources of capabilities:

experience in making and marketing a product line, or providing a service

the developing strengths and weaknesses of the individuals in the firm

the degree to which individual capability is effectively applied to the common task

the quality of the coordination of individual and group effort

Identifying strengths: The distinctive competence of an organization is more than what it can do; it is what it can do particularly well. Start by defining the functions served by the firm. Examine also the skills that underlie whatever success has been achieved; for example:

new product development

marketing services

distribution methods

new quality-price combinations

creative merchandising

Matching opportunity and competence: This is what establishes a company's economic mission and its position in the environment. Aside from distinctive competence, the principal resources found in any organization are money and people—technical and managerial. "At an advanced stage of economic development, money seems less a problem than technical competence, and the latter less critical than managerial ability."

Uniqueness of strategy: "In each company, the way in which distinctive competence, organizational resources, and organizational values are combined is or should be unique."

Discussion Questions

1. How does the definition of strategy given here relate to those given in other readings?

Andrews's definition of strategy relates well to three of the five definitions Mintzberg gives in his Chapter 1 reading "Five Ps for Strategy." Given the emphasis placed, in Andrews's reading, on deliberation and formulation, the definition relates strongly to strategy as plan—a consciously intended course of action, made in advance of that action, and developed purposefully. Andrews prescribes a systematic look at external threats and opportunities and internal strengths and weaknesses, taking into account the values of top management and the firm's ethical responsibilities. He also encourages detailed "summary statements" of strategy (i.e., plans).

But Andrews also uses the word "pattern" quite often in his definition and discussion. He seems to acknowledge that a series of resource allocation decisions speaks louder than the words of a document. This is clearly related to Mintzberg's "strategy as pattern."

Andrews goes on to say that the pattern "defines the central character" of the company. He talks about how this will change only slowly, and he gives examples such as commitments to quality or high technology or good labor relations. These are all related to the concept of "strategy as perspective."

Lastly, he says that the pattern defines "the position [the company] will occupy in its industry and markets." In other words, his definition also relates to "strategy as position."

2. What does Andrews mean when he says that we should not "separate goals from the policies designed to achieve those goals?"

He means that you should not be doing something (a policy) unless you can say why you are doing it (an objective). Otherwise it is difficult for the organization to make a meaningful contribution. He puts it eloquently:

"It is the interrelationship of a set of goals and policies that crystallizes from the formless reality of a company's environment a set of problems an organization can seize upon and solve."

3. How can it be said that "deciding what strategy should be may be approached as a rational undertaking?"

This is a pure value judgment by Andrews, one with which many, particularly Mintzberg, would disagree. What he is saying is that he thinks it is possible to sit down and rationally decide what

28

strategy *should* be. One should, he says, examine threats, opportunities, weaknesses, strengths, managerial values, and social responsibility. One should then match opportunity and competence and formulate a unique strategy.

4. Andrews says that strategy formulation is a four-way balance among what a firm might do, can do, want to do, and should do. What do you think of this idea?

Most students will agree with this statement. It is really nothing more than Andrews's idea that one should examine threats and opportunities (might do), weaknesses and strengths (can do), managerial values (wants to do), and social responsibility (should do). Some students may disagree with the very logical, almost cookbook quality of the model.

5. In what sense can it be said that structure follows strategy, but that strategy also follows structure?

Andrews calls the first part of this statement a "logical proposition." In other words, strategists should examine the structural requirements of any strategy and design or adjust the organizational structure accordingly. The second part of the question is "organizational reality," says Andrews. What he means is that a firm's existing structure is likely to shape its future strategy, in at least two ways. First, the structure should be well-suited for the strategy for which it was designed, so there is a bias for continuing that strategy. Second, the existing structure is one of the elements shaping the way people in the firm think, which also biases action in favor of strategies consistent with the status quo.

6. To what extent can it be said that "if purpose is determined, then the resources of a company can be mobilized to accomplish it?"

This statement is typical of the attitude of thinkers in the strategy formulation school. In their view, the most difficult thing about strategy is formulating it, i.e., determining purpose. Once you've done that, they assert, implementation (mobilization) is straightforward.

As the readings by Wrapp (in the previous chapter) argued, this is at best an oversimplification. At worst it ignores the incremental nature of forming strategy from a synthesis of the pieces floating by in the stream of action in which the firm is immersed.

Talking about the formation of purpose as an activity that *precedes* mobilization is inaccurate on its face, according to Wrapp. He talks about how the best objectives are not "formulated" in a strict sense. They "evolve over time from an indescribable mix of operating decisions." In other words, the action or mobilization occurs first, and the purpose is determined later.

7. How can it be said that if members of an organization can reach a consensus even subjectively, about the organization's core competence, then its application to identified opportunity can be estimated?

If an organization can figure out what is its core competence, it has a chance to make a contribution, to solve some problems or fill some needs. It can do this by seeking out opportunities and problems which its distinctive competence can exploit or solve. If it doesn't know what it's good at, it can make no such moves. Andrews's point is that this self-knowledge is essential; the method of attaining it is not. Even if strategists discern their organization's competence in a subjective way, that is adequate.

8. What are the implications of the statement that "the insight required to identify the essential strength justifying new ventures does not come naturally?"

Andrews is saying that a firm which is very good at something often comes to take its skill for granted. It may not even know what is the underlying strength beneath the skill. The implication of this is that strategists must devise ways to penetrate that barrier of familiarity. Andrews offers only the "recognition of the need for analysis." Others have offered things like the Devil's Advocate and dialectical inquiry techniques, or the notion of counterbalanced prescriptions.

9. What do you think of the author's assertion that "money seems less a problem than technical competence, and the latter (is) less critical than managerial ability?"

This question is designed to stimulate discussion and to open the eyes of students to an interesting point made by Andrews. Most students assume that the biggest resource constraint facing organizations is financial. They further assume that managerial and technical talent is about balanced in importance. Andrews argues that the most important resource constraint is management talent. Technical talent is the second most important, and money is last in importance. As evidence he points to the many instances of diversification where the money to diversify was there, but the talent to manage the new parts of the company was not. When one reviews the points made in the previous chapter, about the skills needed by strategic managers, one realizes just how rare they are.

Rumelt, "Evaluating Business Strategy"

Summary of Reading

When a firm is either formulating or adjusting strategy, strategy evaluation is needed. The latter is an attempt to appraise the fundamental factors and trends that govern organizational success.

The challenge of evaluation

Strategy evaluation must answer three questions:

1. Are the objectives of the business appropriate?

2. Are the major policies and plans appropriate?

3. Do the results obtained to date confirm or refute critical assumptions on which the strategy rests?

These are difficult questions; insight and a reasonable store of situation-based knowledge are required. It complicates things that strategy is unique for each firm. Also, strategy is concerned with the selection of goals and purposes, which are easier to set than to evaluate (partly because people are better trained in problem solving than in problem structuring). Lastly, there are problems of conflict, usually concerning who is competent to evaluate strategy.

The principles of strategy evaluation

Strategy: "a set of objectives, policies, and plans that, taken together, define the scope of the enterprise and its approach to survival and success. Alternatively, we could say that the particular policies, plans, and objectives of a business express its strategy for coping with a complex competitive environment."

Strategies must be submitted to tests, which will fall into one of four categories:

Consistency: The strategy must not present mutually inconsistent goals and policies.

30

Consonance: The strategy must represent an adaptive response to the external environment and to the critical changes occurring within it.

Advantage: The strategy must provide for the creation and/or maintenance of a competitive advantage in the selected area of activity.

Feasibility: The strategy must neither overtax available resources nor create unsolvable subproblems.

Consistency

This may be a problem if the strategy has evolved or if a formulated strategy contains compromises. Consistency is needed to provide coherence to organizational action. Here are three indicators of strategic inconsistency:

Conflicts persist despite changes in personnel.

Success for one department means, or is interpreted to mean, failure for another department.

Operating problems continue to be referred upwards (despite attempts to delegate) for *policy* resolution.

There must also be consistency between objectives and top management values.

Consonance

The basic mission or scope of the firm must match its environment over time; this is called *generic strategy*. Critical threats from without usually threaten an entire group of firms. The key to evaluating consonance is understanding why the business exists at all, and how it assumed its current pattern.

Advantage

Competitive strategy focuses on the differences among firms rather than their common missions. It is the art of creating or exploiting those advantages that are most telling, enduring, and most difficult to duplicate.

Competitive advantage can normally be traced to one of three roots: (1) superior resources; (2) superior skills; or (3) superior position. The first two are obvious. The third comes from intelligent arrangement of resources, to enhance their combined effectiveness.

Positional advantage tends to be self-sustaining and defensible. That means that it (1) returns enough value to warrant its continued maintenance, and (2) would be too costly to capture, so rivals are deterred from attacks on the core of the business.

The two most common manifestations of positional advantage come from size and scale. Some type of uniqueness is a prerequisite. Successful trade names are another type of positional advantage. Here are some other sources:

Raw material sources

Geographical location

Service leadership or experience

Full-line production capability

Good reputation

Feasibility

Can the strategy be attempted within the physical, human, and financial resources available? Financial resources are the most easily quantified and are normally the first limitation against which strategy is tested. The less quantifiable but actually more rigid limitation on strategic choice is that imposed by the individual and organizational capabilities that are available.

Assessing capability is helped by answering these three questions:

Has the organization demonstrated that it possesses the problem-solving abilities and/or special competencies required by the strategy?

Has the organization demonstrated the degree of coordinative and integrative skill necessary to carry out the strategy?

Does the strategy challenge and motivate key personnel and is it acceptable to those who must lend their support?

Conclusions

The political structures of firms make strategy evaluation an implicit process that is difficult to separate from planning, reporting, control, and reward systems. It is less an intellectual task, more a continual organizational process:

"Ultimately, a firm's ability to maintain its competitive position in a world of rivalry and change may be best served by managers who can maintain a dual view of strategy and strategy evaluation—they must be willing and able to perceive the strategy within the welter of daily activity *and* to build and maintain structures and systems that make strategic factors the object of current activity."

Discussion Questions

1. What does the author say is the whole point of strategy? What is your assessment of this statement?

He says that "the critical factors determining the quality of results are often not directly observable or simply measured, and that by the time strategic opportunities or threats do directly affect operating results, it may well be too late for an effective response." He continues, saying that strategy evaluation should appraise "those more fundamental factors and trends that govern success in the chosen field of endeavor." In other words, in Rumelt's view, strategy evaluation should be very much forward-looking.

Students will react to this in various ways. It's difficult to disagree with the statement. But it is certainly possible to wonder about how one goes about fulfilling Rumelt's prescription. No one has a crystal ball to examine the future. Recall, too, that in an earlier reading Quinn pointed out that strategy deals not only with the unpredictable, but with the unknowable. This makes forward-looking strategy evaluation difficult.

2. What are the implications of strategy evaluation's needing "a reasonable store of situation-based knowledge and more than the usual degree of insight?"

The first of these points implies that strategy evaluation must be done by people intimately familiar with the situation being evaluated. It is not an abstract analytical activity that can be done by anyone, e.g., a consultant. It must be done by people who are so familiar with the business, and all the conditions surrounding it, that they can make an informed evaluation. The second point implies that the evaluators must nevertheless be able to detach themselves from the strategy and the situation, so that they can examine it thoroughly and "see" things that might be hidden if they keep their perceptual filters on.

3. Strategy evaluation rests on situational logic. How might this be a problem, if at all?

It is a problem only if one is looking for universal solutions to strategic problems, as an outside consultant might. Universal solutions in management have been discredited for a long time. Rumelt is saying here that it is possible to strategically succeed in many ways. It is up to the well-informed strategy evaluators to have the proper "feel" for whether a given approach is appropriate for the given firm. Rumelt's thinking here is certainly consistent with Wrapp and Mintzberg, who argue that successful strategy will develop over time as highly-involved managers carefully nurture it.

4. What is the difference between problem solving and problem structuring? Do we overemphasize the former, leading to difficulties?

A problem is a condition where the decision maker is not achieving her or his desired state. Problem solving means returning to normalcy by taking action to achieve that desired state. Problem structuring means identifying the problem in the first place. It is much more difficult than problem solving.

Rumelt says that people find it easier to set goals than to evaluate them. Goal setting is a problem-solving activity—we specify the desired state we wish to achieve. Goal evaluation is a problem-structuring activity—we try to figure out which are the best goals, or whether the goals we have are good or not.

There is little question that in most business education programs, problem solving is taught better than problem structuring. Many excellent tools have been developed to facilitate problem solving. There are virtually no tools for problem structuring. In this reading, Rumelt is suggesting some problem structuring tools—his four tests. Rigorous, and successful, use of his tests would help strategists decide whether goals were adequate: Are the goals consistent? Do they confer an advantage? Are they adaptive to environmental demands? Can they be achieved given our skills and resources?

5. Is there a tendency to confuse values with objectives? If so, why does this create problems?

Rumelt makes an interesting assertion here. He argues that people confuse values (fundamental expressions of human personality) with objectives (tools for directing organizational action). There is probably no right answer to this question. Some people will agree that people get too bound up in their value systems when they are setting or evaluating objectives. Others will disagree.

If organization members *do* confuse values and objectives, then evaluating objectives becomes very difficult. They will find it difficult to be unbiased about objectives which they feel cut right to the heart of their value systems. This is similar to the point Selznick made about institutions having value and being difficult to change.

6. If we reject Rumelt's definition of strategy, what does that do to the validity of his four tests?

Rumelt's definition of strategy fits squarely into the idea of strategy as <u>plan</u>. He says that the set of objectives, policies, and plans that guide its approach to success is the strategy, or they are the expression of it. As Mintzberg pointed out in Chapter 1, this is only one way of looking at strategy. It may be defined in at least three other ways—pattern, position, and perspective.

If we reject Rumelt's definition, his four tests, with the possible exception of consistency, are still valid. Even if the strategy is mostly emergent, chances are that the strategists agreed upon the pattern because it was consonant with what the environment wanted. Or it fit the capabilities of the organization (it was feasible).

Similarly, the advantage test fits with the notion of strategy as position. Whether a firm's management chose particular strategies because of deliberate attempts to gain advantage, or things just emerged that way, is not as relevant as the existence of the advantage.

Mintzberg's ideas about deliberate and emergent strategy really deal only with intentions and realization. They do not get to soundness or "goodness" of the intentions or the realized strategy. Rumelt's four tests, by contrast, go directly to the question of whether or not a strategy (intended or realized) is a good one.

7. A key function of strategy is to provide coherence to organizational action, but how truly necessary is it to state the strategy clearly and explicitly?

This is somewhat of a trick question. Rumelt says that a clear and explicit concept of strategy "can foster a climate of tacit coordination that is more efficient than most administrative mechanisms." At first glance this seems to contradict Wrapp, who advised against explicit statements of strategy. But actually Rumelt does not advocate an explicit *statement* of strategy, only a clear and explicit *concept* of strategy. Wrapp would probably agree, saying that policies should be transmitted to organization members over time as part of the mix of operating decisions. In the organization conjured up by Wrapp, Rumelt would find his clear concept of strategy. Only it probably wouldn't be written down; it might not even be possible to easily articulate it. But members would "know" what it was; it would provide "tacit coordination."

8. What is the point of the author's discussion of values and strategy?

If one is formulating strategy, one must take managerial values into account. If one is evaluating strategy, the same is true. The strategy in either case must be consistent with management values. If it is not, it is generally the strategy that must be changed, not the values (which are usually close to immutable). Rumelt cautions, though, that strategists must be careful when making these adjustments; they must give "special attention to a firm's competitive position."

9. How is the distinction between generic and competitive strategy related to Mintzberg's five Ps of strategy from Chapter 1?

In his discussion of strategy as position, Mintzberg discussed how most uses of this concept focused on the idea of competition. This would fit with Rumelt's advantage test, which is associated with competitive strategy.

But Mintzberg also said that the view of strategy as position could be based on the achievement of any viable position, whether or not directly competitive. This fits with Rumelt's consonance test and the notion of generic strategy. As he puts it:

"The role of the evaluator in this case is to examine the basic pattern of economic relationships that characterize the business and determine whether or not sufficient value is being created to sustain the strategy."

10. How difficult is it to know "why (a) business exists at all," in order to "study the consequences of key trends and changes?"

Examined from one perspective, it is very difficult to know why a business exists at all. Those closest to a full knowledge of the business are for that very reason often unable to have an objective view of the firm. Their reasoning ability may be overcome by their emotions or other non-rational ties.

As Rumelt means it, though, knowing why a business exists at all is much more possible. He means it from a purely economic standpoint. He is arguing that if strategists can get "a good grasp of the basic economic foundation that supports and defines the business," it becomes possible to focus on the relevant economic trends and other data.

11. In discussing position, the author proposes two kinds of advantages—those related to size, and those related to uniqueness. How does this mesh with the Porter readings in the next chapter?

Positional advantage based on size is related to Porter's *Cost Leadership* strategy. This is because size has had a tendency to be associated with economies of scale, which in turn lead to lower costs. Advantage based on uniqueness is related to differentiation. Actually, differentiation *is* advantage based on uniqueness.

12. Rumelt says that individual and organizational capabilities are "more rigid limitations on strategic choice," than the more quantifiable resources. How could this be? How does this jibe with the Andrews reading?

It takes a long time to modify "individual and organizational capabilities." People have to be trained, retrained, or hired outright. Organizations have to be redesigned. Work groups have to be formed, reformed, or modified. Technology has to be transferred, and so forth.

Quantifiable resources, especially cash, are extremely flexible. There are at least four ways to get money: make a profit; borrow it; get people to invest; or sell assets. Some of these ways can be very fast—getting loans secured by inventory, for example.

This point is closely related to Andrews's point that "money seems less a problem than technical competence, and the latter (is) less critical than managerial ability."

13. Given the way he discusses them, how related does the author see consistency and feasibility?

Rumelt sees consistency as a way of creating organizational skills that could contribute to making more strategies feasible. He says that one of the sub-tests of feasibility is the degree of coordinative and integrative skill extant in the organization. Earlier, he argued that consistency facilitated coordination, integration, and the firm's ability to mobilize its resources. So consistency, if it can build these skills and abilities, is related to feasibility.

He also says that managers must be motivated by the strategy. If they are not, then it fails in a major way. One could argue that this relates to his earlier comment that strategy must be consistent with the values of management.

14. So, is strategy evaluation a purely intellectual task or an organizational process? Which should it be? What are the implications of each alternative?

The key word is "purely." Rumelt is saying that strategy evaluation has an intellectual component, but it is too important to be an abstract, "ivory tower," *purely* intellectual exercise. He argues that it is tied up in the everyday processes of the firm. It is reinforced by the organization's other systems (e.g., information, planning, reward), but it is one of them, not something apart. He sounds much like Wrapp in arguing that strategy evaluation is something that happens all the time, because it is built into the activities in which the members of the firm engage.

Quinn and Hilmer, "Core Competencies and Strategic Outsourcing"

<u>Summary of Reading</u>

Two strategies allow managers to leverage skills and resources:

> Concentrating on a set of "core competencies" to achieve advantage and provide unique value to customers

> Strategically outsourcing activities where there is no strategic need and no special capabilities

These allow for leverage in four ways:

> Maximize returns through concentration on distinctive skills

> Create barriers to entry by rivals

> Full utilization of suppliers' investments, innovations and special expertise (too expensive or difficult to develop internally)

> Decreases risk, shortens cycle time, lowers investments, increases responsiveness to customers

Three questions must be answered:

> What exactly is a core competency? Too many definitions are tautological.

> Which non-core activities should be outsourced?

> How should relative risks and benefits of outsourcing be assessed, and how should risk be contained when outsourcing occurs?

<u>CORE COMPETENCY STRATEGIES</u>

We have known since 1974 that unrelated diversification and vertical integration rarely yield high returns. More focused approaches are generally considered superior. But cutting back product lines and "sticking to the knitting" increases systematic risk.

Moreover, some firms (Sony, Mitsubishi, Matsushita, 3M, Hewlett-Packard) are highly successful yet have wide product lines with little vertical integration. They redeploy key skills from market to market but contract out significant support activities. The term "core competency strategies" was used to describe these and other strategies centered around a central set of corporate skills. But there is little theory or consistency about what "core" really means. The solution: think in terms of specific skills needed to create value, but do so by going well beyond traditional product or functional approaches. Instead, look at "the fundamentals of what the company can do better than anyone else."

36

The essence of core competencies

What then is really core? Effective core competencies are:

1. Skill or knowledge sets, not products or functions. Look to the intellectual skills or management processes that create a maintainable competitive edge. Products can be back-engineered, duplicated or replaced by substitutes. Competencies tend not to be functional, but are skills that cut across functions. Examples: product or service design, technology creation, customer service, or logistics. These are based on knowledge, not physical assets or even intellectual capital per se. "Knowledge-based activities generate most of the value in services and manufacturing." Services make up more than three-quarters of the economy in the United States, and virtually all value added is knowledge-based. The value chains of manufacturing companies are dominated by knowledge-based activities, e.g., R&D, product design, process design, logistics, market research, advertising, distribution, and customer service.

2. Flexible, long-term platforms—capable of adaptation or evolution. It is a mistake to focus on narrow, product-centered skill. Companies must build dominating skills that will be valued by customers for a long time. "Flexible skills sets and constant, conscious reassessment of trends are hallmarks of successful core competency strategies."

3. Limited in number. "Most companies target two or three (not more than five) activities in the value chain most critical to future success." Increasing complexity makes it difficult to excel at more than two or three value chain activities. Skill sets require intensity and dedication that cannot tolerate dilution.

4. Unique sources of leverage in the value chain. To be effective, companies must seek out places where they are uniquely qualified to fill gaps or market imperfections. They should seek areas where intellectual investments can be leveraged.

5. Areas where the company can dominate. "Companies make consistently more money than their competitors only if they can perform some activities . . . more effectively than anyone else. True focus in strategy means the capacity to bring more power to bear on a selected sector than any competitor can." Firms must scrutinize their values chains to see which parts they can do better than anyone. Strategic analysis changes from industry analysis to a broad analysis of all potential providers of a value chain activity, regardless of the industry in which that provider supposedly operates.

6. Elements important to customers in the long run. At least one core competency should relate directly to understanding and serving its customers.

7. Embedded in the organization's systems. Don't depend on one or two talented stars. Embed the competencies into a reputation or culture. If the strategies depend on creativity, personal dedication, initiative or attracting talented people, it is especially important to capture the core competencies in the company's systems.

8. Preeminence: The key strategic barrier. Companies must ensure preeminence in core areas, even if it means defensively operating in non-core areas. They must block competitors from core competencies and must avoid any outsourcing that could give others knowledge of them. Over time, knowledge-based core competencies become harder to overtake because they grow exponentially. "Core competencies are the activities that offer long-term competitive advantage and thus must be rigidly controlled and protected. Peripheral activities are those not critical to the company's competitive edge."

STRATEGIC OUTSOURCING

In efficient markets, everything would be outsourced. But supplier markets are not efficient, and they carry risk for both sides. Outsourcing also carries transaction costs that may be too high. When considering whether or not to outsource, managers must answer three questions:

1. What is the potential for obtaining competitive advantage in this activity, taking account of transaction costs?

2. What is the potential vulnerability that could arise from market failure if the activity is outsourced?

3. What can we do to alleviate our vulnerability by structuring arrangements with suppliers to provide appropriate controls yet provide for necessary flexibilities in demand?

If 1 and 2 are high/high: high control needed, usually means producing internally.

If 1 and 2 are low/low: low control needed, company can buy "off the shelf"

Intermediate points: find a balance between independence/incentives for the supplier and control/security for the buyer. Extend outsourcing first in less critical areas. Outsource to non-competing companies as you gain experience. Sometimes the desire to gain specialized skills results in more complex alliances, even with competitors.

Competitive edge

Key strategic issue: Ability to achieve maintainable competitive advantage by insourcing on continuing basis. Sources of advantage: doing it more cheaply, better, faster, or uniquely. If any of these is critical to customers and can be done well, keep activity in house. Bad reasons to do something internally: history or seemingly integral nature of activity. Benchmarking against suppliers often reveals that internal capabilities are significantly below those of best-in-world companies.

Transaction costs

Always include internal and external transactions costs. Insourcing requires sustained R&D, personnel development, and infrastructure investments. Other costs to remember: laggard innovation and nonresponsiveness by internal groups that have ready-made markets; headquarters and support costs; and executive time spent on peripheral activities. Internal costs tend to be much higher than first assumed, but are often ignored because external costs are easier to calculate.

Vulnerability

Large number of suppliers typically means that outsourcing will be worthwhile. A small number of suppliers can hold buyers hostage, unless there is no depth in that market. In that case, the small number of suppliers will not provide the range of products and innovations that are needed. Insourcing would be better. Lack of information may also hurt, e.g., suppliers have special knowledge of labor shortages or raw material problems, or have unique information capabilities.

Degree of sourcing control

Range of outsourcing arrangement goes from full ownership, through partial ownership, joint development, retainer, long-term contract, call option, to short-term contract. The issue is how to structure insourcing versus outsourcing on an optimal basis.

Strategic risks

Outsourcing creates opportunities but also risks:

1. Loss of critical skills or developing the wrong skills. If a company makes a mistake and outsources what turns out to be a vital skill, it may find later that the supplier is no longer willing to make the parts. By this time the original firm may no longer have the needed skills to reenter that area. Companies may become dependent on suppliers for new product introduction, reducing their strategic flexibility.

2. Loss of cross-functional skills. Cross-functional interactions can be rich sources of innovation. The potential loss of this can be alleviated somewhat by requiring that workers interact frequently with outsourced experts.

3. Loss of control over a supplier. Non-matching priorities between a company and its suppliers can be real problems. Management must keep in contact with both shop-floor people and top management at the supplier.

New management approaches

Most companies already have sophisticated outsourcing techniques. Also, much can be learned from industries with considerable outsourcing experience, such as natural resources, construction and finance. Other useful middle management adjustments: (1) setting up professional and highly-trained purchasing/contract management group, and (2) enhancing logistics-information systems.

Conclusion

Substantlal leverage can be obtained by:

1. Developing a few well-selected core competencies of significance to customers in which the company can be best-in-world.

2. Focusing investment and management attention on items in #1.

3. Strategically outsourcing many other activities when they cannot be or need not be the best.

There are risks in outsourcing, but also in insourcing. These can be overcome through the application of a genuinely strategic framework. "When intelligently combined, core competency and extensive outsourcing strategies provide improved returns on capital, lowered risk, greater flexibility, and better responsiveness to customer needs at lower costs."

<u>Discussion Questions</u>

1. What is your assessment of the authors' list of four ways to create leverage through focusing core competencies and outsourcing most everything else?

At this relatively early point in the course, students may grasp the significance of some of these concepts, but not all. For example, the idea that a firm could maximize returns through concentration on distinctive skills is straightforward. But many students may not know about barriers to entry. In this instance, these mean that the distinctive skills developed by the firm pursuing core competency strategies are so hard to duplicate that other companies are discouraged from entering into competition with it. The third item on the list, "full utilization of suppliers' investments, innovations and expertise," essentially means getting benefits but having somebody else pay for the needed investments—this is fairly straightforward.

The fourth item may require some explanation, except for investments, which are lowered because of the dynamic just mentioned. Risk will be decreased for a related reason—a firm that outsources things at which it does *not* excel will likely do so with a firm that *is* competent in that activity. The supplier bears the risk, which is lower because of its skill, and the buying firm carries less risk when it avoids something it doesn't do well. Lastly, if suppliers are really best-in-class at something, they can move faster at that something than the buying firm can. Presumably the buyer will move faster at the things *it* does well. With both parties moving quickly at their respective competencies, cycle time is reduced.

2. What is a better answer than simply focusing on a core business?

At first glance, focusing on a core business seems sensible. It is less "scattered" than unrelated diversification and less rigid than pulling together many operations in vertical integration. But there is still "systematic risk" involved, since the firm may be putting all its eggs in one product basket. It is vulnerable to rivals who introduce better, or even just competitive, products. It is better to look at the "fundamentals of what the company does better than anyone else." In other words, focus, but not on product. Focus on key skills, skills that customers value and that are difficult for others to do. This reduces systematic risk because one skill set may be applied to many different products.

3. What is significant about considering core competency as skill sets, not products or functions?

Products might be replicated by rivals. They might be back-engineered, duplicated or even replaced by substitutes. Skills will be much more difficult to replicate. This is particularly true for intellectual or knowledge-based skills. These types of skills can be sustained because they are hard to copy and they create a competitive advantage because they make up the bulk of value added by a firm. Examples are: R&D, product design, process design, logistics, market research, advertising, distribution, and customer service

4. Why should companies not focus on product-centered skills?

Skills that are centered on products are tied to the lives of those products. But most products have short life cycles. So the advantage granted by product-centered skills is fleeting. A better approach is to develop skills that dominate and that are valued by customers for long periods. For this to happen, the skill sets must be flexible and adaptable and must evolve as needed.

5. The authors think that core competencies should be limited in number. What do you think?

Students look at large complex organizations and assume that they are good at many things. And it *is* true that these firms *do* a lot of things. So students may balk at the idea that firms should concentrate on only two or three core skills. But the authors' point is that even if firms do many things, they can only truly be excellent at a small number. That allows them to intensely focus their management and organizational learning efforts on the most important skills. They can competently do a few others that are needed to support the core, and they can outsource everything else.

6. The authors say that "the basic nature of strategic analysis changes from an industry analysis perspective to a horizontal analysis of capabilities across all potential providers of an activity regardless of which industry the provider might be in." What do they mean, and why is this significant?

In recent years strategy scholars have prescribed industry analysis as a, possibly as *the*, primary way to do strategic analysis. However, many types of activities cut across industries, e.g., customer service, product development processes. The authors suggest that in trying to figure out where it can dominate, a firm must examine *all* practitioners of a given activity, *regardless of industry*, to see who does it best. If there is no way to "catch" the best practitioner, the firm might consider outsourcing to it. If it can be beaten, the firm should decide whether it wants to make the commitment needed to become dominant in that activity. All of this is quite different from the traditional industry analysis.

7. What is significant about core skills being embedded in the organization's systems?

We have already seen how skills embedded in products is non-defensible because of the relative ease of duplicating products. Perhaps even more precarious are skills embedded in specific individuals--they can retire, be lured away (which is worse) or become incapacitated in some way. To be maximally sustainable and difficult to copy, core skills should be deep-seated in the organization's structure and management systems and most importantly in its culture. These are what the authors mean by "systems."

8. In what way do knowledge-based core competencies grow exponentially?

A good analogy here is compound interest. On an investment with compound interest, you get *interest on the interest* as the investment matures. By the same reasoning, an investment in knowledge puts you at a higher knowledge level, and you build *from that level* when you make subsequent knowledge investments. A similar dynamic works with regard to attracting talented people. If you add some, they will work on and solve the most interesting problems. This will tend to generate high returns, allowing you to hire some more people with talent, and the cycle will repeat.

9. What is this concept of "vulnerability to market failure" that the authors discuss, and why is it significant?

If a market is well-structured, a firm could outsource an activity to firms that occupy it and be assured of two things: (a) adequate supply of the activity (b) at a reasonable price. If a market fails, one or both of these conditions will no longer hold and the firm will find that its decision to outsource has left it quite vulnerable.

The benefits of outsourcing (in concert with building on core competencies) will be lost. Risk formerly borne by the supplier will now be assumed by the buyer. This risk may be accentuated if the buyer has not "kept up" its skills in that activity. Money saved by letting the supplier make investments will be lost, and then some. Advantages gained through utilizing the supplier's innovations and special expertise will also evaporate. Cycle times will rise dramatically in the short run as the buyer seeks to rebuild its skills or find new suppliers. Responsiveness to customers will suffer for the same reasons.

10. What are the inadequate reasons for insourcing an activity, and why are these reasons inadequate?

The two reasons are that (1) historically or traditionally the firm has done this activity and (2) the activity seems integral to the business. These reasons are potentially flawed for the same reason—neither is a guarantee that the firm is the activity's best performer. Some other firm, perhaps not even in the same industry, may be world class at the activity, while the focal firm is run-of-the-mill. The authors' paraphrasing of the typical response to management findings is instructive: "We thought we were best in the world at many activities. But when we benchmarked against the best external suppliers, we found we were not even up to the worst of the benchmarking cases."

11. What is your reaction to the authors' list of internal transaction costs?

It's an interesting list. It contains things relatively easy to quantify, like sustained R&D, personnel development, and infrastructure investments. But it highlights other costs that are often forgotten in the calculations: laggard innovation and nonresponsiveness by internal groups that have ready-made markets; headquarters and support costs; and executive time spent on peripheral activities. Internal costs tend to be much higher than first assumed, but are often ignored because external costs are easier to calculate. This question should really provoke students to think differently about insourcing and the viability of outsourcing.

12. What is the risk inherent in losing critical skills through inappropriate outsourcing?

It can happen that a firm outsources some activity that turns out to be core. If the supplier goes out of business, the firm must "re-tool" its skills, which have probably atrophied. If the supplier breaks off the relationship and starts performing the activity for the highest bidder, the firm is hit with a "double whammy"—it must re-tool *and* compete against its former supplier. Even if nothing happens to the contractual relationship, the supplier who controls a core activity may end up in the position of being able to dictate product introductions or other innovations.

Porter, "How Competitive Forces Shape Strategy"

Summary of Reading

The essence of strategy formulation is coping with competition. Competition in an industry is rooted in its underlying economics. Competitive forces go well beyond established combatants, and include customers, suppliers, potential entrants, and substitute products.

A strong set of competitive forces means poor long-run profitability prospects. The weaker the forces are collectively, the greater the opportunity for superior performance. The strategist's goal is to find a position in the industry where the company can best defend itself against these forces, or can influence them in its favor.

CONTENDING FORCES

Threat of entry

The seriousness of the threat of entry depends on the barriers present and the reaction from incumbent competitors. There are six major sources of barriers to entry:

Economies of scale: forces aspirant to enter on large scale or accept cost disadvantage

Product differentiation: brand identification (fostered by advertising, service, longevity, or product characteristics) forces aspirants to spend heavily to overcome customer loyalty

Capital requirement: high needs for financial resources (for plant, up-front advertising, R&D, customer credit, inventories, and start-up losses) create a high barrier for potential entrants

Cost advantages independent of scale: learning curve effects, proprietary technology, special access to raw material, government subsidies, good locations, all create hard-to-overcome barriers.

Access to distribution channels: the more limited the wholesale or retail channels are, the higher is the barrier faced by aspirants.

Government policy: license requirements, limits on access to raw materials, regulations—all of these limit, or even foreclose, entry to certain industries.

Aspirants must take at least four things into account with regard to potential retaliation from incumbents:

Have incumbents lashed out at entrants in the past?

Do incumbents possess substantial resources to fight back?

Do incumbents seem likely to cut prices?

Is industry growth slow?

Actions by large segments of the industry, as well as other changing conditions, may affect entry barriers.

Powerful suppliers and buyers

Suppliers can exert bargaining power by raising prices or reducing quality. Buyers can force down prices, demand higher quality or more service, and play competitors off against each other.

A *supplier* group is powerful if:

It is dominated by a few companies and is more concentrated than the industry it sells to

Its product is unique or well-differentiated, or if it has built up switching costs

It is not obliged to contend with other products for sale to the industry

It poses a credible threat of integrating forward into the industry's business

The industry is not an important customer of the supplier group.

A *buyer* group is powerful if:

It is concentrated or purchases large volumes

The products it purchases from the industry are standard and undifferentiated

The products it purchases from the industry form a component of its product and represent a significant fraction of its cost

It earns low profits (incentive to lower purchasing costs)

The industry's product is unimportant to the quality of the buyers' products or services

The industry's product does not save the buyer money

The buyers pose a credible threat of backward integration

The choice of suppliers and buyers should be viewed as a crucial strategic decision.

Substitute products

Substitutes limit the profit potential of an industry by placing a ceiling on prices. The more attractive the price-performance trade-off offered by substitutes, the firmer the lid. They also reduce the bonanza during boom times. The most important substitutes are those that are subject to trends improving their price/performance trade-off.

Jockeying for position (intra-industry rivalry)

The most common tactics used in situations of rivalry are price competition, product introduction, and advertising slugfests. Rivalry is intensified by the presence of certain factors:

Competitors are numerous or are roughly equal in size and power

Industry growth is slow

The product or service lacks differentiation or switching costs (so buyers are not locked in)

Fixed costs are high or the product is perishable

Capacity is normally augmented in large increments

Exit barriers are high

The rivals are diverse in strategies, origins, and "personalities."

Companies can counter these things by strategic shifts like creating switching costs or differentiating the product.

FORMULATION OF STRATEGY

The strategist now has the tools to identify the strengths and weaknesses in the company's posture vis-à-vis the competitive forces. There are three types of choices:

Position the firm for its best defense against the forces

Influence the balance among the competitive forces to improve the company's position

Anticipating shifts in the factors underlying the competitive forces and trying to exploit these changes

"The key to growth—even survival—is to stake out a position that is less vulnerable to attack from head-to-head opponents, whether established or new, and less vulnerable to erosion from the direction of buyers, suppliers, and substitute goods. Establishing such a position can take many forms . . . ."

Discussion Questions

1. How is it that "the essence of strategy formulation is coping with competition?"

This question is intended to stimulate discussion. Some students will say that, of course, competition is the most pervasive of the things facing strategists. They will agree that the most important thing the strategy must address is the competition. Porter makes a convincing case.

The problem that some students may identify is that this is a limited view of strategy. It is rooted almost entirely in the idea of strategy as position. Porter's model is a wonderful tool for understanding part of the firm's environment, but that's about it. It does the best job, of all available models, of addressing Rumelt's advantage test. But it is not as good at the consonance test, and really doesn't address the feasibility and consistency tests. Yet the factors examined by these tests (environmental fit, company strengths and weaknesses, the existence of a central vision of strategy) are also part of the "essence of strategy."

2. How does the author define an industry?

One of the problems with this reading is that Porter does *not* define industry, at least not explicitly. In some places he is quite vague. For example, he describes the "producers of fiberglass insulation" as an industry when he discusses substitutes like cellulose, rock wool and Styrofoam. Yet one could make a good case that all four of these products are in *one* industry, insulation.

Any analyst using this model should first be explicit about the boundaries of the industry, remaining consistent with this choice throughout the analysis. Used this way, Porter's model is obviously very useful.

3. The author discusses entry in a reverse way, by talking about barriers. How useful is this to strategic managers?

This question is designed to stimulate discussion. Some students will have a difficult time visualizing entry as "overcoming barriers." They will adopt the perspective of the incumbent firm that wants to know what its *specific rivals* are going to do. These students will be unimpressed by a discussion of barriers.

But Porter's model is designed to give strategists insight into economic conditions in the *industry*. This is related to Andrews's comment that strategists must learn what are the underlying economic conditions in the firm's industry. Viewed from this perspective, analyzing barriers to entry in the industry is extremely useful. Strategists can take a systematic look at the role of economies of scale, product differentiation, capital requirements, cost disadvantages independent of scale, distribution channels, and government policy. Even if the strategist doesn't get a good prediction about the behavior of a *particular* aspirant, doing this analysis would be of great benefit.

4. How important do you think switching costs are?

Switching costs seem trivial to most students. But they can be powerful shapers of competitive behavior. High switching costs increase the power, relative to the industry, of a supplier group. This could lead to higher prices or lower quality for the industry. Low switching costs increase rivalry within the industry, because buyers are not locked in. This may result in price competition and advertising slugfests to lure customers away from rivals. Companies spend a lot of resources trying to create switching costs to prevent these things from happening. The point is, switching costs are much more important to competitive strategy than most students think.

5. What is the "price/performance trade-off?"

It is the comparison, on price and quality, of a product and its substitute. If the price of the product gets too high, the consumer may elect to purchase its substitute, as long as the quality of it is not too low relative to the product. Similarly, if the quality of the product declines, the consumer may purchase the substitute, as long as the price is reasonable. A related scenario occurs when the price of the substitute drops dramatically and its quality remains constant, suddenly making it a more attractive alternative. As Porter says, "Substitutes often come rapidly into play if some development . . . in their industries . . . causes price reduction or performance improvements."

6. How important, and how common, are exit barriers?

Porter's discussion of exit barriers would indicate that they are both common and important. They include things like specialized assets, large investment in fixed assets, and management loyalty to a particular business. These are fairly common phenomena. One result of high exit barriers is excess capacity, which intensifies rivalry, primarily manifested by price wars (to keep fixed assets productive) and advertising battles (to unload excess inventory). Clearly, these are important consequences of exit barriers.

7. The author says that strategy is "finding positions in the industry where [competitive] forces are weakest." He also says that "the key to growth . . . is to stake out a position that is less vulnerable to attack . . ." So shouldn't his approach be called "avoiding competition?"

Porter never claims that his model helps firms engage in head-to-head competition. The perception that competition means "head-to-head" is part of our commonplace way of thinking about the concept. We tend to assume that competition is related to war or sports rivalry, which is characterized by head-to-head confrontation.

Porter's model is actually closer to population ecology models, which say that organizations must adapt to the conditions extant in their environments. One of the best ways to do this is to find protected niches. This is similar to how animals in the wild make specialized adaptations to their locales, which ultimately result in species. The majority of competition in the world is of this "protect yourself, adapt to your local environment" kind. Porter's implicit point is that business is no different.

Mintzberg, "Generic Business Strategies"

Summary of Reading

This article seeks to outline in an orderly fashion the families of strategies widely represented in organizations, divided into five categories:
Locating the core business

Distinguishing the core business

Elaborating the core business

Extending the core business

Reconceiving the core business

Locating the core business

Strategies of stage of operations:

Upstream business strategy: functions close to raw material (e.g., mining, basic material processing)

Midstream business strategy: takes a variety of inputs, gives out a variety of outputs (e.g., canoe manufacturing)

Downstream business strategy: takes in and sells a wide variety of inputs (e.g., department store)

Strategies of industry: trying to find the commonality among a group of firms called an industry (SIC coding)

Distinguishing the core business

Functional areas:

Input sourcing strategies (procurement, recruitment, financing)

Throughput processing strategies (process development, fabrication, assembly, product research, product development)

Output delivery strategies (distribution, promotion, pricing, sales, service)

Supporting strategies (legal, control, training, MIS)

Value chain

47

Primary activities:

  Inbound logistics
  Operations
  Outbound logistics
  Marketing and sales
  Service

Support activities:

  Procurement
  Technology development
  Human resource management
  Firm infrastructure

Porter's generic strategies: firms that wish to gain competitive advantage must make a choice from among these—"being 'all things to all people' is a recipe for strategic mediocrity and below-average performance." "A firm that engages in each generic strategy but fails to achieve any of them is 'stuck in the middle.'" Generic strategies include:

cost leadership (broad competitive scope, competitive advantage sought through lower cost)

differentiation (broad competitive scope, competitive advantage sought through differentiation)

cost focus (narrow competitive scope, competitive advantage sought through lower cost)

differentiation focus (narrow competitive scope, competitive advantage sought through differentiation)

Strategies of differentiation: acting to distinguish one's products or services from others'

Price differentiation strategy (having a lower price)

Image differentiation strategy (create a distinctive perception of the product)

Support differentiation strategy (having better sales, service, or related products)

Quality differentiation strategy (making the product better)

Design differentiation strategy (offering something that is truly different)

Undifferentiation strategy: "To have no basis for differentiation is a strategy too, indeed by all observation a common one, and in fact one that may be pursued deliberately."

Scope strategies: distinguishing the extent of one's products and services

Unsegmentation strategies: "one size fits all"

Segmentation strategies: virtually limitless possibilities

Niche strategies: focus on a single segment

Customizing strategies: each customer is a unique segment

Elaborating the core business

Given a core business with a distinguished competitive posture, what generic strategies are available to extend that core business?

Penetration strategies: using existing products in existing markets to get more share

Market development strategies: promoting existing products in new markets

Geographic expansion strategies

Product development strategies: new products in existing markets

<u>Discussion Questions</u>

1. How useful, for locating a business, is the framework given by the author? Would you add anything?

The answer to this question depends on what you mean by locating. Mintzberg's scheme tries to show where a business is in the chain of production. Is the business upstream (early in the production of the products in question), midstream (takes in lots of inputs, throws off lots of outputs), or downstream (many products sold in one distribution mode)? He also discusses the notion of identification of industries (e.g., Standard Industrial Classification codes).

The framework assumes that "locating" a business means identifying the spot in the production chain to which it belongs, or the industry to which it belongs. This is a very content-oriented sense of the word identifying. But identifying could also mean figuring out which general approach a firm is following, regardless of where it is in the production chain. Used this way, Porter's generic strategies can be used to "locate" a firm, i.e., which strategy is it using compared to other firms in the industry? This is related to the notion of strategy as position, from Chapter 1.

2. What is the basic concept behind Porter's value chain?

The value chain breaks down all the activities performed by a firm, and how those activities interact. He distinguishes between primary value activities and support value activities. Primary activities involve "the physical creation of the product and its sale and transfer to the buyer as well as after-sale assistance." Support activities provide "purchased inputs, technology, human resources, and various firmwide functions."

Each activity (and each interaction) is examined to show how it adds value for the firm's buyers. The point of value-chain analysis is to increase the firm's profit margin. Porter defines margin as "the difference between total value and the collective cost of performing the value activities."

3. What are the four generic strategies proposed by Porter?

Porter's four strategies are based on two factors. The first is the source of competitive advantage which is being sought; this could be either lower cost or differentiation. The second factor is the desired competitive scope of the firm; this could be either broad or narrow.

Firms with broad competitive scope who base their sought-after advantage on lower cost follow a strategy of *Cost Leadership*. Broad-scope firms with an emphasis on differentiating themselves are using *Differentiation*. Narrow-target firms seeking lower cost are using *Cost*

Focus; similar firms relying on differentiating themselves follow the strategy of *Differentiation Focus*.

4. *Mintzberg places the value chain and Porter's generic strategies in the category of "distinguishing the business." What do you think of this?*

This question is intended to stimulate discussion. It is akin to question 1, designed to make students think about the terms Mintzberg is using to describe his five categories of generic strategy.

Firms which follow value-adding strategies, or which follow one of Porter's four generic strategies will, if they succeed in operationalizing the strategy, distinguish their business. But this framework could also be used to locate the business (in the sense of an outside observer's identifying the firm's approach).

All of this is related to the notion of strategy as position, from Chapter 1. Porter's framework could be used to characterize the approaches used by all the various firms in an industry, in a sense "locating" them. From the standpoint of the firm, the particular approach it used would distinguish it from other firms.

5. *The author says that cost leadership is merely a form of differentiation. What is your opinion?*

This question is designed to stimulate discussion. Some students will argue that cost leadership is not a form of differentiation because firms that follow this approach tend to have plain-vanilla products. They succeed with this strategy because their costs are so low that they can still make a profit.

Other students will agree with Mintzberg. He argues that the point of competitive strategy is to seize competitive advantage, and that can only be operationalized in the marketplace. In the case of a cost leader, that would be operationalized as low price. This low price would distinguish (i.e., differentiate) the firm from its competitors. Hence, cost leadership must translate into price leadership, which is a form of differentiation.

6. *Mintzberg says, "To have no basis for differentiation is a strategy too, indeed by all observation a common one, and in fact one that may be pursued deliberately." What is your opinion of this assertion?*

This question is intended to stimulate discussion. Mintzberg's assertion may strike some as being heretical. Most marketing texts, for example, strongly urge firms to distinguish their products and themselves. Students who buy into this thinking will be mildly outraged by the statement in the question.

Mintzberg is pointing out that when one looks at the realized strategy of firms, there are many which are undistinguished. So any complete listing of generic strategies would be incomplete without including the undifferentiation strategy. Furthermore, some firms may deliberately follow such a strategy, because there is enough demand in the market for them to get away with it, or because their managements are not skillful or energetic enough to distinguish the firm, or both.

Quinn and Voyer,
"Logical Incrementalism: Managing Strategy Formation"

Summary of Reading

Strategy change processes rarely resemble the rational-analytical systems touted in the literature. They are typically fragmented, evolutionary, and intuitive. ". . . Real strategy tends to *evolve* as internal decisions and external events flow together to create a new, widely shared consensus for action. . . ."

THE FORMAL SYSTEMS PLANNING APPROACH

This approach states which factors *should* be included in a systematically planned strategy. It tends to focus on quantitative factors, underemphasizing qualitative, organizational, and power factors. This kind of planning should be just one building block.

THE POWER-BEHAVIORAL APPROACH

Some literature has enhanced our understanding of:

Multiple goal structures

Politics of strategic decisions

Bargaining and negotiation processes

Satisficing in decision making

Role of coalitions

Practice of "muddling" in public management

SUMMARY FINDINGS FROM PRESENT STUDY

Neither approach above is adequately descriptive of strategy processes.

Effective strategies tend to emerge incrementally and opportunistically in a cohesive pattern.

The logic behind this process is so powerful that it may be the best approach to recommend for strategy formulation in large companies.

Because of cognitive and process limits, this approach must be managed and linked together in a way best described as "logical incrementalism."

"Such incrementalism is not 'muddling.' It is a purposeful, effective, proactive management technique for improving and integrating *both* the analytical and behavioral aspects of strategy formulation."

CRITICAL STRATEGIC ISSUES

Even though "hard data" decisions dominate the literature, there are various "soft" changes that affect strategy:

Overall organizational structure

Overall management style

External (esp. governmental) relations

Acquisition, divestiture, or divisional control

International posture/relationships

Innovative capabilities

Personnel motivations affected by growth

Value and expectation changes, and their effects on worker and professional relationships

Technological changes

Precipitating events and incremental logic

Executives reported that no single formal analytical process could handle all strategic variables simultaneously. Various events often precipitated interim decisions which shaped the company's future strategy. Top executives tried to deal with these precipitating events incrementally. Early commitments were kept broadly formative, tentative, and subject to later review. Future implications were too hard to understand, so parties wanted to test assumptions and have an opportunity to learn. Also, top executives were sensitive to social and political structures in the organization, and tried to handle things in a way that would improve the dynamics.

Diversification subsystem

Generating a genuine, top-level psychological commitment to diversification

Consciously preparing to move opportunistically

Building a "comfort factor" for risk taking

Developing a new ethos

Major reorganization subsystem

Avoid negative effects on organizational politics and social structure

Assess the new roles, capabilities, and individual reactions of those involved in restructuring

Train and test new people (perhaps for extended periods)

Modify concept of reorganization as more is learned

Make final commitments as late as possible

Move opportunistically, step-by-step, selectively moving people (events seldom come together at one convenient time)

Articulate in detail the broad organizational concept only when the last pieces fit together

Allow for testing, flexibility, and feedback

FORMAL PLANNING IN CORPORATE STRATEGY

Formal planning techniques serve some essential functions. They discipline managers to look ahead, and to communicate about goals and resource allocations. Long-term planning encourages longer time horizons, and facilitates the evaluation of short-term plans. They "create a psychological backdrop and an information framework about the future against which managers can calibrate short-term or interim decisions." Lastly, "special studies" have a large effect at key junctures for specific decisions.

Planning actually institutionalizes incrementalism, for two reasons. First, most planning is "bottom up," and the people at the bottom have a vested interest in their existing products and processes. Second, most plans are meant to be "living" or "ever green," intended to be only frameworks, providing guidance and consistency for incremental decisions; to do otherwise would be to deny that further information could have value. "Thus, properly formulated formal plans are also a part of an incremental logic."

Total posture planning

"Occasionally . . . managements do attempt very broad assessments of their companies' total posture. . . . [But] major product thrusts . . . proved unsuccessful. Actual strategies therefore evolved as each company overextended, consolidated, made errors, and rebalanced various thrusts over time. And it was both logical and expected that this would be the case."

LOGICAL INCREMENTALISM

Strategic decisions cannot be aggregated into a single decision matrix, with factors treated simultaneously to achieve an optimum. There are cognitive limits, but also "process limits"— timing and sequencing requirements, the need to create awareness, build comfort levels, develop consensus, select and train people, and so forth.

A strategy emerges

Successful executives connect and sequence a series of strategic processes and decisions over a period of years. They attempt to build a resource base and posture that is strong enough to withstand all but the most devastating events. They constantly reconfigure corporate structure and strategy as new information suggests better—but never perfect—alignments. The process is dynamic, with no definite beginning or end.

Conclusion

"Strategy deals with the unknowable, not the uncertain. It involves forces of such great number, strength, and combinatory powers that one cannot predict events in a probabilistic sense. Hence logic dictates that one proceed flexibly and experimentally from broad concepts toward specific commitments, making the latter concrete as late as possible in order to narrow the bands of uncertainty and to benefit from the best available information. This is the process of 'logical incrementalism'. . . . [The latter] is not 'muddling'. . . . It is conscious, purposeful, proactive, good management." It allows executives to blend analysis, organizational politics, and individual needs into a cohesive new direction.

MANAGING INCREMENTALISM

How can one proactively manage in an incremental mode? Executives tend to utilize somewhat similar incremental processes as they manage complex strategy shifts.

Leading the formal information system

The earliest signals for strategy change rarely come from formal company systems. Using multiple internal and external sources, managers "sense" the need for change before the formal systems do.

Building organizational awareness

This is essential when key players lack information or psychological stimulation to change. At early stages, management processes are broad, tentative, formative, information-seeking, and purposely avoid irreversible commitments. They also try to avoid provoking potential opponents of an idea.

Building credibility/changing symbols

"Symbols may help managers signal to the organization that certain types of changes are coming, even when specific solutions are not yet in hand." Highly visible symbolic actions can communicate effectively to large numbers of people. Grapevines can amplify signals of pending change. Symbolic moves often verify the intention of a new strategy, or give it credibility in its early stages.

Legitimizing new viewpoints

Planned delays allow the organization to talk through threatening issues, work out implications of new solutions, or gain improved information base. Sometimes, strategic concepts that are initially resisted can gain acceptance and commitment simply by the passage of time and open discussion of new information. Many top executives, planners and change agents consciously arrange such "gestation periods."

Tactical shifts and partial solutions

"These are typical steps in developing a new overall strategic posture [when] early problem resolutions [need] to be partial, tentative or experimental." Tactical adjustments or a series of small programs typically encounter little opposition, while a broad objective change would encounter much opposition. These approaches allow the continuation of ongoing strengths while shifting momentum at the margin. Experimentation can occur with minimized risk, leading to many different success scenarios.

"As events unfurl, the solutions to several initially unrelated problems tend to flow together into a new synthesis. When possible, strategic logic (risk minimization) dictates starting broad initiatives that can be flexibly guided in any of several possible desirable directions."

Broadening political support

This is an essential and consciously active step in major strategy changes. "Committees, task forces or retreats tend to be favored mechanisms. By selecting such groups' chairmen, membership, timing, and agenda the guiding executive can largely influence and predict a desired outcome, yet nudge other executives toward a consensus."

Overcoming opposition

This is almost always necessary. Unnecessary alienation of managers from an earlier era should be avoided; their talents may be needed. Preferred methods are persuasion, co-optation, neutralization, or moving through zones of indifference.

Successful executives honor and even stimulate legitimate differences. Opponents sometimes thoughtfully shape new strategies into more effective directions. Sometimes they even change their views.

Occasionally, strong-minded executives may need to be moved to less influential positions, or stimulated to leave.

Consciously structured flexibility

"Flexibility is essential in dealing with the many 'unknowables' in the total environment." This requires:

1. Active horizon scanning

2. Creating resource buffers

3. Developing and positioning champions

4. Shortening decision lines

"These—rather than pre-capsuled (and shelved) programs to respond to stimuli which never occur quite as expected—are the keys to real contingency planning."

Trial balloons and systematic waiting

". . . Strategists may have to wait patiently for the proper option or precipitating event to appear."

"Executives may also consciously launch trial concepts . . . in order to attract options and concrete proposals . . . . Without making a commitment to any specific solution, the executive activates the organization's creative abilities."

Creating pockets of commitment

Often needed for entirely new strategic thrusts. Small projects, deep within the organization, test options, create skills, or build commitments for several possible options. The executive provides broad goals, proper climate, and flexible resource support, without public commitment. This avoids attention on, and identification with, any project. Yet they can stimulate the good options, make life harder for the poorer options, or even kill the weakest ones.

Crystallizing focus

At some point, this becomes vital. Early commitments are vague. But once executives "develop information or consensus on desirable thrusts, they may use their prestige or power to push or crystallize a particular formulation." This should not be done too early, as it "might inadvertently centralize the organization, preempt interesting options, provide a common focus for otherwise fragmented opposition, or cause the organization to undertake undesirable actions just to carry out a stated commitment . . . . When to crystallize viewpoints and when to maintain open options is one of the true arts of strategic management . . . ."

Formalizing commitment

This is the final step in formulation. It usually occurs after general acceptance exists, and the timing is right. The decision is announced publicly. Programs and budgets are formed. Control and reward systems are aligned to reflect intended strategic emphases.

Continuing dynamics and mutating consensus

Advocates of the "new" strategy can become as strong a source of inflexible resistance to new ideas as the advocates of the "old" strategy. "Effective strategic managers immediately introduce new foci and stimuli at the top to begin mutating the very strategic thrusts they have just solidified—a most difficult but essential psychological task . . . ."

Not a linear process

"While generation of a strategy generally flows along the sequence presented, stages are by no means orderly or discrete." The process is more like "fermentation in biochemistry, rather than an industrial assembly line."

"The validity of a strategy lies not in its pristine clarity or rigorously maintained structure, but in its capacity to capture the initiative, to deal with unknowable events, to redeploy and concentrate resources as new opportunities and thrusts emerge and thus to use resources most effectively toward selected goals."

Segments of major strategies are likely to be at different stages of development. They are integrated in the minds of top executives, each of whom may nevertheless see things differently. Also, "the process is so continuous that it may be hard to discern the particular point in time when specific clear-cut decisions are made."

INTEGRATING THE STRATEGY

The process may be incremental, but it is not piecemeal.

Concentrating on a few key thrusts

Effective strategic managers constantly seek to distill a few (six to ten) "central themes" that draw the firm's actions together. These maintain focus and consistency in the strategy.

Coalition management

The heart of all controlled strategy development is coalition management. Top managers act at the confluence of pressures from all stakeholders. These stakeholders will form coalitions, so managers must be active in forming their own. "People selection and coalition management are the ultimate controls top executives have in guiding and coordinating their companies' strategies."

CONCLUSIONS

Recent managerial approaches emphasizing formal planning have failed because of poor implementation. This is the "classic trap of thinking about strategy formulation and implementation as separate sequential processes . . . . Successful managers who operate logically and proactively in an incremental mode build the seeds of understanding, identity and commitment into the very processes which create their strategies . . . ."

Discussion Questions

1. In what sense are most issues that trigger strategy formation not amenable to quantitative modeling or even formal financial analysis?

One has only to examine a list of the factors listed by Quinn to see that quantitative analysis is difficult, maybe impossible. Changes in overall organizational structure have implications that are not quantifiable. The nature of overall management style at an organization is almost by definition qualitative. External (especially governmental) relations are riddled with so many problematic and unpredictable areas that quantitative analysis would be very burdensome, at best. Questions of acquisition, divestiture, or divisional control would seem to be amenable to quantitative analysis (e.g., formal criteria for acquisition candidates), but in practice such things are almost always social, organizational, or political. To a large extent, issues related to international posture or relationships turn on cultural questions, which are not quantifiable. Innovative capabilities rely to some extent on investment decisions, but they also require non-quantifiable changes in skill

56

levels. Personnel motivations affected by growth, or even "regular" motivations, have always been tricky. Even more tricky are value and expectation changes, and their effects on worker and professional relationships. Lastly, it may be true that technological changes can be predicted, but they never have been with the kind of precision hoped for with quantitative modeling or forecasting techniques.

2. What is your opinion of the authors' assertion that "no single formal analytical process could handle all strategic variables simultaneously on a planned basis?"

This question is intended to stimulate discussion. Some students will disagree with the assertion, arguing that well-designed and well-implemented planning processes should be able to handle large number of strategic variables simultaneously. Indeed, they will argue, that is what operations research (or management science) is all about—handling problems with large numbers of variables.

Others will stress that strategic variables are not the same kind of variables well-handled by analytical procedures. They are inherently ambiguous, and usually not quantifiable, as the list in the preceding answer showed. Moreover, many strategic issues can only be handled by the passage of time—e.g., creating "comfort factors," learning, building consensus.

3. Why is it so important to deal with "precipitating events" in an incremental fashion?

Quinn points out that no organization can possibly foresee the timing, severity, or even the nature of all precipitating events. Also, there might not be the time, the resources, or the information to do a full formal analysis. Yet decisions made under these conditions can have profound implications—new thrusts, precedents, lost opportunities—that can be difficult to reverse later. The most logical response is to proceed in small steps that can be assessed, reviewed, and changed, until decision makers have a better idea of what is going on.

4. What do you think of the notion of "comfort factors?"

This question is designed to stimulate discussion. Some students may be confused by this concept. They may view changes in strategy as being pretty straightforward—once you know what the "right" (determined through analysis) thing is, do it. Quinn's point, recognized by some students, is that any major change must take into account the individual and organizational stakes that people have in the status quo. Before an organization can undertake a major strategic change, people have to understand it and be committed to it. They will be neither until they feel comfortable with the proposed change. That is why it is often important to let some time pass (or do other things) to create a feeling of comfort with a new idea.

5. Can "formal planning practices actually institutionalize incrementalism?"

There are two reasons why planning practices might actually act as a spur for incrementalism. First, most planning is "bottom up," and the people at the bottom have a vested interest in their existing products and processes. Consequently, managers need to proceed incrementally to overcome some of these vested interests. Second, most plans are meant to be "living" or "ever green," intended to be only frameworks. If this is true, then plans will be changed often as the organization learns. The plans will still be good for providing guidance and consistency to the incremental decisions. Thus, formal plans used as frameworks can be a good support mechanism for incremental logic, and actually encourage it. These are the things Quinn means when he says that formal planning institutionalizes incrementalism.

6. *What do you think of the authors' statement that it was "logical and expected" that major product thrusts would fail, and strategies would actually evolve "as each company overextended, consolidated, made errors, and rebalanced various trusts over time?"*

This question is intended to highlight one of the most important, and provocative, points made in the reading. By now, most students will grasp that this text is taking a radically different approach to teaching about strategy making. If there are any holdouts, this statement will provoke them. It is saying that strategies are not analytically formulated, but instead evolve as organizations learn, through trial and error. This will be a real eye-opener for most students. Furthermore, Quinn says that most managers *expect* this, and find it *logical*. It is only in the traditional textbooks that the all-knowing strategic manager still exists. In real-life organizations, people expect many bumps along the way as they learn.

7. *How can "process limits" be just as important as "cognitive limits?"*

The cognitive limits that constrain individual decision makers have been getting much attention for many years now. If strategy making is seen as primarily an individual activity, then these cognitive limits are very important. Quinn's point in this part of the reading is that process limits are equally important, because he views strategy making as an organizational (i.e., multi-individual, collective) activity. It may not be possible for an individual to process large quantities of data simultaneously. But it is at least as difficult for managers to make large numbers of people aware of the need for change, make them comfortable about it, develop consensus among them as to the proper actions, train them in new skills, etc.

8. *What are the implications of the statement that "strategy deals with the unknowable, not the uncertain?"*

Uncertainty means that several future events are possible, but that the decision maker cannot assign probabilities to their occurrence. Quinn's point is that it is not even realistic to expect decision makers to think of the possible future events, let alone probabilities. It is simply not possible to know what the future will bring, at least not in the kind of long-term time frame which characterizes strategic decision making.

The implication of this is that managers should strive to make their organizations as flexible, responsive, and adaptive as possible. That way, no matter what happens, there is the chance for an appropriate response. Part of this capability involves using logical incrementalism—proceeding in small steps, going from the broad to the specific, waiting for as long as possible.

9. *How can it be said that "the rationale behind [logical incrementalism] is so powerful that it perhaps provides the normative model for strategic decision making?"*

Quinn makes this statement at the beginning of the reading, and he spends most of his time in the reading trying to justify it. The essence of his argument is as follows:

Strategy deals with the unknowable;

There are large number of factors that must be taken into account when developing strategy;

Process and cognitive limits restrain what strategists can do;

Therefore, strategic factors cannot all be treated simultaneously.

Given these realities, Quinn argues that the normative (or recommended) approach is to proceed incrementally, learning as you go, building awareness and commitment as you go; this is far superior to trying to plan everything out in advance, and then trying to implement those plans, i.e., the formal systems planning approach, which is what most of the literature recommends.

10. In what way is logical incrementalism not muddling, but conscious, purposeful, productive, good management?

If a strategist were to proceed incrementally, but without knowing what she or he was doing, without tying everything to an overarching sense of direction, without being aware of the political and social structures that exist in the organization, without trying to build awareness and commitment to what he or she was trying to accomplish—*that* would be muddling. But the *logical* incrementalist is proceeding in small steps *because* she or he is aware of these issues. Accordingly, logical incrementalism is conscious, purposeful, productive, *good* management.

11. What do the authors mean when they say that managers should be "leading the formal information system?"

Students often misinterpret this phrase. It does not mean "being in charge of the formal information system." It means "being ahead of it." The earliest signals for strategy change rarely come from formal company systems. Using multiple internal and external sources, effective managers must "sense" the need for change before the formal systems do.

12. What is surprising about the statement that, in early stages of strategy formation, "management processes are rarely directive?"

In the context of most of what has been discussed in this text, there is little that is surprising in this statement. It is only surprising in the context of the mainstream strategy model.

13. How effective and important is the manipulation of symbols?

Students may differ on this, but the evidence shows that symbolic manipulation is both effective and important. Symbols may help managers signal to the organization that certain types of changes are coming, even when specific solutions are not yet in hand. Highly visible symbolic actions can communicate effectively to large numbers of people. Grapevines can amplify signals of pending change. Symbolic moves often verify the intention of a new strategy, or give it credibility in its early stages.

14. What is the purpose of planned delays?

Planned delays allow the organization to talk through threatening issues, work out implications of new solutions, or gain improved information base. Sometimes, strategic concepts that are initially resisted can gain acceptance and commitment simply by the passage of time and open discussion of new information. Many top executives, planners and change agents consciously arrange such "gestation periods."

15. How does the discussion of "tactical shifts and partial solutions" differ from the "mainstream" strategy formulation model?

The mainstream model prescribes that the strategy be developed by top management, as an integrated whole, using analytical techniques, prior to any action's taking place. Implementation is by lower level participants.

What Quinn suggests in this section could not be more different. Top management encourages others to undertake many small, low-risk projects. These are unlikely to attract opposition, the way a large-scale proposal might. Progress is made, but it is partial, tentative, and experimental. As events unfurl, the solutions to several initially unrelated problems tend to flow together into a new synthesis.

Note the differences. Action occurs first. The strategy comes in pieces, not an integrated whole. Synthesis is used instead of analysis. The sources of new strategy are organizational members, not top management. It is impossible to distinguish formulation from implementation.

16. How can a CEO gain broader political support for an emerging thrust, and why is it important?

Committees, task forces or retreats tend to be favored mechanisms. By selecting such groups' chairmen, membership, timing, and agenda the guiding executive can largely influence and predict a desired outcome, yet nudge other executives toward a consensus.

17. What is surprising in the idea that "successful executives tend to honor and even stimulate legitimate differences in views concerning . . . major directions?"

This is a trick question, because there is nothing surprising in this. This behavior is exactly the kind of thing Mintzberg had in mind when he said that politics can be the challenging force for change. It is the kind of thing Starbuck and his co-authors had in mind when they said that firms should adopt contradictory prescriptions and tolerate some irrationality.

18. What is the idea behind "trial balloons?"

A trial balloon is a concept launched in order to attract options and concrete proposals. It is usually launched by someone other than the executive; this prevents him/her from being pinned with blame if the balloon is quickly punctured. It usually attracts lots of attention and reaction. By floating a trial balloon, and without making a commitment to any specific solution, the executive activates the organization's creative abilities.

19. What is significant about this statement: "Despite adhering to the rhetoric of specific goal setting, most executives . . . were careful not to state many new strategic objectives in concrete terms until they had carefully built consensus among key players?"

The statement is totally congruent with Wrapp's point about avoiding policy straightjackets. It also evokes his point about needing to be aware of the power structure in an organization. The executive provides broad goals, proper climate, and flexible resource support, without public commitment. This avoids attention on, and identification with, any project. Yet small projects, deep within the organization, test options, create skills, and build commitments for several possible options.

20. What is your reaction to Quinn's assertion that "when to crystallize viewpoints and when to maintain open options is one of the true arts of strategic management?"

The first reaction is that he is probably correct. The second reaction is disappointment, because the statement offers no guidelines about how to practice the art. The third reaction is the realization that that is what this text has been about—strategy is not formed or managed in a vacuum. Strategic managers must become engaged in their organizations' activities, much like the potter in Mintzberg's "Crafting Strategy" reading (see next page). Only after a long period of intimate involvement with their organizations will strategists be able to practice this "true art."

21. Why is mutating the consensus "a most difficult but essential psychological task?"

It is difficult because it goes against the organization's natural predisposition at this point. As Mintzberg, and Tushman, Newman and Romanelli pointed out, what usually happens after an upheaval is a long stable (or convergent) period. The organization wants to become re-obsessed with its strategy.

It is important because mutating the consensus is one way to avoid the "contamination" Mintzberg mentioned in his reading earlier in this chapter. Most of the organizations where logical incrementalism would be used would be machine organizations. That form of organization is prone to being contaminated by over-standardization. Mutating the consensus would help minimize the effects of this.

22. What is significant about how the incremental process is not linear and "is so continuous that it may be hard to discern the particular point in time when specific clear-cut decisions are made?"

What is significant is how dramatically this differs from the mainstream strategy model. In that, the point at which a clear-cut decision is made is unmistakable. Everything is neat, orderly, rational, and sequenced. The strategy is formulated as an integrated whole in advance of any action. Usually the responsibility for the strategy can easily be fixed on someone in top management.

23. Why is it important to "concentrate on a few key thrusts?"

Too many managers and strategists dissipate their energies by trying to do too many things. Also, it is more difficult for the people in an organization to follow a large number of thrusts. As the authors put it, the few key thrusts "help maintain focus and consistency in the strategy. They make it easier to discuss and monitor intended directions."

24. How does the section on coalition management, especially the two quotations, relate to the notions of (a) strategy as perspective and (b) process strategy (both from Mintzberg's Chapter 1 reading)?

The person in the first quotation says, "If good people share the same values, they will instinctively act together." This is as good a description of strategy as perspective as one could find. The speaker is saying that the shared values, which Mintzberg called ideology, will guide strategic action.

The second speaker says, "How do you manage the strategic process? It all comes down to people: selecting people." This is one aspect of process strategy, which was the indirect control of strategy by control of organizational processes.

Mintzberg, "Crafting Strategy"

Summary of Reading

Planning strategy brings to mind orderly, analytic thinking. But the metaphor of *crafting* strategy evokes traditional skill, dedication, perfection through mastery of detail. Instead of thinking and reason, what springs to mind are involvement, intimacy and harmony with the materials, long experience and commitment.

61

The thesis of the reading is that "the crafting image better captures the process by which effective strategies come to be. The planning image, long popular in the literature, distorts these processes and thereby misguides organizations that embrace it unreservedly."

The reading compares strategists to potters. Managers are craftsmen and strategy is their clay. Like potters, they sit between a past (of corporate capabilities) and a future (of market opportunities), and they should bring an equally intimate knowledge of the materials at hand.

Strategies are both plans for the future and patterns from the past

People tend to define strategy as planning, but they describe a firm's strategy as consistency in past behavior. These patterns in action are not difficult to find in organizations. But it is often difficult to find statements of intention that we can trust. We need to go back to the intimate connection between thought and action.

Strategies need not be deliberate—they can also emerge, more or less

Most things written about strategy say that first we formulate, then we implement; first we think, then we act. But a potter will get ideas about different objects after she starts working, perhaps because of slight problems or other events that happen, even if she had some different initial idea. Action has driven thinking. The same thing may happen in a company. Salespeople will learn things from customers, which lead to product changes, which may lead to whole new strategic thrusts.

The point is that strategies can *form* as well as *be formulated*. "A realized strategy can emerge in response to an evolving situation, or it can be brought about deliberately, through a process of formulation followed by implementation."

While it may be true that organizations could formulate smarter strategies, it is also true that organizations could be smarter by "allowing their strategies to develop gradually, through the organization's actions and experiences. Smart strategists appreciate that they cannot always be smart enough to think through everything in advance."

Craftsmen don't think one day and work others. Yet organizations try to separate the work of minds and hands, severing the feedback link between the two. "The notion that strategy is something that should happen way up there, far removed from the details of running an organization on a daily basis, is one of the great fallacies of conventional strategic management."

Strategies that appear without clear intentions are called *emergent*. Emergent strategy fosters learning; deliberate strategy tends to preclude it. But strategy making uses both approaches. Learning must be coupled with control. Deliberate and emergent strategies form the ends of a continuum along which real-world strategies may be found.

Effective strategies develop in all kinds of strange ways and places

Some strategies are *personal strategies* of talented individuals in firms. In the grass-roots approach, strategies grow like weeds in a garden, taking root anyplace where people have the capacity and resources to learn.

With *umbrella strategy*, management sets broad guidelines and leaves the specifics to others. In the *process strategy*, management controls strategic processes and leaves actual content to others. Each of these approaches is *deliberately emergent*.

Strategic orientations happen in brief, quantum leaps

The conventional view of strategy claims that change must be continuous, which is ironic, since the essence of strategy is *stability*—to set direction, to lay out actions, to elicit commitment from members. "No stability means no strategy . . . . Indeed, the very fact of having a strategy . . . creates resistance to change!"

Reconciling the forces for stability and for change is a fundamental dilemma for strategy making. Research indicates that it is resolved by having long periods of stability punctuated by brief (and rare) periods of significant change. Success is achieved as the firm exploits its strategy during the long periods of stability. As the firm gradually moves out of synch with its environment, it must go through a "strategic revolution," which is followed by another long stable period.

Research shows that this pattern is particularly applicable to large firms. Smaller, more creative firms have shorter stable periods and more frequent changes. In either kind of firm, success seems related to attending first to one force, then to the other. Failure seems related to either mixing the two, or focusing too much on one or the other.

To manage strategy, then, is to craft thought and action, control and learning, stability and change

The popular view is the strategist as planner or visionary. The view offered here is of the strategist as a pattern recognizer or learner, one who manages a process in which strategies can emerge as well as be deliberately conceived. The strategist may also be the "collective entity made up of the many actors whose interplay speaks an organization's mind."

The words associated with craft are "dedication, experience, involvement with the material, the personal touch, mastery of detail, a sense of harmony and integration." *Managers* who craft strategy are "involved, responsive to their materials, learning about their organizations and industries through personal touch, . . . [and] sensitive to experience . . . ."

Managing stability. Managing strategy is mostly managing stability, not change. It is making the firm as effective as possible at existing strategy. It is not promoting change, but knowing when to do so.

Strategic planning is "a means, not to create strategy, but to program a strategy already created . . . ." It is analytic (i.e., based on decomposition), while strategy creation is *synthetic* (i.e., based on putting pieces together). It typically leads to extrapolating existing strategy or copying from competitors. Planning can, though, play a useful role.

Detect discontinuity. The real challenge in crafting strategy lies in detecting discontinuities that are important to the firm's future. There are no techniques for doing this, only "a sharp mind in touch with the situation." This sharpness tends to atrophy during the long periods of stability mentioned above. So the effective strategist must be able to manage during the stable periods, yet detect discontinuities.

Know the business. The knowledge needed for strategic management is not intellectual, but personal. It means having an intimate understanding, equivalent to the craftsman's feel for the clay. The author calls it wisdom, which is not promoted in modern bureaucracies, which distance leaders from details. Craftsmen and managers must train themselves to see things others miss.

Manage patterns. A key to managing strategy is detecting emerging patterns and helping them take shape. Don't just preconceive strategies, but recognize their emergence elsewhere, and intervene when appropriate. Create a climate where a variety of strategies can grow.

Reconcile change and continuity. Keep the quantum theory in mind. Learn to sense when to exploit an established crop of strategies, and when to encourage new strains to displace the old.

"While strategy is a word that is usually associated with the future, its link to the past is no less central. As Kierkegaard once observed, life is lived forward but understood backward. Managers may have to live strategy in the future, but they must understand it through the past.

"Like potters at the wheel, organizations must make sense of the past if they hope to manage the future. Only by coming to understand the patterns that form in their own behavior do they get to know their capabilities and their potential. Thus crafting strategy, like managing craft, requires a natural synthesis of the future, present, and past."

Discussion Questions

1. The author says that "the crafting image better captures the process by which effective strategies come to be." What is your opinion of this assertion?

This question is intended to stimulate discussion. Some students will balk at this statement. They will not understand the analogy, or they will prefer not to accept it. So much of business education is oriented toward analytical techniques, some students simply want to believe that the techniques extend to strategy formulation.

Other students will welcome the different metaphor. As Mintzberg describes it, crafting has many desirable aspects—involvement, intimacy and harmony with materials, long experience, and commitment. Other words he describes as associated with craft are "dedication, experience, involvement with the material, the personal touch, mastery of detail, a sense of harmony and integration." This is also related to Peters and Waterman's notions of "hands on, value driven" management.

2. How does this reading relate to previous readings?

This reading is closely related to Mintzberg's Chapter 1 reading on "The Five Ps of Strategy," which actually elaborates on the continuum of strategies mentioned here. There are also elements of the reading that related to Quinn's model of logical incrementalism.

3. The author points out that most writing on strategy says that first we formulate, then we implement; first we think, then we act. Then he rhetorically asks, "Why would anybody want to proceed differently?" How do you answer this question?

This question is intended to stimulate discussion. Some students will ask, "Why, indeed?" They will agree with the traditional model that for coherent strategy to occur, it must be thought through first. Others will answer that there are other ways to proceed. Lots of times people act and get ideas, good ideas, from their actions. In other words, they learn. This happens for potters and other craftsmen. Why shouldn't it also happen for strategists?

4. Mintzberg says that "smart strategists appreciate that they cannot always be smart enough to think through everything in advance." What is your opinion of this? How does this relate to other readings?

Students may differ on this. Some will think that the strategists who work for large corporations should have the resources available to them to successfully think through everything in advance. Others may not be so sure, and will agree with Mintzberg's assertion. This point is very closely related to Quinn's reading on logical incrementalism. Quinn argues that one of the reasons why logical incrementalism is the preferred approach for developing strategy is because of the impossibility of identifying all factors in advance, not to mention the difficulty of trying to deal with all the factors simultaneously.

5. What is your opinion of the author's discussion of the severing of the link between thought and action? To what other readings is it related ?

How students react to Mintzberg's discussion should differ. Those who strongly believe in the value of analysis will disagree with him. They will argue that good analysis is needed in large organizations. That may be true. The problem to which Mintzberg alludes is when this attitude is taken too far. People in general need to be able to act, then think about their actions. They also need to be allowed to think, then act on their thoughts. Just thinking, or just acting, is not enough. Mintzberg's discussion is related to Wrapp's comments (Chapter 2) about the manager needing to be involved in operating detail.

6. Mintzberg asserts that deliberate strategy tends to preclude learning. What is your opinion of this statement?

This question is intended to stimulate discussion. Some students will argue that there is nothing about good strategic planning processes that precludes learning. Indeed, they will say, good planning processes are set up to monitor the environment, constantly learning about it. But Mintzberg's point is that *deliberate* strategy, by definition, means going from intention to realization with *little or no deviation*. In other words, a deliberate strategy fulfills the plan, no matter what new information is gained along the way. So, a purely deliberate strategy *would* preclude learning.

7. The author says that the essence of strategy is stability, and that "the very fact of having a strategy . . . creates resistance to change!" What is your reaction to these ideas?

Some students may disagree, saying that good planning processes make for adaptability. Others may be confused by the statement; it implies that there is a downside to strategy, and most students think of strategy as a good thing. Still others may buy into this statement. The evidence seems to indicate that strategies do create stability and resistance to change. But these are not bad things, especially during those long periods of strategic stability. As Mintzberg points out, those are the times when the firm usually has the most success.

8. What is your reaction to Mintzberg's description of the typical strategy cycle, i.e., long stable periods punctuated by brief, quantum leaps?

Students may wonder why firms can't do things differently. Why do they wait so long, until they are out of synch with their environments, before they make changes? The main reason is that frequent change would be too expensive, monetarily and in human terms. Firms find it more lucrative to live with a slightly-out-of-alignment strategy for a while, than to change frequently. Another point that should be raised is that smaller, more creative firms have shorter stable periods and more frequent changes. There is a movement toward making even large firms more like these small firms. This is the "thriving on chaos" idea popularized by Tom Peters.

9. Which view of the strategist do you prefer—the strategist as planner or visionary, or the strategist as a pattern recognizer or learner?

Students may be disappointed that Mintzberg implies that the planner/visionary is not accurate. One the other hand, the description of the "craft" manager is a compelling one:

Managers who craft strategy are "involved, responsive to their materials, learning about their organizations and industries through personal touch, . . . [and] sensitive to experience . . . ."

They are also characterized by "dedication, experience, involvement with the material, the personal touch, mastery of detail, a sense of harmony and integration."

10. What is the "analysis vs. synthesis" distinction the author makes between strategic planning and strategy creation?

Analysis means taking something and breaking it down into its components. Strategic planning excels at this. The problem is, as Wrapp pointed out in his Chapter 2 reading, management consists of taking a variety of "pieces" and trying to figure out how they might fit together. Putting many things together in a holistic way is called synthesis. It is what management is all about, and planning is its antithesis.

11. What is your opinion of the five "management pointers" the author gives at the end of the reading?

Of course, students will have a range of opinions on these points. "Managing stability" will seem pretty strange to students, who may have come into this reading thinking of strategic management as change-oriented. Some may not find the "detect discontinuity" advice particularly helpful—the author says that "there are no techniques for doing this." They may, on the other hand, agree with the idea that managers should "know the business." "Managing patterns" is another way of saying that firms need to become more flexible and innovative, and most students probably favor this. Lastly, "reconciling change and continuity" will probably still seem strange to students who wonder why firms wait so long before changing strategies.

Pascale, "The Honda Effect"

Summary of Reading

"Strategy" seems like an innocent noun, but in fact it embodies an implicit model of how organizations should be managed, i.e., by top management, with empirical models and concepts, using strategic planning processes.

Words often derive meaning from their cultural context, and that is true for strategy. The Japanese are interested in the concept not for itself, but to learn about our peculiarities. They distrust single-minded approaches that detract from peripheral vision. American companies in mature industries, who were wedded to the portfolio concept (like Baldwin, Textron, and AMF), were outflanked by Japanese competitors (like Yamaha, YKK, and Honda).

HONDA: THE STRATEGY MODEL

From 1959 to 1966, Honda went from 0% to 63% of the American motorcycle market. What accounted for this phenomenal success?

The Boston Consulting Group's (BCG) 1975 report to the British government became the standard "strategy model" explanation for what happened. Honda is portrayed as a firm dedicated to being the low price producer (by utilizing its dominant Japanese market share to accumulate volume), using that dominant domestic position to force entry into the U.S. market, expanding that market by redefining a leisure class (using the "Nicest People" advertising campaign), and exploiting its advantage via aggressive pricing and advertising.

THE ORGANIZATIONAL PROCESS PERSPECTIVE

The explanation given by the six Honda executives responsible for the company's entry differs from the BCG's. Mr. Sochiro Honda, the company founder, was an inventive genius who secured the firm's industry leadership with brilliant design innovations (not volume production). By the end of 1959, Honda became the market leader in Japan because of the 50cc Supercub, which was well-designed and affordable because of its lightweight engine. Demand was so great that the company invested in a new 30,000-unit-per-month factory (not completed until mid-1960).

In late 1958 the company sent two executives to investigate the American market. They found some things discouraging: substandard dealers, poor inventory, motorcycles sold on consignment, retailers provided consumer financing, and poor after-sales service. On the other hand, there were 450,000 motorcycle registrations every year, and 60,000 motorcycles were imported from Europe each year. The Honda people thought it was reasonable to shoot for ten percent of this import market. Other than that, "In truth, we had no strategy other than the idea of seeing if we could sell something in the United States," said one executive.

After getting a grudging currency allocation from the Japanese government, Honda rented a run-down warehouse in Los Angeles in July, 1959. The three executives they sent shared an $80 per month furnished apartment, with two sleeping on the floor. They stacked the crates and swept the floors themselves. By spring of 1960, they had forty dealers, who mostly sold the larger 250cc and 305cc bikes. The Honda people did not push the small, 50cc Supercubs; instead, they used them for transportation around Los Angeles.

In April disaster struck when the large bikes developed oil leaks. While the engineers back in Japan tried to solve the problem, a Sears buyer called about the Supercubs. Realizing they had no choice, they decided to let the small bikes go. They were phenomenally successful.

The "Nicest People" campaign was the result, in the author's words, of "an inadvertent sequence of events." It was conceived in the spring of 1963 by a junior advertising major at UCLA as part of a course requirement. He sold the idea to an advertising firm, which tried to persuade Honda to use it. The company's management team was badly split, but after much discussion, the Director of Sales convinced his peers that it was the right campaign.

By 1964, one out of every two motorcycles sold in the United States was a Honda. Late that year, the company announced that it would no longer ship on consignment, but would require cash on delivery. Even though every dealer reacted to this, none gave up its franchise.

THE "HONDA EFFECT"

In hindsight, these pivotal events—the engine designs achieved by Mr. Honda, the decision to go with the Supercubs, the "Nicest People" campaign, the cash delivery policy—all seem ho-hum common sense. But each day, as organizations live out their lives without the benefit of hindsight, few choose so well and so consistently.

"Western consultants, academics, and executives . . . tend to impute coherence and purposive reality to events when the opposite may be closer to the truth. How an organization deals with miscalculation, mistakes, and serendipitous events *outside its field of vision is often crucial to success over time.*"

Most Japanese products initially did poorly. For example, "The Japanese did not from the onset embark on a strategy to seize the high-quality small car market. They manufactured what they were accustomed to building in Japan and tried to sell it abroad . . . . Success . . . did not result from a bold insight by a few big brains at the top, [but from] senior managers humble enough not to take their initial strategic positions too seriously, [and from] the cumulative impact of 'little brains' . . . all contributing incrementally to the quality and market position these companies enjoy today.

"The Japanese don't use the term 'strategy' to describe a crisp business definition or competitive master plan. They think more in terms of 'strategic accommodation' or 'adaptive persistence,' underscoring their belief that corporate direction evolves from incremental adjustment to unfolding events . . . . 'Strategy' is defined as 'all the things necessary for the successful functioning of the organization as an adaptive mechanism.'"

1. *What do you think of the author's discussion of the word strategy in the first two paragraphs of the reading?*

This question is designed to stimulate discussion. The author is clearly criticizing the standard "planning" model of strategy. Some students may disagree with these criticisms, arguing that firms need the discipline imposed by strategic planning. They may also like the top-driven nature of this model, as well as its extensive use of empirical analytical tools. Other students may agree with the author's criticism, arguing that the planning approach is too laborious, too abstract.

2. *In summarizing what Honda did, the author says, "As organizations live out their lives without the benefit of hindsight, few choose so well and so consistently." Why was Honda so good and so consistent?*

Partly because they were flexible, but mostly because they were willing to learn from what was going on, whether it was good or bad. First, Mr. Honda was persistent in seeking lightweight, flexible, affordable designs. Second, when things went poorly with the bigger motorcycles which the company had hoped to sell in the United States. Honda was willing to shift to an emphasis on the Supercubs when that opportunity presented itself. Then, they seized on the "Nicest People" campaign when that came along. Lastly, having learned about their strong position in the market, Honda could insist on the cash-on-delivery policy.

3. *What would be your next course of action if you received a copy of the BCG report? What if you received a copy on what actually happened at Honda?*

This question is designed to highlight the differences in the two approaches. Recipients of the BCG approach would probably want to continue to analyze things. They would take the report back to the office and study it. This is almost the opposite of what the Honda executives did. They *acted* on the information they observed when they tried to sell their products. This is the crucial difference—the planning approach encourages analysis (reflection), but the Honda effect encourages *action*.

4. *What do you think of the author's notion of "big brains" and "little brains?"*

This question is designed to stimulate discussion. Some students will dislike the criticism of the "big brain" approach. Many of these students still think of managers, particularly top managers, as very powerful, very incisive thinkers, as "commanders." Other students will recognize that it is unlikely that only the top management of a firm will generate the ideas needed to keep the company moving forward. Ideas must come from as many sources as possible. These students will agree with the validity of the "little brain" approach.

5. *How useful is the term "adaptive persistence?"*

Of course students will differ on this question. Some will find it somewhat meaningless. Others will see the point Pascale is making. Success in forming strategy is a matter of being persistent (in the sense of always trying to improve), but also making sure to adapt and change as the organization learns what works and what doesn't.

6. *What do you think of the author's definition of "strategy" in the last sentence?*

He defines it as "all the things necessary for the successful functioning of the organization as an adaptive mechanism." This will strike some students as messy; it's not a "clean," crisp definition. But that is the point. As this and many other readings have said, strategy is not the precise statement of intentions, but the realization of whatever it will take to make things work. This kind of activity is probably going to be messy (but ultimately successful).

SECTION I CASES

EDWARD MARSHALL BOEHM, INC. TEACHING NOTE

Overview

This case is an excellent vehicle for introducing the basic concepts of corporate strategy, the structure of strategy, niching, and certain relationships between values and corporate strategy choices. It should be used early in a business policy course. As a short case, it literally can be read in class on the first day, if necessary. It allows the professor to begin the class with a discussion orientation, yet obtain rather complete closure on a complex strategy issue. The case itself concerns the positioning of a high quality, porcelain, art objects company. It goes well with readings on strategy formulation, value chains and differentiation, and the entrepreneurial context.

Session Structure

The case can be used to allow students to arrive at a definition of strategy empirically by formulating a strategy in their own words. The question "What should the strategy of Edward Marshall Boehm be?" tends to be an adequate opener. On the blackboard, the professor can then capture and catalog the comments of the students as they come forward, using any of the many structures provided in the book that he or she finds useful. A series of more structured questions (which follow) can be used to bring out different aspects of strategy.

Since this is a small company, it is normally useful to develop the strategy functionally, while emphasizing the interactivity between the functions. The marketing strategy deserves special attention, but should not become isolated from the production strategy, organization strategy, finance strategy, personnel strategy, or R&D strategy. These can be clearly related by using a category such as "corporate strategy" or "company concept" to show how the overall strategic concept drives and holds together the various component strategies.

Marketing Strategy

Normally, executives or students immediately dive into the marketing strategy by defining the product as "a high quality art objects line." Some students will want to limit the line severely and increase its price. Others may want to exploit the line's potential by large scale production. Others will want to develop a multiple product line, accomplishing several objectives for the corporation by using different product lines for each goal. Following are some of the more important issues from a marketing viewpoint.

Product Strategy: Should the company present a collector's art line? A limited line? A high quality gift line? High quality porcelain products? Functional products such as plates? Strictly art items? Multiple product lines? What degree of diversity is desirable in the product line? Just porcelain products? Paste <u>and</u> bone china? Birds and flowers? Other nature objects?

Pricing Strategy: What should be the pricing of the larger pieces vs. smaller pieces? Margins at retail and wholesale? Pricing relative to other porcelain? Pricing relative to other art objects? Should pricing be based on costs? Should potential speculation gains in market value be shared with customers or absorbed by Boehm? How should each line be priced? Each product within the line? Should Boehm or its retail distributors determine ultimate pricing? Why?

Teaching note copyright © 1987 by James Brian Quinn. This note prepared by Professor Quinn and Penny C. Paquette, Research Associate.

Advertising Strategy: This should depend on the product positioning taken. Should Boehm use electronic media? Printed media only? Which selected media? What message should be carried? How should the ads be formatted to differentiate the product? To whom should the ads be targeted? How should they attract attention?

Promotion: What kinds of promotions should Boehm use? Contests? Auctions? Gifts? Shows? Museums? Non-paid promotions (e.g., articles)? Talk shows? And so on? How can these be stimulated?

Distribution: Should distribution be broad-based? Selective? Exclusive? What are the advantages and disadvantages of each? If selective or exclusive distribution is used, what types of retail distribution outlets? How many per city? How many cities? Should mail order be used? Should selling be direct? Or through wholesalers? How many wholesalers/distributors? National or international? What controls should be maintained over distribution channels? How can this be done?

Marketing Research: How can Boehm determine what products will be successful? It is notably difficult to forecast sales for art objects. The company can use sales records from previous customers to identify patterns. But much will depend upon the intuition of Boehm's management. Little research on a particular product's potential is useful until the product is actually produced and demonstrated to customers.

Overall Company Concept

The marketing strategy leads naturally to a discussion of the overall concept of the company and the goals of Mr. and Mrs. Boehm. More astute students will suggest that one should very quickly talk to the Boehms and see what their personal goals and values are. These should be used to obtain a balance among various overall corporate goals. The Boehms were interested in: (1) having Mr. Boehm's art recognized and honored in the art world, (2) supporting nature and wildlife causes in a significant way, (3) and being very wealthy as a result of their company's success. Students will try to determine distinct priorities among these. Point out that the Boehms wanted to meet all three goals. But Mr. Boehm was more interested in art and nature. Mrs. Boehm was more interested in art and profitability. Both were interested in wildlife causes. This sets the stage for a discussion of the multiple goals of corporations and the impact personal values have in selecting the balance among such goals. Profit maximization alone would not be an appropriate goal in this situation. Students must then consider optimization vs. maximization.

Manufacturing Strategy

Manufacture of porcelain requires first the development of artistic sketches of the product. These must then be rendered in clay. The clay renderings are then rough cast in porcelain. The porcelain must then be finely sculptured into a positive master. The positive master casting must be very carefully designed, oversized relative to the ultimate casting, to allow for differential shrinking during kiln baking. Much hand work is needed both in the initial sculpting process and in later painting and glazing processes.

It is very difficult to automate a kiln for a wide variety of products. Balance of the size and shape of products within the kiln is a highly judgmental process. This raises the question of what skills are needed to expand production, in what sequence they should be obtained, and whether or not production should (1) purposely remain hand work to keep each product relatively unique or (2) be as mass production-oriented as possible. One can raise questions as to how to train workers when the output is a highly artistic piece. What kind of controls, motivation systems, inventory controls, etc., should be used?

Once the master negative molds have been made, a large number of similar castings can be made with relatively little further capital cost. Mr. Boehm could perhaps design one major piece per year (like Fondo Marino), plus perhaps one intermediate sized creation (like that in the picture) per month, plus a large number of the small "fledglings" if so desired. The distinctiveness of the ultimate product is clearly dictated by the sketch design and by the sculpturing, casting, and coloring techniques used in the final product.

Initial molds for the "large art objects" might run well over $100,000. Molds for the intermediate line might run $40-75,000; molds for the fledglings might cost only a few hundred dollars. Variable costs depend primarily on the complexity of the product and the degree of coloring and glazing they require. Variable costs per unit for the major art line might run multiple thousands of dollars. Variable costs for the intermediate line would run a few hundred dollars. Variable costs for the fledglings were tens of dollars. If a limited line strategy is adopted, approximately how many should be run in each category? Should the molds be broken?

Research and Development Strategy

Given the marketing and production strategies, what should R&D concentrate on? New clays? Cost reduction? Diversification? Quality control? Should the company seek patents or practice secret art? Its porcelain formulation is probably patentable. Processes are generally open art. How large should the R&D program be? How should it be staffed?

Personnel and Organization Strategy

What kinds of people should be sought? In what sequence? Where would you find the needed skills? What is the most crucial aspect of personnel policy? How should employees be motivated? How can Mr. Boehm's skills be transferred over to other people? How should the company be organized? Why?

Diversification Strategy

In what directions should Boehm diversify? Why? What portion of Boehm's revenues should be devoted to the bird line vs. diversification into other products? How should this diversification be sequenced? Guided? Motivated?

Financial Strategy

How should Boehm's proposed strategy be financed? Internally? By banks? Through a stock issue? Through venture capitalists? What should the Boehms' long-term financial concerns be? How can they maintain adequate control over the company in the long-term future? How can they get their own money out of the company? How rapidly can the company realistically grow? What will they do with it as they begin to age?

Policy and Limits

The case offers an interesting opportunity in each area to define the specific policies (rules or limits) that give focus to a strategy. These are crucial to a niche or focus strategy. In military strategy terms, the company can concentrate its forces in a single segment and become the dominant factor in that segment. As the company dominates, it produces higher margins through relative scale economies, can reinvest more than its competitors, and thus increase its dominance even more. To do this, it must limit distribution, limit its use of media very selectively, set strict rules on pricing, retailer control, image control, production and quality control, personnel hired, and so on. Each of these policies in the functional areas should be consistent. If they are, they create an additive, or synergistic effect, which gives them even higher impact. The case provides an ideal vehicle for discussing the difference between policies and goals, policies and programs, and the use of policy in strategy.

Sequence of Actions

It is very productive to ask the students at a certain stage what actions they would take first, second, etc. This brings up the use of sequencing to conserve resources and gain focus in strategy. In this case, probably the first step is to gain better insights through certain market information sources, then build the name of the company through careful promotion and advertising, rapidly create a replacement for Mr. Boehm, develop support skills in the organization for production, then change the distribution channels to match the selected concept of the company, develop extremely careful quality and cost controls during the buildup period, and later diversify the line slowly, diversify internationally, and plan for a transition in management toward at least some percentage of professional management.

Overall Strategy

The discussion should at certain crucial stages address who potential competitors may be. Just porcelain manufacturers? All porcelain manufacturers? All art objects producers? By clipping some advertisements, it is interesting to demonstrate the different positions of competitors in this marketplace. Boehm has to define its basis for distinctive competitive advantage. Is this just in design? Design and porcelain? Design, quality production, and porcelain material? Design, quality, porcelain, distribution and image? If a high end focus strategy is taken, each element in the company's value chain should support this. Using the Porter structure one can carry this through very thoroughly. To integrate all these functional strategies, a very interesting discussion can be developed on how one conceptualizes the difference in appearance between Boehm's birds and those of perhaps Mrs. Dowdy (in England), Royal Copenhagen, or other specialty porcelain groups. How does one build on Mr. Boehm's unique strengths in achieving this conceptual focus?

SUMMARY OF OUTCOMES

Students should not be asked to second-guess the actual decisions of management. Nor do such decisions provide right or wrong answers to a case. Nevertheless, a brief summary may be helpful to both professor and students in considering their own analyses.

Mr. Boehm died shortly after the date of the case. Fortunately, an extremely talented younger artist had been working with him for some time. This man had begun to share some of Mr. Boehm's own personal values concerning wildlife art and had developed substantial skills in the design of porcelain art objects. Mrs. Boehm, however, was the driving entrepreneur behind the future history of the company. Over a period of time, she did the following things. She first concentrated on developing a firm reputation for a limited line of collectors' porcelain art objects. The major art objects were largely used as promotional pieces to extend the reputation of the Boehm line. The mid-sized birds were used as the major cash generator of the business. The fledglings were kept to sell to younger people, to extend the reputation of Boehm to a wider marketplace, and to train artisans for the company.

To establish the name of the company on a permanent basis, Mrs. Boehm called it "The Studio of Edward Marshall Boehm" just as there was a Studio of Rubens, etc., in the past. She then got Richard Nixon, who was then President of the United States, to let the company design a Boehm statue as a gift of state for a significant occasion. Mr. Nixon chose a Boehm mute swan as a symbol of peace for his impending visit to China with Mao Tse-tung. This extraordinary piece began to symbolize the continuing capabilities of the Studio of Edward Marshall Boehm.

Mrs. Boehm in earlier years had used as promotions sales of Boehm products to major museums. She had arranged a gift of Boehm porcelain from President Eisenhower to Prince Philip and from President Eisenhower to Prime Minister Diefenbaker of Canada. She was also very talented in placing articles in major art and "living" magazines about the Boehm product and company. She also had obtained interviews on the major television talk shows, etc. Along with Mr. Boehm, she had developed near the Trenton Boehm factory one of the world's finest private aviaries. She created a museum of Boehm art next to the factory. The factory itself is a showpiece to help interest people in Boehm porcelain.

When the name Boehm was sufficiently established, she cut the distribution of Boehm products to approximately 50 retail outlets. These were very carefully selected to be the premier department stores in their areas. The company very carefully controlled the way in which the product was displayed, sales clerks were trained, compensated, etc. Boehm maintained a careful control list of those who owned major Boehm products in order to ensure that no one cornered the market. The product was priced well above its competition. Nevertheless, Mrs. Boehm saw to it that purchasers obtained the major benefit of any appreciation in value on the products. This supported their positioning as collectors' items in the art market.

The Boehm's did not want to lose control over their product or concept. Consequently, with some minor exceptions, they financed the operation internally. As the company's profitability grew, its capacities to borrow grew. At key junctures, the company also financed itself by encouraging its large, well-known customers to pay on relatively short terms to maintain cash flows for the company.

In its technological strategy, Boehm tried to avoid disclosing its processes or formulas for porcelain through patent publications. It tended to practice its porcelain art quietly to avoid competitive incursions. As the Boehm birds became more successful, the company diversified its product line into other art objects such as flowers, special art displays having to do with a geographical area (such as Egypt or China), and into thin porcelain pictures. The latter product represents perhaps the most difficult of all porcelain arts. Casting a thin porcelain picture with square edges, and maintaining key dimensions during firing, is most difficult. The company has done very well. Boehm further diversified by an acquisition of a bone china company (Malvern) in England. And its products are now recognized worldwide. Mrs. Boehm is now beginning to face the difficult question of what to do with the company in the long run.

GENENTECH, INC. TEACHING NOTE

Overview

Genentech was the most successful IPO of its era, and its success launched an entire new industry. The Genentech case should normally be placed early in the course sequence. It deals with the start-up of a new enterprise, venture capital strategies, and the early positioning strategies of a truly entrepreneurial company. The case can also be used as a vehicle for discussing values and their impact on corporate strategy and the desired structure of goals in a large organization. Genentech goes well with readings on strategy formulation, the entrepreneurial context, culture, the innovation context, and adhocracy structures. Genentech set the pattern for start-up financing in long-term, high-tech fields for several decades. Because biotechnology is such an exciting and current field, the case tends to have strong interest for executives and students. One collateral set of issues in the case has to do with the regulation and control of the biotechnology industry. This portion of the discussion ties in with the Mintzberg article on power.

Session Structure

We usually begin the case discussion by looking at the nature of high-tech start-ups, Genentech's pre-start-up strategy (before 1976), then move to the venture capitalist's strategy (1976-77), the early positioning strategy for Genentech, and then the longer term strategy for developing Genentech for the future. Fairly frequently, we insert a discussion on values and corporate goals just after the discussion of the venture capitalist's strategy. This outline will follow the latter approach.

Basic Research Strategies

Prior to 1976, the biotechnology field primarily consisted of groups either funding or performing basic and early applied research in a rapidly moving scientific field. Such a field is characterized by the following dimensions:

A. <u>A highly diffuse grouping</u> of technical centers performing the research. Strategies are dominantly guided by individuals' technical backgrounds and interests, funding availability, and publication opportunities.

B. <u>Very long time horizons</u>. From Watson and Crick's definition of the structure of the DNA molecule until the first introduction of a product, 26 years elapsed (from 1958 to 1984). Even from the first laboratory demonstration of the recombinant DNA phenomenon to the marketplace, 12 years elapsed (1972-1984). Scientific expertise, inquisitiveness, and persistence are the critical success factors during this time period.

C. <u>Network strategies</u> are necessary to keep up with the field at this time. One acquires knowledge by working the nodes among the highly diffuse centers at which knowledge is generated. Because the probability of any single project's advancing to commercial success is very low (1/1,000) and time horizons are so long, it is difficult for companies to develop products from a basic research stance. Consequently, they tend to form flexible "listening" strategies designed to keep up with the field and to move in a timely fashion as the technology begins to move toward applied or development phases.

Teaching note copyright © 1996 by James Brian Quinn. This note prepared by Professor Quinn and Penny C. Paquette, Research Associate.

D. <u>Support for the field</u> tends to come from government, foundation, or university funds. One can ask some interesting questions about why governments should sponsor such research when corporations cannot or will not. Is it truly economical for the country? Since the whole society can ultimately capture the benefits of such basic research (while a single company could not): it may make economic sense for the society to support such research, even though it might not be economically sound for a company to do so. When one realizes that many of the frontier discoveries in biotechnology were made during inquiries on small creature genetic structures (such as frogs' eyes and moths' lungs), one can develop a greater understanding of: (1) why it is so difficult to judge the worth of basic research, (2) why politicians might have to support such research without very careful controls, and (3) why allocating national resources to this kind of work is so judgmental.

E. <u>"Unplanned" random spurts of progress</u> are common in such a field. Any reader of Watson and Crick's book (or any other major technological history) will be struck by the fact that science moves forward in fits, spurts, and frustrations, rather unpredictably. Trying to plan such work in a linear fashion is not good strategy. An effective strategy recognizes the randomness of the process and sets up appropriate listening, networking, exchange of information, etc. strategies to deal with and exploit the process as it actually occurs. This kind of problem faces many large companies today; they cannot conceivably cover all these sciences potentially relevant to their futures.

F. <u>A focus on individual researchers</u> is essential. A few researchers tend to lead in basic research fields and are in the best position to gather and trade information at the "nodes" of the field. Supporting and listening to these few researchers offers high leverage on one's investment dollar.

Venture Capital Strategy

An interesting set of issues underlies a venture capital group's method of operating during the period when it is investing only $100-200,000 in seed capital—as in the early stages of Genentech's development. The professor can ask, "What should the venture capitalist's strategy be? What are the primary things the venture capitalist is looking for? How should the deal be structured? Why was this particular structure chosen in the Genentech case?" Following are some of the more interesting issues presented:

A. <u>A Large Upside Potential</u>. The venture capitalist looks first at the nature of the opportunity. He expects to see a "big" opportunity. This means tens to hundreds of millions of dollars in sales potential over a five-year time frame. One can ask whether marketing research is of much use at this stage. Clearly only very broad numbers are relevant. Even with 6-7 years of hindsight, one cannot yet estimate the true market for many of Genentech's biotechnology products.

B. <u>The Payoff</u>. Venture capitalists tend to look for very high returns. Currently, venture capitalists look for ten times their money back in five years or five times their money back in three years. One can ask how this kind of structure contrasts with the expectations for investments in large corporations. What would be the effect of putting such "hurdle rates" on certain types of projects?

C. <u>The People</u>. Venture capitalists tend to spend more time evaluating the people involved in the project than do other capital sources. They want to have the finest team of people in the world working on their project. If there is a large business opportunity and the most competent people in the world are working on it, the venture capitalist has the highest probability of achieving a positive return. Venture capitalists want not just technical expertise and business expertise, but intense personal commitment to be apparent. To ensure this, most venture capitalists spend much of their time evaluating people. The values and drives of individuals are most important in this evaluation.

D. <u>The Deal</u>. Only after a basic look at the business opportunity and a careful evaluation of people do venture capitalists look seriously at the financial numbers. In this case, it is worthwhile to ask why convertible preferred stock is used. There are several reasons. First, the venture capitalist wants some protection if the investment goes sour. Since there are likely to be few salable physical assets, the "preferred" position gives the venture capitalist access to any <u>technology</u> developed, prior to common shareholders' interest. However, equally important are the peculiar characteristics of preferred stock. Preferred does not require repayment of its face value. Interest payments can be delayed or abrogated by the parties upon mutual agreement. Consequently, the company is not committed to the same level of cash payouts that it would be if convertible debentures were used. In addition, convertible preferred stock (like convertible debentures) allows the investor to gain the "upside" benefits of a truly successful project. Moreover, preferred stock is looked upon as equity by banks, consequently it can be leveraged with other loans. Yet, common shareholders tend to look at preferred as debt, not interfering with their equity positions until it is converted.

E. <u>The Value of the Company</u>. It is interesting to ask what value the venture capitalists are implicitly asking the other investors to place on the company. Since they are seeking $500,000 for 11% of the company, implicitly an investor must place a $4.5 million value on the total company. Is this an appropriate value? One can look at the projected net incomes three years hence of $3 million. If such an income is achieved and a price earnings multiple of 15 is maintained, the company would then be worth $45 million or ten times the original evaluation. This seems like a reasonable return for this type of situation.

F. <u>A Private Placement</u>. One can question why the initial offering is done as a "private placement." This allows much more flexibility in dealing with investors, lowers the cost of making the placement, and brings in people who are more likely to provide "patient money" than a public stock offering would. Private placements keep owners from seeking early payouts of dividends. The professor should note that there are severe restrictions on private placements under state and SEC regulations. Only a small number (usually interpreted as 35) of "knowledgeable" or "qualified" investors may be contacted about the placement. Such investors must have a sufficient capability that if the investment goes bad, they can absorb the loss. There are specific requirements under each state's "blue sky" laws to protect innocent, small investors from being fraudulently deceived by private placement brokers. The professor may wish to look up private placement requirements in a financial handbook.

G. <u>Control</u>. Most sophisticated venture capitalists do not seek 51% or greater financial control at this stage. They are afraid that such control would lessen the motivation of the founders of the company. Instead, they insist on board positions and access to internal company records so that they can track and monitor their investments well. They want sufficient board representation to be able to replace or guide incompetent managements.

H. <u>The Early Plan</u>. In return for the initial $100-200,000 investment, venture capitalists would expect the co-founders to: (1) develop a clear business plan, (2) demonstrate that they could manage both the research process and an organization, (3) attract good people to work with them, and (4) achieve (if possible) laboratory "proof of principle" for the new technique. The latter may or may not be possible within this low level of funding, but the venture capitalist would want to know that no insurmountable obstacles could be identified.

I. <u>Decreased Downside Risk</u>. The venture capitalist also moves to decrease downside risk by: (1) developing a risk portfolio for its investments in which some investments are "sure bets," others offer high probability of reasonable gains, and some are high risk but with high gain potentials; (2) insisting that venturers not invest heavily in fixed plant or fancy facilities; (3) making sure that the management team is the "best group in the world"—if they fail, anyone else probably would; (4) using some preferred stock or debentures in the structure; (5) obtaining other venture capitalists' support in the project to spread risks; (6) releasing the money in small pieces, i.e., $100,000 units at a time.

J. A Way Out. Venture capitalists want to see a way to get their money out of the enterprise, typically by going public or a partial or total sellout within a reasonable time.

The above are the critical elements in a venture capitalist's strategy at this stage. A very interesting discussion of these elements usually results. The professor will have to lead students through the financial portions of the transaction, since they are typically not knowledgeable in this area.

Corporate Goals

One can then ask what seem to be the goals of Genentech, Inc. These fall out directly from quotes in the case. They include the following:

A. To commercialize recombinant DNA and be the first to bring the benefits of this powerful technology to society.
B. To build one of the finest scientific teams in this field and to be a continuing contributor to the scientific community.
C. To build a major integrated, profitable company.
D. To integrate both the scientific and business aspects of the recombinant DNA field.
E. To create a truly innovative research organization.
F. To remain on the leading edge of the technology.
G. To develop and select products in great demand.
H. To be an attractive company in terms of investment returns over five years.
I. To be controlled by the company's own management.
J. To have 1980 sales of $15 million and profits of $3 million with sales of over $100 million in the late 1980s.

The class can then critique this particular goal structure. Should the company consider only "maximizing profits for shareholders?" Why does the company develop or need multiple goals? Are the goals adequate in specificity and coverage? If not, what types of goals are needed? How can a company manage to meet such a wide variety of goals? Should the goals be made consistent? If not, how does one obtain consistency among them?

One can point out that there are many different stakeholders in the company other than shareholders. Any adequate set of goals would reflect a conscious attempt to consider the interests of all stakeholders including customers, employees, the scientific community, investors, management, suppliers, and so on. They tend to address the following points: (1) the overall mission of the company, (2) the distinctive competency of the company, (3) people development, (4) areas for innovation and improvement, (5) degrees of market penetration, (6) the company's image, (7) financial results sought, (8) ownership, growth, and productivity goals. Although in total, Genentech's stated goals may not have enough specific dimensions to them, they do offer overall guidance, they do help attract people to the company, they do help make the company attractive to investors and to the local community, and they do state the overall mission of the company relatively well.   More specificity is needed, however, in product market scope, geographic areas served, managerial development, physical plant and resources, and productivity relative to competitors.

The case allows the professor to develop or utilize whatever specific framework for goal setting he or she finds most useful. Checklists for the nature and structure of corporate goals are easily found in any reasonable policy text. We suggest that the professor present a balanced choice among these to ensure that students approach strategy problems with a concept of the breadth of goals needed by an enterprise and the difficulty of establishing these in ways which do not overly conflict. If the goal structure is found to be inadequate, students should be asked to complete the goal statement after analyzing the next section on Genentech's early introduction strategy.

Early Introduction Strategy

The case provides an excellent vehicle for developing the concept of a niche strategy. We usually break Genentech's strategy down into a series of functional strategies integrated by an overall concept statement. A structure of this sort follows. There is no right answer to the case. The pros and cons of different postures can be pursued. However, in a niche strategy, one is trying to obtain maximum consistency among the different functional strategies and (to the extent possible) the synergy of each functional strategy supporting other functional strategies in specific ways. We usually build the functional strategies first and then (as they begin to interact) develop a corporate concept statement which embraces the specifics developed in each functional area. Consequently, the following structure will start with functional strategies and end with a concept statement. Obviously, some other sequence could be followed. Following are the critical questions to raise relative to each of the functional strategies:

A. Technological Strategy

How can Genentech attract the high quality researchers it needs to fulfill its goals? How can it be more attractive to researchers than a university? Than its large competitors? Should it offer stock to attract people or give stock upon completion of specific technological targets? Can it offer greater freedom than the universities? Better laboratory facilities? Publication support?

The question of publication policy is an important one. High quality researchers will not come to Genentech without being allowed to publish results in professional journals. Such publication can, however, be made after a patent application has been filed without impinging heavily on the rights of the individual. A progressive publication policy will soon be seen to support marketing strategies, financial strategies, and personnel strategies. This is a major point of synergy.

How can Genentech best join in the networking process needed to stay "on course?" In joint ventures with universities? Should it license its technology to others, or should it practice the technology internally? Can patents really be obtained on new life forms? How can early stage research be financed? Since expected lead times will be 3-7 years, this is a very difficult and important question.

B. Marketing Strategy

The overall marketing strategy is made up of several component strategies:

(1) Product Strategy. Product strategies will ultimately depend upon which research projects are undertaken and which succeed. These in turn will depend upon the skills and interests of the particular researchers selected. In the early stages, Genentech should probably pursue: relatively simple compounds, with the shortest possible time to the marketplace, with a very broad market application, products which are currently being made by others, but for which recombinant DNA can lower costs significantly. While concentrating on a relatively few such molecules in the early stages of development, Genentech should probably disperse its bets a little in order to improve its probability of success—i.e., it should undertake 2-5 projects in parallel. In fact, these included somatostatin, insulin, human growth hormone (HGH), and thymocin Alpha1 and several different types of interferon. Later, Genentech also developed a hoof and mouth disease vaccine for animals.

One of the early questions was whether the company should concentrate on human health, animal health, plant biology, or biotechnology for the chemicals industry. There are pros and cons for each area of concentration. However, it is helpful to note that concentrating on human health meets several goals simultaneously: (a) it matches the interests and values of key researchers like Boyer, Itakura, and Riggs, (b) the products of human health research are glamorous and can achieve greater publicity, (c) if successful, such research can help the company obtain very high price earnings multiples, (d) by concentrating on chemicals/drugs already in the marketplace, Genentech could shorten the FDA drug clearance process—the major negative to a "human health" strategy, (e) human health products often had a very large potential for cost reduction.

(2) Customer strategy. Should Genentech attempt to sell directly to doctors, hospitals, other health providers? Or should it sell to pharmaceutical manufacturers? If it chooses to sell to pharmaceutical companies, should it sell its technology? Products? Processes and nutrients? Genentech chose to split its line, selling certain products requiring mass distribution capabilities in bulk through large pharmaceutical companies and also targeting a few specialty products which could be sold directly on their own merit by a relatively small sales force to doctors, hospitals, etc.

(3) Promotion should probably be done largely through scientific papers, conferences, and newsworthy articles which increase the credibility of the company and its products in the process. The scientific community, professional investors, and the general business community should be targets. Note how this hinges to the publication policy described above.

(4) Advertising should probably be directed on an institutional basis to financial concerns and to potential customers, pharmaceutical companies and health providers. Much more emphasis should be placed on scientific publication and general publicity than formal advertising, whose impact is likely to be diffuse.

(5) Distribution will vary according to the product strategies chosen. Products sold through the pharmaceutical companies would be sold in bulk for a royalty, with Genentech perhaps providing early batch manufacturing. Products sold directly by Genentech will require a highly specialized sales force "detailing" the product directly to health providers. Such a sales force is expensive to develop. Genentech needs to develop special incentives to attract professional salesmen for this purpose. Stock bonuses and incentives may be appropriate for this purpose.

It should be pointed out how expensive it is for Genentech to develop its own sales force, vs. the logic of its other early strategy to present its product to the market through pharmaceutical companies. For the latter segment, an important question was whether Genentech should use the largest producer of the existing product or a somewhat smaller competing producer who might give Genentech's products more aggressive sales emphasis. Genentech chose to go with the largest existing producer in order to minimize potentially destructive pricing competition.

(6) Pricing strategy. How should Genentech price its new products relative to the benefits they brought its collaborators? Should it take just a royalty? Should Genentech require that collaborators make "front end" investments in its R&D projects? How can Genentech protect its royalties if a new biotechnology approach (like using yeast instead of bacteria) comes along to produce for the market at a lower cost? How should the producer of the drug price it in the marketplace? Relative to cost? Relative to other products? Relative to potential benefits?

If competitive biotechnology processes are developed, these will force costs and prices down to approximately 1/100th of what they are currently. Then even a large market like insulin will seem small. If initial prices are kept too high, this will encourage competition. Some initial "skimming" followed by a steady decline in market prices will help protect Genentech's position. How should this be negotiated with collaborators? How should Genentech price the bulk materials it sells to pharmaceutical companies for their preparation and distribution? How should this be related to the royalty structure?

(7) Finance strategy. What will be the major financial needs of Genentech? How should it finance these? If it develops joint ventures with large pharmaceutical companies, will the latter pay for initial research? Drug clearance? Major facilities investments? How can Genentech finance its own long-term research and development efforts? Is there an opportunity to use research and development limited partnerships? Clinical limited partnerships? If Genentech goes public to support its own internal research, what should determine the timing of releasing the issue? How would one price the issue?

Note that the major financial commitments for a new drug were in the $10-20 million range (now $50 to $200 million) necessary to conduct clinical trials and get FDA clearances and in the manufacturing facilities to produce it. Establishing a major distribution network would also run in the high $10s of millions. Genentech needs to concentrate its own internal financing on what gives it greatest leverage, i.e., development of new drugs through biotechnology, new biotechnology processes for producing these drugs, and research on new methodologies for producing biological entities. These activities are probably best financed with equity capital, while clinical trials and FDA clearances and production facilities can be financed by limited partnerships or joint ventures.

C. Production Strategy

Should Genentech be manufacturing products at all? Should it do only small scale batch processing? Should it do enough production to make sure that it stays au courant in basic production knowledge? Can it use production technology to maintain its royalty streams with its customers even after the initial patents or technologies become obsolescent? These are crucial strategic questions. If Genentech does not maintain control over production processes, it is likely to become technologically obsolescent itself. On the other hand, if it develops small scale batch processes and maintains a strong production research group, it can control a crucial factor for the success of its customers—and thus maintain its long-term royalty stream.

D. Organization Strategy

In order to develop its special competency behind such research endeavors, Genentech needs to provide an attractive atmosphere for research. Key to this are good laboratory facilities, a great deal of research freedom, high morale, and perhaps stock incentives for accomplishing the first expression of new biotechnological agents. In addition, there are some crucial top level management questions. Who should follow Swanson as CEO? Who should be COO? This person should undoubtedly be production and marketing oriented. Who should direct research, since Dr. Boyer does not wish to do so? What should Boyer's role be? Emphasis in this discussion should be in keeping the organization informal, flat, attractive to young biotechnologists, yet also having a few premier personalities like Boyer or Goeddel available for consultation and stimulation inside the company. Open access should be provided to university research laboratories and to major discussion forums. Note how these policies support those in other areas.

E. Diversification Strategies

After Genentech is successful with the cloning of a few biotechnological proteins, it should begin considering how widely to diversify its line. Should it go into animal health as well? Chemicals? Plant sciences? Note that the data in the case show that the chemicals and plant markets are among the largest in the world for biotechnology products. Should Genentech niche and concentrate its resources solely on the human health field? If so, why? If not, why not?

F. Overall Company Concept

After developing these functional strategies, one should show how the marketing strategy can support the financial strategy, technology supports marketing, personnel and publicity strategies support financial and marketing strategies, and so on. By making policies in each of these value chain areas consistent, Genentech can develop a high technology niche or focus strategy. It can also get synergies from the interactions of its functional strategies.

A final set of questions involves, "What should the overall company concept be? Should Genentech be a research company? A research and manufacturing company? A fully integrated research-marketing company? A human health company? A diversified biotechnological products company?" Students should be asked to relate this selection to the available resources of the company, i.e., what fields can Genentech dominate with the resources it has at hand? How can this initial niche be related to the future potentials of the company as it grows its research base? Should Genentech be a U.S. company? A world company? What differences do these two definitions make? This is a good point at which to ask the students to write a mission statement for Genentech and to discuss what the structure, purpose, and content of such a mission statement should be. Students should have enough information in hand to do a thorough job at this stage.

Long-term Strategy

What should the long-term strategy of Genentech be? What sequence should this occur in? What are the key dimensions of such a strategy? Probably the following are the most crucial elements—somewhat in the sequence they should, or are likely to, occur.

A. Build a base of technology and credibility about the technology.
B. Build resources of people, patents, and finances through royalties.
C. Build coalitions with customers to exploit research results and to leverage resources.
D. Concentrate on human health first with some side bets in other areas if FDA does not approve drugs rapidly or if reactionary forces do not allow patenting of recombinant DNA products. Options perhaps in animal health and plant science would seem most appropriate. Chemicals would seem a bit far afield.
E. Develop process capabilities in support of biotechnological entities which have been created in the laboratory. Emphasize small scale batch processes and extreme flexibility.
F. Perform biotechnological research for others on a royalty basis, if successful. Use royalties to finance research.
G. Develop a strong patent base; constantly lobby for full patent protection for biotechnological entities and processes. Actively engage in the public discussion of patents in this field. This is crucial to the company.
H. Defend the company's technological integrity by maintaining absolute quality standards on products and plant safety issues. Join in coalitions with universities and leading thinkers to develop safe methodologies for producing and experimenting with biological agents.
I. Keep Wall Street and scientific journals informed of progress. Because Wall Street does not understand biotechnology, become a source of information for investors.
J. By allowing researchers to publish and maintain interactions with universities and other leading biotechnological information sources, maintain a network to be in a leadership position in research into new health arenas.
K. Wait until the company has definitely produced several attractive biotechnological agents which can demonstrate the technology, then go public. This should maximize multiples. The timing of the issue is important.
L. Develop a professional organization, especially at the top management level, to support Swanson and Boyer. Elements of this have been described above.
M. Undergo a phased development of products, dominating each market sector entered. Maintain a high profile in publication circles to create the special competencies in research and development on which Genentech depends.

National Policy Issues

There are a number of national policy issues which can be investigated with interest and benefit. Chief among these are the following:

A. Patent rights. Should the country allow patenting of human biological materials cloned by recombinant DNA? What are the pros and cons? If such entities were first created in a university laboratory or under a federal grant, should an exclusive license be allowed to ensure that a company would be willing to develop and produce these agents? What are the effects of patent policy on research? Development? Early exploitation? Economics? University structures?

B. Public Safety. How can public safety be ensured? How dangerous are biotechnological entities? Can the research process be made "inherently safe?" How can plants be designed or monitored to secure safety? Who should set standards? Don't the people who will be setting the standards have an interest in seeing the technology exploited? How does one make the trade-offs between public benefit and public risk? Should these be local regulations or national regulations? Why?

C. What is the likely impact on university structures of a growing biotechnology "industry?" If professors are allowed to participate in companies and make large amounts of money from recombinant DNA technology, will they be willing to teach and develop new talent in the field? If not, won't the industry eat its own "seed corn?" How does one ensure the scientific objectivity necessary for high quality academic research when such research can lead to very high profitability?

D. Secrecy vs. Publication. What should national policies be relative to publication of results under federal grants? University research activities? How can one allow the maintenance of enough of a proprietary position to encourage a company to take the risk of introducing a new product?

E. Responsibility. Who is responsible if an error is committed? The researcher? The institution doing the research? The government for permitting the research to go on? Science in general for not understanding what could happen? The public for undertaking a risk which caused a particular individual's pain? This is a major issue in national research policy and could be pursued at some length.

F. Clearance of Drugs. The FDA is often criticized for taking 6-10 years to clear drugs. U.S. drug clearance standards are higher than those in most areas of the world. This means that the U.S. population does not have access to some of the most current research results. How can FDA policy be made responsive to both the potentials of alpha and beta errors in drug clearance?

G. Irresponsible Press. How can the press be kept from misinforming the public by emphasizing the more terrifying aspects of recombinant DNA however improbable they may be as opposed to its more likely potential benefits? What rights should companies have when their integrity and profitability are threatened by a press or media presentation which unfairly presents the risks of their technology? How should companies manage relationships with the media to improve outcomes?

H. Short Time Horizons. Why did larger companies not develop this technology? What keeps larger companies from undertaking long-term research and development like this? Are there any appropriate remedies for this shortcoming? Why could small companies undertake such ventures while large companies could not?

I. What important moral or ethical issues does recombinant DNA pose? How should these be resolved within a policy structure of government? Companies? Individuals and universities?

All of the above pose fascinating and rich areas for discussion of the interface between corporate strategy and national policy. If the country leads in recombinant DNA research, it can potentially maintain a leadership position in the chemical and health care industries. If it does not, the public may suffer in terms of health care, and many industries may lag in next generation production technologies. Yet the issues posed above are very real and should not be simply set aside as "other issues" or values issues which cannot be discussed or reconciled within some type of policy forum.

SUMMARY OF OUTCOMES

While the actual actions and strategies followed by a company do not indicate correct or incorrect solutions to a set of problems, they may be helpful to the professor in raising issues or leading the discussion.

Genentech followed a strategy of developing new products and biotechnological processes dominantly for the human health field. The human health focus combined the interests of Dr. Boyer and the young biotechnologists who were attracted to Genentech with the advantages of a potentially high margin field which could obtain high publicity if solutions were achieved. A genuine demand existed for lower cost or more widely available products in the ethical pharmaceutical field. In some cases (such as insulin or interferon), new solutions could be achieved only by revolutionary new production processes or through biological processes which produced the desired chemical agent directly from gene sources. After achieving some initial successes in the human health field, Genentech did some joint research with the Department of Agriculture to develop a hoof and mouth disease (HMD) vaccine. However, it later withdrew from non-human health fields.

Genentech's basic strategy was to create an environment which was attractive to first-rate scientists and researchers and gave them incentives to develop frontier state-of-the-art biotechnological solutions to human health problems. Genentech started with a relatively simple series of proteins, notably somatostatin, insulin, and human growth hormone. It proved the principle of the new technology on the simpler compounds and then (with the knowledge developed) moved toward more complex compounds. It constantly tried to select as targets compounds: (1) which would have far-reaching therapeutic benefits (2) where biotechnology could lower costs significantly, (3) which could be sold through partnerships with large pharmaceutical companies, or (4) which (in some cases) could be sold with a very limited sales force to a highly specialized marketplace.

The early products Genentech chose to create (like somatostatin and insulin) were chemicals already cleared for human use by the FDA. This shortened the clearance process and decreased the risk and expenditures associated with bringing the drug to the market. For entities which were already on the market, Genentech usually chose a co-partnership with the largest existing producer of that entity. The co-partner helped support the initial research on the biotechnology solution, handled the clearance of the drug through FDA, and invested in the large-scale production facilities necessary to bring it to the marketplace. This avoided Genentech's having to invest in large facilities, a clinical research group (to oversee drug clearances), or a large marketing and detailing sales staff. Royalties from the sale of these entities supported further research by Genentech. Later, Genentech developed research clinical partnerships for the clearance of drugs, thus expanding its own capital capabilities enormously.

In addition, Genentech targeted a few products which it thought would have very important therapeutic effects, would require only a small specialized sales force, and could be defended through patents. For these products Genentech maintained total control over development and built up the required clinical staff to clear the drugs. At the crucial moment, it built in a sales staff of experienced salesmen, recruited from the larger pharmaceutical companies using valuable stock bonuses.

To recruit the kinds of researchers it wanted, Genentech created a very attractive research atmosphere. (See details below.) It rewarded well people who worked for Genentech. If they achieved target milestones of accomplishment, they could be given stock. Dr. Boyer did not want to be a full-time employee, but was available as a stimulus for researchers and a person to whom they could refer. Later, Genentech was able to attract several very well-known researchers to its staff to provide a critical mass of knowledgeable people who would be available for advice, stimulation, and counsel to its young research teams.

To create identity and morale among its researchers, Genentech developed a series of unique practices, including a "DNA cheer" used when a new protein was biotechnologically synthesized. It developed informal get-together sessions called the Friday afternoon "ho-hos." Its researchers worked in very small teams, and agreed to apply for patents in a fashion that would protect the company's interest at the time of publication of results. The company allowed publication within these rules to help stimulate the researchers and to attract the quality of people it sought.

Early Developments

In June 1979, Genentech announced the successful bacterial production of human growth hormone using molecular biological techniques. Somatostatin had 14 amino acids, insulin 51, and HGH 191 amino acids. This indicates the degree of scaling up and complexity which occurred after the company had demonstrated early successes with somatostatin and insulin. In December 1979, in a joint project with USDA's animal disease center, Genentech created a new vaccine for hoof and mouth disease. This was the first time that a Class 5 pathogen, a potentially deadly disease agent, had been synthesized by biotechnological techniques. Later (March 1980), it announced thymocin alpha1, which held promise for the treatment of brain and lung cancer. At the same time it announced that it had created human pro-insulin, offering the prospect of much greater production yields in insulin itself. In early 1980, Genentech also announced it had produced two new types of interferon (human leukocyte and human fibroblast). From this point on, Genentech became a leading source of breakthroughs in the reproduction of human health agents through biotechnological means.

In a historic decision on June 17, 1980, the Supreme Court ruled 4-5 that new life forms created in the laboratory were eligible for patents. This was the last major policy break which was necessary for pharmaceutical and biotechnological companies to exploit rDNA techniques, and created a very favorable situation in the stock market for public offerings by new biotechnology companies. Genentech created the market itself in October 1980 when during its initial public offering its stock exploded to a peak of $89 before subsiding to $72, almost twice its expected introduction price. Genentech's timing was superb. Before going public, it had demonstrated its capability to develop biotechnological entities and the credibility that it could continue to do so, and had become slightly profitable. Its public offering provided the capital for other major research endeavors by Genentech.

The corporation entered into a joint venture with Eli Lilly for the development of insulin and with Kabi for the development and production of somatostatin. Similar relationships were entered into with large pharmaceutical companies when they had premier positions in existing pharmaceutical products for which Genentech was developing biotechnological alternatives. Other biotechnology concerns' stock soon appeared on the stock exchange. However, none enjoyed the number of technical successes that Genentech did. This probably comes back to the very careful thought Genentech gave to its personnel policies to attract, motivate, and hold first-rate biotechnological talent. The research atmosphere produced by Genentech was crucial to its entire strategy.

To develop recombinant DNA technology safely, Dr. Cohen (along with others) led a far-reaching discussion among biologists to create careful standards and controls for research in the field. One crucial element was to develop a bacterium for experimental use which would make it essentially impossible for life-threatening recombinant DNA products to get out of a laboratory environment and survive. As a result of their work, the National Institute of Health set up the Recombinant DNA Advisory Committee (RAC) to approve any scale-up facilities or experimental regimes involving biotechnology. By 1985-86, the first major biotechnological products were entering the marketplace. The first human health product was Genentech-Lilly's insulin. Genentech's product Prototropin (HGH) for hypopituitary dwarfism was soon available to treat some 10,000-15,000 children. The FDA gave rapid clearance to the product (just 23 months) because of the tragic nature of the disease. The prospects for the market expanded as new applications were found and the cost dropped. The potential market for HGH was estimated to be some $100 million by 1988.

Late 1980s Development

However, the most important mid-1980s development for Genentech was a tissue plasminogen activator (TPA), a substance that dissolves blood clots in heart attack victims. Analysts estimated a probable market for this product (called Activase) of some $500 million per year in the near future. To develop its organization, Genentech hired as COO Dr. Rabb, an experienced M.D. with pharmaceutical management experience.

By the late 1980s, many products were available for diagnostic purposes. Therapeutic agents such as alpha interferon, beta interferon, interlukin, and tumor necrosis factor were in clinical tests. Human insulin and HGH were on the market. And several new animal health care vaccines were anticipated. Through biotechnological techniques, much had been learned about the way in which disease occurs in human beings and new therapeutic approaches were being proposed. Among the more interesting of these was a potential vaccine for hepatitis B and the possibility of a new approach to the treatment of AIDS. In tests performed with laboratory animals, Genentech had found a protein which provoked a disease fighting response against AIDS in a methodology which had not been identified earlier. But much clinical research was still needed to prove its safety and effectiveness.

While Genentech's blockbuster product was expected to be Activase, it was also introducing a new biotechnological method of producing Vitamin C which could have large profit potentials. It was developing a product, Inhibin, which was a potential contraceptive for both men and women. It had also developed (through its subsidiary, Genencor) detergent enzymes using biotechnology. These were initially intended to be used in biotechnology production itself, but could have wider chemical applications later. In 1985-86, Genentech sold off its exclusive rights to certain veterinary products to Ciba-Geigy of Switzerland as a portion of consolidating its line for the more competitive future it expected in the manufacturing and marketing arenas for human health products.

During the decade of the '80s, Genentech invested more than 40% of its revenues in research and development for long-term growth. By 1989 it had completed preclinical studies on a lung surfactant for infant respiratory distress syndrome, TFF-Beta for wound healing, a tissue factor for hemophilia, a nerve growth factor for Alzheimer's Disease, Inhibin for sickle cell anemia, and monoclonal antibodies for ovarian cancer. It had completed phase I clinical trials for Relaxin (a childbirth assisting drug) and an insulin-like growth factor for nutritional support and wound healing. It also had several treatments for preventing transmission of AIDS to newborns. Its human growth hormone (HGH) had completed phase III clinical trials, as had its Actimune which had a wide variety of potential uses. However its Activase drug, which was being targeted for several different specific treatments, was still in phase III trials. A special preparation for pulmonary embolism was approaching approval.

Activase had been so spectacular in its early clinical tests that the FDA had allowed it to move rapidly through the various phases towards the marketplace, without the usual full array of tests. Genentech suffered a setback in mid-1987 when a special advisory committee to the FDA requested additional data on Activase's effects on mortality before issuing the final NDA. However, after an initial euphoria, cardiologists moved the drug into practice much more slowly than anticipated. A growing professional debate developed as to whether Activase was better than competing products, especially streptokinase eminase, which cost considerably less than the $2200 per dose price of Activase. Medicare and some other public medical associations advised using the cheaper drugs, which appeared to be almost comparable in their effects. By the late 1980s Genentech stated that Activase held 65% of the U.S. thrombolytic market, with the remaining 35% going to streptokinase. Unfortunately, only 30% of eligible heart attack victims were receiving the thrombolytic therapies.

In 1990, a major international study comparing Activase and streptokinase (still at approximately 1/10 the price) began to suggest that Activase was no more effective than streptokinase in saving lives, although later studies were to show that it was more effective in relieving the initial stress of heart attack. In early 1990, before the March announcement of this study's results, Hoffman-LaRoche announced that it would buy a controlling position in Genentech. Genentech announced that "Roche Holdings (the parent company of Hoffman-LaRoche) will invest more than $2 billion in Genentech, while allowing it to move ahead independently doing more of what we do best—delivering the dream of biotechnology. Roche's direct equity investment in Genentech will be almost $500 million, giving us new resources to accelerate the pace of our ongoing research and planned new product introductions. The proposed transaction is structured so that we have the ability to continue as a separate, autonomous, public company with the same entrepreneurial independence, scientific traditions, priorities, and corporate culture as before."

At this time Swanson stepped down as CEO. Some thought Swanson was removed because he insisted on plowing 40% of revenues back into R&D, while Raab was unhappy with this percentage. A stronger link to Hoffman-LaRoche meant increased scale and marketing power, something that manager Raab appeared more interested in than entrepreneur Swanson. The financial capabilities of Hoffman-LaRoche were very important to Genentech because of a series of large-scale drugs that might need extensive development and applications support. These included its AIDS therapy called CD4, Relaxin for easing childbirth pains, new applications of gamma interferon, etc. While LaRoche appeared willing to give Genentech its independence initially, the larger partner reserved the right to purchase the rest of the stock of Genentech should the company's independence not pay off.

Under Hoffman-LaRoche, Genentech continued as a strong developer of biotechnology products. However, it no longer enjoyed the preeminence it had once had. The biotechnology field became very large and complex with numerous independent smaller companies developing new products. As they arrived at their needs for large capital infusions, they usually formed some form of alliance with a larger company. Biotechnology stock prices oscillated wildly as market preferences changed on the stock exchanges. Genentech's Activase finally received an overwhelming endorsement in late 1995, when investigations showed that TPA had been extraordinarily effective in reducing the clots of thrombosis. Genentech's persistence and Hoffman-LaRoche's continued investments seemed about to achieve very high yields.

Overview

This case offers an excellent opportunity to integrate three aspects of the strategy formulation and formation process. It deals with the strategists themselves, dominantly MacArthur and Roosevelt. There are definite aspects of strategy formulation. However, the famous island hopping strategy actually emerges from a series of decisions and interplays between various powerful forces. Hence, the case allows one to raise the key issues of power and politics in strategy. The case deals with the way in which the most spectacular strategy of World War II, island hopping in the Pacific, was simultaneously developed and implemented.

It allows the professor to bring out many of the classic principles of strategy as they emerge from the military/diplomatic field and suggests how they can be used to evaluate strategies. Executive audiences find this case very powerful. They tend to empathize with the kind of thinking that goes into strategies on this scale and see the business utility of military strategy concepts. The case, based on William Manchester's book, *American Caesar*, debunks many of the myths about MacArthur, offering a further opportunity to query students or executives about their own perception screens concerning MacArthur as a leader. Their initial views are often distorted by myths, misinformation, hearsay, etc. The case goes well with readings on the strategist, strategy formulation, strategy formation, power, bureaucratic strategies, and evaluation of strategies.

Session Structure

We usually begin this session by asking the students to define in their own words what the Allies' strategy was in World War II. This allows the professor to introduce different levels of strategy: global grand strategy, U.S. political strategy, and the Pacific campaign strategy. The Allies' global strategy was to concentrate on what was the greatest perceived threat, Nazi Germany, first and destroy that force. In the meantime, sufficient forces were deployed to Southeast Asia to "contain" the Japanese threat. Then, after the defeat of Germany, all forces were to be concentrated in the Pacific area to finish off Japan. The Allies hoped to form a more stable post-war world based upon more democratic governments in all of the areas conquered by Germany and Japan. The conflict in goals between the Western Allies and Russia—and the need to compromise goals and strategic thrusts to accommodate these differences—can be brought out in the discussion, as can the trade needs and aspirations of each party in the post-war world. This provides a broad framework for the overall Pacific campaign strategy.

However, it is also worthwhile to note the dominant influence of U.S. political strategies—especially the need for Roosevelt to be re-elected and the fear that MacArthur's popularity would make him an overwhelming opponent in such an election. The visions and conflicts of Roosevelt, MacArthur, Marshall, and the joint chiefs of staff may also provide an interesting focal point. This level of strategy can be brought out as an adjunct to the discussion of the Pacific campaign strategy, if so desired.

Defining Strategy Itself

Rather than providing a canned definition of strategy, it is useful to have the students define in their own words what the strategy in the South Pacific really was. As the description

---

Teaching note copyright © 1987 by James Brian Quinn. This note prepared by Professor Quinn and Penny C. Paquette, Research Associate.

comes forward it will contain several major goals, i.e., to capture a series of key islands as stepping stones; free the Philippines to avoid being flanked in any attack on the main Japanese islands; neutralize the Japanese fleet by a steady war of attrition; control the air above all major military action areas; cut off the supply lines of the Japanese in the south, capture weak areas and use these to sortie against the Japanese supply lines; obtain bridgeheads close enough to the Japanese mainland to launch a full-scale bombing attack; weaken Japan's production capabilities so that an invasion could occur; obtain unconditional surrender.

A series of major policies (rules or limits) will also tend to fall out of the discussion. Chief among these policies are: concede the Asian land mass to the Japanese; bypass the Japanese great strengths on the mainland and in their own most fortified island strong points; avoid massive frontal attacks; move rapidly to avoid exposure during movement; sacrifice materiel not men; utilize the overwhelming production capabilities of the United States to produce materiel; never leave air cover unless absolutely necessary; form coalitions with liberated governments in order to avoid having to leave strong occupation forces behind; and so on.

Finally, there is a rather distinct sequence which develops in the strategy. This sequence includes delaying the Japanese advance during an initial fall back to gain time enough to bring superior air and naval forces to bear; regroup using Australia as a base and begin moving north, bypassing Japan's concentration of strength on the mainland; stop the Japanese advance at sea; capture a few key islands; cut the supply lines of the Japanese; starve and isolate the remaining troops; create forward bases at the Philippines and at Okinawa nearer to Japan; soften up Japan through bombing; obtain a Russian coalition to force Japan to fight on two flanks; invade Japan; achieve total victory; be magnanimous in victory.

Sources of This Strategy

One can ask what were the determinants of this strategy? Clearly, the U.S. value system influences many choices, notably the belief in the value of human life, the capacity to squander material resources, the belief in the superiority of the U.S. cause, the confident outlook of U.S. leaders, etc. Next, of course, are the leaders' (Roosevelt's and MacArthur's) own values and power needs as highly charismatic leaders. MacArthur had seen the dreadful waste of life in the stalemated trench warfare of World War I and was determined to avoid such a situation in the Pacific. He felt a moral obligation to return to the Philippines and liberate the Philippines. He was knowledgeable about the Japanese situation and felt he could make more sensible choices than those leaders isolated from the Far East. Political needs clearly determined the strategy. Roosevelt and MacArthur both constantly balanced the amount of action given to the different services, making sure each had a high enough profile role to maintain their morale and political support. Roosevelt needed to show concrete progress before an election. MacArthur had to deal with the realpolitik in the United States MacArthur undoubtedly saw himself as a political candidate for the presidency and worked his public relations skills to maintain a high profile. This also allowed him flexibility for action in the field. MacArthur also understood his opponents' political situation in Japan and was able to modify the overall strategy to accommodate this, moving rapidly and flexibly at the end of the war to save lives and resources on both sides. Politics and strategy are intimately intertwined.

Situation Analysis—Strengths and Weaknesses

Beyond these more qualitative points, one can analyze the relative strengths and capabilities of the Japanese vs. the United States. The key weaknesses of Japan were its necessity to import all raw materials, the sheer number of people in the combined armies of the Allies, the extensive land mass Japan was trying to control with a relatively small army, their less extensive and more vulnerable production facilities, their inability to modernize their aircraft and ships as rapidly as the United States, the fact that the United States could read all of the Japanese codes and know their major alignments, etc. The strengths of the Japanese situation

90

lay in their control of extensive areas with key resources (like tin and rubber), their highly disciplined culture and armies, their experienced field commanders, the attacker's advantage of surprise, some excellent equipment designs, the population intensity and loyalty of its citizens if Japan itself were attacked, a number of forward bases from which to attack to the South and East, and so on.

The Allies aligned their strategies much more carefully to the opportunities the post-war world offered in former colonial countries. The Allies for the most part very carefully targeted their propaganda and political approaches to the most important emerging trends in the worldwide political scene. Chief among these were the emergence of nationalism, anti-colonialism, a deep resentment of the cruelties of the Japanese, the disintegration of the European economic dominance, empires, and colonial "special concessions" or areas of influence in the Far East. The United States in particular recognized the emergence of Russia as a dominating world power, the importance of high technologies (air, chemical, and nuclear) to nations with small manpower bases, the importance of developing countries as sources of raw materials and as possible future markets, the need to neutralize possible communist expansion, etc.

It is very useful to show how the strategy was influenced by the dominating perceptions of these various factors in the United States at the time. A most significant weakness of the strategy was the failure to see the people of emerging countries and their political needs as coequal with those of the Western nations. Perhaps most poignant was the willingness of the United States and the Allies to write off China as a desirable focal point for direct military or political energies. Instead, China was handled through a weak coalition partner, not having a strong popular base, and the U.N. was conceived as a bastion for maintaining existing power arrangements in the post-war world.

Evaluation of the Strategy

After describing the strategy and classifying its components in a fashion which helps the professor develop his or her particular view of strategy, it is desirable to ask, "Why was this an effective strategy? What are the characteristics of an effective strategy? What can we learn by looking at this most successful strategy of World War II?" Perhaps the following are the things that stand out most strikingly:

A.   U.S. leaders had a relatively clear vision of the post-war world they wished to achieve and the role of the United States in that world.

B.   The goals of the strategy were clear and decisive.

C.   There was a careful evaluation of the relative strengths and weaknesses of the contending parties.

D.   There was a careful and constant evaluation of the enemy's changing potentials and its leaders' intentions.

E.   The United States extended its own resource capabilities by forming coalitions with China, the occupied countries, and the other Allies.

F.   The strategy was based on the careful use of intelligence derived from reading the Japanese codes, local native guerrillas, and formal intelligence gathering bodies.

G.   Much attention was paid to the full logistics (oil, ammunition, food, etc.) necessary to support the advance.

H.   Careful attention was given to the motivation and morale of the troops and supporting groups in Japanese-occupied countries.

I.   When the organization was unified, the results were much more effective; however, unification of command was not always achieved.

J.   Communications among the services and the Allies were a constant challenge. While it worked amazingly well between the Allied countries, this aspect of the strategy was not always well carried out between the U.S. services themselves.

K.   The strategy used the overwhelming U.S. strengths of its undiminished production base, its constantly strengthened Navy, its capacity to outproduce Japan's aircraft industry, its better command of high technologies, the capacity for mobile fast striking forces, independent action, etc.

L.   Strategy offset weaknesses of the United States, particularly in numbers of troops which could be committed in the southeast Asian sector.

M.   The strategy used surprise and speed of movement to leverage resources and obtain higher impact with limited resources.

N.   The strategy protected the flanks of the advance, thus avoiding the Japanese cutting off the supply lines of the United States.

O.   The strategy attacked the weaknesses of Japan, i.e. places where there was local guerrilla activity, command or small garrisons, etc.

P.   The strategy used minimum resources (particularly human lives) to achieve its goals.

Q.   The strategy was internally flexible to changes in the environment, notably in its decisions concerning the attacks on Formosa and Luzon.

R.   The urgencies of timing were constantly kept in mind (both at the political level and in the need to arrive at the Philippines before the Japanese could reinforce them).

S.   Concentration of overwhelming resources at chosen points (the 700 ship Armada was the largest ever assembled in the Far East).

T.   The use of synergy (i.e., the additive effects of air, land, and sea forces when coordinated).

U.   The strategists anticipated the opponent's' moves. MacArthur worked back and forth in his own mind the various "what if" contingency plans until he had thought through all major alternatives.

V.   The strategy split opponents' strengths and enabled the Allies to attack key points piecemeal.

W.   The Allies were able to maintain the initiative and thus leverage their own resources by making the Japanese respond at points selected by the Allies.

   The main weaknesses of the strategy were:

A.   Key leaders did not really understand their opponents.

B.   There were misassessments of various environments (the weather and soil conditions in the Philippines).

C.	There were communications breakdowns especially in the Navy's handling of the battle of Luzon and the Surigao Straits.

D.	There were intelligence failures in understanding the internal collapse of Japan's military and economy.

E.	Periodically, the Allies would attack strong positions unnecessarily (e.g., Buna and Okinawa).

F.	Because of MacArthur's ego needs, he sometimes announced victories prematurely or misassessed the situation.

G.	MacArthur periodically exceeded his authority —which could have been disastrous if a failure had occurred.

Following this evaluation, it is useful to ask, "What could the Japanese have done better in light of the strategy which MacArthur did adopt? If they had taken these counteractions, how should MacArthur have responded?" Some items are fairly clear. The Japanese overextended their resources by trying to attack as far south as Australia. The attempt to conquer all of China would also have used up more resources than Japan had available. Clearly, there were also tactical errors, e.g., not coming into Leyte Bay and staying there; the U.S. fleet could possibly have been seriously damaged at that point. The Japanese lost the support of local countries by the atrocities they committed and their excessive use of violent control techniques. An earlier withdrawal to a perimeter and concentration on U.S. sea and air forces within that perimeter would have made it very difficult for the United States. Obviously, there are other strategic possibilities. Each of these can be analyzed in the same fashion.

How was the Decision Made?

There is much information in the case on the decision process itself. It is clear that the "island hopping" strategy did not burst forth from MacArthur's brain in a single brilliant flash. At first, the Pacific strategy was dominantly a delay and containment strategy until the Allies could bring sufficient forces to bear at key points to stop the Japanese advance. At the time, later stages of the strategy could not be clearly conceived because information about later conditions was not available. In the early stages, the Japanese maintained the initiative, had overwhelming forces, and could strike essentially at will throughout the southwest Pacific area. Only after the containment strategy became successful was the "advance" strategy marked out. Even then, MacArthur had to see at first hand the devastating effects of trying to advance in force through the jungles against a well-trained and positioned enemy. In such a battle situation, the United States could not bring to bear its most significant strengths, i.e., air power and heavy fire power. The professor may want to note that these same limitations later hampered, if not destroyed, the military strategy in Vietnam. Even then "island hopping" was not clearly planned in advance. There were experiments which worked. From these the overall pattern and strategy emerged.

One can ask "Who decided on the island hopping strategy? Who originated the idea?" Answers to both questions are murky. Roosevelt had to approve of the strategy; but then again, so did MacArthur and King or it would not have been acceptable. MacArthur clearly championed the strategy and led others to his conclusion. However, it is interesting to note that the strategist in this case had to persuade the commander-in-chief of his viewpoints. The strategy does not come from the top, i.e., Roosevelt, down to MacArthur. Even after the grand strategy was agreed upon, MacArthur still had to persuade Kenny and King about key elements in the strategy, and major decisions were made by Sutherland, Truman, those who chose to build and drop the atomic bomb, and others who modified the strategy at key points.

The Hawaii Conference provides an interesting vehicle for investigating how such decisions were made. Roosevelt used the conference to obtain some of his other goals, personal publicity, headlines, and identification with MacArthur. He also used the meeting to bypass the

Pentagon bureaucracy and get an independent view on strategy. At the meeting, MacArthur won in part because he was both better informed than Nimitz and was arguing for himself. Nimitz was not as articulate, was arguing for King, and was not as prepared on the politics of the issue. In essence, the result of the meeting was a coalition between MacArthur, Leahy, and Roosevelt that bypassed the Pentagon's power base. Instead of acting as a line officer giving commands, Roosevelt acted as a chairman leading a debate. When the decision involved variables which are not easily measurable, MacArthur moved the argument to the "values" level, bringing in unarguable concepts like honor, promises kept, moral issues, etc., which others cannot really debate.

Finally, as the strategist, MacArthur obtained the best advice he could from his subordinates. He consciously pitted the subordinates against each other to maintain his own power base and to improve the quality of the information he had. He went to the front to obtain information personally, making sure it would not be biased by the perceptions of intermediaries. He consciously chose commanders who had different command styles and attitudes toward risk than he did. The result was a series of checks and balances on his own judgment. MacArthur constantly updated and changed his views as new information became available. He was even forced to allow certain actions which he did not support to go forward. These included the attacks on Okinawa and Iwo Jima which cost heavily in casualties.

The students should notice how symbols and dramatic flair help implement a strategy. The best examples are MacArthur and Roosevelt before the Hawaiian conference, MacArthur and his staff wading onto the Philippines beaches, and finally, their unarmed appearance in Japan.

The students should be asked to consider how MacArthur's and Roosevelt's broader world views affected the actual outcomes of the war. Without linking the Pacific campaign ultimately to strongly held higher values, the United States could have won the war and lost the peace. Instead, MacArthur, Marshall, and Roosevelt converted the peace itself into the true triumph by rebuilding and modernizing the nations that were conquered. Thus they avoided the very mistakes that brought Japan to its knees.

Strategic Principles

After the discussion, it is useful to ask students what strategic principles can be drawn from this case. Military strategists would point out the following:

A.   Clear decisive objectives allow local commanders to act independently, yet coordinate their actions toward the desired strategy. Objectives must be as simple as possible, understood (whether written or not) and decisive (i.e., if achieved, they must assure victory). This is the basis of decentralization in organizations.

B.   A good strategy maintains the initiative and choice of points at which contact will be made with the enemy. This choice allows one to obtain greater gains for a given commitment of resources, i.e., to leverage resources. This is a corollary benefit of having a distinctive competitive edge. Those who are determining events find it easier to maintain morale, and morale itself helps to utilize resources more effectively—i.e., with limited resources one obtains a higher effect. Defensive strategies tend to become reactive and to make it difficult to maintain morale. Because the defender cannot determine the point of attack, he must spread or disperse resources, losing the advantage of concentration.

C.   A well-designed strategy concentrates more force at selected points than the enemy can possibly deal with. This ensures a series of local victories. The local victories build morale and bring new resources under the control of the victor. Concentration and resource building are among two of the most important principles of strategy. These are the reasons behind the emphasis on a distinctive maintainable competitive edge and the highest market share concepts in industrial strategies.

D.   <u>Concession of certain positions</u> is necessary to obtain concentration. In business strategies, this is a most difficult issue to get managements to deal with. They want "to do everything for everyone." In order to achieve concentration and focus, one must set policies limiting commitments to other areas severely. Yet, this limitation must be achieved while leaving sufficient force to protect the flanks of the area of concentration.

E.   <u>Planned flexibility</u> is another key element in strategy. Since by definition a strategy deals with a set of forces whose power, interactions, and ultimate outcomes are unknowable, one needs to design conscious flexibility into the strategy. This allows one to use later information and intelligence either to anticipate new modes of attack or to take advantage of developing weaknesses in the enemy's position, which might not have been expected in the initial strategy. To obtain such flexibility requires maintaining reserve resources, flexible communications channels, a fast response organization and support capabilities, and the full logistics necessary to move forces into new positions quickly. Opportunistic moves leverage resources through timing advantages. Overplanning or loss of flexibility can waste resources by maintaining commitments to obsolete goals or policies.

F.   <u>A coordinated command</u> is necessary to achieve maximum effectiveness from resources. When commanders disagree on what should be done, much effort is wasted and the strategy can be undermined. The Okinawa campaign is an example of this as was the split in battle fleets at the battle of Leyte. Similarly, lack of a working consensus among members of a top management team can waste resources and confuse the entire organization.

G.   <u>Surprise</u> leverages resources. When the enemy is not prepared, one can achieve greater results with fewer resources. A good strategist consciously tries to hit the enemy where he least expects it. This is one of the great failings of the "formula approaches" to strategy formulation in businesses. Many of the most successful enterprises develop totally unique postures that accomplish goals in a new way.

H.   <u>A secure base</u> for operations is an essential element in strategy. One must have a set of resources that is essentially unassailable from which to launch other ventures. This is the principle of having a "cash cow" or a large raw material or installed product base in business organizations. In warfare, it means having a secure production base or land mass where production and training can occur. As soon as the mainland of Japan could be attacked, it lost this crucial position, while the United States was fortunate to maintain a secure base during the entire war.

Utilizing the criteria developed for evaluating a strategy given above and in the Edward Marshall Boehm, Inc. case, one can develop a series of "principles of strategy" which provide useful memory triggers and strategic concept structures for executives and students. Executives particularly like to think in these terms. They find the analogy very useful in designing corporate strategies. And strategic planners or consultants find the analysis useful in critiquing or recommending corporate strategies. Most strategies fail because they violate one or more of these key principles.

Overview

The New Steel Corporation case is intended to be a short case for use along with some other materials the professor may wish to lecture or present through audiovisual media. But the case can be used as a full discussion case, if one extends it into the realm of the "competitiveness" issue in the United States. New Steel Corp. can be used to bring out issues of: (1) competitive analysis, (2) a niching strategy, (3) establishing specific goals through "figures of merit," (4) emergent strategies, and (5) "U.S. competitiveness." The case deals with the start-up of a new steel company in the early 1980s by a group of young—but experienced—steel executives from one of the major U.S. steel companies. Those companies, for documented reasons, had entered a long period of decline. These young executives tried to stimulate their employers to meet the new competition in a totally new, innovative attack mode. Because of their fixed investments and past cultures, the large steel companies did not wish to respond. This case deals with the question of how a new steel company could be successfully positioned in the dismal steel markets of the United States in the early 1980s.

Session Structure

The case lends itself to a fairly straightforward structure along the following lines: (1) How can a new U.S. steel company obtain competitive advantage in the early 1980s? (2) How should the company position itself on each of the critical cost factors affecting a steel company? (3) What organization structures and motivational concepts must go with this positioning? (4) Why did U.S. Steel (and other old line manufacturing industries) get into their current difficulties? What can government policy do to improve the competitiveness of smokestack industries like steel? Why shouldn't the country simply leave these industries to the workings of the marketplace?

How to Position a New Steel Company in the United States

We ordinarily open by asking, "How would you like to have started a new steel company in the United States in the early 1980s?" There is usually a humorous and negative reaction. Then we ask, "Let's suppose that you were these young steel executives. How would you conceptualize an approach which might be successful? How would you position a start-up steel company in the early 1980s?" There are a number of data provided in the case both on trends and on the relative cost positioning of the U.S. steel industry at that time.

1. Overall Positioning. Given the amount of capital it would take to start a fully integrated steel company, and the competitive slump in basic steel, this is probably not a feasible positioning for a new company. However, a positioning in a regional specialty steel marketplace might be feasible. Specialty steels have slightly higher margins, can be produced in smaller batches, can allow certain regional locational cost advantages, and may be niched to avoid the enormous capital and retaliatory powers of a basic steel industry utilizing a cut-throat price policy as it thrashed its way downward.

2. Positioning Against Foreign Competition. It helps to obtain focus in the discussion by asking fairly quickly, "Specifically, how can we position a new U.S. steel company to beat its foreign competition? Since this was the big issue in competitiveness discussions in the late 1970s and early 1980s, let's focus on this issue first."

Teaching note copyright © 1991 by James Brian Quinn. This note was prepared by Professor Quinn.

Specific Positioning of New Steel Corporation

One can open this next phase of the discussion by asking, "Are there any areas in which a U.S. company would have some inherent competitive advantages vs. foreign-based competitors? How might we parlay off of some of these advantages?" Students and executives will very quickly identify one or two areas where the United States has distinct competitive advantages vs. the Japanese and Koreans. These generally include energy costs, raw materials, and transportation advantages. As each of these is put forward, we try to pin down the discussion with questions like, "How much of a competitive advantage do we have here? How would you measure it?" One should acknowledge that the data in the case are averages and might not apply to any specific company or location. Instead one should concentrate on, "How can we be sure that New Steel Corp. has at least parity with its foreign competition in this respect? What measures could you use to ensure that this parity is attained?"

1. Energy Costs. This is usually the first positive competitive cost factor identified. One should ask for what forms of energy does this advantage exist? Clearly, Japan buys all of its coal from overseas (much of it from the United States). The United States has the largest supplies of coal in the world. The large Western coal fields allow very low cost production. But the United States also enjoys much lower cost electricity than Japan or Korea. It has much greater hydroelectric supplies. Its old nuclear plants (especially those in the South) can sell off-peak power at extremely low rates. Electricity in Texas is available from such sources at about 4¢ per kilowatt hour as opposed to 8-12¢ in Japan. Pinning down the nature and scale of the energy cost advantage tends to set the tone for further discussions.

2. Raw Materials Cost. The audience will frequently cite raw materials cost as a second major advantage. Yet the numbers in the case indicate $37 per ton as an average cost advantage for Japan. There is a frequent misconception that the United States still has extensive reserves of low cost iron ore. The students should be reminded that the large reserves in the Mesabi Range involve secondary and even tertiary recovery processes. Japan has access to the huge iron ore capabilities of Australia, but with a significant transportation cost. On the other hand, the United States produces more scrap than any other nation in the world, and its scrap prices tend to be the lowest in the world. Note that electric arc furnaces using scrap have an $117 per ton of materials cost. There is a genuine cost advantage available to anyone who uses scrap in their processes in the United States.

3. Transportation In. Since the bulkiest and most expensive materials for the steel process must—at a minimum—be transported into Japan from other countries, U.S. companies have a significant "transportation in" or "incoming logistics" advantage. This advantage will depend, for any particular company, primarily on its choice of location relative to raw materials and energy sources. However, since materials are a large component of cost, there should also be the possibility of significant savings in inventory vs. the Japanese, because one does not have to carry as much in terms of buffer stocks for unexpected variations in delivery.

4. Transportation Out. Clearly, a U.S. steel company has a significant cost advantage in terms of its outgoing shipping costs vs. Japanese or Korean steels which must be transported into the United States across the Pacific. U.S. companies can exploit this and the other advantages of being physically closer to their customers.

5. Customer Responsiveness. If the New Steel Corp. locates itself well relative to its customers, it should be able to respond better to their needs—especially for specialty steels—than any firm operating at the great distances of Japan or Korea. However, it should also be possible for a U.S. operation to understand the nuances of each customer's needs better than a foreign-based operation. If the company actively makes customer responsiveness one of its key strategic weapons, there is no way—other than by inventorying large amounts of steel in the United States—that a foreign operator could possibly achieve comparable flexibility advantages. One might go into the specific services involved in "increased responsiveness" and how to ensure primacy.

6. Specialty Steels. Such responsiveness is especially important in the specialty steel field. Here, orders are smaller, very carefully defined steel-chemical structures are essential. Customers are willing to pay a slight premium to have lower inventories, more assured supply, and greater understanding of their precise needs by the supplier. If New Steel Corp. links its operations directly to those of its customers by the most sophisticated computer techniques, it can maintain close contacts with these customers that no one else could improve upon.

7. Steel Processes. Fortunately, specialty steels also lend themselves to relatively smaller steel producing processes, notably the basic oxygen process and the electric arc process. In basic oxygen processing, a mixture of scrap and ore is melted and reduced by inserting a lance containing pure oxygen at the top of the bath. Smaller scale converters, looking very much like Bessemer converters, are the core of this process. Electric arc processes use large carbon electrodes to melt the bath. Because the chemistry of electric arc processes is highly controllable, it lends itself well to specialty steels. Highly pure steels can be developed by either BOP or electric arc processes.

However, as is pointed out in the case, basic oxygen process technology had tended to level off in its experience curve characteristics. Electric arc technology was undergoing another spurt forward in the early 1980s, especially for use in specialty steels. Clearly, New Steel Corp. could invest in "the world's best technology" for either process, ensuring that its processing technologies were close to world standards from the beginning. Whichever process is undertaken, New Steel Corp. must also hire a few "best-in-world technologists" to make sure that its processes are both using the most current operating methodologies and also can be improved as quickly as possible in the future.

Continuous casting techniques (allowing one to move from the initial melting of steel in either the electric arc or BOP processes, directly to rolling, forming, or other intermediate fabricating processes) had been debugged by the early 1980s. These avoided numerous heavy investments in pigging, pickling, and reprocessing of ingots after the initial melt. These processes were associated with older Open Hearth and Bessemer processes. Thus, New Steel Corp. could avoid some of the expensive intermediate processes its older competitors had to have. Again, it would be essential for New Steel Corp. to obtain some best-in-world technologists familiar with continuous casting, if it chose to use this process.

8. Capital Costs. One of the major costs of making steel is the cost of the capital tied up in the business. If New Steel Corp. buys current equipment, it should be able to obtain a comparable throughput and an equipment price that is close to that of its most serious competitors. In this sense, its capital cost per ton should be no greater than its competitors. However, both Japan and Korea have national policies which give their companies average capital costs that are 1/3 to 1/2 those of the United States. One should ask, how can New Steel Corp. offset this national policy disadvantage? There are several major possibilities. (1) New Steel Corp. can obtain lower investments in inventories by being closer to both raw materials and markets. By eliminating intermediate processes as continuous casting would, New Steel Corp. can keep its aggregate capital investment to a minimum. (2) It can undoubtedly buy some good quality, current steel equipment from some companies that are in severe stress. (3) If it can demonstrate a very rapid potential growth rate and return on investment, New Steel Corp. could get low cost equity funds. A 30 times PE ratio would give it funds at essentially a 3% rate. (4) It could raise money through industrial revenue bonds or other tax breaks which local communities or states might offer. (5) It could lower its total plant costs by innovative design of processes itself.

Individual companies have used each or a combination of the above methodologies to lower their capital costs. However, most of the new steel companies which formed in the early 1980s did rely on some form of local capital support. This could be through tax holidays, guaranteed local bank support, etc. In fact, New Steel Corp. found a location with severely depressed employment conditions, a state treasury which was strong at the time, and presented a plan to some venture capitalists which gave it low equity costs, allowing higher leverage through local bank and industrial revenue loans.

9. Overhead Costs. Another major cost in manufacturing steel is overhead. The large steel companies in the United States built up enormous bureaucracies during their long histories. Their managements also allowed themselves significant perks, including large recreational facilities in the West Virginia mountains, etc. Japanese companies' overheads are also reasonably high. By targeting the lowest possible overhead, as a new company, New Steel Corp. could keep from building up these elaborate bureaucracies. In fact, companies like Nucor and Chapparel ultimately were able to operate at the billion dollar level with only a few people (less than 20 in one case, and less than 100 in the other) at the corporate level. These companies refused to let overheads grow from the very beginning. Chapparel had less than 3 people in its personnel department, for example. All these companies made extensive use of outsourcing specific overhead costs—like payroll accounting, personnel searches, etc.—when this was advantageous in the long run. In addition, by operating with non-union workers, they were able to get workers to perform multiple tasks, which the larger unionized companies could not. For example, even night watchmen were expected to be computer programmers and to perform emergency repairs. Managers' offices were kept "bare bones" and were located right at the steel manufacturing floor to remind everyone that the company had to operate with lowest feasible cost.

10. Quality Costs. The New Steel Corp. had to recognize from the outset that high quality costs less in the long run. Consequently, facilities were designed with quality in mind. Workers hired were trained immediately in the most advanced quality techniques and wherever possible new workers—with no bad habits from past jobs—were hired. Foremen were given direct line responsibility for quality control, with only a small highly technical quality assurance department at the corporate level. Contacts on quality issues went directly from the customer to the factory floor, rather than through a marketing intermediary. The most advanced monitoring and sampling techniques were used directly in the melt baths.

Service response times were emphasized, measured, and monitored constantly. If necessary, everyone was expected to work overtime to ensure delivery promises. Quality teams were set up around various processes and prizes given for maximum quality performance on a monthly basis. Everything possible was done to directly involve workers and first-line management in the quality process. Foremen actually wrote the quality manuals and trained workers in quality control. Foremen answered the telephone when customers called on quality issues and were responsible for the company's response to quality inquiries.

11. Labor Costs. If students wish to discuss this issue early, the professor should consciously say, "Let's hold that one until last. It is obviously a major problem and we need to deal with it explicitly." If the professor has covered all other potential cost issues (as outlined above) and indicated that New Steel Corp. can obtain at least parity—and in many cases a distinct competitive advantage—at each cost level, then he/she can ask, "If New Steel Corp. has been able to achieve at least parity in all of the above costs, can we set a target 'figure of merit which must be met for labor costs? How would one attack doing this so that we could be sure New Steel Corp. would be in a lowest possible cost position if the 'figure of merit' were met?"

This case brings out the figure of merit idea quite clearly. By using numbers in the case or querying at each stage of the discussion above how could one benchmark each factor to make sure that New Steel Corp. was at least equal (and preferably ahead) of best in world foreign competitors? One can get across the idea of benchmarking as well as figures of merit. A figure of merit is a performance level, which—if achieved—ensures dominance or success in that factor. If New Steel Corp. has achieved at least parity in all of the above costs, one can ask, "Below what cost must labor costs in New Steel Corp. fall to ensure business success? If achieved, how can we be sure New Steel Corp. will win?"

Students may begin by suggesting that one could drive the cost of labor down to $0 per ton. This might be achievable but only at an elaborate investment cost. However, by meeting or exceeding best in world performance in other factors, one does not have to achieve zero labor cost in order to be assured of success. (1) One can benchmark lowest cost per ton of labor in Japanese or Korean mills and stay constantly below that level. (2) One can set a target of "less labor cost per ton than the trans-Pacific cost per ton of shipping steel." If New Steel Corp. can hit either of these, it can have a low cost, high flexibility, quality policy that no foreign company could meet. Again, it is important to note that this is not a "generic strategy." New Steel Corp. is seeking low cost, service, flexibility, and quality at the same time.

In fact, New Steel Corp. set as its figure of merit reducing labor costs per ton below trans-Pacific shipping costs per ton. Given the fact that New Steel could prove "parity or better" on all other costs, this meant that Japanese or Korean mills would have to have negative labor cost in order to beat New Steel Corp. It was prepared to go to court on the grounds of dumping, if it encountered pricing that indicated costs below this level. However, it was extremely important that laborers buy into this target as realistic. If New Steel Corp. simply set the target arbitrarily, it probably could not have achieved the desired result, nor could it have obtained a constantly improving cost ratio for labor.

Instead, New Steel Corp. asked its labor force to help design the plant. It opened its books to labor so that laborers would know the exact cost of steel made by the company as well as just the labor cost itself. The company shared any improvements in labor cost productivity with the labor force. Management agreed to invest heavily in productivity improvement, setting aside up to 50% of all profits for this purpose in the early years. By carefully containing its own overhead costs and allowing open information exchanges, especially on cost factors, New Steel Corp. was able to obtain the trust of its workers. The workers were non-union and remained so. However, their wages were as high as union wages for comparably senior people. They simply were expected to work on multiple tasks and to contribute to many aspects of New Steel Corp.'s operations.

The Issue of National Competitiveness

While New Steel Corp. was very successful in more than matching its overseas competitors' cost and performance parameters, many people (including many U.S. academics at the time) claimed that it would be impossible for American steel companies to ever again compete with foreign steel producers. This offers an excellent opportunity to raise a series of questions about the whole competitiveness issue and what U.S. national policy approaches can do relative to this issue. What does competitiveness mean? If exchange rates are allowed to float freely, why wouldn't a country's import-export balances equalize over a period of time? The industries in which the country had relative comparative advantage not absolute cost advantages would be where it exported. In fact, economic theory says this must happen in a free market situation. Further, if an industry is not one in which the country has a comparative advantage, why should it be continued? What is the difference between comparative advantage and competitive advantage? These are issues concerning which most U.S. students and executives are woefully ill-informed. Since these issues are too complex to outline completely here, we will only suggest some of the major discussion points.

1. <u>Defining Competitiveness</u>. How does one define competitiveness in an industry? Is productivity per person in that industry a good measure of the competitiveness? Relative cost? If so, at what exchange rate? Relative quality? If so, which marketplace defines quality? For example, a simple, long-running, easy-to-repair automobile may define quality for a frontier country—while an urbanized affluent country may demand luxury fittings, special features, ease of parking, etc. Does a positive balance of trade in an industry equal competitiveness? If so, all countries are competitive in the long run, since they must balance their payments—and according to economics—their trade balances.

Isn't a country's steel industry competitive if its multinationals produce abroad and ship to competitor nations or to the parent country itself? What then is the real issue in competitiveness? If foreign countries were to build steel mills in the United States and produce steel here, would it increase U.S. competitiveness? If a company produces and sells steel at lower margins, attains higher volumes than another country's steel industry, is that industry more competitive? If one country's steel industry is subsidized by heavy national R&D contributions, military subsidies, or capital subsidies (including risks assumed by the government), is that industry more competitive? How can these subsidies, including social security costs and pensions, be sorted out?

2. <u>Is Competitiveness in Some Industries More Important than Others?</u>. A great deal of concern has been expressed in the United States about the loss of its "smokestack" industries. Why should the United States worry any more about buying steel from the Far East than buying shirts or software from the same areas? Since 77% of all U.S. jobs are in the services industries, shouldn't the United States be more concerned about its competitiveness in those industries than in the manufacturing industries which employ only 18% of its work force? If steel has become a commodity and U.S. workers are only willing to work in steel plants if they are paid premium wages, why should the country seek to force its people into jobs they seemingly do not want? Should it follow the same policies in textiles as in steel? In computers? The value added to gross national product (as measured) is approximately the same for the financial services industries as for all of manufacturing. Why then shouldn't the United States be more concerned about competitiveness in the financial services sector than in manufacturing?

Even the concept that balance of trade in an area measures its competitiveness can be challenged. When the United States sells a ton of steel or an automobile abroad, it credits the full wholesale <u>price</u> of the item sold to the U.S. balance of trade account. Yet the United States has lost forever the ore, energy, and other raw materials content in the product sold. Another country now gets the benefit of that raw material (by using the steel or automobile) rather than the United States. By contrast, if the banking service is sold abroad—having the same value as the shipment of steel—only the profit or fees associated with that sale are considered credits to the U.S. trade balance. Yet no raw materials have left the country. All of the jobs and value have been created in the United States, and no externalities (like air and water pollution) have been created. What then do we mean by competitiveness? What industries should we be sure to maintain? Why?

3. <u>Why not an Industrial Policy?</u> It is popular to deride the concept of "industrial policy" in the United States today. With so many of our major trading partners actively espousing industrial policies and directly supporting selected industries, are we in the United States not simply turning over some important industries to other countries? The example of Japan's targeting such industries as electronics, semiconductors, chemicals, steel making, shipbuilding, and automobiles (to a lesser extent) are well documented. Europe has targeted the large commercial aircraft field with its Airbus. European countries are also targeting biotechnology, superconductors, and other technologies believed to be important in the future. If their companies can compete with substantial subsidies—which lower their costs—in these areas, how can our "private enterprise" system hope to maintain its position?

It is a fact of life that U.S. companies now have to compete against coalitions of governments and companies operating abroad. In order to protect jobs, future competitiveness, and important technologies in the United States, why should we not actively try to develop industries important to our current competitiveness and to our future economic growth? The usual answers are that competition and free markets allocate resources better than governments can "target" such activities. Further governmental support is claimed to be inefficient, it discriminates against one taxpayer in favor of another, it may in fact be deeply wrong in its allocation, damaging future competitiveness more than it helps the targeted industries. Stimuli to particular industries arbitrarily distort the marketplace (and presumably individual's free choice in their purchases) by shifting costs from one sector to another. Students and executives will tend to latch on to such arguments readily.

To stimulate discussion, however, it might be desirable to point out that the United States has long had a "de facto" series of industrial policies. While these policies generally do not "target" industries in the same sense that Japanese and European policies have, they have nevertheless had very similar effects. For example, the mining and energy industries were stimulated for many decades by depletion allowances which gave owners of such properties tax shelters. Housing and construction has been subsidized by making mortgage payments tax deductible. And so on. However, a large number of other industries were actually created by government stimulation. Among these were the aerospace, computer, biotechnology, aircraft, vaccine, specialized health equipment, satellite communications, railroad, and other industries.

A large number of U.S. industries have actually been heavily subsidized by government. These include the automobile industry (by construction of highways and roads), agriculture (by subsidizing prices and massive research and extension activities), the airlines industry (by subsidizing airport construction and aircraft control systems), the health care industry (by heavy research, development, experimentation, and public data expenditures), home building (by underwriting low-cost loans), communications (by allowing AT&T to operate as a monopoly for many years). And so on. In fact, there are relatively few industries today that have not been supported by some form of government help at a crucial juncture in their development.

In addition, the Federal Government has long pursued a number of consistent actions (emergent policies) that made the United States more competitive across whole industrial classes. Among these were allowing large-scale immigration, keeping interest rates low by regulating banks, creating the land grant universities and subsidizing graduate research programs, supporting high standards of public education, developing transportation and communication infrastructures, establishing standards for purity of foods and drugs sold through mass distribution systems, establishing safety standards for workers and products, creating a 200-mile limit for fishing rights along the shorelines of the United States, subsidizing agriculture and high standards of public health. And so on. The United States led other countries in these types of policies for many years. In fact, most of the Japanese policies today are mirror images of similar policies in the United States during the 1800s and early 1900s. If such policies worked well for the United States in the past, why should they not be used now?

4. What Government Policy Changes Would be Most Important for U.S. Competitiveness? The point should be made that the U.S. government currently does have a series of industrial policies. However, they are a hodgepodge. There is not consistency among these policies. Consequently, they often are conflicting, wasteful, and confusing for industrialists. The simultaneous attempt to improve trade balances and yet not tax oil is a classic case in point. There are many others which will occur to the professor. One can ask why there is no greater consistency in our policies? The clearest cause is, of course, the highly fragmented power structures of the U.S. Congress. Each of the legislative and appropriations committees has extraordinary power within its own realm. Yet there is no central coordinative capability in the Congress, except a full vote of the Congress. Each agency is pushing its own programs, in parallel with its legislative and appropriations committees of the Congress, with the result that there are few counter pressures for coherence. The Office of Management and the Budget (OMB) and the Congressional Budget Office (CBO) try to provide data for disciplining allocations, but neither has the line authority to take action. All of this is of course rooted in America's great distrust of centralized power. Hence any really cohesive industrial policy is unlikely to be articulated or enforceable. Nevertheless, certain actions could assist U.S. competitiveness. Asking the students to recommend and prioritize these can be very interesting.

Alleviating the much publicized high cost of capital in the United States will be an interesting point to raise. While many agree that this is a serious problem and needs to be addressed, there are few practical solutions one can offer. Ask the students how they would increase savings rates? Lower capital costs in an integrated world capital marketplace? Influence interest rates? And so on. They will find this most difficult to deal with, except by lowering the deficit of the national budget. This, of course, decreases demands on available capital. It could also decrease the total share of government expenditures as a portion of GNP, with some potential efficiencies. However, the Congress has been completely unwilling to face up to this issue. Consequently, it becomes moot as a policy suggestion. Another approach, however, is to offer further incentives for capital expenditure vs. current consumption. Shifting the balance of consumption taxes upward and taxes on capital downward could have some significant effect. A 3-4 year holding period for reducing capital gains taxes—or a continually lower tax rate, the longer an investment asset is held—could shift "savings" ratios at the margin as could eliminating the double taxation on corporate incomes. However, it has proved to be very difficult to get action on such priority shifts.

Sudden changes in regulatory or tax rules have also created enormous uncertainties for industry. Such uncertainties implicitly increase the cost of capital. By .requiring that all regulations—except those representing true emergencies—to be promulgated 2-3 years ahead one could decrease many of these uncertainties. A shift within the government budget from income transfers to true investment items (like airports, bridges, highways, roads, schools, etc.) could also shift priorities from shorter term to longer term horizons—implicitly forcing savings. If such investments do lower social costs, they create higher incomes for later taxation and lower public costs to help with competitiveness. In fact, public infrastructure expenditures are probably the most feasible single item the Federal Government can influence to assist in national competitiveness.

Excessive government regulation is a common excuse put forward for loss of competitiveness. This assertion should not be left unchallenged. First of all, any products sold in the United States—whether made by U.S. companies or foreigners—must meet U.S. regulatory requirements. If anything, therefore, our product standards create more problems for foreign companies (which must meet the standards in their own countries and in the United States) than for U.S.-based companies operating only here. One should also note that European and Japanese environmental standards are in most cases higher than those in the United States There are, of course, some absurd examples of overregulation in specific sectors of the U.S. economy. These will affect individual industries, but the overall level of U.S. environmental and market regulation is probably less severe than in our competitors' countries.

Antitrust laws, particularly for joint development efforts, are another common point of attack suggested. One should note that joint development among companies is expressly allowed under the 1984 Technology and Trade Acts. Although a number of development consortia (like Sematech) have been formed, few of these have been effective in the United States. In general, the U.S. governmental environment has probably been more favorable to business than its major competitors' environments in recent years. For example, patents on pharmaceuticals have now been allowed to begin only after FDA approval of the drug, extensive cooperative arrangements have been allowed among industries to increase their international competitiveness, tax rates in the United States are among the lowest in the world, and so on. Finding new, specific initiatives to improve competitiveness through government policy is very difficult.

5. What is the Real Competitiveness Problem? Most of the major studies reluctantly conclude that American management itself is the major problem. Because of short-term pressures by their owners and the restructurings forced by capital markets, managers have tended to underinvest—especially in longer-term projects. Although many management techniques such as Total Quality Control, cross-functional design groups, self-directed teams, etc., were first initiated in the United States, American managements were slow to pick up on these techniques. The U.S. steel industry is an excellent case in point. It continued to ignore new technologies, to operate fully depreciated facilities because of lower accounting costs, to exploit the protection ocean shipping of steel imports gave to the U.S. industry, to regard workers as tools rather than problem solvers, and to stick with large vertical hierarchical organizations long after they were economically sensible. The industry also ignored the potentials that smaller-scale, faster customer response, and the use of integrated electronic production and inventory control systems allowed. The application of these new approaches was much more extensive in the Japanese steel industry than in the United States.

Until managers like those in New Steel Corporation began to take major new initiatives, the U.S. steel industry was in difficult shape. However, now, according to international studies, U.S. steel companies using techniques like those suggested in the case have the lowest cost structures in the world.

ACTUAL RESULTS AND UPDATE

Companies like Nucor and Chapparel followed these practices very successfully. Since this is a disguised case, specific results cannot be indicated with precision. However, through 1989 New Steel Corp. grew at a 35% annual rate, it obtained approximately 35% ROE, and became one of the top ten U.S. steel companies. It located in a Sun Belt area, with low energy costs, high unemployment because of the oil industry's decline, available local support to lower its capital and tax costs, and a growing local steel fabrication demand. It kept its overheads to a minimum, emphasized fast service response to its customers, and drove for lowest total cost by benchmarking its competitors' costs effectively worldwide. It uses primarily electric arc steel, direct casting, and TQL practices to serve a growing regional specialty steel market. It has linked itself directly to customers by EDI and "in-house design team" connections. Yet it still has only approximately 25 people in its headquarters facility with sales of well over $1 billion.

Its aggressive use of employee consultation and cooperation plans has made it a leader in new management techniques in the United States. New Steel Corp.'s management is often cited as one of the most progressive in the United States.

INTEL CORPORATION TEACHING NOTE

Overview

This case can be used for a variety of purposes. The first portion provides an ideal entrepreneurial niching strategy case. The case is also an effective vehicle for strategic analysis, strategic mapping, and some competitive and industry analysis. It also provides an excellent basis for evaluating strategies at different stages in the growth cycle of a business. It develops interesting insights on the nature, uses, and development of corporate culture. Finally, it poses some complex organizational questions as well as international competitive policy questions. We would recommend its use after introductory cases like Genentech, Inc., New Steel Corp., and Edward Marshall Boehm. The case goes well with readings on: strategy analysis, strategy formulation, organization, culture, systems, the entrepreneurial context, the innovation context, and adhocracy. The section portion of the case provides a context for students to consider the evolution of a technology strategy, the process of strategic renewal, and the relationship between a company and its environment.

Session Structure

We recommend developing the first part of the case in several stages: (1) start-up issues, (2) early strategic niching, (3) organization for the strategic niche, and (4) Intel's strategy for the future. Some professors may want to start with an industry analysis, competitive analysis, value added-chain analysis, and so on.

The Start-up Phase

An interesting set of opening questions is "Why was Intel started and why was it structured as it was?" Noyce and Moore were classic "breakaway" entrepreneurs. They had been successful in running a company for someone else. However, they were frustrated with the problems of large company management. In addition to profits, they wanted independence, control, a chance to develop a new technology to its utmost, and an opportunity to gain personal recognition. This offers an opportunity to bring out the multiple goals involved in most entrepreneurial start-ups and the importance of personal values in these situations.

A second set of questions has to do with the way Arthur Rock operates as a venture capitalist. The interesting questions are as follows: Does Rock want control of the company? No, he wants the entrepreneurs totally committed to "their" company. Why does he not attempt to master the technology? He knows he cannot be as expert as the founders. His job is to judge people and the business potentials, if they are successful. How does he evaluate a venture opportunity like this?—(1) by probing the founders' experience, values, commitment, and (2) by deciding whether there is a "big" potential for the business if it is successful. What does he expect of Noyce and Moore?—total commitment, the capacity to attract people, knowledge and dedication. How can a venture capitalist develop a strategy for this early stage of seed capital development? See the Teaching note for the Genentech, Inc. case for more detailed analysis of venture capitalist strategies.

How long does it take to get back the initial capitalization?—(6 1/2 years). Why do they use convertible debentures?—to leave equity control with the founders, gain some preference in liquidation, or gain more if all goes well. Why is a private placement used for this type of investment?—to obtain patient money, knowledgeable investors, more flexible and lower cost financing. How does one estimate a market at this stage of a new venture?—the product has never been sold, hence intuition and understanding the basic opportunity are crucial. This is a good point to relate to some of the concepts developed in the innovation and entrepreneurial context chapters of the book. It is very interesting to inquire why the large companies in the vacuum tube field were unsuccessful in penetrating the semiconductor market. They had to split their resources between tubes and semiconductors. They were not totally committed to semiconductors and hence willing to take the long-term risks involved. Because of their faith in the old technology (tubes) they couldn't believe the potentials of semiconductors. Semiconductors would have destroyed their existing investments. And so on. (See Quinn article on "Managing Innovation: Controlled Chaos.")

The Initial Niche Strategy

The second stage of the case should ask "What are the critical factors for success in the early development of Intel?" Some major strategic actions to consider are the need to:

1. Maintain a narrow product line with a wide usage base.

2. Concentrate more talent on semiconductor memory than anyone else in the industry.

3. Dominate volumes and timing in the sectors chosen to obtain experience curve advantages.

4. Achieve product reliability and delivery reliability unsurpassed in the industry.

5. Create commitment among the people who must carry out both the initial innovations and their later production.

6. Eliminate all mistakes in the production process (manufacturing costs are dominated by error costs).

7. Use the critical technical advantage of Intel's founders (the silicon gate).

8. Leapfrog competitors in design in order to obtain early profitability and experience curve advantages.

9. Develop a balanced technology, manufacturing, marketing capability which no one else had.

10. License second sources to maintain control over the technology, yet satisfy customers' needs for a guaranteed supply.

Organization for the Niche Strategy

This is an excellent opportunity to show the conflicting requirements for an effective organization in each of the functional sectors. One can first inquire how to maximize the value chain contribution of each function. Then the instructor should get the class to draw an organization chart to accommodate these different needs. An analysis will generally proceed as follows:

A. In manufacturing: What are the critical factors for success? How can these be realized through organization form and systems?

1. The experience curve is crucial. Concentrate on high standardization and large product volumes.

2. Make each unit identical to all others, so that customers can reliably use them as components.

3. Produce in precisely designed and measured modules to ensure maximum repetition and minimum start-up errors.

4. Build a large plant with open space structures so that new modules can be created to increase production (do not expand existing lines).

5. For expansion, duplicate existing lines exactly (the "MacIntel" approach).

6. Hire new people two months ahead of production to obtain thorough training and indoctrination.

7. 100% test all products (no defects can be shipped out).

8. Keep modules small and personal to obtain identity and to maximize information exchange.

9. Provide awards for superior performance on timing and quality.

10. Automate to the maximum extent possible and measure everything to ensure consistency.

11. Have a sufficient planning horizon to anticipate when new plants will have to be available without the need to disrupt ongoing production operations.

B. Engineering: Critical Factors for Success

1. Maintain small sized ad hoc groups to maximize the identity, communications effectiveness, accountability, and motivation of design groups.

2. Attract the very best people in the world (establish a value system, organization, culture, style, and atmosphere which attracts them).

3. Offer special stock options to obtain critical people and reward internal entrepreneurs with equity participation.

4. Obtain a direct interface between designers and customer needs.

5. Maintain maximum flexibility and fast movement capabilities in design units ($250,000 in capital spent with no signatures).

6. Mix spectacular new engineering graduates on teams for new product design with experienced manufacturing people (mix vertically and horizontally).

7. Keep engineering physically close to manufacturing to be aware of and sensitive to the quality and reliability needs of production.

8. Allow great flexibility in lateral movement (or conversely rotate assignments) so that engineers become intimately aware of marketing and production needs.

C. Marketing: Critical Factors for Success

1. Recognize customer wants absolute reliability in delivery and quality.

2. Realize Intel's product is a minuscule percentage of the cost of the customer's product, but crucial to its performance, hence absolute attention to customer needs is essential.

3. Make sure design and production understand precise quality and reliability needs.

4. Avoid quotations or proposals when reliability specs cannot be assured.

5. Go beyond the customer to the customers' customer for market information; this is the ultimate user.

6. Become selected customers' electronics research unit (increase switching costs).

7. Get highly qualified Intel marketing engineers into customers' design groups (have Intel "specced" into the customer's product).

8. Focus on selected industry groups and large customers to obtain high volume and to create entry barriers.

9. Develop inventory policies to ensure absolute customer delivery satisfaction.

10. Develop personnel incentives to achieve the above.

D. General Management: Critical Factors for Success

1. Develop an overarching goal or philosophy which can attract the kinds of people desired.

2. Develop a style of openness and trust which allows delegation and freedom, yet concentration and control.

3. Develop a style of constructive confrontation where open factual discussion is essential.

4. Develop small units to obtain maximum personal identity.

5. Measure "absolutely everything" to obtain maximum consistency in product.

6. Install incentives at all levels for creativity, consistency, and identity with the company.

7. Develop a collegial relationship (no privileges, no walls, 20% solution, all share).

8. Develop a matrix adhocracy with MBO measures to support all goals and to obtain consistency.

E. Overall Organization

After developing the critical factors for success in each functional area, it is fascinating to ask the students to draw an organization chart. Marketing needs to be oriented to customers and industry classes, engineering needs to be oriented toward project clusters and disciplines, and production needs to be developed on a modular basis. The pros and cons of a variety of organizational configurations can be brought out in this discussion. If the Intel case is used later in the course, one can ask what management controls appropriately belong with each organization structure.

Intel's Future Strategy

At the decision point in the case it is useful to have students discuss Intel's future strategy and ensure that they know enough about Intel's development to handle the issues raised in the second portion of the case. Given all the above, what should the future strategy of Intel be? What are the crucial factors for its future success? Some critical issues are summarized below:

What should the <u>company's concept</u> be ,given that rapid advances in the technology are taking place at the same moment that individual lines are maturing? Can Intel develop one of the three generic strategies (focus, differentiation, or low cost) in order to guarantee its success? Is Intel's "leapfrogging" strategy still viable? If not, does it have the scale to compete? If it continues its innovation strategy, is this a sufficient point of "differentiation?" Or should it "focus" as well? If a focus strategy is followed, what target markets should Intel attack? What should its unique competency be? How can it win at innovation against the large research and development capabilities of NEC, IBM, and AT&T? Is a less innovative, production-oriented strategy realistic given Intel's size or acceptable to the Intel culture?

<u>Market positioning</u>: Where should Intel concentrate its marketing endeavors? The memory market is becoming "commodity oriented." The microcomputer and application-specific VLSI markets look attractive. Can Intel jump to a next generation technology in memories (i.e., 4 megabit RAMs or bubble memory)? Does Intel have the necessary software capability to move downstream toward microcomputers themselves? IBM is increasingly emerging as a dominant customer. How can Intel deal with this? Can Intel penetrate the Japanese market? How?

<u>Diversification</u>: Note the high cyclicality in Intel's sales and profits. What can it do to offset this? Can it diversify through its customers' countercyclicality? Can it afford to move downstream and compete with its own customers? If so, how? Where? Can it use world markets for diversification? If so, how does it offset the Japanese strategies and advantages? What should its product portfolio be? What will provide its growth markets? Cash generators? Harvest sectors?

<u>Organization Issues</u>: How can Intel organize to carry out a more focused market orientation? Greater profit orientation? Long-term innovation investments? Finding new specialty markets? How can it deal with the attractions Intel's own engineers find to spinning out and forming their own companies? How can Intel maintain the required secrecy to give it a product edge? How can it motivate its people in its increasingly large organization to be continuously innovative? How can it obtain the closeness to customers necessary to maintain a design edge? What changes in organization form from its earlier niched form are necessary now?

<u>Dealing with the Japanese</u>: How can Intel use its U.S. strengths to deal with Japanese incursions? How can it increase its innovation rate? How can it provide service support superior to the Japanese? How can it develop and protect proprietary software positions? Could Intel develop close contractual, equity, or organizational arrangements with individual customers to give it a "special relationship" with them? Can Intel form creative coalitions with the military or

INTEL STRATEGIC MAP
MAIN STRENGTH OF COMPETING FIRMS

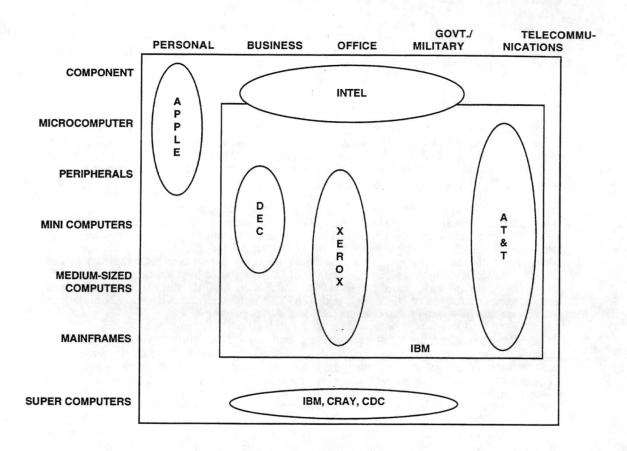

other large user groups to give it a leading edge position in selected markets? How can it deal with the high capital cost structure of the United States vs. Japan? How can it deal with the developing countries' increasing manufacture of semiconductors as the Japanese move "offshore" to obtain labor cost advantages?

Financial Needs and Strategy: What are the crucial issues facing Intel in the financial area? What can it do about these? If it continues its 35% per year growth rate, Intel will be a $3.2 billion company in 1985. This will require an increased capital investment of some $2.4 billion at the current-assets-to-sales ratio. Given its current profitability problems, how can Intel generate needed capital? How can Intel avoid a takeover by an aggressive outside company? Should it seek a friendly merger? If so, with whom and at what price?

Intel Changes

Because of competitive pressures, particularly price pressures, Intel began to move its product mix away from memories toward microprocessor related products. In 1982, the product mix was 61% microcomputer-related, and 39% memory-related. In 1985, the mix was 77% microcomputer-related, and 23% memory-related. However, within the memory line, there was a significant shift toward EPROMs, where Intel enjoyed advantages due to its own discovery of both EPROMs and E^2PROMs. By 1985, Intel was the number one producer of EPROMs with 21% of the total market followed by Hitachi with 16% and Advanced Micro Devices with 14%.

Intel had introduced a new 1 million bit (megabit) NMOS EPROM. It had developed a distinctive new strategy for this chip, standardizing on 3 different pin designs (28, 32, and 40) which allowed the chip to be modified for different applications. Although the industry had standardized on a 28-pin socket, the diversity of applications for megabit EPROMs demanded other possible configurations. Intel had also invented a KEPROM (keyed access EPROM) which prevented unauthorized access to computer systems and prevented illegal copying of proprietary software stored in the KEPROM. Intel had entered a dumping suit against the Japanese in EPROMs. There was a ruling that the Japanese had been dumping. Negotiations on the implications of this across all semiconductor lines were still ongoing in 1986. However, by mid-1986, Intel had been able to increase its prices of EPROMs by 25%.

In 1985, Intel had introduced a scientific supercomputer (the iPSC) priced at more than $500,000 which embodied new "parallel processing" techniques in its Hypercube architecture and used more than a hundred microprocessors.

In mid-1986, Intel began volume shipping of its soon-to-be-famous 32-bit 80386 microprocessor. Although Motorola and National Semiconductor had entered the market already, Intel's 80386 had the advantage of being the only one compatible with existing MS-DOS systems (used on IBM PCs and IBM-compatible micros) as well as other operating systems such as AT&T's UNIX. Analysts predicted that Intel would eventually have the largest share of the 32-bit market. This market was expected to grow to over $100 million ($500 million including associated peripheral components) by 1990 and to be the longest lasting of the microprocessor generations.

In terms of specific markets, Intel had targeted the micro communications and automotive markets. In 1986, Intel and Nissan jointly developed a 16-bit microcontroller for electronic engine management. EDS and Intel had entered into a joint relationship to develop a "speech recognition terminal" for industrial work stations (allowing instructions to be conveyed by wireless voice transmission).

Technology/Manufacturing Changes

As the lead time Intel could obtain when it "leapfrogged" to new design and process technologies grew shorter and shorter, it began to emphasize cost reduction from a manufacturing efficiency standpoint as well. In its 1985 Annual Report, the company stated that its manufacturing objectives were "Make it fast, make it cheap, and make it good since superior technology and close customer relations will do little good if we can't manufacture products over their life cycles in a cost-effective, efficient manner." A heavy emphasis was also placed on quality control. Each year Intel's quality performance improved markedly. The company had one of the lowest defect rates in the industry. As a result, many customers had completely eliminated incoming inspection for Intel products.

The mainstream production technology was moving towards CHMOS and away from NMOS. CHMOS (complementary high performance metal oxide semiconductors) was becoming the mainstream technology for high density VLSI because of its low power using characteristics. Over a six-year span, the portion of Intel's components fabricated in CHMOS grew from 0-80%.

Two other major technology shifts should be noted. Design rules had moved to 1.0 M (microns) and below. Intel began to make 6-inch wafers vs. its standard 4-inch wafer. This allowed a doubling of the number of chips that could be made per wafer with no increase in labor cost. It might also provide the precursor technology for wafer-scale integration, which could allow a completely new structure of computers by 1990. However, the cost of the first chip for these new technologies had moved up significantly. Development costs for the 30386 chip exceeded $100 million. However, integrated design and production technologies had allowed Intel to improve the predictability of yields to the point where the first 30386 chip run produced by Intel yielded good chips.

In May 1986, a trial began in which Intel was suing NEC to protect its copyrights on microcode. Such code translated computer software into the binary digits in which microprocessors operated. The key issue was whether the microcode could be classified as software and be copyrighted for protection. NEC had had a license from Intel as a second source provider of its microprocessor chips. Later, when NEC came out with its own design for a new chip, it seemed to duplicate Intel's microcode in the operation of that chip. The interpretation of whether microcode was software or an integral part of the hardware design (which could only be protected by patent) was crucial to all semiconductor, computer, and software producers.

In 1983-84, IBM took a 12% equity position in Intel. This grew to approximately 20% by 1985. It is important to note that these were new shares, which brought capital into Intel. In early 1986, IBM began to reduce its holdings in Intel by selling some $300 million in Eurobonds, which were convertible into IBM's Intel shares. Analysts interpreted the move as a strategic weakening of the links between IBM and Intel, since IBM had been increasingly relying on making its own semiconductor chips. Yet, at the same time, IBM signed a 5-year technology exchange and licensing agreement with Intel. The details of this agreement are not publicly available.

STRATEGY FOR THE 1990s

Introduction

The second part of the case presents Intel's strategic situation after the 1985 decision to exit the DRAM (dynamic random access memory) business. The decision marked a critical transition point for Intel since the company invented DRAMs and had historically viewed itself as "the DRAM company." The case explores the subsequent evolution of the company and provides the student with the context to consider critical strategic issues facing the company in 1990. The case focuses on technology strategy and its evolution throughout the company's history, but it also develops key themes of corporate strategic renewal and the relationships between the company and its environment. The major themes of the case concern:

1. the DRAM situation in 1990,

2. the rationalization of technology strategy with changing industry dynamics and paradigms,

3. the continuing implications for corporate strategy of tensions between commodity and proprietary businesses: EPROM and Flash,

4. changing modes of corporate intrapreneurialism and strategic renewal: RISC vs. CISC, Flash, and

5. forward integration and the future of Intel.

Preparation Questions:

1. What are the long-term implications of Intel's exit from the DRAM business? How did Grove handle the situation? Would you support U.S. Memories?

2. Do you agree with Intel's decision to re-market DRAMs from Samsung Semiconductor? What are the benefits and risks of that arrangement?

3. What are the key differences between the DRAM and EPROM businesses? Should Intel exit the EPROM business now that it no longer produces DRAMs?

4. Compare and contrast the arguments of Chou, Parker, and Barrett regarding "technology drivers." Are these arguments mutually consistent? If not, who is right? What are the implications for Intel's technology strategy?

5. Does the strategy articulated by the marketing manager for Flash differ from the corporate strategy. If so, how? Should Intel continue to invest in Flash? As the Flash manager, how would you defend your position to senior management?

6. How did Kohn succeed in developing a RISC chip? What are the dangers, if any, of Intel developing the i860? What are the benefits? If you were Grove, would you support Kohn?

7. Is Intel still a technology leader?

8. How well do the three corporate macro strategies outlined in the case serve to guide Intel through the 1990s?

DISCUSSION OF MAJOR THEMES

The Decision to Exit the Dram Business

The decision to exit the DRAM business in 1985 can be viewed as the ratification of a decision the organization had already made. All the logical reasons for maintaining the DRAM business had disappeared over the previous four years, yet managers were still clinging to the "self-evident truth" that DRAMs provided Intel with a crucial competitive advantage. The strategies for maintaining the DRAM business had grown unfocused, and regardless of technical arguments about the DRAM's overall importance to the company, the product was in such low volume that it was providing Intel with little competitive advantage.

This perspective can lead to a rich discussion of the role of senior management and particularly of the CEO in a changing environment. Grove's perspective argues that the CEO must be able to question the self-evident truths posed by the organization. At the same time, he implies a subtle difference between CEO as strategic recognizer and ratifier vs. CEO as strategic forcer.

The role of senior and middle level managers in the strategic planning process should be viewed in the context of the company's evolution. In the early days, senior management was intimately familiar with the scope of Intel's technologies, products, and customers. In a relatively small company such as Intel in the '70s and early '80s, senior managers could develop the firm's strategy without extensive informational input from middle management; they knew the business intimately. As the company grew, the complexity of its operations increased to the point where senior management had to rely on middle managers for their expertise.

The initial reaction to the firm's growth and increased complexity was to create smaller decision-making units with a "bottom-up" planning process. The weakness of the strategic planning process derived from its lack of overall direction and integration. The "task relevant maturity" of middle managers was not sufficient to create an effective strategy-making organization. Major decisions were not directed from the top; they emerged from the bottom in a process which tended to build a bureaucracy and create self-perpetuating strategies. Grove realized that he could not expect the DRAM managers to recommend their own obsolescence. Senior management was in the unique position to make such a judgment.

In Grove's view of strategic planning, a critical success factor derives from forming effective communication paths between middle level and senior managers. In an environment which encourages communication, senior management can evaluate middle managers' positions of advocacy in the overall context of the business.

The unfolding of the DRAM decision implies that the marketing group's perspective on DRAM importance proved to be correct. The marketing group had suggested that DRAMs were a critical component in the sales product mix. Intel's agreement with Samsung, albeit two years later, can be seen as vindication of this viewpoint. It can also be seen as a strategy to help develop competitors for the dominant (Japanese) DRAM suppliers.

New events since the initial draft of the case: Recently, key events have added to the DRAM story. The U.S. Memories venture eventually failed due to lack of corporate sponsorship in early 1990. Soon thereafter, Intel signed an exclusive marketing and technology agreement with NMB Corporation in which it agreed to market 100% of NMB's output in exchange for automation technology transfer. NMB is the Japanese ball bearing maker who entered the DRAM business with no previous semiconductor expertise. This alliance appeared to be significant for Intel from two perspectives: first, since NMB's business strategy is to participate in commodity businesses, it has no long-term interest in the microprocessor business (unlike Samsung); second, NMB has sophisticated automation technology which could significantly enhance Intel's long-term cost position in its businesses (e.g., EPROMs and microprocessors). Note, however, that NMB might well have an interest in entering the EPROM business.

The Rationalization of Technology Strategy with Changing Industry Dynamics and Paradigms

The contrasting quotations from Chou, Barrett, and Parker present a rich context for discussion regarding Intel's current technology strategy and its evolution over time. While these three senior managers appear to represent significantly different viewpoints, a more detailed analysis reveals common threads in their logic and an evolution in the strategic position of the company.

Chou argues that Intel does not need to have a high volume product to continue learning and to remain a technology leader. He argues that learning is "time and engineering constrained, not number of wafers constrained." He asserts that enhanced learning techniques can take the place of the historical "brute force" techniques of volume production.

Chou's position contradicts the traditional model of learning in which cost reduction is related to cumulative volume. The cumulative volume model of learning-dominated thinking at Intel before the DRAM was abandoned. In fact, it was a critical argument for maintaining a position in the technology.

Chou does not offer an explanation for what makes the cumulative volume model less appropriate in the late '80s than it was in the early '80s. He asserts that the difference lies in an attitude towards process improvement that transcends volume: "You have an intuition about what to do [to improve process yield]. You just fix everything you can think of." Parker, the Vice President of Technology Development (Chou's immediate superior) presents a different perspective.

Parker suggest that the "industry paradigm" has shifted. Cumulative volume still drives learning, but the learning accumulates more at the equipment vendor and less at the semiconductor manufacturer. Thus, the cumulative volume of the entire industry becomes more important than the volume of any single vendor.

In this view of the world, high volume semiconductor producers "learn" more quickly than low volume producers by virtue of their purchasing power and their enhanced linkages with the equipment vendors, not because they have more wafers on which to learn. They get the benefits of each generation of equipment first. Nikon (a vendor of photolithography equipment) derives learning from the entire industry (in the form of feedback from its customers), but then tailors its most advanced product offerings to Toshiba (rather than Intel) because Toshiba, as the largest DRAM manufacturer, is Nikon's largest customer.

The implication of Parker's view is that from a process technology perspective, Intel is a technology follower. While some of Intel's managers may view the company as participating at the leading edge of technology development, its position is limited by its relatively weak linkages with equipment vendors. Parker's view of the changing industry would suggest that a strategy of fostering enhanced relationships with equipment vendors would lead to an improved technology position.

Parker's view of learning through industry equipment vendors differs significantly from Chou's view where learning is decoupled from equipment vendors. According to Parker, Intel watches what the equipment manufacturers are doing for the DRAM companies and makes sure that Intel's future process plans will be compatible with the new generation of equipment. Still, there is a six-month lag when the DRAM manufacturers have the latest technology and other companies do not.

Barrett suggests that Intel's processing improvements have accelerated since the DRAM exit. He attributes that trend to improved engineering techniques, not to advances in process equipment, as does Parker. In Barrett's view, Intel has not become a technology follower.

Barrett adds another dimension to the discussion of Intel's technology position. He bolsters Chou's arguments by suggesting that high volume processing is not critical to success, although he simultaneously asserts that Intel stayed in the EPROM business to maintain high volume product. He says: "We were late waking up to the fact that we did not need to run volume in order to learn." Then he says "When we got out of DRAMs, we were concerned that we might suffer from the lack of volume. We tried to address that concern by selectively staying in the EPROM business. . . ."

An attempt to reconcile the apparent contradiction in Barrett's view of the importance of "volume" products yields an important insight. Barrett says: "We chose to stay in those commodity businesses partly because it does 'keep us honest.'" He believes that EPROMs are critical not because they provide scale advantages for learning, but because they provide a critical linkage between Intel and its competitive environment.

These three senior managers have different views of Intel's technology position and the changing nature of the industry's structure. Parker emphasizes that there has been a fundamental change in the "industry paradigm," which means that Intel is now a technology follower. Barrett does not concede that change. Instead, he suggests that Intel must continue to maintain a position in low margin products to sustain a tight linkage with cost trends in the rest of the industry.

These two viewpoints have different implications for Intel in the future. Parker's view suggests that a volume product such as EPROM is not necessary for Intel's portfolio, since process improvements will come from equipment suppliers. Barrett's viewpoint suggests that EPROMs are necessary only to support the microcontroller business in the short term and to keep the microprocessor business on an efficient cost reduction curve in the long-term.

On the evolution of Intel's technology strategy: Chou's discussion of the changing role of process technology and the new challenges presented by Intel's microprocessor business provides background for a discussion of where Intel should focus its technology development investments in the future.

Chou argues that the critical success factor in the microprocessor business is in creating and exploiting close linkages between the processing and the design capabilities. In the previous era, Intel's advanced processes were developed on DRAMs and then transferred to other products. Now, new processes must be developed exclusively for microprocessors, presenting challenges in the relative timing of process and design development. Both design and process must now be developed simultaneously rather than sequentially in order for Intel to maintain its technology position.

Given the argument supported by Parker, Intel is a technology follower in the absolute terms of the major DRAM manufacturers. However, Intel may still be able to sustain a critical advantage in microprocessor processing technology if it focuses process development there and improves its ability to introduce new processes and new microprocessor designs simultaneously. By exploiting close linkages between process advances and new microprocessor families, Intel may be able to protect its position in "performance" microprocessors against newcomers.

The Implications for Corporate Strategy of Tensions between Commodity and Proprietary Businesses

The theme of tensions between commodity and proprietary businesses runs through Intel's development. The consequence of Intel's exit from the DRAM business has been to further narrow the processing capability of the company. Before 1985, Intel had three process technologies. In 1990, it supports only two, the microprocessor technology and the EPROM/microcontroller technology.

While the actual processes are not intrinsically "commodity" or "proprietary," the products which each supports are: he EPROM process supports primarily commodity products (except for microcontrollers) and the microprocessor CMOS process supports proprietary logic products. The tension between commodity and proprietary products continues to exist at Intel.

A key discussion question surrounds the future of commodity products at Intel. In retrospect, the exit from the DRAM business appears to have been a good move for Intel. Its sole sourcing strategy and focus on proprietary products has led it to a very profitable position (see Exhibit 1 in the case). Why not take the next step and eliminate EPROMs, given that they are so much less profitable than microprocessor products?

Some evidence indicates that the process of exiting the EPROM business has already started. In the discussion of the sole sourcing strategy for microprocessors, the case states: "In order to support the sole sourcing strategy, Intel converted their new Israel facility, originally designed for EPROMs, to make microprocessor products." Thus, in the ongoing capacity battle, commodity products continue to lose at the margin.

It is clear, from the example above, that there are several forces (profit driven) which will tend to favor microprocessors over EPROMs. Only active management intervention will prevent EPROMs from going the way of DRAMs. From a profit perspective, it appears to make more sense to invest in the higher margin business at the expense of the low margin business.

Barrett articulates the key reasons why he believes that Intel should continue to participate in the less attractive commodity segments. He says that participation in the EPROM business enables participation in the microprocessor business ("helps amortize R&D expenditure"), and that overall, the discipline afforded by the marketplace keeps the manufacturing operation lean and always learning.

While Barrett's arguments have internal consistency, they may be subject to argument. Having strong environmental linkages (playing in the commodity market) ensures discipline in manufacturing, but so might another incentive system. Should Intel decide to exit the EPROM business, it would have to develop internal mechanisms to ensure the same assiduous attention to cost reduction that currently exists.

Note: The figures provided in the case suggest that while EPROMs have positive margins, they may not be profitable, given the high cost associated with the EPROM technology development group. Intel is still the world leader in the EPROM business, but growth is relatively slow and capital investment intense.

Changing Modes of Corporate Intrapreneurism and Strategic Renewal in Large Corporations

This case presents a rich context in which to examine the role of corporate intrapreneurship in Intel's strategic renewal processes. Gordon Moore (Chairman), while discussing the invention of the EPROM, suggested that the current-day Intel was much less capable of developing a product without a clear market than the Intel of 1972. Moore asserted that today's Intel was likely to kill an effort like the EPROM before it had a chance to prove itself. Indeed, the complexity of the business has grown to where the introduction of a new product requires the concentrated effort of hundreds of people.

This case presents two situations in which corporate intrapreneurs appear to be emerging from within the corporate structure. The first case involves Intel's entrance into the RISC processor marketplace, the introduction of a product which can be seen as modifying the company's core strategy. The second case is somewhat more subtle, and has not yet completely played out. Again, however, the key middle manager involved supports a view of Intel's strategy significantly different from the mainstream view and is pursuing ways to bring his vision to fruition.

The i860 story: The story of Intel's entrance into the RISC processor business details the emergence of new product family which may ultimately challenge Intel's core microprocessor products. It illustrates the ability of an astute technologist, Les Kohn, to test the boundaries of the currently articulated corporate strategy and to modify them.

As Gordon Moore suggested, new products in this industry are complex and require the support of a large organization in order to come to fruition. Les Kohn concurs when he says that his product was way too big to be developed in a "skunk works." Kohn had been attempting to get Intel into the RISC processor market since he joined the company in 1982. As he puts it: "RISC was not an existing business and people were not convinced a market was there." In fact, the strength of the organization's aversion to RISC architectures is demonstrated by the corporate jargon, YARP, for "yet another RISC processor."

117

Kohn's comments in the case are somewhat understated, but a careful reading reveals a deliberate strategy which could be viewed as subversive. From a technical standpoint, Kohn believed that RISC (reduced instruction set computing) architecture had intrinsic advantages over CISC (complex instruction set computing) architecture. However, he had learned from several more straightforward attempts at the product approval process that an approach which supported rather than challenged the status quo would be more likely to yield success.

His solution was to disguise his product. He proposed a co-processor for the 486 chip rather than a stand-alone processor which would have been perceived as competition. In effect, he decided to sell his RISC architecture within Intel as a peripheral chip to enhance the performance of Intel's core processor product. Rather than compete, Kohn close to enhance. Kohn says he made sure that the chip's financial justification would rest solely on its role as a co-processor.

In contrast to the internal selling strategy, the actual design of the chip focused on making a stand-alone part: "We designed it as a stand-alone processor, but made it very useful as an accessory to the 486." Kohn's success in developing the i860 suggests that senior management likely did not realize what Kohn was up to (a consequence of the highly technical, diverse and specialized businesses Intel is in). By the time senior management realized what their "co-processor" was, Kohn had already lined up a customer base for the stand-alone processor, a base he suggested was different than the companies who purchase the 486 chips. Thus Kohn could demonstrate that he was broadening Intel's business rather than cannibalizing it.

Intel's participation in the RISC processor business ultimately carries the danger of undermining its highly profitable x86 business. And, Intel does not have proprietary ownership of a dominant RISC architecture. However, the RISC marketplace had been growing and posed its own threat to Intel, regardless of Kohn's product.

Kohn's team, unburdened by the belief that x86 architecture was the best strategy for Intel, developed a strategy to show senior management that RISC was a viable alternative. Intel senior management eventually decided it was better to participate in the RISC market than to remain aloof, as it had for several years.

Flash Memory: The second story of corporate intrapreneurship is much more subtle than the i860 story and has not yet reached a conclusion. Nevertheless, the story of Flash may be used as another example of how a middle manager who does not fully share the corporate strategic vision may find ways to develop proof of his alternative strategy.

The middle manager in charge of Flash has plans for that technology which ultimately would have implications for the microprocessor business. Internally, however, he sells the technology as a way to protect current market position in the EPROM business. While EPROM replacement will clearly be the first application for Flash technology, this manager believes that it will have significantly more impact. He sees Flash as a way for Intel to reenter the memory business: "The best way to compete with the Japanese is the change the game."

Through a technical argument, which suggests that in the next several years Flash memory will become cheaper than DRAM, this manager believes that there is an opportunity for Flash to undermine the DRAM business. However, for this to happen, the basic structure of microprocessors would have to change to suit the functionality of Flash memory. In other words, a new microprocessor architecture will be required to take advantage of Flash's cost reduction potential.

In a more radical long-term view, he sees Flash as ultimately providing a way to develop neural network computers. Neural network computers would again challenge Intel's corporate view of the best technology for microprocessors. Thus this middle manager has a view of Flash that is radically different from the corporation's original view of EPROM: EPROM started at Intel as an enabling technology for microprocessors; Flash (EPROMs successor) may ultimately be a replacement technology.

Note: Exhibits 5 and 6 in the case suggest that Flash devices are still more expensive than magnetic memory devices and may continue to be so.

Forward Integration and the Future of Intel

The last section of the case describes the recent growth in Intel's systems' business. This section serves to underline the diversity of Intel's operations and to present the obvious path for Intel's next growth phase.

The case provides the context for a discussion surrounding the benefits and risks of Intel's apparent forward integration strategy. Intel appears to be uniquely positioned to participate in the personal computer business, particularly since it has a lock on the microprocessor market. This strategy is very bold since it fundamentally involves competing with customers.

Intel's sole sourcing strategy for the 386 and later microprocessor generations allows it significant latitude in developing a systems business that competes with its customers. However, that strategy is still not without risk. Regarding the sole sourcing strategy, Barrett points out a significant risk: "Everyone is gunning for you. They are either making clones of your product or substitutes."

Intel's forward integration strategy will likely create additional negative sentiment among some of its customers. Those customers will be predisposed to switch to alternative technologies as the clones and substitutes become available. To the extent that clones can access the installed software base that runs on Intel's microprocessors (a technical problem), Intel will suffer significant competition, particularly at the low end of its business.

The discussion regarding forward integration should recognize that clones are being developed anyway as a response to Intel's sole sourcing strategy. Competitive processors will likely be developed regardless of Intel's forward integration moves, so forward integration may simply accelerate a process that is already in motion. Given that clones and substitutes are already being developed, forward integration can be seen as a strategy to provide Intel with a way to extend the life of its processors.

SUMMARY OF OUTCOMES

In July 1993, Intel celebrated its 25th anniversary. In a special publication, it outlined 25 events that have defined Intel as a company. In that publication, it stated the following: "As Intel enters its second quarter-century, the company is once again leading the computing industry into a revolution. 'We see incredible opportunities in the area of business communications—making the PC a truly full-functional, real-time communications tool,' says Andy Grove. 'The PC has the ability to obliterate time and space barrier in dealing with information.' . . . 'Once again, we're leading with our chin into a brand new arena. . . .Historically, it's our best mode.'"

In late 1995, "Intel planned to unveil server technology designed to throw the fast-growing parallel-processing market into hyperdrive, with a low-cost commodity structure similar to that of PCs—and with Intel as the leading supplier. That, combined with Intel's growing influence among enterprise server manufacturers, put Intel in a whole new league. . . . Central to Grove's long-term vision for Intel is direct involvement in the building of servers and server components. Next month the company will unveil a four-processor motherboard that employs the next-generation Pentium Pro chip. . . . By 1997 Intel expects to incorporate high-speed interconnects that will let the company link thousands of these boards to build low-cost, high-performance, massively parallel enterprise servers. . . . Intel, by supplying highly integrated motherboards and helping build full systems will control the computer technology that corporate America will buy."

"Intel also has a joint venture with Hewlett Packard to develop microprocessor technology that combines CISC and RISC capabilities. This partnership could free it from its dependence on Microsoft. Intel officials predict that Windows NT will eventually become the predominant operating systems for clustered Intel-based servers. But Intel's link with HP in the Unix camp, as well as the company's key role in establishing a new applications programming interface (API) for Unix, gives Intel a leg up in enterprise systems."[1]

---

[1] "Intel's Bold Power Play," *Informationweek*, October 23, 1995.

APPLE COMPUTER, INC. (A) TEACHING NOTE

Overview

This short case provides a brief look at some of the critical policies which shaped Apple Computer in its early years. It contains the exciting story of Steve Jobs's and Steve Wozniak's early actions in forming the company. The story has become a classic of modern entrepreneurship. It allows a discussion of the conditions which allowed this success story to occur. More importantly, however, Apple Computer (A) offers the first really thorough example of strategic outsourcing as a basic strategy. It shows how: (1) by concentrating on its "core competency" of designing software at the user interface and (2) "outsourcing" essentially all else, Apple could leverage both its capital and intellectual resources enormously. The case provides a very useful infrastructure for discussing the nature of core competency and its use with strategic outsourcing. It matches up well with the Quinn and Hilmer, Andrews, and Mintzberg articles. The case works well alone or as a combined assignment with Apple Computer 1992. The two cases were designed to link together and to allow students to bring the discussion up to current date. However, Apple Computer (A) can be used alone as an excellent opening conceptual case, since students know many of the background facts—or at least think they do.

Session Structure

We usually open this case by asking what the critical environmental factors were in Apple's start-up. We then move on to a discussion of core competency and how one thinks about the "skills based" and "best-in-world" aspects of core competency. Next we open a discussion of what such an extensive outsourcing strategy entails. This allows one to raise questions of both risks and benefits and to begin challenging students on how to offset the risks of core competency-strategic outsourcing strategies, while realizing their great potential gains. A third question that stimulates much discussion is how a venture capitalist could have evaluated the Apple start-up. How would one "price" such a start-up? What would be the essential ingredients to ensure its success? What, if anything, could others have done to subvert Apple's success? How should Apple have responded? How does this opening strategy affect Apple's future positioning in its marketplaces?

Core Competency With Outsourcing Strategy Summary

One can start the case with the broad question, "What critical factors led to Apple's early formation and initial growth?" Perhaps most important among these are the following:

A.   Advances in Technology: The miniaturization of chip technologies and the standardization of memories made it possible to package a reasonably powered computer in a few chips. The cost of the chips had dropped to the point where they were not the dominating cost factor in product entry. Production problems were primarily of an assembly nature and did not require large fixed investments. The main contributor to value was software.

B.   Determined Risk Takers: Wozniak and Jobs were willing to put their entire assets on the line, contribute their own energy and intellectual capital, and to bring in key partners like Markkula to start the enterprise. Jobs had a vision of producing a readily accessible computer device, and was willing to put in the necessary years of risk and frustration to bring it about.

Teaching note copyright ©1996 by James Brian Quinn. This note was prepared by Professor Quinn. The bulk of this note consists of the teaching note prepared by Professor William Davidson to accompany the original Apple Computer Company case, copyright © 1983 by the Sponsors of the Colgate Darden Graduate School of Business.

C.   IBM Ignores the Market: Apple was able to start-up because IBM did not choose to use its enormous power to develop this marketplace. It concentrated on its then existing strengths, in the mid-line central processing marketplace, directed toward mid- to large-sized companies. Before IBM responded, Apple was able to establish a clear market position and uniqueness.

D.   A Strict Software Focus: Jobs and Wozniak were superior software designers. With their vision and skill, they could dominate a small segment of the computer marketplace. They concentrated all of their own energies on producing a user-friendly interface between the customer and the screen. With their own talents, they could dominate this segment of the value chain.

E.   Customer Need: Customers had been frustrated by the complexity of access to IBM-dominated equipment. They welcomed a simpler format using computer graphics potentials. Jobs and Wozniak added the fillip of humor to their software using gulping trash cans and highly simplified menu-driven screens. They were fortunate in that external software programmers came up with very useful routines, like spreadsheets and word processing just as their equipment hit the marketplace. This added enormous value to an otherwise relatively useless computer.

Core Competency with Outsourcing

Reinforced by the company's resource scarcity, Apple's early strategy focused on its unique intellectual strengths in software and leveraged its resources to the maximum extent possible through outsourcing. Note that the outsourcing strategy was not Jobs's creation. Michael Scott, Financial Officer of Apple, put it into place. This is an excellent point at which to ask the question, "What was Apple's core competency? What is a core competency? How did Apple reinforce it?" This quickly brings out that the company's core competency was not its product (i.e., a computer which anyone else could have assembled at that time) but the founders' software skills which enabled creation of a totally new value concept for computers. From this one can develop the crucial concepts of core competency. Core competencies tend to be knowledge-based skills. To be a company's core competency, the company must be best-in-world at that activity. If it is not, then it is someone else's core competency and not that of the company. A single company can be best-in-world at only a few things. It can leverage its resources most by focusing its investments on those few things and maintaining control of those activities which support the core competency. The core competency provides a strategic block between outsourcing suppliers and the marketplace. At least one core competency must be intimately in contact with customers and provide a flexible platform for future changes. Clearly Jobs and Wozniak were best-in-world at the software interface linking users and the computer screen. This was supported by their unique "user groups" who provided customer inputs. As long as Apple could dominate this interface, it could create a unique value concept.

Apple leveraged this capability enormously by opening its software structure sufficiently for outside applications programmers to innovate uses for the computer. This tapped into the intellectual capabilities of thousands of people Apple could not have afforded itself. By outsourcing all of its component production, Apple both avoided those heavy investments and tapped into the innovation stream of all of the suppliers it utilized. It avoided the risks inherent in backing any single approach in a rapidly advancing field of technology. It shortened its cycle time to market by not having to invent and reduce to practice all of the components itself. It thus lowered its risk as well as increasing the value of its products to customers.

However, Apple went well beyond merely outsourcing its component parts. It became one of a new wave of companies outsourcing many activities formerly considered to be integral to the company. Thus it outsourced marketing to Regis McKenna, stylistic design to Frogdesign, and distribution to companies like Computer Land. This leveraged the value output of its limited capital resources enormously. The result was that—with its limited resources—Apple could dominate a key sector of the value chain in the computer market. As long as it could dominate that portion of the value chain, Apple was successful. Only when an outsider, Microsoft, began to

122

provide an even more extensive value package at the customer-screen interface did Apple run into serious difficulties.

One can next ask, "What are the inherent risks of this kind of strategy for a smaller company." The biggest are: being whipsawed by a supplier, having a supplier jump over the company to its marketplaces, not being able to obtain desired priorities from the supplier, and loss of control if a competitor decides to duplicate the strategy. All of these are largely offset if the company itself has a true core competency, i.e., it produces something important to customers in a uniquely high value fashion. Thus, the software innovation capabilities of Jobs and Wozniak become a strategic block between Apple's suppliers and the marketplace. Later, as the Apple name becomes known and supporting programs designed by others become widely available, these become a further block to suppliers jumping over Apple. The mutual interests of all these parties provide a set of strategic alliances that is doubly powerful. As Apple gains in scale, it can exercise increasing power over its suppliers. However, the most important thing Apple did was to develop a phenomenal EDI system and process for tracking its suppliers' capabilities. It held on to the assembly process for the computer, not to lower costs but to ensure coordination and control of all interrelationships among component parts. Just this portion of the case can make for a lively discussion which is applicable to a wide variety of companies. However, the Teaching note by William H. Davidson which follows brings out other interesting aspects of the early history of Apple Computer. This Apple (A) case may stand on its own or be used in conjunction with the Apple Computer 1992 case—explaining many of the strengths and exposures Apple faces in 1992.

Why was Apple so successful? One common response suggests that they just happened to be in the right place at the right time. A follow-on question is what was it that made Apple distinctive? What did they do that others didn't. Some of the important point to elicit are listed below. Each of these points is important to set up other parts of the discussion.

Source of Success

- right place and time
- ease of use
- user-friendly
- retail mass marketing
- marketing skills—promotion, image, public relations
- open specs/software
- fresh vision
- ambitious, aggressive, think big
- willingness to seek help, use outsiders, hire management
- packaging of technology

A brief discussion of each of these points is warranted. Apple's approach in all of these areas stands in marked contrast to prior practice in the computer industry. It is worth discussing how Apple's approach compares to existing computer companies. What did they do differently? For example, their documentation was non-technical, their name and image were fresh and accessible. They attempted to demystify and "detechnify" the computer, and to sell computers to mass markets. Publication of the Apple II specifications was a key and unprecedented step. Formerly, specifications and operating systems were strictly proprietary. By publishing the specs, Apple stimulated massive production of software by hobbyists, hackers, and professionals. Visi-Calc is the key result. Availability of a range of software was the driving force behind adoption of microcomputers by new user segments.

Apple's management had a fresh vision of how computers could be used. They took all the appropriate steps to design, support, and sell microcomputers to a new, latent market segment. That vision, and Apple's aggressive commitment to it, should take tangible form during this phase of the discussion. Apple is dedicated to changing the way people live by making computer technology available to the average person. An image of fanatical zeal can be developed here—an image that is useful for later reference.

After 15 minutes of discussion on sources of success, a transition to a strategy review should be made. A standard strategy statement format can be used for this phase of the discussion. The transition can be best achieved by referring back to Apple's marketing skills. Let's take a closer look at their marketing strategy. Several of the initial points also can be used to focus on Apple's concept (bring computer technology to the masses, user-friendly, mass marketing). Either approach can be used to effect the transition.

In developing a strategy statement, (see later part of the note), I would spend only a few minutes on marketing policies. Establish the fact that Apple built the distribution channel, with service, support, and cooperative ads for dealers (who were almost all new venturers themselves). Apple focused on primary demand development via pull advertising. Apple was the first computer maker to use a consumer marketing approach. Its target market was not a data processing manager, but an average person. Apple sells to individuals rather than organizations; and not just to professionals. Apple did what Honda did for motorcycles—made them acceptable and accessible to the average person. It is important to ask, however, whether Apple is using penetration pricing to develop this market, as Honda did. Some students may say yes. If so, respond by asking what level of gross margins is typical for firms using penetration pricing. You can leave the point unresolved for now; it will later become apparent that Apple is skimming—they are in fact "selling share" in this business by 1983.

It is possible to spend a fair amount of time on Apple's marketing policies, but I would limit this discussion to just a few minutes. After establishing the general thrust of Apple's marketing efforts, the next step for the instructor is somewhat complex—developing an idea that Apple management calls "the leverage principle."

The Leverage Principle

Assessment of Apple's manufacturing, finance, and R&D approaches all drive the discussion towards identification of Apple's leverage strategy. This element of Apple's approach is central to their business concept.

There are several ways to guide the discussion. Under manufacturing, "What is Apple's plant-and-equipment-to-sales ratio? 5%. Low or high?" Under R&D, what is Apple's R&D to sales ratio? Is that low or high for the industry? For an emerging company? Under finance, how has Apple financed its growth?

Regardless of the approach, I like to use a standard cash flow/business cycle chart to illustrate the key point. If students have seen it, just put it up; if not, it can be developed by just asking what the cash flow would look like for a new business and why. The point, of course, is that Apple has positive cash flow virtually from day one. The next question is: Which approach is better, Apple's or the Boston Consulting Group's?

Cash Flows for Emerging Businesses

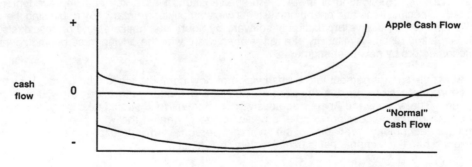

124

Then, how can Apple pull this off? First, they don't invest in plant and equipment. Second, they don't spend much on R&D. Third, they have an interesting working capital cycle.

Working Capital Cycle Analysis

One of the more useful pieces of financial analysis that can be developed in this session focuses on Apple's working capital cycle. The case tells us that Apple is paid by its dealers 15 days after shipment, but pays its suppliers after 60 days. This fact, with some retrievable margin data, permits the following analysis of the working capital cycle for an Apple II unit as of early 1983.

Apple II Financial Structure

Retail	$2,000
Factory	$1,000
Cogs	$ 450
Gross Margin	$ 550

It is then useful to ask the students what part of the $450 is 1) purchased parts, 2) direct labor, and 3) overhead (including quality control, testing, materials management and factory overhead). They should be able to deduce that direct labor is very small (it is in fact less than two man-hours for assembly). Factory overhead is also small, but indirect costs for QC, testing and materials management are very important. A reasonable breakdown might be $200 for purchased parts, $50 for direct labor, and $200 for "overhead and indirect costs." With these numbers—which can also be used to give us important insights into other aspects of Apple's strategy—we can now trace the working capital cycle.

Board Plan

Day 1. Purchase parts @ $200 in accounts payable

Ask students how long these parts are in inventory before they are assembled and shipped. With excess demand for Apple IIs and with real constraints in supply of many parts, these parts are going to be shipped quickly. If you calculate inventory turns from the case, you have more than a 1-month turn cycle; that is misleading because the inventory level is tied to current sales, which are running 2-3 times what they were over the past year. I would argue that these parts might be shipped in 15 days, but would settle for shipment in day 30.

Day 30. Ship Apple II @ $1,000 in accounts receivable.

Day 45. Receive payment @ $1,000 of accounts receivable paid.

Day 60. Pay for parts @ $200 of accounts payable paid.

This exercise points out one of the key reasons why Apple violates the expected cash flow pattern for emerging businesses. We are now ready to go on to the next phase of the discussion.

At this point, we should have a strategy statement on the board that looks something like the following:

- Goals: leader in microcomputers

- Concept: bring computer technology to mass markets
user-friendly, ease of use
consumer marketing, packaging
leverage

- Product/Market: little segmentation, general market thrust

- Target Users: individual purchasers (as opposed to organizational)

Marketing	Manufacturing
dealer network development	final assembly and test
service	QC effort
training	plant and equipment=6% of sales
high margins	sourcing from Japan, United States
primary demand development	heavy reliance on suppliers
advertising, public relations	no vertical integration
packaging/design focus	
pricing=skimming or penetration?	

Finance	R&D
cash=$150 million, no debt	software done outside
use of venture capital equity	R&D=6-8%, R or D?
working capital management	source of technology?
high margins	are they innovators?
no dividend	willingness to use outside ideas
review other ratios	engineering or marketing company?
	reliance on suppliers
	packaging of technology

We are now ready to begin the most complex phase of the discussion. The transition can be accomplished by referring to the leverage principle—"Apple doesn't really do any manufacturing or software development; it doesn't really do any basic research, and the bulk of sales and distribution effort is done by the independent dealers. All Apple does is make money." It's not a bad idea. Are there any problems? The ensuing discussion can be readily structured within a Porter industry analysis framework and a supplier-user map.

Industry and Competitor Analysis

Apple's position is so clearly attractive it will draw a host of imitators. Are there any barriers to entry to limit competition? Apple's cost and price position are certainly not a barrier, nor are its technological abilities (in the Apple II market). Further thinking about barriers can be stimulated by putting the class in the position of the new entrant. Two important issues emerge. To compete in the same mode as Apple, (we'll explore other modes in a moment) a new entrant will need to convince a) dealers to carry his product, b) software developers to write programs for his machine, and c) consumers to buy it.

These are very tall orders. This market is characterized by very high purchaser uncertainty and anxiety. Consumer brand recognition, and more importantly, consumer brand "comfort" will be very difficult to achieve (with at least one exception). Software writers will write only for machines with large installed or expected unit sales. There is a Catch 22 here—you need a lot of software to sell a lot of units, and vice versa. Dealers will carry only those products that solve the above problems and offer total margins that are at least as attractive as Apple. Access to shelf space, software support, and brand differentiation are important barriers for Apple. At least one company, IBM, can readily overcome these barriers.

The next step in the discussion can focus on other modes and rivals. We have identified at least one company that can play Apple's game. There are other possible approaches to the market as well. One way to develop these other approaches is to ask the class to list other competitors. The list should be assembled as shown in the table. (This list will become part of a supplier-user map.) How do these other companies plan to make a profit? This discussion can be stimulated by asking: How does Apple make a profit? Apple makes profits on hardware sales. There are several other identifiable approaches that are common to groups of firms. These generic strategies, which are developed in the case, can be developed in discussion.

Possible Strategies

Generic Strategy	Firms	User Segments						
		Home		Education		Business		
						Stand-		
		Low	High	Low	High	Alone	Network	Professional
Razor and Blade	TI	XXX	XX	X	X			
	Atari	XXX	XX	X				
	Commodore	XXX	XX	X				
Hardware Package	Apple		XX		XX	XX		
	IBM		XX		XX	XX	XX	
	Tandy		XXX		XXX	XX		
Knock-Off	Franklin		XXX	X	X	XX		
	Pineapple		XXX	X	X	X		
	Compaq		XXX	X	X	X		
Hitech	Hewlett-Packard						XX	XX
	Convergent Technology						XX	XX
Hardware and Software	Apollo					X	XX	XX
	Daisy					X	XX	XX
	Lisa					X	XX	XX
Portable	Osborne					X		X
	Kaypro				X		X	
Smart Terminal	ATT						X	X
	Televideo						X	X
Dual processor	NEC						XX	XX
	DEC						XX	XX

127

Some discussion of user segments can follow analysis of various competitors. Where do each of these firms focus on target segments? How much overlap is there? A simplistic set of user segments appears in the preceding diagram. Further development of user segments can be done by discussing the needs, concerns, and sensitivities of various user groups, and positioning suppliers against identifiable clusters of users. The key objective here is simply to show the diversity of the competitors, the increasing segmentation of the market, and the trend towards convergence of the various supplier strategies across user segments. Are there mobility barriers, or will Apple face growing pressure from a variety of competitors?

As you look at these various strategies, do any of them pose significant threats to Apple? One in particular deserves special discussion. The razor and blade strategy is very important. These companies give away the hardware and plan to make profits on subsequent sales of software and peripherals. As a result, they offer significantly lower prices on hardware. The Commodore 64 has more memory and features than the Apple IIe and sells for less than half the price, for example. This approach stands in dramatic contrast to Apple which has always acted as if software were and should be a free good. Apple has made profits on hardware packages alone. Take a minute to develop the implications of a confrontation between these two approaches in the market.

Which is a more effective strategy? This discussion can lead to the supplier section of the analysis. The razor and blade approach requires a controlled supply of software. Can they have a large software base and control profits on software sales at the same time? This is a fundamental issue. Take a few minutes to develop it. Why did TI lose so much money in PCs? On a broader scale, how can any PC-maker capture software profits? Are the bulk of future profits in this industry tied to software sales? Who will get these profits?

Two pieces of analysis flow from these questions—substitutes and segmentation of the software industry. The primary substitute for the PC maker is alternative distribution of software. Software can be distributed direct to end users via mail order, direct to retailers or independent intermediaries. Attempts to control software distribution will require understanding of the types of software producers and distribution alternatives.

Supply Chain

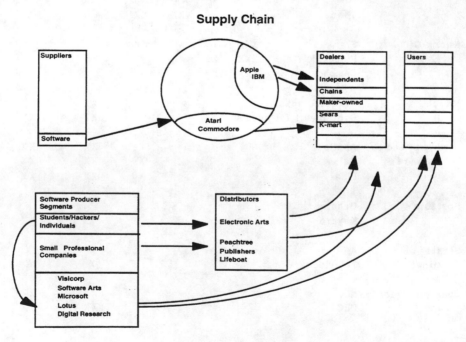

The big software firms are aiming to establish their own brand identity, direct distribution, and multi-machine capability. They will be very hard to control. There may be better opportunities to secure controlled sources of software from individuals or small companies. Still, substitutes in the form of publishers, clearing houses, and other intermediaries are rapidly emerging for these programmers. Software strategy is a vital issue for all PC makers.

Some closure on the industry analysis can be gained simply by reviewing the forces at work here. What are the prospects for Apple in this environment? What should they be doing in response to the issues that have been raised? This question, and a specific question about Apple's strategy for the home computer market will focus preparation for the next phase of discussion.

We have developed an understanding of what made Apple successful and begun to develop some of the current issues facing the company. We concluded that Apple was now facing significant competitive threats of various forms. How has Apple responded to these threats? Let's evaluate their most recent moves—the IIe and Lisa. What were they all about?

IIe	Lisa
enhanced, extended II line	radical technology
memory from 32 to 48k	extreme ease of use
keyboard features added	new target market
screen columns from 40 to 80	integrated hardware and software
prices reduced $400	skimming?
custom chips—costs reduced	can they succeed in the office market?
defensive or aggressive?	
clear cash flow, skimming strategy	

Let's put the IIe and Lisa in perspective in two ways. Refer to the supplier-user map, and develop a simple price-performance grid as below. Performance here is just hardware horsepower—we can expand this definition later.

Price-Performance Grid

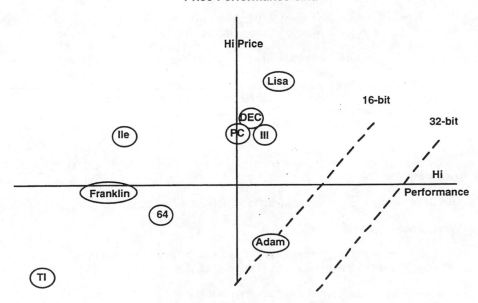

129

Price-performance standards in the industry are rapidly moving away from the II series. Can Apple continue to maintain a price premium of up to 100% over comparable models? It can certainly support a premium, based on its servicing dealer network and brand name (both key to reducing cyberphobia), and its huge software base. However, the premium is getting much larger over time, and Apple's competitive advantages can be eroded. The performance enhancements and price reduction incorporated in the IIe are a temporary effort to close some of the gap, but the II series, which is tied to an old 8-bit microprocessor and operating system, is going to be surpassed by the new 16-bit and 32-bit systems described in the case. These new products offer quantum leaps in price-performance. What can Apple do about this inevitable development? The class may suggest introducing a 16-bit system, but it is important to suggest that it will be very difficult for Apple or any company to dominate successive generations of technology in this industry. (A bright student might suggest skipping the 16-bit generation and jumping to 32-bit— Lisa's M68000 microprocessor has a 32-bit internal architecture.)

Technology Cycle

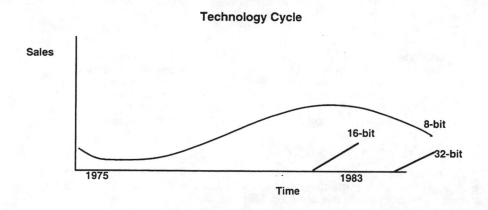

The Apple II is a fantastic cash cow that is still growing at a remarkable rate (the faster it grows, the more cash it throws). Why and how to replace it? Very slowly. Apple is almost forced to be defensive in order to minimize profits from the II series. At this point in the discussion, raise the issue—Does Apple want to be the leader in micros, or does it want a lot of money?

What do you want to do with the II series? If Apple doesn't replace it, someone else will. But how to replace it most effectively (i.e., profitably)? One answer is to continue moving it down and right in the price-performance grid, but only as required by competitive developments. A more aggressive approach involves using the II series as Alan Oppenheimer's home computer entry.

In discussing the future of the II series, many points will emerge. Some of the stronger ones, to my mind, include:

• It's better to replace it ourselves than to let someone else do it

• We can do it gradually.

• In some segments we may not have to replace or migrate the II at all. Let's begin to focus and differentiate the II series in terms of segments.

• It is better to replace from above than from below.

130

This last point is important. Macintosh is the next generation equivalent for the II. A perceptive student may suggest that Apple is skimming from Lisa at $10,000 to Lisa at $8,000 down to Macintosh at $2,500. Isn't that the right way to introduce a new product? What does this imply for the home market? Apple would be violating one dimension of its past if it introduced a "Lisa-like" home computer immediately—the financial dimension. But, where can Apple compete best—in the office or in the home? There is a lengthy discussion to be had here if the instructor has the time. Set up key success criteria, using customer characteristics and concerns and competition in the two sections, and compare to Apple's strengths and weaknesses. If you have time, this can help drive the class towards recommendations for the home market, within the context of a larger corporate strategy. Ask the students not only what they recommend but what they think Apple will do.

Be sure to leave some time for update and summary points. There will be many updates. Some of the more important at this time (December 1993) are the price reductions on Lisa, TI's withdrawal (Apple had always maintained that you couldn't be profitable with that approach), soaring demand for the IBM PC and PC Junior, and Apple's faltering financial performance in late 1983. Note that Apple's plant and equipment, marketing and R&D expenses rose dramatically in 1983.

Apple 1992 is set in March of 1992 with John Sculley posing the following question to his staff: have we gone far enough to alter or influence the competitive structure of the personal computer industry? By posing this issue, Sculley allows us to confront three central issues in the formulation of strategy:

1. How can firms mold or shape the character of their industry;

2. How can firms position themselves for superior performance in a deteriorating industry structure; and

3. The evolution of industry structure over time, and its implications for positioning.

The case can also be a vehicle for examining the role of standards in competitive strategy. The different approaches to standards, especially the closed, proprietary systems of Apple vs. the open standard introduced by IBM, had dramatic implications for the long-run viability of both firms as well as how the industry was ultimately structured. The case also allows for some rough calculations of the economics of standards. A critical question for Apple and all firms in industries where standards play a central role is whether there is enough room for more than one standard to exist.

Structure of the Case

The case begins with an overview of the personal computer industry's declining profitability. Despite the fierce increase in competitive rivalry, Apple Computer has been able to maintain above average, and by many definitions, superior performance. However, John Sculley, Apple's chairman and CEO, suggests that if the industry structure continues in its present form, Apple will not be able to maintain its position. He therefore poses the question to his staff: can we change the nature of competition and how? And are there other alternatives available for Apple?

The case then proceeds with a brief history of Apple. The purpose of this history is to demonstrate that Apple has largely shaped the history of the personal computer industry since its inception. Apple brings to the party some unique competitive advantages that are unmatched by competitors in the United States and elsewhere. It is the second largest PC company in the world, with an ROE almost three times the average of U.S. manufacturing, yet for some reason, Apple management believes that its position is not sustainable. What is especially noteworthy about Apple's view of the world is that management saw they were "on a glide path to history" while their profitability and balance sheet were among the strongest in the industry.

The problem, of course, relates to a fundamental shift in the structure of the industry; this is laid out in the early part of the case. There are two pieces to the story on industry structure: first, the case examines three phases of the industry's evolution; and second, the case explores the economics of PCs as of 1992. This section allows students to see that industry structure problems must be broadly defined: it is not just rivalry or barriers to entry, but there has been a shift in the bargaining power in the industry from the competitors to suppliers (Microsoft and Intel), which has induced severe rivalry, a collapse in the barriers to entry, more buyer power (through the creation of standards and new channels). There is also the prospect of substitution (new technologies), which might represent even more pressure in the future on the industry structure, or the prospect for greater growth and profitability in less competitive arenas.

I categorized the industry structure into roughly three phases over 15 years, which look like they fairly closely approximate the product life cycle of a typical manufactured product. The first phase of the industry looks like a classic emerging business: there is explosive growth, very low barriers to entry, almost chaotic competition, and only one clear leader—Apple. Yet, despite Apple's role as a pioneer, it did not dominate the business. On a worldwide basis, we see in Exhibit 4, that Apple had only 8% of the units and 8% of the revenue in 1981, prior to IBM's entry. Nonetheless, Apple prospered because of the very rapid growth. The second phase begins with IBM's decision to change the rules of competition by entering the industry with an "open" system. IBM's decision to release the specifications of its machine to encourage third parties to write software is a relatively well-known story. What is less often discussed is what alternatives did IBM have in 1981? IBM's real mistake, which should emerge with the later discussion of Intel and Microsoft, was not that it created an open system for application software, but that it did not demand exclusive rights to the operating systems software of Microsoft and x86 microprocessors of Intel. Even though IBM was playing catch-up to Apple in 1981, neither supplier was in a position to deny IBM an exclusive arrangement. (For example, Microsoft, which in 1992 had a market capitalization greater than General Motors and almost 50% of IBM, had only a half done employed a few million dollars in sales in 1981.) No one understood that operating systems software and microprocessors would be so central 5-10 years later, but this simple contractual change would have altered the industry's landscape, and especially IBM's position.

The second phase of the industry was one of relative consolidation around one standard, with IBM commanding the leadership. During this period of 1981 to 1985, PCs were still a relatively immature product, customers were not very sophisticated, and channels were not well developed. The result was relative concentration in the competitive structure and in the channels of distribution. There was limited shelf space and the three premium brands—IBM, Apple, and Compaq—which made the most margin for the computer dealer, captured the space. The hundreds of clones had to compete for the last one or two spots on the computer dealer's shelf. Apple's competitive advantage during this period was in transition: the IBM PC was a superior computer to the Apple II (more computing power at a comparable price), so Apple tried to change the playing field with the introduction of the Macintosh. Apple managed to stabilize its market share around 10% during this period, while IBM moved into a dominating position with 30% of worldwide revenues and units. Within the IBM standard (which unfortunately you cannot directly observe in Exhibit 4), IBM's share was almost 60%.

During the third phase, IBM tried to shift the terms of competition again by creating a "more" proprietary system, the PS/2. However, Compaq and other clones decide to maintain the old IBM standard by buying standard components from Intel and Microsoft, defeating IBM's effort to create a new standard. The result was that hardware become a commodity, especially as new channels of distribution exploded. With mail order and mass merchandisers selling PCs, the computer dealer was no longer an entry barrier. And, as the technology became standardized, it was very easy for any entrepreneur anywhere in the world to make PCs for a minimal investment

($1 million in capital). Apple largely escapes from the problems of the MS-DOS/x86 world until prices of hardware collapsed in 1990 and Microsoft introduced Windows 3.0. Suddenly, Apple must confront the reality of the PC industry with less technical differentiation.

The final portion of the case explores Apple's response to this dilemma. The question for the classroom is: has Apple responded appropriately to defend its position, alter the industry structure, or both? Is Apple's position defensible in 1992, and what should Sculley do?

TEACHING PLAN

Study Questions

1. Does Apple need to change the character of the personal computer industry in 1992 to retain its competitive advantage? Why/Why not?

2. Evaluate Apple's strategy since 1990; how will it affect Apple's competitive position and the structure of the industry?

3. What should Sculley do in 1992?

Teaching Questions

I begin with the following questions:

1. What are Apple's competitive advantages?

2. Why has Apple outperformed the industry to date?

3. Why have the dynamics of the industry change threatened that position?

Start at the left side of the front board

- Apple's historical competitive advantage:
  - unique, proprietary software
  - user-friendly interface (GUI)
  - graphics and education software
  - networking, multimedia
  - "system" solutions for the desktop

Since Apple is technically not a "PC" and has a proprietary technology, I ask: "Does the structure of the PC industry matter to Apple? Why is Sculley so concerned about the structure of the PC hardware industry? Why is the structure so lousy?"

- Rivalry: becoming fierce
  - declining differentiation in hardware
  - declining leadership (IBM provided price leadership in the past)
  - slower growth (maturing product); more head-to-head competition. Historically, double-digit growth rates were normal in both revenues and units. Unit growth declined in 1991 (see the first page of the case).
  - no proprietary technology in the MS-DOS world

-everyone is imitating quickly (Compaq imitates IBM; Dell imitates Compaq; Packard Bell and ALR imitate Dell, etc.)

- Buyers: growing much more powerful and price sensitive
  - switch to MIS departments
  - more knowledgeable, less sensitive to brand
  - require less service
  - operating under tight budgets—more price sensitive
  - no apparent loyalty

- Barriers to Entry: virtually nonexistent in 1992
  - $1 million in capital to build an MES plant; if you want to make less than 200,000, you can enter for a few thousand dollars
  - no technology; PCs are a pure assembly business, almost anyone can enter, anywhere in the world
  - channels exploding; mail order, superstores, mass merchandisers and VARs make it easy for anyone to get access to the ultimate customer
  - brand unnecessary as long as you conform to industry standards
  - no loyalty among customers and no switching costs, as long as you conform to industry standards

- Threats of Substitutes: serious possibility of new products
  - Workstations are increasingly moving into the PC product space
  - Palm-tops, pen-based computers, computer players (Sony) have the potential to threaten the growth of PCs

- Suppliers: appropriating virtually all the value being generated in PCs
  - two types of suppliers: commodity and sole sources—commodities have no power
  - how much profit are Intel and Microsoft earning? Almost 50% of the entire PC industry's profits! The two companies earned roughly $1.2 billion in 1991 vs. 4% ROS for the entire industry (see the first page of the case), which equals about $2 billion

Why?

-This is a complicated question, but it revolves largely around two key features of OSs and microprocessors: first, a standard has been established around MS-DOS, which runs only on the Intel x86 microprocessor. Forty billion dollars in software has been purchased for these machines, in addition to more than one hundred million dollars of hardware. The switching costs for the user to change OS and therefore microprocessors (assuming 1992 technology) is prohibitive. Not only would users have to buy new hardware and software, it would cost millions of dollars for a typical firm to retrain workers.

-In addition, the barriers to entry in both microprocessors and OSs are much higher than PCs: intellectual property protection is better (though not airtight in either area), and the scale economies are very high in both arenas (e.g., a state-of-the-art microprocessor plant in 1992 cost $1 billion). The case states that next generation OSs will cost $500 million; the case also states that IBM spent $1 billion on OS/2. Through 1991, both Intel and Microsoft have been sole sources for most of the products available on the market.

Once the industry structure has been explored, the instructor should return to Apple. The most important question is: so what that the PC industry's structure is deteriorating? Isn't Apple immune from the problems of PCs, given its proprietary technology? I then lay out on a side board a discussion of the "Defensibility of the Mac."

- Differentiation of the Mac vs. the PC is diminishing

- Even though the Mac is still a superior product, Windows 3.1 has significantly narrowed the gap

- Apple's installed base is so small relative to the PC world, it is reducing the attractiveness of the Mac for independent software vendors (ISVs). ISVs write for the largest installed base. These numbers can be determined from Exhibit 6, the shipments of Intel-based systems vs. Motorola: 91 million vs. 12 million, respectively. The instructor can add that projected numbers for 1992 were that 30-35 million x86 processors would be sold.

The growing installed base of DOS and x86 machines raised a serious problem of scale economies in writing operating system software, which should be explored below

- Apple's core differentiation depends on ISVs writing advanced applications for the Mac
  -who is the leading vendor of applications for the Mac?
  -Microsoft! Where will Microsoft innovate in the future—for Windows or the Mac? Obviously, Microsoft would prefer that leading edge applications would go on MS-DOS and Windows-based machines before they work on System 7.
  -Apple's cost structure represents a mixture of hardware and software companies—it is losing cost competitiveness to more focused competitors.

This is an opportunity to force students into some simple calculations, which dramatically reinforce the severity of Apple's dilemma. I use the other side board for these numbers.

Economics of Software

Microsoft receives $15 per OS ($30 for MS DOS and Windows); if we assume $500 million in development costs and 0 marginal costs of production (a very reasonable assumption in OS software), Microsoft must sell 33 million units to break even. Put another way, Microsoft has to reach about 33% of the installed base (91 million units) of x86 machines to recover its upfront investment. Or, Microsoft can break even within 1.5 years if it bundles its OS with each new X86 computer sold (roughly 20 million per year).

For the purposes of public information in the case, I have oversimplified this analysis. In reality, Microsoft receives about $5-$10 per machine every time MS-DOS is sold, and a little more every time Windows is sold through an OEM. Roughly, Microsoft will receive about $30 when the two get bundled with a retail computer sale. When these software products are sold through retail, Microsoft's wholesale price is also in the range of $20-$25 apiece. The vast majority of DOS sales, however, go through OEMs, and the average price is roughly $15.

If Apple sells its OS with each new Mac, it is selling about 3 million per year (the number of Motorola microprocessors being sold) and assuming that Apple incurs the same $500 million development expense, Apple's implicit price is about $165. Alternatively, if Apple sold its OS for $15, it would take 11 years to recover the investment. With a product cycle of roughly 5 years, this is impossible. Also, while Microsoft sells their OS and GUIs as upgrades through a retail channel, Apple historically bundled their products with their machine and charged little or nothing for upgrades. How can Apple get a premium price? Note: there are several variations on these calculations. Students' estimates range from $90 to $175 for the added premium Apple must charge. The precise number is not important. The main issue is that Apple must charge a substantial premium over Microsoft, and that will be possible only by bundling their software with their hardware and charging a premium for their hardware. The key question for Apple management is: Is it feasible for Apple to continue charging a premium, given the new industry structure?

Herein lies the heart of the problem: we just said that Windows 3.0 had caused Apple to lose much of its differentiation, which had allowed it to charge premium prices in the past. In addition, if Apple is losing ISV attention, it needs to gain market share, which again is inconsistent with a premium price strategy. At this point, one should ask students:

Is this a serious problem for Apple?

The answer should be, without big changes, "This company is on a glide path to history" (second page of the case).

I now make a transition to Apple's response to this situation by asking: "Has Apple's strategy since October 1990 adequately addressed these problems? Will Apple's moves alter the structure of the industry?"

I then lay out Apple's major moves and ask students to evaluate how each move will impact Apple's competitive position in the PC market and whether it will influence the structure of the industry.

Low Cost/Low Priced Strategy

• High volume strategy, designed to make Apple a mainstream player with enough share to attract ISV attention and change the economics of Apple's business

IMPACT ON POSITION: Apple is pursuing a low cost, low priced strategy when it is not even close to being a low cost producer; Apple's overhead and R&D will never make its relative cost position favorable with the clones.

IMPACT ON INDUSTRY: Apple claims publicly that it has gained enormous share; however, the doubling of share described by Apple is only in the U.S. dealer channel—the declining channel in the U.S. market. On a worldwide basis, we see in Exhibit 4 that Apple has gained only 0.2 of one share point. Therefore, it cannot be regaining ISV attention. Apple is also selling low powered Mac classics to gain share: ISVs do not like to write for the last generation machines. What excites a software vendor is high volumes of the most current products, which allow the user to utilize the most advanced software. Apple's low-priced machines could cannibalize its high-end sales.

Apple is also reinforcing price competition in the industry with its Mac Classic strategy, not remolding rivalry away from price.

Hit Products Strategy

• Bring out new products with rapid cycle times to reinvigorate the Mac business

IMPACT ON POSITION: Leverages Apple's superior technology and allows Apple to generate increasing revenue at a time when the industry's growth is slowing. However, is it sustainable? Apple is proud of its new products every six months to a year; Dell Computer is now bringing out products every three weeks! Dell's oldest product is 11 months! What if Apple missed on one hit product?

IMPACT ON INDUSTRY: No sustainable impact unless its increases Apple's share dramatically.

The hit product strategy is probably the best option available to Apple in the short run. It allows the company to leverage its capabilities in software and hardware design, and probably earn premium prices until competitors copy the hardware. The Powerbook, Apple's first "hit" product, was a spectacular success. It sold $1 billion in 1992; estimates suggested that 300,000 units were sold to Mac users and 100,000 to x86 users. The real issue is sustainability: can Apple replicate the Powerbook every year?

- Claris

Unlikely to impact either Apple or the industry. For teaching purposes, this is not worth much discussion.

IBM Joint Venture

- This action is worth some time and analysis. While we cannot go into too much detail, the logic of the JV and its potential impact are important elements of the strategy.

IMPACT ON POSITION: Potentially, the JV could be very good for Apple; it does give Apple greater legitimacy in the MIS community, especially by facilitating better communication (interoperability) between Apple and IBM hardware.

-It gives Apple a new source of microprocessor technology, with a second source. Apple's reliance on Motorola was running out of steam and had cost Apple dearly in 1990.

-Apple could not afford to spend $500 million to develop "Pink." Apple was continuing to develop its own OS (System 7); with its small installed base, it could never hope to recover an investment of $1 billion. IBM effectively is underwriting Pink and has given Apple another 15% of the market to sell it to automatically.

-Multimedia (Kaleida) is unlikely to have a big impact, and there is not adequate information in the case to explore it.

IMPACT ON THE INDUSTRY: This is the critical issue: will Pink kill Microsoft? Will the RS6000 kill Intel? The problem with Pink for both Apple and IBM is that they must migrate the buyers from their existing OS to Pink; otherwise they will not change the structure of the industry. Pink will provide a migration path for people that will be using the then current Apple technology (System 7) and OS/2—NOT Windows! The irony for Apple is that Pink can change the structure of the OS part of the industry only if IBM is successful in using OS/2 to beat Microsoft's Windows. However, Windows has 10 million units as of the time of the case, and is selling 1 million units per month. If IBM cannot stall Windows momentum, Microsoft will sell 50 million units of Windows before Pink is released!

Whether the RS6000 will kill Intel is a matter of speculation. The only information in the case is that Intel was investing aggressively to counter any performance disadvantages it might face from RISC technology.

Joint Ventures with Japanese Manufacturers

This is really a diversification strategy into the new products. Beyond getting students to understand that, there is not enough detail in the case to explore this facet of Apple's strategy. The major issue is whether this type of diversification is consistent with Apple's strategy in its core business and whether a computer company like Apple can successfully define its core while attacking entirely new segments in consumer electronics. This may be a very good strategy for Apple; however, it will take at least 2-3 years before any of these products will generate enough volume to offset some of the problems in the Mac business.

At this point, I ask students to step back and evaluate Apple's situation. I think it can be succinctly:

Apple is trying to defend its core Mac business and keep it alive as long as possible by attacking costs, increasing share as much as possible, and hopefully forestalling ISV defections as much as possible. The strategy is largely a holding action, hoping that either the IBM JV will help Apple defeat Microsoft and Intel, or hope that the new products that will be jointly developed with the Japanese will generate a new business for Apple.

The question then becomes: What should Sculley do in 1992? If his current strategy is very risky with low probability of success, are there any alternatives?

I suggest that three generic options are worth discussing:

1. Attach the industry structure problem directly:

   • move or "port" Apple's OS to x86, go head-to-head with Microsoft and/or

   • license the Mac hardware, allowing low-cost clone companies to increase Apple's share of the overall market

Either strategy suggests that Apple's real competitive advantage is software, and it will focus on being a software company rather than an integrated hardware and software vendor. There may be some confusion about porting Apple's OS to x86. The case notes that System 7 was written explicitly for the Motorola chip; the case later notes that Apple was rewriting System 7 to be able to run on multiple microprocessors, such as the IBM RS6000. This last point is to let the students know that while technically very difficult to port Apple's OS, it is not impossible.

2. Bet the company on IBM and Pink:

   • status quo

   • hope that Pink will revolutionize the software and hardware business

   • requires nonstop hit products to keep the Mac core alive

3. Bet the company on new technologies and the Japanese JVs

   • Milk the Mac business, use Mac cash flow to fund new activities

   • Recognize this is a diversification from the core PC business, requiring new different skills and technologies.

After the options are explored, the instructor can show a brief (five minute) film of John Sculley addressing the ISMP students in the summer of 1992. The film shows Sculley discussing the big mistakes he made during his tenure as CEO. He said that his biggest mistakes were: 1) not taking control of Apple's strategy and technology earlier on in the history of the company; 2) not making Apple's OS available on Intel's X86 platform. This was a mistake, says Sculley, because Apple could have written a better "Windows" GUI than Windows, and that, by itself, could make enough money to fuel an entire company; and 3) not making Apple's "imaging" business (scanners, printers, etc.) more open and available in the x86/DOS world.

Summary

There is no clear answer to this case (in the spring of 1992). But, I hope that students will draw some very important lessons from the discussion:

1. Product advantages, per se, do not necessarily translate into competitive advantages. Apple had clear product advantages over the MS-DOS/x86 world, but that is not enough to guarantee the success of the company. Competitive advantage involves a much broader array of advantages, ranging from controlling the standard to influencing the structure of distribution.

2. Dynamic changes in industry structure can overwhelm a firm's competitive position, even if that firm has proprietary technology and significant advantages in various parts of the value chain. On the surface, Apple looked immune to the PC industry's troubles, but this analysis should show how industry structure can undermine firms even at the periphery of an industry.

3. If a firm wishes to mold industry structure, it must find substitutes, or reshape the most powerful elements of the industry. Apple was failing to reshape the industry because it was not willing or able to take on Microsoft head to head. As long as Microsoft controls the OS and sets the standards for the industry, Apple would be at a continual disadvantage. However, at least through mid-1992, Apple was unwilling to go after Microsoft by becoming a much more aggressive software company.

4. In standards battles in technology-intensive businesses, competitive advantages or competitive gaps must be very large to be sustainable. VHS was able to beat a superior Beta format in VCRs when the differences in product technology were relatively close. Beta was only viable as an alternative as long as its product advantages were very large. Similarly, Apple was viable as an alternative standard as long as there was a huge gap between DOS and Apple; as soon as Windows narrowed the gap, Apple's position weakened dramatically and perhaps fatally—EVEN THOUGH IT STILL HAD THE BETTER PRODUCT.

Apple's Historical CAGR and (%) of sales figures

	10-yr. CAGR	% of sales				
		1991	1990	1989	1988	1987
Total Revenues	0.33	1.00	1.00	1.00	1.00	1.00
Cost of Sales	0.34	0.53	0.47	0.51	0.49	0.49
Research & Development	0.39	0.09	0.09	0.08	0.07	0.07
Marketing & Distribution	0.41	0.28	0.28	0.25	0.22	0.25
General & Administrative	0.25	0.04	0.04	0.04	0.04	0.05
Operating Income	0.19	0.07	0.13	0.12	0.15	0.14
Net Income	0.21	0.05	0.09	0.09	0.10	0.08

	1986	1985	% of sales 1984	1983	1982	1981
Total Revenues	1.00	1.00	1.00	1.00	1.00	1.00
Cost of Sales	0.47	0.58	0.58	0.51	0.49	0.51
Research & Development	0.04	0.05	0.06	0.07	0.07	0.06
Marketing & Distribution	0.25	0.25	0.26	0.23	0.21	0.15
General & Administrative	0.07	0.06	0.05	0.06	0.06	0.07
Operating Income	0.14	0.07	0.06	0.13	0.17	0.20
Net Income	0.08	0.03	0.04	0.08	0.10	0.12

Comments: Apple's margins are starting to erode; Apple's SG&A is the highest in the PC industry; Apple's "low cost strategy" is not yet apparent; and Apple's R&D spending keeps going up to keep up with Microsoft.

Comments on Exhibit 2

Apple's historical advantage is being eroded by clones.

Comments on Exhibit 3

New channels have destroyed the old barriers to entry—anyone can now sell/make PCs.

Comments on Exhibit 4

Apple never had a commanding market share. IBM steadily lost share from 1984 onward. Apple's high volume strategy has gained it only 0.3 share points—this will not attract ISV attention.

Comments on Exhibit 5

IBM spends on R&D what Apple's revenues are.

Compaq spends more than most on R&D but is not getting differentiation. Like Apple, Compaq was a clear leader in the mid-1980s but began feeling the pressure earlier than Apple.

Apple has much higher margins but also much higher expenses than clones with margins of 47%, R&D at 9% of sales, and SG&A of 32%.

Dell Computer spends 3.7% of sales on R&D while Apple spends 9%. How much of a premium does the extra 5% R&D buy? Dell's return on sales fell dramatically in 1988 indicating that the new structure of the industry permits much smaller margins, even for the most successful competitors.

Intel and Microsoft made about $1.3 billion in profit vs. $2 billion for the entire PC industry in 1991. As a percent of sales, Microsoft spends more on R&D so as Microsoft grows, its R&D will grow also thus increasing its advantage.

Comments on Exhibit 6

While Apple's market share grew faster in 1991 than previously, the absolute numbers make the X86 a more attractive platform for ISVs.

Comments on Exhibit 7

Operating profits are clearly higher in software but Apple is trying to span both worlds.

Comments on Exhibits 8 and 9

This exhibit and Exhibit 9 allow for a discussion of vertical and horizontal scope. Sculley suggests in both pictures that the relevant industry is much broader than PCs and Apple must work with others to appropriate the value.

Case Overview

Microsoft Corporation (A) traces Microsoft's evolution from its origin in 1975 through 1994. Starting with its entrepreneurial formation, the case highlights the firm's competitive maneuvering to position its major products in both the U.S. and European markets. The case ends with a competitive positioning analysis vs. Borland, Lotus, and Novell in the 1993 marketplace. It provides insights into both coalition behavior and into the management style which has both made Microsoft successful and created enormous controversy around it. It poses many of the questions of hypercompetition, innovative management, and coalition behavior posed in the readings. It is an excellent case for illustrating strategic learning, the development and fragility of strategic alliances, competitive positioning in a dynamic marketplace, and inter-organizational politics.

The case describes Microsoft's alliances with hardware producers—particularly IBM and Apple—in operating systems (MS-DOS), electronic spreadsheets (Multiplan), and word processing (Word). It traces Microsoft's efforts, throughout the 1980s, to position these packages in both the U.S. and European markets. By the mid-1980s, Microsoft's focus shifted to development of a graphical user interface (Windows). This led to friction with Apple, resulting in a lawsuit over patent infringement. Then, relationships with IBM became strained, and the PC giant began increasing its own software development efforts to reduce its reliance on Microsoft. By the end of the case, Apple and IBM had begun a joint venture to develop an entirely new PC standard. Microsoft faces the combined threats of Apple's lawsuit, IBM's integration into software, the IBM-Apple joint venture, and the development of Internet and network-oriented software companies.

Session Structure

One can begin the case discussion by asking why was Microsoft successful in its early years? What was the unique confluence of forces that made this company come into being? One can bring out the unique combination of personal characteristics, adventuresome style, lack of anything to lose, wide open new marketplaces, and shortages of a key ingredient for a major product's (PC's) success (i.e., software) as peculiar at the time. What characteristics of Bill Gates and Tom Allen made for corporate success and what problems might they produce later? What external events contributed to the company's success? This includes the emergence of critical software like spreadsheets and word processing to build the market for micro computers. It also includes the unique need of IBM to catch up with Apple in a marketplace where its ponderous style would not have succeeded. One can next ask what are the critical factors for success in this early marketplace? These include superior personal knowledge, fast response, placing multiple bets, keeping teams small, personal commitment, capability to attract top talent, willingness to constantly counterpunch and maneuver, extending one's capabilities through alliances, and very clear-cut hard-nosed self interest. A series of questions to develop this portion of the case appear under the caption Key Issues which follows. One can then focus on the strategic issues at the end of the case.

Teaching note copyright © 1996 by James Brian Quinn. Parts of this teaching note, as indicated, were written by Professors G.W. Danforth, R. McGrath, and G.J. Castrogiovanni of Louisiana State University to cover the extensive portion of the case which they developed.

Industry Structure*

After dealing with the early stage entrepreneurial questions outlined above, one can ask what is the structure of the industry Microsoft is in? What is its industry? Who are its competitors? Quickly, it develops that Microsoft's biggest customers, notably IBM and other computer producers, are also its biggest competitors. In addition, it faces competition not just from independent software producers but from all those in other industries who wish to have proprietary software of their own. This includes everyone in the specialized services businesses, telecoms, entertainment, and foreign country software businesses. How can Microsoft define a continuing competitive edge in this environment? How can it develop this edge in such depth that it remains unassailable? What are the limitations set upon it by Mr. Gates's style? Because these questions are so complex, it is useful to start off with a broad SWOT analysis of the company's position in 1993.

SWOT Analysis

Strengths:

- Proprietary products,
- IBM alliance,
- User orientation,
- Adaptive organization culture,
- Loyal employees; low turnover,
- Intellectual capital; very creative staff,
- Bold management; visionary leadership,
- Strategic learning (willingness and capacity to adapt).

Weaknesses:

- Limited financial and marketing resources relative to IBM,
- Some evidence of overconfidence due to past successes which could impede strategic learning in the future.

Opportunities:

- New applications software developed into "suites,"
- Demand for improvements to existing software,
- Graphic user interfaces. Entertainment and games software,
- Network software and applications,
- Groupware and communications software.

Threats:

- Management style of Gates,
- Crumbling alliance with IBM,
- Apple's lawsuit,
- IBM-Apple joint venture,
- Maturing PC market (flattening of software demand),
- Possible loss of Intel Pentium dominance.

---

*This section of the teaching note is copyright © 1992 by George W. Danforth. This teaching note written by Professors George W. Danforth, Robert McGrath, and Gary J. Castrogiovanni, Louisiana State University.

Key Issues:

1. <u>How should Microsoft address the deterioration of its alliance with IBM?</u>

The case describes how Microsoft buckled to IBM's pressure to gear its spreadsheet program to the IBM 64K machines. Shortly thereafter, sales of larger (256K) machines took off. Because it was geared toward the smaller machines, Microsoft's Multiplan lost out to Lotus 1-2-3 in the battle for dominance of the U.S. market. The case emphasizes that Microsoft's Bill Gates learned an important lesson from this experience: he should position according to long-term industry trends rather than submit to the short-term pressures of a key partner (e.g., IBM).

Presumably, this is why Gates resisted IBM's preference for focusing on the newly developed OS/2 system. When OS/2 sales proved lower than expected, Microsoft focused on continued demand for MS-DOS, and catered to this demand with a new version (DOS 5.0). Microsoft's shift in emphasis (from OS/2 to DOS) parallel's IBM's earlier shift from 64K machines (and Multiplan) to 245K machines (and Lotus 1-2-3). Apparently, Gates learned from the Multiplan experience and decided to play the same game against IBM this time around.

It is questionable whether Microsoft wants to use its financial and marketing muscle to fight IBM. Furthermore, IBM offered a credible threat of integrating into Microsoft's software domain. This is evidenced as early as 1983 by IBM's venture into graphical interface (TopView). Microsoft does not have the countervailing potential to threaten expansion into IBM's hardware domain.

Evidently, Gates forgot how friction with IBM had hurt Digital Research several years earlier, leading IBM to abandon Digital's CP/M operating system (then, the industry standard) in favor of Microsoft's DOS. Microsoft may be setting itself up for a decline similar to that experienced by Digital. Although Microsoft enjoys a strong position within the industry and demand continues for its major products, Gates would gain by repairing relations with IBM. But this could alienate other rapidly growing PC producers.

2. <u>What should Microsoft have done in response to the lawsuit by Apple?</u>

This is a high risk decision. If Microsoft loses, it might have to take all current versions of Windows off the market and pay royalties to Apple for past sales. To prepare for this possibility, Microsoft could have increased its cash reserves or established lines of credit to cover the royalty payments that might be required. This, however, would have reduced Microsoft's ability to negotiate for a lower settlement by credibly threatening to go bankrupt if required to pay Apple the full amount. On the other hand, Apple might not settle for less, preferring instead to force Microsoft into bankruptcy in order to reduce competition and enhance its long-term profit position. Conversely, Microsoft could attack aggressively, pointing out that Apple's own software was really in violation of Xerox PARC's inventions and patents. At the same time, Microsoft needs to quickly develop alternate products to replace current versions of Windows in the event that Windows has to be pulled from the market.

3. <u>How should Microsoft respond to the Apple-IBM joint venture?</u>

Keep in mind that the joint venture (JV) may not work. Under a worst-case scenario, however, Microsoft has two basic options. One would be to take actions that improve Microsoft's relationships with IBM and Apple. For example, Microsoft can reemphasize its development and support of OS/2 in order to pacify IBM. It might also reach an amicable out-of-court settlement of the Apple suit. These and related actions could enable Microsoft to participate in the joint venture, perhaps as the contracted supplier of software for the JVs new generation of personal computers. If the JV is unsuccessful, these actions would serve to maintain the alliances that so heavily contributed to Microsoft's past success. If the JV is successful, however, IBM and Apple would have considerable bargaining power over Microsoft, and this could be used to squeeze Microsoft's profit margins.

Another alternative would be for Microsoft to minimize dependence on its linkages with IBM and Apple, even going so far as to take steps that would defeat the potential market success of the JV. Many clones were more powerful than IBM's original PC. Continued advances in computer chip technology would lead to further increases in the computing power of these machines. Microsoft may want to form alliances with one or more clone manufacturers (possibly in their own joint venture) to support PC clones so powerful that they could devastate IBM without Microsoft's software. Since the latter would continue to run on MS-DOS, Microsoft could concentrate on further improvements to that operating system, and additional DOS-based applications. Aside from technological feasibility considerations, the success of this alternative hinges on the following assumption: because of their considerable past investments in DOS-based applications, users would not want to incur the switching costs that would arise with purchases of the IBM-Apple (joint venture) computers—especially if new Microsoft software would enable other DOS-based computers to do the same things.

Discussion Questions

1. What were the characteristics of the PC industry in 1980 compared to 1990? What changed? Why was Microsoft successful during the 1980s? What should it do to ensure continued success through the 1990s?

2. Trace Microsoft's marketing strategies for its various products (MS-DOS, Multiplan, Word, Windows). How did these change as the firm entered European markets? In general, did they evolve as the company grew and its environment changed, or did each one differ because of the unique aspects of the products offered and situations encountered?

3. Why do you think alliances in the computer industry change so rapidly? Is this a strategy, or does it result from the lack of one? From a long-term perspective, is it better to maintain stable alliances, or to be willing to shift alliances as (short-term) situations and needs change?

1993 Situation

By late 1993, Microsoft had become so powerful that many considered it a threat to the entire industry. While investors loved Microsoft, it had many detractors in the software, user, and computer fields. Bill Gates's style and determination to dominate the industry had alienated many. There was a real question as to whether Microsoft could continue to form the alliances that had been so important to it in the past. This became especially troublesome as software moved from freestanding applications into the more complex worlds of groupware and network software. There is a fascinating question which could dominate the entire case discussion, "How should Microsoft reposition itself in the new software world of the mid-1990s?" Clearly no single answer is possible. And it is likely that Microsoft's only true strategy can be to select a few segments of the marketplace for dominance while maintaining a very flexible compatible posture for the remainder of the market.

Microsoft's Windows software had been an outstanding success, projecting it into a new dominating position for PC software. However, Microsoft had outraged competitors by allegedly hiding sets of instructions in its operating system software. It had purportedly kept a few secrets concerning its software details available only to Microsoft programmers for their applications. This created some problems as Microsoft tried to enter coalitions with other applications software providers. Recognizing the power of specialized applications in certain marketplaces, Mr. Gates began to acquire outstanding applications software companies in specific fields. This gave Microsoft a base for broadening these specialized bits of software into "suites" for broad ranges of applications (such as office use). Competitors brought a number of antitrust suits against Microsoft. However most of these were dropped in a complex agreement made between Microsoft and the Justice Department. As of this time, that relationship had not been completely clarified. In 1995, new companies exploiting Internet had become darlings of the software marketplace. Programs like Netscape and JAVA had become powerful competitors. Microsoft was attempting to co-opt these by making them available through its Internet Information Server in versions of Windows AT.

The case provides enough data for the student to segment the emerging software market and determine (1) which pieces seem to fit with Microsoft's strengths, (2) which can be combined into reasonable suites, and (3) which must be accessed by alliances. Microsoft (B) provides a very useful second case to pursue the detailed organizational implications of any decisions made in the (A) case.

As one wraps up this case discussion, the question should be asked, What is Microsoft's unique competency today? Can anyone maintain a competitive edge in software? How? What markets must Microsoft dominate in order to maintain its "share of market?" What is the pertinent marketplace for Microsoft to be considering? Would it be better served by breaking itself up into a series of competitive, freestanding, self-financing units in a starburst form? What value does the corporation itself add to the value of its individual software writing units? Is it time to break away from Mr. Gates's highly personalized style? If so, how would one describe the new style, organization, and coalition positioning of Microsoft? Because of Microsoft's highly controversial posture, one can get very lively discussions on virtually any position in this case.

Fortune, December 11, 1995 summarized the company's position at the end of case as follows, "From all appearances, 1995 was Microsoft's year. Not only did Bill Gates and company manage the biggest, noisiest launch of a product since New Coke, but the software, Windows 95, has done fine. Its instant ubiquity is helping Microsoft prolong its growth by selling updates of popular applications programs and is enabling Gates to extend his dominance of the PC software business. The company's on-line service, Microsoft Network, premiered with Windows 95 and looks to be taking off. And a scary shadow went away: Microsoft made peace with Justice Department trust busters, defeating a last minute effort by a renegade Federal judge to force investigators to reopen the case. Yet the real sensation of computerdom in 1995 is the Internet . . . [which] is demonstrating vividly what the elusive and overhyped information superhighway really means: that your primary vehicle on it will be your PC rather than your TV, and computers soon will be as indispensable to everyday life as telephones, and that it will transform leisure time as much as work."[1]

---

[1] B. Schlender, "Who's Internet," *Fortune*, December 11, 1995.

Overview

The Gallo Winery case can serve many functions. It is an excellent example of: (1) a mature industry strategy, (2) an industry or competitive analysis positioning, (3) a generic low cost strategy, (4) some of the major problems in managing a family-owned concern, (5) the development of a truly dominant marketing position, with significant outsourcing of a major component material. The case goes well with the Mintzberg article on generic strategies, and the chapters on maturing industries and diversification. The case gives a lively view of how Gallo developed its absolutely dominating position at the lower end of the table wines industry, developed a lowest cost position in the industry, and has had some real difficulties in shifting its image upward in order to use its low cost advantages in higher priced marketplaces. The focal point of the case is on how a company develops a truly integrated low cost strategy and the problems of breaking out of that strategy once it is thoroughly developed. The end of the case is positioned in the late 1980s.

Session Structure

We usually open this case by asking, first, What have been the critical factors in the past success of Gallo? Why did Gallo undertake this approach? How do the Gallos' personal values affect the strategy? Second, we ask, how does size help Gallo in its strategy? What unique power does size give to Gallo? Third, we ask, how does Gallo develop its power relative to other competitive forces? This leads to a rather full-fledged Porter-style "five forces" analysis. One can ask how Gallo might increase its power further relative to any of these five forces. Fourth, we look at the "model of a low cost strategy" and how each element in that model reinforces all other elements. Fifth, we ask what important changes are occurring in the marketplace? How will these affect Gallo's position? Sixth, what should Gallo's strategic response be to these changes? What should its new distinct competency be after these moves? Seventh, we ask how others might attack Gallo's position? What should Gallo's planned response be to these potential moves? Finally, we ask what rigidities a generic strategy builds in for its managers? How can one break out of a low cost strategy, once a completely configured positioning is achieved? What should Gallo's future management do? How should Gallo transition to this new position?

What are the Underlying Reasons behind Gallo's Strategy?

This question opens up the issues of the basic values of the Gallo brothers that drive this company. Although the students may tend to skim and describe some of the policies the Gallos used to obtain dominance, one should probe the more important question, "Why did they choose this particular approach? Why did they not choose some other approach?" If necessary one can even use the prompt, "How did the Gallos' values affect the strategy? Where did these values come from?" This is a key point.

The insecurity created by the Gallos' father's failures, murders, and suicide had to create a lasting impression. The harshness of the Depression and their family situation undoubtedly created an insecurity and a desire to make things as certain as possible under all circumstances. This led to their psychological need for dominance, control, and perfection. It also undoubtedly led to Ernest and Julio's personal styles. Each needed the security of his fiefdom. The need for control led to a push, not leadership, strategy.

Teaching note copyright © 1991 by James Brian Quinn. This note was prepared by Professor Quinn and Professor Richard D'Aveni.

These values led to further elements of the strategy, i.e., a suspicion of outsiders, the drive to obtain the stability of market share, the more certain approach to marketing offered by cost and price reduction, the ruthlessness with which the Gallos often treated outsiders (particularly non-successful distributors). The same values also fed their tendencies toward a highly centralized organization, non-communication within the organization, the tendency toward security through specialist knowledge, and many of the future problems the company must face. One can note how the very strengths of the company in the past (i.e., controls, attention to details, specialist knowledge, push techniques, centralization, etc.) automatically create some serious problems for the future. However, these should not be pursued at this point.

How Does Volume-Size Help Reinforce Gallo's Strategy?

Properly utilized, size allows Gallo to have very high leverage over its distributors, have better information about the total marketplace than anyone else, parlay off its high volume products to introduce or support lower volume products, achieve purchasing economies of scale, obtain better advertising buys than anyone else, accept very thin profit margins (yet have very high personal profits). This is a good point to emphasize that economies of scale are not simply in the production area. Some of the most important economies of scale are from the information which Gallo has. It can support a larger research endeavor than any other winemaker. It can demand that suppliers meet its quality standards, it has the capital to invest in highly efficient plants, and it can afford an advertising plan no other company in the industry can.

One can ask, "How did Gallo get into this high volume-low cost position?" Again, the problem is to avoid simply repeating the case. As each concept comes forward ask, "<u>Why</u> did this work? <u>What alternatives</u> were available? What were the explicit costs involved in this action? What special policies would be necessary to make it work? Why couldn't others duplicate this element with success?" Concepts like concentration only in wine; concentrating on low cost jug wines; making distributors highly profitable and hence good coalition partners; initially integrating vertically to capture profit at various levels of the value chain; heavy investment in plant and equipment; later willingness to move out of the vineyard business with its associated costs and risks and rely on grape suppliers; focusing on a sales strategy rather than a high cost advertising strategy at first; emphasizing simple repetitive themes like "Thunderbird is the word"; cutting costs by ruthless attention to detail all deserve special focus. (See Model of Low Cost Strategy chart.)

It is important to note how different this strategy is from most other American companies. The Gallos are willing to work for <u>very long time horizons</u>, do not have shareholders to satisfy, can emphasize production and distribution volume, are more concerned about share than current profitability, etc. One should note that these are the very characteristics which have made Japanese industries so potent. One should raise a basic challenge as to why this kind of strategy—though so successful when used well—is not attractive to many American companies. Most managers and shareholders do not have the same needs and values for long-term success, control, stability, nor do they have a disdain for current profits, glamorous images, etc. It largely is the Gallos' values which drive the strategy to success, and shareholder and management values which have driven their competitors into oblivion.

How has Gallo Increased its Power Relative to Other Competitive Forces? How Could it Increase this Power Further?

This allows the introduction of a rather thoroughgoing five forces analysis of the Gallo structure. This is in the attached diagram. Although one should keep pounding the question, "How could Gallo further increase its power relative to each of these forces?" The answer is, "Not very easily." Probably the main way in which Gallo could increase its power is by increasing

MODEL OF LOW COST STRATEGY

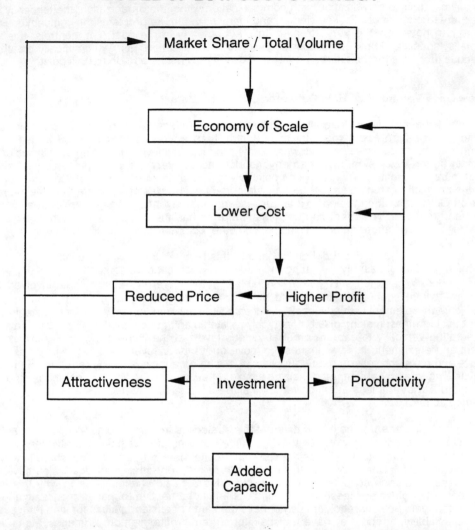

Source: William C. Wandell, *The Outline of Strategy*, The Planning Forum, Oxford, 1986, p.55.

The Mature Industry Trap

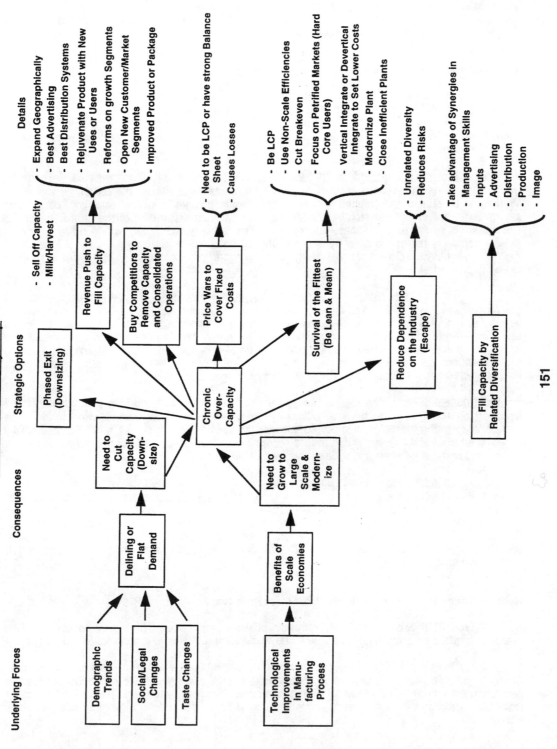

volume and/or increasing its leverage over distributors by broadening its line. This becomes a focal point for the latter portion of the case. We urge the development of a Michael Porter-style diagram of the sort illustrated either on the blackboard or on an overhead viewgraph. One can also use this same diagram to ask, "What current trends are causing power shifts among these forces today? What should Gallo do about these?"

What is Changing in the Industry? What Threats are Created?

There is ample industry information available to define certain very important trends. The changing technology of the industry has made it possible for other competitors to enter the U.S. market. The tastes of consumers are changing, as are other important demographics. There has been a major industry consolidation into large competitor companies. Gallo has to position against all of these.

1. Technology Has Changed the Nature of Competition. Almost all competitors—except the most exclusive wines—have moved over to Gallo's stainless steel production technologies. Wines can be stored and shipped great distances, making wines from low labor cost countries a real threat. University research has led to much greater understanding of the characteristics of grapes, soils, weather conditions, and processing chemistry that make wines better. Thus a private company has more difficulty in maintaining a competitive edge through sheer knowledge of the technology. Other consolidating, large competitors can quickly catch up to Gallo's technological edge.

2. Demand Shifts: Total Volume of Wines Consumed is Decreasing—Growth in table wines has slowed to about 5% per year. More people are drinking non-alcoholic drinks. The absolute volume of the very low price wines, Gallo's strength, has been falling. Driving while intoxicated laws have tended to slow all wine growth. Affluence has pushed tastes toward more expensive wines, while fitness trends have slowed consumption of cheaper wines. All of these factors place real pressures on Gallo's basic low cost wines. Gallo will have to move out of its strongly established niche, if it hopes to exploit any of the major growth trends.

3. The Upscale Market Fragments. Many of the upscale wines are imported premiums. These account for about 20% of the $1.6 billion in foreign imports. The upscale wine market has fragmented among the different imported brands, into special niches created by the varietals, with a heavy emphasis on brand and vineyard recognition. This raises the interesting issue of how Gallo can leverage its strengths against this kind of fragmentation.

4. Distribution is Shifting. In most states, wine distribution has shifted toward supermarkets and supermarket chains as well as state liquor stores. All of these groups are becoming larger with more power relative to Gallo. Gallo's competitive edges of size and point-of-sale presentation are considerably less significant, the latter being taken over by the mass distributors themselves. Gallo's relative leverage in using its low priced brands to introduce higher priced premiums, therefore, may be rapidly decreasing. Consequently, it needs to move quickly to meet this competitive shift.

How do These Pose a Threat to the Low Cost Producer?

Each of these major market trends poses some special problems to Gallo. This discussion offers an opportunity to show some of the vulnerabilities of a generic low cost strategy.

1. Volume Needs. Many of Gallo's competitive advantages stem from its volume position. Anything which threatens that position threatens the entire strategy. Gallo could lose its relative purchasing power and hence control over its suppliers, its capacity to invest heavily in fixed plant and R&D, and its relative marketing power vs. distributors. It could also lose its capacity to use

its margins on its low cost lines to implement selective "penetration pricing" strategies among specialized wines where it might want to introduce or expand in upscale markets.

2. Power Relative to Suppliers. Suppliers will begin to see opportunities to form new coalitions. They could move to other large scale producers, move into specialty wines, or attempt to form growing and wholesaling coalitions to counter the pressures of Gallo. If other competitors obtain higher volumes in specific wine classes, it may be difficult for Gallo to maintain its low cost strategy across the board in the future. Because of the pressures on total wine volumes, certain vineyards might become desperate and be willing to cut prices on good (but not top) grapes to competitors. Consumers' moves toward specialty wines and varietals cannot help but increase the power of these specific suppliers.

3. Production Capacity Issues. Maintaining and filling Gallo's huge plant capacity is very important to its strategy. If wine volumes in the lower segment fall, Gallo will have to carry enormous fixed costs on the remaining limited volume. This could be exacerbated if suppliers and competitors begin desperation pricing of their wines or grapes as lower volume wine sales drop. Anything that decreases Gallo's production cost advantages will impact its relative competitive power in all fields, i.e., its capacity to pressure distributors through across-the-board selective price decreases, to maintain its huge sales force, to advertise more than its competitors, etc.

4. Improvement R&D. Similarly, if Gallo loses volume in its main lines, its guaranteed cash flows for R&D would be threatened. Since this is one of the main bases for Gallo's information power and low cost production power, volume losses of any significance could seriously threaten Gallo's relative technological knowledge position—with feedback effects that will injure its low cost positions further, causing secondary positive feedback losses in position. Fortunately, Gallo is already the largest distributor of premium wines in the world, and can obtain synergies between its basic knowledge of wines and grapes (from its older lines) and the sophisticated fine tunings needed for the desired characteristics of an upscale wine.

5. Market Information Advantages. One of the major advantages Gallo has had is the market information it can gain from its preeminent presence in the marketplace. Because it is so strongly represented by its sales force and shelf space, Gallo has more knowledge of competing brands' shelf positions, volumes, prices, promotions, etc. than any competitor. Consequently, it can more finely tune its position in the market. If Gallo begins to lose volume, its sales force may decrease in absolute size as will its power over advertisers and others who help Gallo gain information. Hence its capacity to utilize its other advantages to the fullest may be threatened. The importance of market information in high volume, low cost strategies should be stressed.

Foreign Wines

Foreign wines pose some special threats to Gallo. Perhaps these are the most important opportunities and threats for Gallo in the emerging marketplace.

1. Lower Costs. Because of lower labor costs, foreign wines can potentially achieve much lower costs than Gallo. Both vineyard cost and winery costs can be affected. Because the technology of production (especially stainless steel production) has been widely disseminated, Gallo can no longer depend upon this for lower costs, except in those areas where it might have much higher volumes.

2. Image Implications. The foreign wines have long enjoyed a halo effect in terms of image. Domestic wines tend to be downgraded in the "snob" market. Good foreign wines with low labor cost support could block Gallo's moving upscale with its California wines. But there is perhaps an even greater threat. Italian wines are growing very rapidly because of their combinations of low labor costs, good growing conditions, and unique grape and soil combinations (especially the "grappa" table wines). These could mount a strong attack on the traditional focal strength of

Gallo in the lower cost, high alcohol content, wine market. If the Italians can obtain substantial distribution, this could be a major threat.

3. New Technologies. These have made it possible to store and ship wines over much longer distances. This has made not just the European wines, but the Australian, and potentially less developed country wines into possible threats. Cooling technologies, stainless steel production, and stainless steel storage make it possible to ship wines inexpensively in bulk and then repackage them domestically. This offers potential opportunities to Gallo, as well as potential threats. Gallo clearly could purchase its wines abroad, using its mass distribution and volume capabilities for leverage there in the same fashion it has in the United States.

In addition, growing technologies have improved enormously. Yields per acre have increased substantially, diseases are more controllable, and the relationship between soils, grapes, and weather conditions is much better understood. Combined with improved distribution technologies, this makes it possible to source wines virtually anywhere in the world and maintain quality. This means that Gallo could conceivably use its technology advantages (if it can maintain them) to improve production, productivity, wine quality, or to source from (or acquire and upgrade) big name vineyards in other countries where labor costs are inherently lower.

4. A Few Big Companies. The industry has been consolidating in mass distributed wines toward a relatively few large companies, including Huebleins, Seagrams, etc. These large scale producer-distributors can bring a new technological and market sophistication to the marketplace that Gallo has not encountered previously. If they chose to make wines a major portion of their broader foods or alcoholic product lines, they could put substantial research resources up against Gallo. Gallo needs to move to preempt the power of these major competitors vis-à-vis potential overseas sources.

Gallo's Future Strategy

Given these major market and technological changes, what should Gallo do? How should it position its line? What should its new distinct competency be after any moves it undertakes? There are some very strong inherent conflicts in Gallo's current powerful position vs. the new marketplace.

1. Marketing Position. One of the biggest opportunities in the current marketplace is the relatively low U.S. consumption of wine per person. If Gallo can reposition its low end wines to pick up the young college students and other new entry consumers (with inexpensive, but elegant wines), it could slowly expand the wine drinking base in the United States. This requires a primary market strategy. One can ask students how they would approach this market opportunity.

Another major opportunity is to use the knowledge of grapes and wines that Gallo has. Unknown to most people, Gallo is also the world's largest producer-distributor of premium wines. From this distribution position and the information it provides—if it can maintain the cash flows of its lower priced wines—Gallo can leverage itself slowly upward in the emerging market for upscale wines. It should probably attack growth niches within this marketplace. Of special interest are the varietals, where no overwhelmingly strong market positions exist for other producers. Gallo could also move upscale into sherries and other heavier wines. However, crucial to any "extension strategy" is the maintenance and utilization of a better information base about the marketplace than any of its competitors. This is a good point to introduce questions about how to develop and leverage information as a competitive weapon. Could Gallo go as far as McKesson or SuperValu have, and lock its distributors further to Gallo by providing them with accounting, inventory control, and/or personnel software packages that help the distributors but tie them ever more closely to Gallo?

Gallo can diversify into related specialty areas. It has already achieved a major position in coolers. It could move to dominate the low cost coolers market. It has made a major success of André as a sparkling wine. From this, it could move upward into champagnes, especially with an acquisition of some good French vineyards. It might also introduce a special variety of "ultralight wines" for those who like the wine taste but do not want as much alcohol.

Students will tend to look at other products which could go along with wines. Some suggestions will be snacks, cheeses, beers, or even liquors. However, in any of these marketplaces, Gallo will meet very strong established companies, with better knowledge bases. These companies probably block Gallo from serious nonrelated product expansions, although Gallo might carry some such items merely for service purposes to small distributors. This might be a way to resolve the family problem with Joseph Gallo.

Perhaps a much better positioning would be for Gallo to invade major foreign markets. Japan with its growing affluence offers an intriguing opportunity. Some questions can be raised as to how Gallo could obtain access to this marketplace. Europe continues to offer major opportunities, if Gallo can extend its technology capabilities there, yet use local vineyards or wine names as its entry points. The higher volumes consumed per person in these marketplaces could give Gallo the kind of added volume Gallo needs to maintain its domestic dominance. Its biggest problems will be political—obtaining permits and distribution in what will certainly be a hostile marketplace. Growth in foreign markets is clearly a longer-term strategy.

However, Gallo could buy foreign wines and import them to the United States, using its existing strong distribution capabilities. It could buy wines, vineyards, or producers. Alternately, it might license the use of important brand names in the United States and try to leverage its own wines into these or related marketplaces. Foreign wines are growing (at 6.5%) faster than U.S. wines in the domestic marketplace. And they provide 24% of the total market. If Gallo can obtain a substantial segment of this market, it both blocks potential competitors and increases its own volume. Both are important competitive considerations.

There is a significant question as to whether Gallo should milk its existing lines for profits and divert these cash flows into totally new product areas. However, one must realize the strategic importance of share to Gallo's basic strategy. If it gives up share in its lower price markets, many other elements of its strategy tend to fall apart. It should certainly maintain share in these marketplaces at almost any cost in the short run, until it can build sufficient volumes in other markets to give it the kind of power it currently has in its more established lines.

2. Production Strategies. Maintaining volume is crucial to the production aspects of the Gallo strategy. Because the facility has been built to operate almost like a refinery, any lowering in volume will increase overhead costs substantially. Essentially, the problem is to keep the production facilities filled. This would be simple, if the facilities could be easily converted to produce various wine lines in smaller volumes. However, given the way in which the plants were developed—to be lowest cost for high volume, low cost wines—this looks improbable.

With a major technology investment, it might be possible for Gallo to lower its breakeven position on existing plants. Perhaps more important as a longer-term strategy would be the development of a much more flexible process to produce multiple wine lines through the same facility by automating key steps and the set-up processes for converting from one line to another. While this would help for its new wine lines, Gallo cannot give up its lowest cost production approach for its low price lines. This might argue for a dual or multiple facility approach, separating production for the different lines, but this brings added costs and fewer of the scale economies which are Gallo's strength. Note the communication problems this will cause between Ernest and Julio.

Another aspect of production strategy might be for Gallo to acquire capacity from its dying competitors. On the one hand, it might be possible to do this at low cost. On the other, this could ease the exit barriers for these competitors and make them less likely to do desperation pricing as they decline. Some very low cost capacity might be obtained for specialized wines. Another key element to consider is how much production Gallo might feasibly do overseas for its new lines. Any production strategy, of course, has to follow the selected line positioning for Gallo—and it has to deal with the realities of coordinating Production and Marketing in a more complex geographical and product realm.

3. <u>Financial Strategy</u>. Although specific data are not available, Gallo undoubtedly has the current cash flows to finance almost any strategy. Its biggest portfolio problem is to redeploy these cash flows before its "cash cow" lower priced lines turn sour. The biggest problem in finance, however, is what happens when Ernest and Julio begin to transfer ownership over to their children or grandchildren? If the stock is broken up into packages representing each of the 26 grandchildren, serious problems of continued family control will occur. Should the stock be placed into a trust which controls all voting, key appointments, etc.? Should "B shares" held there be partitioned out among the junior members of the family? Should the Gallos sell out and realize the capital gains themselves? How should they handle the taxes implicit in any disposition of the company?

In the end, this decision will come back to the basic values of the Gallo brothers. They may prefer the security and control of the trust, rather than the potential of outside parties breaking up their empire. On the other hand, they may choose simply to sell the whole enterprise to some major corporation, giving themselves (and presumably their heirs) an enormous cash position to deploy. This might represent a lower risk to the Gallos' minds than passing the operating company over to other people they presume would know less about its operations than they do. On the other hand, they might enjoy the enhanced power implicit in linking the company up with a major player in another segment of the beverage industry, i.e., Coors or Huebleins. Or they might be unable to work for anyone, even in a transition mode.

Overall Strategy

The Gallo brothers have to pick a major strategic positioning. They are caught in a classic mature industry trap. (See attached chart.) Once one achieves a low cost, high volume status, this can be maintained so long as the industry itself is growing at a rapid enough rate. Should total demand begin to decline or remain flat, overcapacity will develop—as it has in the wine industry—and present the company with the major strategic options posed in the chart. Each option carries with it specific risks and opportunities. There is a major question in this case as to whether the aging Gallos can carry out the revenue push, capacity filling strategy. This may be the time for them to capitalize on their gains and move out of the business themselves. The diagram makes an excellent point of departure for a final discussion and summary.

Whatever happens, if the company is to continue, the Gallos must handle the succession problem. This is an extraordinarily difficult issue. Neither individual has confidence in his own progeny. Consequently, continued management by the family is probably not a real possibility. More disturbing than this, of course, is the organizational split which has survived only because the Gallo brothers themselves have had such a long-term relationship. Each one of the major—Production and Marketing—units has its own internal focus. There has been relatively little cooperation between the two units. Information and control systems undoubtedly have been built around each unit. This will make it extraordinarily difficult for Gallo to shift its organization structure to a more decentralized form. Any successor management will have to immediately install a whole new control system, on top of the existing system, yet maintain the strengths of the existing controls which are a key competitive advantage for Gallo.

Despite Gallo's strong current market positions, the internal organization problems may make it impossible to sell the company to others. This is such a major dilemma that it requires a significant portion of the final wrap-up strategy discussion. It should be pointed out that the unwillingness to transfer power is a constant plague in closely held family companies. Many of the students will recognize this in their own parents' companies.

How can Competitors Attack Gallo?

A company with deep pockets could begin to undertake a series of "nibbling" strategies designed to decrease Gallo's volume edge. Companies with a wide wine line could selectively decrease costs on their lower price lines creating a "sting" strategy which could cost Gallo a significant amount of money, while costing the perpetrator a relatively small amount, unless Gallo retaliated against their higher level wines—more difficult for Gallo to do because of the fragmentation of the upper-priced wines.

Such a company could begin to buy growers or small wineries at low costs in the currently depressed marketplace and blend these into its own low priced line. Similarly, others could import low cost wines, attach a U.S. distribution name and perhaps beat Gallo at the "low cost game." Such a strategy would be facilitated by hiring a few of Gallo's second line managers, who must be distressed at the possibility that they would not be considered for the top positions at the company. In particular, Seagrams might seek to consolidate a number of brands in the above fashion, in anticipation of a management change at Gallo in the near future.

Any other competitors could of course target the lines where Gallo is not strong, emphasize a foreign image, emphasize the quality that only a specialized company can offer. The industry has long used rumors and lawsuits to force Gallo to defend itself. Courts have ruled that Gallo must identify itself on any bottles of premium wines that it presents to the marketplace. This suit might be overturned, but at some cost. Similarly, rumors were spread widely that the Bartles and James characters were actually Julio and Ernest Gallo. Competitors will do everything possible to link any upscale Gallo wines to its old "Thunderbird" image.

What Should Gallo's Response Be?

Most importantly for Gallo, the large growing upscale market will soon not remember the old "Thunderbird" name. Gallo can play on the younger sophisticated, smart buyer who shows sophistication by choosing excellent taste at low cost. To support this concept Gallo can either integrate its operations internationally or import good wines from abroad at low cost and repackage them for the U.S. market. It can work on its image using sophisticated upscale advertising at the institutional level. It has already successfully positioned several wines in this fashion. Emphasizing the youth market, it can feature "spritzes," like Reunite. And most importantly, it can use its distribution and advertising power and its knowledge base about the wine industry to position its products very, very carefully vs. competitors.

However, students should not forget the verity that 7% of consumers consume two-thirds of the table wines sold in the United States. Gallo is in an excellent position to target these heavy drinkers in the five states of California, New York, Florida, Texas, and Illinois, which consume one-half of all table wines sold in the United States. By a very careful selective geographical and premium product line strategy, springing off its existing high volumes and knowledge bases, Gallo should be able to resist the onslaught, if it can handle its very complex organizational issues.

HOW GALLO INCREASED POWER

```
┌─────────────────────┐
│  POTENTIAL ENTRANTS │
└─────────────────────┘
           │
           ▼
```

GALLO'S POWER POSITION

Coalition with Distributors
Low Price-Tight Margins
Full Scale Economies
Strong Production Technologies
Aggressive Response to Entrants--"Stings"
Controls Shelf Space
Wide Product Line No Openings Available
Strong Niche Position
Dominates Knowledge about Grapes and
   Distribution
Private Ownership

```
              ┌──────────────────┐
              │  GALLO'S RIVALS  │
              │  IN THE INDUSTRY │
              └──────────────────┘
```

GALLO'S POWER POSITION

Own as Many as Possible
Use Exclusives
Committed Sales Force
Need Gallo for Impulse Sales
Seek Hungry-Committed
   Distributors
Make Distributors Rich
Train Distributors--Best
   Trained Sales Force in
   Industry
More Information about
   Market than Anyone
Coalitions with Buyers-
   Distributors
Advertise Direct to Customers
Aggressive Control of Dis-
   tributorships
Ruthless Cutting if Not
   Performing

GALLO'S POWER POSITION

Outsources to Avoid Volatility
Avoids Weather Risk
Maintains Maximum Flexibility
Size Increases Supplier Dependency
Suppliers Fragmented vs. Gallo
15-Year Contracts for Selected Suppliers
Huge Storage Capability
Own Trucks Avoid Supplier Integration Forward
Suppliers Locked into Grapes Gallo Wants
Suppliers Can't Integrate Forward
   Because of Gallo Distribution and Advertising
Gallo Knows Growing Technologies and
   Quality Better than Suppliers
Gallo Supports R&D to Maintain Lead

```
┌───────────┐            ┌──────────────────────────────────┐           ┌──────────┐
│ Suppliers │            │ Gallo's Power Position            │           │ Buyers-  │
│           │ ─Rivals→   │                                   │ ←Rivals   │ Distrib- │
│           │            │ Strong Brand Recognition          │           │ utors    │
│           │            │ Dominates Shelf Space             │           │          │
│           │            │ Size - 3X, 5X Nearest Competitors │ ←─        │          │
│           │            │ Marketing Knowledge               │           │          │
│           │            │ Attention to Distributors         │           │          │
│           │            │ Vertical Integration              │           │          │
│           │            │ Largest Industry R&D              │           │          │
│           │            │ More Information from Market       │           │          │
│           │            │ Thin Margins Long-Term View       │           │          │
│           │            │ Concentration on Wines            │           │          │
└───────────┘            └──────────────────────────────────┘           └──────────┘
                                         ▲
                                         │ Rivals
```

GALLO'S POWER POSITION

Appeal to Lightness Preferences
Move Upscale Incrementally
Use Low Cost Wine in Coolers
Try to Change Image

```
              ┌──────────────┐
              │ SUBSTITUTES  │
              └──────────────┘
```

Overview

This is a powerful case for investigating how a strategy actually comes into place in a large complex organization. At the time it occurred, the IBM 360 was the largest single private investment ever made, the equivalent of about $50 billion today. The first part of the case provides a superb basis for discussing strategy formation. The case goes hand-in-glove with the Wrapp reading on "Good Managers Don't Make Policy Decisions." It should be used after the initial concepts of strategy and strategy analysis have been discussed. It points out many of the limitations inherent in the more structured analytical processes of strategy formulation, especially in innovative situations or in those requiring major changes across multiple divisions of large organizations. The latter portion of the case shows how the 360 decision dominates the position of IBM up through 1983 and causes IBM to ignore important problems in the strategic environment. The 1983 case endpoint poses exactly the problems that Mr. Gerstner faced when he took over in 1993. IBM again had not been able to restructure itself around the enormous changes in the marketplace. Its product line offerings had become unfocused, incompatible, and bureaucratized. In short, IBM needed to undergo once again the same kind of major change process that it did in the IBM 360 decision. The specific dimensions of the new need are spelled out at the end of the case, leading to the final question, "What should IBM have done next?"

Session Structure

We would recommend first investigating the process through which the 360 decision was made at IBM. Second, there is an interesting opportunity to look at Mr. Learson's management style and how it fits this kind of process. His style is process-oriented, highly political, and incremental. Finally, there is an opportunity to analyze how outside parties took advantage of the IBM 360 decision and how IBM later needed to re-evaluate its overall strategy in one of the classic strategic breakdowns of the era. The later part of the case provides a superb combination of a company falling back into the very same patterns that had once threatened it—i.e., bureaucracy, incompatibility of products, and lack of responsiveness to new market changes. These factors pose the exact questions that Mr. Gerstner faced when he took over IBM in 1993. This part of the case also provides an interesting portfolio and organizational structure case, whose issues are as valid in 1995 as in 1983.

The Decision Process

We have found it very useful to ask the students, "When was the IBM 360 decision actually made?" The initial response is to select a particular point like the March 1964 final assessment conference or the public announcement of the 360 series. One can then inquire whether or not the decision did not have to be made substantially prior to those events and whether these were mere confirmations of a process that was already irreversible. Then one can begin to inquire, "When did the decision become essentially irreversible?" This then raises other key junctures in the decision process which we outline on the board in temporal order so the students can see the whole process. Then we ask, "What were the critical management processes involved in each step?" We outline the two side by side, roughly as follows:

Teaching note copyright © 1996 by James Brian Quinn. This note was prepared by Professor Quinn and Penny C. Paquette, Research Associate.

Date	Key Event	Management Process
1959	Learson heads General Products	Choose key people and Data Systems
1960-61	Lines overlap, feeling of proliferation	Listen, low level clues
1960	Begin manufacturing internally	Partial decision
1960-61	MIT meeting, Spaulding Report	Increased awareness
Jan. '61	8,000 presentation	Kill options
1961	"Blanket the market," kill SCAMP	General concept
May '61	Stretch fails	Freed resources, consider new options
mid '61	Start NPL	Begin new options
mid '61	Logic committee	Involve key players
Aug.-Oct.'61	Begin strategic dialogues	Create participation
Nov. '61	SPREAD Committee: Control Leadership	Choose committee
Jan '62	SPREAD Report	Dimension concept
Jan '62	"All right. We'll do it."	Partial commitment
mid '62	Authorize production facility	Capital commitment
late '62	Ski lodge conference	Reassessment
late '62	Evans in charge	Champions empowered
1963	San Jose objects	Use power
1963	World Trade joins in development	Co-opt opposition
late '63	Honeywell introduces line system	First signal from control
Jan. '64	Shoot out—401S/360-30	Kill options
Feb. '64	Remove Haanstra	Remove opposition
Mar. '64	Final assessment "Going, going, gone"	Formal approval
Apr. '64	Public announcement	Public commitment
late '64	Time sharing—G.E.	Reassess technology
Apr. '65	Delivery	Field implementation

Date	Key Event	Management Processes
1965	Announce 90, 44, 67, 20 Not all compatible I/O Memories, etc.	Tactical shifts
1971	Learson CEO	Management succession
1972+	Architecture influences 370 Cash flows through 1970s	Technology persists Long time horizons

The professor can then inquire, "Why were these steps essential or important to the decision process?" From this, the student begins to understand: (1) that all the information needed for the decision is not available in its early stages or at any one time until quite late in the process, (2) political forces are sufficiently powerful to upset the decision until momentum is well established, (3) the needed organizational commitment is not there to carry out the decision until late in the process.

The professor can now begin to inquire about different aspects of the process itself. Some useful questions are: "When did the decision process begin? Why? What triggers a major strategy change in such a large organization?" The students' initial response is to say that market pressures forced the decision. However, one should point out that the first measurable market signal which might have started the decision was in late 1963. Had IBM waited until that date to start its decision process, the 360 series might have been 3 years too late for the marketplace.

Another interesting question to ask is, "Who actually makes the IBM 360 decision?" The students' usual response is Mr. Learson. However, one can quickly demonstrate that Learson is guiding the decision process, rather than actually making the decision. A number of people are essential in making the actual decision. One of the more exciting observations is that most of the people who are crucial to the decision are quite young. These people, including Fairclough, Brooks, Evans, etc., are at ages 28-35 determining the future trade patterns of major countries.

Another interesting question is, "How does one manage this kind of decision process? Where are the 'planners' in the process?" This allows one to suggest that the early stages of the decision process were quite diffuse because of lack of information about the technology or the marketplace. At these stages Learson and Watson are managing processes of "awareness building" and "information gathering." Later, through the "strategic dialogues," the SPREAD Committee, and later intermediate conferences and meetings, they are managing the "consensus building" process necessary to provide the information and momentum for the decision to work. One can inquire, "How do they manage risk in this project? Why is there resistance in the organization? Why wouldn't this kind of strategy have come out of the formal planning process?" Neither major division would have dared to replace its own product line and a sister division's with one that "blanketed the market."

Next ask, "Why do Watson and Learson use the 'shoot out' process, rather than a formally planned 'systems analysis' or 'system evaluation' to design the optimum computer on paper and then proceed with only the best alternative design?" Shoot outs improve the motivation, timing, and information for decisions. They lower risks by making final decisions close to the marketplace. As one pursues these questions, it becomes clear that this is a continuous, evolutionary, political, consensus-building process, with substantial "bottom up" contributions rather than a single "top driven" decision. One can inquire, "Why is this kind of process appropriate or inappropriate to this particular decision situation?" When the marketplace is changing rapidly, when long time horizons, many experts, and multiple organizations are involved, this kind of process uses the organization's best talent, decreases risk, increases commitment, and makes the final decision as close to the marketplace as possible.

A number of interesting questions surround the time span of the decision. Inquire, "When did the IBM 360 decision actually begin? When does it end?" The professor can then point out the important early decisions in 1959 and 1960—appointing Learson and building the technology base—and then note that the decision does not end even with the 1965 announcement of the 360 line. Different products are added, compatibility is dropped for certain lines, peripheral systems are developed around the line, etc. Nevertheless, the architecture of the 360 series determines the development of the 370 series, and the line provides the cash flows the company builds on through the 1970s. In fact, the dominance of the IBM 360 architecture gives the company its premier world market position throughout the entire 1970s.

The professor can then note that a complex strategic decision in a healthy organization like IBM will often span 3-5 years, affect performance for a decade, and be reshaped as new information and competitor responses develop during this cycle. This leads to a discussion of the need to manage this process, to maintain flexibility, and to consciously involve key people to stimulate commitment in large organizations. Most of the readings in the strategy formation chapter of the book are directly applicable to this case as are those in the innovative section, particularly the Quinn article, "Managing Innovation: Controlled Chaos."

The Learson Management Style

This section of the discussion can begin with the general question, "Was Mr. Learson a good manager?" The answer is overwhelmingly yes. The next question can be, "What makes him a good manager?" Students usually respond with answers having to do with his personality. One can then inquire what management techniques make Learson an effective manager? At this point, the Wrapp article makes an excellent outline for the discussion.

Mr. Learson does not seem to express explicit goals. He seems to keep his goals broad and flexible. He knows what he is trying to achieve, but makes only a few goals explicit at any given moment. One can then inquire why keeping goals "vague" as suggested by Wrapp or Quinn can be a useful technique.

One can then raise some questions about Mr. Learson's style of "short-circuiting" the formal organization. One can inquire when this technique is useful and how it must be managed to be effective. One can develop the realization that information filters develop readily when one doesn't use this technique. One can then inquire, "Why does a manager like Learson use the 'questioning' technique rather than giving formal orders?" One can also investigate the impact of the Learson style of carrying such questions to the point of being "almost an inquisition." What effects does this have on individuals, on the organization, and how must this process be managed to be effective?

One can then inquire about whether Learson and Watson are operating directly or indirectly in this decision process. They seem to operate to a large extent by what Wrapp calls "the hidden hand." One can ask, "Why are they not much more visible in making specific decisions?" One can inquire about how they handle opposition in the decision process. It is also worthwhile to investigate why the divisions are not <u>ordered</u> to cooperate in the design of the 360 rather than having its major development be carried on <u>outside</u> the normal business activities of the divisions.

A number of interesting questions can be asked about the "shoot out" process used by Learson in this case. As used in IBM, the process allows those who are championing different alternatives to obtain high level exposure, makes the final decision on major new products as late as possible consistent with information, ensures that any decision actually made will already have strong support by an operating group to carry it through, improves the information available for evaluating different alternatives, maintains maximum flexibility until the last sensible moment, and so on.

Finally, the case allows one to inquire about the essential nature of leadership. The "team" of Watson and Learson is strongly complimentary. Which is really "the leader?" What characteristics or actions of Learson constitute leadership? What does one have to do to keep his somewhat impatient, domineering style from being destructive? Is Mr. Learson or Mr. Watson really "manipulating" this decision? If so, is this destructive? How could they possibly have managed the process better? Is Learson a Theory X or a Theory Y manager?

The case allows some intriguing investigations into how a top manager deals with power in an organization. Haanstra is clearly a major player in IBM and must be dealt with carefully during the decision process. What political moves seem to have been made by Watson and Learson? Why do they not push the whole package of the 360 at first? How do Watson and Learson develop the information which allows them to manage a system which has more information than they have? What are the key points for intervention in this process and how do Learson and Watson manage them?

The case allows both the student and the professor to weigh the pros and cons of "muddling with a purpose" as Wrapp calls it, in large organizations. It demonstrates how essential is the process of maintaining flexibility, involving the key players in the decision, dealing with both political and informational issues, and making sure that emotional commitment to the new decision is implanted at the time the decision is actually announced. It is clear that the strategy is not first arrived at analytically and then implemented.

The Strategy and Its Evaluation

If time permits, it is worth asking, "What was the IBM 360 strategy?" After some probing, one can come to the conclusion that the "360 strategy" was a basic new technological/marketing/product/organization concept that refocused the organization in new directions. This allows one to pursue the idea that making that concept clear and having it understood in the organization has significant merit for obtaining focus of resources, organizational commitment, personal commitment, etc.

One can then inquire about each element in the strategy itself. Why was it essential to have a single line? Compatible? Standard interface? System which blanketed the marketplace? Provided duality between business and engineering functions? Was announced simultaneously to the marketplace? And generated entirely new markets? One can relate these back to the unique strengths of IBM at the time of the 360 decision. Each of these conceptual factors had significant impact on IBM's later capacity to create entry barriers to other computer companies. Among other things, it created switching costs which were insurmountable to customers, provided a full "life cycle" product line for IBM customers as they grew, gave IBM economies of scale which only it could exploit, avoided excessive investments in a wide variety of incompatible software, allowed IBM to dominate the "center line" of the marketplace and integrate its systems in this central range, while conceding only temporarily the upper and lower ends of that marketplace. One can analyze why this was an appropriate strategy for IBM, but would have been inappropriate for any other player in the marketplace. One can use either the Rumelt or Quinn criteria for evaluating the strategy. One can also inquire whether the IBM 360 strategy neatly fits into one of Porter's three generic strategy categories. It does not! Does this mean it is a poor strategy? Not if it meets the other criteria suggested.

Responses and Countermoves

Another interesting branch to the discussion is to ask, "How could outside groups have taken advantage of the IBM 360 strategy?" Some possible responses are briefly cataloged below:

1. Develop a high end niche (as Control Data and Cray Research did).

2. Develop a low end niche (as DEC and Apple did later).

3. Jump over IBM's "hybrid" technology to integrated circuitry.

4. Develop software or systems installation competencies (as EDS did).

5. Make IBM-compatible input/output, or peripheral equipment. (Many did.)

6. Develop the communications interconnections necessary to utilize this powerful new equipment at remote points. (AT&T and EMI did.)

7. Develop time sharing or service bureau activities where IBM cannot compete. (GE and Control Data did.)

8. Develop leasing services to take advantage of the fact that IBM will have to price the 360 series for relatively quick sale in order to cover its $5 billion investment. (S. Stienberg did.)

9. Develop a supplier relationship to IBM (as Intel and Texas Instruments did).

10. Use the new equipment to develop significant new applications for computing.

11. If you are a foreign competitor, form coalitions with other companies or countries to gain advantages vs. IBM.

12. Attack IBM through antitrust suits (as Control Data did).

13. Exploit the price umbrella and confusion that will occur as IBM tries to introduce such a complex line.

14. Develop a business to handle the returns of old IBM equipment and sell it in a second market.

15. Hire disenchanted key people like Amdahl, Haanstra, or Fairclough, etc.

Given these possible modes of exploiting or attacking IBM's new strategy, what changes should IBM make or have made in the strategy? Unless significant improvements can be identified by the student group, one must conclude that the IBM strategy was an effective one for its purposes.

A NEW INDUSTRY

At the end of the case is an open-ended decision. We usually begin this stage of discussion by asking the questions, "What are the most critical factors with which IBM's strategy must deal if the company is to be successful in the future? What actions should be taken relative to each of these?" The section opens with a "positioning strategy" issue, moves on to portfolio issues, and ends up with a discussion of the organization needed by IBM to support its strategy. During the "positioning strategy" portion of the section, we try to indicate how a large company like IBM can gain leverage by relating its strategy in each of several areas to other elements of strategy. Students will tend to bounce back and forth between various functional elements in the strategy. It is very helpful to frequently ask, "How does the strategy in this functional area support strategies in other areas? How can IBM obtain leverage from that decision in other realms? What alternatives exist? How would each of these affect other elements of the strategy?" This analysis fits well with Porter's value chain concepts.

This teaching note will be developed—for lack of sufficient horizontal space as one might find on a blackboard—in a sequential fashion. However, the discussion is unlikely to develop in this sequence. Students will see relationships as they go along and will begin to move from one element of the strategy to another as they see ways of reinforcing each significant factor.

Changes in the Marketplace

To open the discussion, it may be useful to ask, "What are the most important changes which seem to be taking place in the marketplace?" Some of the most important are outlined below:

A. In the early 1980s, computers were entering a maturing phase in their life cycle. Some portions of the computer industry were approaching commodity status. Competition was therefore shifting more toward a low cost, high volume, pricing-oriented strategy. This was particularly true of the home computer, personal computer, and "low end" segments of the market.

B. As microcomputers grew in power, they were beginning to press the "middle line" mainframe computers. Micromainframes and microsupercomputers were soon to be anticipated. These would clearly put significant pressure on IBM's traditional strength, "its mid-line computers."

C. Plug compatible machines and "IBM look-alikes" were moving into the marketplace, depressing margins. Central Processing Units (CPUs) accounted for a decreasing share of "computer system sales."

D. Distribution channels were changing rapidly. IBM's superb "Big Blue" marketing force was no longer necessary to sell to major segments of the market, i.e., sophisticated users of small computers, and was too expensive to use for small companies and home users. To reach these markets, it was necessary to move through distributors and retailers. Sophisticated systems houses and value-added distributors could provide many of the services formerly provided by IBM's salesmen. In a maturing marketplace, superior distribution, along with low cost and volume, would be the key to success.

E. Software was becoming an increasing portion of the total cost of a computer installation (often representing 3-5 times the hardware cost). Both independents and customers were doing their own software development. Many customers were becoming frustrated with the incompatibility of various systems, especially when they had DEC, Wang, Apollo, or other sophisticated CAD/CAM or office automation systems which could not be interfaced with those of other manufacturers.

F. Interconnectivity or communications interfaces were becoming more important to customers. This was especially true of large national accounts or multinational companies. The competitive capacity to connect stand-alone installations with each other and with other elements in data base, local area networks (LANs), or value-added networks (VANs) was becoming a crucial competitive factor. In trying to satisfy these customers, IBM would be running headlong into powerful communications companies like AT&T, NEC, NTT, etc.

IBM's SNA software offered both some strategic advantages and some problems. SNA was a strong element rendering compatibility to IBM's own line. However, in 1982 it did not allow compatible interfaces for machines that were not "IBM look-alikes." A major issue existed as to whether IBM should stay with SNA or move to some more "open architecture" or "compatible architecture" like Unix which would allow IBM systems to interface easily with those of other manufacturers.

G. World markets—Competition was increasingly occurring on a worldwide basis. IBM's large customers wanted to communicate with their foreign markets and foreign operations effectively. Many customers wanted to tie into worldwide data bases, communications systems, etc.

H. Market segmentation was increasing rapidly. A series of small niches representing specific applications were appearing in the marketplace. Many of these required application-specific software and servicing capabilities. A most important strategic problem for IBM was how to develop the volumes it needed for efficient manufacture and at the same time serve all of the fragmented niches that were developing in the marketplace.

I. Where value could be added in the value-added chain in the new marketplace was an important issue. Machines were becoming more "look-alike" and similar in performance capabilities. Value was often added in how well they served particular application segments. This was often a software issue, or an issue of designing a machine for a particular purpose such as engineering design, cash register work, work station controls, etc.

J. Finally, IBM was competing significantly against itself. IBM's line had become fragmented and overlapping. Any new IBM entry was likely to cannibalize as much of IBM's own line as it might take away from competitors' sales. Purchasing vs. lease strategies were becoming very important. The case indicates how hard it was for IBM to estimate what volume of sales it could achieve on a new product line. The market was very price sensitive and buyers could be shifted easily between leasing and buying by pricing strategies. Whether IBM wanted more leasing vs. direct sales was an important strategic question, given the large investments it then faced.

Comment to the Professor: It is interesting to point out to the students that price performance ratios were changing so fast that on average every 10 years, one could buy 10 times the computing power for the same dollar price. One could buy 20 times the storage capability every 5 years for the same dollar amount. Thus, if IBM was to continue its traditional 13% dollar sales growth rate, it would have to sell 35 times the installed power each decade that it sold the preceding decade. One can ask, "Where do the market niches exist for such enormous computing power?"

Technology Changes

Along with these enormous changes in the marketplace were technological changes of perhaps even greater significance. Every year, semiconductor producers were able to put approximately twice the number of components on a chip that they could the preceding year. This meant that computers were becoming extraordinarily small, that personal computers (PCs) could provide as much power as mainframes in an earlier generation. Small computers could be built directly into appliances. Small home computers could be programmed to do an enormous range of functions. The Japanese had moved strongly into the semiconductor field and had been successful in pre-empting the 64K RAM and 256K RAM storage markets. Japan was no longer copying U.S. technology, but was doing its own advanced research, and had undertaken larger technology programs emphasizing artificial intelligence and parallel processing. What were some of the most important implications for IBM? Some of the more interesting issues follow:

A. IBM needed to maintain access to frontier research in semiconductors and communications systems. This meant that it needed a substantial investment in basic research to be able to "listen" and "understand" what was going on in basic research fields worldwide. In a very clever move, IBM was able to negotiate with the Japanese government to obtain patent access for any of the programs Japan developed in its "Fifth Generation" and "Super Computer" projects.

166

B. In order to maintain flexible access to first production runs of new semiconductors, IBM purchased a minority equity interest in Intel. At one point, it owned as much as 20% of Intel's stock. Once the development of the 32 bit 80386 chip it needed for its PC-AT was announced, IBM decided to sell off about 1/3 of its stock in Intel.

C. The first cost for new chips was huge, $100-200 million. Consequently, IBM had to pick its technological thrusts very carefully. Targeting these investments might mean considerably more coordinated planning than had existed at times in the past.

D. Because of the large software investments being made by independent groups and customers, IBM's own software investments had to increase sharply. In addition, it had to decide whether to maintain an open architecture which let others support IBM systems with their own proprietary software, or to maintain a certain amount of secrecy in software to increase switching costs to customers.

E. IBM had to decide whether to continue its practice of being somewhat conservative in technology—but with an overwhelming market presence—or to take a stronger leadership position in technology so that it could obtain the benefits of "experience curve" cost reductions by being the first entrant to a new marketplace.

F. IBM's software had become relatively incompatible among its various lines. This was beginning to multiply IBM's costs for software development, just as it had at the beginning of the IBM 360 process. Should IBM allow this to continue in order to better attack the very fragmented specialized niches it had to serve? Or should IBM begin to consolidate its software into 2 or 3 clumps or major groupings which would give it some economies of scale in software development?

G. How should IBM prioritize investments in manufacturing technology vs. product technology. Should process technology be developed separately or integrated into its product development units?

H. To what extent should IBM perform its research internally? Join in consortia with other semiconductor suppliers or researchers? With communications companies?

Production Issues

If IBM was entering a maturing market era, how should its production function be organized? What would be the critical factors for success? How would this impact its product lines? How could IBM simultaneously obtain the needed economies of scale and experience curve advantages which large volumes permitted, yet serve the fragmented niches that now represented the marketplace?

A. IBM needed to be on the frontier of flexible automation technologies. This was necessary to obtain maximum scale economies for itself, yet allow flexible lot production to serve many niches in the marketplace.

B. To the extent possible, IBM needed to standardize its lines and componentry. However, there were significant trade-offs between such standardization and the flexibility demanded by the marketplace.

C. IBM needed to invest heavily in its production facilities and maintain a leadership position in those facilities at all costs. Notice that by doing so, it automatically had a leadership position in CAD/CAE/CAM technology which could be sold in the marketplace.

D. IBM was the largest user of componentry in the world. As such, it had a natural "in-house" market for its semiconductors. To what extent should it sell outside? Should it try to do this as a purposeful portion of its strategy to increase economies of scale and volume gains for experience curve effects?

E. If IBM were able to achieve extremely low cost production, would this expose it to even more antitrust action? If so, how should it organize its production to avoid a potential breakup by the Justice Department?

Organization Strategy

Based upon the information in the case, one can draw a rough organization chart of IBM at the time of the case. The professor can then query, "What changes in IBM's organization are necessary to support the strategy concepts developed above? What are the most important organization issues facing IBM? What should it do about these?" Some of the more important of these are briefly outlined below:

A. Increasing Size of Operations: Because of its size IBM runs the risk of increased bureaucracies, inflexibility, lack of innovation, lack of entrepreneurship. How can IBM attack these crucial issues? Did Learson's style create an environment conducive to entrepreneurship and innovation? Can this be continued in IBM's new competitive situation? If not, why not? If so, what are the main features of what it should continue?

B. Marketing Organization: What are the critical factors in marketing? How should marketing be organized? Should the total marketing organization be centralized? Or should it be broken up and assigned to different SBUs or IBUs? The key strategic element in marketing is to focus IBM's full marketing power on its customers. IBM needs to present a consistent face and not have a number of competitive salesmen calling on the same customer. How can this be done? Is a special sales force needed for very large customers with international operations? Is a different kind of sales force needed for the distributor network of IBM? Can IBM continue to afford to use its Big Blue salesmen with increasingly sophisticated mid-sized company buyers? Or can this group be better served by the distributor network? Should IBM's marketing strategies be worldwide product strategies? Regional strategies? Segment strategies? These issues can lead to a great deal of lively debate.

C. Technological Organization: IBM needs to continue its flexible, fast moving, highly competitive, ad hoc method of product development and technological development. How can this be structured to interface effectively with customer needs defined by marketing? With the needs of manufacturing for highly sophisticated, reliable, low cost, high volume technology? Should manufacturing engineering be split off as a separate function to obtain attention and effective top management focus on this element of the business?

D. Matrixing Issues: Given the needs for coordination across marketing, production, componentry, technological groups, etc., to what degree should a matrix structure be put in place? How could this be organized? Where should decision powers lie? What should be the primary organization of the company? What should the basis of the SBUs be? Product Groups? Markets? Regions? What should the structure of independent business units (IBUs) be? How should these differ?

E. What kind of performance measurements and control systems are needed to make the new IBM organization work? Where should the profit centers be? What can IBM do to avoid the building up a very large centralized bureaucracy? What items should be centralized? Decentralized? Why?

F. In light of antitrust pressures on IBM, should IBM's organization structure be integrated together? Set up as separate businesses? Matrixed to handle all possible contingencies? What are the gains and losses of each type of primary organization?

Financial Issues

How should IBM finance its future operations? What are its likely capital needs? How should it think about its portfolio of products and services? How can it allocate between these various sectors? Some basic calculations need to be made by the students in order to understand IBM's situation. If IBM continues its historic growth rate of 13% per year, what are the implications? Some of the more interesting issues are developed below:

A. Capital Needs: If IBM grows at 13% per year, it will double its size in approximately 5.5 years. This means that in 5.5 years it will have to double its assets. The average amount of increase in assets per year over this period will be $5.9 billion. On an exponential buildup basis, it will need $4.2 billion of incremental assets in 1983.

B. IBM's cash flows in 1982 are approximately $9 billion ($6.1 billion operating income plus $2.9 billion depreciation expense). It has been investing capital at the rate of $6.8 billion in recent years. One can conclude that, if IBM can maintain adequate margins, it can continue to finance its growth internally and still pay significant dividends.

C. One can then calculate the required hurdle rate for IBM to grow its assets at an annual increase of 13%. By using the classic Boston Consulting Group formula (see below) one can see that this takes an average hurdle rate of 21.8%.

Growth Rate of Assets	=	Debt Equity	(Hurdle Rate	-	Interest) Rate	•	Percent of Earnings Retained	+	Hurdle Rate	x	Percent of Earnings Retained
G	=	$\frac{D}{E}$	(H - i)	x	P	+	H	x	P		
.13	=	.14	(H-.05)	x	.54	+	H	x	.54		
.13	=	.075H	- .004	+	.54H						
21.8%	=	H	=	Required Average Hurdle Rate							

D. Portfolio allocation: One can now ask the students to allocate resources to the different product areas and establish appropriate hurdle rates for investments in each of those areas. Obviously, there is no correct answer to this issue. However, one might look at IBM's current organization and ask what should be the portfolio role of each of the divisions as outlined on the next page.

Have the students define what hurdle rate would be appropriate for each of these investments in IBM's portfolio and why. (Examples shown below.) Differential hurdle rates may be required in specific situations because returns are inherently lower in those businesses, i.e., satellite systems or semiconductors. Others may require higher hurdle rates because they represent very high margin businesses with greater risk, i.e., software development, services, etc. Some (like SNA) might be undertaken as a support system investment so that IBM can present a full system interface to its customers. Personal Computers might be asked to return high initial rates to cover their early capital investments, then shift to a penetration strategy emphasizing lower returns to build an installed input-output (I/O) base with IBM equipment. And so on. This exercise can give the students an interesting experience in trying to decide how to allocate a very large capital budget like IBM's.

Division	Possible Portfolio Role	Possible Hurdle Rate
Federal Systems (Govt. Contracts)	Service/Tech	Capital Cost+ 7%
Instruments	Near Growth	25%
Education	Long-term Growth	22%
Semiconductors	Security, Low Cost	15%
Peripheral Equipment	Near Growth	30%
Personal Computers	Near Growth-I/O	20%
Satellite Systems	System Support	15%
SNA	System Support	15%
Software	Near Growth	35%
Supplies	Stability	20%
Computer		
Middle-small	Cash Cow	35%
Large-complex	Cash Cow	35%
Other Services	Stable Growth	30%
Marketing		
Software-services	Star	35%
National accounts	Cash Cow	30%
Distributor accounts	Future Growth	22%
Research and Development	Planned Cost	--
Acquisitions	System Support	30%
World trade	Stable Growth	35%

Overall Company Concept

After looking at each of these components of strategy, one can ask: In light of the above, how should IBM restate its mission statement? Its distinct competency? Or its other major goals? Should IBM continue to be a systems vs. a components company? Why? Is it an "information systems" company? A "computer" company? A "computer/communications" company? What markets does it intend to dominate?

What will be IBM's distinct competencies in the future? Its marketing-distribution skills? Its low cost production skills? Its advanced technology skills? Its service to its installed base? What can IBM reasonably be expected to accomplish over the next decade? If it continues its 13% growth rate, in 10 years it will be a $128 billion company. Is this feasible? Should it be a full line company? If not, where should it specialize? What markets should its growth focus on? How should it best accomplish this growth?

SUMMARY OF OUTCOMES

While the actions of IBM must necessarily be highly summarized and do not necessarily provide a guide to correct or incorrect action, they may be helpful to the professor. It is very difficult to summarize so complex a company as IBM. These are highlights, rather than summary descriptions.

By 1986, IBM had at least 9 major computer architectures or internal designs in its active product line. To simplify its line and make it easy to move applications among different computers, its senior vice president of development and manufacturing said the company would in the future emphasize three architectures to the exclusion of everything else. These were the "370 Line" (comprising all IBM mainframes), the "System 36 minicomputer line," and the "PC family." The 370 mainframe architecture (derived from the 360) was used in the 4300 line, the 3080 line, and the new 3090 (Sierra) line.

While IBM increasingly emphasized communication networks to interrelate its free-standing machines, it found that it could not operate a satellite system profitably. Consequently, it sold the satellite system to MCI for 37 million shares of that company's stock. In essence, by selling its SDS unit to MCI, IBM obtained ownership in an even larger communications unit. In addition, it had earlier purchased ROLM to obtain a technology entry in communications.

To combat the problems of bureaucracy, inflexibility, and slowing innovativeness, IBM continuously tried to decentralize its operations. In addition, IBM began a series of entrepreneurial activities to give it an added presence in rapidly growing "applications segments," like the medical care and delivery area, factory automation, retailing, etc. To coordinate its marketing power internationally, IBM World Trade stayed centralized. Within IBM World Trade, the organization structure was regional with groups for the Americas, the Far East, Europe and Africa.

By the mid-'80s, however, IBM had acknowledged that it might not be able to meet the ambitious historical goals. Growth for big mainframes had slowed from more than 10% down to about 3%. Users had begun to rethink their information management strategies to deal with networking issues.

Mr. John Akers became CEO in 1985 and began a very strong pruning and chopping program. Nevertheless, as competition increased throughout the industry, IBM's grip on the computer market (in percentage terms) weakened considerably. Although many customers were moving to smaller supercomputers and workstations, IBM continued to push its giant mainframe computers hardest because they were the company's major profit center. In the late 1980s, Akers began to turn that strategy upside down. He began pushing smaller, high powered units referred to as "open system workstations." By encouraging easier communication links between these smaller computers and IBM's big models, Akers hoped to exploit this booming market while supplementing sales of mainframes. The open systems market was growing annually at 30%. Nevertheless, there was a risk that the line of new computers known as RS/6000 could cannibalize IBM's existing line. Key to the strategy was a new set of software programs called SAA, designed to interlink IBM's disparate computer lines.

Each year IBM spent more on R&D than any four other computer companies put together. It had the most salesmen and technicians on a worldwide basis, and it had the broadest product range.

In the late 1980s, Mr. Akers began to push its strategy toward obtaining "economies of scale in information gathering and services." This stood to completely refashion IBM's concept of itself. It had thought of itself dominantly as a producer and seller of information system boxes. However, by 1990 not only was 90% of the cost of developing a new system in software, customers found that over 60% of their continuing costs were due to software maintenance and update. With the largest installed base in the world, IBM could obtain some economies of scale, not available to anyone else, in servicing this installed base. By 1990, *The Economist* noted that while IBM held half the world market in mainframes it had only about 15% of the minicomputer market, and 10% of that for personal computers. Consequently, linking and servicing its computer base became the core strategy of IBM. The key question was, "How could IBM develop a distinctive competency in the services?" Mr. Akers set up some meetings between his top managers and large customers. The customers "lambasted IBM" for its arrogance, its unwillingness to listen, and its inability to adapt to customer needs. To change this image and make IBM a truly "service-oriented" company became the main theme of IBM's customer presentations in the 1990s. To meet its customer demands, IBM has had to share more information about its systems and to make them more compatible. It published its Systems

Application Architecture (SAA), which allowed users to share information across many computer systems. To extend its integration capabilities further, IBM entered a large number of alliances (see Exhibit 1). Key among these was its relationship with Microsoft, the world's biggest supplier of software for personal computers, which helped to create DOS and OS/2 for IBM. It also entered into an alliance with Steve Jobs's new company NeXt to jump ahead to what it thought of as the next generation of personal computers. However, many of these alliances proved hard to manage. IBM was never able to achieve the desired results from ROLM. Microsoft became upset with IBM and turned its attention from OS/2 to Windows. Nevertheless, in mid-1990, IBM in a startling move brought Ross Perot (founder of EDS) back into the fold with an alliance with Perot's Systems Company to expand its presence in the $5.9 billion systems management market.

In the competitive marketplace, two things were happening of great importance. Given the extraordinarily high power of super-mini and super-microcomputers, the network connecting these computers essentially became the computer itself. The workstations and databases into which a system connected merely became nodes in a computer system. Elsewhere, most of the major U.S. mainframe companies had merged. Burroughs and Univac/Sperry Rand had merged into Unisys, as had NCR and AT&T, Honeywell, GE, and Bull, and so on. However, the fastest growing companies in the industry were those associated with mini and microcomputers like Compaq, Sun Micro Systems, etc.

The Japanese computer companies had tried to invade IBM's mainframe stronghold, and IBM had to adjust its Japanese strategies. Japanese heavyweights Fujitsu and Hitachi were selling IBM-compatible mainframes at cheaper prices. IBM decided to reverse the game. It re-engineered its mainframes to mimic Fujitsu's and Hitachi's machines which together commanded 44% of the Japanese market. It moved aggressively both to defend its $9.5 billion, 25% share of the Japanese mainframe market. But it also pinned down Hitachi and Fujitsu in their strong home market, thus weakening their attacks abroad. It also lined up joint ventures with twenty-three major companies, including a large commitment with NTT Corporation in Japan, and it was offering huge discounts (up to 90%) for educational users of IBM equipment in Japan.

While these highlights do not adequately reflect the true complexity of IBM's strategies, they are helpful guidelines in leading a discussion of IBM's position and strategy in the 1990s.

COMPETING GLOBAL NETWORKS: IBM AND AT&T

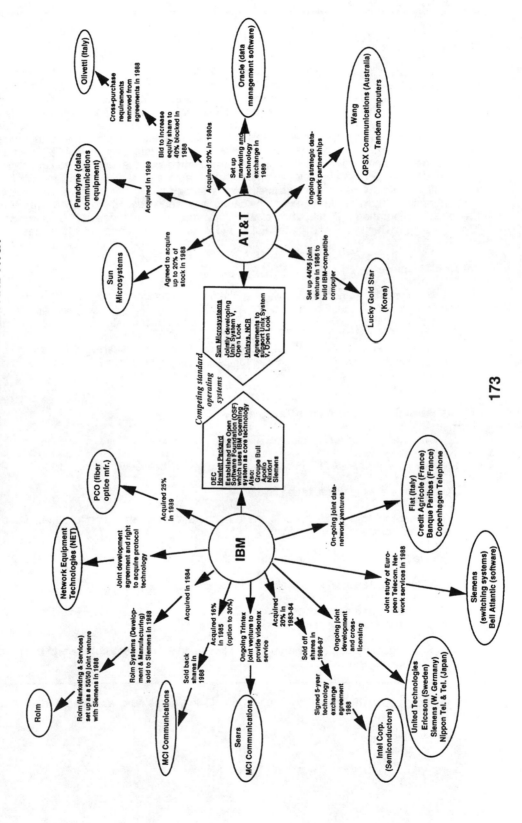

173

Overview

This is a superb process case. In one of the most widely publicized large company successes of the last several decades, Robert Allen undertakes a series of steps to lean down and refocus AT&T. The case sets forth the important steps in that process. It then provides the basis for analyzing what new organizational and control system changes will be needed. The case has a strong international focus, deals with the management of change and the building of a new leadership team, and provides a basis for discussing the advantages and disadvantages of product-oriented, regional, SBU, and matrix forms. It contains the new AT&T performance measurement system, which it widely discusses and introduces the students to economic value-added (EVA) as a performance measurement tool. The case ends with the issues AT&T faces in 1994. The company has reformed itself from a stodgy public utility into a very competitive national entity. It now needs to extend its capabilities worldwide. It works well with Mintzberg "Beyond Configuration," Tuschman's et al, "Convergence and Upheaval," Bleeke and Ernst, "Collaborating to Compete," and Baden-Fuller and Stopford "Crescendo Model" articles.

Session Structure

We would recommend beginning with the general question, "What were the critical issues Mr. Allen faced when he took over AT&T?" A natural follow-on is to ask why Mr. Allen undertook the various steps he did in the sequence he chose. Next, one can ask, "What would the students have changed, if they had been in a position to do so? What are the critical issues facing AT&T domestically? Internationally? What critical steps need to be taken in the future? In what sequence? How should AT&T organize for its European presence? Chinese opportunity? United States? The rest of the world?"

Key Issues at the Time of Allen's Takeover

What were the critical issues Mr. Allen faced when he took over?

- Morale was terrible. AT&T had laid off 73,000 people between 1984 and 1986.

- Costs were still high despite the layoffs.

- AT&T's personnel were used to the bureaucratic world of a comfortable, prosperous, regulated company.

- People had lost their self-confidence and did not know how to compete.

- AT&T's organization was basically functional and bureaucratic.

- The company had never operated extensively overseas, except as an interconnection point with other telecom suppliers in host countries.

- Top management contained a number of key people who were not used to operating in a "profit-oriented" environment.

- The company had been forced to split off all of its local and regional telephone companies and a major portion of its Bell Laboratories group.

- Deregulation had brought a number of new competitors, and technology was making it possible to compete against AT&T's Long Lines operations through wireless means and use of fiberglass.

- Foreign telecommunications companies could invest in the new U.S. telecom competitors, but their host countries would not allow AT&T to invest in telecom units abroad.

Mr. Allen's Sequence of Actions

Why did Mr. Allen utilize the sequence of steps that he did? Here the problem is to avoid the students' merely repeating the facts of the case. The professor could constantly ask, "Why did he do this? First? Later? What would you have changed?" It is best to begin this discussion in 1986 while Mr. Olson is still alive.

(1)   Creating a New Vision: After a series of cutbacks, people feel like losers, are disoriented, need a positive future to look forward to. Old fiefdoms need to be overridden by a common cause that encourage cooperation with other groups. To make a new vision work, however, top managers must be willing to make some positive investments and to provide a real basis for hope. This was the crucial role of the digital technology investment made in this "down" period. The investment symbolized that management was looking forward, was willing to take risks, and was offering a basis for a more positive view of the future.

(2)   The $6.7 Billion Write-off: The time to take a write-off is early and completely. Once the write-off is finished, all profitability becomes incremental and is not burdened with the overheads from a previous era. Managers generally want to take "one bite from the cherry" and not nibble at it. Otherwise, write-offs continue for a long period, depressing operations and people for years.

(3)   Business Units: The formation of the business units served several purposes. First, they gave power to market, rather than regional, units. They provided a basis for training managers in profit-oriented operations. They provided a basis for driving down responsibility from the centralized top of AT&T. Each unit became more manageable than the whole of AT&T. It became possible to identify where real problems did and did not exist. To support this, the entire information systems structure of AT&T needed to be changed. Such changeovers tend to take 1-2 years. It was important that this process begin as early as possible. If this pushed the organization too far toward short-term profit orientation, that swing was probably necessary and desirable to change the culture.

(4)   Staff Functions: It was essential to send signals that the corporate staff would not be untouched by these changes. AT&T had built up a huge staff bureaucracy, which was very capable, but too bureaucratic for the new system. The "customer-supplier relationship" sent the proper signals to staff units. Although these actions were not initially successful, "What else should Mr. Allen have done?" raises a proper question for the students. "What do you think of the dual reporting structure of controllers?" is an excellent question to ask at this stage. Why not do the same thing with other corporate staff functions? How can one measure staff performance? The professor may note that when it is impossible to measure performance directly, "market mechanisms" like those proposed by Mr. Allen tend to be a reasonable solution.

(5)   Business Groups: Why were Business Groups necessary at all? Didn't they merely leave elements of the bureaucracy in place? What do you think of the break-out of "immediate performance" characteristics for the Business Units? Why should planning, allocation of resources, and opportunity scouting be at the Business Group level? Why shouldn't this be an activity of the Business Units? If it were left at the Business Unit level, how should it be

implemented? Shouldn't Business Group activities be subject to the same customer-supplier relationship programs as corporate staff?

(6)   Bell Laboratories: AT&T really could not deal with the Bell Laboratories issue until it had formulated the broad structure of the operating groups. First, the courts had to decide how much of Bell Laboratories would be allocated to the RBOCs and what an acceptable breakdown between the activities of BellCore and the Bell Labs might be. Secondly, in order to make Bell Labs more customer oriented, the customers (divisions) themselves had to be reorganized. What do you think of having 80% of the Labs' employees compensation paid directly by the Business Units? This creates a tighter technology market linkage. However, it undermines the basic strength of Bell Laboratories, which was its enormous cross-discipline research capabilities. The thought was that the 20% of Bell Laboratories budgets remaining at the centralized level would serve this function. Implicitly, 80% of Bell Labs was to be customer oriented. Interestingly, this was not a large shift from the earlier structure when the "Development" portion of the Bell Labs accounted for at least 80% of all expenditures, and was allocated on the basis of projects by a Research Committee which contained representatives of the regional operating units, Western Electric, and AT&T corporate staffs.

After about five years of "great turmoil" the Business Unit structure began to settle down sufficiently to move to the next stage of its development. It would have been inappropriate to benchmark the divisions against best-in-class competitors until 1991. AT&T had neither the internal data nor the appropriate competitive positioning data to make such benchmarks reasonably accurately. The more important thing in the early stage was "a learning system" where people began to respond to market needs, profit requirements, and the need for faster response. Although they apparently wanted accountability and responsibility, they had to learn to operate in this type of environment. The best-in-class benchmarking provided a second stage check on their progress. Not surprisingly, this led to an additional downsizing of about 50,000 employees. It would have been unfair and probably unwise to undertake so much downsizing until AT&T management had both the market and performance data to determine who should stay and who should leave.

Similarly, it was probably unwise to begin the softer discussions of leadership and revitalization until the "numbers" had become available to evaluate performance. The first great culture change had to be a much more numbers-oriented management style. Once that began to be in place, it was appropriate to talk more about leadership styles and teamwork. It was essential during the preceding five years to build up a tight identity with the Business Units and to let them work mostly on their own problems. One can ask, "Did it really take five years to do this? Might it have been better to begin these discussions earlier? Were the steps that Mr. Allen took at this time appropriate? Why did Allen begin with the Strategic Forum? What is the main function of such a forum? Is AT&T ready to arrive at a strategy? Or is it to bring people together, give them a chance to interact, participate, and feel an identity with a larger group?" Note, Allen brought in only the top 60 managers. In two days time, they could easily begin to recognize each other's faces, personality quirks, biases, etc. This would make later communications easier. In essence, the Forum was an awareness building experience setting the stage for further actions. A good question at this stage is, "What do you think of the AT&T mission statement appearing on page 242?" The professor can lead the discussion toward what elements make a mission statement effective. Most executives find that a single sentence or short paragraph (not two pages or so) is preferable. The mission should state: (1) What makes the company attractive to all its critical stakeholders? (2) What its unique competency will be. (3) How the company creates unique value for its customers? Is the mission statement specific enough? Why does it not contain any numbers? What would be the effects, disadvantages of being more specific? The Quinn article on incrementalism provides an excellent framework for this portion of the discussion.

Next, one can ask what is the use of a values statement like *Our Common Bond*? Why didn't Mr. Allen undertake this before the mission statement? Why wasn't this put into place in 1986 before the Business Units were formed? It might have provided an excellent framework for them. However, it might have perpetrated the earlier public utility, bureaucratic values that Allen and Olson wanted to overcome. By 1991, the new business realities and organizational structures would have begun to inculcate some desirable new values, and the survey in 1992 indicated that there was a genuine need for this type of value statement. Its primary purpose is to bring cohesion and tolerance among the groups within AT&T, without losing their increased focus on competitiveness. Ask the students, "What do you think of *Our Common Bond*?" Many will respond that it is "useless motherhood." Are such statements really meaningful? What makes them meaningful? Until management acts in congruence with the values, they will not be accepted. Generally, unless there is some reflection of the values in the performance appraisal system of the company, there will be no response. It is notable that AT&T tried to institutionalize both behaviors. First, it allowed subordinates to evaluate their "bosses." The evaluation started at the top. Mr. Allen tried to inculcate appropriate behaviors and to teach managers appropriate behaviors as *Our Common Bond* was rolled out through the organization. He participated in the "Values Deployment Program" himself and provided a role model for expected behaviors.

The Performance Evaluation System

The AT&T performance evaluation system has been widely discussed. There are many management articles which include detailed clues on its structure and utilization. Note that Allen had to start the process with a relatively simplistic measure, i.e., measured operating income (MOI). This started his managers focusing on profitability at a time when the culture handled the other values relatively well. He was trying to create a distinctive change in mindset, without destroying the old values completely. However, one can increase operating income by making enormous investments that may not be appropriate from a long-term financial viewpoint. This led to the development of AT&T's much copied EVA (Economic Value-Added) system. This system charges the divisions with a capital cost of the capital tied up in their operations. The capital costs can be varied according to different risk discounts for the different divisions or a single risk discount for the entire company. Which would be preferable? Why? What problems would you expect from each? This measure encourages managers to get rid of capital investments that are not productive in their overall portfolio.

However, as one might expect, simple financial measures quickly caused divisional managers to undercut longer-term development activities. The People Value-Added (PVA) measure was intended to offset one aspect of this. Customer Value-Added (CVA) was expected to offset another. Ask the students what they think should be measured in either category. Why? How? How does one measure increases or decreases in these characteristics from year to year? Probably the best single evaluation would reflect the market value of the division: if it were sold to a third party, if it were replicated from scratch, if it were bought on the outside, or if the market knew the true anticipated present value of cash flows. One can raise some very interesting questions as to how to make these measurements. This is an area of intense interest and opportunity for students.

The People Value-Added skills can be approached in a different fashion. How much is a person worth after certain types of training, experience, upgrading? How would you approach this in a fashion which is different from the old "Hay Point" systems, which focused on levels of formal training, responsibilities, numbers of subordinates, etc. What one really wants is "a market value of the person" year by year. How can this be accomplished? Is it necessary to put a dollar value on this set of characteristics? If not, what characteristics should be evaluated? By whom? How does one obtain objectivity in these measurements?

Customer Value-Added (CVA) is an area which has more objective measures available. Several are mentioned in the case. Many companies have found that customer surveys, product comparisons, direct measurements of service performance levels, and comparative surveys made by consulting firms offer excellent guidance as to the degree to which customers perceive value-added from the company. More important than the dollar value of value-added is the nature of why customers think that the company adds value or does not perform as required.

Note that AT&T intends to give equal weighting to EVA, PVA, and CVA. Is this wise? What would you substitute? How can the company overcome the bias to use financial measures, since they appear to be more "precise" than the other measures?

1994 Challenges

At this stage, it is appropriate to begin asking what the future strategy of AT&T should be. It is probably best to break this down into domestic and international strategies. Although Allen and the MEC have stated that AT&T was to be a major player in "all aspects of the infocom business," does this give adequate direction? Is it feasible? Can AT&T in fact dominate the full range of generating, processing, storing, and transmitting all forms of information? If not, where should AT&T's focus be? What can it do to provide unique value to customers?

An extremely important issue is, given the intense competition which would force lower prices and commoditization of the information products, how could AT&T create higher value than its competitors? What should its core competencies be? What should it do at best-in-world levels? The quote on page 244 poses this issue well. To date, the infocom businesses have found it difficult to capture value at the distribution level. As overcapacity gets even greater in the "distribution system," how can AT&T protect itself from price erosion? What portion of the "distribution business" will allow it to have unique profits? If the courts allow the RBOCs to enter the "Long Lines Business," as well as Sprint and MCI, what happens to AT&T? What can it do about this? Can AT&T do anything that is unique? Mr. Allen recognizes AT&T's crown jewel to be its telecommunications network of wire, computers, fiber optics, and software. He has added to this the wireless spectrum and the cellular market. How should AT&T participate in the high margin "software" portion of the business? Should it form alliances with entertainment companies, game companies, computer software providers? If so, what should its priorities be?

AT&T's Western Electric Division has long been a superb producer of telecommunications equipment. However, margins on this equipment are dropping as more and more producers enter the marketplace, and Western Electric's monopoly on sales to the RBOCs declines. As noted, by both selling equipment to the PTTs in Europe and attempting to obtain distribution and/or alliances with these crucial distributors, AT&T is in a conflict situation. Should it continue to develop and sell equipment? If not, how can it maintain its technological edge? Is Western Electric still significant to the strategic development of AT&T? Should it be spun out? Why? Why not?

What should be the three or four major thrusts of AT&T domestically in the future? How should it organize for this purpose? Should it seek any high priority acquisitions? If so, what are the criteria for these acquisitions? Is there any preferred sequence for them? Should it enter the cable business? If so, how? How should it develop its acquisition of McCaw Cellular Communications for maximum effectiveness? From a national policy viewpoint, how should the RBOCs be separated conceptually from AT&T? Does it make sense to have all of these large, well-financed companies trying to compete for the same sector of the U.S. market? How could the government ensure adequate competition, without massive duplication? What should AT&T's posture be in national discussions? More importantly, how should AT&T restructure its major divisions around its future strategic needs? Around providing its existing services on a best possible basis to domestic customers?

International Expansion

While the domestic telecommunications market is growing at some 10%, international communications groups are growing much faster. What do you think of the way AT&T has organized to attack these marketplaces? What can it bring uniquely to them? Its initial entries were based on U.S. multinational company and world traveler needs. While this allowed AT&T to obtain knowledge about these marketplaces, what does it need in the future? It already has facilities in 120 countries. What should its role in host countries be? How should it cooperate, compete with local units? Mr. Allen has set a goal of approximately 50% for non-U.S. revenues by the year 2000. Is this realistic? How could he approach it? Does the international marketplace require a regional strategy to deal with the individual countries? If so, how can AT&T bring to bear its enormous capabilities in technology, distribution knowledge, connectivity to bear? Should the China experiment be extended? If so, where? Where not?

Mr. Allen has tried to organize worldwide around certain critical strategic thrusts. However, the case defines many of the problems of doing this. What organization form is required? What new management practices are required? How would you implement them? These are the critical questions for this section of the case. Cross-unit cooperation is, obviously, one of the most important issues facing any international company trying to provide a "local presence" or "thinking internationally, operating locally." There is no single solution to this problem. This case—along with the Andersen Consulting case—offers a marvelous vehicle for discussing these issues. AT&T has an enormous depth in technology, perhaps the best in world capability in its industry. This obviously should be the basis for its international thrust. It also has the largest "connectivity" to the U.S. market. These two core competencies should provide the basis of its international extension. It also has a very favorable financial record, allowing it to participate in large-scale projects anywhere it pleases. It probably dominates all other telecom companies in these respects.

How does one use these core competencies to roll out a number of new services, nationally, internationally? Should AT&T use these great strengths by centralizing them and then operating the rest of the enterprise on a "network-alliance basis?" Does it need to have command and control structures throughout the world? If it implements a network structure how does it change AT&T's modus operandi? How can it develop the management talent it needs to operate in this mode? Are its five existing divisions (communication services, communication products, network systems, NCR, and AT&T capital) an adequate basis for this worldwide venture? The following section specifies what AT&T has done to date.

1995 UPDATE

On September 20, 1995, AT&T announced a plan to undertake the largest voluntary breakup in business history. It split itself into three parts: a $49 billion-a-year communications services company that would continue to call itself AT&T; a $20 billion-a-year maker of communications equipment (mostly the old Western Electric Company); and an $8 billion-a-year computer company (mostly the NCR group bought by AT&T in 1991). Each company would have its own board and its own stock. AT&T shareholders would receive shares in all three. Under the plan, the historical AT&T would cease to exist on January 1, 1997. On the date of its announcement, the new AT&T would still rank #12 on the Fortune 500 list. Its chief source of revenue was its Long Distance Business, holding a 58% share of the U.S. market against Sprint and MCI. The main rationale for breaking up the company was the problem of selling equipment to the same phone companies against which AT&T as a distribution company competed. CEO, Bob Allen, felt that each division was often reluctant to act for fear it would hurt the other parts of AT&T. The old Global Information Solutions Computer Division had never done well under the AT&T umbrella and had drained cash from the other divisions.

The change was partially in response to a pending communications reform bill which would allow local phone companies to keep their existing monopolies, while allowing them to invade the long distance business. AT&T hoped to counter by moving more substantially into the local distribution business. A large portion of this would be based on its McCaw Cellular Communications acquisition, which gave it the largest presence in that business. Mr. Allen said, "I was probably as frustrated as I'd ever been trying to coordinate across our various businesses."[1] The stock market reacted very well to the announcement, immediately pushing up share prices by about 10%. The new AT&T would be headed by Alex Mandl, described as a bit "brash, flashy, and even loud." Its new businesses would include long distance, wireless, the Universal Credit Card, and a brand-new business called AT&T Solutions which sought to compete against EDS and Andersen Consulting in the information technology and systems integration field. Mandl would be supported by two very aggressive executives running the consumer and the business portions of his operations: Joseph Nacchio in Consumer, and John Petrillo in Business. After spending some $1.7 billion in PCS auctions, AT&T could provide cellular service to 80% of the potential cellular market. Wireless, long distance, and credit cards would be the main thrusts of the new AT&T. Credit cards would try to create a permanent bond with customers. The other elements would offer the world's most fully integrated telephony product offerings to consumers and business.

While handling some of the coordination problems illustrated in the case, the breakup left most other issues unresolved. Its basic strategies for attacking the world marketplace, coordinating Bell Laboratories, integrating Wireless and Long Lines, forming and managing cross-functional teams, and developing new alliances were still undefined. Mr. Allen still emphasized the independence and profit orientation of the Business Units, with the caveat "make sure you contribute to the success of the core telecommunications network." How this balance was to be achieved was an open question. AT&T's Universal Card had made AT&T into the second largest credit issuer in the United States (after Citicorp). Yet earlier, Mr. Allen had said that he would not convert this division into a full financial services unit. Mr. Allen was still emphasizing his goals of greater nimbleness, "leadership wearing two hats," and a 50% international presence. He wanted AT&T to promote continual communication for customers and within itself. To promote this, the MEC members' bonuses were based on roughly equal proportions for the performance of their group and for AT&T as a whole. Interestingly, AT&T had lost a powerful element of horizontal integration, when it split off its hardware divisions. The standards set for and by the hardware forced integration across the entire business. No substitute for this was yet evident. Meanwhile, the Bell Laboratories (spending $3.5 billion annually) had been more integrated toward the operating divisions. Eighty percent of its employees reported to the Business Units, which paid their salaries. But a similar lateral orientation among operations had not yet been achieved. Both integration and internationalization would be demanded if Allen was to meet his goal of a 10% annual earnings growth for the rest of the decade. In its 1994 Annual Report, it emphasized that "with 5% of a $1.5 trillion global information industry, AT&T is a small fish with lots of room to grow."

AT&T's 1994 earnings per share were $3.01, margins were 41%, and gross revenue growth was $5.7 billion. AT&T's revenue growth alone exceeded the annual revenues of 80% of the companies on the 1994 Fortune 500 listing. AT&T had won the prestigious Baldridge Award for quality for the third time, a feat not accomplished by any other company. It had added more trans-Atlantic telecommunications circuits in the past three years than in all its previous history. One of AT&T's major problems and opportunities was the expansion of Internet which now connected some 25 million people worldwide. In a startling pattern of growth, one out of every ten AT&T people was engaged in software development, indicating the nature of the new AT&T. The company noted that "There may not be cable companies or phone companies or computer companies, as such [in the future]. There will be information conduits, information providers, information appliances, and information consumers." AT&T seemed to be positioning itself clearly in the conduit marketplace. Was this a proper strategy? In its 1994 Annual Report, AT&T defined its role in the rapidly expanding marketplace as follows:

Infrastructure Equipment and Systems ($150 billion—9% growth): AT&T's role included hardware, software, and systems integration supporting global networking of voice, data, and video. This includes micro electronics, switching, transmission, wireless, satellite, and operating systems; massively parallel and scaleable computing; database management; fiber optics and applications software.

Communication Services ($750 billion—7% growth): AT&T's role here included traditional and emerging voice, data, and video communications services. It encompassed U.S. and international long distance; mobile, air-to-ground, paging, messaging, voice processing, language interpretation, and interactive voice, data, and video services; electronic mail and electronic data interchange.

Products and Systems ($400 billion—7% growth): AT&T designed, manufactured, and serviced communications, computing, and other equipment for consumers and businesses worldwide. It included corded, cordless, and cellular communications devices; multimedia personal computers; desktop videoconferencing systems; answering, audio processing, and messaging equipment; modems; and retail, financial, and other business systems.

Integrated Solutions ($100 billion—12% growth): AT&T provided systems integration, network management, transaction-management and other end-to-end solutions and professional services that bring together the benefits of numerous technologies for customers so that they can concentrate on their businesses.

Content/Content Handling ($50 billion—12% growth): AT&T was involved in the development and management of interface systems and software that help people navigate a wide variety of information and entertainment choices from content providers.

AT&T's 1994 Annual Report also noted that revenues from operations outside the United States grew at more than 31% in 1994. AT&T now has more than 50,000 employees outside the United States. It seemed well placed to exploit the much-discussed opportunities of the new information marketplace.

CORPORATE RENEWAL

In a paper (co-authored with Chris Bartlett of HBS) entitled, "Rebuilding Behavioral Context: A Blueprint for Corporate Renewal," Professor Ghoshal puts the changes at AT&T in a new perspective. He describes how the Economic Value-Added systems became the basis of an organization-wide consensus on and commitment to the standards of performance required to move AT&T into its new competitive operating environment. And how in order to provide substance to the norms of empowerment and to validate the redeployment of assets and resources, senior managers had to step back from their historic role as the organization's chief planners and controller, and redefine their core responsibilities in more support terms. . . . they needed to provide more coaching and guidance. . . .The People Value-Added measure was designed to help spread this management model.

He continues by writing, "For most companies, the initial tightening of ongoing operating performance is only the first stage of a long transformation process towards becoming a self-renewing organization. For while this rationalization phase can improve the productivity of a company's resources, some very different efforts and abilities are required to restart its growth engine. At AT&T, for example, while the fragmentation of the organization into disciplined business units allowed the company to reduce waste and cut expense, it also led to the creation of 21 highly autonomous units run by what one manager described as 'a bunch of independent SBU cowboys.' Yet, to grow—whether by expansion into the dynamic new infocom business growing at the intersection of the computer, communications, consumer electronics, and entertainment industries, or by exploiting the fabulous potential of the emerging Chinese market—the 21 entities would have to operate as one AT&T. . . . Between 1993 and 1995, AT&T struggled to tun around the momentum of its highly successful rationalization process by creating the integrating mechanisms necessary for the revitalization phase [including a new regional management structure, cross-business unit project teams, *Our Common Bond*, etc.]. . . . Yet, after two years of effort, the company was finally forced to abandon this effort and to break up the company into three separate entities, demonstrating the enormous difficulties of managing the transition from the rationalization to the revitalization phase."

NINTENDO CO., LTD. TEACHING NOTE

Overview

The Nintendo Company Limited (NCL) case provides a superb base for discussing hypercompetition, managing intellect, and the emergence of software as a dominating form of competitive strategy. Because Nintendo is a Japanese company, it allows an opportunity to challenge some of the stereotypes about the Japanese management style. It is an excellent vehicle for discussing strategic outsourcing and the controls that are essential to make such outsourcing effective. Nintendo must both manage its own software internally and the development of software externally. This allows a focus on two of the most interesting strategic issues facing management today, i.e., how to attract and manage intellect internally and externally. Nintendo's unique strategic position established the format of the computer games industry and allowed Nintendo to become the most profitable company in Japan. It started subsidiary industries in both semiconductors and software. Nintendo created more millionaires than any other company in Japan's history. Nintendo and its actions forced responses by companies as diverse as Apple Computer, Atari, Intel, and movie producers. In a short time its Mario Brothers characters became better known than Mickey Mouse, as Nintendo revolutionized the entertainment field. The dynamic interplay of the forces surrounding Nintendo make for a fascinating discussion of the cross-competition among industries and whether and when the concept of industry analysis makes sense anymore. The case traces Nintendo through its start-up phase to the point where it became perceived as a genuine threat to the American electronics and entertainment industries—and indeed family values. A number of social values issues surround the case . Embedded in the case is a fascinating second case (the start-up of 3DO). This is an entrepreneurial positioning case asking the questions, "How would you position a new company entering in competition with an established power like Nintendo? How should Nintendo respond?" The case has many unique entrepreneurial and management features.

Session Structure

The case lends itself well to a three-phase approach. First, we usually open by asking the students to evaluate Nintendo's past strategy. Why could Nintendo make such high profits? What were the critical factors in managing for success in this industry? Who are Nintendo's competitors? How do these fit the model of hypercompetition? What do strategies in a hypercompetitive environment look like? Second, we focus on the NTG/3DO entry. This allows a very interesting discussion of how 3DO should position itself, what its core competencies are, how it can have a best-in-world continuing presence? 3DO was one of the most successful initial public offerings (IPOs) of the early 1990s. How could one evaluate 3DO? What should Nintendo's response be to 3DO? Third, now that Nintendo is attracting major competition from other game companies, the computer companies, and the entertainment industry, how should it change its strategy for the future? How can it maintain a distinctive competitive edge? Can others copy its strategy with success? How can Nintendo reposition to outmaneuver its new competitors? What issues does Nintendo face in the emerging markets of the world? Where should it go in the future? How can one create a competitive edge when intellect is the primary asset that a company must control to be successful?

Nintendo's Past Strategy

Why could Nintendo make such high profits? What were the critical factors for success in this industry's early years? It is helpful to ask the students to evaluate Nintendo's past

Teaching note copyright ©1996 by James Brian Quinn. This note was prepared by Professor Quinn and Professor Phil Anderson.

strategy. The key question is, "Why were Nintendo's actions successful? What criteria would you use in evaluating success?" Many others undoubtedly tried the same general strategy, but did not succeed. What differentiates Nintendo's strategy? Since Nintendo is developing a new primary market, a Porter-style five forces analysis is not very instructive. Other more useful strategic criteria are as follows:

1. <u>Vision</u>: Mr. Yamauchi provided a clear continuing vision that there would be a "games market in the new electronic world." Even though his first endeavors were not successful, the consistency of this vision, its breadth, and its attractiveness provided coherence for the strategy.

2. <u>Values</u>: Mr. Yamauchi set standards for high performance, high imagination, family-based values, and whimsy that gave Nintendo its early and continuing attractiveness. These values attracted people to design for the company.

3. <u>Clear Limits</u>: Mr. Yamauchi set consistent policies to maintain quality, to control critical aspects of the operation, to reject items not up to standard, to make all licensee contracts equal, etc. These rules provided the consistency and trust in the organization which built alliances and corporate value over time.

4. <u>Use of Strengths</u>: From the beginning, Nintendo used its enormous strengths of name recognition and distribution in Japan. Its distribution capabilities were core to its leverage, as was Yamauchi's knowledge of the distribution channels. This provided the <u>quid pro quo</u> for obtaining new software from licensees.

5. <u>Concentration</u>: After a few misfires, Yamauchi concentrated his resources on electronic games, eschewing other potential spin-offs. He concentrated internal resources on the skills of Yokoi and Miyamoto and external resources on building and maintaining the most powerful distribution channels in Japan and then North America. Because of its distribution power, Nintendo was able to acquire low cost units and create new operating synergies.

6. <u>Full Logistics</u>: Mr. Yamauchi developed logistics controls over the entire value chain from concept to marketplace. At crucial junctures, this allowed him both to leverage the company's resources significantly and to build its resource base by outsourcing substantially.

7. <u>Organization</u>: The organization was highly centralized around a few critical personal skill sets: Yamauchi's capacity to choose games, Yokoi's creativity and capacity to attract creative talent, and Mr. Miyamoto's remarkable capacities to manage all elements of creative game design. Unlike most creative organizations, Nintendo was highly centralized internally in its early stages. Yet Yamauchi was wise enough to allow his R&D people special status and much freedom. What particular policies made his combination "loose-tight" style work effectively? Through the limits set in its contracting relationships, and its strong distribution potentials, NCL was able to outsource software creation extensively.

8. <u>Coalitions</u>: In its outsourcing, Nintendo created strong alliances with software producers. It gave them access to the marketplace and high personal returns. As its brand name developed, it gave preferences for high-demand products to those who offered strongest distribution potentials. It built the potential for future coalitions through the "network capability" built into Nintendo machines.

9. <u>Communications</u>: Nintendo concentrated on communications with its customers through its *Nintendo Power Magazine* and extensive answering services, the first and still the most extensive in the industry. This decreased customer frustration, increased identity, and leveraged the new products of the company enormously.

10. <u>Motivation</u>: Through its licensing policies, Nintendo created more millionaires than any other Japanese company. This allowed it to tap into a much larger intellectual resource base than any competitor. Creating such private wealth for new companies and entrepreneurs was not common in Japan at the time.

11. <u>Planned Flexibility</u>: Through its strategic outsourcing, Nintendo was able to leverage its capital and intellectual resources enormously while decreasing its own risks. Its licensees had to pay Nintendo to produce their software, further decreasing Nintendo's risks and investments. By utilizing software outsourcing, Nintendo could keep flexible touch with the infinite number of changing possibilities in its industry. In addition, it did not stick to any single form of game: i.e., shooting, legend, or interactive. It could opportunistically attack whatever marketplaces seemed to be opening. And Mr. Yamauchi's style made fast decisions possible.

12. <u>Selecting Key People</u>: By careful selection and control over his key people, Yamauchi could determine the direction, style, and flexibility of the company. In any creative enterprise, the creative managers are the crucial elements in success. Despite his centrist style, Yamauchi appeared willing to decentralize the actual creative processes to both his trusted key people internally and to outsourced software vendors.

13. <u>Multiple Approaches</u>: In an unknowable marketplace, it is essential to have multiple approaches and to allow the customer to make selections. By having numerous (well controlled) software offerings available, Nintendo could build on its brand concentration and distribute its risks.

14. <u>Attack Weakness</u>: Nintendo attacked the weakness of existing games through much improved graphics, more sophistication in game content, and consistency in its offerings. Through its technological capabilities, Nintendo was able to jump over the limitations of earlier game programs and provide its product at lowest cost.

15. <u>Time Horizon</u>: Note that it took 8 years before Nintendo really began to build a worldwide presence. Donkey Kong was the product that provided this presence in the United States. Although relatively profitable in its early years, Nintendo continued to be willing to invest in new risky game creations and wider worldwide distribution throughout this long period.

16. <u>Reuse Resources</u>: Once Nintendo had established a concept, it reused it for future offerings. This was true of the "legend games," Donkey Kong characters, the Mario Brothers, etc. Such reuse decreased the investment of both Nintendo and its users.

Because of the interactions between software, chip technologies, computer technologies, television, and other games, the marketplace or industry for Nintendo is virtually impossible to define. New players will appear constantly. Consequently, the conditions of "hypercompetition" apply. Constant flexibility, reserved resources, coalitions, counter punching, concealment, and other elements of guerrilla warfare strategies make much sense. The case ties in well with Bruce Henderson's articles on "Competitive Maneuvering" and Richard D'Aveni's writings on "Hypercompetition." The key to strategy in these situations is concentrating one's own resources on a few core competencies until a clear dominance is achieved—then utilizing this core competency as a strategic base from which to sortie out and to punish others who attempt to encroach, as well as a basis for negotiation and expansion into new territories. An interesting question is, "What are the crucial dimensions of strategy in the world's new cross-competitive, hypercompetitive, marketplaces? How do these differ from the old structural guidelines provided by classical industry analysis?"

The NTG-3DO Strategy

How should NTG develop its position? What should NTG's core competency be? Should it try to finance its growth alone? Should it use venture capitalists? A series of coalitions? A large public offering? If it takes the latter, what steps are essential before it should make the offering? What is the critical timing parameter for such entry?

In many respects, NTG was trying to do exactly what Nintendo successfully accomplished in its early stages. It concentrated on a true "step function" advance in the hardware technologies—which when combined with superior software would allow faster response times, picture quality graphics, and totally new game perspectives (such as zoom effects). Once these hardware capabilities were developed and demonstrated by NTG on a technical basis, its primary problems became attracting software developers to use the NTG system, acquiring sufficient capital to achieve major distribution, and preemptive timing in introducing its new system. All of these argued for an early coalition strategy with a major successful graphics and entertainment partner, open access for game software designers interested in new effects, holding key elements secret or obtaining such strong proprietary protection that these features could not be replicated by others, and controlling the concept development carefully by using an outstandingly talented, small, self-integrated team. This is what David Morse tried to do with NTG. Later, the coalition with Electronic Arts provided the entertainment software connection which was essential before further expansion. At this stage, a pros and cons analysis of the differing partnership and financial possibilities makes for an extremely useful discussion.

The NTG Strategy *

The NTG section of this case provides, among other things, a discussion module on leveraging the competencies of other firms. One can use this to introduce the question of when to make, buy, or partner. The discussion questions are:

1. What are NTG's core competencies? What other core competencies would NTG or some combination/partnership it joins need to have to challenge Nintendo successfully?

2. Clearly in this industry software drives hardware sales. Does NTG need to match Nintendo's in-house software development capability? What would you do to ensure that the new machine has available the compelling software that gives game-players a reason for buying it?

3. What should Morse do?

   a) Raise more venture money and proceed with development?
   b) Accept the Medio partnership proposal?
   c) Search out some other partner?
   d) Form a consortium?
   e) Sell out to some other firm and exit the business?

Discussion of the first question can begin with a competitive analysis of the video game industry highlighting where Nintendo is vulnerable to attack. It becomes clear that there is an opportunity to establish a web of relationships with suppliers and channels disaffected by Nintendo's policies. It also becomes clear that NTG needs to get to market quickly with a technically superior product that will take far more capital to develop than NTG has.

---

*This section of the teaching note was written by Professor Philip Anderson, of Dartmouth's Amos Tuck School, who developed the case on which the NTG-3DO sections of the case are based.

The second question initiates an interesting discussion of the way complementary technologies fit together into systems. The students usually conclude that NTG does not have competencies in software development, and they come up with a variety of incentives to attract third parties that can develop software for the new system. This provides a nice platform for discussing alternatives to vertical integration in hardware/software systems. The difference between NTG and Nintendo is that there now exists a solid base of software providers, which Nintendo did not have at its inception. Nintendo couldn't sell systems unless it developed a best-in-world game programming capability; NTG does not face the same constraint.

Student opinion is usually split fairly evenly over whether Morse and Hart should continue development with more venture capital or seek a partner. Few suggest exiting the business at this point. As it turns out, Morse and Hart formed Medio with a nondilutable 25% stake. This move made them tens of millions of dollars. The competencies Trip Hawkins brought to the table were: (a) a gift for publicizing the system and gaining momentum for it, critical in network technologies; (b) connections and relationships that allowed him to attract partners such as Matsushita and Time Warner. Medio briefly became a partnership called San Mateo Software Group, which was renamed 3DO when the firm was taken public. The IPO was hugely successful, and in fall 1993, Trip Hawkins was the person *Time* magazine put on its cover for a story about the coming multimedia revolution. One reason why the IPO was so successful is that Hawkins positioned the 3DO system as a video game machine which could also be the heart of a set-top box for a "500 channel" broadband multimedia environment. In fact, 3DO did land a contract to develop set-top boxes for US West.

The third question explores a subtle point that usually gives the students an "a-ha" experience. Morse withdrew from day-to-day management of Medio (though his partners were key to building the machine). He founded a new company called Crystal Dynamics, which became the premier software developer for the 3DO system. Crystal Dynamics gained a high profile by hiring Strauss Zelnick, the head of Fox Motion Pictures, as CEO, and within 18 months of its founding, it was conservatively valued at $50 million. Morse recognized that his core competence is starting companies and "filling in the black boxes." Trip Hawkins was the perfect person to get strong allies and lots of publicity, putting a great deal of momentum behind 3DO. Morse profited hugely from the IPO, yet was able to create an entirely new revenue stream by focusing on what he does best instead of trying to turn NTG into a Fortune 500 company. The answer to question 2 turned out to be that software could create more value than hardware, but the vehicle for creating that value was a company separate from NTG that drew upon Morse's distinctive skill, his ability to get a focused company off the ground and attract the best people in the world for its specific domain.

The 1993 Situation

Now that Nintendo has attracted major competition from game companies, computer companies, and the entertainment industry, how should it change its strategy for the future? Although Mr. Yamauchi tends to discount the "hardware" producers, one should be reminded that his own early success was dictated by Nintendo's capacity to "jump the J-curve" in technology. How should it meet the threats of new hardware providers? PC-based games? Interactive network games? The strategy might well be broken down into several elements.

Technology: Should Yamauchi give up the protected, semiconductor-based, machine designs that have made it so successful? Could it adequately protect CD-ROMs from piracy? Can it now hope to keep ahead of all of the hardware innovators worldwide, especially since Sony seems to be targeting this marketplace? Should it discourage entry by regarding and pricing its hardware as the "razor" portion of the business and essentially give its machines away at cost? This would help to discourage new entries but might not affect SEGA, which has a large installed base. Must Nintendo somehow stay at the cutting edge of hardware graphics technologies? If so, how? In fact, how does it develop a competitive edge? Is it important that earlier machines and software are not compatible with later entries?

Software: What special strategies can Nintendo use to lure software producers away from SEGA and the improved graphics technologies of 3DO? What special support can or must Nintendo acquire to somehow stay abreast of the cutting edge of hardware-graphics technologies? How can it do this? What can it give to software producers to offset the hardware capabilities of competitors? Is Yamauchi correct that only 20-30 software producers are worthwhile? How can it effectively tap into the new worldwide sources of games? Should this be coordinated from Japan or decentralized worldwide? What can Nintendo do to discourage the pirating of its software? Will the PC platform become the only really important platform for games? If so, how can Nintendo develop a competitive edge?

Do new networking potentials, with the Famicom and with PCs, make this into a major new marketplace for Nintendo? Are there any peculiarities, opportunities, or threats this new competitive mode poses? How should Nintendo exploit this trend? How can Nintendo have a quality edge if the PC becomes the dominating platform for all games? How can one manage game creation internally for maximum advantage? Externally? What kinds of guidance should Yamauchi give game designers? Should Nintendo have a "family of concepts" which distinguish it from other producers? Should it continue to avoid excessively violent, pornographic, etc. game creations? How would you describe Nintendo's software "special competency?" How can this be further extended? Defended?

Diversification/Alliance Potentials: Should Nintendo begin to look toward some new alliances? If so, with whom? Could it join Sony to advantage in a major hardware-software coalition? What would be the advantages? Disadvantages? Should it perhaps join with Disney to fill its own amusement park and "on-line" gaps? How should it position relative to the competitors listed in Exhibit 6? Should Nintendo form a strategic alliance with some outstanding entertainment software technology group (like Silicon Graphics or Dreamworks)? An excellent way to enter this discussion is to ask the question, "What should Nintendo's distinctive competency in the future be?" Since the games marketplace is changing so rapidly, the students will tend to second-guess based upon recent events. This is a good point to ask why or why not questions. Clearly, new options will open constantly for new game formats. Is it possible to have a distinctive competency when the entire production unit is essentially ephemeral human intellect?

Antitrust and Social Issues: What should Nintendo do about the types of social issues expressed near the end of the case, which are very popular with the American press? Can it remain clear of these accusations if it screens its games properly? Will it have to give up too much potential if it does not produce graphic violence like *Mortal Kombat*? Have people's tastes changed so much that Yamauchi's values are no longer realistic? Who should be the final interpreter of these values for Nintendo? Can Yamauchi transfer this to another level of management?

Do Nintendo's practices in restricting competitor's access to magazines, distribution, and its own equipment represent violations of the antitrust code? If so, what should Nintendo do about them? Are there other ways in which Nintendo can create barriers to entry that do not encounter antitrust problems? For example, can it excel in communication-response capabilities for its customers? Highly sophisticated adaptations of games for particular marketplaces: by age, demographic, ethnic, geographical, etc. preferences? What should it do about the internationalization of the games business? How can it handle the need for many different languages? What should Nintendo's goals be in this new marketplace? If you were to write a 1993 mission statement for Nintendo, what would it look like?

Overview

The magnetic levitation train is one of the most startling potential major innovations of the Twenty-first Century. As automobiles jam highways and airways become too crowded for safety in highly populated areas, magnetic trains allow an opportunity to literally "fly" at 350 miles/hour between city centers with very little fuel or pollution cost. The technologies exist for such transportation, and the case describes both their development and current state-of-the-art. Magnetic levitation trains have operated on an experimental basis in Japan for some years, and a large-scale operating test track is under consideration. The case raises some very interesting issues concerning the limitations of markets in their capacity to optimize investment, innovation, or economic growth. Although requiring public investment, the levitation train, if successful, would itself be a major product for the Japanese to export. Its subsidiary technologies—notably superconducting magnets—could provide a national competitive edge in other areas.

The maglev train can decrease social costs enormously both in terms of pollution and time expenditure. From the nation's viewpoint, it would help decrease importation of fossil fuels, and hence improve balance of payments. As numerous areas of Japan and the United States become overpopulated, the magnetic levitation train appears to be more and more economical in cost terms relative to other alternatives: automobiles, short hop aircraft, and other very fast trains running on rails. The Japanese appear willing to use public mass transportation. But in the United States both individual consumers and producers externalize their costs—i.e., pollution, deaths, injuries, and balance of payments problems for oil imports—onto the public at large. Analyzing the alternatives available in terms of total social costs, government's proper role in the economy, and how its actions affect competitiveness poses some interesting challenges. The case raises basic questions as to whether investments in "public markets"—such as the government's aircraft, communications, computer, software, canal, railroad, electrical distribution, road, and public health investments of the past—may not yield higher social and competitive payoffs than unfettered private markets that develop trinkets, fashion goods, and entertainment for individuals. The decision is complex and real.

Session Structure

Since this case intends to jar some of the preconceptions students may have, it is best to open with the question, "What are the payoffs from having an effective high speed transportation system for intensely populated areas?" This leads to a more realistic evaluation of payoffs at both the personal and national level. Successful high speed train systems decrease the travel times of people, increase transportation reliability, lower fuel costs and imports, decrease pollution, increase safety, lower production costs for manufacturing, and provide jobs in an urban setting. If successful, Maglev's operating cost is demonstrably cheaper than investing in new superhighways, fast trains, or airlines for transportation in highly populated regions. If one looks at the marginal costs of <u>increasing</u> capacity in other modes, the payoffs are enormous. Yet no one company or consortium can create a market for Maglev. An interesting question is, do such "public markets" (like dams, hospitals, road structures) create any lesser opportunities for profit, capital investment, jobs, Keynesian multipliers, and technological multipliers than do private markets? If a nation had $5 billion to invest, would it be better to invest in Nintendo-like computer games or in Maglev type transportation systems? Why? Finally, there are two decision questions: (a) should the Japanese continue their development of the Maglev? (b) what should the U.S. position be? Again, it is helpful to note that the present U.S. dominance in aircraft, computers, pharmaceuticals, energy, telecommunications, software, semiconductors, electrical equipment, large-scale engineering design, etc., were all induced by major government market creation. The case provides an excellent basis for showing that what look like externalities from a company or individual consumer viewpoint are genuine gains or losses from a national viewpoint, affecting the wealth potentials and competitiveness of all industries.

This case allows analysis at several different levels: (1) the national level, (2) the corporate level, (3) the international competitiveness level. And finally, (4) why would one want to pursue maglev technology vs. other technologies? It helps for the discussion to clarify the national level payoffs early. Students are quite interested in the technology. The problem is to get them to understand the possible economic implications as an opportunity, then to try to see how to exploit it in the national and corporate interest.

Why Japan?

The first question should normally be why should Japan support the development of the maglev train? Japan is a highly urbanized, very densely populated country with short distances between its major cities. In Japan, traveling from central cities to airports, between airports, and back to center cities takes far longer than traveling by rail between central cities. This same situation is rapidly developing in the densely populated belts of the United States—the Northeast Corridor from Washington to Boston; the California Corridor, San Diego to San Francisco; the Florida Belt; and the Midwest Great Lakes Belt. In Japan, however, limitations will be felt earlier than elsewhere. These include the following:

1. Japan's population density is so great that expanding travel by air is not a serious option.

2. Construction of new infrastructures for Shinkansen "bullet trains" or highways will be extremely costly.

3. Shinkansens are rapidly approaching their maximum speed limits (set by the buildup of an air layer between wheels and rail, and the extreme vibration of very fast motion).

4. One can expand capacity on existing tracks only by going faster. Land costs are too high to condemn more land for rails or airports.

5. Population density is likely to increase.

6. Japan leads in the maglev technology and can export it.

7. Maglev will drive important new technologies (like high density magnets and superconductivity) which could open new industries.

8. Maglev maintenance costs are 20-30% below those of Shinkansens.

9. Maglevs will use considerably less energy than air, autos, or Shinkansens.

10. Japan must import all of its energy sources.

11. Japan has a large installed base of nuclear power, making electricity the optimum fuel for public transport.

12. Maglevs produce less air pollution and noise pollution than any other transport mode. This is important in densely populated Japan, where weather "inversions" are common, causing serious amounts of respiratory disease.

Japan is the second largest user of energy in the world. Its energy use per unit of population is as high as the United States. Japan must import all its energy. If it can avoid spending its money to import energy, it can use the same funds to improve the skills and infrastructures of Japan, capturing the capital value of the energy use. Japan's pollution problems are so great that health and agricultural difficulties are very real. As Japan's wages rise, time saved in travel becomes a major competitive advantage, lowering costs for companies throughout Japan. Japan is intensely interested in exports to Southeast Asia and helping those countries develop their infrastructures. Many of the Southeast Asian countries are also densely populated with people packed in cities close together. Maglev could be a natural export for Japan. Japan lacks the military-defense expenditures which can drive high technology in other areas. Maglev offers some unique opportunities in this regard.

Why National Support?

Virtually all the arguments posed for Japan apply equally well to the heavy traffic corridors of the United States. As opposed to autos or planes, maglevs and very fast trains (TGVs or Shinkansens) are clearly <u>cost</u> effective in operating terms for travel of 300 miles or less. When one includes externalities like pollution or time saved, the <u>costs</u> are even less. However, unless governments purchase or support such transportation infrastructures, there will be no market. Consequently, no private company can afford to undertake the enormous costs and risks of developing such a system. Disregarding (for the moment) the question of whether maglev or TGV is the preferred mass transit technology, how might one justify the expenditure on a fast train option from the national viewpoint? What data does one look at for this kind of decision from a national viewpoint? If one had complete data on all transportation forms, what portion occurred at the 300 mile or less interval, what percentage of total energy went into this sector of the marketplace, and the actual times saved by center-city-to-center-city transport rather than going to airports, one could make an accurate calculation. However, with the data in the case, one can demonstrate quickly why an investment in maglev makes sense for Japan. Using the Osaka-Tokyo run, one can make the following observations:

Miles Osaka-Tokyo	300
People per hour transported	10,000
Hours per year of use (12 hours/day)	4,380
Hours saved per trip vs. Shinkansen or air	2
Hourly wage (or time value equivalent)	$20
$ billions saved per year	$1.75
Investment ($ billions) in 300 mile system	$7.4
Return on investment	23.6%
Breakeven at government bond interest of 7%	2966/hr. (or less than 1 year)

Obviously, one could question any single assumption, but the magnitudes are right. However, several observations are worthwhile. Note the $7.4 billion investment is not incremental. If expansion is necessary and TGV or highway costs are at least as high (as they are in Japan), the net marginal investment for maglev is actually zero. Hence the actual return on investment for Japan would be infinite: i.e., the gains would be achieved with no marginal investment.

The same marginal argument applies in the United States. If the United States has to invest in either more highways or railroads to carry heavy traffic in highly urbanized areas, the net investment in maglev would be minimal. For example, the "44-lane highway" Senator Moynihan described for Miami to Ft. Lauderdale would cost $440 million per mile. Such costs obviously overwhelm the costs of public transportation, both TGV and maglev. In the United States, the relevant figure for a marginal investment in maglev vs. TGV or an urban highway would be $6.5 million per mile. For a 300-mile system, this would be $495 million. At a $20 per hour saving, this would require only 250 million passenger total use. Since aircraft now carry about 50,000 people per day in these major corridors, the savings would be 100,000 hours or $2 million of wages per day. The payback time would be approximately 250 days on this marginal investment for the Boston-New York to Chicago routes or the Los Angeles-San Francisco routes. Consequently, it is not difficult to make a reasonable economic case that: "If more transportation infrastructures are needed in a highly dense population area, maglev could pay for itself on savings vs. the other transport systems." One can further argue that maglev could be introduced incrementally: i.e., each area could find that maglev pays for itself incrementally. As the experience curve develops, costs would be lower. To the above, one should add the following economic benefits for a $7.4 billion maglev project:

(a) Lower actual costs of operation (i.e., 1/3 to 1/7 the cost of air or highway transportation).

(b) Fewer highway deaths and injuries.

(c) Decreased pollution costs.

(d) Energy savings of 2/3 x the barrels of oil used for other transit modes x $20 per barrel.

   Note: in using the energy exhibits, there are 5.8 million BYUs per barrel of oil.

(e) New jobs created by the maglev and its supporting industries (150,000 person years of wages).

(f) Increased taxes (or decreased investment costs) from maglev industries ($18 billion x 20%) = $3.6 billion per year.

The sum of these economic gains is formidable. One can even question the applicability of the full investment cost—since the projects will require labor in urban areas to build the infrastructures. If one could employ "currently unemployed" people on these projects, the marginal costs of their employment would decrease total investments by as much as two-thirds and the country would have an asset worth billions of dollars in addition to having employed people and taught them skills. It is important to note that projects of this sort (dams, waterways, canals, airports, roads, etc.) have traditionally been used to decrease unemployment. The interesting tradeoff is that instead of merely giving money to people who are able to work, the society would receive in return an asset at least equal to the value of the cost it has incurred. One could argue that (again) the marginal costs of such investments are practically zero. If one adds the actual payback potentials of the system and the high probability of creating some new major export industries (as Japan plans), the costs of investment in this technology and its development quickly disappear. The returns on this kind of investment are significantly obscured by the way we keep books on national accounts. The fact that autos appear to be beneficial is largely an artifact of not charging the industry with the full cost of its operations, i.e. roads, pollution, congestion, traffic injuries, deaths, the balance of payments problems due to oil imports, and so on. The structure of transportation in the United States depends largely on whom the government chooses to subsidize and how. All of this can create a very interesting discussion—and probably an argument or two—on the validity of such public investments as a strategy.

There is a common mythology that the government cannot create wealth, and therefore the concepts of strategy—except loss minimization—do not apply. At this point, it would be worthwhile for the professor to note that most of the major export industries in the United States—

including those in which it is now most competitive—have been created by a substantial infusion of government capital. These include a variety of industries in which the United States has a dominating world position, such as: aircraft, nuclear power, computers, semiconductors, software, telecommunications, agriculture, biotechnology, pharmaceuticals, aerospace, health care products, advance materials, environmental systems, and even automobiles. Students tend to forget that the United States' success in automobiles, electric power equipment, electric appliances, and a variety of other products was strongly supported by government investments in roads, dam systems, power distribution systems, etc. Maglev is just another example of an area where government investments could help create large new industries. But the probability and exact size of these industries is not calculable in specific terms. Similarly, no one could have forecast the explosion of industries stimulated by government support of biological research, energy development, computers and software. The returns from these industries dwarf the amounts of government support that helped create them. As populations become more dense throughout the United States, land costs will increase, any investments in infrastructures will become more expensive, and the cost of inadequate transportation systems in terms of lost productivity will increase enormously. Such events affect the real wealth of people in the United States and the productivity of individual companies.

The United States Situation

The above analysis for Osaka to Tokyo could be replicated for each of the dense population areas of the United States. However, the problem is not so much justifying the maglev in economic terms as justifying it against a dogma that assumes that only private companies and free markets create value. However, there are many circumstances in which market imperfections are so great that government intervention is required to optimize investment patterns. The clearest example is in the environmental area where private companies could continue to benefit by polluting their environments. In essence, the nation, and private individuals, had to absorb these costs which the companies considered externalities. However, what is an externality to a company is a genuine cost to the society. The same is true when people choose to drive automobiles, causing large health, accident, and roadway infrastructure costs which get externalized onto other parties. Innovation forgone is also a cost of market imperfections. Clearly, without the government's support, many medical technologies would not be available, nor would aircraft, computers, etc. The alternative cost of non-investment in these advanced technologies is the loss of these entire industries—or at a minimum the industries being dominated by other countries. The benefits of one successful industry (supported by government) such as aircraft, computers, or communications so far outweighs the government's net initial investment in these industries as to be ludicrous. From a private industry standpoint, the government's investment in education, transportation, and communication infrastructures lowers costs and increases value for the entire society. The result is greater efficiency and competitiveness for private companies—and consequently higher profits. The big problem is how to analyze and deploy such expenditures on a reasonable basis. This may be the largest issue in the strategy field today and needs to be approached analytically.

Unfortunately, the U.S. structures for political support and taxation have made a rational allocation of resources by government more difficult. Each specialized polity has access to and the capacity to influence many power players. They can substantially distort economic decisions for the country, while optimizing their own private gains. This type of distortion has become a major cost for the United States. It has especially affected the nation's capacity to invest in areas in which history proves government to be effective, i.e., (1) fields with time horizons longer than corporate time horizons, (2) early stage-lower probability scientific studies, (3) large-scale, high-risk projects beyond the capacity of individual companies, (4) systems requiring coordination for standards or mass market development, (5) markets in which the government is the sole possible purchaser (i.e., space, weapons, bridges, tunnels, water supplies, etc.), (6) systems requiring international cooperation (such as pollution control, space use, health cooperation, anti-terrorism, law enforcement, etc.), (7) systems requiring reliable enforcement of rules to achieve safety and equity, such as pure foods, contract enforcement, fair labor practices, intellectual property, etc., rules.

As world competition becomes more complex, foreign governments increasingly take a role in supporting their own country's industries. Japan has used such capabilities to great advantage for the last several decades and is now exporting its techniques to Southeast Asia. Since U.S. companies will increasingly have to compete against government-supported coalitions throughout the world, students and executives need to understand better the interaction between government and industry in creating new markets (like maglev). U.S. companies and their government have often joined together to economic advantage in the past. Some very interesting discussions can be undertaken on where and how this kind of cooperation increases economic opportunities and wealth. This requires some assessment of the committee structures of Congress, the access of private lobbying groups, the use of private monies in elections, and genuinely increased amounts of information to the public on the alternatives available. One should focus on whether and how a genuine strategy is needed, how it could be created, and what its form might be. The maglev project can provide an excellent vehicle for this discussion.

Maglev vs. TGV vs. Conventional Transportation

At this stage, it is probably unwise to either go whole hog on maglev or to choose a single maglev technology for government support. The technology is developing along many different dimensions. Keeping multiple options in play is highly desirable under these circumstances. Consequently, the government—if it supports maglev—should probably consciously support several different systems at the developmental level. While seeming to be more expensive, this process will lower long-term costs. Users should be involved in the design from the outset. And systems should be brought on stream as early as possible to learn about practical operating issues. Thus the use of trains for center-city-to-airport, very high-density single-track intercity, or theme-park transportation purposes could drive the technology and be very useful experiments, while paying for themselves.

Even using conventional analysis, the data indicate that maglev is very close to competitive for use against TGV (very fast train) alternatives. The main advantages of TGV are its slightly lower initial investment cost and the known nature of the technology. However, its speed limits will rapidly be reached. Next-generation mass transport technology cannot rely on such systems. Similarly, airlines are a very high cost transportation system for distances of less than 300 miles. From an efficiency viewpoint, one could stratify transportation systems as follows:

Less than 50 miles	autos or standard mass transit
50-300 miles	TGV or maglev
Over 300 miles	aircraft

One very interesting facet of analysis should be the use of TGV-maglev systems to transport packages to the center city. Companies like UPS point out that package pickup and delivery in cities is enormously expensive. Their costs could be dropped substantially by delivering and picking up packages from a center city location on TGV-maglev systems connecting to cities up to 500 miles away. Most of this transportation could be accomplished at night when the transit systems of most cities are heavily underutilized. (See chart at end of case). If one considered the potential advantages of package shipment by TGV or maglev systems, the payoffs would become much higher. However, to date, none of the national studies has even considered this commercial aspect of the benefits rapid rail could offer to the public.

Any analysis of maglev vs. other systems should be made on an incremental basis. This involves comparing the relatively minor increases in infrastructure investment for maglev (vs. highways or rail transport systems against the enormous time and energy benefits of maglev. The incremental investment in maglev should not be considered simply the full $7.4 billion for a

300-mile system. The true incremental cost is $7.4 billion minus the $5.8-12 billion investment which would have to be made in highways or other transportation systems in any event. Once this investment base adjustment is made, maglev becomes highly competitive with these other systems.

A STARTLING CHALLENGE

This case presents a truly unusual chance to challenge students' thinking about resource allocation at the national and corporate level. It can lead them into some very interesting discussions on competitiveness, public vs. private investment, national gain vs. private gain, and the genuine meaning of externalities. Note that the society gains the full cost per barrel of oil that it does not buy from a foreign source—if it can invest the same funds internally in capital projects that cover more than the cost of capital. The country achieves both the savings from oil imports and gains the value of the infrastructures which will be available permanently in the future. Unfortunately, in the current economic climate, policymakers tend to overlook these verities. They do not look at marginal costs to the full society, but at marginal cost to individuals. We do not tend to look at the feedback loops created by government investment in new areas which private companies would not consider or could not develop on their own. One can expect some real fireworks if this case is used properly.

FORD: TEAM TAURUS TEACHING NOTE

Overview

The Ford: Team Taurus case can serve several functions. It is an excellent example of (1) an emergent or incremental strategy, (2) a major strategic change process, (3) an outstanding innovation in a large organization, and (4) a macro change in product and organization strategy. Thus it can be linked with readings by Quinn on incrementalism, Mintzberg on emergent strategies, and articles in Chapter on the innovation context. The case offers a thorough overview of the process through which Ford Motor Company broke out of the problems its car line had in the 1970s and early 1980s and began to compete on favorable terms with the Japanese and Europeans. The case provides an excellent opportunity to look at multinational strategies, particularly at Europe '92. It also deals with major strategic alliances and is a superb example of outsourcing strategy.

The focal point of the case is how one of the United States' major smokestack-industry companies managed a successful turnaround and created the most financially successful automobile line of the 1980s. The end of the case is positioned for the early 1990s.

Session Structure

We usually begin by asking <u>first</u>, how did Ford get into so much trouble? Ford was, and is, one of the great companies of the world. What happened to it? Why did the turnaround not occur earlier? <u>Second</u>, we ask what management concepts made the new system work? What is different about Ford's Team Taurus approach and other concurrent design or simultaneous design approaches? These are core segments of the discussion. <u>Third</u>, we ask what issues would you expect the Team Taurus approach to raise? Specifically, how would you solve each of these issues? <u>Finally</u>, we ask how this process has changed strategy for Ford and the auto industry. How does its emulation elsewhere affect the strategies of other major players in the automobile industry? What should Ford do in the future, particularly about Europe '92? The case can be kept lively and up to date by using or quoting commentaries on the automobile industry from current publications.

What Happened to a Great Company?

In this section, it is important to dislodge the student (or executive audience) from simply talking about poor quality or high labor costs in the automobile industry. These are just symptoms, not causes. The key set of issues is <u>why</u> did the industry decline? <u>Why</u> did Ford in particular decline? It will probably be essential to prompt the audience to think a bit more deeply about these issues. Some suggested prompts follow:

1. <u>What structural issues contributed most to Ford's problems?</u> Ford's functional organization and the protected (oligopolistic) U.S. market tended to mask the severity of its problems. It is extremely difficult to measure the effectiveness of centralized functional organizations like Ford's, because output and productivity measures are so difficult to establish for each function. The functional power structure of the company also made it very difficult to share information horizontally. Oligopolistic competition in the automobile industry and the fact that the Japanese chose not to compete at the higher end of the market further masked the great difficulties Ford was in for many years, as did the tendency of managers and investors in the industry to appraise company performance solely by short-term financial indicators.

---

2. <u>What were the effects of Ford's management style?</u> Henry Ford II's management style was extremely authoritarian, preventing the development of lower level managers, experimentation, or competing ideas at these levels. Henry's style and the vertical organization structure tended to filter the information that went to the top and created conservative, second guessing in management decisions. Without highly decentralized performance measures it was difficult to discern problems early or to spotlight good or poor management performance (other than costs) at lower levels. The company thus became cost driven. But even worse, when Henry II chose some wrong directions, the whole company went wrong—there were few counter-balances.

3. <u>Why did U.S. autoworkers' productivity drop so much relative to Japan's?</u> The long use of Frederick Taylor's type of methods engineering and detailed work measurement at the worker level; and presumptions about management's infallibility and labor's essential nature as a non-thinking commodity further prevented more modern management and motivational techniques from being developed. This led to a feeling of helplessness and hostility among laborers and to a strong and militant union geared to protect workers' jobs. Compensation structures, emphasizing detailed job categories, further made labor very inflexible and committed to defending each job, rather than seeking broader job responsibilities, more efficiency, and greater security through such efficiency. The vertical, functional organization structure also developed a group of management and technical specialists in each area, whose security depended upon defending their particular specialty and its bureaucracy rather than contributing to the overall company's prosperity.

4. <u>What major changes in technological structure had the company ignored?</u> The tendency of the industry to think in terms of economies of scale and marketing gimmicks as modes of differentiation ignored the changing nature of the marketplace itself. Economies of scale were moving toward components and subsystem fabrication—and away from large assembly plants. Suppliers had become increasingly sophisticated and powerful relative to the assembling automobile companies. Yet by simply running their depreciated large-scale plants for more years, automobile companies could still make short-term profits without investing extensively in new technologies. Supplier overcapacity had made it possible to whipsaw suppliers in the purchasing process, despite the ultimate dependency of the automobile industry on these suppliers. Consequently, the U.S. industry stayed with its vertically integrated (internal sourcing) structures too long and cut itself off from the innovation, flexibility, and cost reduction that better relationships with outside suppliers could have generated.

5. <u>Why didn't Ford's management modify its car lines and production practices earlier?</u> The short-term, inward looking, orientation of top managements (defending current profitability and ROI) tended to undercut investments in new markets, major technological advances, and risky innovations. Note Henry II's decision to continue exploiting existing car lines rather than investing in front-wheel drive, smaller cars, or more efficient engine technologies during the 1970s. Smaller cars were perceived as cannibalizing more profitable large-car sales, and not as a major long-term threat (or much less an important opportunity) offering foreign companies experience curve advantages that would later let them attack large-car markets.

Copycat designing was rampant in the industry. If companies like Ford and Chrysler merely replicated the designs of GM, they could not be too far off in the large-car American marketplace. Hence their shares would not shift too radically, and designers and executives would be secure in their jobs. The few examples of earlier radical change attempts (notably the Chrysler "Air Flow" car and Ford's Edsel) had been disasters. Managers naturally wished to avoid such major "career terminating mistakes."

6. <u>Why didn't Ford and the U.S. industry respond earlier to demands for better quality?</u> The exceedingly large, stable nature of the U.S. marketplace also masked the need for change. Large volumes and profits could be maintained in larger cars even if some share of the market was lost. By exploiting old designs and old equipment, the automobile companies could avoid innovation risks, obtain high cash flows, show profitability, and keep investors reasonably comfortable. As long as only U.S. companies competed in the larger car markets, quality choices

were not available. This was exacerbated by Detroit's tendency to ignore the smaller car end of the market, and thus avoid head-to-head competition with foreign companies on quality.

This allowed Japanese companies to move well down the quality experience curve on compact and sub-compact cars before the U.S. companies responded. By then, the Japanese had developed a "perceived quality" advantage in the marketplace, and U.S. companies had to pursue competitors who were both (a) ahead on quality technologies and (b) had an absolute need to emphasize quality in order to survive. In order to support their automobiles in the United States—without excessive warranty, repair, and distribution infrastructures—the Japanese had to focus on quality, while U.S. companies emphasized power, price, and features which masked other quality differences. When the oil shortage suddenly shifted consumer demands toward small cars, U.S. companies did not have time to make an orderly transition to the new market.

7. <u>What strategic errors did Ford and the industry make in appraising the power of outside competitive forces in the industry?</u> Believing that manufacturing was no longer a major competitive weapon, neglect of the manufacturing function became rampant throughout the industry. Promotion to top levels came through marketing or finance, rather than from production or design experience. Errors from poor practice in manufacturing were passed through to dealers to correct. In the short run, this saved the companies apparent costs. In the long run it alienated both consumers and the distributors—i.e., both levels of the market that U.S. automobile companies should have been cultivating, and where they could have created a maintainable competitive edge.

Meanwhile, the addition of foreign cars, notably Japanese, enabled some dealers to grow to mega-size. These dealers began to have much more market power and capability to influence customers at the point of purchase. Although U.S. automobiles had higher unit margins, they also required much greater post-sale expense. Consequently, dealers' net profits were often diminished by focusing solely on U.S. automobiles. Hence they both carried and pushed Japanese and European cars to increase their profits and leverage vs. U.S. brands. By not thinking strategically, industry leaders had overlooked major power shifts among three of the leading forces affecting them—their suppliers, their potential competitors, and their customers.

8. <u>Other than small cars and quality, what major strategic opportunities did U.S. companies overlook, particularly Ford?</u> In a peculiar set of strategic mishaps, Ford Motor Company did not use the major economies of scale and innovation that its strong European operations allowed in design, in developing manufacturing techniques, and in sensing important marketplace changes. Much of this was due to the isolation at the top created by its aging top management, its functional organization, its closed "Detroit culture," and the authoritarian management style during this period. Ford's very success and financial strength bred inflexibility, isolation, and strategic blindness.

One should not dwell too long on this first section. Students and executives will tend to shoot from the hip and bring out their favorite complaints. It is essential to drive for some depth in understanding as to what the real issues were and not just skim the surface as usually presented by the popular press. One should be aware of the high labor cost and high capital cost arguments one is likely to incur. A good query is, "Did Ford really lose position because it could not acquire the capital to invest in its automobiles or because it could not afford to manufacture them overseas?" The answers to these questions are obvious. One can also ask why labor costs in this industry rose to such an extent. The alienation of the workers, the geographical isolation of the industry, and its tendency to operate as a protected oligopoly need special emphasis. In the past, labor monopoly, oligopoly, and isolated markets—not efficiency—had led to high wages and profits. While these factors had changed, industry strategies had not. Virtually all the studies of loss of competitiveness in autos show that it was management practices, not labor or national policy issues, which were primarily at fault.

Why did the Team Taurus Management Concept Work?

Again, there is a problem in keeping students or executives from skimming or simply repeating back the case. One should be prepared with a number of prompts to get at the underlying issues. Following are some questions about key issues which may be helpful:

1. Vision. What was there about the new vision of Messrs. Petersen and Caldwell that made Taurus/Sable work? Of major significance would be the following. The positioning of the product as "best-in-class in the upper middle market" clearly broke with the past, was attractive to all parties, positioned the product uniquely within its defined price bracket, and offered a set of potential benchmarks for measuring results. Yet the goal itself was left sufficiently open so that a variety of creative approaches could be used. Creating a distinctive car had a similar effect. Caldwell and Petersen constantly reinforced both goals by asking, "Why should I buy this product from Ford?" This kept the emphasis on comparative quality and value. The concept was reinforced by putting the quality goal into the number one position in the Mission Statement.

2. Figures of Merit. How was the vision made explicit enough to be operational? By breaking down the product into 400 subsystems and specifying in numerical terms what best-in-class meant (using 18 quality measures) the Taurus/Sable group was able to create precise and challenging goals for quality improvement. This anchored the broad vision statement in ways that made it operationally useful. The figures of merit the team set, specifying need and best performance on each individual subsystem, gave substance to the broad goals of the vision. Without these, the vision would have been empty. Clear challenging goals helped coordinate the project and motivate people.

3. Radically Redesigning the Car. Why were people willing to take the risks to join Team Taurus despite Ford's past conservatism? Radically redesigning the car allowed the Taurus/Sable team to achieve an internal status which a mere redesign would not have achieved. People who worked on the project became an elite and obtained a unique identity within Ford—in the same sense that those on GE's "Hawthorne Project" earlier did at GE. This special status led to high morale and visibility if successful. The radical repositioning also allowed engineers to challenge traditional wisdom and thus come up with totally new solutions which might otherwise have been ignored. Such a radical redesign might not have been possible if Ford had not incurred substantial losses in two years.

4. The Top Level Team. Other than the presence and vision of Caldwell and Petersen, what factors in top level organization were crucial to success? The top level team had to be balanced enough in skills and political power to make a thoroughly integrated decision. The team included competent operating people who understood the problems of redesign in-depth and hence were more comfortable with the risks associated with a radical repositioning. Rotation of management from foreign operations and non-traditional units made sure that objectivity was present. Caldwell and Petersen were themselves committed, giving the program the credibility it needed to bring about changes throughout the organization. And the inclusion of all functions in decisions diluted the power of the key functions (Marketing and Finance) which had dominated in the past. Without any one of these, the process would probably have failed.

5. The Process Designed the Car. Why was such a radical organization design (and chart) used? What did Veraldi et al. mean by the phrase: "the process designed the car." By having everyone work on the car simultaneously, the suboptimizations which each functional group would have introduced because of its particular goal bias were avoided. The chart itself signaled a shift from a centrist style to cooperative, and from order-giving to information-seeking in the design process. The circular chart implies that all necessary power is inside the group. The Team Taurus group had to stay together long enough to complete the cycle of design. It had to create a new management process as well as an automobile line. Key to this were long-term continuity and a complete enough process to avoid what had earlier been a complete redesign at final stages (the latter probably would have occurred again, if the Taurus design had to be handed off later to successor groups who had not been intimately involved in the process).

The simultaneous design process avoided the problems of passing each step in the design ahead without its having been cleared by the next "user group." This lowered error costs and avoided conflicts and time previously lost when the project required returning for rework by a preceding element in the design sequence. On-time performance tends to improve with simultaneous design. With a sequential design concept and with over 20 elements in the sequence, if each group has a 95% probability of being on time, the probability that the whole system will be on time drops to about 37%. Similarly, the probability that an error in earlier stages will show up later (even with a very low error rate at each stage) balloons with sequential design. If the design process was right, many benefits were almost automatic.

6. Worker Incentives and Perceptions Changed. Why were workers willing to join in the process? Mr. Veraldi's approach, saying "How can we make your job easier?" gave the workers a reason to join in the design. The employment guarantees took away the risk of participation. Immediate feedback to workers, by showing that suggestions would be accepted, created believability for the program. The trust that Pete Pestillo and Don Ephlin were able to introduce through working together decreased potential formal conflicts. Taking Mr. Ephlin to Japan to look at the competition helped Mr. Ephlin see how serious Ford's problems really were. Introducing a number of experiments before asking workers for full approval increased their trust and sense of participation in the process. Training workers in quality control and then trusting them to use and develop the systems further made workers genuinely a part of the process. Asking workers for "tremendous trifles," which they could imagine and engineer themselves, allowed them to see their creativity in the product or in the workplace.

It is important to note that this was a step-by-step or incremental process which allowed a major shift in corporate culture to occur at all levels. None of this could have happened if the process had been suddenly introduced in its totality. Workers themselves had to break with their past patterns, obtain an identity with the program, and overcome a vast distrust of the company. This case makes an excellent vehicle for the discussion of incrementalism and the simultaneous design and implementation of strategy.

7. Quality Emphasis. What were the most crucial elements in creating the new quality focus? Again, the process was incremental. Caldwell and Petersen changed the decision flux and made key symbolic changes at the top, as was noted above. But other incremental steps were also crucial. The quality emphasis was clearly reinforced throughout the organization. The use of "tremendous trifles" made the idea visible to all and let each person contribute to it. The commitment to a totally new car broke people away from many specific technical errors of the past. The setting of figures of merit on each part and subsystem was crucial—providing clear targets and progress measures—as was the continuous best-in-class benchmarking and questioning of "how you would design it if you started all over?" each year. Producing an entire set of prototype cars with manufacturing-level parts allowed for a complete quality adjustment of the car before its final release to production. Taguchi methods provided a systematic means to measure and (more importantly) justify improvements in quality. Without this, there would have been endless arguments as to how far quality should go. Reducing the number of suppliers, entities under construction, and individual parts in final assembly helped to improve the amount of automation which could be put into place and the experience curve benefits on each part. Modular assembly meant that complete subassemblies could be pretested and responsibility clearly assigned for quality throughout the system.

Errors were captured early rather than late. Bringing the legal and safety people in early meant that these features were not add-ons likely to create problems later. Benchmarking best-in-class gave specific targets and incentives for both suppliers and subsystem producers. By tracking these objectively, Ford had a way of measuring whether it was indeed meeting its quality goals. Getting suppliers to coordinate full systems increased accountability, decreased the number of potential error points, and increased suppliers' capacity to invest in needed automation and quality systems. Finally, developing information systems to tie suppliers' production processes directly to Ford's production floor in real-time allowed suppliers to know immediately if they were producing errors and to correct them before they became a problem in the customers' hands. But critical to the entire process was Caldwell and Petersen's continually asking the question, "Why should I buy this product from Ford?" This kept an emphasis on a quality _edge_ and made designers justify their changes on a quality basis.

8. Leadership. What characteristics do leaders have to possess in this kind of system? Top level leaders, Caldwell and Petersen, provided _vision_ and constant _discipline_. They selected a person they trusted, who had the right values as well as experiences for the new system. The coordinating leader, Veraldi, had to be _acceptable_ to virtually all functions alike. He was one of the few people in the company who had been allowed to have the relevant cross-functional experience in design and manufacturing. Veraldi's leadership style had to be _coordinative_ and _persuasive_ to keep up involvement and momentum for the 5 years of the project. Yet he also had to be able and willing to _force and resolve_ issues personally, when necessary. Charm alone would not have worked.

At the divisional level, Veraldi's team had to rely more on leadership with _expert knowledge_. This was extremely difficult, since the past culture had emphasized cost cutting, rather than design and quality. The "bean counter" mental set and control of power points had to be replaced by group decisions, like "consensus purchasing." All existing power centers were threatened. Although the appearance of Caldwell and Petersen at the top clearly changed the management balance and style, there was enormous resistance to change from the established power centers below them in the organization. This took both _pressure tactics_ and _symbolic leadership_ at the top. It also required constant _detailed follow-through_, bypassing of established power bases, building of partial consensus, pockets of support, and process management from the top. _No single management style would have sufficed throughout._

If Ford had not undergone the $1 to $ 1 1/2 billion losses in each of the preceding two years, the needed massive changes in organization culture might not have been possible. They certainly would not have occurred without the persistent follow-up of the top team. They had to take a number of steps to break the "chimneys of power" and entrenched attitudes of the divisional groups without losing their support. What steps would students recommend? What could management do to preserve the dignity and genuine expertise of these groups? This is an excellent place to develop the various models of change management introduced in various readings.

9. New Control Systems. What control system changes were essential to bring about changes? If Ford had stuck with its old "knock dollars out of the design" approach rather than a value-added approach, designers never would have been able to implement the key changes in Taurus/Sable. Workers would not have participated if output per hour standards had been maintained and detailed and visible quality standards had not been installed. Similarly, the "profit-center-by-car-line" approach had to be modified. Strong line executives of the individual car lines (Ford, Mercury, Lincoln) would not have participated if the project had not been pulled out on a separate corporate budget which did not hit their operating budgets during this period. The Board also had to exhibit a patience not too apparent in the past.

Formal organization controls had to change. Team Taurus had to be given decision-making authority over all of the trade-offs and cross-functional balances which were necessary. If such decisions had been forced to go all the way to the top, the process would have been so slow as to be impossible. Some of the main control shifts were to shorten communication lines, involve people across all functions in new goal relationships, shift measurement criteria throughout, and bring those with knowledge about those criteria as close as possible to the top. Perhaps the most important change in controls was from authoritative, engineering-based and financial-based measures to personal and group measurements. What problems would you have expected during this change?

What Problems Would You Have Expected During the Change?

One of the most fruitful approaches for generating discussion is to bounce back and forth between the "why did it work" question and the issue of "what problems might you have expected to encounter? What would you have done about this?" This keeps the students from skimming with a list of good points followed by lists of questions. Some suggested issues follow:

1. <u>Where would you have started this process? Why?</u> Clearly the selection of leadership for the program had to be paramount. Establishing the authority of this leadership relative to the very powerful heads of the functional groups was also crucial. Developing and articulating a clear credible vision also has to be among the first possible steps. But this probably could not have occurred without a period of sensing, analysis, and probing of what would be possible and acceptable within the existing structure. The early vision had to be clear and stimulating, but not imply a criticism of the power players who had to join in.

2. <u>What forms of resistance would you have expected? How would you overcome these?</u> The functional heads, who had held all power in Ford in the past, would clearly resist breaking out a major portion of their responsibility. These groups were so strong as to be known as "chimneys of power" inside Ford. Caldwell and Petersen had to undertake a number of chimney breaking exercises. At various times, Caldwell and Petersen were reported to have come directly to the functional heads and said, "If you can't resolve this problem (with an adjacent division), I will find someone who can. You must deliver your management on this project."

The functional heads at first tended to assign their fourth or fifth best person to Team Taurus. Caldwell and Petersen let it be known that they wanted the highest quality person within each functional division. And they let the division heads know they knew who that person was. There are many stories about how this chimney breaking portion of the change was actually implemented, including Caldwell or Petersen saying to division heads, "How would you like to work for Mr. ____, (the head of an adjacent division in the design process)?" When the top functional executive would express surprise, they would reportedly respond, "That is exactly what is going to happen if you do not give me your very best person—and I know who that person is." Other methods of chimney breaking were also essential, such as changing the criteria for evaluating functional performance. Some interesting questions can be raised around this point, and the pros and cons of various change process techniques can be discussed. Some role playing of various interested parties (staff people, workers, suppliers, etc.) can be very lively and keep students from generalizing too glibly.

3. <u>What new expenses would you have expected to result from the Team Taurus approach? Would you have expected design cost to go up or down? Why?</u> This allows one to pursue the relative costs of more complex communications, of making changes early (vs. later) in a design process, the risks of mis-estimating consumer demand and freezing designs four years ahead of release date, the risks of making errors and having to correct them later, and the relative costs of designing and building quality into subsystems vs. releasing poor quality to the field.

In fact, the old Ford system had relatively few Engineering Change Orders in the early stages of design, an apparent saving. They peaked just before Job #1 was produced. Then after the product was in the marketplace, there was another high secondary peak which only tapered off 3-5 years after the car was in the marketplace. This meant that extremely costly changes were made after full-scale production tooling was in place—or had to be performed expensively in dealers' repair shops. During the Team Taurus project, almost all engineering design changes were made early in the process, when it is less expensive. Even if the same number of Engineering Change Orders were made in both processes, the excessive costs of making these with manufacturing tooling vs. design tooling strongly favored the simultaneous design approach. In addition, simultaneous design eliminated the costs of allowing each receiving group to send back an improper design to the preceding stage, with its associated costs of duplication, time lost, and communications errors. The advantages of eliminating time lost and having decisions made as close to the release date as possible needs special emphasis.

4. <u>What types of communications problems would you expect?   How should they be approached?</u> Communications among the design groups. Simultaneous communication among such a large core group posed some significant difficulties. Keeping this group in close physical proximity, meeting frequently, and working constantly on a culture of open, problem-oriented communications was key, as was developing a language and methodology for measuring net value-added. Pursue these issues with explicit questions to get depth. Setting up the functions and activities chart to coordinate the timing of decisions was an enormous help.

However, it was important that, in addition, a whole new infrastructure of electronic communications be set up within Ford and with its suppliers. Since suppliers were all over the world, this required a new global approach to logistics systems. These had to extend directly into suppliers' design groups and on to their production floors throughout the world. Everything that could be measured had to be specified in detail and electronic designs had to be kept constantly updated in a command center for the project. Without this capacity to have real-time communications, things could easily have slipped out of control. By breaking the product up into 400 subsystems, coordination at that level by the subsystem teams became much more feasible. Key to the control process is the distinct definition of each subsystem and the coordinating standards subsystems have to meet to match other subsystems. The latter has to be centralized in Team Taurus.

5. <u>How could the company avoid a copycat design with so many people working on the project?</u> The normal effect of a large committee is to achieve a series of compromises, not a dramatic new design. It was only Caldwell and Petersen's insistence on something really different, a distinctively best-in-class performance, and the drive of some new key people to produce the new "aero look" that made this possible. In addition, Caldwell and Petersen eventually gave Veraldi almost czar-like power to enforce a design configuration once the basic car design was agreed on. Insistence on value-added calculations tended to support more radical changes vs. incremental ones which would have been more difficult to justify. Although the decision to manufacture in existing plants made some process changes more difficult technically, Ford made a conscious choice to produce in or near existing facilities in order to reduce pressures for worker layoffs. This enabled Ford to obtain more labor cooperation than it otherwise could have.

6. <u>What issues would you have expected in benchmarking best-in-class performance?</u> This is a very interesting issue. How does one get suppliers to participate in designing a new product? How does one make trade-offs between different quality levels in a component system? Between component systems? How does one forecast what best-in-class will be at the time the product is released? Can market research really help determine the value of a design change at the subsystems level? Various techniques are useful to mention here. Using trends in quality performance and projecting trend lines is useful. Recognizing the exponential nature of technological change is crucial. Introducing experience curve concepts at the component systems level is also crucial for cost and quality estimation. Setting up a trade-off matrix, looking at relative performance levels for each function of the subsystem is very helpful. One can then use a ranking system, rather than a dollar system, to rate the importance of various component performance characteristics. Getting the students to talk about how they would design and implement such performance grids is very enlightening.

The issue of making comparisons between the <u>elements</u> of performance in one subsystem vs. the elements of performance in another subsystem is very important. While one expert team may fairly easily array the relative importance of component characteristics in a single subsystem, one cannot really compare those elements vs. individual elements in another subsystem—because the performance comparison really occurs only at the level of the full subsystem not at the component performance level. That is, it is very difficult to compare tightening a piston clearance specification vs. a more aesthetic cushion design for a bumper. Comparing the <u>overall</u> cost/performance and efficiency of an engine system with the relative cost, aesthetics, and shock absorption capabilities of a bumper system is much more feasible.

7. Why doesn't Mr. Veraldi use standard ROI measures on design changes? Why do they agree not to measure the benefits of their Employee Involvement Program? ROI measures will tend to emphasize those things which can be quantified in dollar terms. It tends to underemphasize quality changes and intangibles, the very things that best-in-class would mean to customers. Utilizing ROI measures is more appropriate after the overall design balance has been achieved and one is talking about specific production process investments where things are much more measurable. Earlier cost/benefit and feature trade-off matrices better match the accuracy of the data available and the goals of the process. Veraldi was trying to introduce a new mindset to the entire design process.

Similarly, Pestillo and Ephlin were afraid that any attempt to measure benefits of the Employee Involvement Program could have proved negligible gains for all parties in the beginning and probably would have created real counterpressures against the move. More concrete measures would probably have been quickly converted into new performance measures—using the same old techniques—by the very strong controllership groups inside of Ford. Workers would have interpreted these as another tightening of the screw and would have refused to participate. To stimulate change required an early flexibility and experimental mode of operation. In time, a complex set of quantitative and qualitative measures focused more on quality were required—rather than simple cost center, investment center, profit, or ROI measurements.

8. Why didn't Ford automate its processes and focus on technological solutions? Although Ford did introduce some of the most advanced automation in the field, it thought that the real problems were motivational and performance-oriented rather than limited by technology. It felt (based on the data available) that managing the production process better (in terms of inventory levels, quality levels, absenteeism, worker suggestions, etc.) had a much higher potential payoff. Ford did not think that technology was the primary factor limiting its quality or cost improvement. Ford felt it could add technology to the process as time went on, but that it was very important to get worker/management attitudes and process of production right first. Other companies had made the common error: to automate a process before it had been completely revised and made as efficient as possible. The result was that these companies had "automated in" a number of inherently bad practices and thus created even more intransigent long-term problems for themselves.

9. Who should be in the Team Taurus core group? What happens to those who are on Team Taurus? What would you expect to happen to them? The people on Team Taurus had to have high technical credibility within their own organizations, yet be willing to cooperate with outside groups. They had to be able to command resources within their functional organizations and have sufficient formal authority or personal clout that, with the backing of Team Taurus, they could obtain responses within both their divisions and the top management group. Yet it was crucial that they be able to interrelate with the other functions and not look at the problem solely from a specialist viewpoint. Each individual had to have a large enough network inside his/her own functional division (or in the major line divisions within Ford) to find the right people to solve specific problems as they occurred. A major problem was balancing the team with both experienced executives and those who could bring new ideas. Too radical a group of "young Turks" would not have been successful. Getting balanced functional representation kept the core team at 10-13 people, larger than most would have liked.

After the project, it was essential that team members be given high visibility positions. A few headed the functional divisions remaining, a few took on leadership of the next versions of the Team Taurus approach used for the Continental, and other lines of cars. Soon the upper levels of the company could have been seeded with people who had been in such cross-functional groups, and the power centers (and the entire culture) of Ford could have been shifted. Unfortunately there is emerging evidence that the functional culture maintained much of its power, and the company lost a great opportunity to revise its whole structure. One of the main problems of creating strong task forces of this sort is that members may build up strong antagonisms in their own groups in order to make needed compromises. Without a major cultural shift it became difficult to return to one's "home base" after such a project. Lesson: Top managements need to plan future career paths for those who succeed on such teams and to facilitate total cultural changes for the organization.

10. <u>What problems would you have expected in introducing the cars in competition with Ford's other cars?</u> Marketing the new line in competition with the cash cow cars of the existing functional groups posed some unique problems. One had to avoid downgrading the existing divisions and their employees while introducing Taurus/Sable as a totally new look for Ford. This posed important strategy issues for Ford. Should Taurus even be used as an international auto entry or be regarded as simply a U.S. car? If introduced internationally, should the car have been produced in the United States for international shipment or produced abroad in Ford's existing facilities? Should future lines abroad reflect the same "aero car" family look? In the end, Ford did ship Taurus/Sables throughout the world and received high acclaim for the car. The cars caught on in Europe and were introduced (slightly modified) there as a "European car" (Scorpio). Other American Fords followed the aero look in stages to establish a family of cars and recognition as such.

11. <u>What problems would you have expected with suppliers? How could these be dealt with?</u> Ford had enjoyed a contentious relationship with its suppliers. It took several years of building trust and placing long-term contracts to overcome this negative image. On investments that suppliers considered to be risky—if Ford withdrew its contract—Ford had to co-invest. Both groups had to agree to coordinated information systems, definitions of costs, quality, length of lead times, etc. Standards had to be built into information networks for instant feedback in both directions. Ford had to insist that suppliers produce prototype parts using "production metal" before Job #1 to be absolutely sure of fit, color, etc. Elaborate technology sharing and protection agreements had to be inaugurated to avoid suppliers selling unique proprietary items to others and to ensure that Ford could not pass suppliers' proprietary knowledge on to other competing suppliers. Since all factors could not be covered in contracts, it was important to build a whole new relationship with suppliers based on mutual trust. Try to get executives and students to define exactly how to do this.

12. <u>Why did Ford encounter quality problems in its early Taurus/Sable cars?</u> Actually, the first production series of Taurus/Sable was well received and relatively stable from a quality viewpoint. Later (1986) cars did have quality problems that developed after the cars had seen extensive use. However, it is important to introduce the idea that when one puts out a new system—with 95% new parts—it is almost certain that there will be failures. One simply cannot foresee all the interactions of parts, driver performance, wear, etc.. until a car has been used in the field for some time. Ford's quality performance is remarkable given this fact. The second year of Taurus/Sable cars (1986-87) had more quality problems as workers lost the initial exhilaration of producing a new and better car, and as small improvements in the automobile meant that new fits were not as closely controlled from a system viewpoint. However, Ford later reestablished continuous total system control for the automobile and the 1988-89 Taurus/Sables reacquired their fine quality reputation. The 35-miles-per-hour front-end collision problem remained, although this is probably more an issue of testing methodology than it is of real quality. One can raise some very interesting issues as to what affects real quality in an automobile and how to measure that. What portion depends on design, manufacture, maintenance, customer perception vs. reality, etc.?

What was Different about the Taurus/Sable Approach from All Other Forms of "Simultaneous Design?

Since simultaneous engineering or concurrent design has become more common in the last couple of years, it is important to ask what is different about the Ford approach to these issues. How does it apply to other companies?

1. <u>The completeness of the process is probably most important.</u> No one else had carried simultaneous design as far as involving all suppliers, suppliers' suppliers, workers, regulatory people, repair men, insurance companies, etc. Further, the process extended all the way from

204

the CEO throughout the organization to assembly floor workers. The entire culture had to be changed radically. The entire mission of the company was restated. The process tapped all potential sources of change and advance. This is a superb case of innovation in a large organization, coupled with introducing a much flatter organization concept, more rapid response times, and employee involvement and empowerment at all levels. There is a broad literature on innovation in small business environments and in R&D. The case provides an opportunity to see what variables large-scale manufacturing innovation creates.

2. The scale of the project after its introduction is important. The design investment was $3 1/4 billion. The Taurus became one of the largest selling and probably the most profitable single car of the 1980s era—certainly for U.S. manufacturers. In terms of technological scale, suppliers, the production floors, marketing departments, dealerships, and repair shops were all directly connected by technology. As soon as quality failures appeared in the marketplace, it became directly apparent to the production group in Ford assembling that subsystem. If the item was outsourced, repair information went directly to the suppliers so the product could be immediately corrected. This kept response times for component redesigns and replacements to an absolute minimum. This is extremely important when the interactions of all systems under extensive field conditions cannot possibly be predicted.

3. Product teams emerged throughout the company. These were cross-functional teams within each of the 400 subsystem design groups as well as within Team Taurus itself. Designing and managing these teams became a crucial portion of the culture. Old concepts of line authority had to give way to ad hoc team—or self-directed team—decisions, yet these had to be disciplined in new ways. The figures of merit and the key events schedule were crucial and had to be kept constantly up to date. Asking how all of these subsystems and 1500 key events could be kept coordinated raises some interesting questions of information system design. The system is only as good as its inputs.

4. User-customer orientation throughout the process is extremely important. The concept that the next person or group in each stage of the design concept was defined as a user or customer was crucial. This meant that there had to be simultaneous lateral discussion of any decisions. This predisposed later stages to accept changes and help make sure that these changes were correct. It is also apparent that if each "user" had to sign off before a change could be implemented, the entire system had to be onboard before a major change could be made. Although this appears time consuming and conservative in impact, it forces discussions which should take place as early as possible. The entire process, therefore, becomes customer, not technology, or engineer or finance driven. Ultimately, this ensures higher value added at each step.

5. Extensive outsourcing became a much more important element in Ford Motor Company. It is interesting to note that profitability of U.S. automobile companies in recent years has become inversely related to their degree of vertical integration. This implies that economies of scale have moved to the supplier level and that significant economies can be achieved by outsourcing. A number of interesting questions can be raised about the outsourcing strategy. How does one coordinate it, what are some of the dangers? Why has this type of alliance or outsourcing strategy only recently become popular? How does one analyze one's competition under these circumstances? It becomes clear that companies compete as networks of suppliers, assemblers, and distributors, rather than as individual companies. The functional capability within each company has to be compared with the same functional capability within other companies to ensure best-in-class capability. If one is not best-in-class at a function, then one is giving up strategic advantage. The implications of this need to be pursued with students.

6. A design focus is crucial to effectiveness. Only some 20% of a new product's investment is in the design itself. Yet this can solve many of the problems encountered and create savings throughout the entire set of succeeding investments in production and marketing. Asking the customer-oriented question, "What can we do for you?" at each level of the design process—including asking line-workers—is very important. Not only does this ensure lowest cost, it means

205

that each group is willing to participate in implementing the new design and it significantly lowers costs as well as time and information costs in introduction. The closer one can be to product release time at the moment of design, the better the information, the lower the risk and the higher the perceived quality can be for the product.

Notice that the Taurus/Sable came in one-quarter billion dollars less in development costs than was budgeted. Similar successor projects have reduced the design cycle to 4-4 1/2 years and allowed the design process to occur ever closer to the marketplace. One of the most significant (though unmeasurable) benefits of simultaneous design is the improvement in responsiveness to the marketplace, quicker product cycle introduction, and less risk of the market moving away from the design after it is established. The flatter organization (required by simultaneous design) further improves the quality of future design changes and response times. It also allows one to "de-layer" an organization and thus decrease its overhead costs.

7. Multiple level cooperation was emphasized throughout Taurus/Sable. Many other concurrent design projects merely involved the management of groups in engineering, research, design, and/or marketing. Getting all levels involved requires a much more thoroughgoing process, starting with a clear culture shift at the top and accompanying mission statements backed up by control systems compatible with the new concept. Most important of these for Taurus/Sable was the emphasis on quality as #1 and quality of work life as #2 in the change. For a company that had been bottom line driven, this was a radical departure. Numerous questions can be introduced as to how one can cause the organization to respond to these two goals as opposed to traditional ROI or profit goals. What needs to be measured in order to ensure that these goals are met? How does one tie this in to the next round of benchmarking?

8. Integrated CAD/CAE/CAM systems are crucial to this kind of process. In implementing simultaneous design systems, companies should expect substantial increases in their information systems and logistics functions. Worldwide sourcing tends to up logistics costs by a factor of 10-20%, but lowers production and quality costs by factors of 30-80%. Integrating worldwide sourcing requires reconsideration of the portfolio of customer countries one serves, places where assembly takes place, and supplier locations. With gigantic fluctuations in exchange rates, many billions of dollars can be made simply through sourcing strategies for a company like Ford through its MIS systems. Tying MIS systems completely to suppliers, to customers, and to repair shops is an essential leverage in this type of concurrent design process. However, this is rarely implemented sufficiently by most companies.

9. A New leadership mode has to emerge to back up this type of system. In Ford, the leadership was changed at the very top as well as in a single major project accounting for 40% of the corporation's sales. This is a massive change in any organization, even more so in one as big as Ford, especially as conservative as the company had been. This is a case where a massive organization change, restructuring, culture change, and a shift from a conservative functional to a more integrated marketing, design-oriented company was needed. To do this, leadership is needed (1) at the corporate level, (2) at the program level, (3) at each of the major subsystem levels, and (4) within each of the functions. All of these people have to begin to share an entire new set of goals and measures, as well as information and power on a scale they never had to before. It is important to note how the figures of merit and Taguchi methods make such measurements possible and help one shift from mere financial standards to true quality and performance standards. Without being able to relate engineering standards to financial or figures of merit (quality) standards meaningful to the other functions, the latter can defend their turf much more successfully by simply claiming superior expertise.

Ford's Future

Although this is clearly primarily a process case, one should ask, "What would you expect the impact of the Taurus/Sable to be on Ford's future? How will competitors respond? What should Ford's next steps be?"

1. Immediate cash implications. The Taurus/Sable had consumed $3.25 billion in cash. Clearly, Ford had to maintain good margins on the cars' pricing during the first few years in the marketplace. The Taurus/Sables, if successful, could eventually be enormous cash cows. Should Ford attempt to hold its plant sizes, create a mild shortage, and up its Taurus/Sable prices? Build Taurus/Sables overseas and lower costs? In fact, the car was an enormous success in the upper middle market. Ford's cash flows reversed in short order and Ford began looking for new investment opportunities. Where should Ford focus? Should it expand its Ford Financial arm even more? Consolidate and strengthen dealerships? Drive for volume and penetration? Move for maximum automation? Focus on bringing its other car lines into coherence with Taurus/Sable? Start at the top (Lincoln) or bottom (Tempo, etc.)?

2. European implications. Ford's very strong European position indicates this as a primary target area. Given the impending unification of Europe, how should Ford organize for the European marketplace? It had a powerful German subsidiary and somewhat weaker operations in the United Kingdom. Should it concentrate in one location? Specialize in different locations? In Europe, however, this raises the question of how much the Ford auto line should be standardized across international boundaries. Should it have a standard Eurocar or appeal to national preferences and pressures? Should automobiles be designed for worldwide introduction or introduction into single geographical areas or countries? If so, where should various cars be produced?

3. Decentralization vs. centralization. Notice that the data in Exhibit 5 show that Japanese cars are designed with 82% unique parts as opposed to 62% in the United States. This suggests that the economies of scale in production are no longer the most important economies. Economies of scale have shifted to design capabilities, marketing capabilities, data bases, technologies, etc. This would suggest that Ford could profit by internationalizing its design capabilities more and decentralizing its parts and assembly as much as possible. Ford decided to develop a series of "centers of excellence" and unified platforms for a line of cars which would be introduced worldwide, yet modified in certain respects locally. How can it define policy for such "localization?" Each geographical area can now adapt the surface configurations and features of its cars to the personal taste of its domestic marketplace. The centers of excellence were to develop technologies in-depth. Each center had a selected set of special competencies which were to be utilized by other divisions throughout the world to obtain economies of scale in technology. How can these be defined to obtain the desired results, organized to overcome local jealousies and power plays, etc.?

4. Gaining further downstream leverage with the marketplace. Ford still suffered a volume deficit vs. GM and individual lines of Toyota. To gain some volume control, Ford participated in a management LBO of Hertz Rent-a-Car. This gave Ford access to the world's largest fleet purchaser of cars. This helped stabilize volume. Although it could have used this as a very sophisticated base for continuously testing and upgrading the quality of its cars once in service, there is little evidence to date that this synergy has been developed. In a further move downstream, Ford expanded its Ford Finance Group, later buying up a number of consumer finance companies including First Nationwide Financial Corporation. Should it eliminate, buy out, or control some of its distributors? Increasingly, power is shifting toward large distributorships. Should Ford at least operate a few on its own to understand their problems better? Perhaps consciously increase the average size and automation of dealers as Exxon has? Undertake other downstream strategies?

5. Flexible automation of the Taurus/Sable processes. After its processes had been debugged under a more personnel-oriented system, Ford began to more extensively automate its processes. Yet—because of union contracts—such automation could not be phased in any more rapidly than at one-half the pace of Ford's attrition losses. Ford had agreed to replace one person for every two attrition losses in its employment maintenance contracts. It also agreed that if technology eliminated a job of relatively high skill, it would supplement the affected employees' wages until new jobs calling for similar wages came into being. Nevertheless, Ford was able to

undertake a major flexible automation and CIM program over the next several years, using the cash throw-off of the Taurus/Sable. Establishing line balances with its policies of workers being able to stop the line and no on-line inventories made this essential.

6. Extending its core competencies. Ford had a very strong market share in trucks. By focusing on this marketplace and applying similar simultaneous design principles, Ford could leverage itself and its core competencies of integrated design and technology even further. There was an especially attractive and underdeveloped market (with only 8.2% and 6.4% of the non-UK market) for Ford trucks in Europe.

7. Positioning Ford's car line. Repositioning Ford's line relative to Japanese and European competitors was another major issue. Although Honda had proved that it could manufacture small cars in the United States and ship them back to Japan at a profit, U.S. companies were still focusing 83% of their development projects on medium to large cars. Europe was focusing 64% of its efforts on medium-sized cars. With its strong European presence, Ford had an opportunity to develop a high quality small car in Europe for presentation in the United States and perhaps Japanese markets. In 1990, the developing micro-mini market was totally untouched by U.S. competition. This, too, offered an interesting opportunity to utilize Ford's new concurrent design capabilities.

If U.S. producers like Ford could "get on the experience curve" before the Japanese were too strong in these new marketplaces, and while they were suffering from the relatively strong yen, U.S. companies might be able to preempt positions in these emerging marketplaces. If Ford could develop either the Taurus/Sable or a European-American small car of high quality, it could also partially preempt the Japanese in Europe '92. A crucial question was how to organize for this type of international development and obtain the organizational and emotional commitment to see it through, despite Ford's previous Detroit biases.

8. Competitive response. Given Ford's success with the Taurus/Sable concurrent design process, one would expect competitors to adopt similar processes in the near future. This would prove somewhat more difficult for companies with a large number of individual divisions (like GM). On the other hand, the Japanese could easily adapt the same complete system approach to product development and attack Ford's competitive edge. How should Ford respond? It can expect the Japanese companies to move upward from their small cars into the Taurus/Sable marketplace shortly.

Ford's main defense against this can be: (1) using its volume in the Taurus/Sable line to drive down its costs through experience curve effects as rapidly as possible and (2) being prepared to sting Japanese entries into that marketplace as soon as they are introduced in the United States—before the Japanese can build volume there. Real and perceived quality has to be a continuing concern; the perception of Japanese quality is very high, after years of performance and image building. There is increasing evidence of consumer tolerance of quality problems in Japanese cars because it has become fashionable not to mention them and because repairs are genuinely faster in Japanese automobiles. While sticking with the well-tested quality basics of the Taurus/Sable, Ford could make a planned series of cosmetic or feature changes in the car for the next 7-10 years which gave it the feeling of newness while improving its actual (below the skin) performance slowly and steadily. Simultaneously, through expanded dealer programs and its MIS systems, it could push the quick repairability it had built into the cars.

However, at the top of its line, Ford should also exploit the perceived weaknesses of Chrysler and Cadillac. Ford might further increase the perceived quality of its Taurus line if it can subtly associate Taurus and Continental. In fact, Ford had used the same process to redesign its Continental line and had created a smashing success, selling more of the new Continentals—before their initial release—than its entire planned model year production. Once secure at the upper middle and top of the line, Ford's next attacks should be at the smaller European car and upper-end-small-car markets in the United States. It needs to block the upscale moves of the Japanese in its markets. It should be able to hurt its Japanese competition by selectively pricing to prevent their attaining high volumes and profitability in the United States as Japanese internal costs rise due to exchange rates.

Ford has the United States and world volume to position itself strongly against the Japanese and Europeans, if it can change its quality image. While GM is suffering greatly in this respect, Ford can gain back enough U.S. market share to perhaps achieve market dominance. An excellent challenge for the class is, "What would it take for Ford to achieve market dominance?"

9. Organizational issues. How should Ford's organization look in future years? If Ford seeds the top of its various functional organizations with people from the Team Taurus group, it can expect more cross-functional cooperation, but only if it changes its internal performance measures and traditions. This could ultimately lead to performance standards for each team by car line. Should Ford go all the way to a series of worldwide product divisions, i.e., Continental, Taurus/Sable, Tempo, etc.? Should it divisionalize only at the level of its well-known marketing names (i.e., Ford, Mercury, Continental)? Should it align its marketing, R&D, and production by auto line or by brand name?

Internationally, how should its European affiliates be blended into this? Should Ford invade Japan directly or with a partner? How? Should there be common worldwide designs for component systems (like engines, suspension systems, etc.) and if so, whether by product (Tempo, Taurus, Continental) or by major trademark (Ford, Mercury, Continental)? Alternately, should Ford consider a geographical structure, (i.e., U.S., Canadian, European, Asian Pacific divisions dominating)? Or should it have a matrix organization with production and/or marketing under either trademark or geographical controls? Or should it simply operate with car-line teams? In each case, if so, how? Should it integrate design under a separate rubric or attach it to the selected divisional structure? Since economies of scale have now shifted to the supplier level, should Ford have a centralized purchasing and logistics system or should this be decentralized to the operating levels?

If Ford gives several more design teams the kind of cross-functional power it gave to Taurus/Sable, its traditional power structures will substantially erode and its series of worldwide brand lines could decline unless these are purposefully reinforced. Organization charts for the various proposed structures can be most illuminating. For each structure, students should be asked what kinds of control metrics they would propose. How would they ensure quality? Hedge against highly fluctuating exchange rates? Avoid over-reliance on a single currency? What should be the role of corporate (vs. the divisions) in enforcing a worldwide location and currency portfolio for Ford?

10. Alliances. Should Ford form a series of alliances with Japanese suppliers or Japanese auto companies? Should it widen its alliances in Europe? What can it offer? What does it need? Who are its best potential partners? At what level should alliances be made? What are the risks? How can these risks be best avoided? Controlled? Professors should emphasize potential supplier, marketing, and production levels of alliances; and not just joint ventures, but contract, non-contract, and technology alliances. A whole case discussion could be developed on just the issues and potentials of alliances. However, most will find the case most helpful in: (1) illustrating that organizational design and process management are equally as important as analysis in the generation of strategy, (2) discussing how major organizational changes and strategic repositionings can come about in very large organizations, (3) the importance of simultaneous design and team management in large organizations today.

The Trotman Era

Alex Trotman, Ford's new CEO, was considered its most visionary leader since Henry I. His approach was to pull together Ford's scattered worldwide operations to create an integrated company that could still serve each market individually. Under the aegis of a program known as

209

Ford 2000, Trotman proposed to merge its many engineering centers into five. Ford would revolutionize the way it designed the 70+ lines of cars and trucks it sold in over 200 markets. It hoped to save more than $4 billion a year from volume purchases and reduce duplication of effort, doubling the $3.8 billion profits from automotive operations in 1994. If it could do that, it would match Royal Dutch Shell as the most profitable company in the world. It was already clearly the most profitable automobile company.

In its quest, Ford had fewer than half as many models as GM, with 80% of GM's volume. Its trucks were highly ranked and among the ten best sellers in the United States. Its market share climbed from 20% in 1980 to 26% in 1995, while the Japanese brands remained relatively constant. Ford's sales volume grew from $5.3 billion in 1991 to $6.7 billion in 1994. But its share price did not reflect these successes. In a strong stock market, it was selling at a P/E multiple of only 6.

Ford 2000 eliminated Ford's separate North America and European engineering operations and replaced them with a structure organized around five vehicle development centers—four in Dearborn and one in Europe. The European center was to design the basic platform for all "small-car" vehicles throughout the world. Each of the Michigan centers would have a separate global mission: (1) developing large front-wheel drive cars including minivans, (2) developing rear-wheel drive cars including Jaguars, (3) designing off the road vehicles and smaller trucks, and commercial trucks. Manufacturing and assembly would continue at hundreds of factories throughout the world. With sales relatively level in North America, Europe and Japan, Trotman began to focus more on the developing regions of the world. However, the challenge was to do this with relatively few car designs while satisfying the major markets in the advanced markets. Ford's much touted "world car," the Contour, did not take off well. Learning from that experience, Trotman proposed that the inner components of cars sold everywhere in the world would be the same, but the outer skins would look different in each market in order to satisfy local needs.

To carry this off, Trotman introduced a global design cycle plan identifying every new car and truck Ford would introduce in every market from 1995 through 2003 and estimating the resources needed for each. Ford intended the reduce the number of basic platforms from 24 to 16, yet increase the number of models over those platforms by 50%. The big problem everyone anticipated was obtaining the dual focus needed to pull off this concept. Like many other large companies, Ford had built up a large middle management bureaucracy known as "the layer of clay." There was still large resistance on both sides of the Atlantic to Trotman's plan. Nevertheless, he proposed to move 25,000 employees to different offices and different bosses. Getting Ford's 338,000 employees to follow was a major challenge. Trotman proposed that each Ford manager have two bosses: a functional boss and a product line boss. This classic matrix structure posed significant problems. The relative power of the local units to influence design was still wide open. Critics were afraid that the new cars would be "McFords" pleasing no one. Similarly, cars sold globally would have to meet the world's toughest regulatory standards regardless of where they were sold.

Trotman and Jacques Nasser (a Lebanese who headed Operations) argued that the auto industry is a worldwide enterprise, not a national or regional business. Ford's five design centers would shepherd cars from the drawing board all the way to the show room in each of the world's marketplaces. The target was to cut development time from 37 months to 24 months, thus equaling industry leaders Toyota and Honda. Analysts said that Ford was shooting for a startling 30% reduction in costs from these processes. In 1995, Ford introduced its new Taurus line, a much downsized version of the earlier Taurus, which had become heavier and more complex as time went on. The new Taurus once again provided a startling look, giving Ford products a uniquely recognizable appearance. It continued the basic aero flow design first introduced in the original Taurus. However, its smaller, lighter platform made it more adaptable for the world's many changing and emerging marketplaces.

1994 Operating Highlights

	1994	1993
Factory sales (in thousands)		
Sales of cars in North America	2,250	1,950
Worldwide sales of cars and trucks		
United States	4,276	3,824
Outside the United States	2,363	5,965
Sales and revenues (in millions)		
Automotive	$ 107,137	$ 91,568
Financial Services	21,302	16,953
Total	$ 128,439	$ 108,521
Operating income (in millions)		
Automotive	$ 15,826	$ 1,432
Financial Services	2,792	2,712
Total	$ 18,616	$ 4,144
Net Income (in millions)		
Automotive	$ 3,824	$ 940
Financial Services	1,484	1,589
Total	$ 5,308	$ 2,529
Capital expenditures (in millions)		
Automotive	$ 8,310	$ 6,714
Financial Services	236	100
Total	$ 8,546	$ 6,814
Assets (in millions)		
Automotive	$ 68,371	$ 61,737
Financial Services	150,983	137,201
Total	$ 219,354	$ 198,938

ARGYLE DIAMONDS TEACHING NOTE

In the Argyle Diamonds case, management is confronted in 1991 with a major and complex strategic decision. Its initial contract with the Central Selling Organization (CSO) is coming up for renewal and it must decide whether to persist with its efforts towards more independent marketing of diamonds, or leave its marketing to the cartel and sacrifice its independence for the security that presumably offers.

The case also illustrates a number of strategic issues which can usefully be discussed in class:

1. It is a relatively rare example of active marketing in the mining industry where the full range of the marketing mix is used.

2. It is about a newcomer establishing itself in a market place dominated by a monopolistic cartel. The company uses a mixed strategy of co-operation and competition.

3. It can also be used to illustrate the importance of controlling or at least being able to influence the key power points along the value system in strategy formulation.

Case Description

The case describes the discovery and development of a substantial diamond deposit in the remote northwest of Australia. The mine was developed by a joint venture led by CRA, Ltd., the Australian listed member of the Rio Tinto group of the United Kingdom. The production capacity of the mine is large in world terms. Within three years the mine was operating at capacity, producing about 30 million carats per annum or 40% of world output of diamonds by volume. The quality was, however, mediocre and the mine accounted for only about 5% of world sales by value. The relatively low value was due partly to the relatively small proportion of gem quality diamonds compared to near gem and industrial diamonds. In addition, the mine produced a high proportion of colored diamonds, particularly of yellow and brown hues. It also produced small quantities of pink diamonds which are very scarce and can command high prices. Its pink diamonds were of a deeper shade than found elsewhere and this was a special feature of the mine. However, it did not produce sufficient pink diamonds to compensate for the low grades of the rest of the production.

The diamond industry is controlled by the world's most durable and successful cartel, run by De Beers Ltd., a company registered in Kimberly, South Africa. De Beers spokesmen deny that it is a cartel, preferring to call it a marketing arrangement with benefits to all involved, including the consumers who would not wish to see the value of their purchase decline. The cartel was formed during the early part of the century and has survived several attempts by mines and countries, such as Zaire and Russia, to break away from the cartel and do their own marketing. In almost every case, these producers eventually returned to the organized marketing of the cartel. Marketing is done through the De Beers subsidiary, the Central Selling Organization, which is registered in London. The De Beers group has stabilized the supply/demand balance by absorbing excess production during economic downturns, and controlled release during times of high demand. De Beers/CSO was able to operate the stockpile and the cartel because of its access to very substantial financial resources, as well as its unwavering faith in the merits of maintaining an orderly diamond market.

Teaching note copyright © 1992 by André Morkel.

Note: all dollar figures are U.S. dollars unless otherwise indicated.

CSO was known for its sophisticated marketing of diamonds. It literally created markets for near-gem stones where none existed before. Its early successes were in the United States and the United Kingdom and Commonwealth countries where it popularized diamond engagement rings and other jewelry. More recently it created similar markets in Japan and Germany.

The Argyle joint venturers negotiated a deal with CSO whereby about 75% of its production would be marketed through CSO leaving them the freedom to market the remainder themselves. This was a unique arrangement, allowed to no other producer in the cartel. The Western Australian and Australian Federal Governments were involved in the negotiations. Getting concessions from De Beers was possibly helped by pressure from the Australian union movement not to deal with De Beers because of its association with South Africa and its apartheid racial policies.

Argyle embarked on a vigorous campaign to enhance the value of its colored diamonds. Diamonds are graded according to size, lack of flaws, and lack of color. White, or colorless diamonds have traditionally been valued much higher than diamonds with yellow and brown tints. Pink, blue, and green diamonds were very rare and formed a special highly valued category. By far the most common collocations were tints of yellow and brown and this decreased their value dramatically. Argyle promoted yellow and brown diamonds as champagne and cognac diamonds and commissioned high profile and extravagant exhibits such as Fabergé style eggs and other "objets" which they displayed at international exhibitions to promote the value and sales of colored diamonds.

At the end of the case, the five-year contract with De Beers was due to be re-negotiated.

Questions for Discussion and Assignments

1. What is the basic problem facing management of Argyle Diamonds and how would you go about resolving the problem?

2. What are the alternative courses of action open to Argyle Diamonds in its relationship with CSO?

3. Why is the CSO so strong? Why have companies and countries such as Zaire, Botswana, and Russia failed to establish rival marketing systems for diamonds? Is there any reason to believe that Argyle would do any better?

4. Sketch the value chain for diamonds and identify Porter's competitive forces for the players in each step. Where do CSO and Argyle concentrate their efforts?

TEACHING PLAN

The Argyle Diamonds case can be taught as a normal interactive strategy case. It can also be used for an examination or as a take-home assignment. There is a clear problem facing management and the case discussion can be built around this as a focus.

The case can also be used to:

(a) discuss strategies of mining companies and the growing importance of marketing in the mining industry; and to

(b) examine the nature of the CSO cartel and why it has been more successful than other attempts at international commodity cartels (OPEC, copper, tin, wool). In exploring this theme it is useful to bring home to students the reality of economic power held by a group such as the CSO. Several companies, and indeed countries, attempted to break away in the past and were unsuccessful. Would Argyle be able to do any better?

The Problem

In the case, management of Argyle Diamonds is faced with the challenge of identifying and establishing a suitable marketing relationship with the CSO cartel established and managed by De Beers for orderly marketing of diamonds throughout the world. The choice is more complex than a simple yes or no decision. Even though it has spent a very substantial effort on developing its own marketing strengths, the Company has been selling only a quarter of its production on its own. The remainder is sold through the CSO cartel.

The question is thus not simply one of going with the cartel or breaking away completely, but rather which of a range of options to negotiate:

(a)   to renew the contracts on more or less existing terms;
(b)   to seek more independence incrementally;
(c)   to take a bolder step towards marketing independently (which could include a complete breakaway); or
(d)   to fully rejoin the CSO cartel and dispense with the costs associated with its own marketing efforts.

The company is operating in three major market segments, i.e., gem, near-gem and industrial diamonds, and it may decide to follow different strategies in each of these markets.

The Central Selling Organization (CSO)

The CSO is one of the most successful and enduring cartels of modern times. It sells gem and near-gem diamonds in many countries throughout the world and has kept a firm grip on the diamond market ever since the early 1930s. The marketing of near gem diamonds is a remarkable story of creating mass markets for luxury goods where none existed before.

Throughout history diamonds have been associated with kings, sultans, potentates, and the very wealthy. It was considered the rarest and most desirable of all jewels. The situation changed with the discovery of the rich Kimberly diamond fields in South Africa in 1871, five years after the first diamond was found in that country. A diamond rush was on, similar to the gold rushes of that period: California (1849), New South Wales and Victoria (1850s), and later the Transvaal (1880s) and Western Australia (1880s). Large numbers of fortune hunters flocked to the diamond fields to dig for their fortune. While some diamonds fields were alluvial and could be handled by individual diggers and small syndicates, the Kimberly deposits consisted of an ancient volcanic pipe which went down far deeper than the diggers could go. As the diggings went deeper, the small operators were forced out by large syndicates with the capital and organization for large-scale deep mining.

The volume of diamonds produced in these new mines threatened the market value of a product which depended very much on perceived scarcity to maintain its desirability. The price of diamonds fluctuated wildly during this period.

Some of the influential mining groups sought to stabilize prices through various sales agreements with only partial success. Eventually Sir Ernest Oppenheimer mobilized the financial resources of London financiers behind the De Beers/CSO cartel to create an organized market for diamonds which has endured up to the present time. It involved consolidating the supply of diamonds, creating orderly distribution channels, and being able to stockpile as many diamonds as necessary to create stable pricing regimes for the products. His son, Mr. Harry Oppenheimer, and other members of the family have carried on the family tradition and led the cartel since the

Second World War. The family also controlled the giant Anglo American Corporation which is the largest producer of gold in South Africa and is involved in a wide range of other mining and industrial activities.

The cartel has been amazingly durable in spite of many difficult years. It is worth discussing in class why it has lasted, and why it has not broken down like so many other cartels of the past. The De Beers group appears to have kept the cartel together with a combination of determination and persistence, diplomacy, financial strength, shrewd business dealings, and a proven track record of success. They have tirelessly promoted the idea that it is in the interest of all the parties involved to stay within the group rather than compete with it. To be successful, the cartel concept takes unshakable faith and enormous financial reserves to buy and stockpile diamonds in order to stabilize prices in tough economic times. It is not a game for the faint of heart or those in danger of running out of money. The biggest investments to mop up supply must be made at a time when the market and the world economies are depressed, and most experts are advising against such investments. It is a game where you must see the strategy through to the next upswing in the economy in order to realize a return on your investment. The advice of "not throwing good money after bad" would lead to certain losses by selling in depressed times and driving the prices down even further. The strategy works only if the cartel can successfully control supply and pricing, if demand returns on a cyclical basis, and no true substitute is developed. If any of these assumptions do not hold true, the result could be disastrous.

The depression of the 1930s was the early testing time for the cartel and it managed to survive that difficult time under the leadership of Sir Ernest Oppenheimer and his son, Harry. Difficult times were experienced more recently in the late 1970s, early 1980s, and also at the time of writing, in 1992. According to Nicky Oppenheimer, (46 in 1992), the crisis in 1981 was particularly severe. Ironically the 1980s crisis was triggered not by a fall in demand, but rather by a rapid increase in diamonds prices. Dealers, cutters, and investors, with bank financing, sought quick profits through speculative buying, building stockpiles and seeking to bypass the CSO channels. When the bubble burst, followed by a recessionary downturn in sales, bankers foreclosed on stocks and ended up with control of big holdings of diamonds outside the orbit of CSO. CSO had to do a lot of convincing to keep the banks from dumping their stocks, thus averting the first downturn in prices since the cartel was formed.[1]

Many producers have also tried over the years to bypass the cartel and market their production independently. Zaire as a large producer of industrial diamonds, Tanzania with gem diamonds from the then Williamson mine, and the Soviet Union have all tried at various times to break out of the cartel arrangements without success. In the end they realize that co-operation is more profitable than competition. Perhaps they also found the markets more sophisticated and the distribution channels harder to break into than it would seem initially. The achievement by the cartel is all the more remarkable considering that it is a capitalist monopoly with its home base within the apartheid regime of South Africa. It is hard to imagine a more unpopular mix of political and ideological associations for some of the supplier countries who co-operated in the cartel. It violates the anti-trust legislation of the United States, and to avoid arrest and prosecution, it is said that De Beers/CSO executives never visit the United States.

A cartel works best if it has closed ranks, and the presence of a large independent competitor could upset the delicate balance. Initially CSO sought to control sources of supply. This has become increasingly difficult as more and more sources of supply have become available from mines in different countries. Smuggling and illicit trading further enhanced the problems of controlling supply. The massive output of the Argyle mine, for example, must have been decidedly unwelcome within the industry.

The cartel's control within the industry has increasingly shifted down the value chain to key components in the distribution channels, as much as supply. The cartel had a major role in stimulating demand. Creating the tradition of a diamond engagement ring in the United States and other English-speaking countries was an early marketing success of the cartel. The case describes the more recent campaigns in Japan and Germany. De Beers managed to create mass markets (mainly for near-gems) while still retaining the perception that these are rare and very special jewels with mystique and romance. Significantly, they also managed to create a market where the product is bought but seldom re-sold. Selling an engagement ring would be unthinkable in a stable relationship and even where the engagement was broken off, it was not common to sell the diamond. When trying to sell a diamond back to the trade, one is confronted with the realities of the high markups and sales and luxury taxes characteristic of the industry. The jeweler can buy the same quality diamond at wholesale without the retail tax and would not be keen to buy from a private vendor unless it was a very special diamond, or sold cheaply. The perceived high value of diamonds is best not tested in the reality of resale markets. "A diamond is forever" became true in more ways than one for many owners.

With CSO having created a market for the product, an independent producer can then opportunistically enter the market as long as it has access to distribution and retailing channels and its volumes are not so large as to upset the dynamics of the market. The Aredor mine of Guinea has followed this strategy with considerable success as described in the case. However, CSO has managed in the past to lure most of the breakaway efforts back into the cartel. While the industry is clouded in secrecy, it appears that De Beers/CSO uses a complex approach to managing the cartel. It has a very urbane and sophisticated presence appropriate to the trade in luxury goods and the high levels of financial dealings of the "City" in London. It combines this with skillful and street smart haggling characteristic of the jewelry trade. The comment in the case by CSO director, Anthony Oppenheimer, son of Sir Philip, as the new negotiations are about to commence, hints of their approach to managing the industry. Finally it is said that CSO will also exercise brute force and power where appropriate. The proverbial iron fist in the velvet glove.

In Argyle's case, CSO accepted a position, negotiated with the government and trade union backing, where the bulk of the production was sold through the cartel while allowing Argyle to develop its own independent marketing channels.

Argyle's Marketing Strategy

The value of diamonds is determined by size, lack of color, and lack of flaws. It was in colored diamonds where Argyle had to depart from the established marketing image for diamonds created by CSO. A substantial percentage of Argyle's output is colored and consisted mainly of what the trade classified as inferior "Cape Yellows" and "Cape Browns." For Argyle, a system based on gradings of white and blue-white would seriously limit the prices they could command for their products. For them, the payoff in creating a special market for colored diamonds was high, and the cartel was not going to do it for them.

There had been earlier attempts to upgrade the image of the yellow colored diamonds and Argyle was not the first to use terms such as champagne for light yellow stones. However, they seem to be the first company to have put in the necessary effort and resources to credibly upgrade the image of colored diamonds.

A bold departure from tradition was called for. Naming the stones "champagne" and "cognac" diamonds was only the beginning. Most diamonds are mounted in gold jewelry where the golden color of the metal is reflected and diffracted in the facets of the gems, no matter how good their white or blue white ratings are on their own. Argyle built on this as an advantage and it emphasized in its promotions the interplay of color between white, champagne, and cognac diamonds mounted in gold settings.

The Company commissioned Stuart Devlin, the Queen's jeweler, to design a collection of jewelry with a large extravagant Fabergé style egg as its center piece ("or objet"). The Faberge egg's association with the excesses of the Czars was part of the image-building process. The collection was exhibited around the world at jewelry fairs and national exhibitions and created considerable interest in the trade and with the general public. It placed colored diamonds and Argyle Diamonds on the map as new and interesting. Argyle also established itself as a sophisticated and credible supplier of gem diamonds in a very traditional and clannish trade. The Devlin egg was sold for a good price after it had served its role in promoting colored diamonds. Thus the marketing costs associated with these extravagant pieces of jewelry are not as high as it would appear on first sight.

Mining Strategies

Given the importance of mining in the Australian (and several other countries') economy, it is worth reflecting on the nature of strategy in that industry. Strategy is usually concerned with how firms position themselves in the marketplace. In mining, competition between firms tends to lie elsewhere. Marketing in mining usually consists of negotiating long-term supply contracts with downstream processors. While these contracts have to be won in competition with their rivals, the familiar marketing emphasis is not the main focus of strategy in mining.

For mining companies, competitive positioning comes more from the supply side, that of finding and securing rights to good economic deposits rather than differentiating its goods in the marketplace. Thus exploration or the acquisition of suitable tenements from existing owners form important parts of mining strategies. Thereafter, the companies concentrate on achieving the best possible mining and extraction efficiencies at lowest costs (i.e., cost leadership strategies), and negotiating the best possible sales contracts for their product.

The Argyle case illustrates the importance of securing the mining lease tenements and achieving production efficiencies. In this sense it follows the normal pattern of mining companies. However, it is the emphasis on sophisticated marketing which makes the Argyle case unusual and interesting.

The instructor can gainfully explore with the class whether mining companies ought not to devote more of their energies to differentiating themselves in the market place. The potential gains from successful marketing can be enormous, considering the existing practice where the industry largely relies on bargaining skills to gain small increments when negotiating long-term contracts.

Value-Added Chain

The value-added stages after mining and recovery of rough diamonds are comprised of a sequence of trading, polishing, and setting into jewelry as in Figure 1. Trading is a highly formalized system organized and regulated by the CSO. Recognized dealers are invited to "sights" where they inspect priced parcels of diamonds assembled by CSO and reflecting to a certain extent their requirements. In the past, their only option was to accept or reject the offered sights. They could not change the composition of a parcel and no haggling about prices was permitted. In recent years CSO has become less arrogant and sight holders can now place orders ahead with CSO trying to match their needs.[2]

With the majority of its ornamental diamonds in the lower near-gem category, the bulk of Argyle's production is distributed via cutters in India and other Asian countries. The development of a diamond-cutting industry in China also fits a strategy of developing channels for lesser near-gems. A relatively small number of top quality gems are cut and polished in Perth at the headquarters of the company. While the exact reasons are not stated in the case, it is reasonable to assume that processing some gems in-house is part of a strategy where the company is fully knowledgeable about each step of the value chain of its product. Information about the various activities within the value system is important to the company when setting its prices and working with its customers. It is also a source of added profits and there would also be some political advantages of being engaged in downstream processing within Australia.

Rather than seeking to progress one step at a time down the value chain, the company leapfrogged the intermediate steps to concentrate on marketing and creating a separate market for its products. It concentrates on the early production stage and final marketing stage while supporting existing and new players in the intermediate stages, doing only a very limited amount of it in-house. The company thus concentrated its efforts to control the key power points in the value system, i.e., control over the resource and control over marketing. With many diamond cutters to choose from, the company can decide whether to do some of this in-house or not, without affecting its essential power position in the industry. Diamond cutting is essentially a cottage industry and the small companies have a relatively weak bargaining power when dealing with large companies. It makes sense for the producers to work within this structure rather than attempt to displace it.

Note that the value chain for Argyle differs from the one for De Beers/CSO in two significant ways, as shown in Figure 2. For the latter, diamonds are delivered not only from their own mines, but from virtually all other mines in the world. Second, De Beers maintains the very substantial stockpile which acts as a sink or buffer to even supply and demand. The maintenance of the stockpile requires resources which are well above the capacity of most producers, including presumably, Argyle.

What should the Company Do?

Having made a substantial investment in the marketing of its own diamonds and developing a separate image for colored diamonds, it is likely that the company will continue to market at least some of its own diamonds. Thus the present arrangement, perhaps with more favorable terms, would be attractive to the company. There is little to be gained from a direct confrontation and price war with CSO. It is more likely to be a process of high level negotiations where the desired outcome for Argyle would be an incremental step of marketing an increased share of its output. With so much at stake, the company should invest a substantial effort in the negotiation process, using the best counsel and tacticians available. As a subsidiary of the large CRA Group of Companies it will be able, to some extent, to balance the economic and professional power of the De Beers/CSO group.

SUBSEQUENT EVENTS

The five-year contract with CSO was re-negotiated during the first half of 1991. From a media report of an interview with David Karpin, MD of Argyle, it appears that Argyle managed to negotiate a number of key points in its favor.[3] The new five-year sales agreement (from July 1, 1991 to June 30, 1996) was signed with CSO's Swiss arm, De Beers Centenary Corporation AG, and it gives Argyle total control over its pink diamonds and new marketing powers for its other colored diamonds. CSO's share of revised share of the gem and near-gem stones will increase from 75% to 78%. The agreement also continued a rare short-term escape clause giving Argyle the option to terminate the contract before June 30, 1992 if the company were not satisfied with the way its diamonds were classified and valued by CSO to establish its 10% sales margin. Because every diamond is different and stones vary from mine to mine, the valuation process is complex, and prices are generally set against a mutually-agreed standard sample held by CSO. The sample can comprise a mixture of any of the 5000 categories of gems. The escape clause appeared to reflect Argyle's concern of some years ago that it was not receiving the fairest possible deal from CSO. Part of Argyle's human resource strategy was to train its sorters to the levels where they could challenge the sorting judgments of CSO sorters. This was crucial to its profitability as the price obtained for its diamonds from CSO depended on the skills and judgments of the diamonds' sorters.

Mr. Karpin stated that both Argyle and De Beers were happy with the agreement. The new deal does not allow for caps on production levels, although CSO has the right to defer purchases if the market weakens. The big bonus for Argyle was CSO's decision to allow it to retain all of its production of pink diamonds and as much as 20,000 carats of other gemstones for further processing. According to the report, this compared favorably with a flat 60,000 carats specified in the previous deal.

The company continued to promote colored diamonds very actively in the marketplace. According to David Karpin, the company increased the value of pink diamonds from a previous price of tens of thousands of dollars a carat to as high as a million for the best quality.[4] The Devlin collection with the Fabergé egg as its center piece was very successful in enhancing the interest and exposure of yellow- and brown-hued diamonds in the market place. The company sold the Devlin egg and other pieces at a profit and commissioned a second large 700 mm tall Kutchinsky "library" egg with an estimated value of A$13 million and containing about 435 carats of diamonds. It weighed 23 Kg. and used 15 Kg. of gold. A feature of the library egg was the extensive use of some 20,000 pink diamonds, mounted together with champagne and cognac diamonds. By combining the valuable pink gems extravagantly with white and yellow tints, the company sought to upgrade the image of its champagne and cognac diamonds.

Market research done by the company indicated that the consumers were interested in colored diamonds and that the problem lay with the conservative attitudes in the trade. The company then embarked on active campaigns to persuade the U.S. retailers that colored diamonds were an exciting new adjunct to their business. The company was careful to avoid cannibalizing the existing trade for white diamonds and sought to develop new markets for its colored products. According to the company, the retailers in California who participated in their promotional campaign were delighted with the results, and experienced higher sales than they had anticipated. With a decline in sales due to the recession, an additional line of diamond products was welcomed. Whether these experiences can be duplicated and sustained in the many cities of the world is still to be seen, and would likely require sustained and expensive marketing efforts by the company. Argyle spent about A$6 million on marketing in the U.S. diamond jewelry market (a $12.5 billion retail market). In 1992 the company allocated A$7 million for marketing with a focus on the $12.5 billion Japanese and $8 billion European retail diamond jewelry markets. In comparison, De Beers budgeted about A$164 million on marketing in 1992.[5] The wholesale market for diamonds as sold by CSO and Argyle was $3.9 billion in 1991, the first time in four years that sales had dropped below $4 billion.[6]

According to one media report, part of Argyle's campaign for upgrading the prices paid for colored diamonds was directed at improving the cut Indian cutters and polishers gave these diamonds. There was a vicious cycle at work with colored diamonds. As long as these sold at 60% less than the colorless products, they will likely be cut by the less proficient cutters, which in turn makes it hard to command higher prices for the final products. Only when the colored diamonds are cut at equivalent standards to colorless diamonds will Argyle be able to command higher prices for its products.[7]

Argyle has been sufficiently bullish about its future to announce major expansion plans to commence in mid-1992.[8] Under the plan, A$100 million will be spent on new ore handling and processing equipment and special high pressure roller crushers. Output from the mine will be increased by one third to 8 million tons of ore per annum (t.p.a.). (The mine commenced in 1980 with a capacity of 3 million t.p.a. capacity. This was increased in 1990 to 6 million t.p.a.) The company will be able to maintain production at about the present rate of about 35 million carats per year, despite the decline in grades as the ore body deepens. Exploration drilling in 1991 established proven reserves for at least 15 years of mining at 15 million t.p.a. The mine will remain an open pit with alluvial top-up for at least the next ten years, after which it will go underground. Production for the year to December 1991 amounted to 34.96 million carats, compared to 33.78 million for the same period in 1992.[9]

Until fairly recently there was little public response or comment from the De Beers/CSO group regarding Argyle's efforts to enhance the image of colored diamonds. The big question for CSO must be whether Argyle's marketing has created a new market for colored diamonds or whether it is cannibalizing the market for colorless diamonds, i.e., whether it is a positive or zero sum game. If it is truly the creation of a new market, the De Beers group would stand to gain very substantially, as the production of yellow tinted diamonds from the world's mines at 40% is very similar to that of Argyle's. However, there is also likely to be a level of skepticism and nervousness in the CSO camp. Their whole marketing approach to diamonds over the years has reinforced the old trading traditions of the enhanced value of colorlessness. According to a media report,[10] De Beers has commissioned a research project in the United States and Japan to judge whether the brown diamond campaign expands the diamond market or acts as a substitute to the colorless diamond.

At the time of writing, the diamond market is adversely affected by the economic recession of the early 1990s. According to Nicky Oppenheimer the group has become more knowledgeable about the downstream activities in the marketplace. "In the past where, as long as the cutting centers (of Antwerp, Tel Aviv, Bombay, Thailand and Brazil) were okay and we could sell alright there, that was fine. We were never really too concerned about what happened beyond there, through the pipeline all the way to the retailer. . . we now realize that the (diamond) trade is an integrated unit. We've got to know what happens all the way down and we've put a lot of knowledge and effort into discovering what happens."[11]

The company is also displaying less arrogance to its customers. In the past, CSO determined what the dealers needed, sometimes putting hard-to-move diamonds in an otherwise suitable quality parcel. It also made its own assessment of diamond demand in determining the size of parcels offered to sight holders. Any dealer who twice refused parcels was not invited back. Sight holders now assess their market requirements and order ahead of the London sights and the CSO tries to match their needs. Refusals are rare and lead to discussions rather than Coventry.[12]

De Beers suffered a 15% drop in sales from $2,084 million for the first half of 1991 to $1,787 million for the same period in 1992. With a 26% drop in attributable earnings in the same period, the company reduced its dividend to 24.7 US cents per De Beers/Centenary linked unit for the first half of 1992 compared to 25.1 cents in 1991. While this reduction may appear small to an observer in a period when many once mighty corporations were struggling to survive, the reduced dividend sent shock waves through the investment community in the United Kingdom. De Beers had been seen as a bastion company which could be trusted to increase its dividend steadily over the years. It had cut its dividend in the past only once, in 1981, and the new dividend cut damaged the stock's reputation with investors. De Beers also announced that it had imposed a 25% quota reduction on all producers supplying the CSO cartel. The company gave two reasons for this drastic action: low retail and rough diamond sales due to weaker than anticipated upturns in Europe and the United States, and a continued slowdown in Japan, and a dramatic increase in illicit diamond supplies from Angola. CSO had managed to mop up much of this trade, but some of it was still being marketed outside the cartel.[13] In spite of the downturn in sales, smuggled volumes were on the increase. The illicit diamond sales from Angola commenced in volume after the peace accord early in 1989 in that country. An estimated 50,000 private diggers are at work and their numbers are swelling daily in the drought-ridden country. To add to the glut, De Beers itself was opening a new diamond mine, Venetia, in northern Transvaal province of South Africa, with an estimate capacity of 6 million carats per year. There were rumors that illicit diamonds were also being traded out of Russia, in spite of the $5 billion agreement the CSO had signed with the Russian gold and diamond organization, Rosalmazzoloto. Two Belgian trading firms who have had many years of dealings with the Russians were punished by being temporarily excluded from attending CSO's sights. Mr. Harry Oppenheimer, now 84 years of age, and his son Nicky visited Russia in 1992 to personally cement relationships with the Russian producers.[14]

Thus much is happening in the diamond industry, and it will be interesting to monitor how the recession of the early 1990s will affect the relationship between Argyle and the De Beers/CSO group.

References

[1] Peter Maher, "Sight for Sore Ice," *The Bulletin*, Sydney, March 17, 1992, pp. 32-33.

[2] Maher, "Sight for Sore Ice."

[3] Tim Treadgold, "Argyle Joins the Big League," *Business Review Weely*, Sydney, January 31, 1992, pp. 16-18.

[4] Philip Rennie, "Argyle Hits the Chapagne Trail," *Business Review Weekly*, Sydney, August 9, 1991, pp. 36 & 39.

[5] Katherine Teh, "Marketing Battle Looms over Brown Diamonds," *The Australian*, Sydney, May 13, 1992, p. 31.

[6] Treadgold, "Argyle Joins The Big League."

[7] Teh, "Marketing Battle Looms."

[8] Treadgold, "Argyle Joins The Big League."

[9] Treadgold, "Argyle Joins The Big League."

[10] Katherine Teh, 1992, op. cit.

[11] Maher, "Sight for Sore Ice."

[12] Maher, "Sight for Sore Ice."

[13] Philip Gawith, *Financial Times*, London, August 12, 1992.

[14] Kenneth Goodwin, *Financial Times*, London, August 28, 1992.

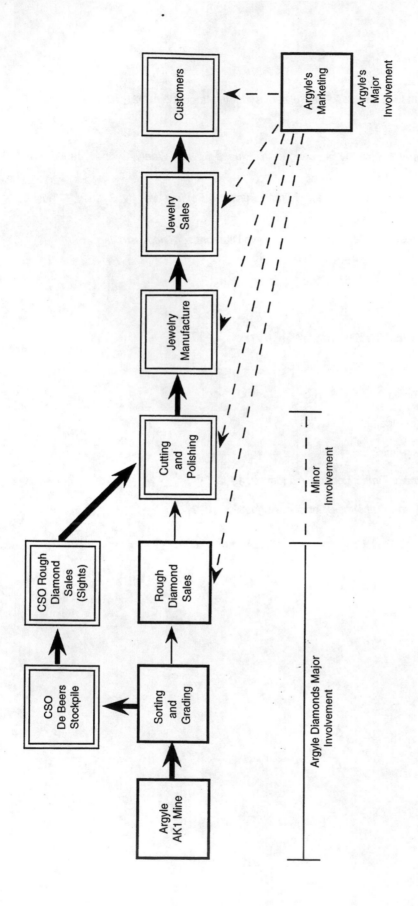

Figure 1. Argyle Diamond's Involvement in the Value Chain

222

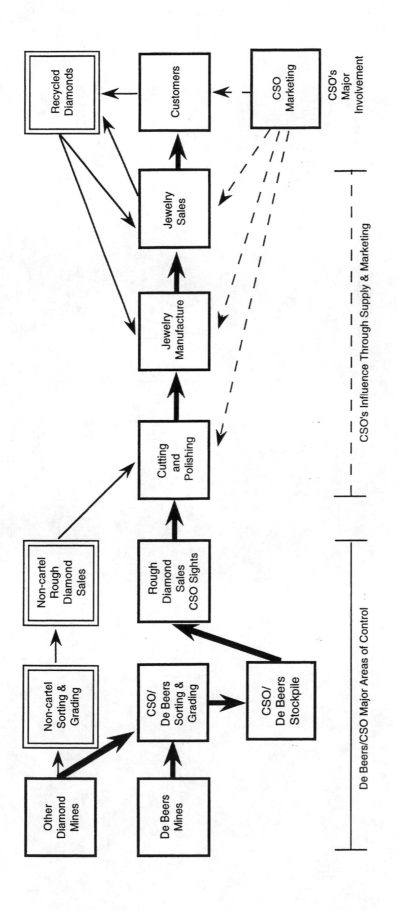

Figure 2. The Diamond Industry Value Chain from the CSO Perspective

SECTION II: ORGANIZATION

Galbraith, "Strategy and Organization Planning"

Summary of Reading

Recent models of organization planning convey two key ideas: (1) organization is more than just structure, and (2) all the elements must "fit" to be in "harmony" with each other. Also, successful strategy requires a fit between strategy and organization. The organization planner must aid management in choosing an appropriate strategy for the existing organization, or a new organization for the new strategy.

I. STRATEGY AND ORGANIZATION

Recent work has illuminated how different strategic change patterns lead to different structures, systems, and cultures. The key is the organization having a center of gravity or driving force. The center of gravity of a company depends on where in the industry supply chain the company started.

This chain has six stages:

> Raw material extraction
>
> Primary manufacturing
>
> Fabrication of commodity products
>
> Product production
>
> Marketing and distribution
>
> Retailing

The first three stages are called "upstream," the last three "downstream." The upstream stages add value by reducing the variety of raw materials into a few commodities. The downstream stages add value by producing a variety of products to meet customer needs. This downstream value is added through advertising, product positioning, marketing channels, and R&D.

The upstream/downstream distinction is important because of the fundamental differences in success factors, management experiences, and organizational forms; these differences are rooted in where the company began in the chain. Here are some of the differences:

Upstream	Downstream
Standardize/Homogenize	Customize/Segment
Low Cost Producer	High Margins/Proprietary Positions
Process Innovation	Product Innovation
Capital Budget	R&D/Advertising Budget
Technology/Capital Intensive	People Intensive
Supply/Trader/Engineering	R&D/Marketing Dominated
Line Driven	Line/Staff
Maximize End Users	Target End Users
Sales Push	Market Pull

"Companies can be in the same industry but be very different because they developed from a particular stage of the industry . . . . The firm develops an integrated organization (structure, processes, rewards, and people) which is peculiar to that stage and forms the center of gravity."

II. STRATEGIC CHANGE

The first strategic change that an organization makes is to vertically integrate within its industry. This does not change the center of gravity because these forward or backward stages are operated for the benefit of the center of gravity. (These concepts are illustrated using the paper industry.)

One of the first diversification moves made by a vertically integrated company is to sell byproducts from the points along the industry chain. This changes neither the industry nor the center of gravity.

Another strategic change is diversification into new industries but at the same center of gravity. This is called "related diversification."

A third type of diversification is moving into new industries and new centers of gravity, but maintaining some link among the various businesses (e.g., a primary producer of paper products, which owns woodlots, moving into wood products and wood-byproduct chemicals). This is called linked diversification.

A final type of strategic change is to diversify into unrelated businesses. This would involve moving into new industries and different centers of gravity, but with little relation among the businesses.

A last possibility for change is for the firm to remain in the same industry but change its center of gravity in that industry. An example would be a chemical company's moving downstream into the manufacturing of higher margin, proprietary products.

III. STRATEGY, ORGANIZATION, AND PERFORMANCE

Here is the current view of the relationship between strategy and structure:

Strategy	Structure
Single business	Functional
Vertical byproducts	Functional with profit centers
Related businesses	Divisional
Linked businesses	Mixed structures
Unrelated businesses	Holding companies

There has been no work done on the structures, or performance differences, that result from changes in center of gravity. But there is evidence about the effects of the other structures on economic performance.

Using return on equity, the highest performers are the related diversifiers. This may be because of the industries they are in, or it may be because they have learned a set of core skills and know how to design an organization at a particular center of gravity. In other words, they get a diversified portfolio of businesses, but each with a system of management and an organization that is understood by everyone.

Unrelateds have to learn both new businesses and how to operate at a new center of gravity. The latter is the most difficult to accomplish.

The poorest performers tend to be vertically integrated byproduct sellers. These companies make up "Smokestack America." They have done poorly because their organizations were set up for upstream stages, and they were unable to change for downstream businesses.

228

It appears to be very difficult to change centers of gravity, because this requires dismantling of the power structure, rejection of parts of the old culture, and all-new management systems. Related diversification works for exactly the opposite reasons—it involves minimal changes in power structure and accepted ways of doing things. Changes in center of gravity usually occur by new start-ups at a new center of gravity, rather than a shift in the center of established firms.

Most research has been done on diversification. Little has been done on center of gravity change.

Discussion Questions

1. Exactly what does the concept of "center of gravity" mean, and how useful is it?

Galbraith says that the center of gravity is similar to Tregoe and Zimmerman's concept of "driving force." The driving force of a business is the area which governs whenever a strategic decision is made. For example, in a company with a driving force of sales growth, any important decision would be made on the basis of how it affected potential for sales growth.

Center of gravity is a little more specific than driving force. Galbraith identifies six stages in the industry chain. A firm's center of gravity is the stage on the chain that is most important for it, the stage where it had its initial success, where it has learned the most lessons. For example, a firm might be primarily a raw material extractor, even if it has some primary manufacturing capability. Or it might be primarily a retailer, even though it has some product producing capability.

Students will differ on how useful the concept is, but it seems to accurately characterize firms, especially when the coarser concept of "upstream/downstream" is used.

2. The author says that what distinguishes upstream from downstream companies is differences in "factors for success, lessons learned by managers, and the organizations used . . . ." Rank order these by importance.

Of course there is no hard-and-fast answer to this question. Some students will argue that regardless of management and organization, the factors for success in the industry will determine effectiveness. Others will argue that skillful managers can "read" environments and understand success factors, or that managers who learn the wrong lessons can fail to adapt to changing environments. This makes lessons learned by managers the most important factor. Still others will assert that organizations are either adaptable or not, depending on their structure, and so organization is the most important factor.

3. How do related and linked diversification differ?

These two forms of diversification are the same in that both involve moving into new industries. How they differ is in the way center of gravity is handled. In related diversification, companies operate at the same center of gravity in both their old and new industries. An example would be Procter and Gamble, which diversified from paper into soap and food, but was a marketer/distributor in all three industries. In linked diversification, firms enter their new industries at a different center of gravity from their original one. A good example here would be Union Camp, which diversified paper into wood products and chemicals; in its original industry, it was a primary manufacturer, but in the wood products industry it was a raw materials extractor, and in chemicals it was intending to operate from a product producer center of gravity.

4. How can a company really expect to change its center of gravity?

As the author points out, this is extremely difficult to do. A center of gravity shift requires a dismantling of the current power structure, rejection of parts of the old culture, and establishing all-new management systems. The management lessons learned at the old center of gravity are worse than useless—they may actually impede progress at the new center of gravity. The structure that was so successful previously will most likely be inappropriate now. And the success factors that loomed so large at the old center of gravity may now be less important.

There are really only two ways to succeed at center of gravity changes. The first way, mentioned by the author, is to establish a start-up subsidiary at the new center of gravity, and then invest and divest in such a way that the overall firm ends up at the new center. The other way is to proceed incrementally, and over a long period of time, until the wrenching changes have been accomplished.

5. *Which explanation do you prefer, and why, for the success of related diversified companies?*

   a. They are all downstream companies in high margin businesses.

   b. They can apply skills learned at a center of gravity in one business to the same center of gravity in another business.

   Students will probably differ on this question. Some will argue that it is the high margin businesses in which the "relateds" happen to compete. They may argue that if one could control for industry, there would be little difference between the relateds and the unrelateds. Of course, this reasoning begs the question, mentioned by Galbraith—"If the unrelateds are good acquirers, why don't they acquire high-margin businesses?"

   The second choice above will get its advocates. They will argue that the relateds would excel regardless of which industry they entered, because by staying at the same center of gravity, they can apply all the managerial and organizational lessons they learned in their original business. This explanation gets around the problem of which businesses are acquired, because it is center of gravity that is important, not industry. If upstream companies diversified into other industries, but in upstream stages, they would do well. The evidence shows that most upstream companies tried to diversify into downstream stages, and this presented them with control and organizational problems.

6. *How does change in center of gravity differ from diversification?*

   Diversification means switching to a new industry. Change in center of gravity may occur with or without diversification. It involves moving the primary focus of the company from one industry chain stage to another. It is more than mere forward or backward integration. In trying to change its center of gravity, a firm has to alter the way it sees the world and approaches the world. It requires cultural, organizational, managerial, and political change.

Mintzberg, "The Structuring of Organizations"

Summary of Reading

Management theory has evolved from "one best way" to "it all depends." This reading argues that a third approach, "getting it all together," is better. This means that elements of organizational design should logically configure into internally consistent groupings.

SIX BASIC PARTS OF THE ORGANIZATION

Operating core: the people who perform the basic work

Strategic apex: top management, which oversees the whole organization

Middle line: a hierarchy of authority between the operating core and the strategic apex

Technostructure: staff which plans and controls the work of others

Support staff: staff which provides internal services to others

Ideology: the traditions and beliefs which distinguish an organization from other organizations

Another part of the organization is **politics**.

SIX BASIC COORDINATING MECHANISMS

Mutual adjustment: coordination through informal communication

Direct supervision: one person coordinates by giving orders to others

Standardization of work processes: the direct specification of the content of work (procedures)

Standardization of outputs: specification of results (is usually manifested as financial targets)

Standardization of skills: standardizing workers by teaching them a body of knowledge; typically takes place outside the organization (e.g., in a professional school)

Standardization of norms: achieving coordination by sharing a common set of beliefs

ESSENTIAL PARAMETERS OF DESIGN

1. Design of the individual positions:

   Job specialization: the number of tasks in a given job, and the worker's control over those tasks

   Behavior formalization: the extent to which work content is written down

   Training: the use of formal instructional programs for skill and knowledge transfer

   Indoctrination: programs and techniques used to standardize norms

2. Design of the superstructure:

   Unit grouping: how positions are combined into units, and those units into larger units; boils down to either *functions* or *markets served*

   Unit size: the number of positions (or units) contained in a single unit

3. Design of linkages:

   Planning and control systems: used to standardize outputs

   Action planning: specify the results of actions before they are taken

   Performance control: specify the desired results of whole ranges of actions after the fact

Liaison devices: mechanisms used to encourage mutual adjustment

Liaison positions: created to directly coordinate the work of two units; little formal authority

Task forces: temporary groups designed to bring units together

Standing committees: permanent groups designed to bring units together

Integrating managers: liaison personnel with great formal authority

Matrix structure: designed to formally balance between two or more bases of grouping (e.g., functional and market)

4. Design of decision-making system:

Decentralization: the diffusion of decision-making power

Vertical decentralization: delegation of formal power down the hierarchy to line managers

Horizontal decentralization: delegation of formal power outside the hierarchy to nonmanagers

Selective decentralization: dispersal of power over different decisions to different places

Parallel decentralization: dispersal of power over the same kinds of decisions to the same place (e.g., all division managers have the same set of decision powers)

ORGANIZATIONAL SITUATIONAL FACTORS (Translated)

Age

In older organizations, the jobs are more specified (i.e., formalized).

Organizations in older industries have organizations that are more formalized.

Size

In larger organizations, the jobs are more specified (i.e., formalized).

Larger organizations are more specialized and have a greater proportion of administrative personnel.

Larger organizations have units that are larger, on average.

Technical system

Technology that controls the work of the operators leads to specified jobs and bureaucratic structure.

Complex technology leads to larger, more professional support staff. That staff tends to get more decision-making authority. The use of liaison devices goes up.

Automating the operating core lets the management structure be more organic, less bureaucratic.

Environment

Fast-moving environments are associated with organic structures.

Complex environments are associated with decentralization.

Diverse markets lead to market-based divisions.

Bad times lead to temporary centralization of an organization's structure.

If the environment has a lot of diversity, the organization is encouraged to distribute decision-making authority in a diverse way.

Power

If an organization is controlled by outside forces, it will become bureaucratic.

If there is conflict among the outside forces, there will be more politics internally, and vice versa.

Managers adopt some organization structures because those structures may be fashionable. This will sometimes happen even if that structure is the wrong one for that firm.

THE CONFIGURATIONS

A limited number of configurations can help explain much of what is observed in organizations. There are seven pulls emanating from the seven parts of the organization:

Pull to lead: emanating from the strategic apex

Pull to balkanize: emanating from the middle line

Pull to professionalize: emanating from the operating core

Pull to rationalize: emanating from the technostructure

Pull to collaborate: emanating from the support staff

Pull together: emanating from the ideology

Pull apart: emanating from organizational politics

Depending on which pull dominates, the organization is drawn to design itself as a particular configuration.

1. **Entrepreneurial organization**: relies for coordination on direct supervision; dominated by the strategic apex; no formalization; operates in dynamic environment

2. **Machine organization**: prime coordinating mechanism is standardization of work processes; consequently, key part of the organization is the technostructure; very formalized; environment tends to be simple and stable

3. **Professional organization**: its key, the operating core, is made up of professionals who coordinate using standardization of skills; training occurs mainly outside the organization; stable yet complex environment

4. **Diversified organization**: is really a set of independent entities (usually divisions) connected by a loose administrative structure; key part is middle line, who are coordinated using standardization of outputs (usually financial outputs)

5. **Innovative organization**: the highly skilled support staff succeed in collaborating with other parts of the organization, becoming its key part; coordination is achieved using mutual adjustment; complex and dynamic environments

6. **Missionary organization**: so called because of its members' identification with its *mission*; ideology, achieved through standardization of norms, is the key part; not very formalized; tend to be old (it takes time to build an ideology)

7. **Political organization**: is dominated by politics; has no particular key part or prime coordinating mechanism

Discussion Questions

1. How much does the "getting it all together" approach really add to the "it all depends" approach?

It adds quite a bit. The contingency ("it all depends") approach says that you should design your organization to fit environmental contingencies; e.g., if the environment is turbulent, you should have an organic structure. The configuration ("getting it all together") approach says that we know that many design elements actually should go together, i.e., they should not be picked individually.

A decision to build a machine organization is really a decision to put many elements together—narrow (rather than broad) job specialization, action planning (not performance control), centralized (not decentralized) decision making, many small units (instead of a few larger units), functional (as opposed to market-based) grouping. This argument is similar to the one Waterman, Peters and Phillips make in their "7-S Framework" reading—everything interrelates and fits (or *should*).

2. What's your assessment of the author's definition of ideology?

Some students will question Mintzberg's definition of ideology. He calls it a "strong culture," encompassing the traditions and beliefs which (1) distinguish an organization from others and (2) infuse life into its "skeleton." Critics will wonder why he feels it necessary to introduce a concept in addition to the already-familiar "culture." If a firm has a strong culture, then it has an ideology. But what if it has a weak culture? Does that mean it has a weak ideology, or *no* ideology?

3. What is your opinion of the idea that the term bureaucratic applies to any structure that relies, for coordination, on any form of standardization?

Students will find this a bit odd. The terms "bureaucracy" and "bureaucratic" have negative connotations, so few people will question the use of the terms with regard to the machine organization. This will probably also be true for diversified organizations, which tend to be large and formalized. But this assertion implies that professional organizations and missionary organizations, which rely on standardization of skills and norms, respectively, are bureaucratic, too. Many students will question this. But it is true that professional standards can be very strict, and organizational norms can be very strict. So those two types of organizations can be as restrictive as organizations burdened by many rules.

4. What is the distinction between training and indoctrination?

Training is aimed at imparting skills or knowledge. It is a key design parameter in professional organizations. It is a substitute for formalization in obtaining standardized behavior. Indoctrination, by contrast, is aimed at standardizing norms. It is a tool for socializing organization members, and is usually more psychologically intense than training. It, too, is a substitute for formalization, in this case the standards being internalized as deeply rooted beliefs.

5. In what sense are function and market the only two real bases for unit grouping?

Functional grouping, based on what is done in the work process, is a familiar basis of unit grouping. It is always available to the organizational designer. So the root of this question is whether or not market grouping in indeed the only other basis. Mintzberg mentions three possible bases—product, client, and geographical area. His argument is that each of these is simply a surrogate for market. Products are targeted for particular markets. Clients, in the aggregate, *are* the market. And geographical areas are markets. So, market is the only other basis for grouping.

6. How does action planning differ from performance control?

Action planning specifies the actions of workers *before* they do them. It is an important design parameter in machine organizations. Performance control specifies desired outcomes, and leaves the necessary actions up to the workers. It is an important design parameter in diversified organizations.

7. How do the concepts of liaison positions and integrating managers differ?

Liaison positions are considerably weaker than integrating managers. Liaison positions are jobs created to coordinate the work of two units. Those who serve in them must use their powers of persuasion and negotiation to bring the two sides together. Integrating managers have formal authority over the units they link. They are liaison positions, only with authority.

8. What is the distinction between vertical and horizontal decentralization?

Decentralization means the diffusion of decision-making power. Vertical decentralization means that formal power is diffused by top managers to lower-level managers. Horizontal decentralization is the diffusion of either formal or informal decision-making power to non-managers, such as operators, analysts, and support staffers.

9. What is the distinction between selective and parallel decentralization? How useful is this distinction?

Selective decentralization refers to the dispersal of power over different decisions to different places. An example would be giving the organization's staff attorneys power to make legal decisions, but giving its real estate experts the power to make real estate sale or purchase decisions. Parallel decentralization means the dispersal of power over various decisions to the same place. The best example is the position of division manager in a diversified organization. Each division manager is given the same set of decision making powers—e.g., how much can be invested, how much can be granted in pay increases, the amount of latitude in business planning, etc.

10. What are the implications of the "age and size" hypotheses?

The implications are straightforward—as an organization gets older and larger, it gradually becomes a machine organization. It is characterized by the dominance of standardized work processes (formalized rules) and the prominence of the technostructure (which writes the rules). The rules allow the organization to have larger units. Lastly, the organization is more specialized. All of this adds up to machine organization.

11. What are the implications of the five "environment" hypotheses, taken as a whole?

The more "difficult" is the environment, the more adaptable must be the organization. Adaptability means organic (the opposite of bureaucratic) structure, i.e., coordination is not based on standardization. It also means the dispersal of decision-making power to places closer to where the decision should be made, i.e., decentralization. And it means being "differentiated," i.e., divided up in ways as complex as the environment, including specialized divisions for specialized markets.

The one hypothesis which doesn't fit these implications is the one which says that bad times lead to temporary centralization of an organization's structure. This means that when things go wrong, top management takes the reins a bit more tightly. The quickest responses can come from organizations run by one person, or a small number of people, and this is frequently what is needed in a crisis.

12. How can fashion affect the choice of structure? Is this good or bad?

Organizational structure, like other aspects of management, has its fads and fashions. A few years ago, matrix structure was very fashionable. Many organizations adopted a matrix form, even though it was not appropriate for them. Today, many organization designers denigrate formalization, even though it is widely recognized that rules can be very effective, in the proper circumstances. Most students will agree that this is a bad thing. Organization design should be based on the situational factors of age, size, technical system, and environment, and on how the parameters fit together into a proper configuration.

13. What is your opinion of the "seven pulls on the organization?"

Students will differ on the usefulness of the "pulls" concept. Some will say that it adds little to the seven parts and six coordinating mechanisms discussed earlier in the reading. Others will argue that it is these pulls that lead the organization to finally end up in one configuration or the other. They are the driving forces behind the formation of configurations.

14. How can the operating core of an entrepreneurial organization be organic?

The term "organic" has positive connotations, and is usually reserved for describing organizations whose workers have lots of freedom and decision-making power. These attributes are not typical of entrepreneurial organizations, whose strategic apexes tend to reserve most power to themselves. But Mintzberg uses the term "organic" as the opposite of "bureaucratized." In that sense, the entrepreneurial organization *is* organic, since it has no standardization. The entrepreneurial organization does not rely on any form of standardization for coordination; its prime coordinating mechanism is direct supervision.

15. In what sense is the diversified organization not a complete structure?

The term "diversified organization" applies to only part of the structure of such firms. It describes only the structure of the overall corporation. It does not describe the structures of the various divisions. In theory, each division could have a unique structure. (In practice, they tend to be machine organizations.)

Quinn, Anderson and Finkelstein, "New Forms of Organizing"

Summary of Reading

Hypercompetition is the competitive situation where traditional sources of dominance—cost, quality, timing, know-how, competitive strongholds, and deep pockets—are constantly being eroded. Hypercompetition compels the end of static competitive advantage. "No cost or quality advantage is sustainable, [but] the skill of generating new cost and quality advantages is sustainable."

Hypercompetition and Organizational Forms

Some of the forces causing organizational structure innovation: hypercompetition, customization, globalization, rapid technological change, deregulation and shifting work force demographics. There seems to be a transformation from command-and-control to information-based organizing.

The term "network organization" has become a catch-all, but a common theme is debureaucratization. Lateral relations are more important than vertical ones, and hierarchies are flatter or nonexistent. No one "network organization" will prevail as the dominant type.

These forms are rarely pure and rarely exist across the entire organization. Their evolution is not driven by their presence among new firms. Rather, they are forms of organizing embedded within larger organizations. "The organization of the future will not be a hybrid, but will be polymorphic, containing within itself sub-units whose fundamental ways of bringing intellect to bear upon problems are vastly different from one another." There will be five basic types of network organizations that differ mostly in how they deploy and develop intellect.

THE NETWORK ORGANIZATION

It has been known for a long time that organic organizations perform better in turbulent environments. But hypercompetition is more than turbulence. Under hypercompetition, firms cannot emphasize only one advantage and they cannot afford to fall behind world-class standards. Successful firms will combine organic and mechanistic elements.

There are two schools of thought about the future of network organizations. One is that organizations will substitute lateral ties for vertical ones, with very flat organizations and with cross-functional teams emerging as the building block. The other school stresses the replacement of command relationships by quasi-market mechanisms. The authors contend that the first of these is but one way of organizing encouraged by modern technology, and they question whether cross-functional teams will emerge as the building block. They contend that, unlike the second school, they do not focus on any one control mechanism. They have three other contentions: "(1) bureaucracy will not disappear; (2) hierarchy in the broadest sense . . . will continue to be the dominant mode of organizing; and (3) the core problem that network organization must address is the effective deployment of intellect."

Bureaucracy

Bureaucracy will continue because of the coexisting demands of flexibility, efficiency, reliability, independence, and compliance. Bureaucracy is good for stable units that need to be consistent, accountable, and incremental.

Hierarchy

Hierarchy, in the sense of "a structure composed of interrelated subsystems that ultimately rest on a small number of fundamental building blocks," will characterize organizations that face hypercompetition. Hierarchy will survive to help resolve disputes and allocate resources, but also to facilitate learning. The latter happens more easily in stable sub-units. This is important because "learning is the fundamental challenge facing organizations under hypercompetition—the methodology for continually generating new advantages while old ones are eroded away."

Networks, Speed and Intellect

Networks are touted for their purported ability to integrate efficiency, speedy response, and innovation. But a more basic reason is that networks help firms to develop and deploy intellect. This responds to an epochal change in capitalism, *from* mass production *toward* innovation-mediated production "where the principal component of value creation is knowledge and intellectual capabilities." This ends up making services the critical link in the value chain. Over three-fourths of all economic activity is now delivery of services and intangibles. Much of this involves capturing and distributing intellectual outputs to the point of their consumption or use. This is even true in manufacturing contexts. It all means that "dominance" must be rethought. It now means "being able to bring more talent to bear on an activity critical to customers than any rival firm can. This occurs when (1) a company has the most effective presence in the specific service activities its segment of the market most desires, and (2) it can capture and defend some special experience or specialization benefits accruing to that activity share."

DIFFERENT ORGANIZATIONS FOR DIFFERENT PURPOSES

Firms will "mix and match" different forms of network organization to meet their needs. The following sections examine five such forms. Four dimensions distinguish the five forms:

- *Locus of intellect*, the principal domain(s) within the organization where deep knowledge of its fundamental disciplines reside(s).

- *Locus of novelty*, the principal location(s) at which intellect is converted to novel solutions.

- *Mode of linkage*, the direction of flow of information and how the locus of intellect and the locus of novelty are connected.

- *Source of leverage*, how the enterprise leverages its know-how base.

The "Infinitely Flat" Organization

These are so called because there is no inherent limit to their span. The locus of intellect is the center of the organization. The center has a highly specialized form of intellect, e.g., operations knowledge in a fast food firm, or a huge body of data and analysis in a brokerage firm. The nodes are individuals, and they become the locus of novelty. Linkage is mostly one-way, from center to nodes. The source of leverage is multiplicative. There is theoretically no limit to the number of nodes that can be linked to a center. Each node can make information about the outside world useful yet can still rely on the center for knowledge about the firm's cumulative experience. The number of nodes observed has ranged from 20 to 18,000. Examples are fast food, brokerage, airline, shipping or mail order operations.

Little direction is given by the center to the nodes, nor do the nodes communicate among one another. Central authority becomes a source of information or a communications coordinator. Nodes look to the center for information leading to better performance, not for guidance. For example, Merrill Lynch uses its information technology to allow its 17,000 brokers to connect directly into headquarters for all their needs.

Infinitely flat organizations work best when the activities of nodes can be broken down into minimum repeatable elements and measured that way. They also function best when each node is totally independent of other nodes. The center is a resource for improvement, a way to tap into the firm's experience curve. These characteristics allow firms to pursue maximum responsiveness and maximum efficiency, which allows them to function well in hypercompetitive environments.

Management problems:

- Lack of career path

- Need for pay based on individual performance

- Dependent on isolated professional management.

- Difficult to transfer people from nodes to center and vice versa.

- Need to maintain system flexibility; too easy for system to become rigid over time. This is true for both "technical" and "cultural" linkages.

The Inverted Organization

Here, the "major locus of intellect is the nodes contacting customers, not the center." Examples are hospitals, medical clinics, therapeutic care-giving units, or consulting engineering firms. Novelty is created at the nodes because of the unique adaptation and delivery of services to customers. Since the nodes are professional and self-sufficient there is no formal linkage. Know-how diffuses informally. Leverage is distributive, with the center providing logistical or administrative support to unburden the nodes. The center may also be a repository of some useful information.

The line hierarchy supports instead of giving orders. Line managers break bottlenecks, develop culture, communicate values, develop special studies, consult upon request, expedite resource movements, and provide service economies of scale. "What was line management now performs essentially 'staff' activities."

The inverted organization works best if servicing the customer at the point of contact is the most important thing, and if the person at the point of contact has the most information about the client's problems and their potential solution. "Quite often this form is restricted to only certain units in direct contact with customers; however, in some intellectual aristocracies, such as law firms, medical clinics, or colleges, the inverted organization may pervade virtually all departments. [Accordingly,] inverted organizations should be used sparingly . . . . Their proper functioning depends on the genuinely superior knowledge of the contact people." Line managers contribute as analysts and arbiters and in long-term activities like resource building and public policy participation.

Management problems:

- Loss of formal authority for line managers

- Need for continued professional training for contact people

- Great attention to personnel selection

- Need to simultaneously empower and control contact people at nodes

- Need for powerful information systems and constant reinforcement of operating norms

The "Spider's Web" Organization

This is a true network. There is often no intervening hierarchy or order-giving center. Locus of intellect is highly dispersed, residing in the nodes. Point of novelty is project/problem requiring interaction among nodes or between nodes and others possessing needed knowledge/resources. Know-how is latent until a project materializes it through connections. Information linkages are complex as knowledge moves among nodes in temporary collaborations. Leverage is exponential—with even a modest number of collaborating nodes the number of connections mounts rapidly.

Spider's webs emerge when highly dispersed nodes must interact to serve customers. Nodes may have no hierarchical relationship and interaction may be voluntary, done only to capture scale or scope economies. Authority interactions occur through ad hoc committees. High coordination needs may necessitate the use of a project manager. Purest example of spider's web is the Internet. Other examples are open markets, securities exchanges, library consortia, and political action groups.

Spider's webs are actually not new, but "they enjoy selective advantages in hypercompetitive environments because they can simultaneously accommodate high specialization, multiple geographic locations, and a disciplined focus on a single problem or customer set." Particularly useful for dispersed customers who need diverse services.

Management problems:

- Need to foster communication without overloading the system

- Need to foster sharing

- Tendency for "dawdling"

- Managing competition across nodes by solving problem of assigning credit for intellectual contributions

The Cluster Organization

Superficially resembles spider's web because of knowledge transport from node to node. But locus of intellect here is in loosely formed clusters which carry out somewhat permanent activities (e.g., staff analyses, technical innovation, customer relationships) that require deep competence. Subclusters may form to solve specific problems. Members stay in proximity. Temporary teams may occasionally be pulled together from the various clusters. These teams are not this organization's defining characteristic. The cluster organization's "essence lies in [how] the team members are cross-trained to help with enterprise-wide tasks, but spend most of their time in clusters of people who handle useful daily problems for the enterprise while they continue to build depth in their particular specialty."

Specialized units create knowledge, teams assemble expertise into larger packages. Novelty occurs when a team forms to address a problem. Information moves from cluster to team. There is usually a clear authority figure to head the task group. Leverage is additive, as "teams . . . package together the sum of the clusters' know-how." Members return to their clusters, to build specialized know-how, when the team's work is done.

Cluster organizations are effective when organization-wide tasks require deep knowledge beyond that possessed by any individual or group. They combine specialization in the clusters with diverse skills on the teams. Scale economies can be had when the clusters have stable base loads of activity, even more so when the clusters can be geographically centralized. Routine or geographically-dispersed activities are not good candidates for cluster organizations.

Management problems:

- Individuals face dual pressures from clusters (for in-depth knowledge) and cross-cluster teams (who need contributions from diverse disciplines)

- Dependent on quality of leadership, breadth of training, and motivation of participants

- Assignment, not volunteerism, is common, posing problems of equity, identity and reentry to the cluster.

- Takes several years to become acculturated to this form

The Starburst Organization

This form is observed when markets are very diverse. Technically this is an inter-organizational network, but the units are under shared ownership of some form. Often they are creative organizations that peel off from the core competencies of parent organizations, like "shooting stars." Subsidiaries remain partially or wholly owned by the parent, but may raise funds independently. Control is market-based. Examples are movie studios and venture capitalists.

The locus of intellect is divided. The center retains deep knowledge of common technology or knowledge base. The nodes are business units and contain specialized market and production knowledge. The nodes are the locus of novelty—the center spins a node off to exploit a new core competency. Movement of intellect is typically from the center outward toward the nodes. Each node draws from the center, but the center does not try to consolidate the diverse knowledge of the nodes. Market knowledge moves laterally among the nodes. The source of leverage comes from applying core competencies to local opportunities.

Starburst organizations differ from more traditional diversified forms "because they maintain a cohesive intellectual competency center." The center is maintained and recharged by assessing the nodes a fee. The nodes get the benefit of economies of scale and new opportunities offered by a large knowledge base. "The corporate center primarily helps raise resources, invests in maintaining the core competency, manages the culture, and sets priorities by selecting people and letting them bid for resources."

These work well when a strong center knows it cannot micromanage the spin-offs, and where entrepreneurship is even more important than mere flexible response. Ambiguous environments where market tests are needed to assess the outcomes of actions are also fertile ground for starburst organizations.

Management problems:

- Need to keep faith in shooting stars in patient way

- Need to balance autonomy and control; either live with quasi-market control or spin off

- Need to generate significant resources, particularly in a way that does not overtax the core

- Tends to work best in smaller scale, lower investment, opportunities

POLYMORPHISM

These are forms of organizing, not organizational forms. Firms facing hypercompetition will combine them in various ways, even including old-fashioned bureaucracy. Therefore "a key challenge for top management will be integrating these disparate structures into an intelligent enterprise." Advances in software design provide a good analogy as to how this will happen. Programming is moving from a "line of code" orientation to an "object" orientation. "Under the object-oriented approach, managers model real-world business processes in terms of prepackaged data 'objects' which can then be used ubiquitously in many specialized operating models." One result is that "more than ever an organization's intellect will be embodied in its information systems, particularly its software . . . . The organization's data systems will contain the essence of its way of viewing the world and its competitive capabilities." Another effect is that "object-oriented systems will not only facilitate but render imperative the process of learning from highly decentralized experience. The essence of the new paradigm is flexible re-usability, continuously creating new programs from the basic building blocks of previous ones. Those firms which develop the most effective data collection systems and dynamic models about what they know will be able to outpace firms whose data and models are less robust and less representative of their experience."

CONCLUSION

Purpose of article is to stimulate debate. Search for other forms should continue.

Discussion Questions

1. What is hypercompetition, and why is it important?

Hypercompetition is the competitive situation where traditional sources of dominance—cost, quality, timing, know-how, competitive strongholds, and deep pockets—are constantly being eroded. It is important to recognize hypercompetition because the only enduring advantage is the ability to generate new advantage.

2. What is the distinction between "forms of organizing" vs. "forms of organization?"

"Forms of organization" implies organizational structures, like the familiar functional, divisional or matrix forms. There is a structural, somewhat static connotation to this term. "Forms of organizing," by contrast, is a much more dynamic term. It implies processes, actions, and approaches, not static structures.

3. What is the key to hypercompetitive survival?

Since hypercompetition erodes traditional sources of advantage, the only way to counter it is by being able constantly to generate new advantage. The best, perhaps the only, way to do that is to develop and deploy intellect within the firm. That is the key to hypercompetitive survival.

4. The authors contend that "bureaucracy will not disappear." What is your reaction to this?

Some students may be surprised by this assertion, thinking that "new" forms of organizing will drive out old-fashioned bureaucracy. But the authors' point is that bureaucracies are good at efficiently providing large quantities of goods or services. Hence, they will always have a place as specialized production units.

5. The authors contend that "hierarchy . . . will continue to be the dominant form of organizing." What do you think of this?

Both students who have accepted that bureaucracy has its place and those who haven't will be confused by this assertion. The former will say, "Of course," since hierarchy is typically associated with bureaucracy. The latter will continue to think of hierarchy as a bad thing, like bureaucracy. The authors' point is that hierarchy is "stably interrelating sub-assemblies," layers that "nest" into one another. Hierarchy has been observed in virtually every natural, self-organizing system. It is a neutral concept that seems most visible in bureaucracies, but is definitely not exclusive to them.

6. How does hierarchy help organizational learning?

Organizations don't learn if they are either too rigid or too flexible. Excess rigidity snuffs out learning because the organization refuses to change, and learning implies change. Excess flexibility dissipates learning because there is no place for the learnings to be "deposited." Hierarchy allows for the creation of locations in the firm for depositories of expertise that can then be disseminated and augmented.

7. Which is more important, speedy response or development of intellect?

Many students will opt for speed in answer to this question. Textbooks and the business press are always talking about the need to do things faster, to reduce cycle time, and so forth. But speed is a source of advantage that can ultimately be eroded as other firms speed up their responsiveness. Intellect is more difficult to erode, and high levels of intellect can generate (1) more intellect and (2) other, less erodible, sources of advantage.

8. What is your reaction to the authors' claim that services are "the critical links in the firm's value chain?"

With all the emphasis that has been placed on improving the quality of manufacturing operations, some students may be confused by this assertion. But the improvement in manufacturing quality actually has accentuated the need to improve services. As product quality differences narrow, the need to differentiate on the basis of services increases. And since the economy is overwhelmingly services anyway, the reliance on services is especially high. Also, when you look at the value chain of a manufacturing enterprise, only one of the primary activities—manufacturing—is non service. The others—marketing, sales and service—are services, as are all of the support activities. Of those, research and development may be crucial and is definitely an information-generating service of the kind the authors emphasize in this reading.

9. What are the four "intellectual dimensions" that distinguish the network forms?

The authors provide an interesting framework for distinguishing among "network organizations." The distinctions are based on differences in *locus of intellect*, *locus of novelty*, *model of linkage*, and *source of leverage*.

- The locus of intellect is the point in the organizational form where the intelligence resides. It could be the center (e.g., corporate management) or the nodes (e.g., individual practitioners or clusters of practitioners), or both (as in starburst organizations, where each has different knowledge).

- The locus of novelty is the point in the organization where innovation occurs. This could be in the nodes, as in the inverted organization, or it could be in the overall combination of nodes, as in the spider's web.

- The mode of linkage is the direction of information flow. It could be from center to nodes (infinitely flat organization) or node-to-node (spider's web) or non-existent (inverted organization).

- The source of leverage is the way the organization increases its intellectual capacity. Each of the five forms discussed in this reading uses a different form of leverage—multiplicative, distributive, exponential, additive and synthetic, respectively.

10. *What are the key characteristics of the "infinitely flat" organizations?*

There are just two levels: the nodes (typically individuals) connected only to the center. The center contains the knowledge, but the nodes apply it. Information flows from the center to the nodes, but it is the latter who exercise creativity or novelty as they apply the organization's knowledge to interactions with clients and customers. Leverage is multiplicative because there is no limit to the number of nodes that could be linked (there have been as many as 18,000 in some organizations) and the center can assemble the knowledge gained by all the nodes collectively and make it available to individual nodes.

11. *What is the role of the center in infinitely flat organizations, and what is your reaction to it?*

The central authority usually becomes an information source, a communications coordinator, or a reference desk for unusual inquiries. It tends not to give direct orders, since lower organizational levels connect to it to get information to perform better. In a sense, this is a form dominated by what Mintzberg, in the previous reading, called technostructure. The central authority designs the nodes' jobs, provides them with the information they need to do those jobs, and that's pretty much it. It is likely that students will react negatively to this. Even though bureaucracy should be a neutral term, referring only to standardization of work processes, the term has over the years acquired negative connotations. The infinitely flat organization, even though it does not have the number of levels of hierarchy typically found in machine organizations, is nevertheless a kind of machine organization. The nodes *do* have some latitude, but only under the considerable constraints of the firm's structured work processes and information systems.

12. *What do you think is the biggest management challenge with the infinitely flat organization?*

The authors mention three problems. The first is an overly-short career path. There is a correspondingly greater emphasis on individual reward systems and a greater variety of intangible rewards (e.g., different job titles, personal development opportunities). But this is not likely to be the greatest problem, since details like this are usually resolvable.

The second problem is that management development is difficult. The roles of the nodes and the center are so different that it is difficult to develop people by transferring them between the levels. People at the center need in-depth analytical knowledge; people at the nodes need to be skilled at service provision and customer interface. This is a serious problem with no easy answer, but some answers are possible through sophisticated development programs.

The third problem is that this form can quickly become as dehumanizing as older versions of the machine organization. To avoid this, the organization's information systems must somehow capture the qualitative as well as quantitative aspects of service provision. The firm needs to create support teams that gather specialized knowledge, not only about the technology but also about the "outside world" facing the firm. Otherwise the firm's systems can become overly rigid and non-responsive. Because of the number and complexity of problems in this area, this may be the most challenging problem facing management in the infinitely flat organization. But students may be able to make viable arguments for any of these three problem areas.

13. *What is your overall reaction to the concept of the "inverted organization?"*

Students will likely react differently to this form. Some, particularly accounting students, may view it as desirable, since they will be entering a profession characterized by inverted organizations. Many others will focus on what is undoubtedly the form's biggest problem—the excess individualization of the nodes which could lead to lack of control and suboptimization. This form, by the way, is very close, perhaps identical, to Mintzberg's "professional organization" from the previous reading. When students realize this, and when the authors' reference to colleges as a type of organization where the inverted organization "permeates all departments," they may react a bit more negatively as they think about individual professors they've had who have been too isolated, or who have not kept up their development.

14. What is the trickiest thing about making inverted organizations successful?

The authors mention several problems. The structure is difficult to control, relying as it does on the skills of its "contact people," the professional service providers. As mentioned above, this requires continuous professional development for the professionals. It also requires very stringent personnel selection (which is why, for example, hiring, and later tenure, decisions are so crucial in colleges and universities), and constant reinforcement of organizational values. This latter point is crucial. It is very easy for professionals in this form to become highly individualized, not at all interested in organizational rules and norms. So the trickiest thing about managing these organizations is probably the need for powerful information systems and constant reinforcement of operating norms.

15. The authors say of the spider's web form that "often there is no intervening hierarchy or order giving center." What is your reaction to this?

Of all the concepts that have become associated with network organizations (and the spider's web is perhaps the most prototypical of the latter) the one with which students struggle the most is the idea that there is no central authority. No doubt many students will be puzzled by this, particularly since (1) hierarchy in the form of bureaucracy is still so prevalent and (2) even these authors argue that it will linger for a long time. But the key thing to remember is that there are organized entities that do not need a central authority. The best example is the human brain, which is organized and very effective, but which is a network of neurons with no "central neuron" to control things. Ant and termite colonies are also highly organized but have no central *directive* authority. The best answer to give puzzled students is that organization in a spider's web comes from the *relationships* among the nodes, not from any given node.

16. What makes the spider's web so adaptable in hypercompetitive environments?

The authors point out that, while old, spider's webs have advantages in modern hypercompetitive environments. They are able to accommodate, at the same time, high levels of specialization in the nodes, activities at multiple geographic locations, and, by acting in concert in a network, achieving a disciplined focus on a single problem or customer set. The authors point out that they are particularly adept at solving problems where customer sets are dispersed and when highly diverse specialties need to be tapped.

17. What are the biggest challenges to managing the spider's web?

A network whose members do not communicate is almost not a network. Shared information is more important than the information stored in the nodes. So maintaining communication is vital. But good communication can beget other problems: flooding by trivia, resistance to screening and control mechanisms, dawdling (as nodes focus excessively on their own specialties while ignoring solution of the common problem), and difficulties in assigning credit for intellectual contributions.

18. What is the essence of the cluster organization? How does it differ from the older matrix organization?

In the cluster organization, people belong to clusters whose members develop in-depth knowledge in a given area, but who are cross-trained to join and contribute to temporary cross-functional teams that work on enterprise-wide tasks. In a matrix, members always simultaneously belong to project teams and functional specialties. In the cluster form, members "help with enterprise-wide tasks, but spend most of their time in clusters of people who handle useful daily problems for the enterprise while they continue to build depth in their particular specialty." The difference is that the dual memberships are not strictly project/function. They are cluster/team, which may be project/function, but which may also be something else.

19. What is the biggest management challenge in the cluster organization?

"The tension between demands to build deep, cluster-specific competence to service their normal clientele and pressures to contribute to cross-cluster teams." Exacerbating this problem is that membership on cross-cluster teams is usually by *assignment*, not by volunteering. This commonly raises issues of equity (fair treatment for all members of clusters and teams, regardless of their "home" origin), identity (to whom does the member owe allegiance, cluster or team?), and reentry to the cluster (is there something for the returning team member to do in the cluster, has her/his skills eroded or fallen behind since they left for the team assignment, and so forth?).

20. In what sense is a starburst organization an inter-organizational network?

The starburst begins with the "star," the company whose technologies and other skills are spun off, or "burst," into other enterprises. In a strict sense, these spun-off entities are separate business units, which makes the starburst an inter-organizational network. But since each of the spin-offs is still owned by the original star (or *its* parent), this qualifies as an organizational form.

21. The authors say that the locus of intellect in starburst organizations is divided. What do they mean?

Each part of a starburst—the center or "star" and the nodes or "bursts"—possesses some distinctive intelligence. For the center, it typically is "deep knowledge of some common technology or knowledge base." This is akin to the notion of "core competencies." The nodes possess "specialized market and production knowledge."

22. What is the starburst's classic problem?

In this form, management often loses faith in its free-standing "burst" or "shooting stars" and tries to consolidate functions to gain efficiencies. The problem with this is that the nodes are so different that not even sophisticated information systems are able to help management run all the nodes from a central location. There are only two alternatives in this case: live with quasi control, or fully spin off the troublesome business units.

23. What is the basic point of the section on "polymorphism?"

In the face of hypercompetition, firms will possess different combinations of these, and older, forms of organizing. This is really just an extension of Lawrence and Lorsch's idea of differentiation to match environmental demands. The authors give the example of NovaCare, a provider of rehabilitation services. Within NovaCare "there are centralized functions (accounting), cluster (acquisitions), geographical hierarchical (hospital), inverted (therapy), and spider's web (professional knowledge exchange) structures."

24. What is the management challenge posed by polymorphism?

By far the biggest challenge is "integrating these disparate structures into an intelligent enterprise." The authors assert that much of this integration will occur through information systems, which will have to become much more sophisticated than they typically are now.

25. What is the point of the analogy of new forms of organizing to "object-oriented programming?"

In object-oriented programming, programs are written as combinations of building blocks of code, called "objects," that contain their own instruction sets and can be combined in numerous useful ways. The authors suggest that old and new forms of organizing are like "objects" that managers will be able to combine in many useful ways. They also believe that there is a direct link between object-oriented programming and network organizations. The "modularization" of the organizations can be matched by the modularization of the firm's information systems. As they put it, "The essence of the new paradigm is flexible re-usability, continuously creating new programs from the basic building blocks of previous ones."

Bleeke and Ernst, "Collaborating to Compete"

Summary of Reading

Flat-out, predatory competition is over. Head-to-head competition is too exhausting financially, too depleting intellectually, and leaves companies too vulnerable. In place, companies are learning they must collaborate to compete. Companies can selectively share and trade control, costs, capital, market access, information, and technology. Companies should compete only in those areas where they have an advantage or where they must compete to preserve power or capture value. Ability and willingness to collaborate is particularly important for companies that want to reach across borders.

THREE THEMES

The number of cross-border alliances is increasing. Some contributing factors are globalization, "Europe 1992," the opening of Eastern Europe and Asia, and the need to get foreign sales to offset high fixed costs. Trying to go it alone is too expensive, too time-consuming, and too likely to be ineffective. Yet only half of cross-border alliances succeed. Three themes emerge from a study of these alliances:

- Companies are learning they must collaborate to compete.

- Alliances between potential competitors represent an arbitrage of skills, market access and capital between them. Maintaining a fair balance is essential for success.

- It is important to see cross-border alliances or acquisitions as a flexible sequence of actions, not a one-shot deal.

Success must be measured against the scarcest resources, including skills and access, not just capital. Willingness to learn from companies with a different approach is often the only way to succeed in this sense. Flexibility in terms of willingness to fine-tune the relationship is another hallmark of successful collaborations.

ALLIANCES AS ARBITRAGE

Because not all companies are equal, they benefit from trading the "chips" of market access, management skills, information and financing across borders. This global arbitrage takes place more slowly than it does in financial markets, but the mechanism is the same. "Each player uses the quirks, irrational differences, and inefficiencies in the marketplace as well as each company's advantages to mutual benefit."

Successful alliance partners approach negotiations as "win-win" situations. They also build in mechanisms to resolve conflict, like strong boards and clarity about roles. Since the value of the "chips" will change over time, partners must maximize their bargaining power but be ready to renegotiate as needed. Predetermined timetables for evaluating the partnership are often helpful.

Note: See the table in the text for a listing of Kenichi Ohmae's "Tips for Collaboration."

A SEQUENCE OF ACTIONS

Cross-border alliances and acquisitions need to be seen as a sequence of actions, not "on-off" transactions. "Companies that take a purely financial, deal-driven approach to cross-border alliances and acquisitions usually wind up in trouble." This method helps build useful experience. It also helps build economies through integrating operations and eliminating overlapping functions.

WILLINGNESS TO RETHINK

Since things change over time, be ready to rethink the situation constantly. It is the only hedge against things going wrong, which is the rule, not the exception. Alliances should be viewed as intermediate arrangement. Always be thinking about "what's next." Since most alliances dissolve by having one of the parties buy it, think early on about likely role as buyer or seller. Companies that can bring the most short-term benefit are also likelier to be long term competitors. Therefore, if selling the alliance is not an option, a more complementary, but perhaps less synergistic, partner needs to be found at the outset.

POSTSCRIPT: A LOOK AHEAD

Global companies will look like amoebas, "always changing shape, taking and giving with the surroundings, yet it always retains its integrity and identity as a unique creature." When entering a new market, managers must ask how things are different and what it is they need to learn. They can help answer these questions by finding appropriate partners. "In the fluid global marketplace, it is no longer possible or desirable for single organizations to be entirely self-sufficient. Collaboration is the value of the future. Alliances are the structure of the future."

The result is very complex management with no standard approach possible. Firms must be slightly schizophrenic—maintain identity but stay open to different ways. Organizations wedded to the "old ways" and to standardization will be inflexible and confrontational, unable to work with the outside world. "These companies may survive because they are large and powerful, but they will cease to be leaders."

Discussion Questions

1. What is your reaction to the authors' contention that "the days of flat-out, predatory competition are over?"

So much emphasis in strategy courses is placed on competitive strategy models that students may well be surprised to read a statement like this. It is important to realize that the point these authors (along with Hamel and Prahalad and Quinn and Hilmer earlier) make is a different paradigm from the straight competitive strategy model. Porter's model of competitive strategy focuses on all the negative things that can happen in an industry, things like rivalry, supplier and buyer power, and threats of entry and substitutes. But Porter's other famous model, the value chain, points to the position taken by these authors—do the things competitively that you do better than anyone else, and either outsource or form alliances to do the rest.

2. What is the essential point behind the notion of "collaborating to compete?"

The authors put it succinctly: "Instead of competing blindly, companies should increasingly compete only in those precise areas where they have a durable advantage or where participation is necessary . . . . [In other areas,] the best approach is to find partners that already have the cash, scale, skills, or access you seek . . . . When a company reaches across borders, its ability and willingness to collaborate is the best predictor of success."

3. What is so important about willingness to learn and to be flexible?

The authors claim that the only way for a firm to maximize its success in the global marketplace is to be willing to learn from firms that are very different. The implication is that the resulting greater variety and knowledge is what will give the firm its edge. This idea is consistent with the notion that learning and development occur at the "edges" of what already exists.

Flexibility is needed for dealing with the ups and downs inherent in any relationship. The authors point out that it is very unlikely that an alliance will remain exactly the same over its lifetime. Many things will change, including things like market demands, technology and the geographic scope of the alliance. They say that "the success rate for alliances that have changed their scope over time is more than twice that of alliances where the scope has not evolved. Alliances with legal or financial structures that do not permit change are nearly certain to fail."

4. What is arbitrage and why might it be a good metaphor for collaboration?

According to *The American Heritage Dictionary* (3rd ed., 1992, p. 94), arbitrage is "the purchase of securities on one market for immediate resale on another market in order to profit from a price discrepancy." The analogy to cross-border alliances is pretty good. A North American firm with, say, good manufacturing technology, but with limited access to, say, an Asian market, "trades" its technology to an Asian firm with weak technology but good Asian access. In a sense, the North American firm has "purchased" its manufacturing technology on the North American market and "sold" it in the Asian market at a profit. For the Asian firm, the transaction is a mirror image of this.

5. What is the significance of a "sequence of actions" approach versus an "one-off" transaction approach?

The arbitrage discussed in the previous question is obviously not risk-free. Like all analogies, it is not perfect. One obvious problem is that when one buys a security in one market and then sells it in another, that is the end of it. The securities are now in someone else's possession and were used only to make the profit. In the case of a strategic alliance, the "securities" remain in the possession of the respective parties, they are shared rather than merely disposed of. So the relationship, unlike a stock sale, cannot be treated as a one-shot transaction. There will be evolution in the alliance over time, so there needs to be an ongoing, evolving relationship. This implies a thoughtful sequence of actions to improve and refine the alliance.

6. How important is "willingness to rethink?"

Because of the evolution mentioned in the answer to question 5, willingness to rethink is very important. The authors point out that trouble is the rule and that the initial set-up may not be meaningful in a few years. To keep the alliance going, all partners must be willing to rethink the situation on an ongoing basis, and be willing to renegotiate changes as needed. Alliances should be considered "intermediate" strategic devices, and their participants should always be thinking ahead to what will come after the dissolution of the alliance. Since many alliances end with one or the other partner buying out the other's share, particular thought needs to be given to how the role of either purchaser or seller should be played. All in all, a willingness to think and rethink the alliance is very important.

7. What is your reaction to the amoebae metaphor?

It should be interesting to see how students react to this metaphor. The amoebae seems like too simple a creature to be interesting to students of business strategy. But the simplicity of the metaphor gives it its power. The essential point is that global corporations need to be simultaneously open and closed. They need to be open in the sense of being willing to learn, to share, to change, to interact with customers and organizations very different from themselves. But they must do all of this while maintaining their integrity and identity, by maintaining their essential "cores" of competence and value-adding capacity.

8. The authors say that "there is no single valid rule book for all markets." What do you think of this?

There may still be some die-hard students who believe that "management is management," regardless of the industry. These authors make the point that many other authors have made in the past fifteen years or so, which is that industries differ so meaningfully from one another that to say "management is management" is untenable. Even *within* an industry there may be great diversity among strategic groups. All of this becomes more salient when one adds cross-border relationships to the picture. It all adds up to the need to become familiar with the "rules" that exist in any given context. What is required, along with some useful models of strategy, is thoughtful management.

Mintzberg, "Ideology and the Missionary Organization"

<u>Summary of Reading</u>

Organizational ideology is the "rich system of values and beliefs about an organization, shared by its members, that distinguishes it from other organizations."

<u>THE DEVELOPMENT OF AN ORGANIZATIONAL IDEOLOGY</u>

Stage 1: The rooting of ideology in a sense of mission

A prime mover identifies a mission and collects a group around him or her to accomplish it. These individuals coalesce because they share some values associated with the fledgling organization. Sometimes there is a "sense of mission," a feeling that the group has banded together to create something unusual and exciting. This is common in new organizations for four reasons:

1.   New organizations offer wide latitude for maneuver.

2.   They tend to be small, facilitating personal relationships.

3.   The founding members frequently share a set of strong basic beliefs.

4.   The founders of new organizations are often "charismatic" individuals, energizing and knitting members together.

   Developing an ideology in an existing organization is possible but much more difficult. The key to the development of an organizational ideology, in any type of organization, is a leadership with a genuine belief in mission and an honest dedication to the people who must carry it out.

Stage 2: The development of ideology through traditions and sagas

As the organization moves forward, it makes decisions and takes actions. These serve as commitments and precedents. Behaviors reinforce themselves, and actions become infused with value. If these forces are strong, ideology emerges. The ideology is strengthened by stories, called "myths," that develop around important events in the organization's past. Gradually the organization establishes a sense of history. All these things—precedents, habits, myths, history—form a *tradition*.   This is captured in a *saga*, "a collective understanding of a unique accomplishment based on historical exploits," which links present with past and turns the organization from an instrument into an institution.

Stage 3: The reinforcement of ideology through identifications

An individual joining an organization with a strong ideology will tend to *identify* with the organization. This happens in four different ways:

1.   *Natural identification*: the new member is attracted to the organization's system of beliefs

2.   *Selected identification*: new members are chosen to "fit in" with existing beliefs; authority positions are filled by people with the strongest beliefs

3.   *Evoked identification*: using informal processes of socialization and formal programs of indoctrination to reinforce natural commitment

4.   *Calculated identification*: individuals conform because it pays them to identify with organizational beliefs

The higher on this list a member's identification tends to be, the more likely it is to sustain, or even promote in the first place, a strong ideology.

THE MISSIONARY ORGANIZATION

The degree of ideology will vary greatly in organizations. Organizations with weak ideologies are called "stylistically weak." Organizations with strong ideologies are "stylistically rich." They can be called *Missionary Organizations*, because they are somewhat akin to religious organizations. Mission counts above all—to preserve it, extend it, or perfect it.

The mission in missionary organizations is typically:

1. Clear and focused, making identification easy

2. Inspiring, so that members actually develop identification

3. Distinctive, creating a unique niche where the ideology can flourish

The organization tends to resist attempts to change the mission.

The prime coordination mechanism in the Missionary Organization is standardization of norms. The key design parameter is indoctrination, to formally promote identification. Decentralization is also high—all full members share in decision-making power.

Control is high, but not through rules. The Missionary Organization captures the members' hearts through shared values: "Teaching new Jesuit recruits to 'love God and do what you like' is not to do what they like at all but to act in strict conformance with the order's beliefs."

The Missionary Organization is an amorphous mass of members all pulling together within the common ideology. There is minimum specialization, differentiation, or status differences. Even managers are hard to distinguish from "workers." The Israeli kibbutz is a good example, with its impermanent office, lack of formal hierarchy, and nonimportance of objective qualifications.

There are several forms of Missionary Organization:

Reformers: set out to change the world directly

Converters: change the world indirectly, by attracting members and changing *them*

Cloister: seek to allow their members to pursue a unique way of life

IDEOLOGY AS AN OVERLAY ON CONVENTIONAL ORGANIZATIONS

The Missionary form may not be appropriate for the large firm which has a strong ideology. That kind of firm tends to overlay its ideological characteristics on a more conventional structure. Best known for this are Japanese corporations, with their lifetime employment, consensual decision-making, collective responsibility, slow evaluation and promotion, implicit and informal control, nonspecialized career paths, and holistic concern for the employee. Some American organizations have adopted a hybrid between these two forms.

Many things have worked against the development of ideologies in American business. But ideology may have an important role to play here, given the enormous success of Japanese firms against large American firms with barren cultures. We might expect more ideological overlays on the conventional forms of organizations in the West.

Discussion Questions

1. What's your assessment of the four reasons given by the author for the existence of a "sense of mission" in new organizations?

This question is intended to stimulate discussion. In general, students will agree with the author. Nothing is "set" in new organizations, so they can maneuver widely, which can be exciting. The personal nature of new firms could make it easier for people to get committed to working together on exciting goals. The strong beliefs of the founders, coupled with their often being charismatic *would* help foster the feeling that the organization was up to something special.

2. How important do you think "organizational sagas" are in business organizations?

Many students will express skepticism about the role of sagas. It will all sound too "anthropological" to them. But in many mature companies, there are stories told about how the company succeeded against great odds. And there is a collective understanding of how the company has had a unique history and unique accomplishments. Viewed in this way, the notion of sagas seems more plausible.

3. How common is natural identification in business organizations?

It all depends on the type of organization. Certainly there are many organizations where natural identification would be scarce. This would be particularly true of machine organizations that were not institutions. But one can think of many business organizations, even somewhat large ones, where one would expect a fair amount of natural identification. Hewlett-Packard, Apple Computer, Sony, Bell Labs, and Genentech are just a few that come to mind. The young engineers who join these organizations really identify with the interesting and exciting work that goes on there.

4. How is selected identification related to Mintzberg's notion of process strategy from Chapter 1?

Selected identification is when people are chosen according to how they will "fit in" with the existing ideology. Process strategy is when top management implicitly sets broad strategy guidelines by manipulating organizational processes to ensure that activity stays within certain bounds. Since strategy in the Missionary Organization flows from ideology, and since ideology is reinforced by selected identification, the latter is a process strategy approach for the Missionary Organization.

5. How reliable are indoctrination and socialization as ways to evoke identification?

This question is aimed at stimulating discussion. Some students will assert that they are very reliable methods, and these students will have a point. Socialization is an almost inevitable process in social situations, and indoctrination is quite common, especially in larger organizations with strong ideologies. Other students will be skeptical. Their argument will be rooted in the very notion of "identification." Identification, they will argue, should not be forced. If people identify with the organization, it should be because it is psychologically compelling to do so. It should not be the result of strenuous socialization, or even more strenuous, and intrusive, indoctrination. Putting their argument at its strongest, they will say that identification should always be natural, and never the result of brainwashing.

6. How is calculated identification even identification at all?

This question gets at the same issue as the previous one, only even more strongly. How can a person truly be said to be identifying with the organization's mission if that person is ready to abandon the mission as soon as a better offer comes along? Some may argue that it is unrealistic to expect that all members of even a Missionary Organization will identify strongly with the firm. Management must therefore rely on all means of gaining productive performance from its members.

7. How is the Missionary form related to Mintzberg's notion of ideological strategy, from his Chapter 1 reading?

This is a straightforward question. Ideological strategy is the form of strategy that is typical for a Missionary Organization. Put another way, if one were to identify the type of organization for which ideological strategy would most likely be found, it would be the Missionary Organization.

8. How applicable is the notion of "Missionary organization" to business organizations?

Students will differ on this. The author offers his answer at the end of the reading. He says that the Missionary form is probably not appropriate for most large firms. For example, things like impermanence of office, lack of formal hierarchy, and the part-time nature of management jobs in Missionary forms would not work in large business organizations. What those firms do is overlay ideology (the key part of the Missionary Organization) on their conventional structures.

9. Examine the Ouchi and Jaeger quotation (at the end of Mintzberg's reading) about the American and Japanese managers who accused each other of being unable to formulate objectives. How does this quotation relate to the reading in Chapter 1 on the five Ps of strategy?

The American managers fit into the concept of *strategy as plan.* Their objectives must be formally set forth, and they must be formulated in advance of action. The Japanese managers are an example of *strategy as perspective.* They do not need formally stated goals; their worldview tells them whether they are doing the right thing or not.

10. In this reading's final quotation, Ouchi and Johnson say that in the American-style Missionary Organization "a new manager will be useless for at least four or five years." To what extent is the development of a Missionary ideology worth this price?

This question obviously has no right or wrong answer. Encourage students to take different side of this issue. Some students will argue that it is better to try to run an organization with rules and policies than to take the enormous amounts of time and energy required to establish and maintain an ideology. Others will argue that ideologies are potentially so powerful that it is worth trying to start and nurture them.

Bartlett and Ghoshal, "Building Structure in Manager's Minds"

Summary of Reading

Managers are losing control of their companies because the companies are organizationally incapable of carrying out the sophisticated strategies they have developed. Strategic thinking has outstripped organizational capabilities. Some managers have responded to this by trying to manage complexity with complex structures.

The matrix seemed ideal as a structure for managing complexity. In practice it proved all but unmanageable, especially in the international context. Dual reporting created conflict and confusion, communications channels were jammed, and overlapping responsibilities produced turf battles and loss of accountability. These problems were extremely difficult to solve over barriers of time, language, distance and culture.

Changes in competitive climate and dissolution of hierarchical structure have led top management to be less like organizational architects. Paradoxically, these pressures have moved top managers to focus on the details of managing people and processes. "The critical strategic requirement is not to devise the most ingenious and well coordinated plan but to build the most viable and flexible strategic process; the key organizational task is not to design the most elegant structure but to capture individual capabilities and motivate the entire organization to respond cooperatively to a complicated and dynamic environment."

BUILDING AN ORGANIZATION

Companies who adopted the matrix correctly recognized the need to have multidimensional structures. The problem was that they defined their organizational objectives in pure structural terms. But structure is like anatomy, and managers need to think too about physiology—"the systems and relationships that allow the lifeblood of information to flow through the organization." Organizational psychology—shared norms, values, and beliefs—must also concern top management.

Many managers felt that changing structure would change interpersonal relationships and decision processes, which would in turn reshape individual attitudes and behaviors. But "reconfiguring the formal structure is a blunt and sometimes brutal instrument of change." But these changes, if they occur at all, will take a long time.

A better way to proceed is "building up an appropriate set of employee attitudes and skills and linking them together with carefully developed processes and relationships." They must build the organization rather than just install a new structure. Successful multidimensional organization builders start with the psychology, the beliefs and norms. Then they enrich and clarify communication and decision processes, which reinforces the psychology. The last thing they do is consolidate and confirm progress by realigning anatomy through changes in structure.

There are no quick and easy ways to affect organizational psychology. But there are three principal characteristics common to those who have managed the task most effectively:

- The development and communication of a clear and consistent corporate vision.

- The effective management of human resource tools to broaden individual perspectives and develop identification with corporate goals.

- The integration of individual thinking and activities into the broad corporate agenda by means of a process we call co-option.

BUILDING A SHARED VISION

Clinging to parochial attitudes is caused by frames of reference bounded by specific responsibilities. To break down this insularity, "develop and communicate a clear sense of corporate purpose that extends into every corner of the company and gives context and meaning to each manager's particular roles and responsibilities." Not a slogan, but a carefully crafted vision that has three characteristics:

- clarity of expression: to make company objectives understandable and meaningful

- continuity of purpose: to underscore enduring importance

- consistency of application: to ensure uniformity throughout the organization.

Clarity

There are three keys to clarity in corporate vision:

- Simplicity

- Relevance, which means linking broad objectives to concrete agendas

- Reinforcement, elaboration and interpretation of the vision to keep it from becoming obsolete or abstract.

Continuity

"Despite shifts in leadership and continual adjustments in short-term business priorities, companies must remain committed to the same core set of strategic objectives and organizational values. Without such continuity, unifying vision might as well be expressed in terms of quarterly goals."

Consistency

Top management must ensure that everyone shares the same vision. Not doing so can lead to total chaos, with different units pursuing different agendas that are mutually crippling. However, a vision will not succeed if individual employees do not understand and accept the company's stated goals and objectives. This is a challenge for the company's human resource practices.

DEVELOPING HUMAN RESOURCES

Top managers have the responsibility to develop and allocate scarce resources. Too often this is interpreted as husbanding finances and technology. This overshadows the development of the scarcest resource of all—capable managers. "But if there is one key to regaining control of companies that operate in fast-changing environments, it is the ability of top management to turn the perceptions, capabilities, and relationships of individual managers into the building blocks of the organization."

Too many companies fail to get their managers to see how they fit into the bigger picture. Managers are often isolated physically and by specialty and consequently become parochial. Taking care of these problems cannot be left to salary and benefits staff—it must be done by top management.

Recruitment and selection

"The first step in successfully managing complexity is to tap the full range of available talent." Companies shouldn't be constrained by historical imbalances in nationality or functional background. They should capitalize on their pool of worldwide talent. They should also develop new criteria for choosing those most likely to succeed. Past success is no longer an adequate criterion.

Training and development

Development, to go beyond skill-building, should have three aims :

- To build common vision and values

- To broaden management perspective. This is "essentially a matter of teaching people how to manage complexity instead of merely to make room for it."

- To develop contacts and shape management relationships.

Career-path management

"Although recruitment and training are critically important, the most effective companies recognize that the best way to develop new perspectives and thwart parochialism in their managers is through personal experience. By moving selected managers across functions, business, and geographic units, a company encourages cross-fertilization of ideas as well as the flexibility and breadth of experience that enable managers to grapple with complexity and come out on top."

CO-OPTING MANAGEMENT EFFORTS

Complexity tends to make managers specialized and isolated and therefore parochially responsive, even in the face of overall corporate interest. Companies must try to counteract this by securing strong and lasting individual commitments to corporate visions and objectives. "In effect, [companies] must co-opt individual energies and ambitions into the service of corporate goals."

THE MATRIX IN THE MANAGER'S MIND

Corporate strategy has become more agile and athletic since World War II. But organizational innovation has not kept pace, and managerial attitudes lag even further behind. "Corporations now commonly design strategies that seem impossible to implement, for the simple reason that no one can effectively implement third-generation strategies through second-generation organizations run by first-generation managers." Successful companies focus less on ideal structures and more on developing the abilities, behavior, and performance of individual managers.

Discussion Questions

1. Why would the matrix be particularly unmanageable in the international context?

Dual reporting create conflict and confusion, communications channels were jammed, and overlapping responsibilities produced turf battles and loss of accountability. These problems were extremely difficult to solve over barriers of time, language, distance and culture.

2. What is your reaction to the authors' assertions about what are the most critical strategic and organizational requirements?

The authors say, "The critical strategic requirement is not to devise the most ingenious and well coordinated plan but to build the most viable and flexible strategic process; the key organizational task is not to design the most elegant structure but to capture individual capabilities and motivate the entire organization to respond cooperatively to a complicated and dynamic environment." Many students will question these assertions, as they run counter to many of the prescriptions found in management textbooks. Planning in an ingenious and coordinated way is often lauded in those books, as is designing elegant organizational structures. The authors are pushing back against these years of "accepted wisdom" and arguing instead for hard, thoughtful management work.

3. What is your reaction to the metaphors of "anatomy" (structure), "physiology" (processes) and "psychology" (values and culture)?

Like all metaphors, this one has its limitations, but one of its strengths is how is gives insight into the difficulties of achieving change using the usual sequencing. As the authors point out, management often tries to change anatomy and then hopes for desirable changes in physiology and psychology. This is much less likely to change the organization than would be beginning at "the far end" of this sequence. The authors make a persuasive case for starting with psychology, moving on to physiology at the right point, and ending with appropriate changes in structure. It should be interesting to see how students react to the metaphors.

4. What is your reaction to the idea that a shared company vision would help overcome "parochial attitudes" among managers?

Students may react with some skepticism about this assertion. Attempts to articulate corporate visions that end up being ineffectual are a dime a dozen. But these authors are talking about long-term work designed to develop clear, continuous and consistent agreement about what the firm is all about. Some firms have actually succeeded in accomplishing this, as the examples of NEC and Philips illustrate. The idea is very similar to Hamel and Prahalad's notion of "strategic intent," a pervasive desire by company members to accomplish some highly motivating achievement.

5. What do you think of the authors' contention that visions should be simple? Of what previous readings does this remind you?

Students who have become accustomed to complexity in their studies may be confused by the notion that a good vision is simple. But that seems most assuredly true. Hamel and Prahalad made essentially the same point in "Strategic Intent." So did Quinn in his Chapter 1 discussion of the merits of concentration in strategy. A simple vision helps focus the minds and efforts of the firm's members.

6. The authors assert that a "key to clarity is top management's continual reinforcement, elaboration, and interpretation of the core vision to keep it from becoming obsolete or abstract." What do you think of this?

Some students will question how a vision can be useful if it keeps getting elaborated and interpreted. But the point is that the vision will constantly come up against day-to-day, or at least year-to-year, reality in the firm. When it does, people will need help in figuring out how to act in that reality yet stay in tune with the vision. Top management will help them decide which concrete actions support the vision, and which will undermine it. It will help them elaborate the vision in light of new realities. Does new technology fit with the vision, or does it require a change in the vision? Do realities in the organization require a rethinking of the vision? These are all things that top management can help with, and, paradoxically, all will help keep the vision shared and alive.

7. What is your reaction to the authors' assertion that the scarcest resource of all are "capable managers?"

Students have a tendency to think, perhaps because of all the finance and operations courses they must take, that physical and financial resources are the most important ones in an organization. But organizations are by definition social entities, and the people who make them up are what makes them distinctive. The managers who run organizations are therefor critically important in determining their effectiveness, and it seems like there are never enough good ones.

8. The authors are critical of "domestically oriented recruiting" and of permitting "historical imbalances" in nationality and functional background to affect recruiting. What is your reaction to these criticisms?

This is a startling, but probably warranted, statement by the authors. Many students will be struck by this statement. What the authors are saying is that, in today's hypercompetitive environments, organizations do not have the luxury of hiring from any particular group. They must hire the best possible people, period.

9. What does it mean to "manage complexity instead of merely to make room for it?"

This comes under the heading "broadening management perspectives." Too many organizations try to "manage" complexity by merely telling their existing management structures to pay attention to it. The authors give the example of the unwieldy three-person management teams at Philips and how they had to be replaced by single general managers with a broader perspective. Complexity is much likelier to be handled by a general manager with a broad perspective than with a "team" of three narrowly-focused specialists.

10. What is so important about "career path management?"

Complex companies know that the only way to develop broad perspectives and avoid parochialism is through personal experiences in many settings. This is also a way to develop the contacts and the network so crucial to management (and therefore corporate) success. Hence it is critically important to rotate promising managers through a variety of functional, product and geographical postings. Much research, beyond even what these authors discuss, has shown that informal networks of contacts and relationships are crucial to the decision-making and information exchange processes of complex companies.

11. What is your reaction to the section on "co-opting management efforts?"

At first blush this seems manipulative and exploitative, and many students will react accordingly. However, a closer reading of the section reveals that "co-opting" managers evidently means giving them more say in controlling their destiny. The North American Philips story shows clearly that a good way to "co-opt" someone is to let them control some important product groups. This sound, and probably *is*, more positive.

12. What do the authors mean by "the matrix in the manager's mind?"

They mean that managers should spend less time trying to come up with ideal structures, and should spend more time building vision, skills and performance. They can then rely on those processes to point the way to emergent structures. In the meantime, they can keep the structures in the minds.

Mintzberg, "Politics and the Political Organization"

Summary of Reading

POLITICS IN ORGANIZATIONS

Organizations function with four systems of influence: (1) authority, (2) ideology, (3) expertise, and (4) politics. The first three are legitimate, the last is not. Political power in the organization is not formally authorized, widely accepted, or officially certified. It is therefore often divisive and conflictive.

POLITICAL GAMES IN ORGANIZATIONS

Political activity can be described as "game playing." The author identifies thirteen games:

Insurgency game: lower-level participants resist authority

Counterinsurgency game: authority fights back

Sponsorship game: lower-level members attach themselves to authority figures to build power base

Alliance-building game: peers negotiate implicit contracts of support to build power base

Empire-building game: managers build power bases with subordinates

Budgeting game: played overtly, governed by rules, to build power with resources

Expertise game: non-sanctioned use of expertise to build power base; experts play by flaunting their expertise; non-experts play by trying to have their work viewed as expert

Lording game: building power by "lording it" over those without it, i.e., illegitimate use of legitimate power

Line vs. staff game: pits line managers with legitimate power against staff advisers with expertise; played to defeat rivals

Rival camps game: played when alliance- or empire-building game evolves into a two-competitor, zero-sum game

Strategic candidates game: individuals or groups play to politically promote their favored strategic changes

Whistle-blowing game: inside information is used to expose unethical or illegal behavior; typically a brief and simple game

Young Turks game: high-stakes game; "Young Turks" near center of power seek to effect change (strategic, ideological, expert/technological, or leadership)

Politics may be present but not dominant, or it may be the dominant system of influence. The latter gives rise to type of configuration called political.

FORM OF POLITICAL ORGANIZATIONS

These organizations are best understood in terms of power, not structure. They have no preferred method of coordination, no key part, no clear type of decentralization. "Everything depends on the fluidity of informal power, marshaled to win individual issues."

Conflict falls into two dimensions: moderate/enduring vs. intense/brief, and confined vs. pervasive. This leads to four forms of political organization:

Confrontation: confined and intense/brief (e.g., takeover)

Shaky alliance: confined and moderate/enduring (e.g., professional organization operating in public sector)

Politicized organization: pervasive and moderate/enduring (e.g., regulatory agencies)

Complete political arena: pervasive and intense/brief (rarely found)

The fourth of these is so unstable as to be very rarely found. The other three endure, one by moderating conflict, the other by containing conflict, and the third by doing both.

THE FUNCTIONAL ROLE OF POLITICS IN ORGANIZATIONS

Dysfunctional influences of politics:

Divisive and costly

Burns up energy

Often used to sustain outmoded systems of power, or introduce unjustified new ones

Can paralyze organization

Functional influences of politics: In general, politics can correct deficiencies in the legitimate systems of influence:

Politics can act in a Darwinian way to ensure that the strongest members of an organization are brought into positions of leadership.

Politics can ensure that all sides of an issue are fully debated, whereas the other systems of influence may promote only one.

The system of politics is often required to stimulate necessary change that is blocked by the legitimate systems of influence.

The system of politics can ease the path for the execution of decisions.

Discussion Questions

1. The author says that "political power in the organization [is technically illegitimate because it] is not formally authorized, widely accepted, or officially certified." What is your opinion of this statement?

Mintzberg says that influence operates in four systems. *Authority* is formally authorized power, by definition legitimate. *Ideology* is a set of widely accepted beliefs that legitimizes influence. *Expertise* is influence that is officially certified by professional organizations or educational achievements. Politics, he says, reflects power that is technically illegitimate, since it doesn't fit into any of the above three categories.

But research has shown that power (the currency of politics) is often gained in informal ways that could nevertheless be characterized as legitimate. Departments that help the organization meet its strategic contingencies usually have greater power. For example, if many departments are *dependent* on a particular unit, that unit will have power. Similarly, if it is difficult to *substitute* for a department's activities, it will have power. Also, if a department is good at *coping with uncertainty* faced by an organization, the department will have greater power. This greater power may be widely accepted, even though it is informal.

2. The author says that politics is inherently illegitimate, particularly in the means it uses. What is your opinion?

The answer to the previous question alluded to the legitimacy of many of the informal sources of power. Beyond that, research has shown that politics is often found in situations where there is disagreement over goals. Under those conditions, if it is not likely that decisions will be made without resort to political processes, is it truly illegitimate to use them? The decisions must be made on some basis, why not a political one? Students will likely differ greatly on their answers to this question.

3. Mintzberg implies that all the political games he identifies are illegitimate. What is your opinion?

Some of the games he discusses are clearly illegitimate. The insurgency, counterinsurgency, expertise, and lording games are of this type. Some are mixed, such as the sponsorship and empire-building games; there may be nothing inherently wrong with trying to get closer to power centers, as in the sponsorship game, or increasing one's authority, which could happen in the empire-building game. But neither game is simon-pure, either. Lastly, some of the other games are not by their very nature illegitimate. For example, is there truly anything illegitimate with forming alliances? Or with playing the budgeting game? (Mintzberg even characterizes the latter as being governed by rules.) And if there are disagreements about goals, why not play the strategic candidates game as a way of resolving those issues? Mintzberg actually concedes the usefulness of games like the rival camps game, which he says can substitute for legitimate power when the latter is weak.

4. What is your assessment of the four functional influences of politics listed by the author at the end of the reading?

This question is intended to stimulate discussion. Many students will come into this reading already agreeing with Mintzberg's gloomy assessment of organizational politics. They may not accept his closing points. On the other hand, there may be students who come into the reading with a more positive opinion of organizational politics than the one in the reading. For them, these points will be most welcome.

The functional influences of politics are important. If there is genuine disagreement about goals, politics can ensure that there is a full discussion of all sides of the issue, and not only the sides favored by the dominant system of influence, be it authority, ideology, or expertise. If the dominant system is retarding change, political activity can stimulate it. And, as the earlier readings by Wrapp ("playing the power game"), Quinn ("logical incrementalism"), and Selznick ("organizational polities") have discussed, politics can be effectively used to ease the path for the execution of strategic decisions.

Henderson, "Competitive Maneuvering"

Summary of Reading

BRINKMANSHIP IN BUSINESS

Behavior in business is not logical. The critical factor is one's emotional bias compared to the emotional bias of opponents. Competition is not impersonal, objective and colorless. Victory is won in the mind of the competitor.

Management must persuade an opponent voluntarily to stop short of maximum competitive effort. This persuasion depends on emotional and intuitive factors, not analysis or deduction. The negotiator should be as arbitrary as needed to get concessions, without destroying the other's motivation for cooperation. Three common-sense rules for this are:

1. Make sure your rival knows what he'll gain if he cooperates or lose if he doesn't.

2. Don't arouse your rival's emotions.

3. Convince your opponent that you are emotionally committed to your position and are completely convinced that it's reasonable.

Friendly competitors

It may seem strange to talk about cooperation with competitors. But it is rarely worthwhile to go all out in competition. It decreases stability of the overall market, and everyone loses. "Utter destruction of a competitor is almost never profitable unless the competitor is unwilling to accept peace." Better to come to implicit agreements that limit competition.

"Cold War" tactics

If both sides persist in being arbitrary, negotiations will break down. Yet negotiators must be somewhat arbitrary, in a kind of *brinkmanship*. In these situations, deciding what to accept is arbitrary and emotional. The key is to convince your opponent that you are arbitrary and emotionally committed, while trying to discover what he'd accept in settlement. Your rival is most handicapped if he acts logically, because he will keep on making concessions until there is no more benefit to him.

Conclusion

The most easily recognized way of enforcing cooperation is to exhibit willingness to use overwhelming force. But it's difficult to convince others that you mean it, without actually using it (which would be expensive and inconvenient). Besides, in business, overwhelming force is rarely available. Each party to a conflict can usually hurt the other. Therefore, the prospects for agreement depend on three things:

1. Each party's willingness to accept the risk of punishment (if you're not willing, and your opponents realize it, you'll almost certainly get either the punishment or worse conditions)

2. Each party's belief that the other party is willing to accept the risk of punishment (what counts is the judgment of probable use of capability)

3. The degree of rationality in the behavior of each party (the less of this you have, the greater the advantage, as long as you don't cross the line of emotionally arousing your opponent)

<u>THE NONLOGICAL STRATEGY</u>

"The goal of strategy in business . . . is to produce a stable relationship favorable to you with the consent of your competitors . . . . *Any competition which does not eventually eliminate a competitor requires his cooperation to stabilize the situation* . . . . There is a point in all situations of conflict where both parties gain more or lose less from peace than they can hope to gain from any foreseeable victory."

". . . The participant who is coldly logical is at a great disadvantage. . . . The arbitrary or irrational competitor can demand far more than a reasonable share and yet his logical opponent can still gain by compromise rather than by breaking off the cooperation." But there is a limit to how arbitrary, etc., one can be, because these behaviors will trigger a like response. "Thus, nonlogical behavior is self-limiting. This is why . . . diplomacy can be described as the ability to be unreasonable without arousing resentment."

<u>RULES FOR THE STRATEGIST</u>

1. Know as accurately as possible what your opponent has at stake.

2. Make sure your opponent knows as little as possible about what *you* have at stake.

3. It is essential that you know the character, attitudes, motives, and habitual behavior of your competitor.

4. The more arbitrary you are, the better—as long as you do not emotionally arouse your competitor.

5. The less arbitrary you seem, the more arbitrary you can in fact be.

Discussion Questions

1. Henderson says that business behavior is not logical, but is instead laced with emotional bias. What do you think of this?

This question may stimulate very different points of view. Some people, particularly those with a logical, rational bent, will object to Henderson's view of things. They will argue that the best business decisions are the logical ones, where all factors are taken into account, where most things are planned and thought through, and where the optimum decisions are taken.

Other students may identify with the author's assertion. Many critics believe that business has gotten too analytical, and that the human side has been neglected. Henderson brings the human, emotional, side squarely to the forefront. There is little doubt that, even if we *should* make decisions logically (and that is not a given), we usually *don't*. This makes Henderson's point an important one.

2. The author says that one must be as arbitrary as possible without eliciting an emotional response from the opponent. What do you think of this approach to competitive behavior?

Students may be able to understand this position, but most will find it difficult to implement it in their own behavior. Most people realize that negotiation requires starting from a position that is unlikely ever to be accepted by the other side. Henderson takes this a step further, saying that one must maintain this attitude *throughout* the negotiations, making sure never to go so far that one angers the other side. Obviously, this is a fine art, as the author implies (but never actually says) many times in the reading. But if you can pull it off, the outcome will be to your side of some "completely fair" result that might be identified.

3. What do you think of the author's discussion of "friendly competitors?"

Some students will have a hard time understanding this point, others will understand it but not accept it, and still others will do both. Henderson's point is basically that going all-out to destroy rivals is too expensive to be worth the effort, unless a particular rival is unwilling to "play the game." In most cases, he argues, it is better to come to implicit agreements that put boundaries around the competition.

Some students will not accept this, arguing that competition must be unfettered if we are to gain its benefits. If a rival isn't "playing the game," that may be helpful to the consumer, because that firm may be driving down industry prices. Students who accept Henderson's view will argue that *consumers* may benefit from competition, but *firms* may not, and Henderson is writing for the managers of firms. They will point out that it is very realistic to expect managers to want to limit competition in order to support the longevity of the firm. Both Mintzberg and Porter mentioned, in earlier chapters, the strong incentive management has to *avoid* competition. Those authors suggested economic approaches; Henderson is merely supplementing that with a political approach.

4. Henderson says that threatening to use overwhelming force is not a good tactic in business because it is rarely available. What do you think?

Henderson alludes several times to the analogy of international diplomacy, war, and deterrent strategy. But in this passage he quite rightly points out that, like all analogies, this one has a limit. Unlike the arena of international superpower politics, in business there is no arsenal of nuclear weapons. There may be examples in some industries of firms which have very large advantages over smaller firms (e.g., IBM in computers). But, in general, there are few "knockout punches" available to most firms, even the large ones, in most industries.

5. *The author says that if you're not willing to accept punishment, and your opponents know it, you'll almost certainly get punished. What do you think of this assertion?*

Henderson is saying that playing the game well implies the risk of sustaining some damage. If you are willing to accept some injury, you will be recognized as someone who will retaliate if attacked. Hence, willingness to accept punishment becomes a deterrent. Conversely, if you are not willing to go to the mat with opponents, they will sense this and make you pay dearly. A second-best approach is to hide your unwillingness to be punished extremely well, so that your opponents will still be deterred.

This is an aggressive reading. Some students will be turned off by this kind of talk. For these people, it is interesting to see their reaction when exposed to this kind of real-world, rough-and-tumble attitude. Some students will respond well to it.

6. *The author repeatedly makes the point that the nonlogical competitor has an advantage over the logical one. How is this possible?*

As Mintzberg points out in the chapter introduction, this reading fits neatly into the "strategy as ploy" concept. Henderson calls the emotional competitor "nonlogical," but in fact that individual is crazy like a fox. His point is that the "unemotional" competitor will want to keep his distance from this "crazy," nonlogical, emotional opponent. The logical opponent will do this, according to Henderson, by adopting a bargaining stance that makes many concessions to the less logical opponent, *as long as logical payoffs are still possible.* In other words, long after an emotional opponent would have angrily said, "That's it! I'm not giving you another thing!" the logical opponent will still be making concessions.

Many students will question this stance, with some justification. There is nothing in the research literature to suggest that logical negotiators necessarily fall into the traps set by their more emotional opponents. A very good "logical" negotiator may be able to see through these ploys.

7. *What is your opinion on the author's point that "nonlogical behavior is self-limiting?"*

It's a point well-taken, one that should actually have more weight in his reading. He argues that if you go too far with your nonlogical behavior, it will become counter-productive. There will be a backlash against you by your opponent. One of the unspoken but critically important elements of Henderson's thesis is that knowing when to stop short of that point is a fine art that *must* be mastered. Henderson may have some good advice here, but he offers no guidance on how to carry it out, short of trying it and learning from experience.

8. *Henderson says, "The less arbitrary you seem, the more arbitrary you can in fact be." How is this possible?*

This is merely the other side of the coin of being as arbitrary as possible without eliciting an emotional response from the opponent. Here Henderson is saying that if you seem like a nice, unarbitrary person, you will get away with more arbitrariness than someone else would. This is a good thing, as he argued earlier in the reading, because it will tend to keep the outcome of the negotiations closer to your desired position than to your opponent's.

Mintzberg, "Who Should Control the Corporation?"

<u>Summary of Reading</u>

Answers to the question "Who should control the corporation?" fall into a continuum. The continuum is not a straight line; it is a horseshoe, because its endpoints ("nationalize it" at the extreme left and "restore it" at the extreme right) are not so far apart. Both call for direct control by specific outsiders—the government in the former, shareholders in the latter.

"Nationalize it"

In the U.S., nationalization is taboo in general, but is often practiced in particular instances (e.g., Amtrak, Tennessee Valley Authority). It does not necessarily help the firm's social record or hurt efficiency. It seems to be most appropriate in two instances:

When a mission is deemed necessary but will not be provided by the private sector

When the activities of an organization must be so intricately tied to government policy that it is best managed as a direct arm of the state

"Democratize it"

This means broadening the governance of the corporation. There are four ways to do this:

1. Pluralistic representative democracy: election of representatives of external interest groups to the board of directors (e.g., "public interest" directors)

2. Worker representative democracy: election of worker representatives to the board of directors (e.g., "co-determination" or worker ownership)

3. Pluralistic participatory democracy: formal and direct involvement by external interest groups in internal decision making processes

4. Worker participatory democracy: formal and direct involvement by employees in internal decision making processes

"Regulate it"

Thought by some to be a clumsy instrument and by others a panacea, it is neither. One obvious place for regulation is to control tangible externalities—costs incurred by corporations that are passed on to the public at large. Regulation may also have a place where competition encourages the unscrupulous to pull all firms down to a base level of behavior. Regulation is a clumsy instrument but not a useless one.

"Pressure it"

This is designed to provoke corporations to act beyond some base level of behavior. Activists bring ad hoc campaigns of pressure to bear on corporations to keep them responsive to social needs. It has proved more effective than the tactics discussed so far at eliciting behavior sensitive to social needs. It is informal, flexible, and focused, so it has been successful. But it is also irregular and ad hoc.

"Trust it"

The argument here is that since the corporation has no need to act irresponsibly, there is no reason for it to be nationalized, democratized, regulated, or pressured. The corporation's leaders can be trusted to attend to social goals. Some have criticized this doctrine as all rhetoric. Others claim that businessmen lack the qualifications to make these decisions. The most far-reaching criticism, from both the left and the right, is that managers have no right to make these kinds of decisions.

The author argues that we have to trust managers for two reasons:

1. Strategic decisions inevitably involve social as well as economic consequences.
2. There is always some degree of discretion involved in corporate decision making; socially, things could be better, but they could be worse.

We must socialize our managers to be trustworthy. Society must aspire to higher standards of conduct. "Without responsible and ethical people in important places, our society is not worth very much."

"Ignore it"

This calls for no change in corporate behavior. It assumes that social needs are met in the course of pursuing economic goals. The argument is that "it pays to be good." But in instances where the status quo is not socially enlightened, "ignore it" actually makes a good case for "pressure it."

"Induce it"

This argues simply "Pay it to be good." The corporation undertakes socially desirable programs only when economically induced to do so. It is the mirror image of "regulate it." It is most appropriate when a problem needs the skills of a specific corporation for solution. A good example might be government payments for job training.

"Restore it"

Adherents of this position believe that managerial control is illegitimate, and must be replaced by the more valid control of its "rightful" owners, the shareholders. Milton Friedman is the most outspoken proponent of this view.

This position tends to be black and white. But Mintzberg believes that it rests on several fallacies:

1. The technical assumption of shareholder control is unrealistic.

2. The economic assumption of free markets, with vibrant competition, unlimited entry, open information, consumer sovereignty, and labor mobility, is debatable.

3. The political assumptions, (1) that the corporation is amoral, merely society's instrument for producing goods and services, and (2) that a free and democratic society does not interfere with the legal activities of businesses, are contradicted by several counter assumptions held by the population (according to polls):

   Large corporations are social and political institutions as much as they are economic ones.

   Society cannot achieve a balance between social and economic needs as long as the private sector attends only to economic goals.

   In a democratic society, ownership control is not necessarily more legitimate than worker control, consumer control, or pluralistic control.

"'Restore it' is the nostalgic position on our horseshoe, a return to our fantasies of a glorious past. In this society of giant corporations, it flies in the face of powerful economic and social forces."

Conclusion: If the shoe fits . . .

We need to treat the horseshoe as a portfolio of positions from which the corporation can draw, depending on circumstances.

First, "trust it," or at least, "socialize it." Without honest and responsible people in important places, we are in deep trouble. Ultimately, what managers do is determined by their sense of responsibility as individual members of society.

Then, "pressure it." The best antidote to the negative forces interfering with social responsibility is the pressure campaign. In fact, "pressure it" is the foundation for the success of most of the other approaches, such as regulation.

After that, try to "democratize it." Many important institutions affect people greatly, yet are hierarchically run. They should be opened up, democratized. This will be difficult.

Only where specifically appropriate, "regulate it" and "induce it." Regulation should work when the corporation can be penalized for abusing its power. Inducement should work when the corporation can be rewarded for doing things only it can do, but may otherwise choose not to do.

Occasionally, selectively, "nationalize it" and "restore it." Nationalization occasionally makes sense, as mentioned earlier. "Restoration" is often appropriate in these circumstances:

- divesting poorly performing attempts at diversification

- "disintegrating" inefficient vertical operations

- reducing the size of non-adaptive organizations

Finally, and above all, *don't* ignore it.

Discussion Questions

1. Why does a "conceptual horseshoe" make sense?

Many students have trouble with Mintzberg's conceptual horseshoe. Some don't understand it, others question why a *horseshoe* is appropriate for this continuum. Mintzberg's point is that the extremes of his continuum *seem* to be far apart, but actually have some similarities. Both call for direct control by specific outsiders. In the case of "nationalize it," the outside group is the government. For "restore it," the "outsiders" who should exert more control are the shareholders.

2. According to the author, what are the two criteria by which the idea of nationalizing a business should be judged? What is your opinion of this choice of criteria?

The first criterion is when a mission is deemed necessary, but will not be provided by the private sector. The author gives the examples of mail delivery and passenger rail service. The second criterion is when the activities of an organization must be so intricately tied to government policy that it is best managed as a direct arm of the state. National defense is the best example; there might be others, in important industries. Students will find it difficult to argue with Mintzberg's criteria, but they may be able to argue that they rarely exist. For example, there are few instances of organizations being intricately tied to government policy. And there are many instances where services offered by the government are being privatized, e.g., parcel delivery, driver and automobile licensing, even prisons.

3. How workable, and desirable, are the four "democracies" outlined by the author?

Worker participatory democracy <u>is</u> workable in the United States, as has been shown by ESOPs. Most students will probably argue that it is desirable, although this may be tempered by the attitude, in keeping with the management perspective that is likely to exist in most business school classes, that it should be allowed to happen only when "regular" ownership fails.

The question of *pluralistic* participatory democracy is much stickier. It would involve much more "outsider" intrusion into everyday affairs at a firm than most management students would like. Its desirability from the perspective of the outsiders is likely to be greater. Depending on how it is handled, its workability would range from poor (decisions stalled by acrimony among disparate interest groups) to good (outsiders giving good information about product ideas).

Worker representative democracy does not seem to work well in the United States. The workers on the board seem to be overwhelmed by management representatives. On the other hand, it could be argued that full-fledged representative democracy, i.e., significant numbers of workers on the board, has not been tried in the United States. It might work. The question of desirability hinges on perspective.

Pluralistic representative democracy has been tried in the United States, and its fate is essentially the same as worker representative democracy. That is, the outside interest group representatives are outnumbered and outvoted. If a more significant number were typically put on boards, the result might be different. And the desirability question depends on whose perspective is applied to it.

4. Why is it that regulation "does not make any firm socially responsible so much as stop some from being grossly irresponsible?"

In some sense, responsibility implies doing the right thing just because it's the right thing. Regulation takes the discretion away from the firm. It says that firms will do the right thing, or else. In that sense, it "does not make any firm socially responsible." Also, in setting up the regulations, it typically establishes a "floor" of acceptable behavior, thereby stopping "some from being grossly irresponsible."

5. What is your position on regulation? Would regulation be applied more appropriately if business took a more enlightened view of it?

It is not clear what Mintzberg means by "applied more appropriately." He probably means "not in waves," the latter being the way it has tended to be applied in the United States. "Appropriate" may mean "fine tuning," rather than the kind of gross adjustments that have characterized regulation in the United States. This point carries some irony, since, as Mintzberg quotes Levitt as having pointed out, regulation has tended to be very good for business. Perhaps this is what Mintzberg means by an enlightened attitude—realize that regulation helps business, and allow it to happen in measured doses.

6. What's your opinion of the author's rosy assessment of "pressure it?"

Mintzberg characterizes "pressure it" as "informal, flexible, and focused." He really likes this approach. Some students may also. One reason is that it implicitly recognizes management's right to make the final decisions. But "pressure it" *does* have the problems of being irregular and ad hoc: Pressure groups form, then they dissolve. They attack particular aspects of a firm's operations, but not others. And "pressure it" is based much more on confrontation than any other approach discussed in the reading.

7. In your opinion, why can managers be trusted to be socially responsible? Why might they be capable of it? How can they be said to have the right to purse such goals?

Students will differ in their answers to this question. Some will argue that managers *cannot* be trusted to be socially responsible, that they are incapable of it, and have no right to aspire to it. These people will argue that managers have the sole responsibility to maximize owner wealth. They do not have the training or the legitimate right to do anything else.

Other students will argue that managers can and should be trusted. They are members of society who carry society's norms around with them as much as any other citizen does. Indeed, the college-educated ones (and many others, too) may have received special training in business ethics and social responsibility. Lastly, as the men and women who direct large enterprises which have great effects on society, managers have every right to pursue social goals.

8. How can it be said that "there is no such thing as purely economic decisions in big business?"

The author makes this point well: "The strategic decisions of large organizations inevitably involve social as well as economic consequences that are inextricably intertwined. The neat distinction between economic goals in the private sector and social goals in the public sector just doesn't hold up in practice. Every important decision of the large corporation . . . generates all kinds of social consequences."

9. With whom do you agree, Friedman or Solzhenitsyn?

This question is *purely* a discussion question. Friedman says that managers must maximize shareholder wealth but play within legal rules. Solzhenitsyn says that "a society with no other scale but the legal one is not quite worthy of man . . . . A society which is based on the letter of the law and never reaches any higher is scarcely taking advantage of the high level of human possibilities." Which side students like best is plainly a value judgment.

10. What should we do to ensure that we can "trust our managers to act responsibly?"

They need to have their consciousness raised about social responsibility issues. One way is to educate managers, either in formal university programs or in their organizations. They also could be helped by indoctrination, and milder socialization, aimed at promoting the proper values. Lastly, organizations might develop ethical codes, which might later evolve into ideologies. These would help managers become more trustworthy.

11. How can we say that "it pays to be good?" Is this always true?

One of the ironies of ethical behavior is that most of the time it does *not* pay to be good. Most worthwhile things come with a price attached. Ethical behavior is a prime example. It is usually cheaper to pollute. It is usually cheaper to discriminate. It is usually cheaper to pay lower wages to women, even for comparable work. Certainly, one could argue that in the long run, each of these practices would come back to hurt the offending firm. But as John Maynard Keynes said, "In the long run, we are all dead." Sometimes, there are public relations benefits to "being good." But these are rare and typically don't add up to much.

12. When would "induce it" be sensible?

As the author points out, this approach works well when the skills of particular corporations are needed to solve particular problems. It makes sense to provide those firms with incentives to perform those tasks. One good example is job training. Another is the establishment of "enterprise zones," areas where businesses are given special tax breaks and other incentives to create jobs where otherwise jobs might not exist.

13. What is your position on the idea of "restoring" corporate control to its owners, the shareholders? On what kinds of assumptions does this notion rest?

As Mintzberg points out, it rests on technical (ownership control can actually be exercised), economic (the perfect competition assumptions of microeconomics), and political (corporations are mere tools, free societies don't meddle inside private-owned enterprises) assumptions that are at least debatable. How students come down on this depends entirely on how plausible they think these assumptions are.

Pitcher, "Artists, Craftsmen, and Technocrats"

Summary of Reading

To change corporations you have to change managers. All else is abstraction. Technocrats with ultimate authority will drive out artists and craftsmen.

HOW TO IDENTIFY A TECHNOCRAT

They like words, charts and graphs, and plans. Here are the words colleagues use to describe them: controlled, conservative, serious, analytical, no-nonsense, intense, determined, cerebral, methodical, and meticulous.

RECOGNIZING AN ARTIST

These are pretty much the opposite of technocrats. Descriptive words for the artist: bold, daring, exciting, volatile, intuitive, entrepreneurial, inspiring, imaginative, unpredictable, and funny.

AND NOW, THE CRAFTSMAN

People trust craftsmen. Craftsmen see organizations as enduring institutions that have lives of their own, pasts and futures. Craftsmen see themselves as custodians of these institutions. Craft is rooted in tradition, experience and practice, all of which lead to judgment. "Apprenticeship is long, frustrating and sometimes arduous." Craftsmen are patient and exhibit judgment. Descriptive words for the craftsman: wise, amiable, honest, straightforward, responsible, trustworthy, reasonable, open-minded, and realistic.

TEAMWORK AND THE TYPES

These three types of people have great difficulty communicating. They have different world views, values and goals. They ask different questions and give different answers. Their conflicts center not on ideas but on character.

Technocrats' cost-cutting programs often cut into what the craftsmen think is the core of the company. Craftsmen see technocrats as too distant and abstract. Technocrats often see profitability as a strategy. "Profitability was not and is not a strategy and it can certainly not inspire anyone as an ultimate goal: 'What do you do for a living?' 'I make profit.' Losing . . . artists, [a] company [loses] vision. Losing . . . craftsmen, it [loses] its humanity."

THE TRIUMPH OF THE TECHNOCRAT

Technocrats make us feel secure when they use their analytical tools. When asked what a manager looks like, students will respond "calm, rational, well-balanced, measured, analytical, methodological, skilled, trained, serious." This is the liturgy of the technocratic school. The technocrat has become the definition of manager.

THE LEARNING ORGANIZATION

The old ways no longer work. Organizations need to learn rapidly and continuously. To do this we need to rely on our visionaries—geniuses, poets, statesmen, leaders, artists. The common thread is "someone who breaks radically with conventional wisdom, someone who sees what others do not, someone who imagines a new order. This is discontinuous learning. We call it imaginative." There is also daily, continuous learning that transforms imagination into the concrete. This is the learning of the skilled craftsman.

Codification of existing learning is done by technocrats. But technocratic knowledge alone can be dangerous. "If [technocrats] have no imagination, they will only mimic the competition—strategy as paint-by-numbers. If they have no skill, they will not understand their markets. If they have no wisdom, they will tear at the fabric of the organization."

<u>VISION, CONTINUITY, AND CONTROL</u>

Leadership consists of knowing how to package these three ways of learning and integrating vision, continuity and control. The first step is to diagnose, but it is made more difficult for three reasons:

1. Artists, craftsmen and technocrats rarely exist as such; they are archetypes. Real people come in complex packages.

2. The task is made more difficult by masquerades. Artists and craftsmen rarely fool us, but brilliant technocrats are able to mimic the gloss of artists or craftsmen. We can be radically misled.

3. Diagnosis is affected by our biases as one of the three types. For example, technocrats might see other, more brilliant technocrats as artists.

The recent call for charismatic leadership will not take the hard work out of managing a business. "You need artists, craftsmen, and technocrats in the right dose and in the right places. You need someone with vision, but you also need someone who can develop the people, the structures and the systems to make the dream a reality."

<u>Discussion Questions</u>

1. What is your reaction to the three types developed by the author?

It should be interesting to see how students react to the types. It is clear that the author likes craftsmen very much, artists a bit less, and technocrats not at all. Technocrats suck the lifeblood out of the organization. Artists are good for providing vision and imagination, but otherwise their heads are stuck in the clouds. Craftsmen are the only ones who seem to have the proper appreciation for the past, present and future of the business as an institution.

It is certainly possible that some students will disagree with the author. As she points out, technocracy is almost a management religion, and it is likely that students enrolled in a business program will see the technocrat as the ideal.

Perhaps older or more experienced students will see the value of the craftsman, a metaphor which almost directly evokes the potter in Mintzberg's Chapter 5 reading, "Crafting Strategy." Of course a good craftsman has a mixture of the technocrat (knowledge of a technology) and the artist (imagination). A good potter, for example, certainly would be skilled in the technique of "throwing" (potting), but would have to have some imaginative ideas about what to throw. That is Mintzberg's, and perhaps Pitcher's, point.

And that is why the artist, much underappreciated, needs to be appreciated more. Without the artist's imagination, the craft would not advance very far very fast.

2. The author says, "Profitability was not and is not a strategy and it can certainly not inspire anyone as an ultimate goal." What is your reaction to this assertion?

Some students may be stunned by this. Shouldn't a firm be interested in making a profit? Of course it should, but making a profit is not a strategy. It is not "a pattern in a stream of action over time." Profitability is an outcome, a goal, of strategic action. A strategy would be something like pursuing differentiation through quality, or price, or service, as we saw in Chapter 4. As for inspiration, even though many people are "turned on" by the prospect of making lots of money, very few people are actually spiritually uplifted by it. Inspiration comes from doing something great, making a distinctive contribution.

3. What are the three kinds of learning, and what is your reaction to the author's comments about them?

The three kinds of learning are: imaginative, daily, and scientific. The first is bold, poetic, and discontinuous. The second is continuous, craft-like, and skilled. The third is study-oriented, diligent, and codifying. It is very clear that the author likes the first two, especially the second, but not the third. She talks about how "our religion" has eliminated the poetic and the craft types of learning. She also talks about how using only the last type of learning will lead to "strategy as paint-by-numbers." There will no doubt be some students who disagree with this assessment of learning, particularly the last kind. Surely there are contributions to be made by "scientific" learning. And it is not clear that craft learning has been eliminated, particularly with the resurgence of "continuous improvement" and its basis in experience and trying new things.

4. What is your assessment of the author's comments about the difficulties of diagnosis?

It is good for students to hear that they are likely to find combinations of these types rather than pure versions of them. Most students will resonate to that. It should be interesting to hear their reaction to the author's second point—the one about "masquerades." The author seems to have a visceral aversion to technocrats, and this section in particular seems to indicate that technocrats are so evil that they can fool people into thinking they are one of the other types. The author's final point is a good one—that what you see depends on where you sit. One's type is likely to bias one's perception of others. This is always a good thing to keep in mind. Perhaps the author should have taken her own advice when it came to technocrats.

Senge, "The Leader's New Work: Building Learning Organizations"

<u>Summary of Reading</u>

Human beings are designed for learning. But institutions seem more intent on controlling than on encouraging learning. People perform for others rather than cultivate their natural impulse to learn. Focusing on performing for others leads to mediocrity, since the only way to sustained success is learning. No one person can learn for the entire enterprise. There must now be "integrative thinking and learning at all levels . . . ."

Adaptive learning and generative learning

Using learning to increase adaptiveness is only the first stage. The true root of the impulse to learn is to be *generative*, to expand our capability. It is about creating, not just coping. "Generative learning, unlike adaptive learning, requires new ways of looking at the world, whether in understanding customers or in understanding how to better manage a business." U.S. businesses tended to use strict inventory controls, incentives against overproduction, and rigid adherence to production forecasts. The Japanese looked at things differently and worked to eliminate delays, which turned out to be a much higher-leverage approach. They were able to do this because they saw the *system*. "Generative learning requires seeing the systems that control events. When we fail to grasp the systemic source of problems, we are left to 'push on' symptoms rather than eliminate underlying causes."

The leader's new work

We tend to see leaders as individualistic, non-systemic heroes. Leadership in learning organizations is subtler and more important. "Leaders are designers, teachers and stewards." New skills are required: building shared vision, surface and challenge prevailing mental models, thinking more systematically. "Leaders are responsible for learning."

<u>CREATIVE TENSION: THE INTEGRATING PRINCIPLE</u>

"Creative tension comes from seeing clearly where we want to be, our 'vision,' and telling the truth about where we are, our 'current reality.' The gap between the two generates a natural tension." We can resolve the creative tension by either raising the current reality to the vision, or lowering the vision to fit the current reality. Creative tension can be a good source of energy for change.

Creative tension will not occur without a vision, and vision will not come from analysis of current reality. No one will make the necessary sacrifices just to get out from under current reality. They need instead to hold a picture of what *might be*—that is where energy comes from. But there needs to be an accurate picture of current reality, too, or members of the organization will wallow in cynicism, not idealism.

Leading through creative tension is different from solving problems. The latter is merely getting out from under some undesirable aspect of current reality. The motivation for problem solving is extrinsic, but for creative tension it is intrinsic, which mirrors the distinction between adaptive and generative learning.

<u>NEW ROLES</u>

Building culture and shaping its evolution are the unique, essential functions of leadership. Learning organizations have three critical leadership roles—designer, teacher, and steward.

Leader as designer

Designer is a neglected leadership role. Being the leader of a poorly designed organization is fruitless. But this design function is not "moving boxes and lines." It involves designing the governing ideas of purpose, vision, and core values. These have enduring impact.

The second design task is of the policies, strategies, and structures to translate guiding ideas into business decisions. These tasks are now more distributed throughout the organization. This is particularly true of emergent strategies and "crafting strategy." "The key is not getting the right strategy but fostering strategic thinking."

The third design task is the creation of effective learning processes. These are "meta-processes" that ensure that the other processes are continually improved.

Leader as teacher

"Much of the leverage leaders can actually exert lies in helping people achieve more accurate, more insightful, and more *empowering* views of reality." Teaching means helping people get more insight. It includes helping them get a better picture of their mental models and to think systematically.

Mental models are mental pictures we carry in our heads about how the world works. "[Mental models] have a significant influence on how we perceive problems and opportunities, identify courses of action, and make choices." Mental models are deeply entrenched partly because they are tacit. But revealing hidden assumptions is only part of the work with mental models. "Leaders as teachers help people *restructure their views of reality* to see beyond the superficial conditions and events into the underlying causes of problems—and therefore to see new possibilities for shaping the future."

Leaders can help people view reality at three levels:

Systemic Structure
(Generative)

Patterns of Behavior
(Responsive)

Events
(Reactive)

"The key question becomes *where do leaders predominantly focus their own and their organization's attention?*" We tend to focus on events, especially short-term ones. Patterns-of-behavior explanations do occur, but are rare. But systemic, structural explanations address the question of what causes the patterns of behavior, so they go much further. All the levels are "true," but the structural level has the greatest power.

Most current leaders focus on events and patterns, which is why most organizations are reactive, at best responsive, but rarely generative. By contrast, learning organizations focus on systemic structure.

Leader as steward

This is the subtlest of the roles, based almost solely on attitude. Greenleaf captured it best in *Servant Leadership*, saying, "The servant leader is servant first . . . . It begins with the natural feeling that one wants to serve, to serve *first*. This conscious choice brings one to aspire to lead. That person is sharply different from one who is leader first, perhaps because of the need to assuage an unusual power drive or to acquire material possessions."

Stewardship applies to both the people led and the purpose that underlies the enterprise. Since people in learning organizations can suffer emotionally, economically, and spiritually under inept leadership, stewardship of people is particularly important there. Stewardship of purpose is important for marshaling people's natural impulse to learn.

NEW SKILLS

Development of these skills requires a lifelong commitment. To be effective, they must be distributed widely throughout an organization.

Building shared vision

How do people come together to create shared visions? The hologram is a good metaphor because each part contains a piece of the whole. In organizations, each person contains a part of the whole organization. When the pieces of a hologram are added up, the image becomes more intense. When many people share a vision, it becomes more real. Here are the skills needed to build shared vision:

- *Encouraging personal vision.* Shared visions emerge from personal visions.

- *Communicating and asking for support.* Share the vision, and ask for feedback on it.

- *Visioning as an ongoing process.* Building shared vision is a never-ending process.

- *Blending extrinsic and intrinsic visions.* A vision predicated solely on defeating a competitor will eventually weaken an organization because it can become overly defensive, as opposed to innovative or creative.

276

- *Distinguishing positive from negative visions.* "Two fundamental sources of energy can motivate organizations: fear and aspiration. Fear, the energy source behind negative visions, can produce extraordinary changes in shorter periods, but aspiration endures as a continuing source of learning and growth."

Surfacing and testing mental models

New ideas often fall by the wayside because they conflict with existing mental models. Few leaders possess the skills to challenge assumptions without provoking defensiveness.

- *Seeing leaps of abstraction.* Our minds move at lightning speed and leap to generalizations that we never think of testing.

- *Balancing inquiry and advocacy.* Advocacy skills that helped a manager get promoted become counterproductive at higher levels where complex problems require collaborative learning.

- *Distinguishing espoused theory from theory in use.* Many organizations purport to believe in something, but their actions reveal something different. Deep learning requires that people in organizations see this.

- *Recognizing and defusing defensive routines.* These are "entrenched habits used to protect ourselves from the embarrassment and threat that come with exposing our thinking." These make it difficult to expose mental models and thereby lessen learning. One way to cut through this is to be more open about one's own defensiveness.

Systems thinking

Seeing the big picture requires systems thinking, which good leaders tend to do intuitively. The field of managerial systems thinking has emerged as a field of practice to suggest some skills:

- *Seeing interrelationships, not things, and processes, not snapshots.* We see the world in linear, static images without realizing how connected we are to each other.

- *Moving beyond blame.* "Systems thinking shows us that there is no outside—that you and the cause of your problems are part of a single system."

- *Distinguishing detail complexity from dynamic complexity.* "Detail complexity arises when there are many variables. Dynamic complexity arises when cause and effect are distant in time and space, and when the consequences over time of interventions are subtle and not obvious to many participants in the system. The leverage in most management situations lies in understanding dynamic complexity, not detail complexity."

- *Focusing on areas of high leverage.* "Small, well-focused actions can produce significant, enduring improvements, if they are in the right place."

- *Avoiding symptomatic solutions.* Quick fixes lead to temporary relief but even greater problems later on. "Sometimes the most difficult leadership acts are to refrain from intervening through popular quick fixes and to keep the pressure on everyone to identify more enduring solutions."

Systems thinking by leaders is very important. Managing at the level of events (as many charismatic leaders do) can lead to an organization whose decision making is dominated by events and reactiveness. People become burned out and cynical. "Visionary strategists" who see both patterns of change and events do a better job, but can end up creating a responsive rather than a generative orientation. Many leaders with intuitive systems approaches cannot articulate their thinking. They often seem authoritarian.

277

"I believe that [a] new sort of management development will focus on the roles, skills, and tools for leadership in learning organizations." Then we will realize an age-old vision of leadership:

> "The wicked leader is he who the people despise.
> "The good leader is he who the people revere.
> "The great leader is he who the people say, 'We did it ourselves.'"
> — Lao Tsu

Discussion Questions

1. "Human beings are designed for learning," says the author. What is your reaction?

The author makes a persuasive case. Infants don't need lessons to walk, talk, or master spatial relations. In short, as he puts it, "Children come fully equipped with an insatiable drive to explore and experiment." Many students will find this compelling. But others will disagree. Perhaps for many of them, sitting in their university classes, "learning" has lost its joy and become a chore.

2. What do you think of Deming's assertion that "our prevailing system of management has destroyed our people?"

It should be interesting to see how students react to this. Deming gives a lengthy list of good things that people are born with—intrinsic motivation, self-esteem, dignity, curiosity to learn, joy in learning. Perhaps some students will argue on some of these points. Many students feel, for example, that workers can be motivated only extrinsically. Some may even argue that there is little joy in learning. But in making that argument they may be thinking of the very things that Deming mentions as "forces of destruction." In schools those are things like prizes for Halloween costumes, grades, gold stars. In organizations people, teams and divisions are ranked and rewards are given to those on top. Those on the bottom are punished. Other organizational practices that destroy intrinsic motivation and the joy of learning are MBO programs, quotas, incentive pay, and business plans. Some students will balk at this list, but others may come to see the deleterious effects of some of these items.

3. In what way can it be said that "performing for someone else's approval" leads to mediocre performance?

This is one of those systems thoughts for which Senge is well known. It goes something like this: Others are concerned mostly with controlling. Performing for those others therefore means being controlled by them. Being controlled by them means making sure not to deviate from dictated standards. This need for surety leads to lack of desire to experiment, lest one make an error. Failure to experiment means that learning will suffer. If learning suffers, performance will suffer (if not in the short run, then in the long run) because superior performance depends on superior learning.

4. The author says that no one person can learn for the entire enterprise. What do you think?

This may violate the assumptions of some students who still cling to the "commander model" of strategic management. The planning and design schools of strategy are based on the idea that some very smart person or small group of people can learn enough to form the strategy of an entire corporation. But, as Pascale says in the reading on "The Honda Effect," this "big brain" approach may no longer work. The "small brain" approach, where everyone in the organization joins in the effort to implement (and learn), is the way to go as complexity increases.

5. In what way is the idea of "generative learning" important for business organizations?

Many students will answer, "In no way." The adaptive learning mentioned by the author is what dominates most conversations about organizations. The "job" of the organization is to fit with (i.e., adapt to) its environment in such a way that it succeeds. The idea of generative learning is too "soft" for many people, students and otherwise. But the author makes an eloquent case for generativity. "The impulse to learn, at its heart, is an impulse to be generative, to expand our capability." Expanded capability is strategically a good thing because it requires looking at the world in a different way. With all the evidence that one cause of failure is the firm's inability to change its business model (its way of thinking about how to do business), anything that helps to change thinking, like generative learning, is good. The author's contrast between Japanese and American manufacturing systems is very apt on this point.

6. What is your reaction to the author's description of the typical Western view of leadership and his suggestions for a new approach to leadership?

The author characterizes this view as individualistic, nonsystemic and prone to hero worship. Many students will resist this characterization, but it is probably an accurate one. The author first mentions here a new approach. Leaders must be teachers, designers and stewards. They must build shared vision, encourage systemic thinking, and surface mental models. At this point in the reading, most students will likely be confused because this approach is so different from the prevailing one. But Senge elaborates on each point and in the balance of the reading makes a compelling argument for his new approach to leadership.

7. What is your reaction to the author's concept of "creative tension?"

This is one of the more mysterious ideas in the reading. Essentially, creative tension is the gap between the desired future (vision) and the present state of affairs (current reality). Senge and his colleague Robert Fritz assert that the mere existence of this gap is enough to motivate behavior toward change. The main job of the leader here is to articulate both ends of this concept. He/she must clearly state the future vision of the organization, but also help its members be honest about current reality. Just doing these things should be enough to motivate change, if the theory of creative tension is correct. It's not clear how students will react to this, but they should be encouraged to keep an open mind about it.

8. How does the principle of creative tension differ from problem solving?

At first glance it may seem not to differ at all. Problems are typically defined as a gap between a desired state and what currently exists. Since creative tension is the gap between future vision and current reality, the analogy seems airtight. But there is a distinction—that the impetus for problem solving loses steam as the problem approaches solution. In other words, the motivation is extrinsic. But in creative tension, there is always a possibly better future vision, so there is no loss of impetus as one moves away from current reality. The motivation is intrinsic. It is to create. This distinction mirrors the distinction between adaptive learning (problem solving) and generative learning (creative tension).

9. In what way is the role of "designer" to be carried out?

It is really an organization-building activity. The first step is to design the organization's governing ideas—purpose, vision, and core values. The second step is to put in place the policies, strategies and structures that translate the guiding ideas into action. This used to be viewed as the bailiwick of top management, but is increasingly seen, with the greater emphasis on emergent strategy, as the work of everyone in the organization. The third design responsibility is to put learning processes in place. In this phase, planners realize that their task is to foster learning, not devise plans. This is where they end up with their greatest impact.

10. In what way is the leader a teacher?

Since so many students see the role of teacher as one of imparting knowledge, many will misinterpret Senge here. He does not mean that at all. Rather, he means that leaders help people with their mental models. Events are driven by patterns of behavior, which in turn are driven by systemic structure. Most people, and most managers, deal with the events of the world. A few better leaders focus on patterns. Both types of leaders create reactive or at best adaptive organizations. But the best leaders must teach their organization's members to see the *systemic structure* underlying behavior and events. These are the organizations that are generative. It is in the context of discussing this question that the notion of systemic structure needs to be driven home to students.

11. In what ways can or should a leader be a steward?

Many students will be intrigued by Greenleaf's idea of the "servant leader," someone whose motivation to lead stems from a desire to *serve*. Other students will be puzzled, because this way of thinking about leadership is so at odds with the traditional, hero-oriented view of leaders. But the case for servant leadership is strong. Senge says that such a person must serve two things. First, he or she must serve the people who belong to the organization. Leaders' decisions can have profound effects on the people who inhabit organizations. This may be particularly true in learning organizations. Second, he or she must serve the organization's larger mission. It is only through a compelling mission or vision that people will be intrinsically motivated.

12. The author compares an organization to a hologram. What do you think of this comparison?

Since few students are familiar with holograms, they may not know how to react to this comparison, which is also used in Gareth Morgan's classic *Images of Organization*. In a hologram, each part contains an intact image of the whole. The analogy in an organization would be that each member would carry an intact image of the organization around in her or his head. This would be a personal vision. When the partial images in a hologram are brought together, the image is sharp and intense. Similarly, when the personal visions of the organization's members are brought together, the shared vision becomes a culture or a strategic intent (a la Hamel and Prahalad). This shared vision is compelling and helps propel the people in the organization away from current reality and toward their shared vision of the future.

13. What items on Senge's list of visioning skills surprised you?

Of course students' answers to this list will vary, but there seem to be some new items mixed in with items that have become "common sense." Among the latter are the ideas that visions must be supported and must be constantly rebuilt. More surprising is the notion that personal vision should be encouraged. Too much of the literature on vision emphasizes the common nature of it, but Senge points out that shared vision must almost by definition involve the blending of personal visions. Another surprising one is the notion of the need to blend extrinsic and intrinsic visions. This relates to his earlier point about the distinction between adaptive and generative learning. People may be compelled for a while with the goal of beating a competitor, but in the long run they will be driven further by their intrinsic desire to create something new. Related to this is the final skill, distinguishing positive from negative visions. Fear is, in the long run, less of a motivator than aspiration. Too many leaders wait until the organization is facing a crisis before pulling the organization together. Once the threat has passed, the urgency to act decreases. This does not happen when the organization's vision is an aspiring, creative one.

14. What is your reaction to the four skills of "surfacing and testing mental models?"

This will be new and unfamiliar material to any student who has not read *The Fifth Discipline* or the work of Chris Argyris. Here is a brief expansion on the four points mentioned in the reading:

The first point, "seeing leaps of abstraction," is related to what Argyris has called the *ladder of inference*. Human beings are sensemaking creatures who are able to make interpretations of even the most puzzling phenomena. The problem is that frequently our sensemaking gear jumps well ahead of "real" data.

The antidote to this is "balancing inquiry and advocacy." Managers must get themselves and their members to ask questions about their assumptions (inquiry) while they are stating them (advocacy). The recent interest in *dialogue* is an attempt to do this.

"Distinguishing espoused theory from theory in use" is analogous to the difference between intended strategy and realized strategy. Talk is cheap; we can state that our philosophy is such-and-such, but it is our *actions* that speak the loudest. Good leaders give us the insight to see such inconsistencies.

Lastly, groups of people in organizations limit their collective insight into mental models by using "defensive routines." These are highly skilled, entrenched habits designed to protect us from the embarrassment and threat that would accompany honest sharing of our views. Defensive routines are what make the "hallway conversations" that follow meetings more meaningful and honest than the meetings themselves. Developing skills in balancing advocacy and inquiry (perhaps through dialogue, mentioned earlier) helps tremendously to overcome these routines.

15. What are the lessons of "systems thinking?"

This material will be unfamiliar to students who have not read *The Fifth Discipline*. Here is a brief expansion on the five points mentioned in the reading:

"Seeing interrelationships, not things, and processes, not snapshots" relates back to Senge's points in the section on the leader as teacher. People in organizations must begin to see events (snapshots) as emanating from patterns of events that are rooted in systemic structures (interrelated processes).

"Moving beyond blame" stresses the point that actors are *part* of the systemic structure they inhabit. Until they and all other participants in the system design a newer, better one, the results are likely to remain the same. The two sides who are part of an escalating arms race are equally responsible for the perpetuation of their system of escalation.

"Distinguishing detail complexity from dynamic complexity" means becoming more aware of how causes and effects may be distant in time and space. Problems an organization is having today may be rooted in decisions it made long ago in locations distant from those experiencing current problems. A good example is the decline of IBM, which can in part be traced to its *success* in the mid 1960s. That success so enlarged IBM that decision stakes went up, driving the company to a conservative, bureaucratic decision-making style that ultimately hurt it in the 1980s and 1990s.

"Focusing on areas of high leverage" sounds easy, but it actually requires somewhat sophisticated modeling of the system in question. Once all the interrelationships in a system have been mapped by the members of the organization, it is possible to simulate the system to discover where the least effort or smallest change will provide the greatest benefit. This is leverage.

"Avoiding symptomatic solutions" is related to a "systems archetype" that Senge discusses at length in *The Fifth Discipline*. The gist of this is that "quick fixes" (i.e., symptomatic solutions) often produce good results; that is why quick fixes are so often used. The problem is that the quick fix works for only a while. When it stops working, the usual response is to use it again, only "more so." This creates the archetypical system "shifting the burden," so called because the repeated use of the quick fix weakens the organization's ability to find and implement a fundamental solution. In effect, the burden of solving the problem has been shifted *away* from fundamental solutions *to* ever-increasing quick fixes.

16. What is the point of the Lao Tsu quotation, "The great leader is he who the people say, 'We did it ourselves?'"

In some ways this related back to the point on leader as *servant*. What is important is *not* that the leader achieve power or gain adulation or reverence. What is important is that he or she *steward* a compelling vision, *design* a healthy system and *teach* people to throw off defensive routines and otherwise be able to see mental models and systemic structure. In doing this the leader will harness the immense collective power of the organization's membership. If he or she is very skillful, the members of the organization may not fully appreciate the leader's contributions, because of their subtlety. Of that leader, the organization's members will say, "we did it ourselves." That would be the ultimate in humble, self-effacing servant leadership.

Sayles, "Middle Managers to 'Do Things Right'"

Summary of Reading

Despite downsizing and restructuring, American business is weaker than ever. Why? Some blame slothful workers, management arrogance, debt, and inflation. "But the evidence suggests that the real problem was management's preoccupation with strategic issues, and its failure to concentrate on everyday performance." Astute managers are saying that in addition to doing the right thing, what is most important is "doing things right."

The shift to operating capabilities

Amar Bhide has found that some companies do not have long-term strategic plans. They succeed by doing well on operating details. Operational capabilities are replacing strategic brilliance as the source of competitive advantage. It is more difficult to copy a well-tuned, effective business operation than it is to duplicate a strategy. The term "operational capabilities" is closely related to the concept of *core competencies*, which "can be defined as exquisitely developed operating capabilities. As a group, these capabilities form a body of accumulated organizational learning on how to integrate dispersed and diffuse technology and activities into a perfectly functioning work system." But aren't these things, running operations, pretty old? Not necessarily.

The new meanings of "operating" and "production"

Many companies improved their efficiency only when forced to do so by external pressures. Operations are difficult for U.S. companies to master.

There are no simple interfaces. The old integrative tasks were relatively simple. Today's have many more elements.

Tasks cannot be precisely described. Other than basic production and clerical functions, most functions defy simple prescription. Professionals and technicians have a lot of leeway. Training, interests, and habit determine how work actually gets done.

Change is almost always constant. Old work stayed fixed for years. New technology evolves constantly.

Organizational coherence is difficult to achieve. Improving customer responsiveness and shortening product-development cycles require groups to be more adaptable and responsive to the outside world and to each other. Well-coordinated groups degenerate over time as parties act autonomously. This creates a "challenge of coherence—of getting the parts to fit together and stay together."

The pivotal position of the middle manager

The accepted wisdom for many years was that good managers were "hands off." "They needed to focus on the future, on planning and bigger decisions." And they would motivate and empower workers to whom they delegated. The result was a focus on developing a strategic vision and gaining loyalty and commitment from employees. Yet upper management has tended to ignore this strategic role of middle managers, cutting them as fat in downsizings. Sometimes it was justified trimming, but often it was not.

This ignores the critical role of middle management in building operating competency. Organizations tend to develop processes that make more difficult the work of subunits. Middle managers are the players who negotiate the needed trade-offs among the diverse elements. "Without [middle management] initiatives, under conditions of modern technology, the real work of the organization will never be performed effectively." This is often painstaking work.

Why middle managers?

These are often tough decisions that are not "win-win" and that require significant managerial intervention. Even when top management must get involved, "it takes a middle manager to get senior management's attention and make the case for change."

Some operations are truly decentralized, but many large organizations are a mixture of centralized and decentralized. These units will often require substantial systems-leadership skill to maintain their operational effectiveness.

Working leaders

"We call effective middle managers 'working leaders.' They focus as much on operations—on getting things done effectively—as they do on maintaining the linkages between top management and supervisors." Their interventions require intimate knowledge of operations and involvement in the work. This is a distinction from traditional managers.

The work of working leaders

Making sure the technology is understood. Documentation rarely tells the whole story. Only intimate knowledge of technology will assure understanding. This usually comes from middle managers.

Continuous improvement. Middle managers tend to be the impetus behind this.

Evaluating trade-offs. Middle managers must be close enough to operations to be able to evaluate the technical quality of their subordinates' decisions.

People management. None of this means that the middle manager's people skills can be ignored. Good middle managers cannot be technocrats or technical lone wolves. They must be able to work with highly diverse people.

Making the system work

"The conventional view that good managers need to remove themselves from the details of work and, instead, manage by results may need revision." It may have worked at one time, but it no longer does in our world of constant product and market change.

Middle managers who try to make things work negotiate contradictions, encourage peers and staff to modify demands or interfaces, persuade upper management to change policies. Most of all they appreciate larger system requirements. They are demanding of others but are willing to make sacrifices. Middle managers who tried to be "hands off" have units that never quite attain high effectiveness and never achieve core competencies.

<u>Discussion Questions</u>

1. What is your reaction to the author's assertion that the reason for the decline in American business is a preoccupation with strategic issues?

This may spark fierce debate among the students. Some, particularly experienced non-traditional students, will agree. But many, influenced by the prevailing tone in management textbooks, will disagree, saying that managers who fail to attend to strategic issues, and who concentrate instead on operations, are making a serious mistake. Doing the right thing, the author asserts, is not as important as doing things right.

Some students may argue an intermediate point that may be the closest to the truth. It is probably necessary to "correctly do the right thing." In other words, organizations and managers should probably blend "doing the right thing" and "doing things right." An overemphasis in either direction is unwise. The author probably overstates his case to offset the overemphasis that strategic thinking has received in the recent past.

2. What is the point of Amar Bhide's findings about how some firms don't do strategic planning?

It is probably *not* Bhide's point that firms should have no strategy. Rather, it is that they should place most of their emphasis on fine-tuning the operating details of their strategies, as opposed to emphasizing the creation of grand strategies through a planning process. As the author points out, "operational capabilities are replacing strategic brilliance as the source of competitive advantage." High quality operational capabilities are more difficult to copy, and are therefore more secure sources of competitive advantage, than strategic capabilities are. The author drives this point home by tying it in to the concept of *core competencies*.

3. What is your reaction to the author's assertion that "operations" and "production" are not the dull routines of old?

The author's points here are good for driving home to students that operations are not what they used to be. There are no simple interfaces anymore, only complex interdependencies. With the proliferation of "knowledge workers," tasks cannot be precisely defined. Change happens all the time, in a sense becoming the only constant. Lastly, organizational coherence is harder to achieve because market needs require greater integration of organizational units, which is harder and harder to coordinate because of complexity and needs for speedy response. Getting the parts to fit together and stay together is increasingly difficult.

4. How do middle managers fit into this picture?

The author points out that the "strategic thinking" bias has created a mental model that holds that middle managers are expendable. But he argues strongly that the conditions he articulated in

284

the previous section of the reading point in exactly the opposite direction. The difficulties of creating operational skill or distinctive competencies in today's world are so great that middle managers are *more*, not less, important. It is the middle manager who works to ensure that the pieces fit together properly, who handles trade-offs among groups, who negotiates and resolves differences in the interfaces among groups.

Sayles goes on to say that many of the decisions made by middle managers are "tough," with no win-win outcomes. Sometimes these decisions even require the intervention of top management. But, he points out, top management is not likely to get involved unless middle managers bring problems to their attention and make a case for change. In complex organizations it is too much to expect of top management that they will have their fingers on the pulse of the far-flung parts of their firms. They need the help of skilled middle managers.

5. What is your reaction to the section on "working leaders?"

The students who continue to be under the sway of "traditional" thinking about management will disagree with much in this section. But Sayles's points are related well to Mintzberg's argument in "Crafting Strategy," which is that strategy develops out of deep understanding of and familiarity with the "materials" at hand. In the case of most organizations, that would be their operations. Only by being intimately familiar with the nuances of their firms will managers be able to distinguish between legitimate requests from subunits and mere posturing on their parts. And work by Jay Galbraith and Joseph Bower has shown that the source of *impetus* for innovation and adaptation tends to come from middle management. In other words, projects tend to be evaluated by top management at least partly in light of the records of the middle managers suggesting them.

6. What is your reaction to "the work of working leaders?"

Many students will be surprised by some of the points raised in this section. The first surprise is the extent to which middle managers are sources of greater understanding about technology. But, often, middle managers are promoted into their slots because of their expertise with technology. It should not be surprising, therefore, that they would be responsible for pushing their subordinates to find the limits of the unit's technology. It is probably not a surprise that middle managers would therefore be the impetus behind total quality or continuous improvement initiatives. Perhaps more surprising is the middle manager's role in evaluating trade-offs, which works toward preventing the "shifting the burden" situation mentioned in Senge's article. Middle managers are the first line of defense for the organization that wants to avoid symptomatic "quick fixes" in the unit's technical decisions. Lastly, it should be no surprise that middle management plays a large role in people management, especially information gathering, information dissemination and negotiation.

7. What is the author's point in the section "making the system work?"

In the "old days," firms had it easy, and running operations was not much of a challenge. Today, running operations in a way that creates excellence and core competencies is extremely challenging. "Actual managerial behavior [shows] peripatetic managers engaging in never-ending lateral negotiations with more insight. Those managers are trying to make things work right." Managers who "managed by results, massaged data, shifted blame and costs to other departments" rarely led their organizations to high levels of effectiveness or core competency. Successful middle managers had an appreciation of what it took to work and negotiate successfully with others, an appreciation of the whole system, and a willingness to make sacrifices while simultaneously being demanding of improvement by others.

SECTION II CASES

THE NEW YORK TIMES COMPANY TEACHING NOTE

Overview

The New York Times deals with a wide variety of very current, interrelated issues. The focal point of the case is on repositioning *The New York Times* newspaper in response to (a) the rapidly changing advertising and media structure induced by electronic technologies and (b) the fragmentation of the printed media field. The case is useful to bring out concepts of: (1) the structure of strategy, (2) strategies in service companies, (3) strategy in the professional context, (4) the impact of technology on strategy, (5) the types of control systems needed in services companies, (6) corporate strategy vs. business level strategies and their interrelating organizational issues. Dated in 1990, the case focuses on the issues Mr. "Punch" Sulzberger faces in his later years as publisher of *The New York Times* and chairman of The New York Times Company. The New York Times Company holds a diverse portfolio of local and regional newspapers, specialized magazines, television stations, news services, and *The New York Times* newspaper. A brief history of the company allows the professor to place current decisions in the context of the enterprise's long-term cultural and values setting.

The case can be used in connection with readings from the chapters on "The Professional Context," "The Structure of Strategy," and "Organization." Sufficient data exist for a careful market segmentation, an industry analysis, and some aspects of portfolio analysis. The case goes particularly well with readings on new organizational forms, such as the Quinn, Anderson, and Finkelstein article and Mintzberg on the professional context.

Session Structure

First, we usually begin the session by asking, "How did *The New York Times* newspaper achieve its preeminent position? What was the past strategic positioning of the company newspaper? Of the company?" This provides an interesting vehicle for a discussion of the structure of strategy. Second, we normally pursue, "What should be the strategic positioning of *The New York Times* newspaper in the future? What is its distinct competency, maintainable edge, desired product market focus? What new policies are necessary to bring focus to this concept?" Third, we ask, "What are some of the more important organizational implications of this positioning? What kinds of new management controls are essential to effect this positioning?" As a portion of this discussion—or in a separate section—one can bring up, "What are the most important technological changes affecting *The New York Times*? What should *The New York Times'* technological strategy be? Why?" (The issue of technological strategy can either be pursued here separately, or as an integral portion of *The New York Times* strategy discussion.)

Next, we ask what The New York Times Company should be, how it should reposition its local newspapers, its magazine groups, and its electronic media activities, to capture the opportunities and meet the challenges of the rapidly changing electronic media marketplace. This brings out some of the important opportunities, exposures, weaknesses, and balances inherent in various corporate strategies. Among other things this discussion can develop such issues as portfolio needs, balancing relative returns and time horizons on different portions of the portfolio, balancing profitability vs. other less financial goals, how to defend *The New York Times* from takeover and some implications of defensive strategies. Finally, one can develop the types of corporate organization or control mechanisms necessary to implement this strategy and their possible implications for *The New York Times* unique culture and value system.

Teaching note copyright © 1996 by James Brian Quinn. This note prepared by Professor Quinn and Penny C. Paquette, Research Associate.

Thus, there is an opportunity for a wide-ranging discussion of very current issues in strategy, organization, control systems, and the use of electronic technologies in the services area.

Analyzing the Past Strategy-Success of *The New York Times*

A few minutes spent on *The New York Times* newspaper's past strategy can bring out some very useful insights concerning the structure of strategy and some of the major components in that structure. By asking, "What made *The New York Times* newspaper successful in the past? What was The New York Times Company trying to accomplish? What led to the past success of these two institutions?" one can develop an exceedingly useful structure of strategy. It is very helpful to break down the discussion to look at the four most important components of strategy: the values served, the goals of the strategy, the policies supporting those goals, and the major sequences of action undertaken. Within each of these segments, one can bring out certain crucial interrelationships.

Values: "The relatively permanent beliefs or principles which a strategy supports" can be clearly brought out in this case. The values which *The New York Times* seems to espouse include impartiality, good taste, courage, truth, faith, rationality, respect for established authority, respect for power, and objectivity. The reinforcement of these values gave *The New York Times'* earlier strategy coherence and focus over a long period of time. They provided a basis for making trade-offs among more subordinate goals. They ensured that the nonfinancial aims of owners were served as well as merely their economic aims. The financial record of *The Times* indicates that these other values had at least as much importance to its owners as current profits. One can have some very interesting discussions as to why optimizing corporate outputs to maximize all of these values and not just "profitability" would tend to increase the total benefits an enterprise provides for its shareholders. If these values are made clear to potential shareholders, they can increase the personal value to them of participating in different enterprises which might otherwise have equivalent financial values—but might vary in terms of the nonfinancial values they produce. Posing the dichotomy between the complex values supported by any real-life organization and simplistic "profit-maximizing" goals can create some very useful and interesting debates.

Values can be defined as strong, relatively permanent beliefs or principles guiding actions of individuals or organizations. To keep this from being just a philosophical (or "poet's") discussion, we tend to emphasize the practical benefits of obtaining clear recognition and reinforcement of a corporation's values. These include: being able to attract better people, higher levels of motivation, higher individual productivity, a longer-term viewpoint, potentials for greater degrees of decentralization (because of shared values), less need for formal controls, easier formation of mergers or coalitions with those who have similar values, and even lower capital costs (because of the willingness of people to compromise some financial returns in order to achieve higher benefits in terms of other values and the greater willingness to trust people with similar values). The list below gives some of the effects of maintaining a strong set of corporation values:

- To weight goals and decision criteria,

- To screen perceptions of opportunity or threats,

- To attract people and create trust,

- To allow efficient delegation and freedom of action within the organization,

- To improve efficiency, motivation, and creativity,

- To ease capital access and simplify mergers,

- To lower legal harassment and community relations costs,

- To foster long-term time horizons, innovation, and high P/E ratios,

- To create identity, maintain morale, and protect confidential materials, and

- To give satisfaction or create frustration.

Goals or Objectives: "The ends toward which the organization strives included: providing all the news, in attractive form, providing it early, presenting it impartially, creating a forum for debate of important public issues, being a record of events, influencing major decision makers, being known as a publishing leader, maintaining independence of operations and editorial viewpoints, etc.—while maintaining adequate returns to shareholders." This array of goals offers an opportunity to discuss the multiple goal structure of virtually all enterprises. One can query whether these are the "right" goals for The New York Times. What makes them so? One can point out the need for qualitative goals, quantitative goals, corporate vs. functional goals, growth vs. preservation goals, vagueness vs. measurability in goals, long term- short term balances, challenge vs. measurement goals, etc. One can critique The New York Times goal structure in terms of clarity, completeness, balance, specificity, measurability, match to owners' values, match to other stakeholder desires, time horizon, consistency, etc. One of the most interesting discussions is whether all goals should be consistent internally? Very often, goals are conflicting within any organization structure. While students will frequently find this rationally unappealing, it is helpful to point out that they probably have conflicting goals themselves. Ask the class about their goals for income vs. lifestyle, or income vs. location preferences. Again, the discussion of goal structures can be very rich as a backdrop for this or other cases later.

Policies: "The relatively permanent rules or limits established to obtain consistent actions or focus in strategy" provide another interesting analytical point in the past strategy. One can point out that all policies can be expressed as negatives, i.e., what it is that one will not do. This underlines the difference between policies and goals. Policies are rules or limits. Goals are desired ends. Some past policies of The New York Times include not setting limits on the opinions presented, not allowing a single partisan viewpoint (a cartoon or editorial), avoiding wit or sarcasm, carefully not allowing opinion (vs. established fact) in news columns, sacrificing cost considerations for full coverage, producing the full text of major pronouncements, not losing family control of the enterprise, etc. One can point out that policies are the rules that provide a balance between conflicting goals. They avoid repeated decisions on recurring important issues. By limiting ranges of actions, they provide focus to strategy. They make values operational, and so on. However, one is left with the question as to whether the policies of the past are relevant in the late 1980s-90s. By 1990, Punch Sulzberger had begun to change some of these policies subtly; others he had left in place. The case raises the issue as to what new policies should replace those which created success for The Times in the past.

Major Sequences: "The step-by-step programs that implement the strategy" are the final elements of past strategy to investigate. These included: (1) the focusing of The New York Times newspaper as a dominant New York, and regional, paper, (2) various experiments (mostly unsuccessful) to enter emerging electronic media, (3) the recent strategy of focused acquisitions in specialized (geographical or subject matter) printed media to diversify The New York Times away from the exposures in its New York base, and (4) current experiments to utilize The New York Times' powerful archival, data, and information-gathering capabilities in new marketplaces. One need not spend too much time on this aspect of the structure of strategy, other than to introduce it so that questions of sequencing come out clearly in the ultimate solutions of the case. Too often, corporate and class discussions of strategy focus dominantly on goal considerations, considerably less on the policy rules or limits to implement the strategy, and even less on the sequence of events needed to carry out the strategy. This structure is very useful when trying to get students to express a strategy in concrete terms, especially in written papers.

Addressing a new strategy for *The New York Times* newspaper or The New York Times Company will imply changes in the values, goals, policies, or action sequences of the company. It is particularly important to have the students explicitly note any changes in values, goals or policies which they are proposing. At some point, one must ask clearly how can *The New York Times* change these elements of strategy when they have been ingrained for so long. These are some of the important elements of implementation involved in the case.

What are the Major Issues Facing *The New York Times* Newspaper's Management in 1990?

There is enough complexity in the case that it is helpful to have the students outline the major issues the newspaper faces and to cluster these under some subheadings for discussion purposes. One can perhaps facilitate this process by asking, "What are the critical factors with which *The New York Times* must deal with in order to be successful in the future?" Or, "What are the key elements of strategy Mr. Sulzberger will have to consider for the newspaper?" Some important issues in formulating strategy might include the following:

A.   Positioning.   How should *The New York Times* be positioned against its competitors? Newspapers? Magazines? Electronic media? Emerging news information formats? Nationally? Internationally? Regionally? In New York City? How should *The New York Times* counter the many negative trends it is encountering in circulation? Advertising? Profits?

B.   Distinctiveness in News.   What policies should *The New York Times* follow to differentiate itself in its marketplace? What is *The New York Times'* distinctive maintainable competitive edge? What rules and limits are necessary to assure dominance in this respect? In what skills does *The New York Times* need to have best-in-world capability? How can it benchmark to be sure that it has this capability? What policies must it implement in the news area to ensure its desired position?

C.   Advertising Strategy.   What should *The New York Times'* distinctiveness be for advertisers? What does it take to make sure that this distinctiveness is achieved? In what priority should advertisers be courted? How can *The New York Times* best obtain the profile of advertisers it seeks? How can it deal with the advertising competition it receives from other media? How should it trade off its various goals for local, regional, national, and international advertising revenues? How can it counter the trends in advertising that all newspapers, and especially big city newspapers, are facing?

D.   Technology Strategy.   What should be the key elements in *The New York Times* technology strategy? Why? What problems would you expect from the Edison plant? What are the bottlenecks in controlling the cost and timing of providing a newspaper for *The New York Times* customers? Delivering it? What role should electronics play in this strategy? Should *The New York Times* continue to be delivered as a newspaper? Become partially electronic? Totally electronic? How is technology likely to change *The New York Times'* strategy in the future?

E.   New Products—Information Strategy.   What other news products can and should *The New York Times* deliver from its existing competency base? How should these be related to the newspaper itself? What conflicts exist in introducing electronic news or data services? To what extent should The New York Times Company be dependent on its newspaper operation in the future?

F.   Organization Strategy.   What changes is technology likely to induce in *The New York Times'* organization in the future? What is likely to happen to the newsroom? The interface between news and advertising? Reporting and editing? Editing and production? The production process itself? The nature of specialist organizations and their relation to "line" news organizations?

G. Control and Incentive Systems: In light of the volume, price and advertising pressures *The Times* is facing, what control and incentive system changes will be necessary for the future success of *The New York Times*? How can one control the "tone" of the newspaper? Its objectivity? Optimize the positioning and value of ads? Cope with late-breaking vs. earlier news? Maintain the style and format of *The Times*? Obtain needed efficiencies without losing the depth of news coverage and analysis desired? Maintain the "look and feel" of *The New York Times* while changing its style, editorial content, and coverage to meet new trends?

The New York Times Newspaper Overall Strategy

The above array of issues is formidable. Hence some structuring of solutions is desirable. We suggest the following for a start. What should *The New York Times* newspaper's overall strategy be in the early 1990s? What distinctive strengths does it have? What should be its distinctive maintainable edge? What should its product market focus be? Why? These are core issues for the overall business strategy of *The New York Times*.

Vision or Mission. What vision should *The New York Times* newspaper espouse? What should its mission be? What should be the nature of the company? What should *The New York Times* newspaper attempt to be in the 1990s? Getting the students to express a clear vision for *The New York Times* can be very intriguing. They will tend to spring off of the past strategy unconsciously. In the vision or mission statement, one should try to get students or executives to rise above the usual "generalized pap" of such statements to provide an exciting beacon which can guide the newspaper's future development. For example: "To be the preeminent, most complete, readable, and widely available printed source of news for key policymakers and decision makers, intelligent and informed readers, and those seeking accurate information about current events" could provide an interesting starting point. One should try to make the vision appealing to all of the relevant stakeholders in *The New York Times*: i.e., customers, potential customers, reporters, editors, employees, investors, local communities, etc. This case offers an excellent opportunity to discuss what the characteristics of a good mission or vision statement should be.

Distinctive Maintainable Competitive Edge. While *The New York Times* has been able to put more reporters on individual stories than any of its newspaper competitors in the past, this is no longer feasible. Other printed sources can focus more power on their individual sectors than can *The New York Times*. What then is *The Times* distinctive maintainable competitive edge? Where in the value chain can *The New York Times* create its greatest value? To analyze this issue, one can explode out the value chain of *The New York Times*. It soon becomes clear that the combination of "gathering and interpreting important news in-depth" may emerge as *The Times* distinctive competency. How it positions this competency relative to the specialized capabilities of its competitors is very important. Perhaps *The New York Times* should be looked at as providing a much greater combined depth and scope of news for its general readers than other printed media, while providing a signaling device about important emerging events for *The Times'* informed readers in their areas of special expertise. The "signals" provided by *The New York Times* can lead the specialized readers to other sources or documents which they can pursue in depth in their own areas when they choose. Further, *The Times* can provide "perspectives" on individual professional fields and how issues fit into a broader context.

Understanding how this special competency can create value relative to other electronic media, printed media, and information sources is crucial to the understanding of the case. To be successful, *The New York Times* must both define this special competency carefully and deploy talents and resources against this special competency in greater depth than any of its potential competitors. Attracting, empowering, motivating, and coordinating these resources toward *The New York Times'* niche is the essence of strategy for *The Times*. These resources should be leveraged to the maximum extent possible by supporting investments in information technologies and training. The case lends itself well to the Quinn-Hilmer reading on core competencies and strategic outsourcing by investigating areas where *The Times* should develop its greatest competency, outsource for efficiency, and form coalitions for higher impact.

Product Market Focus. Within this broader context, *The New York Times* needs to decide whether it is in the information business, the "newspaper" business, the "Northeast regional upscale news" business, the "generating and dissemination of news" business, the "generation and interpretation of news" or some other business. It is interesting to pursue what makes one of these definitions more relevant than others. If *The Times* cannot dominate the definition, given its resources, the definition is too broad. If it could dominate more than the defined sector, it is too narrow. These several levels of defining the overall positioning of *The New York Times* newspaper will help create considerable focus in later discussions of The New York Times Company strategy. If one catalogs or records these elements of strategy—vision or mission, distinctive maintainable edge, product market focus—on the blackboard, they can later be used to discipline the more ephemeral aspects of *The New York Times* discussion.

Implementing *The New York Times* Overall Strategy

This section allows one to pursue how implementing a services company strategy may differ from implementing other strategies. How does one develop a "maintainable competitive edge" for *The New York Times*? How does one "differentiate" the news of *The New York Times* from other news? In what dimensions of news presentation can *The New York Times* expect to create a "maintainable edge?" How does one define, establish, and maintain such an edge? What should the new "vision," distinctive competency, and product market dominance of *The New York Times* be? Although *The New York Times* is still successful, the financial data in the case indicates a real squeeze on volume, profits, and returns. *The Times* and its affiliated newspapers are losing share in a shrinking market. These trends must be reversed.

Vision. How should the Messrs. Sulzberger develop the new vision? To what extent must they change the time-honored philosophies and objectives of *The New York Times*? Can they still present the news earlier than others? Give it impartially? Emphasize truth when the market wants interpretation? Be a reporter's paper? Since the "vision" of *The New York Times* is crucial to attracting the very best reporting staff, can this be phrased in a fashion which will continue the attractiveness of *The Times* to readers, reporters, editors, historians, etc.—yet be appealing to public investors?

Developing a New Distinctive Competency. How does one implement the distinctive competency of *The New York Times*? *The Times* used to be able to put more reporters on a single story than anyone else, but this is no longer feasible because of specialization of other media. If "news gathering" is to be its distinctive competency, how can this be defined and developed? Where in the "value chain" does *The New York Times* add its own maximum value? This would appear to have shifted more toward distinguished editing, and away from "reporting the news." But it may also lie in presentation of the news in formats that are particularly appealing to a specialized demographic, educational, geographic, and power elite. If one defines *The Times* distinctive competency as "completeness" for this audience, how does one develop and bound this concept?

This discussion quickly leads from the goal of distinctive competency into specific policies—rules or limits governing repeated issues of action—for maintaining the chosen distinctive competency. If this portion of the structure of strategy has not been discussed above, it can be entered at this point as a portion of the active discussion of future strategy for *The Times*. One can point out how policies are needed to resolve conflicts between conflicting goals, i.e., a policy of limiting a major story to one-half page (or a similar policy) is a rule of action optimizing between completeness and economy. If news presentation is the selected competency, one needs policies reconciling the desirability of increased ad content and better ad positions vs. more news content and better news positions in the newspaper. One also needs compromises having to do with the presence of color on certain pages which have different forms of news content and so on. It is well to note that "distinctive competency" is developed by putting more resources behind this competency than anyone else. This requires focusing investments, personnel, systems, etc. behind this competency. By definition, this requires limits in order to create such focus.

Product Market Scope. Should *The New York Times* remain dominantly a newspaper? A combination of newspaper and newsprint magazines? A complex of newspaper and newsprint magazines, more plasticized paper magazines, and/or multiple-format printed media messages including ads? Or should *The New York Times* extend into electronic presentations? Within the printed media format, what is there about the appearance of *The New York Times* that would make it distinctive? How should it be distinctive vis-à-vis the *Washington Post, International Herald Tribune, Los Angeles Times, London Times*? Within its selected field of competency, how does one specify the particular news positioning *The Times* would use? How should it appeal to specialists? Policy makers? Educated readers? Persons seeking a record of the news? A highly diverse mix of the above? How does one describe the positioning (and format consequences) of *The New York Times* to its news and reporting staffs? Without some capacity to convey the essence of the "differentiation" of *The New York Times*, it becomes difficult for reporters, editors, make-up people, etc. to operate consistently in creating the newspaper.

Students will attempt to describe *The New York Times* focus in terms of its targeted audience's demographics. There is much good data in the case to push for a specific definition of this market target. But one must push beyond this to ask how can *The New York Times* actually develop a unique format that appeals to this target audience. This is very challenging to do. Even if one can describe this "uniqueness," there is an interesting problem in enforcing this concept across a reporting and editorial staff that now has such a highly diverse background and extends around the world. In former years, when *The New York Times* consisted only of "the world's best reporters" and some senior reporters-turned-editor, the value systems of its people were more predictable and reasonably consistent. However, the paper now includes lawyers, doctors, scientists, nutritionists, environmentalists, etc. writing as reporters. Given the different training and intrinsic biases of people representing such diverse fields, how can *The New York Times* represent itself as "objective" or "balanced" in or among these fields? This latter question will lend itself to some very interesting discussions in the management controls section (to follow later). Perhaps the most important single question is, "Should *The New York Times* develop a strong national newspaper in competition with *The Wall Street Journal, U.S.A. Today*, and certain of the news magazines?" This is one of those places where a high value information newspaper might have a special market niche, not occupied by others. If *The New York Times* expands this newspaper concept, what should it do with its news positioning, its advertising positioning, its overall concept of the present *New York Times*?

Clearly, the positioning and "distinctive competency" of *The New York Times* have to be related to its Regional Newspaper Group, as well. Should the uniqueness of *The New York Times* in any way be transferred over to these papers? To what extent should *The Times* limit access of these papers to its news reporting? Edited column materials? Editorial sections? If it does not limit such access, how can it maintain its own unique posture? If it doesn't share some of these resources, how can it develop any synergy with these other newspapers? Should the sole international representation of *The New York Times* be the *International Herald Tribune*? Should *The New York Times* have an "International Edition?" Should it have a "U.S. National Edition?" If so, how does it develop these papers as unique, complete, and timely? The changing time zones of coverage, (i.e., 20 hours from Europe through Japan), makes it very difficult to provide timely news in each area from the same sources and with central editing controls. Further if *The New York Times* reports in sequence across these areas as the sun rises, it will disclose its own news coverage to its competitors before they release their newspapers in each area. Consequently, *The Times* could well be competing with itself in each of these areas. These are extremely complex questions which can provide some very interesting discussions.

Segmenting News Coverage. Within this structure, to what extent can *The New York Times* ultimately segment its audience? Should it try to segment it simply by regions as it currently does? Should it push further to segment its subscription audience by other demographic characteristics? For example, *Time* magazine can segment its magazine into 40 different editions targeted to people with different demographic, family size, professional, etc. interests. If *The New York Times* does not do this, how can it compete against well-positioned news media which do? Especially, how can it compete against electronic media which may be able to provide a specialized menu of news services tailored to the specific preferences and demographics of individual homes?

Overall, how can *The New York Times* position itself against television? Radio? High quality news magazines? Specialized news magazines? Specialized professional magazines? Specialized electronic information news services? Specialized interest magazines or electronic media (like sports magazines or networks)? Business magazines? Law journals? Medical journals, etc.? How does each of these positions affect the definition of the kind of persons *The New York Times* must seek for its news staff? How do the editors and reporters in each of these specialized segments interact to make sure that their depth, coverage, understanding, sophistication, accuracy, etc. are appropriate to the particular specialty involved? As a special strategy question, can *The New York Times* hope to be as diverse in news as it has been in the past and yet deliver a truly high quality product competitive with the "best-in-the-world" in each specialty? How can it attract the sorts of people who have the special qualifications to recognize genuine merit and news in these specialties? How can it attract people who are able to discriminate amongst the many different (often non-valid) claims made by people in these specialized fields? Issues of the selection and development of the news staff provide some rich grounds for discussion.

Controls for the News Operation. If *The New York Times* wishes to maintain a consistent news presentation, philosophy, style, format, and positioning relative to other media, how can it control its news activities to accomplish this. What should be the relative power of the editors vs. the news reporters? How much editing can be allowed (by various editors without losing accuracy) between the reporter's original submission and the ultimate product? How can the editorial staff maintain quality controls? How can it make sure that news is objectively reported? Written in the style intended? Given the degree of emphasis desired, and so on? If the reporter is truly the expert in the field, then what should be the function, rights, limits of the editors?

Some interesting practices concerning these questions follow: *The New York Times* had a daily "front page" meeting at which the editor of each of its major departments appeared, along with a few of its key reporters, the senior editor, art, photography heads, the publishers, and an interactive voice line to the Washington Bureau. The meeting contained some 20-25 people. Each department was queried in turn as to what its most important story would be for the day. Each department would then put forward 1-3 candidates for the front page. It would rank these candidates. Then the staff would discuss each story briefly. Typically, the publishers and senior editors would have read the draft articles and would query various aspects of the quality of these articles in order to make sure that they met *The New York Times'* standards. Certain rules were developed for doing this. For example, if a person was attacked by a party in print, the party attacked had to be given an opportunity to respond. Any quote had to be verified or checked, two or more sources had to be used to verify controversial facts, the senior editors could raise queries about "taboo" words or concepts. Any reporter or editor similarly could raise quality questions, without rancor.

Managing these meetings was a <u>tour</u> <u>de</u> <u>force</u> for the senior editors. It was through their personal breadth, depth, understanding of the policies of the institution, and conveying the values of the institution that the uniqueness of the newspaper was maintained. At the end of these meetings, the stories selected for the front page, the pictures for the front page, and the relative emphasis within each editorial area would be agreed on. In general, the senior editors then let the editors of each department determine the priorities within their own news areas.

Within each of the news segments (international, sports, national, New York City, entertainment, etc., the senior editor of that section was preeminent. Each had a specified space which he/she could allocate among the stories, photos, and graphics available. After the initial formatting of the front page, allocation was largely left up to the senior editor of each segment. However, increasingly these editors had to work directly in this process with people from graphics, statistics, and photography to balance and enliven their sections. As color came to *The New York Times,* production issues (like producing color back-to-back) had to be introduced to these complex discussions. Pagination became crucial to the entire process in order to visualize exactly what was going on.

In addition, the closing and sequencing times for the different sections was most crucial. Each section of the paper was given a precise closing time, and a control board was maintained in the newsroom showing exactly when each of these segments was finally closed. Those involving less important or less late-breaking news would be closed first. For example, entertainment, science, weather, and living sections could be closed first. However, on any given day a late-breaking news story from any of these segments might require urgent front page coverage and last-minute adjustments elsewhere. Consequently, some final negotiations were often necessary between the managing editors of the newspaper and senior editors in each section.

Complex formulas had been agreed upon between the percentage of a page available for advertising, news, pictorial vs. text content, etc. Increasingly, each of these required the use of self-directed teams who jointly made the final decisions on a page or a segment of the newspaper, willingly balancing their own department's interest vs. those of others concerning needs for style, coverage, interest, and advertising impact. This is a very interesting place to introduce the concepts of self-directed teams and how they can best operate in highly fluid, multiple decision, quick response, high information-content areas requiring rapid decisions. Any form of classical formal organization—maintained rigidly—would fall apart.

Some of the most complex issues are those involving the balancing of headquarters reporters' or editors' viewpoint vs. those of field reporters. For example, Washington Bureau office reporters had real depth and knowledge concerning national news, as did the very experienced reporters at headquarters. How could the expertise of those in the field be balanced against the capacity of those at headquarters to influence copy more directly by their shared presence? Such decisions on a day-by-day basis affected the true centralization or decentralization, the power relationships, and the editorial motivations and balance of the entire newspaper. Those in charge had to be constantly aware of these conflicting forces and consciously balance their decisions between one or another of the conflicting parties as needed to maintain these balances.

Such controls are at the heart of the entire newspaper's management. Students will not tend to understand the complexity of these issues. They will want to deal with controls on much more simplistic terms, but must be led into the right issues. This is a classic example of management in the "professional context" where a reporter's future and reputation depend crucially on whether or not the newspaper printed his/her article with the particular knowledge and viewpoint the reporter represented. If the editors took over too much power, they would undercut the reporting staff. In very short order, *The Times* would not be able to attract first-rate reporters and it would lose its potential for preeminence.

Control over style was exceedingly important. Reporters more recently graduating from journalism schools tended to write with a "looser, warmer" style. While wanting to encourage the use of new language and style, *The New York Times* had to maintain continuity of style among its various departments. This poses some interesting issues. The famous <u>New York Times Book of Style</u> could be updated only periodically. Changes in acceptable word usage, structures of sentences, paragraphs, etc. had to be disciplined on a day-to-day, section-by-section basis for the newspaper. This had to be a constant subject of discussion among all reporters and editors.

Although this is a most crucial aspect of quality control, it is highly subjective and had to be left to negotiated interactions.

The above issues are typical in the strategic management of professional organizations. The focal point of the conflict is between the role of the editors (read senior staff or partners), field reporters (read professional associates), and functional staff (read functional specialists) in the organization. The ordinary rules of line vs. staff simply do not apply. Each group has very high expertise—but in different things—and no single authority structure should control all. As a consequence, one really needs to reach a "team" decision on balancing the value of inputs from each group. Unlike other professions where such balance occurs only periodically as a team completes its project for a customer, such "team decisions" have to be made thousands of times a day in a newspaper. If one needs to reward cooperation, joint expertise, and group decision-making in the environment, how can one also build up the "superstar reporters"—often prima donnas—who have been the backbone of *The New York Times* in the past? Where information has been power in the past, sharing information will be essential in the future.

Advertising Strategy

In advertising, *The New York Times* is bucking a number of countertrends. Key among these are (1) the decline of advertising as a percentage of total advertising and promotion; (2) the decline of newspaper advertising, per se, (3) the advertisers' increasing desire for highly selected targeting to individual demographic segments; and (4) the competition of more highly specialized advertising media targeted to each of *The New York Times'* audiences in depth. In bucking these trends, *The Times* advertising strategy has to be keyed explicitly to its news strategy.

The discussion should begin by asking the students to define to which advertising targets should *The New York Times* give priority? Where can *The Times* potentially offer greater value than its competitors? Its targets probably should include individual consumers in *The Times* selected demographic and original segments, retailers whose locations or lines match those segments, advertisers wishing to provide a message in such depth or detail that electronic media are inappropriate, activities with ephemeral timeframes (like special sales, movies, or entertainment, where repeat messages in other media would be needed to obtain penetration and hence be inefficient), geographically specialized activities (like real estate or job listings). After this opening discussion, it is more feasible to get a reasonable advertising strategy from a class. Note that the strategy has to have two prongs: one which is directed toward which advertisers might select *The Times* and why, the other toward cultivating the right readers and ambiance in *The Times* itself. How does *The Times* develop its content, format, and policies to appeal to both groups?

The New York Times obviously has responded to a number of these issues by providing much more segmentation in its offerings, special sections, magazines, regional editions, etc. The real question is how much further can it go? The ultimate newspaper might be one targeted specifically to each household, containing only the information that household wants. With the new technologies available, how close can *The New York Times* come to this? Can it go beyond what it already offers by combining electronic and print media? Could it offer a special dial-in service to its customers where (through a modem) they could pull off whatever information they wanted each day about the stock market, entertainment, classified advertising, etc.? While this would be very useful for the consumer, it would undercut the desires of advertisers in those sections to contact the random or impulse buyer. The cost savings in such interactive response capabilities for *The New York Times* are enormous. But will the disadvantages to the advertiser offset the advantages to the consumer and *The Times*?

Within its selected niches, how can *The Times* compete against the types of highly specialized "throw away" magazines which have come into the marketplace supported solely by their advertising? How can *The New York Times* combine its news capability and the news capability of advertising itself to accomplish something its competitors cannot? If *The New York*

Times is in a rapidly declining primary market, how can it sufficiently differentiate its product so that it increases its share of that market? How should it position its advertising relative to *The Daily News* and other local and suburban New York papers? Should it discriminate against ad formats that do not meet its image requirements? Should it limit its advertising content by policy in any fashion? If so, how? How can it use advertising to add to the image and information value of the newspaper? Can and should *The New York Times* penetrate new markets for advertising by redefining other items as "news," as it has done with foods, fashions, and books? One can obtain some very creative views in this discussion. These need to be disciplined by asking, "What priorities should *The Times* assign among these targets, and how?"

A Technology Strategy

The technology strategy of *The New York Times* offers a number of interesting points for discussion. One should ask, at the outset, "What is (and should be) the overall technology strategy of *The New York Times*?" *The Times'* strategy in the past has been very conservative. It has chosen not to be the experimental leader in technology. Because of its relative size, the risk of implementing a new technology is very high. Consequently, *The Times* has pursued a "fast follower" strategy. One can ask, "Why? What are the potential gains for *The New York Times*? Losses? What are the key elements in managing a fast follower strategy?" This kind of strategy requires very strong distribution, a high market share, and stabilizing market controls to reduce market risks. By avoiding risks at the developmental level, a company can actually lower its costs during installation. Instead of having to scale up its operation in steps to lower risk, it can move in at full scale from the outset. It can save costs by focusing its attention on production and marketing skills rather than technology skills. And so on. While much attention is given in the current literature to "fast response systems" in technology, this is a case where rapid development might not be a good strategy. Rapid installation might be.

A second set of questions could begin with, "Where are the remaining bottlenecks in the productivity system of *The New York Times*?" Production of *The New York Times* newspaper is almost totally automated, as is its newsroom operation, and these are electronically connected to the field reporting staff. The main bottlenecks are (1) in trucking and physical distribution of the newspaper and (2) in using the full capabilities of the electronic systems which *The New York Times* has for segmenting its markets.

One can get at the former indirectly by asking, "What is the limiting factor on the capacity of *The New York Times* to deliver its news in a most current fashion?" *The Times* can produce a complete newspaper from news input to printing in approximately 6-7 hours. Getting the newspaper from the printing plant to homes or distributors takes another 6-8 hours. How can *The New York Times* attack this issue? If it cannot shorten this time cycle, then how can it position its news to be of value after 12-14 hours? Should it move to an all electronic supplement which would allow its readers a last minute update on their TV screens? Since there is a 32-hour lapse from one day's news closing to delivery of news the next day, should *The New York Times* offer interim editions? A dial-in news update service? Specialized update services for segments of the paper (like stock markets or business news)?

Within the Edison facility—as has been noted above—the "mail room" has become the key bottleneck. This is the point at which the newspapers in their various targeted modes are assembled into packages for distribution to particular geographical and demographic points. This is where trucks are loaded and errors are made; yet this is where the least experienced and least stable workforce is used. As the largest and most complex single "mail room" in the industry *The New York Times* will have to drive this technology itself. How can it think about this development within its overall strategy? This may be a good place for a major strategic alliance, instead of solo internal development.

What opportunities and problems should *The New York Times* expect in the opening of its Edison, New Jersey plant? This is a huge $4.5 billion financial investment. If the unions can shut down the Edison plant at the right moment, they can reassert all of their former power at *The New York Times*. Does *The New York Times* have the cash flows to support a major error? Strike? How should *The New York Times* proceed to minimize this risk? Why does *The New York Times* continue to use the "shape up" system for staffing its production operation? In a thoroughly automated plant like this, why shouldn't *The Times* pay "salaries" to its labor? How can it make the labor into a portion of the "news team" getting the highest quality news to its customers?

Using Electronics to Expand the Product Line

Given the huge amount of information and data that *The New York Times* assembles to produce its newspapers, how can this asset be used to build new product lines? The *New York Times* has a small unit internally which is attempting to build new businesses on an "internal venture" basis. As is noted in the case, *The Times* developed businesses around its information files. It used to have all of these files in a "clipping room" to which it allowed special access as in a library. Increasingly, these are kept on electronic systems. Should *The Times* provide access to this news base for a fee? If so, how should it be marketed? As a portion of developing its own analyses, *The Times* has a large statistical base—and statistical analyses—which it has developed, in addition to its archives. Should it offer access to this statistical base, if so how? Further, through its own operations, *The New York Times* develops a very large amount of demographic information about the New York area. This could be extremely useful to advertisers or political groups. How should this potential be developed? Finally, of course, *The New York Times* has its own huge information-generating capabilities based upon its worldwide reporting staff. Should it sell individual stories, editorial columns, and raw report data, to other newspapers? It is clear that *The New York Times* cannot use all of the information generated for it each day. How could it exploit this information? How can it be organized for potential sale and distribution?

While all of the above represent new business opportunities, there are whole new realms in which *The New York Times* could operate as well. Using its business information service, should it sell special analyses to outsiders? Should it offer an "intelligence service" to major corporations? If it develops an "information resource base" from its archival data, how can it protect the security of its sources? Ensure the accuracy with which such data is used? Maintain the willingness of outsiders to provide information to *New York Times* reporters?

Perhaps most importantly, if *The New York Times* uses its information bases as sources for new business, how does it protect its own operations from the competition this information creates? If *The Times* sells its stories to others, this undercuts the relative value of *The Times'* own offerings. If anyone can use *The Times* data bases, archives, indices, etc., *The Times* own capacity to be unique is diluted. Should *The Times* have a strategy of releasing such access only after one day? Two days? Or on a strictly archival basis (one month or more after events occur)? Should it sell to anyone? Only libraries? Institutional customers under license? In raw data or interpreted form?

Many have asked whether newspapers are not anachronistic. Should *The New York Times* begin to actively develop itself into an all-electronic news medium? If so, how does it conceptualize itself in this marketplace? What can it do that television cannot do better? To date, none of the data text systems has been successful. If the students begin to move toward this solution, the professor should caution them heavily. It seems that television screening of news needs to have a much more lively format than mere print. Print is also extremely slow to present. Consequently, video text is "wasting the time of its readers." However, there are opportunities for interactive services which customers could access once they had an original story. Perhaps they could then tap into a segmented data base for amplifications of particular data within the story. This could be quite compatible with *The New York Times* philosophy of "all the news fit to print on a timely basis." These questions can create some lively discussions.

The New York Times Company Strategy

Once *The New York Times* newspaper strategy is in place, one can begin to ask what the role of The New York Times Company should be? The New York Times Company was originally designed to ensure the continuity of *The New York Times* newspaper and to expand its influence. A number of acquisitions and new ventures compatible with *The New York Times* concept were attempted. Some included radio, TV, and other electronic media networks. To date, The New York Times Company has not been very successful in managing such structures. One can ask what has been the past strategy of The New York Times Company? What appear to have been its success-problem patterns? What unique competencies does The New York Times Company have?

From the data in Table 1 of the case, one can develop a distinctive pattern. The New York Times Company has been most successful in the acquisition and management of strong local or regional newspapers, some highly specialized magazines in the United States, and the development of newspapers in the graying yet growing Sun Belt areas of the United States. It has developed dominating positions in certain areas—i.e., women's service magazines, specialized sports magazines appealing to upper demographic segments, and high quality local or regional newspapers. But it is losing money on these magazines and needs to obtain strategic and operating control. Note that the company has sold off almost all of its earlier electronic media attempts, although it acquired some television stations in the mid-1980s. It has avoided or sold off cable systems. Was this policy wise? Should it be continued?

One has to ask where The New York Times Company should seek growth in the future. The corporation's skills seem highly leveragable in the management of small-regional newspapers. Its strategy of patient development seems to pay off in the long run as compared to competitors' "quick exploitation" strategies. However, all of these policies tend to depress the current profitability of The New York Times Company. This raises the question of whether The New York Times Company is well served by its foundation ownership and its dynastic, succession management. Is maximizing the present value of cash flows or stock prices really the criterion it should pursue in the future? Is it necessary to put more emphasis on this because of recently poor operating results? How? This is a good place to ask, "What should The New York Times Company's goals be for the future?" How should the Sulzbergers implement any desired changes? Again, one has an opportunity to play off profitability goals, short-term goals, longer-term power, influence, stability, risk, and social-information goals against "profit or present value maximizing" goals. Clearly, The New York Times Company needs to reemphasize profit goals in the near future. How much profit does it need? Why? How can it best obtain these profits? A control strategy is needed more than an expansion strategy. In some places this can be a very lively debate.

As the class begins to zero in on the kinds of positions The New York Times Company should seek and dominate, one can increasingly ask for specifics. What other magazines should it seek? What size of town should its newspapers be in? What types of ROI, scale or synergies should The New York Times Company seek in an acquisition program? Should it continue its geographical diversification as a strategy? Should it return to the New York area and increase its dominance there? If so, what types of activities might it undertake? The FCC will have a very strong interest in any potential dominance of electronic media The Times Company might develop in the New York area. However, in other parts of the country—where it was not a dominant news provider—The New York Times Company could probably purchase local stations quite readily. Such an electronic network could give *The Times* a strong secondary use for its news services and perhaps develop the news personalities of some of its staff as being even more interesting to readers. This again could potentially leverage the news capabilities of *The Times*, giving it higher profile. There is a real question, however, whether this fits the "conservative, grey *Timesian*" image that *The New York Times* and New York Times Company have wanted to cultivate in the past. Should this be continued in the future?

Of great importance in The New York Times Company strategy is the issue of what positions it wishes to take overseas. Its news sources obviously allow it to offer some news services abroad. Its prestige should allow *The Times* newspaper to make sales abroad. Should it go beyond the *International Herald Tribune* relationship it now has? If it develops electronic news services should it extend these overseas? What types of priorities should it seek if it does?

Perhaps the most important internal issue for The New York Times Company is its profitability. Note that *The New York Times* has not been as profitable as its major large-scale competitors. Should it shoot for the 25% or 20% margins of the *Miami Herald* or *The Washington Post*? If it does, how can it double its pre-tax earnings? What aspects of its strategic positioning should it be willing to compromise in order to increase margins? Why are profits that important anyway? Its owners are receiving a reasonable return, (+17% CAGR in stockholder equity) in a high prestige business, with very long-term growth and stability characteristics. Since the owners understand the policies of *The New York Times*, they are willingly investing in this venture, hence may have chosen a different mix of values in this investment. Yet one wonders whether these apply to the rest of this portfolio where The Times Company's record is less than spectacular. Still overall risks are relatively low. Takeovers are virtually excluded by the stock structure of The New York Times Company. Is this fair to new shareholders? One can ask whether the society would be well served by increasing The Times Company's exposure to takeover by forcing a single tier of stock structure? Whether society would be served by having *The New York Times* make more profits for its owners at the cost of news coverage? Whether, therefore, maximizing profits is always a socially optimizing function?

The final question of overall strategy is the position The New York Times Company should take relative to the mega-mergers which have been occurring recently. Does Time-Warner create new threats to *The New York Times*? Would a large-scale merger of *The Times* print capabilities and a major TV network (such as ABC which provides more news to people than any other single media) make sense? The scale economies of the newspaper business might support continuous expansions in such areas. But the profitability of electronic media networks have been erratic, and increasingly under attack from small niched operations like the specialized networks, cable networks, etc. What business is The New York Times Company in? The information business? The news business? The newspaper business? The printed media? Or some other business? What should The Times Company's dominance be? What does it take to be dominant in its selective news or media businesses in the future? There are a large number of data in the case which are helpful in discussing these positionings specifically.

The following tables summarize some of the more important data positions. The data do not lead to a clear single solution. Instead, they support certain solutions more than others. This is really a creative case which calls on the students to decide what kind of company The New York Times Company and what kind of newspaper *The New York Times* could or should be. This is largely a value choice question, given the large number of unknowns, but with a real urgency introduced by the short-term need to turn operations around and readjust The Times Company's investment portfolio. An optimum solution can probably be pursued as a "values-driven" or "ends" strategy. Within a broad spectrum, the company could become whatever its owners and managers wish. Its capital structure, cash flows, and breadth of markets served offer few specific constraints.

**Analysis of
Competitor Profiles—Circulation
(in thousands)**

	Daily 1980-89 CAGR	Sunday 1980-89 CAGR
The New York Times	2.24%	1.48%
New York Daily News	—	—
New York Post	1.43	—
Newsday	2.52	2.5
Star Ledger (Newark)	1.46	1.9
Gannett (West/Rck)	Neg.	—
The Record (Bergen Co.)	—	—
The Wall Street Journal	.66%	—
USA Today	N/A	—
The Washington Post	3.32%	3.6%

Source: ABC Audit Data, March 1980 and March 1989; corporate records.

Comment: *The New York Times* growth profile is somewhat stronger than most of its major competitors. However, the notable exception is the *Washington Post*. This suggests that *The New York Times* might increase its penetration of the Washington market by emphasizing a special edition there. It also suggests that further growth is possible with a similar readership profile to the *Post's* in the New York area. Overall, however, *The New York Times* compares favorably with its major competitors in terms of circulation growth. Despite this favorable comparison in circulation, the profitability ratios of *The New York Times* are dropping. This emphasizes a critical problem of management control.

Analysis of
Readership Profile of the New York ADI* and Major
New York Newspapers, 1988
(in thousands of readers)

	Weekday		Sunday	
	NY Times	NY Post	NY Times	Daily News
Total Adults	16.2%	10.6%	21.1%	28.9%
Males	19.7	11.9	23.6	27.2
Females	13.5	9.6	19.7	29.4
Age				
25-54	17.5%	11.6%	23.3%	26.7%
Occupation				
Top Management	31.9%	13.3%	41.3%	19.3%
Prof./Managerial	31.5%	11.2	40.6	21.8
Other Employees	11.3	10.8	14.6	27.0
Education				
College Graduate+	39.5%	11.3%	46.8%	18.5%
Any College	28.8	11.0	36.7	22.8
High School Graduate+	--	--	--	--
Household Income				
$100,000+	32.4%	11.1%	42.3%	19.6%
$75,000+	28.9	11.4	40.6	21.6
$50,000+	24.0	10.4	31.2	23.0
$35,000+	--	--	--	--
$25,000+	--	--	--	--
<$25,000	--	--	--	--
Place of Residence				
New York City	21.4%	17.5%	27.1%	48.8%
Suburbs	12.7	6.2	17.4	15.3

*ADI stands for Area of Dominant Influence as defined by Arbitron rating service.

Source: 1988 Scarborough Report; corporate records.

Comment: *The New York Times* readership profile is clearly superior to its nearest competitor in the New York marketplace, *The New York Post*. If the *Post* folds, *The New York Times* can pick up some substantial portion of the latter's readership. One should note the much higher percentage penetration of *The New York Times* on Sunday and shift advertising strategies toward that higher penetration in the marketplace. One should also note The *New York Times* penetration as being 3 times as high in the top management and professional managerial categories as the *New York Post*. Its Sunday penetration of over 40% in these categories appears unlikely to be increased. Similarly, *The New York Times* penetration of high income groups is extraordinarily high (over 40%). One should note, however, that *The New York Times* penetration of suburban markets is nowhere near as great as its New York City penetration, i.e., 12.7% vs. 21.4% for weekday papers and 17.4% vs. 27.1% on Sunday. *The Times* is also weaker among women. Growth potentials, therefore, would appear to be in the suburban area and weekend advertising sections with a special attention to the female audience.

Analysis of
Demographic and Readership Changes in the New York ADI*, 1980 to 1986
(in thousands of individuals)

	Net Change 1980-1986	
Population	x 1000s	CAGR
Manhattan	139	1.9%
Rest of New York City	47	1.8
New Jersey	233	.9
Long Island	67	.6
West/Rck/Put	31	1.1
Rest of ADI	80	
College Graduates		
Manhattan	115	5.2%
Rest of New York City	231	5.2
New Jersey	292	6.0
West/Rck/Put	74	5.3
Rest of ADI	28	1.7
Professional/Managerial		
Manhattan	133	7.0%
Rest of New York City	192	4.3
New Jersey	353	6.5
Nassau-Suffolk	76	2.7
West/Rck/Put	147	9.5
Rest of ADI	111	6.6
Individuals with a Household Income of $35,000+		
Manhattan	239	18.4%
Rest of New York City	955	18.3
New Jersey	1,380	18.3
Nassau-Suffolk	707	16.9
West/Rck/Put	288	14.7
Rest of ADI	373	17.2
Weekday _Times_ Readership	165	1.2%
Sunday _Times_ Readership	35	.2%

Note: Continues on the following page.

Analysis of
Newspaper Readership
in the New York ADI (Continued)*

		Net Change 1982-1986
Adults		
	Sunday	-4%
	Daily	-4
Men		
	Sunday	-3%
	Daily	-2
Women		
	Sunday	-3%
	Daily	-5%

Employment
in the New York ADI

Adults	+1%
Men	-1
Women	+4

*ADI stands for Area of Dominant Influence as defined by the Arbitron rating service.

Source: 1980, 1982, and 1986 Scarborough Reports; corporate records.

Comment: The above figures suggest that *The New York Times* specific audience is growing rapidly in the New York area. The college graduate and professional managerial groups are growing at 5-7%. High income households are growing at 15.18%. Yet *The New York Times* readership is growing at only 1.2%. Consequently, *The New York Times* is losing percentage readership in its most desired markets. What can be done to reverse these trends? Further, adult readership of newspapers in the New York area is decreasing by about 1% per year. This means that *The New York Times* must increase its penetration in its local market in order to reverse negative growth trends.

Analysis of
***The New York Times* Readership Profile, 1989**
(in thousands of readers)

	Penetration *The New York Times* U.S. Total		Penetration *The New York Times* Northeast	
	Weekday	Sunday	Weekday	Sunday
Total Adults	1.9%	2.0%	6.3%	7.5%
Males	2.2%	2.4%	7.8%	8.9%
Females	1.4	1.6	5.3	6.3
Age				
18-34	1.6%	2.7%	5.8%	6.6%
35-54	2.2	2.4	7.6	7.9
55-64	2.1	2.2	7.0	9.0
65+	1.4	1.5	4.7	5.6
Education				
College graduate	6.0%	6.9%	17.6%	21.4%
<College graduate	0.9	0.9	3.3	3.8
Occupation				
Top Management	3.8%	5.2%	13.4%	21.2%
Professionals/Managers	5.4	5.7	15.6	17.9
Technical/Clerical/Sales	—	—	4.8	6.3
All Other Employed	—	—	2.8	3.7
Not Employed	—	—	4.4	5.0
Household Income				
$75,000+	6.9%	9.3%	17.2%	26.5%
$50,000+	4.6	5.7	12.9	17.2
$35,000+	3.3	3.9	9.6	12.2
$25,000+	—	—	8.8	8.0
<$25,000	—	—	2.3	20.5

Source: Simmons Market Research Bureau, 1989; corporate records.

Comment: *The New York Times* penetration of the total U.S. market is quite small. However, its penetration of the college graduate marketplace is extraordinarily high in both the Northeast and the nation. Points of special interest are that its penetration of the top management group is not as high as the professional managerial group. Some more targeting here could be helpful. *The New York Times* income profile is extraordinarily good, but its weekend penetration of the upper income group gives some idea of its ultimate potentials, i.e., 26.5% penetration. Another very interesting point to note is that *The New York Times* seems to be losing the senior population. Since these people probably were its readers in the past, one wonders how to regain this target audience.

Analysis of
Demographic Trends in Readership, 1976 to 1986
(percentage of population or readers)

	Total U.S. Net Change 1976-1986	Weekday *Times* Net Change 1976-1986	Sunday *Times* Net Change 1976-1986
Male	-1%	-13%	+3%
Female	+1	+13	-3
Median Age	-1%	+1%	+2%
Race			
White		—	+2%
Non-white		—	-4
Education			
College Grad.	+4%	+24%	+21%
Some College		-3	-5
H.S. Grad.		-5%	-10%
Marital Status			
Single	+4%	+5%	+4%
Married	-6	-8	-3%
Div,Sep,Widowed	+2	+3	-1
No. of Children			
None	+5%	+11%	+11
One	—	-1	+1
Two	—	-3	-1
Employed	+2%	+4%	+5%
Males Employed			
Females Employed			
Not Employed			
Prof/Managerial	—	+11	+11
Own Home	+2%	-3%	-1%
Place of Residence			
Metro Central City		-8%	-5%
Metro Suburban		+2	+3
Median Household Income (000)	$12.6	$24.5	$25.9

Source: Simmons Market Research Bureau, 1976/77 and 1986; corporate records.

Comment: In virtually all categories, *The New York Times'* readership is suffering relative to total demographic trends. Part of this is the loss in total readership of newspapers. In some places *The New York Times* is not attacking its potential readership as well as it could. In some areas such as college graduate constituencies *The New York Times* is improving relative to trends. Its weekday *Times* is improving in terms of female readership but rapidly decreasing in terms of male readership. It is losing position relative to homeowners. Its distribution in the central city is decreasing, while there are some favorable trends in the metro suburban areas. The most startlingly different trend noted is that the median household income of *New York Times'* readers has grown almost twice as fast as the demographics it serves. This tends to underline *The New York Times* targeting of college graduate, single, upper income persons. However, it suggests that a strong appeal to the female reader might pay off high dividends.

308

Analysis of
Trends in Annual U.S. Advertising Expenditures
(in millions of dollars)

	Advertising Growth 1980-1989 CAGR
Newspaper, of which	9.1%
National	7.6
Local	9.4
Magazines, of which	8.9%
Weeklies	8.4
Women's	8.6
Monthlies	9.5
Television, of which	10.1%
Three Networks	6.8
Cable Networks	44.3
Syndication (nat'l)	42.5
Spot (nat'l)	9.7
Spot (local)	11.4
Cable (non-network)	51.7
Radio, of which	9.4%
Network	11.2
Spot (nat'l)	8.0
Spot (local)	9.9
Yellow Pages, of which	12.5%
National	13.6
Local	12.3
Direct Mail	12.6%
Business Publications	5.7%
Total National	9.9%
Total Local	9.9
GRAND TOTAL	9.9%

Source: Corporate records, derived from McCann-Erickson, Inc. figures published in *Advertising Age* for various years.

Comment: Although magazines and newspapers are growing at approximately 9% per year, *The New York Times* is not participating in the larger growth areas in advertising, especially television, radio networks, Yellow Pages, direct mail, etc. In fact, the main areas in which the *Times* participates are growing at 9% vs. 9.9% for total national advertising. This can suggest some possible repositioning for *The Times* acquisition program and for possibly developing a larger media presence.

Analysis of
Financial Highlights
The New York Times Company, 1985 through 1989

	CAGR 1985-1989
Revenues and Income	
Revenues	+6.8%
Operating Profits	-4.3%
Income from continuing operations before equity in operations of forest products group	-2.0%
Equity in operations of forest products group	negative
Income from continuing operations	-10.8%
Gain on sale of cable television system and income from its operations, net of taxes	+158%
Net Income	+9.5%*
Cash Flows from Operations	5.9%
Per Share of Common Stock	
Dividends	+31%
Common stockholders' equity (end of year)	+17%
Key Ratios	
Return on average stockholders' equity	Up
Return on average total assets	Level
Long-term debt and capital lease obligations to total capitalization	24%=D/E
Employees	Level
+250/4 Yrs.	

*4 years (1985-88) because of large $198 million gain on sale of TV system in 1989.

Source: The New York Times Company, Annual Report, 1989.

Comment: *The New York Times'* revenues are growing at 6.8%; this is less than the 9% average volume increase in its industry. Consequently, it is experiencing some price erosion. Its net income figures appear to be growing at 9.5% on average. But the unusual gain on sale of cable television systems appears to offset a very bad 1989 income figure. It is important to note that operating profits, income from continuing operations, equity in operations of forest products, and income from continuing operations have all grown negatively over this 5-year period. Growth on earnings per share on continuing operations have been negative. But dividends have been going up at 31%. This suggests that the owners are draining the company of cash for dividends. It will be questionable whether this can continue for long. The company does have a cash flow from operations of approximately $373,000,000. One has to question whether this cash flow is sufficient to cover the huge investments in the Edison plant, or whether that investment has already been covered by earlier cash flows. This is not clear from the data in the case. The financials suggest that the only profit growth over the last several years has come from sales of discontinued operations. Hence the financial condition of *The New York Times* has some very serious problems. Its total segment returns are as follows: newspapers equal 12.5% ROA, magazines equal (loss), broadcasting/information services equal 9.3% ROA. Total ROA equals 12.2%. Hence most of *The New York Times'* earnings still come from newspapers. *The New York Times* has problems in overall earnings, segment earnings, excess payout of dividends, and some very significant potential problems if the Edison plant does not work as planned.

Overall Corporate Organization

Once the strategic positioning of *The Times*, The New York Times Company, and their general dominance, scope, etc. are laid out, other interesting issues can emerge. What should the portfolio relationship be between the regional newspapers, magazines, *The New York Times*, and new electronic ventures businesses be? Short-term growth could come from acquired newspapers and magazines which have been "turned around." Intermediate growth could come from similar acquisitions which become "turned around" over a 3-year time horizon. Long-term growth will probably have to come from a combination of further acquisitions, and increased development of the New York market. (See segment data in the Table 7 in the case.) Next generation growth is the interesting question. How should *The New York Times* play in the new electronic markets? How large can this business be? Should it go into a macro-merger to ensure its long-term growth and stability?

What should the overall organization of The New York Times Company be? Should the individual newspapers be "free standing?" Should the magazines be free standing or organized into a group or groups? If grouped, how will overall strategy be determined? Optimized? At what level? How should the "new growth vector" activity be organized? How does one get sufficient attention to electronic media in The New York Times Company? What percentages of the company's investment portfolio should go to each area? If there are expected to be synergies between *The New York Times* news-gathering force and its various affiliates, how should this be organized? Enforced?

What should be the relationship between the publisher of *The New York Times* and the management of The New York Times Company? Should they be the same person? Why? Since *The New York Times* newspaper occupies the bulk of the investment and revenues of the company, how can and should its power be balanced against the other entities in the company? Should the top management of the company continue to be dominated by newspaper people or should there be a conscious shift away? How much control over their positioning and format should the individual regional newspapers be allowed? Should there be a "family relationship" between the various newspapers in *The New York Times* cluster? How would one establish the goals of each unit within The New York Times Company, measure productivity, measure progress?

Should The New York Times Company bring some electronic technologists into its top management structure? Should it have an overall technology strategy for the Company? If so, how does this affect the overall organization? For example, given the cost of the communications systems, major computer systems, and interfacing needs of software, shouldn't The New York Times Company have a common network strategy for all of its elements? If so, how should it phase this in? How would it deal with the development of these common elements in its strategy? Should The New York Times Company sponsor certain long-term technology programs which cut across all divisions? If so, does it need a headquarters technology group or should this be organized decentrally with only a coordinating "expert" at the center? If The Times Company controls the information system, in this business how can the divisions be held responsible? If the corporate network is open and interconnected internally, how can *The Times* newspaper maintain its own competitive edge?

Within its overall structure, how can management be sure that the various elements of the strategy receive the emphasis they need? The national newspaper? International operations? Electronic systems? The development of new businesses? What controls can and should the corporate management have over each of the divisional groups? Are the usual ROI-profit controls adequate? If not, what other controls are needed, and how can these be implemented?

Is there any way to roll out the scale economies which *The New York Times* expects to achieve from its Edison, New Jersey plant to serve regional newspapers? If so, how should the costs of this investment and rollout be handled? Similar issues exist for the development of satellite systems, pricing of services from such systems, development of new fiber optic information relays for either management or news purposes, and so on.

Thus this case offers an opportunity to pursue organizational issues all the way from macro-structural to self-directed team levels (in the newsroom). It offers an opportunity to question how control systems should be inter-related among the various cultures which will undoubtedly develop within the company. These include the more stately *New York Times* newspaper, the faster moving regionals and locals, the specialized cultures of the niched magazines, the new electronic information culture, etc. The big problem in handling discussions of this case is to hive off discrete sections which can be attacked in detail and avoiding highly generalized "hand-waving" discussions which—while interesting—may not get at the core issues. Fortunately, the case focuses on the many issues which will dominate information-based companies in the 1990s and can be extremely exciting.

SUMMARY OF OUTCOMES

The first five years of the 1990s were difficult ones for The New York Times Company—the economy stagnated, classified advertising volume declined, opening of the Edison plant was delayed for two years while management wrested new labor agreements from unions, and the paper itself experienced editorial turnover. In 1993, The New York Times Company paid $1.1 billion in cash and stock to acquire Affiliated Publications, Inc., parent of the *Boston Globe*, creating the 5th largest newspaper company in the United States and setting up a potential advertising package covering most of the Northeast market.

In 1992, Arthur Sulzberger, Jr., took over from his father as publisher, and one observer noted that the result of his attitude (exemplified by his statement that people should read *The New York Times* not only because it is the best newspaper in the world but also for the fun of it) is a paper that is less substantial and more parochial, subjective rather than objective, a depleted vestige of its former self. *Business Week* in 1993 had an article entitled, "Is *The Times* falling behind the times?" in which it noted that with advertising no longer subsidizing information gathering, it is crucial for newspaper companies to identify what will sell at a premium and that may well be local news and service features—an area that *The Times* is entering belatedly.

In the 1994 Annual Report the company stated that it had made progress in charting its future direction.

". . .Clearly, the Company has changed in ways not imagined a decade ago, but our fundamental identity remains constant—we are an organization involved in the enterprise of journalism, of gathering, interpreting and distributing news and information for the benefit of the consumer, the advertiser, and the shareholder. The skill with which we carry out that process through traditional means or via new electronic systems is our core strength and our competitive edge. . . .We are working on several fronts to develop a better balance between electronic and print media. . . .Over the next several years we intend to expand our portfolio so that about 25% of our profits come from electronics. . . . In all our businesses we are developing new ways to package and distribute the materials we have already gathered."

Mediaweek reported in 1993 that *The New York Times* appeared to be changing its attitude toward the future of media and its diversification into emerging technologies, but most publishers appeared to rush to set up online services while *The Times'* moves have been small. In 1994 it launched *The Times* on America Online. In 1995 it introduced *TimesFax*/Internet edition, an ad-supported online news service based on the 8-page *TimesFax* but in a layout closely resembling the style of the daily paper. The Internet edition has additional features such as a welcoming Web home page and interactive messages from advertisers. The New York Times Company's Information Services Group created an Internet database drawn from the jumbo employment classified advertising section of the Sunday paper. Its latest move was to form a partnership with *The Wall Street Journal* to create and market a news-and-information site for AT&T's upcoming Internet access service.

Financial highlights and segment data are shown below:

	1994	1993	1992	1991
Revenues, total	2,358	2,021	1,774	1,703
Newspapers	1,968	1,538	1,307	
Magazines	280	394	386	
Broadcasting/ Information Services	109	87	80	
Operating profit, total	211	163	135	114
Newspapers	196	114	81	
Magazines	19	12	10	
Broadcasting/ Information Services	25	19	15	
Net income (loss)	213	6	(45)	47
Capital expenditures				
Newspapers	186	72	43	
Magazines	1	3	2	
Broadcasting/ Information Services	6	3	2	
Identifiable assets				
Newspapers	2,718	2,677	1,322	
Magazines	92	248	256	
Broadcasting/ Information Services	116	114	118	

MATSUSHITA ELECTRIC INDUSTRIAL COMPANY 1994 TEACHING NOTE

Overview

The Matsushita case offers an excellent example to bring out concepts developed in a number of the readings. Chief among these are readings on: (1) corporate culture, (2) the mature context, (3) vertical integration, (4) motivation systems, (5) configuration, (6) organization structure, (7) systems. Matsushita Electric is a classic example of a company developing a "strong follower" strategy. It has developed a thorough cohesion among the diverse elements in the "value chain" necessary to carry out that particular strategy. The case explains the culture of the company in great detail. The conflicting pressures that a company using this strategy must deal with are brought out clearly, leaving the student with an open-ended question—how to best organize the company for effective support of its complex national and international strategies.

Session Structure

The session can be structured in several ways. However, perhaps the best way is to start off with an analysis of Matsushita's existing strategy and the key factors for its success. Then, one can develop the importance of shared values in carrying out this strategy. Next is the set of issues concerning how such a complex company can be formally organized. Then one can look at the appropriateness of various planning and control methodologies to the particular configurations chosen. Finally, there are a host of fascinating questions as to what the overall Japanese industrial strategy is and how Matsushita fits into this strategy.

Matsushita's Past Strategy

One can open with the broad question, "What has been Matsushita's past strategy? What are the critical factors for its success: (1) at the corporate level, (2) within each functional area?" From the case, it is easy to derive a mission statement—the purpose of Matsushita is: "to contribute to the betterment of mankind by producing and distributing reasonably priced, high quality, manufactured products which contribute to peace, happiness, and prosperity." One can then investigate whether such a broadly generalized mission statement has merit. If so, how? If not, why is so much emphasis placed on it in the company? What are the effects of such a mission statement?

The distinctive competencies of Matsushita Corporation are: (1) to produce high quality products at a very low cost, (2) to be able to arrive after the initial innovators, yet overwhelm them in the marketplace, (3) to manufacture and distribute a wide range of goods more effectively into worldwide markets than any competitor. Matsushita represents one of the world's best examples of this kind of "quality at a good price" strategy. One can inquire how this strategy relates to Porter's three "generic strategies." It tends to approximate the low cost strategy most closely, but there are several distinctive differences between Matsushita's strategy and that generic strategy.

Critical factors for success at the corporate level include maintaining the long-term investment horizons of the company, obtaining maximum motivation from people, keeping corporate goals clear and concise, integrating all aspects of the company behind the strategy, having superb and wide-ranging intelligence concerning potential markets in many different countries, and maintaining flexibility for fast action to penetrate these markets before someone

---

else can obtain an overwhelming advantage. Why each of these is important and how it can be best conveyed throughout the company makes an interesting set of discussion points.

The marketing strategy's critical factors include: (1) obtaining a very large market share, (2) whenever possible, setting or becoming the product standard in the industry, (3) pricing low to penetrate markets and maintain volume, (4) establishing relatively thin margins in channels to reduce costs, (5) achieving high inventory turnovers (16 times per year), (6) developing and maintaining control over distribution channels, (7) having multiple strong brands in the marketplace to fill various niches and to dominate shelf space, (8) using heavy advertising to pull the product to the marketplace, (9) utilizing well-controlled distribution channels to quickly introduce new products, once decided on. It is worthwhile to bring out all of these different characteristics of Matsushita's marketing strategy and how they interact to give its products a unique value added.

The production strategy embraces the following critical factors: (1) attaining the largest possible standardized production runs, (2) having quality a priority in all production policies, (3) having an integrated components capability, (4) making maximum use of learning and experience curves, (5) continuously lowering costs through heavy engineering and equipment investments for relatively standardized products, (6) maintaining high morale within the production area, (7) getting everyone involved in improving and lowering production cost, (8) maintaining clean and spacious work areas to lower costs and improve quality. Again, one can pursue exactly what policies (rules or limits) are necessary in production to achieve these critical capabilities. How can management monitor to make sure that Matsushita is number one in each area? What policies does the case suggest exist now? What new policies may be needed?

The technology strategy contains the following critical factors for success: (1) maintaining a strong orientation toward process technology, (2) achieving greater depth in process technology than anyone in the world, (3) being able to analyze competitors' positions and surpass them, (4) paying less attention to product innovation than to process development, (5) maintaining a sensitivity to marketing needs in the technology group, (6) obtaining a smooth flow of technology from R&D to operations, (7) achieving fast turnaround times in technology once an opportunity is identified, (8) developing flexible processes that can be upgraded over a significant period of time, (9) investing heavily in factory automation, (10) developing and training workers capable of making technological advances themselves, (11) being willing to invest in technological alternatives before having to commit to them, (12) having massive depth in technology— i.e., more engineers and production laboratories than any competitor.

The financial strategy also contains certain critical factors. To make Matsushita's strategy work, it is essential to: (1) have very low capital costs, (2) keep inventories in the system to an absolute minimum level, (3) control inventories to avoid losses on obsolescent items, (4) maintain stringent cost controls throughout the production operation, (5) keep corporate overheads severely constrained, (6) finance operations as much as possible through customer purchases. Matsushita has an extremely rapid (16 times) inventory turnover, a rigid policy for payment to Matsushita (within 30 days of shipment), and a very limited corporate overhead structure.

Using data in the case, one can develop a series of tight policy statements explaining how Matsushita implements its chosen posture in the marketplace. Because of the thoroughness and care with which this is done, one should ask, "How can a U.S. company compete against Matsushita, when Matsushita has one half the capital cost of a U.S. company, significantly lower production wage rates, and has achieved the degree of focus it has on its chosen niche?" Implicitly, one is asking, "How can Matsushita's position be bettered strategically?"

Corporate Culture

First, one should get the students to articulate what they believe the "corporate culture" of Matsushita is. They will undoubtedly refer to the morning meetings, the exercise programs, company song, rotation during training, and an atmosphere that does not appear to be "high pressure" in the U.S. sense, but is tough and demanding in terms of performance levels. As each of these elements comes forward, one should ask, "Why is this important? Does it have practical implications for the company? What are they?" The exercises, for example, keep workers alert and attentive; the company song helps create a feeling of identity; training allows workers to intuitively integrate their actions; and the less pressured atmosphere allows attention to quality. The trust generated between management and workers encourages suggestions and voluntary improvements; trust also allows the operation to be decentralized yet maintain coherence; the hands-on attitude of management encourages people to work together and builds trust; the acceptability of mistakes encourages a certain amount of risk-taking within the organization.

The emphasis on culture in this discussion should create the awareness that creating a "corporate culture" is not just an exercise in faddishness or philanthropy. It has very positive business results. If the wrong culture is created, even so elaborate a strategy as Matsushita's could be undercut severely.

Organization

The case provides an unusually good vehicle for investigating the complex organization issues that exist in a highly diversified, decentralized company. The case also permits an in-depth discussion of the advantages and disadvantages of vertical integration in such a structure. It should be emphasized that while Matsushita tries to achieve a "direct line" organization as much as possible, the nature of interactions in the company require very complex alignments and "matrix-like" coordination between various operating units.

It is desirable at some stage to ask, "What functions within Matsushita should be centralized and why?" Finance should be centralized to obtain the absolute maximum leverage from Matsushita's position, to allocate resources effectively and to lower capital costs. In a capital-intensive strategy, this is crucial. The controllership function must be centralized to ensure maximum consistency across the organization and to allow the development and sharing of a highly professional control system to reduce costs to a minimum level. Personnel needs to be centralized to coordinate the elaborate interfunctional training programs of Matsushita and to assist in the recruiting of a large number of specialists. The personnel policies of the company have highest priority in management's mind and are essential to the development of the corporate culture which makes Matsushita work.

Engineering laboratories developing generic technologies and background skills for new processes should be centralized to obtain maximum specialist focus. Matsushita's need for patent access and protection in its companies probably argues for centralizing the patent function. Since quality is a central focus of the entire strategy, the quality-monitoring function needs a centralized base. To the extent that the company starts new divisions by creating ventures outside its existing lines, such activities need to be centralized to obtain adequate attention and needed specialist skills. An excellent debate can be generated on whether marketing should be centralized in whole or in part. Another important issue of centralization is whether Matsushita's international presence needs to be coordinated at the corporate level or be left to local or regional heads.

The most important organization question is, "What should Matsushita's primary organization look like?" Should it be organized by product lines, i.e., Consumer Electronics, Industrial Equipment, Business Machines, Home Appliances, Lighting Equipment, Systems Products, Electronic Components, Motors, Batteries, etc.? Or should it be organized by brand name, i.e., National, Panasonic, Japan Victor, Quasar, Technics, etc.? Should it be organized by geographic area, i.e., Japan, Far East, North America, Europe, Africa, etc.? Or should there be a hybrid structure with production organized by product lines and the marketing area organized by either distribution channels or markets? To what extent should the individual brand names be allowed to compete directly against each other? At what level should they be coordinated? How can the organization be established to obtain the desired economies of scale, experience curve advantages, minimum capital costs, necessary distribution leverages, etc. Should each division have its own controllers? If so, what should their relationship be to the central controllership function?

There is no correct answer to this question. Matsushita has experimented for years with different solutions to the problem. The professor should not attempt to lead the students to a particular answer, but to investigate the complexities and advantages of various solutions.

Vertical Integration

Since Matsushita is vertically integrated from componentry to retail stores, this is a good chance to investigate the pros and cons of vertical integration. Among the positive features are the capacities to: (1) capture margins at each level, (2) obtain a fast response throughout the entire system to market or technological changes, (3) reduce costs on a full systems basis in Matsushita's mature markets sectors, (4) control all aspects of quality from design to presentation in the marketplace. Other benefits of vertical integration include the ability to: (1) use the company's full bargaining power to obtain access to key technologies, (2) lock up or dominate channels of distribution and keep competing brands off the shelves, (3) deploy specialized technologies into highly decentralized world markets and thus obtain the full benefits of this economy of scale, (4) develop increased knowledge at each level of integration and to share and leverage this knowledge for cost reduction or quality improvement purposes across all product lines.

Vertical integration, of course, has some significant problems. If markets are highly fluctuating, an integrated system will tend to fluctuate with a greater amplitude than a less integrated one. It may be harder to tap into world sources of technology because various functions tend to get more centralized and perhaps rigid. The company's power is limited to the weakest link in the vertical chain. The company must undertake the capital cost of supporting each stage of vertical integration. Since the company is carrying its own inventories at each interface, this can increase its total costs. The complexity of management is enormously increased, which can lead to the buildup of large central staffs. However, it is important to note that Matsushita has avoided the latter, limiting its corporate staffs to 1.5% of the total company's working population.

Controls and Measurement Systems

Whatever organization structure is chosen, students should be asked what kind of performance measurement system should be used to make it most effective. The case poses some interesting questions directly. Why does Matsushita not use the "portfolio approach" so common in the United States? What are the costs and benefits of this? Why is it desirable to have controllers in the divisions reporting directly to division managers? How does corporate controllership maintain needed consistency, yet allow local controllers to fulfill their functions? Why are divisions forced to operate with "zero cash?" What are the effects of this? How do the policies of keeping managers in positions for seven years affect the control of the corporation? How do the policies of personal visits, advancing young people, and other elements associated with the corporate culture support the needed controls within the company? How much of a division's profitability should it be allowed to keep? Matsushita allows the divisions to keep approximately 40% of their profits. Is this wise? Why?

What should be the key measures in evaluating division performance? Matsushita does not like to use ROI. Given its strategy, what measures are most appropriate to support a high quality, low price, high volume, low margin strategy? Matsushita uses return on sales and sales per unit of assets. Why? (Note: R/S x S/A = R/A). The company uses a peer review system where all division managers get to see their relative performance against critical performance measures. How does this affect motivation, cohesiveness, performance? How can such a system get out of hand?

How can Matsushita make sure that its desired time horizons are reflected in division activities? To what extent can formal planning be used in this kind of atmosphere? Should the divisions be responsible for their future product lines? Or should products new to the company be the responsibility of corporate research and development or venture groups? Matsushita uses a system of controlling to overall plans, not performance measurement on an ROI basis. What dimensions of the plan should be most important to corporate evaluators? How can non-quantitative factors be considered in this type of control system?

Since marketing is so crucial to the company's strategy, what specific measures should be used for this activity? What forms of monitoring are useful in a low margin, high volume, low price marketing strategy? Matsushita focuses heavily on market share, advertising yields, gross margins, and fast response monitoring of signals from the marketplace. It also has an elaborate intelligence-gathering system which includes panel interviews with its distributors, retailers, and customers.

In a vertically-integrated company like Matsushita, it is essential to have transfer prices. How should these be set? How should a division which is heavily capital intensive such as semiconductors have its transfer prices set? What happens when that division's volume goes down, if divisions are allowed to purchase outside? Can short-term pricing strategies by competitive suppliers destroy an internal supplier unit such as the components division? What should be done about this?

There is an excellent opportunity to evaluate the planning system. What is the utility of the 250-year plan? Matsushita uses a 5-year environmental plan and a 3-year plan for new products, capital, and sector development. How can these be developed to be effective? What should each contain? How can managers be held responsible for 3-year plans? What is the role of staff in developing such plans? The next level of planning at Matsushita is a 6-month plan which includes specific targets for sales, accounts receivable, share of market, capital expenditures, profit, head count, inventories, and quality, among other things. Are these the appropriate targets to use? Should an intermediate level of planning be utilized, i.e., a 1-to-2-year plan? If so, what would it do? What linkages are missing in Matsushita's planning system? What should be done about these?

JAPANESE NATIONAL STRATEGY

After developing and discussing the Matsushita strategy, it can be quite interesting to relate this to the Japanese national strategy. One can ask students what they perceive the Japanese national strategy to be? What are the critical dimensions of the strategy? In summary form, the following offers some potential guidelines.

The original strategic goals were to: generate wealth for the total society, stabilize the society, avoid a communist takeover and loss of power by the ruling hierarchy, build a strong industrial base which could maintain Japan's independence and stature in the world, generate a high standard of living relative to other countries, build certain crucial basic industries first (cement, electricity, chemicals, steel) then move to dominate selected manufacturing sectors in international trade.

This was to be achieved through certain critical policies which included the following:

1. Focus on high value-added products which use relatively few imported materials.

2. Focus on exportable manufactures which can generate the currency needed to buy essential raw materials and energy imports.

3. Manufacture quality products, in part because Japan at first could not afford to service lower quality products shipped abroad, in part to increase value added. Emphasize low cost products because of the culture's initial low labor costs, highly disciplined population, and well-educated work force. Drive costs down through imported technology.

4. Help aggregate developmental capital and technological bargaining at the national level through MITI.

5. Develop policies which support a low cost capital strategy: no military expenditures, low national expenditures at the governmental level, a more limited social security program than Western nations, encouragement of personal savings, controlled inflation to maintain low capital costs, close equity-like interactions between banks and major companies.

6. Have the companies take over many of a government's traditional social roles, such as housing, skilled training, social security, etc.

7. Force companies to compete rigorously in the marketplace and manage external trade relationships to help the companies develop domestic markets before they have to compete directly with overseas groups.

8. Provide incentives to capital groups and managers through favorable tax structures.

The professor should note how these policies mutually reinforce each other. Low government costs are achieved in part through low social security costs. Limited social security payments encourage savings and lower money costs. Dependence on the company increases labor's identity with the company and willingness to make improvements and support productivity. And so on.

Reasons for the Strategy

One should inquire, "Why was this strategy arrived at in the post-war years?" Some summary reasons follow:

A. Japan had an island mentality and an enormous need to reestablish its cultural pride after the war.
B. There was a history of government/business cooperation.
C. The youth of the country had been destroyed during the war and employment was essential for those who had survived.
D. Japan had no energy base or raw materials; it had to import all such basic items.
E. Japan had very limited land masses to develop agriculture.
F. There was a traditional devotion to one's organization.
G. The small island culture had created a courteous, cooperative style of personal interaction.
H. Japan was removed from world markets and had to produce relatively standardized products at high quality and low cost in order to gain penetration.
I. Japan enjoyed a relatively homogeneous culture and population.
J. Labor was relatively cheap in the post-war period, and was extremely well educated and disciplined.
K. Japan was technologically sophisticated in a number of basic production areas because of its large war effort and pre-war manufacturing capabilities.

319

Potential Weaknesses in the Strategy

However, there are some serious weaknesses in the Japanese structure. It would be fruitful for the professor to inquire of students, "What are the weaknesses of this strategy? Can the Japanese miracle continue for much longer?" Some items to consider are the following:

1. As Japanese affluence grows, it will be increasingly hard to maintain the same degree of discipline in the workplace or in its cooperative structures.

2. As affluence grows, it will become harder to target sectors, because the economy becomes more "services-oriented" (53% now), and people want to have greater discretion in utilizing their higher incomes.

3. Japan's population is beginning to age rapidly. There is a small labor base to support an increasingly large retiring population.

4. Because there has been a substantial period of full employment, it is likely that layoffs will be necessary to continue productivity gains.

5. Japan's labor cost in its sophisticated export industries is increasing relative to U.S. wages. This is compounded by the yen's current strength vs. the U.S. dollar.

6. Japan's highly diversified major export efforts have made it ever more dependent on world economies and more difficult to protect Japan's own economy.

Japan has developed a three-tier system. The inner or "zaibatsu" tier enjoys many of the advantages often attributed to superior Japanese management. However, the second, or supplier tier which services this inner group, is neither as well managed, capitalized, nor organized. Outside of these two major manufacturing tiers, there is a third tier, exhibiting a great deal of inefficiency and low productivity. This is most marked in Japanese distribution systems and its inefficient agricultural sector. Overall, the U.S. productivity per person is still over 1/3 higher than the average Japanese productivity level.

All of these forces are beginning to converge to create the necessity for a new strategy for Japan. The professor can raise questions as to how this will affect Japanese corporate strategies? U.S. corporate strategies? U.S. national strategy? How the U.S. can exploit some of the anomalies in the Japanese economic system?

SUMMARY OF OUTCOMES

Although the case has been updated through 1994 for this edition, the following information may add to the instructor's understanding of the changes in Matsushita from the early 1980s through about 1990.

Matsushita's goals for the 1980s included a 13% rate of growth in sales, with 50% of revenues to come from non-consumer sales. Matsushita planned to expand overseas production and build up its R&D capabilities to expand further in the more highly technical non-consumer markets. But President Yamashita became increasingly concerned as some divisions began to view themselves as separate companies and sometimes hesitated to cooperate on new product projects, not knowing whether the profits would accrue to their divisions.

R&D activities were split into two divisions: (1) basic and applied research, (2) product development. New groups were set up to develop microcomputer and computer software and optical technologies. Matsushita also began seeking R&D partnerships with outside companies.

It began moving its 800 R&D staff researchers around to different laboratories. The policy became that each researcher was to work in at least 3 laboratories before reaching age 45. In product development, Matsushita was increasingly using a project team approach, combining product development and sales people. The project teams frequently cut across divisional lines to develop "systems" products. Multiple teams of approximately 100 people worked on office automation, robots, video discs, and information-related technologies. Mr. Nakai, head of industrial sales activities, said the four "pillars" of Matsushita's industrial electronics strategy were: factory automation, office automation, electronic components, and audio-visual technology.

In 1986 Matsushita had the following positions:

1. In factory automation, Matsushita had a 10% share of Japan's robot market and planned to grow at 30-40% per year, against an industry average of 25%.

2. In office automation, Matsushita had a 7% market share of the $392 million market in Japan. It was making great strides in facsimile, display terminals and push-button telephones, moving into office automation by building on its communications expertise.

3. In audio-visual technologies, its strongest strategy was in educational applications, but the company was also growing in broadcast systems and building an ultra-large screen color video display system for stadiums, etc.

4. Electronic components now accounted for 1/3 of Matsushita's industrial sales where its competitive advantage was its unmatched production efficiencies and widespread overseas operations to sell to large producers abroad.

By 1990, Matsushita hoped to get to 50% industrial sales overall. Sixty-five percent of this was to be domestic and 35% overseas. To accomplish this, some important organizational changes were made. Corporate overseas management functions were transferred to Matsushita Electric Trading Company Ltd., unifying control of these activities across all Matsushita groups. Matsushita Electric Corporation of America split off a unit (called Panasonic Industrial Company) to specialize in industrial product marketing and established two new manufacturing divisions— Matsushita Electronic Components Corp. of America and Matsushita Communications Corp. of America. Matsushita's overseas production was dominantly in North America and other industrialized countries, but it was increasingly moving toward manufacture in selected developing nations in Asia and elsewhere. In 1990 Matsushita had production facilities in over 25 countries, but concentrated principally in Japan, Southeast Asia, North and South America, and Europe. In those locations it had 343 factories with floor space of some 50 million square feet.

In Japan, its sales and distribution strategies in the mid 1980s were as follows:

1. Consumer products were sold through 120 sales companies (20% or more owned by the company) using 75,000 retail outlets.
2. Residential/non-residential construction products (HVAC, kitchen appliances, etc. and installations) were sold through a sales network of 60 sales companies and some 600 other distributors to 110,000 outlets.
3. Commercial, industrial, and government sales went through a network of 35 sales offices to manufacturers and other commercial users and to wholesalers (including sales companies in which Matsushita owned a portion of the equity).
4. Matsushita established a new electronic component sales network separate from the industrial sales network. This contained 10 sales offices servicing manufacturers and similar large-scale customers.
5. Matsushita had 30 local finance companies to finance its domestic sales. It owned at least 30% of these finance companies.

Yamashita reorganized the consumer electronics division into separate video-audio, television, and "other" units. Each was now run separately and as a profit center. He had earlier transferred responsibility for overseas sales from the product divisions to Matsushita Electric Trading Company, and now Mr. Yamashita ordered each division to develop at least two genuinely new products each year for its own line. He made a personal study of each division's profitability and replaced the chiefs of divisions that were below acceptable levels. Yamashita was said to be searching for joint venture partners in industrial electronics, computers, or telecommunications. He felt a single company could not cover all the necessary areas of technology. While Yamashita wanted to become more multinational in orientation, he hesitated to put significantly more production overseas, because of lost efficiencies and the difficulties of assimilating foreigners into the Japanese management system of Matsushita.

By 1990, Matsushita had established seven strategic businesses as follows: (1) information/communications, (2) factory automation, (3) semiconductors, (4) new audio-visual, (5) automotive electronics, (6) housing-related products, and (7) integrated air conditioning systems. Matsushita's growth during recent years had come primarily from its ability to meet increasing worldwide demand for products based on sophisticated electronics and precision mechanical technologies, like videotape recorders. The company had expanded its activities in non-consumer electronics; areas of emphasis included information and communication equipment, factory automation, and integrated air conditioning systems. In 1988-89, the company restructured its corporate organization to relocate operational control nearer to world markets. Major regional headquarters functions were shifted from Japan to overseas locations in North America, Europe, and Asia.

The company's 1990 revenues by sectors were: video equipment 26.6%, communication and industrial equipment 22.9%, consumer appliances 13.4%, electronic components 13%, audio equipment 9.4%, other 14.7%.

Mr. Akio Tanni had become Matsushita's president at age 57. Known as an excellent listener and coordinator, Mr. Tanni was referred to as "Mr. VCR" by Japan's business press. He saw one of his major challenges as getting Matsushita's 600 companies to cooperate better. While Mr. Tanni increased R&D expenditures to $2.4 billion (5.8% of sales), some questioned whether Matsushita could earn the same profits in its new industrial markets as it did in the consumer markets where its brand names were so well recognized. In September 1990, Matsushita entered into negotiations to acquire MCA, the owner of Universal Studios, a string of theme parks, MCA Records, and the Putnam Publishing House. This followed a dramatic move by Sony to acquire Columbia Pictures for $5 billion. Matsushita spent approximately $7 billion for MCA. This move seemed to be designed to allow Matsushita to capture some of the rapidly increasing "software" side of the entertainment business. However, the business press was quite skeptical. Managing the risky and temperamental entertainment business was not well suited to Matsushita's basic production skills. Some suggested that the entertainment arm of Matsushita might be used (as Sony used Columbia Pictures) to introduce new hardware products like digital audiotape or advanced systems like high definition television. Another potential use would be to introduce high definition television as projection equipment for moving picture theaters throughout the world. Some foresaw elaborate new systems technologies to transmit high definition electronic movies throughout a theater network, without the expensive logistics of handling 35mm film.

Overview

Hewlett Packard is regarded as a very well-managed company. It was prominently featured in *In Search of Excellence* as an outstanding company. It has often been voted "among the top 10 best managed companies in the U.S." by *Fortune* magazine. This case focuses on the strategy and organization changes Hewlett Packard (HP) must make to achieve a better focus on the evolving computer marketplace which now represents half of its revenues. HP has been known for its highly entrepreneurial management style and flexible organization techniques, which allowed it to innovate rapidly in a number of important electronics areas. In the early 1980s, the computer industry was evolving in such a way that HP felt the necessity to coordinate the development and marketing of its products on a "systems basis" across its entire computer line and its various product groups. The case goes well with chapters on culture, organization/systems, the innovation context, and the diversified context.

Session Structure

Because Hewlett Packard is so widely considered a well-managed company, the case may perhaps open with the general question of why the company has been successful in the past. Then the students can be asked to consider why HP felt it needed to make major changes in its organization structure in 1983/84. What is different about the computer marketplace which now supplies half of HP's revenues? If HP's present organization and systems do not fit with the criteria established for success in that marketplace, how should HP reorganize and what changes in management style, planning, incentive systems, etc. need to accompany that reorganization? And finally, how will these changes affect HP's distinctive competency—its entrepreneurial flair?

An Entrepreneurial Company

We tend to open the session with the general question, "Why has HP been so successful in the past?" The portions of the HP Way which are included in the case are useful for this discussion and give an excellent flavor of the company's style up through 1983. A portion of this discussion will undoubtedly bring out the sense of "entrepreneurial flair" which the company has exhibited in the past. One can then ask, "What is entrepreneurship? Why is it important in a company like HP? What characteristics of the company tended to encourage entrepreneurship?"

Among other responses to the above question, one will probably hear at least some of the following:

A. <u>An entrepreneurial top management</u>. Both Mr. Hewlett and Mr. Packard have made $100s of millions from their own company. As co-founders, they understand the drives and necessities of entrepreneurial behavior. They have been willing to delegate authority, support risk-taking ventures, trust people to work on their own, and accept occasional failure as a price for entrepreneurship. It is important to discuss why entrepreneurs at the top of such a company help create the environment. Because they understand entrepreneurial activity, they tend to assess such actions as having lower risk than others with less understanding might.

B. <u>An expanding need</u>. The marketplace for electronic instrumentation, electronic components, computers, test devices, etc. was expanding very rapidly. Large, expanding markets are very forgiving. It is possible to select small niches in such markets and avoid head-on conflicts with existing major players. As the market expands, new small needs appear. One can leverage an existing technical sales force and distribution system to introduce new "stand-alone" items. HP's products were not a significant percentage of the typical buyer's total costs, and new needs for state-of-the-art equipment were constantly emerging. Consequently, a fast moving technical team could innovate and introduce new products with minimum marketing resistance. With market risks thus lowered, one had to contend only with (1) technical probabilities of success and (2) designing genuinely higher performance equipment. HP's organization and style were well adapted to this purpose.

C. <u>An adhocracy</u>. Within the operating divisions, HP encouraged teams to form around a new idea, develop it, and carry it to the marketplace. It did not develop elaborate formal screening mechanisms for these projects. Since many of the products were relatively small scale, it was feasible to let the promising ones enter the marketplace and try to learn quickly from customers how HP's technologies could fit a particular need. Because of the "risk-taking" atmosphere, HP was willing to let people try out new ideas, carry them experimentally to the marketplace, and support the projects, if they were successful. In the early stages of the company's development—and with small scale "free-standing" products—this kind of adhocracy worked well.

D. <u>Small units</u>. Individual divisions were kept down in size. This has several beneficial effects. People tend to identify with the product and with the division's efforts more directly. In addition, there are fewer levels of approval necessary to go ahead with a new project. The people at the top of the division can be closer to the projects and more comfortable with their technologies and potential markets.

E. <u>Product champions</u>. HP's system encouraged champions to create new products, fight the internal battles necessary to get them produced and to the marketplace, and to transfer them over to larger production units when this became desirable. HP rewarded champions both monetarily and with recognition. Mr. Hewlett, especially, was noted for visiting technical groups personally, and setting a climate for support for these kinds of projects.

F. <u>Success fed success</u>. Because there were a number of early successful projects, confidence in the entrepreneurial system was supported. Because top management had experienced technological developments itself, it was tolerant of the time horizons and mistakes necessary for innovation to occur. A portion of the "HP Way" was to create the climate of flexibility and tolerance which encouraged entrepreneurs. In addition, Messrs. Packard and Hewlett have been cited often for providing role models of hands-on, involved leadership. Their style was translated into the corporate culture exemplified in the HP Way.

G. <u>Multiple competing approaches</u>. The corporate style and the highly decentralized organization allowed several projects to proceed in parallel. This competitive approach both increased identity with the individual projects and improved the probability that one would be successful. This style went well with the small independent "line-oriented" units the highly decentralized philosophy HP fostered. When projects became larger scale, the company would form "ad hoc task forces" consisting of members of different functions or divisions to carry them out. These groups were joined together temporarily only and returned to their parent organizations as soon as possible. They were not hierarchically controlled, but were looked upon as peer group efforts. As the company's products became more complex, these task forces sometimes became quite large and were beginning to be unwieldy.

H. <u>The control system</u>. HP's internal control system allowed sufficient slack for new ideas to be tested on a small scale and for department managers to carry them far enough for early evaluation.

I. Corporate goals. HP's corporate goals emphasized the interest of customers, making a needed and profitable contribution to the field, growth, people development, fostering initiative and creativity. The culture therefore was not driven by immediate profits. Instead, there were other qualitative goals which management sought to implement through its emphasis on the corporate culture and the use of evaluation systems which emphasized goals other than just profitability.

J. A good company. An opening or final question for this section could be, "Is HP a good company to work for? Is it truly 'an excellent company?' If so, what makes it a superior company?" In the process, one can bring out students' or executives' implicit criteria for evaluating a company. Generally, these criteria will go well beyond simple growth and profitability to a number of other contribution, organizational, and personal development goals which people really use in evaluating a company.

Why Change Now?

Having praised the company's former structure and philosophy, one should ask, "Why is an organizational change needed now? What is demanded by the changed marketplaces of the early to mid-1980s which HP's present structure and style may not handle well?"

Probably the key is the change in the computer marketplace. Computers now account for about 50% of HP's sales and 43% of its profits. Competition in computers involves larger scale, more aggressive, and better established competitors than the more fragmented test and measurement equipment fields HP has dominated in the past. Critical factors for success in the computer marketplace (which is beginning to mature) are not the same as those in HP's traditional "stand-alone" markets. Desk-top computers were rapidly moving toward a "commodity" status. To be successful, such computers had to be compatible with IBM's PCs, and/or be able to integrate into a wide variety of computer systems which customers already owned. Software and field support activities were extremely important. Margins on small and mid-size computers were dropping. "Clone" or "look-alike" substitutes for IBM's PCs were being produced inexpensively abroad. IBM had automated its production substantially. Increasingly, competition was on the basis of price and distribution. Both of these were heavily volume dependent, in a marketplace where HP enjoyed only a 4-6% penetration.

In these circumstances, the opportunity to innovate distinctive, differentiated products—HP's traditional strength—was severely limited. By definition, any computer would have to successfully interface with IBM and other systems and use generally available software. The capacity to "niche" into higher performance computers was essentially driven by "chip" manufacturing capabilities. Individual chips were becoming so powerful that microcomputers were taking the place of mini-computers and even mainframes. A micro-supercomputer was in the offing. Consequently, anyone competing in this marketplace was automatically in head-to-head competition with IBM, DEC, NEC, Hitachi, etc. In addition to competing on a cost basis, one would also have to face the established marketing and distribution capabilities of these large companies. On the other hand, computers were becoming so essential to the use of "stand-alone" measurement and test equipment that it was questionable whether HP could survive in its traditional fields, without offering a computer line which supported its "stand-alone" equipment. To do this properly required that Hewlett Packard: (1) target its own computer line into areas where it minimized its direct confrontation with its big competitors, (2) integrate the design, production, and marketing of its computer line across all its existing computer activities, (3) develop a systems interface to and from its "free-standing" measurement and test equipment so that these devices could be most easily used as input units for a computer based system—or alternately so that data from computer controlled operations could be fed to them for measurement or test. This required both thorough horizontal integration within the computer divisions and coordination among all of HP's highly diverse product groups and divisions.

A New Strategy for HP?

How should HP adjust its strategies in light of the above major environmental changes? What are the most important issues HP must consider? Some major issues and analytical points can be subtended under four major categories. These follow.

HP's distinctive maintainable competitive edge. There is a question as to whether HP brings to the computer marketplace a capacity for creating a "distinctive maintainable competitive edge." Can HP possibly bring more capability to bear on its selected computer marketplaces than any of its major competitors? Although the Electronic Data Products area is very large and growing rapidly, one has to ask whether this market fits well with HP's demonstrated competencies in innovating rapidly for high performance, high quality, free standing instrumentation. The computer marketplace is entering a period of competitive shakeout with its major players having enormous stakes in the outcome. HP has to either throw enough resources into this market to be successful, niche, or back out. In direct competition with IBM, DEC, Wang, NEC, Hitachi, etc., it is not clear that HP can develop a maintainable competitive edge. Yet, if HP backs out, the growth rate of the company, which has sustained its morale and entrepreneurial style in the past, will decline in the short run. If HP chooses to niche in the computer marketplace, what segment should it choose? In what fashion can it create a special position? Any of the above will require that HP design a compatible, high performance, low price line that can integrate its test and measurement equipment products into computer-dominated systems. This means that many of its successful entrepreneurial, competitive, small team techniques would have to give way to increased planning and standardization of outputs. Meeting product deadlines and designing products which could stand up to inept handling—as opposed to being carefully handled electronic instrumentation—would become important competitive factors. The cost of entering any computer market would be extremely high. This automatically would mean that there would be large scale task forces and a major change in the HP culture. This was a "make or break" decision for Mr. Young.

One should ask, "If HP were to niche, how would it accomplish this?" Given HP's dominant position in quality, advanced technology, measurement and test equipment, this should probably be the strength on which it builds its future position in the computer marketplace. As an adjunct to this market position, the computer line could convert HP into "the world's best, most innovative supplier of quality, advanced technology, measurement and test instruments and systems, providing value added for engineers, scientists, and medical applications." Such a mission statement would give focus to the computer program and allow HP to differentiate itself as an integrated supplier of measurement and test equipment, with full computer capabilities. This would scale down, but not eliminate, computers as a growth vector. However, in 1986, no other company was successfully providing this kind of interface capability. Consequently, HP might be able to convert such a positioning into a new "growth vector." If HP chose such a position, this would mean a strong emphasis on the engineering, scientific, CAD/CAE/CAM and laboratory markets where it had strong positions. It should probably drop its consumer marketing of HP computers and concentrate on industrial and commercial applications to increase its focus.

HP's product portfolio. Depending on what HP's decision is in the computer area, it must adjust the remainder of its product portfolio. The data in the case suggest that there can be two levels of product portfolios in HP. One would be at the group level, another at the individual product division level. Using the data in the case, one can suggest that the Test and Measurement Equipment line might provide strong "near growth" potentials and potentials as input/output devices for computer systems. Test and Measurement Equipment has been growing at 19.8% per year recently and should continue to grow as competitive pressures stimulate new technologies and automation techniques.

Analytical Devices can provide an "intermediate growth" vector for HP. This sector has been growing at 14% recently and has a strong 30% penetration in its marketplace. It can grow continuing the traditional HP entrepreneurial style, somewhat integrated to interface with computer systems. Medical Test Equipment can provide a "future growth vector." Although

Medical has been growing at only 8.2% recently, the biotechnology field offers strong potentials on a somewhat longer time horizon. Computers will probably drop from its strong 23% growth rate under a consolidation strategy. Nevertheless, this division, after focusing on its marketplaces, should both support the other divisions and have strong potentials on its own. A 15-20% growth rate for this division would seem appropriate—given the probable growth rates of the other divisions which it would support. International is a special problem. While International has not been growing as rapidly as the U.S. market (24.6%), Europe has been growing at a 10.9% compounded rate and the rest of the world at 22.2%. Perhaps more focus should be placed on these markets. This presents some interesting questions as to whether HP should use a worldwide product strategy with international activities being components of its major product groups or establish a much more aggressive international group to design products specially for this marketplace.

Following are the cash flow and sales growth characteristics of each of HP's major groups through 1984.

Cash Flow and Sales Growth By Group
($ millions)

1984 Cash Flow	Computers (43%)	T&M (50%)	Medical (4%)	Analytical (3%)
Gross Income	$439	$514	$41	$37
Taxes (~$200 total)	-86	-100	-8	-6
Net After Tax	353	414	33	31
Depreciation	128	68	11	7
Total Cash Flow	481	482	44	38
Dividend ($49 total)	21	24	2	2
Free Cash Flow	$460	$458	$42	$36

Sales Growth

1984	32%	28%	6%	24%
1983	15	12	10	5
1982-84	23	19.8	8.2	14

Financial strategies. HP's finances are extremely strong. But one should raise the question, "Could HP financially sustain its traditional growth rates in the future?" Following are some key financial calculations:

1984 HP Financials

Debt/Equity	2%(81/3545)
Total Assets	$5153 million
Net Income	$665 million
ROA	12.9%
Depr. & Amort.	$237 million
Total Cash Flow	$902 million
Dividends	$49 million
Net Cash Flow	$853 million
3 yr. Growth in Sales	18.1%
3 yr. Growth in Assets	21%

HP Sales Growth by Area

	1984	1983	82-84
U.S.	29%	.0%	24.6%
Europe	16	6	10.9
Rest of World	51	-1	22

Hurdle Rate Calculation

Growth in Assets equals Debt/Equity x Hurdle Rate minus Interest Rate x
Retention Rate plus Retention Rate x Hurdle Rate

$$21\% \quad = \quad .02\,(H-.06) \ .93 + \quad\quad .93H$$

$$.21 \quad = \quad .0186H \quad - \quad .001 \quad + \quad .93H$$

$$.212 \quad = \quad .95H$$

$$22\% \quad = \quad H \ (\text{Average Hurdle Rate})$$

From the above, one can calculate that if HP is to continue to grow its assets at 21% per year, its asset base will double in approximately 3.5 years. This will require additional assets of $5153 million or an average of $1472 million per year. Of this, $853 million can be provided by current cash flows. Thus, HP must either increase its internal hurdle rate for investments to 22% (see calculation) or it will have to obtain capital from external sources. HP can easily borrow substantial amounts based on its low (2%) debt-to-equity ratio. However, it would probably prefer to set a higher target return for its new projects (i.e., 22% after tax) as a challenge for its entrepreneuring groups. A substantial increase in debt would go against HP's long-standing policies. However, such an increase might serve a defensive purpose of dissuading raiders by increasing the stock market's evaluation of HP stocks. Whether additional debt should be used can be an interesting point for discussion—especially among executive audiences.

Organization changes. HP would be at a definite competitive disadvantage if it did not coordinate its computer line and its free-standing products more thoroughly than in the past. This may mean that some of its prior competitive, entrepreneurial, small team techniques may have to give way to increased formal management. A key organization question is whether such coordination, consolidation in the computer group, and interconnection of its "free-standing product lines" may undercut HP's culture and distinctive competency so much that it could not succeed either in its traditional markets or in the computer arena. If computers are maturing as rapidly as they seem to be, this may mean that an entirely different management style is appropriate for that portion of HP's product line—geared more to cost consciousness, repetition, scale economies, distribution economies, standardization, etc. This would require a new management for the computer group. Innovation is perhaps less important to HP in this marketplace where the profile of manufacturing and marketing relative to engineering must be increased. Perhaps, HP can develop a "two cultures" system, with its three traditional product groups operating in its more entrepreneurial mode and the computer group operating in a more controlled mode. Complications of achieving this deserve discussion.

Any integration of HP's product lines will require a higher profile for marketing within the individual groups and at the corporate level. Probably, some "Systems Design and Coordination Division" is called for at the corporate level. Perhaps this function can be provided within groups by the group Marketing Department. It is also likely that the new era will call for a corporate

Planning and a corporate Acquisitions Department. Since HP will have to expand its software capabilities considerably to achieve systems integration, such capabilities may be more easily acquired than built from within. If HP decides to grow its computer division substantially as a growth vector in competition with its major competitors, HP should consider whether to acquire or merge with another company which already has a substantial presence, i.e., DEC, Apple, or Wang. This point can provoke some interesting discussion.

Other important organizational issues are:

1. Where should the international activities be placed? Should international be a component of a product group or centralized for the corporation? How can the corporation best obtain market information from potential international marketplaces? How can it best compete on a price performance basis in these marketplaces?

2. How should R&D be organized? Should anything other than basic research be contained in the central research laboratories? Is Mr. Doyle an appropriate choice for management of central research? Should applied research units be placed overseas?

3. How should the controllership function be managed? Should controllership be within the divisions or groups? Should there be a strong central corporate controllership with divisional representatives of that unit?

4. Should the program manager concept be continued? Is it desirable for coordinating new product designs or should this be in a "systems division?" Should the program manager function be ad hoc or continuing? If the latter, what types of activities should it embrace? How should it be organized? If it is a task force concept, where do its team members go after the program or task force is dissolved?

Although there are undoubtedly other interesting organizational questions, these few should certainly be raised in any thorough discussion of the HP case.

Reorganizations

At this point the professor can display or hand out HP's 1983 and 1984 organization charts, which are included in this note as Exhibits 1 and 2, and ask students to evaluate the changes. "What are the key elements in the organization change? What are these intended to accomplish? What kinds of style, planning, control, measurement, and reward practices must accompany these organization structure changes?" Alternately, students can be asked to propose a new organization for HP and to describe their reasoning in the choice of organization as well as the other changes they would propose.

NOTE: Exhibits 1 and 2 provide not only a graphic representation of HP's 1983 and 1984 organizations, but also a written description of those organizations. These descriptions will provide explanations for many of the terms used by HP to describe its organization. These should be useful to professors in interpreting the charts themselves and in helping students interpret the organization charts given in the case itself.

In either case, an interesting question to end with is whether a company like HP can maintain a "dual culture," with the old HP entrepreneurial flavor where it is practical and a volume and cost-oriented culture in the dominant computer-related sectors. If HP changes its corporate culture to meet the demands of the computer marketplace, what will happen to the culture in the rest of the company?

SUMMARY OF OUTCOMES

While the 1983 reorganization consolidated the various divisions focusing on the personal computer market and realigned the divisions within the computer segment to address the problem of overlapping products and piecemeal approaches to various markets, it left the marketing of computers and instruments separate. The Computer Products Group had responsibility for the development and manufacture of CPUs, operating software, languages, and VLSI; the Information Products Group had responsibility for the development and manufacture of systems peripherals, data communications products, data base resources, print centers, and the software to combine these with systems and workstations to form information networks. The Personal Computer Group had responsibility for the development and manufacture of workstations (terminals), personal computers, and other personal-computation products; the Business Development Group had responsibility for market development and merchandising of HP systems, workstations, networks, and applications software as a set of solution systems for each of HP's major markets; the Computer Marketing Group had responsibility for sales, field marketing, maintenance services, and application support for all HP computer products in all markets.

The 1984 organization reflected the growing interconnections between instruments and computer systems, especially in the manufacturing area, and for the first time created a corporate marketing group. The new organization realigned elements of the previous product group structure into four major sectors. The sectors were: (1) Measurement, Design and Manufacturing Systems—comprised of four product groups responsible for electronic instruments, microwave and communications products, manufacturing systems and computer-aided design and engineering products; (2) Information Systems and Networks—including three product groups responsible for business computer systems, personal computation products, and computer peripherals and networks; (3) Analytical, Components, Medical and Technology—including product groups responsible for analytical instrumentation, electronic components, and medical electronic instruments and systems as well as HP Laboratories, Corporate Manufacturing and Corporate Engineering; and (4) Marketing and International—encompassing world-wide sales and sales administration activities for measurement and computation products, major accounts marketing and other corporate level marketing operations.

The 1984 organization changes also included the appointment of Executive Vice President Dean O. Morton to the newly-created position of Chief Operating Officer. Paul Ely, who had headed the computer area, was placed in charge of the Analytical, Components, Medical and Technology Group and in early 1985 he resigned.

Organization Concept

According to a press release by the company, the new organization structure was designed to bring its product groups and field marketing activities more closely in line with the major markets they served. *Business Week* quoted industry experts as saying that "the changes were not dictated by structural considerations alone . . . a change was badly needed to develop a stronger profile among the company's nontechnical computer customers and to tighten its grip on scientific and engineering markets." In July of 1984, HP took its top managers on a retreat for a week-long indoctrination on the importance of marketing—part of its effort to transition from a company run by engineers for engineers to one with the marketing requisite to reach a wider audience and compete in an increasingly competitive market.

Young commented on the new structure as follows:

"The new organization puts HP in a better position to provide our growing customer base, and especially our major accounts, with fully integrated product solutions drawn from anywhere in the company.

"By adopting a structure that closely reflects our major markets, we are making it easier to focus the full breadth of our measurement and computation capabilities on the needs of our customers. At the same time, we are preserving our well-honed ability to provide single-product solutions in a more traditional selling environment.

". . . the changes signify a further commitment to being the best business partner we can for our customers, while preserving the HP traditions of technical excellence and product quality. The creation of the position of Chief Operating Officer results from the need to draw together and give more active management to the major sectors of our business."

HP's organization change coincided with a major slump in computer markets. In late 1985 and 1986, the company was required to lay off a number of people. There was reportedly a great deal of disaffection with HP and grumbling caused by these moves. Although several of HP's product introductions (notably Spectrum) were later than anticipated, it is difficult to say whether the new organization influenced this in a positive or negative fashion.

The 1986 Annual Report said, "Two years ago, HP began a major transformation from a company driven primarily by technology to one more closely focused on the markets it served." HP was organized according to six areas of emphasis—business systems, engineering systems, manufacturing systems, test and measurement, analytical instrumentation, and medical products. These six core businesses were chosen because of their "linkages"—that is, the technologies, products, applications, and distribution channels they shared. While these linkages allowed HP to leverage its efforts in many different ways, they also made HP an integrated and very complex company. The previously separate instrument and computer sales forces were integrated under a common management. Such changes were to make it possible to provide customers with a combined and focused expertise in measurement, computation, and support. To support this, marketing representatives from each core business were moved into the field to encourage two-way communication between the field sales force and HP's product groups. This consolidation actually made communications more cumbersome. The purpose of its reorganization was to focus more on markets rather than product lines. Despite its short-term troubles, most analysts regarded HP as an outstandingly managed company, with strong long-term potentials, if it could choose its market niches well. The question remains at the end of the case, "Should HP pick its markets to match its operating style? Or should it adapt its style to match markets?" The latter seems to have been difficult. The remainder of this summary focuses on the recent product and operating history of HP.

Net income began to decline in 1985. Some of HP's problems resulted from the general downturn in the computer market. Its introduction of its new Spectrum line also brought with it large developmental expenditures. Although widely anticipated, the Spectrum product did not achieve the kind of impact HP had hoped. The biggest problem was that Spectrum did not seem sufficiently remarkable to replace HP's base of HP 3000 customers, which were relatively unsophisticated companies with regard to computer systems. Although the RISC technology received tremendous technical acclaim, it did not seem to be ready to deliver its full potential at the time Spectrum was introduced.

From 1987 to 1990

From 1987 on, more than one-half of HP's orders were for products introduced in the current and two preceding years. HP routinely put 10% of net revenues into R&D, allocating 85% of that to product development within the divisions. In 1989 HP established science centers in the United States and Europe to do joint research with the leading universities and planned to open another such facility in Japan during 1990.

To strengthen its financial position and to improve its market share, HP undertook two thrusts: (1) it repurchased 32.3 million shares of its stock for $1.7 billion, and listed its stock on four European exchanges to finance its expanding operations there. In May 1989 HP completed a tender offer of $486 million for Apollo Computer. While the acquisition of Apollo was to stem the rapid rise of Sun Micro Systems, the benefits were slow in appearing. HP-Apollo had a combined 31% share of the work station market, which topped Sun's share initially, then fell to 26%—just behind Sun by the end of 1989.

Realizing that both its operations and customer base were becoming increasingly diverse, HP began to supplement its internal efforts by acquiring products and technologies through equity joint ventures, licensing agreements, and a variety of cooperative research activities. It licensed its RISC technologies to Hitachi and Samsung Electronics in exchange for a license to Hitachi's bipolar CMOS technology. These transactions marked the first time HP had opened its homegrown technologies to others. The exchanges were intended to cut product development cycles by up to two years. HP was working with Samsung on a high powered work station to be introduced within two years at a price of $5000.

The company also entered alliances with: (1) Hitachi for precision architecture and chip technologies, (2) Canon for "smart" typewriters and printers, (3) Yokogawa for logic systems, (4) Northern Telecom for micro processor development systems, (5) Sony for digital audiotapes, and (6) Arthur Andersen for management consulting services on computer integrated manufacturing.

HP also became a member of the "Gang of 9"—a group of IBM-compatible PC makers who decided to go nose-to-nose with IBM's PS/2 models in setting the industry standard. The group introduced its own design—avoiding IBM's micro channel bus—and called it the extended industry standard architecture or EISA. EISA allowed computer owners to use older add-on equipment with any make of new computers. HP put out the first EISA machine, the Vectra 486, in late 1989.

The 1989 Annual Report indicated another reorganization, putting all computer product groups under a computer business organization reporting to the COO, Dean Morton. HP's organization as of February 1991 is shown in Exhibit 3.

The 1989 Annual Report also gave the following segment information:

	1987		1988		1989	
	$ Rev	% of Total	$ Rev.	% of Total	$ Rev	% of Total
A.	$3,256	40.3	$3,839	39.1	$4,631	38.9
B.	$2,059	25.5	$2,727	27.7	$3,486	29.3
C.	$1,540	19.0	$1,855	18.9	$2,157	18.1
D.	$ 618	7.6	$ 688	7.0	$ 807	6.8
E.	$ l388	4.8	$ 456	4.6	$ 535	4.5
F.	$ 229	2.8	$ 266	2.7	$ 283	2.4
Total	$8,090	100	$9,831	100	$11,899	100

A. Measurement, design, information and manufacturing equipment and systems—Equipment and systems (hardware and software) used for design, manufacturing, office automation and information processing; general-purpose instruments and computers; and handheld calculators.

B. Peripheral and network products—Printers, plotters, magnetic disc and tape drives, terminals and network products.

C. Service for equipment, systems, and peripherals—Support and maintenance services, parts and supplies related to design and manufacturing systems, office and information systems, general-purpose instruments and computers, peripherals and network products.

D.   Medical electronic equipment and service—Products that perform patient monitoring, diagnostic, therapeutic and data-management functions; application software; support and maintenance services; and hospital supplies.

E. Analytical instrumentation and service—Gas and liquid chromatographs, mass spectrometers and spectrophotometers used to analyze chemical compounds; and support and maintenance services.

F. Electronic components—Microwave semiconductors and optoelectronic devices that are sold primarily to manufacturers for incorporation into electronic products.

Unfortunately, HP's PC market share stayed stagnant at about 2%. It dropped its laptop after a disagreement with Zenith Data Systems. HP had been emphasizing powerful high-end machines but lacked the sophisticated software to go with them. Compaq and IBM knocked HP out of the low-end business by dominating dealer shelf space. In June 1990, HP lost its worldwide PC chief to Apple Computer, and relocated its PC headquarters to Grenoble, France. In 1990, HP was still trying to recover from its organizational problems. While its instrument lines were still doing well, it had yet to find its unique position in the computer industry.

HP continued to be priced as an instruments stock. The biggest product problem was that Spectrum did not seem to be sufficiently remarkable to replace HP's base of HP 3000 customers, which were relatively unsophisticated companies with regard to computer systems.

1990s Update

By 1991, Hewlett Packard's overall organization chart had mutated toward that shown in Exhibit 3. This maintained the smaller divisional structure of the test and measurement systems group and tried to obtain desired economies of scale in computer products, computer systems, and HP's marketing and international groups. Many business publications were becoming critical of HP because of its tendency to try to seize the "professional management" high ground, rather than returning to its old traditions of fast response engineering design in advanced technological products. CEO, Robert Young, had also been criticized for taking part extensively in national policy discussions and the "competitiveness" debate. While the company continued to maintain the very high standards represented by the "HP Way," many thought that it might have lost the lean driving entrepreneurial emphasis that the philosophy was initially intended to inculcate. Clearly, HP had not yet come up with a substitute for the lean profit-oriented structures of an earlier era.

The 1995 Situation

Between 1991 and 1995, HP managed to transform its computer group and become one of the top ten U.S. computer makers and one of the fastest growing. It did so by streamlining decision-making and shortening the product design cycle in all divisions but especially PCs, by sticking with open systems in mid-range systems like workstations and servers, by competing against itself in the printer market and beating the Japanese at their own game, by moving from microwave devices to hardware for the video industry, and beginning the process of collaboration between its two major thrusts—scientific instruments and computers.

In July 1992, Lewis Platt (who at the time was head of HP's Computer Systems organization) took over from John Young as CEO and quickly began the process of figuring out how to take advantage of the company's unique blend of technologies to capitalize on the convergence of computers, communications, and consumer electronics which is rapidly creating a digital future which HP could not afford to ignore. This required the development of all new product categories in which HP could not succeed without the cooperation of several of its notoriously independent divisions. Working with Joel Birnbaum, head of HP Labs, Platt worked to choose three or four potentially big markets for major thrusts and hoped to transform the company over the next 10 years.

Examples of new products included a diagnostic system designed for Ford Motor dealers that combines instruments that monitor a car's internal operations with an HP PC to provide data for later analysis; a printer that can also capture stills from any video source and print them; sensors and devices that monitor a patient, send the data for analysis, and relay the findings to the doctor's computer, etc. Each of these fit into the HP=MC^2 (Measurement, Computing, and Communication) vision and also excited J{ engineers who are known for inventing fundamentally new gadgets. And while HP executives have the right to reinvest the capital their businesses generate and attack markets in their own way based on what they see the customer wanting. *Fortune* in a May 2, 1994 article, pointed out that while HP managers don't like being told what to do, they are not too proud to copycat good ideas from wherever they find them.

Over several years, Platt and Birnbaum succeeded in winning ground from IBM and DEC in midrange computer systems primarily because HP had emphasized open systems and RISC technology. The PC organization under Bob Frankenberg grew through streamlining decision-making, shortening the product design cycle, and targeting such niches as PCs ready to plug into office networks. The old-line Test and Measurement group moved from defense-related work to creating studio equipment and other hardware for the video industry.

In 1995, Platt became the first HP chairman to succeed the founders and described the future in terms of an information utility and information appliances. In August of '95, HP announced a new organizational structure that brought together the Computer Products Organization (which includes the printer and PC businesses), the Computer Systems Organization (which includes UNIX workstations, multi-user systems, and the consulting group), and Worldwide Customer Support Operations into a new Computer Products Organization. In the Annual Report, HP stated that ,"We made this change to help lead a fundamental shift that is taking place in our industry: the convergence of desktop, PC-based computing and enterprise, UNIX system-based computing into a single information technology environment. . . . By unifying our computer activities, we can leverage strengths and deliver the integrated solutions customers are looking for while maintaining the benefits of focused businesses. . . . Clearly, the focus of our previous organization serviced us well. Computer orders grew 30 percent in fiscal 1995 to $25.8 billion—more than twice what we reports as recently as 1992. So it's logical to ask why we made a change. By moving to the new model now, when we're doing well, we believe we're positioning the company to build an even more effective program for customers. The new Computer Organization shows our willingness to challenge the status quo . . . in an industry where rapid, fundamental change is the rule."

Exhibit 4 shows the HP corporate organization as of August 1995 and Exhibit 5 gives selected financial data for the period 1991-95.

EXHIBIT 1

Hewlett Packard Corporate Organization, June 1983

Viewed broadly, Hewlett Packard Company is a highly decentralized organization made up of many business units that offer a wide range of advanced electronic-based products to a variety of markets around the world. Giving the company common direction and cohesion are shared philosophies, practices and goals as well as technologies.

Within this broad context, the individual business units—called product divisions—are relatively small and self-sufficient so that decisions can be made at the level of the organization most responsible for putting them into action. Consistent with this approach, it has always been a practice at Hewlett Packard to give each employee considerable freedom to implement methods and ideas that meet specific local organizational goals and broad corporate objectives.

Since its start in 1939, the HP organization has grown to some 50 product divisions. To provide for effective overall management and coordination, the company has aligned these divisions into product groups characterized by product and market focus. Today there are 11 such groups within five major product segments supported in the field by their own sales and service organizations.

HP's corporate structure is designed to foster small-business flexibility within its many individual operating units while supporting them with the strengths of a larger organization. The accompanying chart provides a graphic view of the relationship of the various groups and other organizational elements. The organization has been structured to allow the groups and their divisions to concentrate on their product-development, manufacturing and marketing activities, while sharing common administrative systems for many of the tasks required of a company doing business worldwide. Normal and functional lines of responsibility and communication are indicated on the chart; however, direct and informal communication across lines and between levels is strongly encouraged.

Here is a closer look at the company's basic organizational units:

<u>Product Divisions/Operations</u>

An HP division is a vertically-integrated organization that conducts itself much like an independent business. Its fundamental responsibilities are to develop, manufacture, and market products that are profitable and which make contributions in the marketplace by virtue of technological or economic advantage.

Each division has its own distinct family of products, for which it has worldwide marketing responsibility. A division also is responsible for its own accounting, personnel activities, quality assurance and support of its products in the field. In addition, it has important social and economic responsibilities in its local community.

Operations are organizations dedicated to particular tasks, usually in support of a product group or various divisions within a group. They also are generally smaller in size than divisions.

<u>Product Groups</u>

Product groups are composed of divisions and operations having closely related product lines. Groups are responsible for coordinating the activities of their respective divisions and of representing their interests in the field and among other segments of the HP organization. The management of each group has overall responsibility for the operations and financial

335

performance of its members. Further, each group has worldwide responsibility for its manufacturing operations and marketing activities. Groups also provide the focal points for creating the common strategies needed in managing product lines that are increasingly interactive, and for developing overall HP solutions to the complex needs of customers. Management staffs of the North American and International sales organizations assist the groups in coordinating the sales and service functions.

Corporate Operations

Corporate Operations management has responsibility for the day-to-day operation of the company. The executive vice presidents in charge of Corporate Operations are directly responsible to HP's president for the performance of their assigned product groups; they also provide a primary channel of communication between their groups and the president.

Corporate Administration

The principal responsibility of Corporate Administration is to insure that the corporate staff offices provide the specialized policies, expertise and resources to support the field divisions and groups adequately on a worldwide basis. The executive vice president in charge of Corporate Administration also reports to the president, providing an important upward channel of communication for the corporate staff activities.

Corporate Research and Development

HP Laboratories is the corporate research and development organization that provides a central resource of technical support for the product-development efforts of HP product divisions. In these efforts, the divisions make important use of the advanced technologies, materials, components and theoretical analyses researched or developed by HP Labs. Through endeavors in areas of science and technology, the corporate laboratories also help the company develop new areas of business.

Board of Directors

The Board of Directors and its chairman have ultimate responsibility for the legal and ethical conduct of the company and its officers. It is the board's duty to protect and advance the interests of the stockholders, to foster a continuing concern for fairness in the company's relations with employees, and to fulfill all requirements of the law with regard to the board's stewardship. The board counsels management on general business matters and also reviews and evaluates the performance of management. To assist in discharging these responsibilities, the board has formed various committees to oversee the company's activities and programs in such areas as employees' benefits, compensation, financial auditing and investment.

President

The president has operating responsibility for the overall performance and direction of the company, subject to the authority of the Board of Directors. Also, the president serves as chairman of the Executive Committee, and is directly responsible for corporate planning and development functions, for HP Labs and for Internal Audit.

Executive Committee

The Executive Committee is the company's primary policy-setting body. It reviews broad issues affecting the company and initiates strategies designed to maintain its direction and meet its goals. Members include the president (acting as committee chairman) and the executive vice presidents for Operations and Administration. All are members of the Board of Directors. Meetings are on a weekly basis.

Management Council

Primary responsibilities of this body are to review and formulate operating policies, and to turn policy decisions into corporate action. The council also reviews performance expectations as reflected in the forward planning of the product groups, and monitors their operating results. Council members serve variously on three committees charged with specific responsibilities for personnel, operations, and the field. Council membership includes the group general managers, the senior vice presidents of Marketing and International, the vice president-Europe, the vice president of Research and Development, the vice president of Manufacturing, the managing director of Intercontinental, and the director of personnel. Members of the Executive Committee also serve on the Council on an ex officio basis.

Source: The Hewlett Packard Company.

EXHIBIT 1 (CONTINUED)
HEWLETT PACKARD'S 1983 ORGANIZATION

#BOARD OF DIRECTORS Dave Packard, Chairman   Bill Hewlett, Vice Chairman
#CHIEF EXECUTIVE OFFICER John Young, President*

#ADMINISTRATION Bob Boniface, Executive V.P.	+INSTRUMENTS Bill Terry, Executive V.P.	+COMPUTERS Paul Ely, Executive V.P.	+OPERATIONS Dean Morton, Executive V.P.**	HP Laboratories
#CORPORATE STAFF	**Electronic Measurements Group**	**Computer Products Group**	**+MEDICAL**	John Doyle
Corporate Controller	Bill Parzybok, Gen. Mgr.	Doug Chance, V.P.	**Medical Group**	Vice President
Jerry Carlson	• Boblingen Instrument	• Data Systems	Ben Holmes, Gen. Mgr.	Research and
Controller	• San Diego	• Computer Systems	• Andover	Development
	• Colorado Springs	•• CSY/Roseville	• Boblingen Medical	
Corporate Services	• Logic Systems	•• Ft. Collins Systems	• McMinnville	Research Centers
Bruce Wholey	• Santa Clara	• Engineering Productivity	• Waltham	
Vice President	• VHP Instrument	• VHP Computer	•• Bedside Terminals	Computer Research
	• Loveland Instrument	• Computer I.C.	•• Medical Systems	
Field Sales Regions	• Lake Stevens Instrument	•• Cupertino I.C.	• Medical Supplies	Physical Research
France	• New Jersey	•• Systems Technology		
Germany	• Integrated Circuits	•• Corvallis Components	**+ANALYTICAL**	Technology Research
General Counsel	Northern Europe			
and Secretary	South/Eastern	**Personal Computer Group**	**Analytical Group**	
Jack Brigham	Europe	Cyril Yansouni, Gen. Manager	Lew Platt, Vice President	**#Corporate Development**
Vice President	United Kingdom	• Roseville Terminals	• Avondale	Dave Sanders
		• Portable Computer	• Scientific Instruments	Director
	Europe	• Grenoble Personal Computer	• Waldbronn	
International	Franco Mariotti	• Personal Office Computer		
Dick Alberding	Vice President	• Vancouver	**+COMPONENTS**	**#Internal Audit**
Senior V. P.		• Personal Software		George Abbott
	Manufacturing	•• Puerto Rico	**Components Group**	Manager
Government Affairs	France	•• Singapore	John Blokker, Gen. Manager	
Bob Kirkwood	Germany	•• Brazil	• Microwave Semiconductor	
Director	United Kingdom		• Optoelectronics	
		Information Products Group	•• Visible Products	
Public Relations	**Microwave & Communications**	Dick Hackborn, Vice President	•• Interface Products	
Dave Kirby	**Instrument Group**	• Boise	• Singapore	
Director	Dick Anderson, General Manager	• Greeley	• Malaysia	
	• Colorado Telecom	• Disc Memory		
Patents & Licenses	• Stanford Park	•• Computer Peripherals Bristol		
Jean Chognard	• Spokane	• Roseville Networks		
Vice President	• Signal Analysis	• Information Networks		
	• Network Measurements	• Colorado Networks		
Personnel	•• Santa Rosa Technology	• Grenoble Networks		
Bill Craven	Center		**#Corporate Manufacturing**	
Director		**Business Development Group**	Hal Edmondson	
	Intercontinental	Ed McCracken, Gen. Manager	Vice President	
Treasurer	Alan Bickell	Systems Marketing Center		
Ed van Bronkhorst	Managing Director	Business Development Europe		
Senior V.P.		•• Information Resources		
	Field Sales Regions	•• Systems Re-Marketing		
Marketing	Australasia	• Guadalajara Computer		
Al Oliverio	Far East	•• Manufacturing Productivity		
Senior V.P.	Japan	• Application Marketing		
	Latin America	• Office Productivity		
	South Africa			
		Computer Marketing Group		
	Manufacturing	Jim Arthur, Vice President		
	Brazil	Sales: N. America/Europe/Intercon.		
	Canada	• Computer Support		
	Japan	• Application Marketing		
	Malaysia	•• Computer Supplies		
	Mexico			
	Puerto Rico			
	Singapore			
			HEWLETT-PACKARD	
	Instrument Marketing Group		**CORPORATE ORGANIZATION**	
	Bob Brunner, General Manager		**JUNE, 1983**	
	Sales: N. America/Europe/Intercon.			
	• Instrument Support		# Corporate & Support Functions	
			+ Business Segments	
	U.S./Canada Sales		• Division	
	Field Sales Regions		•• Operation	
	Eastern		* Chairman, Executive Committee	
	Midwest		** Chairman, Management Council	
	Neely (Western)			
	Southern			
	Canada			
	Corporate			
	Marketing			
	Operations			
	•• Parts Center			

Source: The Hewlett Packard Company

338

EXHIBIT 2

Hewlett Packard Corporate Organization, December 1984

Hewlett Packard is organized to provide its customers around the world with solutions to their increasingly complex measurement and computational needs.

Of the company's four basic business sectors, three offer a wide range of advanced electronic-based products. The fourth encompasses worldwide sales and marketing activities and integrates HP's diverse product lines. Giving the company common direction and cohesion are shared philosophies, practices and goals as well as technologies.

Within this context, the individual business units—called product divisions—are relatively small and self-sufficient so that decisions can be made at the level of the organization most responsible for putting them into action. Consistent with this approach, its has always been a practice at Hewlett Packard to give each employee considerable freedom to implement methods and ideas that meet specific local organizational goals and broad corporate objectives.

Since its founding in 1939, the HP organization has grown to some 50 product divisions. To provide for effective overall management and coordination, the company has aligned these divisions into 12 product groups characterized by product and market focus.

HP's corporate structure is designed to foster small-business flexibility within its many individual operating units while supporting them with the strengths of a larger organization.

The accompanying chart provides a graphic view of the relationship of the various organizational elements. The organization has been structured to allow the groups and their divisions to concentrate on their product-development, manufacturing and marketing activities, while sharing common administrative systems for many of the tasks required of a company doing business worldwide. Normal and functional lines of responsibility and communication are indicated on the chart; however, direct and informal communication across lines and between levels is strongly encouraged.

Here is a closer look at the company's basic organizational units:

Product Divisions/Operations

An HP division is a vertically-integrated organization that conducts itself much like an independent business. Its fundamental responsibilities are to develop, manufacture, and market products that are profitable and which make contributions in the marketplace by virtue of technological and economic advantage.

Each division has its own distinct family of products, for which it has worldwide marketing responsibility. A division also is responsible for its own accounting, personnel activities, quality assurance and support of its products in the field. In addition, it has important social and economic responsibilities in its local community.

Operations are organizational units dedicated to particular tasks, usually in support of a product group or various divisions within a group. They also are generally smaller in size than divisions.

Product Groups

Product groups are composed of divisions and operations having closely related product lines or market focus. Groups are responsible for coordinating the activities of their respective divisions. The management of each group has overall responsibility for the operations and

339

financial performance of its members. Further, each group has worldwide responsibility for its manufacturing and marketing activities.

Business Sectors

Reflecting its increased customer orientation and concentration on major markets, the company was realigned in August 1984 into four major sectors:

Measurement, Design and Manufacturing Systems
Information Systems and Networks
Analytical, Components, Medical and Technology
Marketing and International

These sectors provide the focal points for creating the common strategies needed in managing product lines that are increasingly interactive, and for developing overall HP solutions to the complex needs of customers.

By consolidating its worldwide field marketing and international manufacturing, the company is able to apply its unique range of computational and measurement solutions to the business and technical problems of customers around the world. Management staffs of the U.S. and International sales organizations assist the three product sectors in coordinating the sales and service functions.

The executive vice president in charge of each business sector is directly responsible to the chief operating officer for the performance of the sector's product groups.

Corporate Administration

The principal responsibility of Corporate Administration is to insure that the corporate staff offices provide the specialized policies, expertise and resources to support the field divisions and groups adequately on a worldwide basis. The executive vice president in charge of Corporate Administration also reports to the chief operating officer, providing an important upward channel of communication for the corporate staff activities.

Corporate Research and Development

HP Laboratories is the corporate research and development organization that provides a central source of technical support for the product-development efforts of HP operating divisions. In these efforts, the divisions make important use of the advanced technologies, materials, components and theoretical analyses researched or developed by HP Labs. Through endeavors in areas of science and technology, the corporate laboratories also help the company develop new areas of business.

Corporate Manufacturing

Corporate Manufacturing has responsibility for the coordination of manufacturing activities throughout HP, including the following functions: materials planning and procurement, manufacturing support and standards, quality improvement and assurance, manufacturing information systems, regulatory standards, environmental control, employee safety and health, and corporate physical-distribution systems.

Corporate Engineering

Corporate Engineering is responsible for coordinating the company's engineering activities, with an emphasis on measures to increase engineering productivity through improved design tools, engineering processes, training and development programs and strategic coordination.

Board of Directors

The Board of Directors and its chairman have ultimate responsibility for the legal and ethical conduct of the company and its officers. It is the board's duty to protect and advance the interests of the stockholders, to foster a continuing concern for fairness in the company's relations with employees, and to fulfill all requirements of the law with regard to the board's stewardship.

The board counsels management on general business matters and also reviews and evaluates the performance of management. To assist in discharging these responsibilities, the board has formed various committees to oversee the company's activities and programs in such areas as employees' benefits, compensation, financial auditing and investment.

Chief Executive Officer/Chief Operating Officer

The chief executive officer is responsible for the direction and long-range performance of the company, subject to the authority of the Board of Directors. Also, the chief executive officer serves as chairman of the Executive Committee. Reporting to the CEO are Corporate Development and Internal Audit.

The chief operating officer, who reports directly to the chief executive officer, has responsibility for the day-to-day operating performance of the company. Reporting directly to the chief operating officer are the four operating sectors of the company and Corporate Administration. The chief operating officer serves as chairman of the Management Council.

Executive Committee

The Executive Committee is the company's primary policy-setting body. It reviews broad issues affecting the company and initiates strategies designed to maintain its direction and meet its goals. Members include the chief executive officer (who serves as committee chairman), chief operating officer, and the five executive vice presidents. Meetings are normally scheduled on a weekly basis.

Management Council

Primary responsibilities of this body are to review and formulate operating policies, and to turn policy decisions into corporate action. The council, chaired by the chief operating officer, also reviews performance expectations as reflected in the forward planning of the business sectors and monitors their operating results.

Council members serve variously on five committees charged with policy-setting responsibility for personnel, operations, marketing, computer architecture and networks, and information systems. Each committee is chaired by an executive vice president; in addition, the 22 council members are all group and senior managers of the company.

EXHIBIT 2 (CONTINUED)

Hewlett Packard's 1984 Organization

BOARD OF DIRECTORS
Dave Packard, Chairman
Bill Hewlett, Vice Chairman

CHIEF EXECUTIVE OFFICER: John Young, President
CHIEF OPERATING OFFICER: Dean Morton, Executive Vice President

INTERNAL AUDIT
George Abbott
Director

CORPORATE DEVELOPMENT
Tom Uhlman
Director

ADMINISTRATION
Bob Boniface
Executive Vice President

CONTROLLER
Bob Wayman
Vice President

GENERAL COUNSEL AND SECRETARY
Jack Brigham
Vice President

TREASURY
George Newman
Treasurer

PATENTS AND LICENSES
Jean Chognard
Vice President

PERSONNEL
Bill Craven
Director

GOVERNMENT AFFAIRS
Bob Kirkwood
Director

PUBLIC RELATIONS
Dave Kirby
Director

Hewlett-Packard
Corporate Organization
December 1984

MARKETING AND INTERNATIONAL
Dick Alberding
Executive Vice President

U.S. FIELD OPERATIONS
Jim Arthur
Vice President and Director

Field Sales Regions: Eastern, Midwestern, Neely (Western), Southern

EUROPEAN OPERATIONS
Franco Mariotti
Vice President and Director

Field Sales Regions: France, Germany, Italy, Northern Europe, South Eastern, United Kingdom
Manufacturing: France, Germany, United Kingdom

INTERCONTINENTAL OPERATIONS
Alan Bickell
Vice President and Director

Field Sales Regions: Australasia, Far East, Japan, Canada, Latin America
Manufacturing: Brazil, Canada, Japan, Korea, Malaysia, Mexico, Puerto Rico, Singapore

MAJOR ACCOUNTS MARKETING
Al Oliverio
Senior Vice President

CORPORATE MARKETING
Art Dauer
Director

Marketing Communications
Marketing Operations
Marketing Information Center
Finance and Remarketing Division
Computer Supplies Operation
Instrument Products Operation
Computer Support Division
Instrument Support Division
Corporate Parts Center

MEASUREMENT, DESIGN AND MANUFACTURING SYSTEMS
Bill Terry
Executive Vice President

MICROWAVE AND COMMUNICATIONS GROUP
Dick Anderson
General Manager

Stanford Park Division
Network Measurements Division
Signal Analysis Division
Spokane Division
Colorado Telecom Division
Queensferry Telecom Division
Microwave Technology Division
Queensferry Microwave Operation

ELECTRONIC INSTRUMENTS GROUP
Ned Barnholt
General Manager

New Jersey Division
Santa Clara Division
Boblingen Instrument Division
YHP Instrument Division
YHP Computer Operation
Integrated Circuits Division
Santa Clara Tech Center
Loveland Tech Center
Colorado Springs Tech Center

DESIGN SYSTEMS GROUP
Bill Parzybok
Vice President and General Manager

Fort Collins Systems Division
Logic Systems Division
Colorado Springs Division
Boblingen Computer Division
Lake Stevens Instrument Division
Boblingen Engineering Operation
Fort Collins Engineering Operation

MANUFACTURING SYSTEMS GROUP
Lew Platt
Vice President and General Manager

Data Systems Division
Advanced Manufacturing Systems Operation
Manufacturing Productivity Division
Lake Stevens Instrument Division
Panacom Automation Operation
Manufacturing Test Division
Lyon Manufacturing Systems Operation

INFORMATION SYSTEMS AND NETWORKS
John Doyle
Executive Vice President

INFORMATION SYSTEMS GROUP
Doug Chance
Vice President and General Manager

Computer Systems Division
CSY Roseville Operation
Boblingen General Systems Division
Office Productivity Division
Guadalajara Computer Operation
Administrative Productivity Division
Information Resources Operation
Administrative Productivity Operation
Financial Systems Operation

PERSONAL COMPUTER GROUP
Cyril Yansouni
Vice President and General Manager

Roseville Terminals Division
Portable Computer Division
Handheld Computer & Calculator Operation
Grenoble Personal Computer Division
Personal Office Computer Division
Personal Software Division
Puerto Rico Operation
Singapore Operation
Brazil Operation
Personal Computer Distribution Operation
Personal Computer Group Operation

PERIPHERALS GROUP
Dick Hackborn
Vice President and General Manager

Greeley Division
Computer Peripherals Bristol Division
Disc Memory Division
Boise Division
Vancouver Division
San Diego Division

INFORMATION NETWORKS GROUP
John Doyle (interim)
Vice President and General Manager

Colorado Networks Operation
Grenoble Networks Division
Roseville Networks Division
Information Networks Division

INFORMATION TECHNOLOGY GROUP
George Bodway
General Manager

Cupertino IC Division
Fort Collins IC Division
Northwest IC Division
Information Hardware Operation
Information Software Operation

ANALYTICAL, COMPONENTS, MEDICAL AND TECHNOLOGY
Paul Ely
Executive Vice President

ANALYTICAL GROUP
Dieter Hoehn
General Manager

Avondale Division
Lab Automation Systems Operation
Scientific Instruments Division
Waldbronn Division

COMPONENTS GROUP
John Blokker
Vice President and General Manager

Microwave Semiconductor Division
Optoelectronics Division
Optical Communication Division
Southeast Asia Operation

MEDICAL GROUP
Ben Holmes
General Manager

Andover Division
Boblingen Medical Division
McMinnville Division
Waltham Division
Medical Supplies Center
Health Care Productivity Operation

HP LABORATORIES
Joel Birnbaum
Vice President and Director

Manufacturing Research Center
Design and Measurement Research Center
Distributed Systems Center
Application Technology Center
Technology Research Center
Bristol Research Center

CORPORATE MANUFACTURING
Hal Edmondson
Vice President and Director

CORPORATE ENGINEERING
Chuck House
Director

342

Source: The Hewlett Packard Company.

Exhibit 3

Hewlett Packard Corporate Organization   February 1991

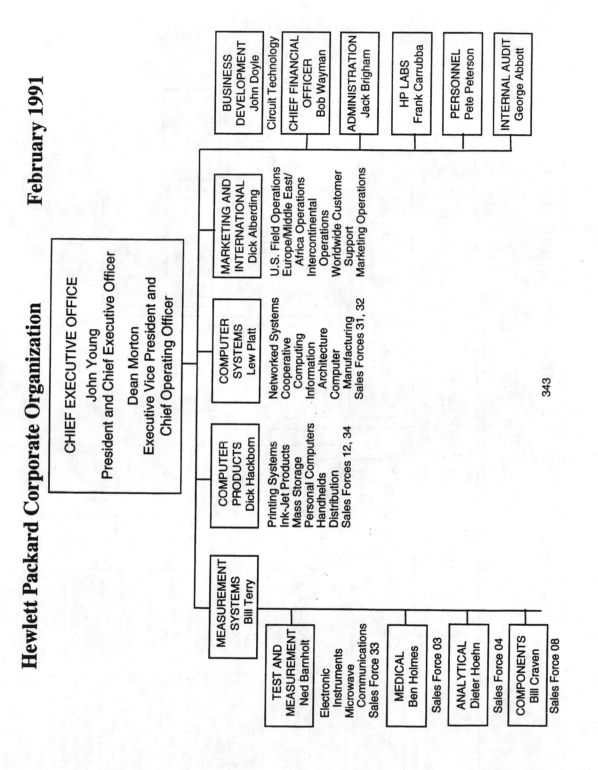

343

Hewlett Packard Corporate Organization

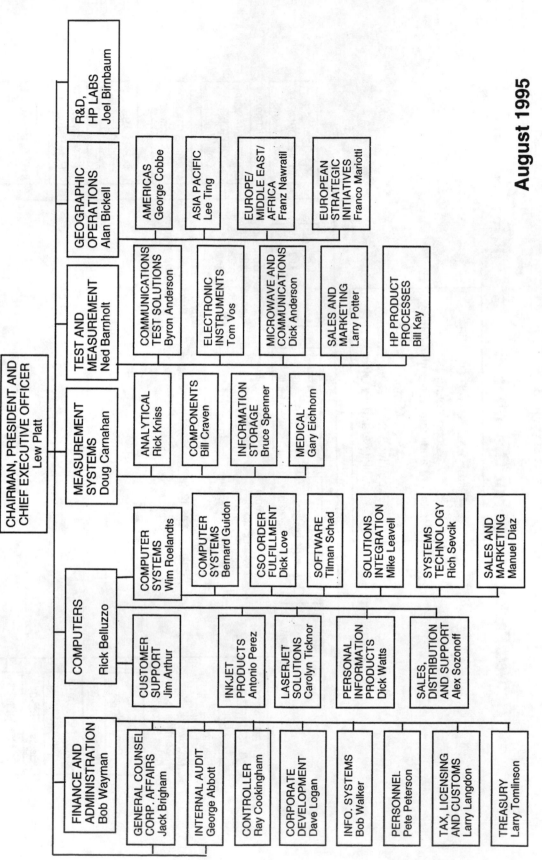

CHAIRMAN, PRESIDENT AND CHIEF EXECUTIVE OFFICER
Lew Platt

FINANCE AND ADMINISTRATION
Bob Wayman

- GENERAL COUNSEL CORP. AFFAIRS — Jack Brigham
- INTERNAL AUDIT — George Abbott
- CONTROLLER — Ray Cookingham
- CORPORATE DEVELOPMENT — Dave Logan
- INFO. SYSTEMS — Bob Walker
- PERSONNEL — Pete Peterson
- TAX, LICENSING AND CUSTOMS — Larry Langdon
- TREASURY — Larry Tomlinson

COMPUTERS
Rick Belluzzo

- COMPUTER SYSTEMS — Wim Roelandts
- COMPUTER SYSTEMS — Bernard Guidon
- CSO ORDER FULFILLMENT — Dick Love
- SOFTWARE — Tilman Schad
- SOLUTIONS INTEGRATION — Mike Leavell
- SYSTEMS TECHNOLOGY — Rich Sevcik
- SALES AND MARKETING — Manuel Diaz
- CUSTOMER SUPPORT — Jim Arthur
- INKJET PRODUCTS — Antonio Perez
- LASERJET SOLUTIONS — Carolyn Ticknor
- PERSONAL INFORMATION PRODUCTS — Dick Watts
- SALES, DISTRIBUTION AND SUPPORT — Alex Sozonoff

MEASUREMENT SYSTEMS
Doug Carnahan

- ANALYTICAL — Rick Kniss
- COMPONENTS — Bill Craven
- INFORMATION STORAGE — Bruce Spenner
- MEDICAL — Gary Eichhorn

TEST AND MEASUREMENT
Ned Barnholt

- COMMUNICATIONS TEST SOLUTIONS — Byron Anderson
- ELECTRONIC INSTRUMENTS — Tom Vos
- MICROWAVE AND COMMUNICATIONS — Dick Anderson
- SALES AND MARKETING — Larry Potter
- HP PRODUCT PROCESSES — Bill Kay

GEOGRAPHIC OPERATIONS
Alan Bickell

- AMERICAS — George Cobbe
- ASIA PACIFIC — Lee Ting
- EUROPE/MIDDLE EAST/AFRICA — Franz Nawratil
- EUROPEAN STRATEGIC INITIATIVES — Franco Mariotti

R&D, HP LABS
Joel Birnbaum

August 1995

344

Exhibit 5
Hewlett Packard Company
Financial Highlights, 1991-95
(in millions of dollars)

	1995	1994	1993	1992	1991
Total orders	$32,510	$25,350	$20,772	$16,761	$14,676
Net revenue	31,519	24,991	20,317	16,410	14,494
Earnings from operations	3,568	2,549	1,879	1,404	1,210
Net earnings	2,433	1,599	1,117	549	755
Net earnings per share, restated	4.63	3.07	2.33	1.09	1.51
Return on average equity	22.3%	17.3%	14.7%	11.9%	11.1%
Employees	102,300	98,400	96,200	92,600	89,000

Overview

The TCG, Ltd./Thermo Electron case provides an excellent vehicle for discussing newly emerging forms of organization. TCG is a highly innovative start-up in Australia, considered one of the country's most successful small enterprises. It has spawned a number of freestanding companies, in a fashion called the "honeycomb" form of organization. Discussion of TCG brings out both the opportunities and problems of starting up a company in this mode. The Thermo Electron company is one of the most dramatic examples of a "starburst" organization in the United States. From a core competency in designing electronic-mechanical devices, Thermo Electron had grown operating income at a compounded annual growth rate approaching 30% in a wide variety of unrelated businesses. The case offers an opportunity to look at entrepreneurial companies growing around a core competency and forming self-financing new entities as its basic mode of growth. TCG and Thermo Electron are not "conglomerates" in any sense. They have both been stock market darlings and have confused investors about their reasons for continuing success. This makes an excellent vehicle for bringing out issues in the entrepreneurial and innovation context. It matches well with sections on organizational adhocracies and corporate culture. It ends with the specification of a strategy for both TCG and for Thermo Electron, and a contrasting of those strategies.

Session Structure

The case naturally breaks itself into two parts. What have been the critical success factors for TCG? How should it approach its current problems? What are the problems of operating in this "honeycomb" form of organization? Does it fit the "starburst" form? What are the key factors in managing companies like this? It is helpful to note that many companies from mutual funds, to venture capitalists, to movie producers operate successfully in the starburst form. Part two of the case picks up with Thermo Electron and asks why has Thermo Electron been successful? Can the success continue in the future? What limits its future possibilities? Why should (or should not) a company like Thermo Electron break itself up into a number of totally freestanding companies and eschew the umbrella of Thermo Electron itself? The case works well with assignments of Mintzberg, "Structuring Organizations," Quinn, Anderson and Finkelstein, "New Forms of Organizing;" and Mintzberg, "The Diversified Organization." The case provides a novel jumping-off point for discussion of a wide variety of new organization forms. Are these "networks" or not? What new skills do managers need in leading these kinds of companies?

TCG Success Factors

TCG follows patterns often utilized by small specialized high tech groups. The case should be relevant for students interested in starting their own companies around a software or service concept. It provides a full cycle view of how incubators work and two success examples from the field. We usually open by asking, "What are the critical factors in TCG's past success?"

1. Special Expertise in Expanding Markets: TCG was a very entrepreneurial, opportunistic company. Its founders had very specialized technical skills. They were therefore able to start with minimal risk by operating on essentially consulting projects with government and

Teaching note copyright © 1996 by James Brian Quinn. This note was prepared by Professor Quinn.

company support. This helped them build even more expertise, while a small team began seeking new markets for the skills they developed. But it was difficult to free up enough time for the "experts" to create whole new businesses when they saw them. Most small companies need to have an initial cash flow because they cannot undertake the long-term investment of a full technical start-up. TCG's consulting activities provided this. TCG served a number of rapidly growing niched marketplaces. The major players in each niche had expertise in operations or marketing, but lacked information technology (or software) capabilities. TCG became an alliance partner, lowering the cycle times and investments for their larger user-partners.

2. <u>The TCG Triangle</u>: A critical concept for TCG was to concentrate its own talents on technology development and opportunity identification—and to immediately seek out a partner in that opportunity's marketplace. The partner was always a user who could finance the project during its critical scale-up phases and provide needed market information. The third portion of the triangle occurred when the partner further leveraged any successful results by seeking out a broader base of customers or alliance partners for wide scale commercialization. The credibility of the partner allowed financing TCG's independent units at low cost, provided needed market input, and created early stability and low risk for each of TCG's innovations. It allowed TCG to develop the technology in depth and to hold on to this know-how, while obtaining a broader base of funds from the licensing and use of the technology itself. TCG's risk was minimized both by its partner's guarantees and the broad portfolio of products and user industries in which it participated. Note that no TCG company went bankrupt during this entire period. Each marketplace was growing so rapidly that TCG had other opportunities to utilize its expanded expertise in its own commercial self interest.

3. <u>The Honeycomb Organization</u>: TCG's unique honeycomb organization provided high leverage for its specialized skills. It (a) lowered overheads for each unit, (b) lowered capital costs, (c) provided needed counsel and advice at low cost, (d) allowed use of consolidated facilities, (e) increased access to low cost "overdraft" funding, (f) allowed members to implicitly offer a wider line of products or services, (g) permitted greater expertise in administrative skills for members, (h) provided some initial internal markets, and (i) provided a basis for research support at low cost. The two most common causes of small company failure are inadequate management skills and timely access to capital and markets. The honeycomb provided both. Perhaps most important is the "credibility" that membership in TCG offered. This saved managers significant time in raising funds, hence managers could devote more time to their own products and expertise. This intangible should not be overlooked. It is a major problem for most small companies.

The TCG "honeycomb" has many attractive features. It essentially attempts to overcome the problems of a small company operating independently, without introducing the rigidities and bureaucracies of a larger company. Can one maintain this desirable posture as the company grows without having more formal controls? What more is needed? Why? What issues would you expect to encounter between the divisions? Between Peter Fritz and the divisions? How can you maintain the desired autonomy, yet get economies of scale? Have the students define precisely what the new balance should be.

4. <u>Unique Policies</u>: The policies which TCG uses to implement the honeycomb concept offer a number of interesting question points, which can best be entered with the general question, "What problems do you see in the TCG organization?" Perhaps most significant among these is, why did TCG itself not take an equity position in its members' organizations? Although Mr. Fritz did take such a position, the benefits might not accrue to TCG as a whole. Other interesting questions include the following:

(A) What rules would be necessary to enforce the non-competition policy?

(B) Did TCG have sufficient power to enforce any of its rules?

(C) How could TCG set fair transfer prices? Should these have been arms-length negotiations? What is the cost vs. benefit of arms-length negotiations or a "pricing formula?"

(D) How can TCG operate without some kind of "approval authority?" How does it keep one of the members from risking the entire organization?

(E) When it was desirable to obtain cooperation among the members on a project which perhaps was not high on individual members' priority lists, how could TCG get the members' cooperation?

(F) What do you think of the lack of a prior agreement on what happens at departure from TCG? What should be substituted for the current "negotiation process?"

(G) How could TCG capture value for the total organization? Partial ownership in private companies is notoriously difficult to evaluate and to convert into liquidity. What arrangements might be made to improve this?

(H) What are the benefits and costs of "network democracy?" What would have been lost by having some kind of central structure? What minimal controls are needed at the corporate level?

(I) What are the benefits and costs of keeping the "extremely flat organization?" Does a TCG member differ from a true franchisee? If so, how? If not, has TCG implemented all the needed relationships of a "franchise organization?"

Public Offering?

At the end of the case, there are some very interesting questions as to the public offering. Should TCG offer the whole structure to the public? If so, how can it do so, since each entity is independently financed? If it does not offer the whole entity, what portions should it offer? Should it offer the "crown jewels" which would give it highest market capitalization? Or hold on to one or two of these? Should it break up each entity and offer it separately? Why? Why not? How will investors respond to the consolidated, vs. individual, offers? Is there any merit in maintaining the TCG structure at this stage? Can it in fact be maintained under a public corporation model? If not, how can TCG obtain the very extensive financing it needs to carry its major projects to their next stages? This poses the basic issues: Can the "incubator" concept move from the early research and development stage into a full exploitation stage without significant disruption?

How would you price the TCG offering? What is the value of the accumulated R&D expenses? TCG appears to be growing approximately 50% per year in after-tax profits. What should be the appropriate P/E multiple for this? Assuming that the offering is made, and successful, what would the company look like post-offer? How could you divide up the gains among the key division people? What would Peter Fritz's role be after the offering? Should the company split itself into two segments, those with rapidly growing commercialization possibilities—and those with development potentials? Can TCG continue its unique organization form and policies after the offering?

In the end, TCG did take the company public in 1993. It took only the three divisions noted. Peter Fritz then brought in a partner to take over operations of the remainder of TCG. Since then, he has slowly withdrawn from an operating role.

THERMO ELECTRON CORPORATION

Thermo Electron has been one of the most interesting phenomena on the U.S. technology investment scene. George and John Hatsopoulos have become quite widely known for their unique concept. George has become a leading spokesman in the area of entrepreneurial finance in the United States, appearing on numerous national panels and as author of a number of well-recognized journal articles. Thermo Electron allows the students to take the small-scale example of TCG and bring it up to a billion dollar scale. TCG's operating philosophies are different from those of Thermo Electron. This can offer an interesting point of contrast. A useful way to develop the discussion is to ask a parallel question to that for TCG, "What have been the critical factors in Thermo Electron's success?" If the professor lists these next to those of TCG, the overlaps and differences will be intriguing. If the professor can do the same thing with the organization portion of the case, an interesting contrast will emerge before the students' eyes.

Critical Past Success Factors

1.   Expertise/Markets: Thermo Electron developed a deep expertise (developed through government contracts) in mechanical engineering, electron flows, and heat transfer capabilities. Unlike TCG, it helped develop the marketplaces for each of these technologies. Its strategies were more technology driven than TCG's. However, like TCG it attacked a number of "niche markets." The areas it chose were larger, required greater depth of technological knowledge, and involved a longer initial build-up time than TCG's. However, its markets were more stable and, once built, could provide a continuing cash flow, while TCG's required constant reinvention. The result was that Thermo Electron could capture profits earlier and longer, and begin to reinvest in growth and in other areas sooner.

2.   Leveraged Financing: Unlike TCG, Thermo Electron looked to the public markets to leverage its financing. Its technique of offering equity in its new divisions was emulated later by other companies, including RCA, GE, and AT&T. The Thermo Electron approach appears to violate some of the generally accepted concepts of corporate finance which suggest investors would rather invest in the individual units. Yet are there good reasons why investors might wish to participate in a portfolio pattern like Thermo Electron's? How does the presence of Thermo Electron Corporation affect the value of its subsidiaries? Why does Thermo Electron maintain a minimum of 80% ownership in most cases? What happens when Thermo Electron drops into a minority position?

3.   The Starburst Organization: Thermo Electron provides a superb industrial example of the "starburst organization" discussed by Quinn, Anderson, and Finkelstein. The starburst allows Thermo Electron to leverage both of its core intellectual competencies (in technology and management) and to leverage its own financial capabilities enormously. The professor should note that this is the same technique used by venture capitalists, movie producers, real estate syndicators, etc. What are some of the problems of operating in this mode? What are the major benefits? How does Thermo Electron "control" its various entities later? The 80% limit normally set by Thermo Electron for its own ownership allows Thermo Electron to consolidate the full earnings of the subsidiary, while benefiting from the various forms of public financing it achieves. Given the benefits which Thermo Electron offers to its divisions, why does the stock market tend to discount the earnings of the individual divisions? If Thermo Electron decreases the risk, as does TCG, why wouldn't the stock market give an increased premium for this?

The Thermo Electron Starburst

One can develop questions about the starburst organization using the Thermo Electron case and the Quinn, Anderson, Finkelstein article. What makes the starburst work for Thermo Electron? Its strong technological core competencies, its culture, and the financial management capabilities of the Hatsopoulos brothers are critical. What is the basis of mutual gain for the "divisions" and for Thermo Electron? The divisions obtain increased capital access, highly developed financial expertise, management planning capabilities, well developed financial and operating control concepts, credibility in the marketplace, continued access to Thermo's developing technologies, the benefits of the Thermo Electron brand recognition, the stability of the Thermo Electron share price, specialized advice in legal, risk management, human relations, investor relations, and shareholder communications as well as tax and accounting capabilities. For this the divisions usually pay a 1 1/2% fee to Thermo Electron. This would appear to be a low cost sourcing opportunity. Note that in contrast to TCG, the Thermo Electron divisions do not tend to be mutually interdependent. They have freestanding market, production, and sourcing capabilities externally. This is a critical difference between the companies.

To Thermo Electron, the divisions bring multiple capabilities. One of these is the capacity to leverage investments through bank borrowings and preferred shares in a manner which might not be possible for Thermo Electron. Bankers or investors can feel more comfortable that they can understand the individual divisions better than they might with the total of Thermo. However, they have the added advantage of security from Thermo Electron itself. Thermo Electron's stock represents the "non operating gains" of increased value in its divisional holdings. If these shares in the individual divisions could be sold independently, why does the stock market discount them in the total Thermo Electron portfolio? What is the basis of the "30% discount on the sum of Thermo's parts?" What are the problems of operating in this mode? What critical actions can the Hatsopoulos brothers take to overcome them?

What Next?

Into what new marketplaces might Thermo Electron extend, given its current capabilities? One of its claimed core competencies is "identifying emerging societal problems and developing technological solutions for them." How can this be leveraged? If one of the principal values Thermo Electron Corporation brings to its divisions is its "corporate culture," how can this be maintained after the Hatsopoulos brothers retire? They are in their early 70s as of the time of the case.

Growth Problems: Can Thermo Electron's cultural competencies be systematized to be independent of the Hatsopoulos brothers? Are there any divisions that will be calling for sufficient capital that they could overwhelm the rest of the divisions? If Thermo Electron sold off a few of its major divisions, would it be able to reproduce its past success with the remainder? What are the keys to the transition to a multiple billion dollar company? What happens when the divisions each become multiple billion dollar entities? Can the entrepreneurial spirit be maintained?

Incentives: Will shareholders be willing to allow substantial stock bonuses or cash bonuses to successful division managers? Must there be wage compatibility and comparable incentives among divisions? What would be the best forms of incentive to use in this situation? Should incentives be based on the performance of individual divisions? The whole company? Some combination? What should be the relative ratio between the two? Should this be provided in cash form? Shares? Options? How will public shareholders view these things? The biggest problem with companies developing in this form has been the tendency to "reassert control" when a division starts to have difficulties. A second is the tendency to lose trust in the independence of the division managers. How can these problems be handled?

Entrepreneurial Spirit: How can Thermo Electron maintain the kind of entrepreneurial independence it wants, yet keep adequate corporate controls? How can it avoid the key problem of having a single non-performing division drag down the entire company? Why should the division managers in performing divisions pay the price of the non-performing divisions, through holding shares of Thermo Electron Corporation? What are the keys to managing in this type of environment? Probably the most important are the establishment of a clear culture, a strong communications network, and thoroughly developed electronic monitoring and control systems. Clearly, commitments (both for capital investment and programs) which would threaten the entire corporation must be cleared by the corporate board itself. If this is not done, the entire enterprise could be at risk. This provides an interesting point to ask again, "What are the critical 'strategic controls' that Thermo Electron Corporation needs? How should these be modified for each of the divisions?"

MICROSOFT CORPORATION (B) TEACHING NOTE

Overview

Microsoft (B) offers an inside look at the way Microsoft is organized to create new software. It is a model of the new highly decentralized "ad hoc" form of organization. It has many controversial features. Case discussion tends to be lively because audiences split on their evaluation of Microsoft as a "highly successful" and "highly desirable" type of organization. The case provides a superb vehicle for discussing the development and leveraging of intellect as a corporation's primary asset. The "Microsoft culture" at first seems very unique. However, one quickly realizes that it applies to almost all highly successful investment banking, consulting, or small-scale innovative companies. While lending understanding to Microsoft's past successes, the case raises questions as to where Microsoft can move in the future. Its organization is both its major strength and major vulnerability. Its highly decentralized, unstructured style may make it difficult to move into the network, systems, and more complex "object-oriented" marketplaces that appear to be the future of software. Microsoft (B) links well with Microsoft (A). However, it stands by itself as a superb organizational case with linkages to many of the types of organizations Maister, Quinn, Mintzberg, and Tushman analyze—and with which business students will work in the future. It fits well into sections on organizational development, learning, corporate culture, innovative organizations, and managing intellect. It ends with a need to assess whether the organization style Gates has created is appropriate to the future challenges of Microsoft.

Session Structure

We open the session by asking what can be planned vs. what must be unplanned in this kind of software development? How does this fit what we know of innovation processes? Microsoft's concept fits well with Quinn's "Managed Chaos," Senge's "Learning Organizations," and Mintzberg's "Innovative Organization".. We then move to what are the most important organizational and structural reasons for Microsoft's past success? This allows one to raise questions about specific elements of its practices, including its highly intense confrontational style, 80 hour per week ethic, small team, independent unit, unique personnel development, and motivational systems. Despite many unattractive features of the Microsoft approach, why do good programmers want to work there? What is the nature of a competitive edge in the software field? How can one develop a competitive edge in intellectual management? Finally, we ask how does the Microsoft style match the future needs of the company? What will it have to change? Specifically, what policy changes would you recommend? How will these affect the very core of Microsoft's past success? Can Microsoft continue to be successful in the future without these changes? How can it continue to develop and leverage its enormous intellectual assets, which have (a) given it one of the highest stock market evaluations in history, and (b) created more millionaires and billionaires than any other innovative company in history? Because Microsoft is so controversial, one must be careful not to go in with preconceived structures into which to "force" the discussion. Instead, raising broad issues and letting students attack them from different viewpoints works well.

The Innovation Process

A good opening question is what do you think of Microsoft's process for innovating new software? This should bring out both pros and cons of the Microsoft approach. The lack of formal tools and structured mechanisms for management will upset some members of the group,

---

while the very lack of structure will appeal to others. If the professor focuses on the question of why Microsoft's actions are desirable or undesirable, rather than just listing the actions, some lively debates occur. These tend to be heavily colored by people's perceptions of Microsoft as a "success" or a "predator." The process Microsoft uses follows the Quinn "planned chaos" model rather well and brings out many of the points in Mintzberg's adhocracy readings. What are the critical focal points?

A.   Strategic Direction: Top management controls the functionality specifications of programs as well as the program interface standards with other Microsoft programs and user interface standards. Why are these not written out more clearly? To what extent should top management set cost specifications? Timing specs? Strategic specifications? If used, what would these look like? How could they be set in this dynamic environment? What will happen as Bill Gates increasingly is unable to cover the details of so many different programs?

B.   The Architects: What is the role of the architects? How do you think they should interrelate with Bill Gates, program managers, user interfaces? What kinds of incentives are appropriate for these people? They tend to deal with platform design and specification, not the specifics of applications program design. At one stage, they controlled 80% of all the lines of code developed at Microsoft. What should be their role in the future? How does one develop "architects" out of the current structure?

C.   Small Independent Units: Why does Microsoft use these tiny 3-5 person units? How can they coordinate with each other? Why does Microsoft not use CASE tools? Why do they not share tools among groups? What are the advantages and costs of this system? Why doesn't Microsoft use a "macro" program to coordinate software development, as Andersen Consulting does?

D.   Documentation: What do you think of Microsoft's documentation practices? Why is this not more formalized? What are the benefits? Costs? Why isn't documentation in the form of the code itself sufficient? Why is so much of the process informal and verbal? What are the gains and losses of this process?

E.   Quality Controls: How is quality maintained? How would you set quality targets for software? In competitive terms? In functionality terms? In cost terms? Flexibility? Compatibility? Responsiveness? Who should set these targets? How? How well do you think the Microsoft process serves this purpose? How could it be improved?

F.   Schedules: What do you think of the Microsoft scheduling process? Who should set schedules? Why do they let programmers do it? How can the schedules of the different subordinated design teams be coordinated? What do you think of the "builds" as quality and scheduling devices? How should one determine strategic scheduling? Update scheduling?

G.   Builds: What do you think of the builds process? How is it superior or inferior to more formalized macros? How does it fit the needs of user testing? How do bug counts play into the quality control system? What are the infrastructures necessary to make this control process work? Common language? Rituals? Checking back against earlier specifications? What disciplines the work? What problems would you expect in this system? Why does it seem to have worked so well for Microsoft?

H.   Planning vs. Chaos: What can be planned in this type of system? Why is chaos desirable? No one has ever designed any of these systems before. Consequently they do not know exactly whether they will work, how they will work, when they will work, what the interactions will be, and so on. The main controls for this type of system are: (1) planning the atmosphere of innovation, (2) selecting and developing people, (3) setting targets and limits, (4) getting independent evaluations (preferably by customers), (5) maintaining small-scale and personal contact in design groups, (6) controlling strategic targets and timing, (7) allowing fast feedback and multiple experiments. Note that the "test suite" designers, internal customers, first use customers, and interactions between different sub-program groups provide much of the discipline, as do the value systems of the company and the programmers themselves.

Structure and Style

In supporting this concept of planned chaos, what do you think of the Microsoft style? Chief among the style elements are:

A.   Hands-On Management: Management must develop trust, know the details, be regarded as expert in the areas they are evaluating. How long can Bill Gates continue his past practice? What can be substituted for this?

B.   Flat Structures: How big can Microsoft become before this structure fails? As it enters a wide variety of new fields, how can it coordinate across them? What alternatives does it have? If you were to change the structure, how would you do it?

C.   Independent Units: Why must the subsystem units be quite this independent? What intermediate possibilities exist between this and Andersen's use of METHOD/1, METHOD/2? Exactly how would you implement an intermediate concept?

D.   Confrontational Style: Why does Microsoft use and tolerate the highly emotional style it seems to allow? Why the shouting, etc.? This probably ensures that no one is afraid to put forward his or her ideas. However, it is a very difficult style to manage. People need to be preselected with the kinds of personalities that work well in this environment, with a safety net for good people who aren't "fighters." What are the good features of the confrontational style? Losses? Alternatives?

E.   Promotion on Technical Merit: To date, promotion has not involved social or organizational skills. Primarily, people move up based upon their programming capabilities. How will this work as the company has to depend more and more on marketing information collected by an independent marketing group? Does program maintenance require the same style as program development? How can this transition be created?

F.   Jumping-Short Circuiting: Bill Gates established a style of jumping around the organization, going directly to programmers' screens. What are the benefits, losses involved in this style? It probably worked well in the early stages and as long as Gates was better technically than any of his people. What happens as the organization grows larger? Should such a style be permitted even at the team level?

G.   Evaluation: What are the appropriate methodologies for evaluating personnel performance under these circumstances? How can one ensure that people are evaluated fairly across the small units? How should they be rewarded? Should rewards depend upon the success of the program in the marketplace? On meeting quality targets? Timing and cost targets? Should they be the same across all units? How will this structure and style work as Microsoft moves into more "systems" or "network" types of programs where interfacing is as important as the functional details of the program?

Managing Intellect

What do you think of the way that Microsoft develops its intellectual resources? What are the keys to intellectual management under these circumstances? How does one evaluate or place a value on intellectual assets? How does a company leverage its intellectual capabilities?

A.   Vision: A company's vision is crucial to this process. It provides the basis for attracting people with like values. It is very important in attracting the most potent talent available. If people believe in the vision, they are willing to put up with a large number of personal inconveniences. If they share values, they will work harder. They are less likely to leak secrets. They are apt to be more creative and flexible. Fewer controls are needed. And so on. This is an ideal place to introduce the question of why companies put so much focus on their vision. Then one can ask whether Gates is making maximum use of this capability. He seems to focus primarily on the technical vision, rather than a market team or organizational vision. Why? Could or should this be corrected?

B.   Recruitment: Crucial to developing intellect is recruitment of the best talent available. People come to Microsoft because they think Gates knows and will establish the future of the industry.   They want to be associated with the very best programmers in their fields. Consequently they "volunteer" to join the company. The processes that Microsoft uses to select and interview these people is fascinating. It is very intense. The result is that they get a reasonably good match-up between personal values and corporate values. This is critical to implementing any vision.

C.   Mentoring: People are immediately put with a mentor on projects. This mentor is a person who is a superb programmer and experienced in the Microsoft system. This allows the person to develop greater connectivity with other people in Microsoft and to develop a feeling for the subtleties of their program vs. the other programs in Microsoft. Mentoring and interaction with the full complexities of real-world problems are critical to the development of individuals, especially high quality professionals.

D.   Eighty-Hour Weeks: Why is this so important at Microsoft? Intellect grows exponentially-based upon the challenges and experiences it encounters. Consequently people become much more valuable in fewer calendar weeks if they work eighty-hour weeks. However, there is a toll to this process. Many do drop out. Is this a bad thing? Microsoft needs to keep a constant turnover and a feeling that those who are there have produced. It is a major mistake to try to save all people in an intellectual enterprise. Up and out has proved to be a very effective technique, and Microsoft utilizes that well.

E.   Continuity: Continuity in teams furthers the exponential learning. It captures in the people on the team their learning experience and holds it for future projects. It avoids the start-up costs of constantly introducing new teams or new relationships. One should question, however, whether there is any encouragement to team managers to either mentor or maintain an atmosphere where people wish to be on their particular team. How could one achieve those goals? What types of incentives might be involved?

F.   Capturing Intellect: An organization must also capture its intellect in its software systems. E-mail is a wonderful way to leverage intellect by sharing. However, as interesting problems are resolved within Microsoft, shouldn't these solutions be shared by utilizing a software package for a particular functionality over and over? There is little evidence of an attempt to capture intellect at this level.

G.   Commitment: Commitment leverages intellect both by motivating people to perform at high levels and by maintaining project continuity. What does Microsoft do to encourage such commitment? How do its incentive plans help or hinder this process?

H.   Leveraging Intellect: What should Microsoft do to further leverage its intellect and to stimulate institutional learning? There is very little attempt in Microsoft's training programs to either teach the culture, or to capture the experience curve of past performance. This is an area needing major attention. The other most significant shortcoming is utilizing software to capture the solutions the company already has so that they may be reused. This includes the experience in managing programs. Andersen Consulting has probably gone too far in this respect; Microsoft not far enough.

Motivation

Throughout the case there are significant questions as to how to motivate professional programmers. The techniques suggested in the earlier section help. Microsoft supports these with high financial rewards. It uses the highly informal atmosphere of its "campus location" to stimulate further identity and informal sharing. Are there other motivational techniques which would be helpful? The professor can lead the students through various questions concerning the reward-performance measurement process. These include:

A.   Use of Huge Stock Options: How do these motivate people? Are they essential? Why are they not individual? All stock options, other than signing bonuses, tend to be team-oriented. Is Microsoft really looking for team or for individual performance? Why would people like those coming to Microsoft want to work in a "team environment?"

B.   Obsessive Perfectionists: The people at Microsoft are described as obsessive perfectionists. They motivate themselves to highest quality and performance. This is a primary function of the recruitment program and the continuous personal monitoring of activity. How can one avoid demotivating people in this environment? What are the key elements in keeping this highly personalized motivational outlook?

C.   Reputation: Most professional organizations use peer reviews because professionals want to be evaluated only by other professionals. How does the outside world know about individual professional's skills? How does the product's performance in the marketplace affect this reputation? How can Microsoft use customer evaluation to further stimulate the obsessive perfectionist characteristics as they apply to users? The perfectionism tends to be targeted toward technical software functionality. What else is needed? How would you change the system?

D.   What to Measure: What elements of performance need to be measured in the different programming units? Usually one looks for professional measurement by peer review, market performance by customers, and process performance by personal evaluations. The "builds" and "bug counts" tend to measure the sheer performance of the software. However, one needs other qualitative observations of how much the individual contributed to this performance, and what customers think about it. The latter needs to be fed back directly to the teams doing the design. How can one facilitate this?

E.   Management Understanding: Much is dependent on the respect with which the top management is held by employees. If they believe that the top management is both fair and extremely competent, professionals will tend to allow evaluation. However, much depends normally on self-evaluation. What do you think of the "self-evaluation procedures" of Microsoft? How could these be improved?

F.   Intangible Rewards: In addition to the huge stock options, what can Microsoft offer in terms of rewards? Most studies indicate that creative people want to be recognized for their personal contributions, desire independence, and want their peers to know of their contributions. How can this be structured to advantage by Microsoft? Students can usually provide some good thoughts on this. The system is implemented by detailed MBOs as well as "objective performance measures." Note that the detailed MBOs are not "profit-oriented." They involve 5-10 major personal achievements that the individual agrees to. How can one best observe, measure, and coordinate experts in a complex system like Microsoft's?

FUTURE ISSUES

The Microsoft (A) case developed many of the future issues that Microsoft faces. Please see that teaching note for amplification of market needs, positioning possibilities, and alliance issues. All of these issues are pertinent to the (B) case. However, the most important relate to the organization structures and motivation systems analyzed previously. One can start with a quick array of what are the critical new factors the organization will have to respond to? How should the organization and its practices be changed to fulfill these needs? What are the limits placed upon Microsoft's market positioning by its organization? How can these be resolved? These questions alone can provide a very lively end of case discussion.

Key Issues

A.   The Effects of Size: What are the limits to size posed by Microsoft's current organization? How can these be averted? How can Microsoft's values and style be maintained in this larger organization context? What will be the impact of much larger marketing, distribution, international, and trouble-shooting operations? These are beginning to change the total number and mix of people within Microsoft. How long can the dominance of programmers continue? How could these new cultures be stimulated? Rewarded? Appreciated? What should the macro organization of Microsoft look like?

B.   Complexity: The complexity of the software marketplace was growing rapidly. In addition to the generic spreadsheets, word processing and graphics packages which all computers now used, some applications had grown into enormous marketplaces for the personal computer. These included specialized programs like Turbo Tax, desktop publishing, games, groupware, education, and database or reference purposes. In addition, the Internet had opened a huge new marketplace for commercial software, browsers, interactive programming, etc. Finally, there were many new markets in the telecommunications structure itself from packet switching through servers to asynchronous transfer mode (ATM) technology. The case provides a variety of data for analyzing different segments of this marketplace. Each segment was large, and most were growing, not only in the United States but worldwide. This led to a number of questions as to how Microsoft should organize for (1) each specialized market it wished to participate in, (2) each national market, and (3) the global market.

C.   Culture-Organization: As the organization grows and becomes more diverse, can Microsoft maintain its uniquely intense culture? Could Gates continue to dominate that culture? If not, how could a new culture be created? To what extent has Gates become a handicap—rather than an asset—in internal management? How should Microsoft be organized under Gates to utilize his great strengths, while offsetting some of the negative effects of his style? Can Microsoft continue to operate dominantly as a U.S. company? If not, how should it restructure to attack international markets? Should it clone its style in each country? Adapt to that country beyond merely having translation capabilities there? How can it tap into the new needs of its different global customers? How do these get fed into the design groups in Seattle? How can international programming be coordinated? Should Microsoft be organized by product groups? Geography? Networks? How can Microsoft attract the quality of people in marketing and support functions that it needs to maintain its position in these emerging marketplaces? What should its new core competencies be? How can it leverage these to greatest advantage? The case notes that the number of marketing and service personnel already overwhelm the computing personnel. How can these people be given status? Incentives? Organized without bureaucracy?

D.   Dominance: In the past Microsoft has dominated PC software. Is this still sufficient? In what markets should Microsoft seek dominance? How is this defined? Against whom? AT&T? Novell? Oracle? Andersen Consulting? EDS? Any other PC software company? IBM? How will this affect Microsoft's mission statement? What will be the effect of large Japanese software producers entering the Japanese market? Asian market? How can Microsoft tap into these marketplaces? In developing its positions, should Microsoft use an "open system" or "proprietary" approach? What are the implications of either position? What should it do to avoid the constant anti-trust suits it has been undergoing? What should the U.S. Justice Department position be on companies like Microsoft? EDS? Andersen? Can Microsoft use its power unfairly? If so, how? What specific action should be taken by regulators? Microsoft? In recent years, Microsoft has grown more rapidly than the sum of all other independent software producers. Can it reasonably continue this process? Nathan Myhrvold points out that Microsoft's growth has just matched the growth of installed computing power. Can this continue? What kinds of growth targets or limits should Microsoft set?

E.   Limits Set by Style: One of the most intriguing questions is what limits Microsoft's style sets on its future growth potentials? Is its style adaptable to the emerging marketplaces? Particularly network computing? Entertainment? Computers are moving from being tools to carrying out functions. At first they merely processed things faster. Now they substitute for reading, communication, and reasoning functions. Is Microsoft's style compatible with these kinds of new functions? Or is it primarily a product design concept for mass manufacture later? Perhaps the biggest question is the movement from micro computers to networks. Costs of communication are dropping to the extent that an international call will cost only about 3¢ in the early 2000s. A computer is no longer just a freestanding object but the entire network itself. In fact, many people view the "network" as the "micro computer of the future." If Microsoft is to maintain its dominance—a characteristic important to Bill Gates—doesn't it have to be a dominant player in this marketplace? However, given all of the decentralization and interconnectivity required for such programs, can Microsoft's style operate in that world? Will Microsoft's programming style work in other countries? If not, how can it achieve a competitive edge there? A very interesting thing to ask is how would you rank the various marketplaces for Microsoft in terms of its probable success? Their importance in the future of software?

Applications
Entertainment
Education
Games
Groupware
Server technology
New generalized PC programs (which ones?)
Networks
Communications Software
Specialized business applications
Expert systems
Large-scale systems
Artificial intelligence

One of the most intriguing characteristics of the case is that Microsoft's style will probably limit its access to many of these marketplaces. Many people have complained about the lack of "bug control" in Microsoft's new releases. Can it handle a variety of marketplaces? Are there some of the above marketplaces where such bugs would be intolerable? Will Microsoft have to change its style in response to these new markets? If so, how should it do so? What will it lose in the process? How must it adjust its support systems to its new needs?

Overview

NovaCare is a $159 million health care company in the rehabilitation business. The case ends with three crucial strategic questions: (1) How should NovaCare reposition itself in the problem-ridden health care industry of the 1990s? (2) How should it develop the information, control, and incentive systems necessary to achieve its goals? (3) Specifically how should it develop NovaNet, its new management information system? The case can be positioned in a number of ways. It offers an excellent vehicle for discussing the impact of values on strategy, multi-stakeholder analysis, service industry strategies, the management of information technology (IT) systems, management of "inverted organizations," and the alignment of control, incentive, and reward systems around multiple stakeholder interests. It fits well with readings by Mintzberg on "professional bureaucracy," Quinn, Anderson, and Finkelstein on "new forms of organizing," and Rumelt on "values in organizations."

Session Structure

The session can be structured with a decision orientation by asking, "What should NovaCare do in 1991?" Or by building up to this strategic question through a series of analytical steps. In either case, the discussion should include the following questions: (1) How do the values of each set of stakeholders affect this strategic decision? (2) How does one manage a radical new organization form like the "inverted organization?" (3) What performance measurement, reward, and incentive structures make most sense in this type of professional organization? (4) What can the information technology (IT) system best provide in support of NovaCare's strategy? (5) What should NovaCare's strategy be for the future?

If desired, one can also introduce a broad range of other issues having to do with the better management of the overall health care system in the United States. The NovaCare case poses many of the pertinent problems of payer control, efficiency, effectiveness, use of paramedics, and so on. Given this backdrop, one can pursue some interesting issues around the question: "Where should NovaCare diversify in the future?"

Values Issues

The NovaCare case offers an interesting opportunity to discuss the management of strategy as a process of finding and optimizing areas of mutual interest among a number of strong players who have conflicting goals and values.

One can open this section by asking, "Who are the company's customers?" With a little probing, one can develop the following as genuine "customers:" (1) the caregiving therapists, (2) the hospitals and nursing homes that manage the care, (3) the directors of nursing within the hospitals and clinics, (4) the doctors who prescribe the rehabilitation care, (5) the insurance and Medicare payers, (6) the patients themselves. Once these are identified as "customers," they clearly become interested stakeholders. To this list, one can add NovaCare's owners, the financial community, and the health care community as interested stakeholders. The success of the enterprise depends upon satisfying all of these stakeholders, and not just the financial community.

One can next ask, "What are the dominating goals and concerns of each of these parties? Where might these interests be congruent? Where are they likely to be divergent? How do these interests affect the actions of the clinician at the point of contact?" A brief summary follows:

- Clinicians-therapists regard themselves as professionals. Consequently, they look to their peers for performance standards and professional approval. In addition, they are highly independent and often strongly motivated by the personal values inherent in "caregiving." They tend to be less interested in profitability and efficiency. Since—at the time of the case—there was a shortage of therapists, they could easily move to other institutions or practice independently. They tended to resist formal organization constraints and paperwork. They tended to be strongly related to the local community and individual patients. Therapists also wanted to have knowledge of the most current and effective clinical practice and the training to implement it in practice.

- Health care institutions tended to be concerned with the quality of care, yet were under increasing pressures to control costs. These institutions wanted truly professional care at lowest cost, and with reliable quality. They wanted to be unassailable in the event of lawsuits. Yet, because of DRG caps, they were very concerned with profitability, capturing available margins whenever ethical, and careful control of costs—with documentation that could hold up upon inquiry. They were interested in filling all available beds and continuing treatment "in-house" as long as that treatment yielded higher margins than others.

- Directors of nursing were interested in providing high quality patient care, utilizing support staff effectively, and having "no hassle" service which kept the patient happy and progressing. They needed genuine professional assistance in assessing patients who needed care, prognosing that care, and delivering it efficiently along with other members of the hospital staff team. They sought professionalism, reliability, and patient improvement with minimum disruption to other aspects of patient care.

- Patients wanted to feel better, be in greater control of their lives, and eventually to get well. Since most of them were covered by hospital insurance, they were not concerned with costs. They also wanted a good personal relationship with the clinician, pleasant treatment, and a minimum of stress-producing conflicts with the care institution or the payer. Their emphasis was clearly on quality of care at a personal level, and not costs.

- Doctors had a strong interest in seeing their patients' well-being improved. They wanted pleasant, effective treatment, but were considerably less concerned with costs because rehabilitation did not typically affect their own billings. They also wanted convenience in overseeing patients, careful reporting, and the assurance that the patient was in truly professional hands.

- Insurance companies were interested in lowest cost total care, genuine effectiveness in any procedures, satisfaction of their client (the insured company), paying company, and ultimately the general satisfaction of the patient. "Hassle free paperwork" was of great value to these institutions. A sizable percentage of their costs were in handling the paperwork surrounding patient care. Any simplification of that process would drop directly to their bottom line. Ensuring that all billings complied with their procedures and coverage was of immense value. Avoiding litigation was a primary concern.

- The health care community was trying to lower total costs. It was constantly seeking to find new ways to measure benefits vs. costs. Some 30% of all medical care costs were in paperwork and administrative transactions. A major portion of costs were due to the overheads of keeping a patient in a formal hospital or clinical facility. There were strong pressures on public groups to lower costs, without causing undue hardship to individuals or to large voting blocks. Of special concern were older people who could not manage their lives without some degree of rehabilitation. The cost of maintaining this latter group was growing significantly.

The Vision Statement

One can develop an interesting analysis of the above by showing which interests are common to all groups, and where conflicts exist. One can then ask, why is a statement of "Vision" and a statement of "Principles" so important in this kind of organization? What do you think of the NovaCare Statement of Vision? What should a vision statement include? Why was such a statement so important at the time? What did it do for NovaCare later? What makes a vision statement effective? What aspects of the NovaCare statement are effective? Ineffective? Why?

Mr. Foster felt that the vision statement was essential after the post-acquisition decline to underline in the clinicians' minds that the company was not interested solely in "the bottom line." The key to the company's profitability was to attract highly qualified clinicians and to motivate them to be productive. The vision statement can be considered a combination recruiting, motivational, and self-control tool. Good people will come to a company which expresses their values and upholds them. They will work harder in that environment. And they can self-direct their own efforts. However, for this to happen, the vision statement must have sufficient "snap" and "glitter" to be attractive. It must express why the company is important to each of its critical stakeholders. It must set forth what makes the company "different" and "interesting" as compared to all other companies. It needs to develop a sense of cohesion and belonging. It also needs to be backed completely by management's own consistent actions and by the performance measurement, motivational, and incentive-reward systems of the enterprise. Hence the vision statement must ultimately be clearly reflected in the metrics of the control system. This point will be reinforced later.

We find it useful to focus on the pragmatics of a well-developed value system, rather than the more abstruse questions of "ethics." Values can be defined as strong, relatively permanent beliefs or principles guiding actions of individuals or organizations. Some of the more pragmatic uses of values management are listed below:

- To weight goals and decision criteria,

- To screen perceptions of opportunity or threats,

- To attract people and create trust,

- To allow efficient delegation and freedom of action within the organization,

- To improve efficiency, motivation, and creativity,

- To ease capital access and simplify mergers,

- To lower legal harassment and community relations costs,

- To foster long-term time horizons, innovation, and high P/E ratios,

- To create identity, maintain morale, and protect confidential materials, and

- To give satisfaction or create frustration.

Strategic Analysis

An interesting opening question for this section is, "What does NovaCare do to create value?" This can play directly back to each of the stakeholders.

- For clinics and hospitals, NovaCare provides more efficient and higher quality service than a small unit could support on its own. It can attract patients to that facility by influencing referrals from non-resident doctors. It can provide inexpensive screening and advisory services. It can indemnify the health care unit from non-payment by third party payers. It can handle all recruitment and training costs. It can avoid overhead fluctuations as patient loads fluctuate. Most importantly, it can handle the expensive paperwork involved in rehabilitation care. And it can ensure world class quality in patient care.

- For the patient, NovaCare can ensure the most current care practice. It can provide better trained and selected people. It can provide monitoring of outcomes to ensure long-term success of treatment. It can ensure that the patient gets a desired degree of attention despite the conflicting pressures on the hospital staff.

- For the director of nursing, NovaCare can handle all paperwork problems, ease the nurses' coordination problems through self-coordination, and provide better quality care and patient support. NovaCare can also save the director's time by handling recruiting and training problems.

- For the facility's owners, NovaCare can increase profitability by increasing or stabilizing patient loads, by providing reliable payments, by lowering risks of malpractice suits, and by including the institution in NovaCare's marketing programs. By capturing the experience of all its many therapists, NovaCare can bring more information to the clinical therapy function than any single facility could.

- For third party payers, NovaCare can make patients more self-sufficient, earlier. Rehab services seem to pay for themselves by a factor of 10 or 20 to 1. Consequently, payers interested in cost containment have a powerful new weapon for the purpose. In addition, with its computer system, NovaCare can provide more accurate billings and save the payer large sums in overhead cost. Finally, NovaCare can capture more outcomes data than any single facility. These data offer highly leveragable potentials for NovaCare in the future and may be the key to its maintainable competitive edge.

What can be NovaCare's distinctive maintainable competitive edge? This question can be approached directly or through a competitor and competitive analysis (as is done below). What are NovaCare's unique strengths? Its size allows it to maintain a recruiting facility no others can touch. It can support this capability with larger scale, more sophisticated training programs to ensure the quality and updating of its therapists' skills. It can provide greater growth opportunities for therapists. By managing its professional clinicians' activities through professionals who are therapists themselves, NovaCare maintains its focus on their professional development. This is an excellent place to note that each of these is a "service activity" and that such "services" are the essence of the company's core competency. Economies of scale do not come from facility size. Instead, they come from obtaining maximum value from developing selective service activities (meaningful to customers) in great depth.

At this point, one could branch into a discussion of the management information system as a primary source of economies of scale. This would lead directly into a discussion of NovaNet and its use as a strategic weapon. In this teaching note, we have separated this discussion under the subtitle NovaNet.

Competitive Analysis

At this point, one could look at each of the "five forces" of Porter and show how NovaCare should deal with each.

362

- Suppliers: NovaCare's suppliers are independent therapists. They are extremely fragmented, lack stability in their patient loads, must finance themselves during substantial delays in direct billing, do not wish to handle administrative chores, find it difficult to upgrade their skills, and may be forced to travel long distances to serve a fragmented client base. Individual suppliers could form consortia and provide similar services to NovaCare. NovaCare's distinctive advantage is its information system and capital base. It can neutralize these consortia by preempting as many facilities as possible.

- New Entrants: Other providers could replicate NovaCare's success and are attempting to do so. NovaCare's most important weapons could be its capital base, recruiting, training, management, and information systems. If it can capture the best practice of all its therapists and feed these back to all its therapists, it can obtain an intellectual advantage that no other company can duplicate. It has economies of scale in the billing and recruiting processes that cannot be duplicated. It also has the opportunity to do more advertising and thus improve its image relative to all others. This discussion should fall back on and help develop the concept of NovaCare's distinctive maintainable competitive edge.

- Customer Power: Hospitals and nursing homes will be attempting to provide their own rehabilitation therapy services. As each unit grows in size, it can be expected to add full-time therapists. NovaCare's defensive weapon is to provide the service at a comparable price to third party payers and yet also provide added information services to its therapists, hospitals, nursing homes, payers, and patients. It might also move downstream into the therapeutic rehabilitation center business as a preemptive move. Such centers would be lower cost than hospitals, and consequently more attractive to third party payers and possibly patients.

- Outside Forces: NovaCare's success will continue to be affected by government regulation, eligibility of rehab services for reimbursement, and the potentials of lawsuits. To deal with these forces, NovaCare needs to have a superb regulatory monitoring capability. Even more important will be its capacities to monitor and prove outcomes, demonstrate higher efficiency than potential competitors, and show that rehabilitation pays for itself. All of these could be functions of the NovaNet system. However, if the government were to undertake a major investment in increasing the number of therapists, this could represent a serious threat to NovaCare's total business. NovaCare would have to reposition its policies very carefully. An interesting discussion can be built around what it would change under these circumstances.

- New Products or Technologies: Some new drugs or electronically controlled therapies might assist in rehabilitation. However, their administration and oversight is still likely to require a trained professional. For its own protection and effectiveness, NovaCare must maintain state-of-the-art knowledge about such potentials, especially combinations of drug and physical therapies. Other classes of therapies could be attractively provided through the NovaCare network. Get students to suggest them.

- New Growth Opportunities: NovaCare should look at each of its stakeholders to see what possible new services it could offer. This can lead to a very imaginative discussion of data services, home care services, operating facilities for a hospital on an outsource basis, new types of contracts where NovaCare would undertake the risks of nonperformance, methods for reaching unserved patients, operating care centers on its own, and so on. One should now begin to ask, how should NovaCare prioritize these opportunities? What programs are necessary to make these priorities come into being? What should be the major new thrusts of NovaCare? Some areas of priority are suggested in the following paragraphs.

- Increased Density in Areas Already Served: This is a thrust which should be undertaken in any event. This allows NovaCare to preempt available hospital and care facilities, obtain better scheduling for its own therapists, avoid the buildup of independent or new competition, and spread the overhead costs of its local and area directors.

- Geographical Growth: NovaCare has been much stronger in the Northern and Eastern quadrants of the United States. Yet the aging population is moving to the South and Southwest. Should the extension into these areas be a conscious element of strategy? If so, how is this best accomplished? Should the main thrust be acquisition? What are the advantages and disadvantages? Should it be internal growth by establishing new offices? Advantages and disadvantages? Are there any of the companies described which would make attractive acquisition or merger partners? What priorities would the students place on these companies? What criteria should be used for acquisitions or mergers?

- Growth in Rehabilitation Services: Are there other rehabilitation services NovaCare could reasonably provide? Why is physical therapy growing, although its margins are lower? Are there other areas of rehabilitation therapy important to elderly people? How should NovaCare attack these various opportunities? Can NovaCare maintain its extraordinary growth rates without moving into new therapies? Following is a table analyzing some of the major trends evident in the data provided by the case.

NOVACARE DATA TRENDS

Item	3 yr. CAGR
Net Revenues	28%
Gross Profit	41%
Operating Profit	358%
Earnings per Share	78%

Key Ratios	Ratio
Return on Assets (1991)	16%
Return on Average Assets (1991)	19%
Return on Equity (1991)	18%
Return on Average Equity (1991)	23%
Cash Flow	$22 million
Debt ÷ Equity	0.3%
Revenues ÷ Assets	119%

Consequently, if NovaCare continues to grow at 28%, it will need to double its assets every 2.5 years, requiring an asset growth in the next year of approximately $50 million. If it merely grows with the industry at 18%, it will double its assets in four years requiring approximately $32 million of asset growth in the next year. Since NovaCare has a cash flow of $22 million, it will have to do some further financing. It clearly has a large debt capacity. It could easily expand its debt base by $30 million. However, with its shares selling at 25-30 times current earnings, equity growth is probably preferable. As in the past, much of NovaCare's growth will have to come from acquisitions. NovaCare clearly has the financial strength to make whatever acquisitions it might wish.

One critical question is whether NovaCare should acquire a few large entities or a number of smaller ones. If it wishes to pursue a preemptive strategy, it should probably acquire a few large units in its area of highest geographical priority. If it wishes to make further preemptive moves, it may wish to acquire entire chains of nursing homes or therapy centers. NovaCare's P/E ratios are clearly based on an anticipation of continued rapid growth. To maintain its growth rates, given the slow growth in each therapeutic category (i.e., 8 to 10%) NovaCare will have to acquire extensively. If one assumes an internal growth in therapeutic treatment equivalent to industry growth of 10%, NovaCare could expand its revenues by only $15 million through internal growth in the next year. This leaves a shortfall of about $35 million in revenues at a minimum.

However, one should ask whether even this amount is sufficient if NovaCare hopes to preempt its developing competition from larger hospitals, hospital chains, and other therapy chains.

Organization Issues and Strategy

One of the unique features of NovaCare is its organizational structure and policies. One can start with a series of questions about the "inverted organization." Why is such an organization desirable in this situation? How does it work? What types of problems would you expect? In what other situations would an "inverted organization" be appropriate? Such organizations work extremely well in truly <u>professional</u> situations. In these organizations, the point person has more knowledge than anyone else in the organization about the delivery of the product itself. Such organizations are common in hospitals, legal firms, research laboratories, investment banking, and so on. They operate best when the locus of intellect is at the contact point, rather than the center—and when there is a truly professional set of standards to maintain discipline.

One can ask, what is the role of executives in an inverted organization? Their role tends to be that of facilitator, expediter, special analyst, and handler of nonroutine problems such as the opening of a new facility. A discussion of the executive's role leads naturally into some of the problems of these organizations. Are there any "orders" given from the center to the contact people? If so, how are these orders given? Typically these are procedural in nature, requiring that the point person fill out certain forms, comply with schedules, prepare plans, and report in a standard fashion on professional activities. Whenever possible, rules and disciplines for these practices are built into the software system. This can be a major function of NovaNet. In a health care operation, many of these rules will be specified by insurance or government requirements—or the dictates of the profession. Interestingly, it is the software professionals who program in such rules, in the process making subtle interpretations which actually influence line action. Note the <u>inversion</u> that "line" has become "staff"—becoming advisors and facilitators. Staff has become line in terms of providing the orders within the system. And what we normally think of as top management now "reports" to what we normally think of as "subordinates."

All of this raises a number of questions. What is the role of local executives? Regional heads? How do we measure executive performance? Is there some way to get the same degree of empowerment without "inverting" the organization? If so, how? If the therapists are indeed the organization's most knowledgeable persons about patient care, how could one have an executive giving them orders? Without a true organizational hierarchy, how does one reward managers? Does one really want to "promote" a high performing therapist into a managerial role? How does one design a compensation system that keeps the good therapists on the task? Perhaps the most important question is how does one attract managers into this climate?

There are a number of other interesting organizational questions. First among these is the issue of turnover. Note the high cost of turnover: $25,000 in recruitment and lost revenue costs. Why is the turnover rate so high? What could NovaCare do to reduce it? How can the organization deal with the "burnout problem?" This is a major issue for professionals dealing with long-term chronic care problems or terminal patients. Most organizations have found that rotation of professionals in these situations is essential. If the organization is truly "inverted," why is it that the company needs a district organization and a regional organization? How do these managers interrelate with their contact bosses?

Even more important is the issue of how to expand an inverted organization. If NovaCare acquires other companies, how can it integrate these into its own operating style? Given the fact that the contact person is a professional in a specific therapy, should that person report on performance to other specialists rather than to a regional manager? What should the overall structure of NovaCare's organization be in the long run? What are the advantages of a regional organization? A specialty or specialist organization in which therapy specialists report only to their specialist peers? If NovaCare moves into operating its own health care units, how can this be made compatible with the existing organization? How large an organization can NovaCare support given its existing policies? How soon will it hit this limit? Note that with a span of control of 15, NovaCare could have a 3-level organization of over 30,000 people (15 x 15 x 15). To keep its organization flat and nonbureaucratic, NovaCare will need to maintain wide spans of control. How can NovaNet facilitate these wider spans? Is it efficient to have a single district manager coordinating 15 people who are specialists in different therapies as opposed to having specialization at the district level?

Finally, one can ask a series of questions about what are the most important long-term problems the organization is likely to encounter. Clearly, the recruiting and motivation of middle management is one of these. Expanding the pool of therapists is another. How to handle the required balance of therapists' activities at the local level is another. How does one encourage therapists to bring new patients onto the caseload? How can they be helped in screening these patients? To what extent should the therapist be dealing with institutions vs. the district managers? How does one maintain the quality of care at the local level and ensure that quality? How does one maintain local differentiation in services? How does one get the therapist to seek out and handle profitable patients rather than those who are most interesting technically? To what extent do financial incentives work with such caregivers? What other incentives might work well? Note that NovaCare's distinctive edge has been its capacity to attract and motivate high quality therapists. What policies will be necessary to support this in the future? Should NovaCare undertake a "therapist apprentice" program? Should it support professional or university programs which train therapists? How can it expand its pool of high quality therapists?

This is a good point at which to raise the question of managing "professionals." What differentiates a professional organization from any other type of organization? The high training and skills of a professional organization's specialists are probably one set of key elements. Another is the fact that professionals develop a code of behavior which is enforced by the profession itself. Consequently, one must make sure that the code of the profession is constantly reinforced and updated for all therapists. To do this, there should be continuing required training sessions, attendance at conferences, exposure to new practices through newsletters, and in-house training. Further, professionals tend to resist performance reviews by anyone but those within their own profession. How then can one review performance within NovaCare? Most professional organizations find they must use a combination of customer-based metrics and professional "peer reviews" to maintain quality control. How can this be accomplished in NovaCare?

A final and vital issue in managing an "inverted organization" is who actually carries out the performance reviews over whom. Most such organizations find that until the contact person begins to rate the "executives" reporting to the contact person, the organization does not become truly inverted. It is merely a public relations sham. What are some of the complications of having contact people reviewing district and area managers? Staff personnel? Top executives? Is this feasible at all? Many organizations have faced this problem and have concluded that a dual review is essential with a balance required between contact person reviews and "center-oriented" reviews. Achieving this should be a critical element in the management control and incentive system.

Control and Reward Systems

All of the above suggests some interesting questions about management control and incentive systems. One can start with the question of what performance needs to be measured at each level of the organization? The most interesting of these is the therapist level. At present, the main focus is on the "billable time" standard. Why is the 25 hours "billable time" standard extant? Should there be other standards tied into this? In particular, how does one measure and control quality of service? The 25-hour standard was actually arrived at by incremental experimentation, rather than analysis. It was intended to allow sufficient time for the therapist to travel, support the nursing director, screen patients, provide extra services at the care facility, and to fill out paperwork. Is there some method of arriving at this analytically? Should it be the same for all therapists? If one wants the therapist to be both caring and thorough, does one want to push the "standard hours" very high? Since one intention of the standard is to give the therapist motivation through bonuses, what percentage of salary should be "base salary," bonus, free time? Most incentive experts agree that about 1/3 of the pay of an individual at this level should be incentive based. One can engage in an interesting discussion as to how to set the precise standard.

Quality measurement is a very important issue. Actual outcomes of patient care cannot be known for some time after the therapy is given. Consequently, one needs a series of procedural and interim benchmarks based on step-by-step physical progress checks. NovaCare has slowly built up a number of discrete progress points to measure progress for each therapy class. To the extent possible, it has also tried to help therapists develop a standardized approach to each observed clinical problem. One can then track both the therapies given and the progress rate in terms of benchmarks. This is very important in maintaining credibility at both the institutional and payer level. NovaCare has gone farther and asked each therapist to set specific goals and measures for progress for each patient. This needs to be reviewed in the weekly performance reports. Is it possible to do this without having personal observation of the results? How can one ensure accuracy of inputs if the therapists are reporting their own performance? This could be one of the important services provided by NovaNet.

How can NovaCare ensure that clinicians spend sufficient time on non-therapy activities? How can it review the effectiveness of these activities? Since one cannot review therapists' activities in detail, the incentive system becomes a method of self-disciplining. In addition, NovaNet could check for many important issues automatically—e.g., eligibility, coverage, and likely success of different therapies. The latter would require that the therapist enter a series of symptoms and "status levels" for each potential patient. Using an artificial intelligence (AI) system, NovaNet could then discern probabilities of successful outcomes given different therapies and display these on a menu for the therapist. The therapist could always override the AI proposal. The hospital or clinic could serve as the control point to see that the therapist actually was present for the times indicated. Real time "clock control" entry from a laptop computer could also offer further controls for accuracy. However, follow-up at the institutional level by area or district managers to ensure satisfaction is a crucial control element.

An interesting exercise at this stage is to get the class to balance the interests of NovaCare in each of its stakeholders. What percentage of time should the clinician put on each goal? One should now go back to the stakeholder analysis to make sure that the director of nursing, health care institution, patient, governmental, and payer interests are properly served. One can make a simple matrix on the blackboard with the stakeholders in the vertical column and the percentage of time and measurement metric shown next to each stakeholder. This reinforces the essential strategy issue of measuring performance in ways that support all stakeholder interests. One can note that if it is properly installed, NovaNet can control many of these important relationships at low cost.

Finally, one can look at the incentive systems which would support these standards and goals. What type of bonuses should be paid? Cash? Shares? Options? For what elements? One can ask what the class thinks about the incentive systems at the different regional levels. Area and division managers receive bonuses based on 50% for profit, 30% for retention, and 20% for other contributions. District managers receive 30% for "productivity," 30% for total billable units vs. budget, 30% for retention, and 10% for other activities. How appropriate are these? Would MBO goals be more appropriate? Why? How measured? To what extent can executives control the elements they are measured against? How should these standards be reflected in the bonuses or standards for therapists? If there is not a congruence at all levels, what is likely to happen? Some lively and useful discussions about the congruence of goals, performance measurements, and incentive systems to match stakeholder requirements can be achieved around these issues.

Because the organization is a professional organization, one should try to design metrics as much as possible to be "customer-based" and "professional standard-based." If these two forces are reflected in standards, one can delegate extensively in a professional environment. In fact, such standards are the key enablers allowing an "inverted organization" to operate.

NovaNet

NovaNet is a critical portion of NovaCare's strategy. As was noted, its information capacities may be NovaCare's most unique economy of scale. A most interesting discussion can develop around the question, "What should be the principal strategic contributions of NovaNet? How can NovaNet be best implemented to achieve these strategic goals?" Students will immediately jump to the operational or efficiency aspects of NovaNet in eliminating clerical time for therapists, accelerating billing cycles, and perhaps even planning transportation and therapeutic programs for therapists. However, if one keeps asking what other truly strategic potentials exist for NovaNet, some interesting suggestions will emerge. Again, one can go back to the stakeholder analysis and show how NovaNet can support each important stakeholder. For the therapist, it can eliminate burdensome paperwork, free up time for patient care, help in time planning, present menus for specific therapeutic ailments, eliminate time-consuming manual systems and telephone call reporting. NovaNet could also track whether therapists were spending adequate time on other "non-therapeutic" activities. And through electronic mail capabilities, it could allow each therapist to communicate successful new approaches for treatment to other therapists.

For the payers, NovaNet would provide accurate documentation, matching treatments to eligibility and coverage requirements, higher accuracy of inputs, and more accurate presentation of data in the form desired. Further, if properly implemented, NovaNet could track progress during the therapy cycle, thus demonstrating that favorable outcomes were actually achieved from treatments given.

From the care institution's viewpoint, NovaNet could provide accurate reports on time spent and results achieved by each therapist. It could eliminate the extremely expensive processes of reporting to all the different insurance groups and give the institution periodic reports on effectiveness against which it could compare its own therapists' performance.

From the investor's viewpoint, NovaNet could offer substantial potentials for profitability. The critical element in NovaCare's profitability is the ratio between billable time and total compensation to therapists. A 35% cushion now exists which could be captured for efficiency purposes by better planning and utilization of clinician time, especially if tied in with appropriate incentive systems.

From the patient's viewpoint, NovaNet could ensure that patients received the most current treatment available, that their progress was adequately tracked, and that new knowledge concerning better procedures was immediately implemented throughout NovaCare's system. This implies that NovaNet be designed to pick up and communicate new procedures throughout the system. It should have built-in artificial intelligence or "applied intelligence" systems which capture actual outcomes throughout the system and compare these with different therapeutic routines. If there were any drugs or other pharmaceuticals administered as a portion of the therapy, NovaNet could track whether these were accurately prescribed, and compare these with hospital records to ensure they were administered as intended.

What other strategic uses could NovaNet be designed to support? Probably the most important of these is the capacity of NovaNet to track outcomes. All health care system payers are becoming more concerned that patients' well-being is improved by treatments. They also want to make sure that the most current and appropriate treatments are provided throughout the system. These are quality control measures of extreme importance. NovaCare can clearly track all of this in the hospital or nursing home environment. If the patient is then sent home, it might be possible to obtain some further measures of progress to justify treatment in the future. Since NovaCare has more such data about its patients than anyone in the world, it should be able to fine-tune its systems better. Consequently, it should increase its capacity to serve patients and its institutional customers with demonstrably higher quality. This could be a crucial strategic positioning issue for NovaCare.

In addition, by measuring and tracking activity in real time, NovaNet should allow NovaCare to have wider spans of control. It is crucial to measure both activities and outcomes at the smallest replicable level in order to be able to plan and control activities while increasing spans of control. Spans can also be extended by decreasing the amount of time area and district managers have to observe performance directly in order to verify activity and quality levels. As NovaCare develops this capability, it might have a service that is salable to its own customers for a fee. Its information bases could allow institutional internal units to benchmark their performance against NovaCare's for a fee. Are there other potential gains from NovaNet? How should the system be designed for maximum flexibility in the future? Clearly, NovaCare cannot anticipate all of the new ailments or procedures which may occur in the future. How can NovaNet be best designed for strategic flexibility, especially the possibility that NovaCare may take on new therapeutic classes. This is a good point for the professor to note that the information system should be designed to capture and automatically update the knowledge base throughout a company's entire system. This tends to provide a competitive edge for larger units, instantly captures experience curve effects, and leverages the intellectual resources of these concerns. If NovaCare has the largest size and does have the highest quality therapists, this adds continuously to its competitive advantage and can provide a distinctive maintainable competitive edge.

SUMMARY OF OUTCOMES

On June 4, 1991 NovaCare and Rehab Systems Company announced a merger in which Rehab Systems' shareholders received 3 million shares of NovaCare common stock valued at $32 1/8 per share. Rehab Systems had filed an initial public offering, which it canceled in response to the NovaCare offer. Rehab Systems' caseload offered a greater diversity of rehabilitation patients to NovaCare and reduced its concentration on Medicare-based revenues to below 70%. It further geographically dispersed NovaCare's distribution system. NovaCare became the largest provider of contract rehabilitation therapy services to the health care industry and the only provider of such services on a national basis.

Net revenues increased 52% for the quarter ended September 30, 1991 (after restatement for the merger with Rehab Systems) to $69,950,000 in that quarter. Gross margin for the quarter increased by 58% to $20,552,000 or a 29% gross profit margin. This improvement was based on the addition of 348 therapists and an extremely high productivity rate. John Foster also noted, "The consolidation of administrative functions, especially human resources and finance, will generate attractive economies of scale." By the end of October 21, 1991, NovaCare had begun operating seven free-standing rehabilitation hospitals and six transitional care units.

On November 18, 1991 NovaCare announced a plan to merge with Orthopedic Services, Inc., which would become a wholly owned subsidiary of NovaCare. Orthopedic Services, Inc. was the largest provider of patient care services in the orthotic and prosthetic rehabilitation segment, operating in 104 patient care centers in 20 states. President Dr. Arnold Renschler of NovaCare said, "The transaction allows NovaCare to broaden its markets to orthotic and prosthetic patients currently served by independent providers at our rehab hospitals and in customers' nursing homes. Moreover, NovaCare's Medicare dependency declined from approximately 76% of revenues to 63% of revenues." At this point in time, NovaCare operated seven comprehensive medical rehab hospitals, one hospital-based rehabilitation unit, and six community-based transitional care programs. Orthopedic Services was the largest provider in the United States. of patient care services in the orthotic and prosthetic rehabilitation segment of the health care services industry. Orthotic rehabilitation involved the design, fabrication, and fitting of custom-made braces and support devices. Prosthetic rehabilitation involved the fabrication and fitting of custom-made artificial limbs.

In early 1992, the Health Care Financing Administration (HCFA) required that all hospital and care units above a certain size have rehabilitation care capabilities which met federal standards. This regulation applied specifically to nursing homes. If the home did not have a resident facility, it had to provide a written plan for such care to HCFA.

In late 1991, *Business Week* noted: "Foster continues to add diversity to his rehab holdings." In August, NovaCare's $100 million acquisition of Rehab System brought with it 7 rehabilitation hospitals. The deal marked NovaCare's entry into the bricks and mortar mainstream of rehab. "Foster Management was also pushing ahead with investments in Rehab Clinics, which plans to build a chain of storefront facilities offering physical and occupational therapy on an outpatient basis."

Business Week continued, "Will Foster succeed over the next decade in assembling his disparate pieces into the Humana of Rehab? Any venture of such ambition faces prohibitive odds. [Yet] not a single one of his limited partners has pulled out of Foster Management's funds. In addition to the time-honored economics of consolidation, NovaCare benefits from low . . . overhead; in essence, it is a company without branch offices. With its large fungible workforce, NovaCare can staff more cost effectively than can health care institutions themselves, pay its employees higher salaries on average than they made on their own, and still earn 35% on equity."

In April 1992, Smith Barney Research noted, "In NovaCare, Foster has created an infrastructure to support and organize rehabilitation professionals who operate in an industry that is characterized by: (1) a high degree of fragmentation; (2) an insufficient supply of certified clinical professionals; (3) inadequate professional management; (4) unsophisticated systems utilization; (5) limited access to capital; and (6) an overwhelming diversity of treatments and technologies. NovaCare has been a pioneer in finding solutions to each of these issues, which historically have been barriers to growth in the industry. The result is that NovaCare benefits all involved parties . . . ."

The year 1995 marked NovaCare's tenth anniversary. Despite the fact that net income before merger and other non-recurring items dropped by 36% in fiscal 1995, management expressed confidence in its ability to make the necessary adjustments to resume the company's growth. The 1995 Annual Report stated that NovaCare was "the leading post-acute rehabilitation company in the United States and the nation's largest employer of rehabilitation professionals. NovaCare's 10,000 clinicians treat nearly 40,000 patients per day in nursing homes, outpatient rehabilitation centers, orthotic and prosthetic care centers, and hospitals."

NovaCare also stated that its long-term strategy was to maintain its position as the largest provider of low-cost, clinically excellent, medical rehabilitation services outside the medical rehabilitation hospital setting. "The company's strategy is based on the belief that: (a) these services will continue to experience steady or growing demand because, in the long term, health care payer cost-containment efforts are likely to drive patients toward lower-cost services outside the medical rehabilitation hospital setting, (b) the continued aging of the population will increase the demand for medical rehabilitation services, as the elderly consume a disproportionate amount of rehabilitation care, (c) purchasers of medical rehabilitation services will increase their emphasis on clinical outcomes in the selection of rehabilitation providers, (d) substantial cost reductions in the delivery of rehabilitation services will result from clinical improvements and innovation, (e) larger providers of rehabilitation services are better positioned to provide clinical leadership, realize economies of scale to contain costs, attract quality management personnel, and train and recruit therapists, and (f) rehabilitation care is not capital intensive, allowing for internal growth without the use of substantial capital resources."

A restructuring of the contract services division in 1994 had destabilized relationships with clinicians, managers, and customers leading to increased therapist and customer turnover and lower therapist productivity. In addition, the industry as a whole faced serious challenges: planned adoption of salary equivalency rates to limit Medicare reimbursement for certain types of therapy, some larger nursing homes choosing to employ their own therapists, managed care payers driving prices and utilization down, and continued consolidation in the nursing home industry. Nonetheless, NovaCare was the largest contract therapy provider to the long-term care industry with approximately 13% share of a $4 billion market.

Through a national network of 400 centers, NovaCare was also the largest provider of freestanding outpatient rehabilitation services in the United States, with a 3% share of a $7 billion market growing at 4-6% per year. In the $1 billion orthotic and prosthetic services market, NovaCare held the largest share (8%) with services provided by 324 practitioners in 125 patient care centers. The company had recently established a separate division focusing on the delivery of management and consulting services to health care and long-term care institutions including subacute program development and management and nursing facility rehabilitation program management and consulting.

During fiscal 1995, NovaCare completed the roll-out of its NovaNet PLUS, which supports therapists, customers, and managers with enhanced analytical capabilities and record keeping, including patient outcomes tracking. NovaCare received extensive national media attention for a breakthrough in prosthetics—a device that gives amputees the ability to feel pressure and sense hot and cold. In April 1995, a little over a year after it had purchased Rehabilitation Hospital Corporation of America with its five hospitals, NovaCare sold its 11 rehabilitation hospitals to HEALTHSOUTH Corporation for $243,000.

The Orbital Engine Company (OEC) case is an example of the lengthy process involved in a major technological innovation. It illustrates the importance of good negotiation skills to secure an adequate return on the sale of intellectual property. It is also a good case to examine the nature of a company's strategy and to ask the well-known question "what business is the company in?" At the end of the case, management has still not succeeded in having its technology adopted for production engines although there are hopeful signs that some of the licensees are close to introducing such cars on the market.

The Sarich saga has been a long one and over the years many observers became skeptical about whether the engine would ever be commercialized. It will be judged an unequivocal success only when the technology is actually used in substantial numbers of car and other engine applications. Sarich and BHP have persevered, and in the 1991 financial year it earned more than $28 million from the sale of intellectual property with the promise of much more to come in future years. It was the best performer on the Australian stock market during 1990 and became the largest company in Western Australia in terms of market capitalization.

Regardless of whether or not students accept the engine as a success, there is much to learn from the case about the process of technological innovation and commercializing intellectual property.

Case Description

In the early 1970s a young inventor, Ralph Sarich, started with a dream of developing a more efficient internal combustion engine based on an orbiting (as opposed to rotating) impeller. His second prototype of the orbital engine was featured on national television, leading to the participation in the venture of Australia's largest industrial company, BHP. The early years consisted of improving the orbital engine and seeking ways to market this invention. Early agreements with Australian companies such as James Kirby and Victa-Sunbeam which produced lawn mowers, were not successful. These companies insisted on duplicating much of his work and went off on what Sarich viewed were unproductive tangents.

After his early experiences with local companies, Sarich became convinced that he had to sign up the large car makers to use his engine first, and then the rest of the industry would follow. Getting through the corporate doors of General Motors and Ford, and getting them to take him seriously, took persistence and hard work. It soon became clear that he would have to develop and test his engine technology to a very advanced stage before they would be interested. He was warned early on that he would need extremely good patent protection on his intellectual property, or else the car makers would bypass him and use the technology anyway. The industry was not used to paying royalties to inventors, and returns on new technology were typically embedded in the price paid for components and equipment sourced by the car makers.

Sarich persisted and built up an outstanding R&D team and a sophisticated automotive research facility. By the early 1980s the orbital engine was refined to a stage where the car makers started to consider it seriously. At this stage the Company developed a novel fuel injection system and associated electronic mixing and ignition controls which, combined with conventional engines, led to technology which was even more attractive than its orbital engine. In particular, a 2-stroke engine using the Orbital Combustion Process (OCP) was significantly superior to the best conventional 4-stroke engines on the market. The new engine was significantly lighter and had greater fuel efficiency than normal engines and could meet tough environmental exhaust emission standards. Because a 2-stroke engine need not use a camshaft or inlet and outlet valves, the new OCP engine also had about 400 fewer parts than a conventional engine, making it cheaper to manufacture and longer lasting.

The cost of switching to the new 2-stroke engine for a car maker would be much less and present fewer uncertainties compared to the orbital engine which was shelved in 1983 with OEC concentrating on developing and selling its OCP 2-stroke engine and the OCP combustion technology.

The case documents the lengthy process of development, testing, demonstrations, and negotiations which formed part of the process the company employed to persuade the car makers to adopt this new technology. The case also hints at some counterplays of stalling, media disinformation, and attempts at bypassing the technology which OEC claimed has been used against it.

At the time of writing the case and these notes, no OCP engine has yet been used in any cars on the market. There are increasing signs that the testing programs of Ford and General Motors are at a stage where they could be introducing the engine into the market soon after 1992. Until this actually happens, the observer must reserve final judgment. OEC has in the meantime generated a substantial income from royalties on its test engines and provisional licenses. Its revenue from royalties in 1991 exceeded A$28 million and its cumulative income to date was more than A$110 million. Management of the company was confident that revenues would rise sharply once the car makers adopted its technology. It was listed on the Australian and New York stock exchanges and the market value of its shares exceeded one billion Australian dollars.

TEACHING PLAN

Teaching Approaches

The OEC case is suitable for class discussions in courses on strategic management, technological innovation, and negotiation. The case can also be used as a major assignment.

Students or groups of students can be asked to prepare negotiation strategies for both OEC and say, a major motor car company, as an assignment or for class discussion. However, the case is not well suited to a major role play exercise. Sarich's persistence through an almost endless series of negotiation sessions over twenty years cannot be replicated in an exercise of gaining the best deal from one or a couple of face-to-face bargaining sessions. A better exercise would be to have groups of students develop and discuss various negotiation strategies for the two sides.

Questions for Case Preparation and Discussion

1. What business is the Orbital Engine Company in?

2. If Sarich asked you for advice in his early days, what would you have advised him?

3. If BHP had not backed Sarich, how would you have advised him to proceed?

4. Sarich insisted on targeting the large motor car companies such as General Motors and Ford. Would it have been better to gain an entry with smaller niche type engines, such as lawn mowers and stationary pump engines?

5. Should OEC become a manufacturer of engines and, if so, to what extent?

6. Is OEC a role model for Australian innovation, or a unique case?

7. To what extent can models of innovation be applied to the OEC case?

What Business is the Orbital Engine Company In?

While it may seem a dated question to ask, it is nevertheless very topical in the OEC case. In Australia much of the media and political debate about Sarich's invention centered around the manufacture of engines. Having invented an engine, it was generally assumed that his aim would be to manufacture and sell engines. However, Sarich was clear from an early stage that he was in the business of developing and selling intellectual property. This has remained his principal aim, while also pursuing a number of supporting activities such as an initial engine manufacturing facility in Michigan and joint ventures for the production of fuel injection devices and electronic chips for his combustion process.

The question remained whether royalties would be sufficient to provide a return for the many years of work and funds invested in OEC. This was the challenge Sarich faced, particularly in an industry where intellectual property often came bundled with the components sourced by the car makers. Much of the case revolves around his efforts to persuade the motor car companies and others such as outboard engine manufacturers to pay an adequate royalty for the technology. In 1989 and 1990 the returns of this strategy started to become evident and the stock market valued OEC shares in excess of A$1 billion.

Sarich did proceed with a medium-sized engine manufacturing plant. He was keen to be involved in some manufacturing, particularly in Australia. However, from the start, the engine manufacture venture was more a pump-priming move to facilitate the adoption process, than to become a major manufacturer of engines. The plant would also give OEC direct information about the process and costs associated with engine manufacturing, which could be used in further negotiations with car makers. Sarich was unable to gain support from the Australian government, and he went instead to the United States where the State of Michigan was willing to provide substantial incentives for the first OCP engine plant.

It is worth exploring with students how far OEC should move into engine manufacture. The capital cost for the Michigan plant is large for the small Orbital Engine Company, and yet its capacity of the plant at 250,000 engines per year is tiny by industry standards. To make a significant impact in the industry, the company would have to obtain and invest huge amounts of capital. In addition, Sarich would be moving away from his core competence of invention and R&D into large-scale manufacturing, a tough competitive area he knew little about. All the major car makers manufacture their own engines. They typically see it as an important part of their core technology. OEC had enough trouble selling its technology and it would be much more difficult to persuade the car makers to stop their own engine manufacture and buy engines from OEC. If Sarich wanted the industry to adopt his technology it would be far better to sell the technology and let them concentrate on manufacturing where they already have the investment and the skills.

For those students who assumed that he should manufacture engines, and that until he did so he was not successful, one might ask, why stop at the engine, why not build a whole car? Most would realize that this would be too ambitious for the small inventor. However, the same argument also applies to the manufacture of engines.

Students should also realize that the relative bargaining power of OEC changes significantly when the engine plant comes into production. On the one hand, it will make it easier for car makers to adopt the engines for minor model lines. The opportunity cost to OEC of holding out for its bargaining terms has now jumped substantially, and management will be under increased time pressure to conclude deals with car makers to adopt the technology. However, OEC now has an opportunity to embed its royalties into the delivered price of its engines, thus bypassing the whole process of pricing and selling the intellectual property separately.

Technological Innovation

The sequence in the development of the orbital engine differs from the typical academic models for technological innovation. The invention did not start in a research laboratory, and it did not proceed in an orderly procession from laboratory bench to pilot plant or prototype to introduction into the market place.

Rather it started from the mind of an inventor who constructed a working prototype using standard machine tools. The laboratory research came at a later stage, once the potential of the invention became sufficiently interesting to attract funds for this kind of work. Research was not the source of the invention, but rather served to make the original invention viable, both technologically and economically.

The sequence, greatly simplified, was this: invention followed by demonstration followed by research followed by negotiation for the sale of intellectual property. The instructor may reflect that this sequence is not uncommon in industry, particularly for the development of many new consumer and industrial products.

It also points to a different role for the scientist and research engineer in industry. It is often assumed that the new inventions and discoveries will originate in the laboratory. Invention and an eye for novelty can occur in any prepared mind, not only those busy with advanced technological research. Many novel ideas occur in boundary-spanning activities where a person encounters problems and opportunities in new settings. The role of the scientist and the engineer in these instances is thus not so much to invent or originate the novel product or concept, but rather to apply professional knowledge and skills to refine and develop it to a level acceptable to the market place.

Displacing the Internal Combustion Engine (ICE)

The motor car industry is a favorite area for inventors, and there is no shortage of attempts to displace or improve on the internal combustion engine (ICE). Steam engines, electric drives, the Stirling heat engine, diesel, turbine, and two-stroke engines have all been tried at various times. The most recent radical engine design seriously considered was the Wankel rotary engines produced for some years by the NSU Company of Germany and more successfully by Mazda for the niche sports car market.

In spite of repeated attempts to displace it, the 4-stroke ICE survives as the overwhelming choice for motor cars. Its basic design has not changed since the early part of the century, and it has constantly been improved over the years.

An interesting exercise for students would be to develop, on behalf of motor car companies, the cases for and against adopting a new engine technology, using the original Orbital and the new Orbital Combustion Process (OCP) two-cycle engines as examples.

The experience curve concept provides a useful framework to understand the immensity of development, refinement, and testing work which has been invested over the years in the ICE. To this must be added the sunk costs and enormous levels of capital committed to the traditional ICE engine, not only by the manufacturers, but also by the many repair and maintenance shops and garages around the world.

The risk for a motor car manufacturer to adopt a new engine design is very high indeed, no matter how good it might appear at the testing stage. If the engine gives trouble in the field, the manufacturer may be liable for very considerable sums in recall and repair efforts, as well as the loss of credibility in the marketplace. The manufacturer could conceivably lose its position in the industry and find it very hard if not impossible to catch up again. In addition, the service and maintenance industry are tooled up and oriented towards ICEs, thus representing a second level of resistance to change. Barriers to entry for a new design are very large indeed.

The development of the Wankel engine was an extremely costly example of an attempt to introduce a new engine design. General Motors is said to have lost about a billion dollars on developing the Wankel engine before they abandoned it, and it is reasonable to assume that they were in no mood to embark on many similar experiments at the time Sarich tried to interest them in his new engine.

The Development of the Orbital Technologies

Sarich started out with the orbital design for an engine. To develop the engine to a stage where the technology could be sold, he built a well-equipped and sophisticated R&D laboratory with a staff of about 200 engineers and technical trades personnel. This group refined the basic engine and were also very productive in developing a range of related engine technologies over the years.

The fortunes of OEC were thus not tied to the success or failure of the original orbital design, but rather to the ability of the R&D team to develop salable automotive and related technology. This change from a single invention to a technological competency enabled the company to shelve the original orbital engine and still continue on course. In this sense it was different from many other "hi-tech" start-up companies of the mid-'80s whose survival depended on the success of one idea or invention.

The fuel injection system was originally developed to improve the performance of the orbital engines. By avoiding the high compression injection mode of existing systems, OEC engineers used air to atomize the fuel and obtain a fine mist with very small particle size of fuel in the fuel/air mixture. Coupled with further work on mixing chambers and electronic controls, this system was able to achieve a more complete combustion of the fuel than in existing engines. This provided dual benefits of improved fuel efficiency and improved emission composition as described in the case. As the case describes, the fuel injection system could be combined with existing two-cycle engine technology to produce advantages very similar to the orbital engine. This became the focus of the company's marketing efforts and it has proved to be much more acceptable to motor car manufacturers.

OEC has continued to develop a variety of technologies around the fuel injection device, including retro-fit devices for two-cycle engines, electronic control units, catalytic converters for emission control of the OCP engine, adapting Orbital technologies to the needs of small engine producers, and the development of multi-fuel capability to use diesel and methanol as fuels in the OCP engines.

Marketing Options

After he had built his first prototype of the radically new orbital engine, Sarich had to decide how best to commercialize his invention. He had several options to consider.

For example, he could have tried to sell his invention as such to a motor car manufacturer for further development. Several well-meaning persons in fact advised Sarich in the early years to take his invention to General Motors Holden or Ford Australia. Chances are that even if they were disposed to purchase what at that time was a very early prototype, it is problematical whether they would have developed it much further. The R&D activities of remote subsidiaries in far-off countries are seldom oriented towards the development of radical innovations, and even if they were, they still had to sell the idea to their parent company. Very few companies have successfully institutionalized innovation and, left to the normal organizational processes, radical ideas from the "provinces" would stand little chance of succeeding in the head office politics of the large bureaucratic car companies.

The support of BHP was crucial to the ability of Sarich to persist with the development and marketing of the engine. Without backing of a large company such as BHP, Sarich would have found it very difficult, if not impossible, to have continued with the development necessary to commercialize the invention.

Even with the support of BHP, options such as full engine manufacture or the development of his own motor car would have been possible only on a small scale as a specialized niche manufacturer with a very uncertain future.

OEC's Marketing Strategy

Sarich decided at an early stage that the best course would be to develop the technology to a stage where he could license it on a non-exclusive basis to the various motor car companies and other engine manufacturers.

He was also convinced that he had to sell the technology in the first instance to a major car maker such as General Motors in the United States. After that he was sure that the rest would follow. Sarich felt very strongly about this strategy and did not seek easier entry routes such as smaller volume specialized applications for lawn mowers or stationary pump engines where the cost of experimentation and failure would not be as high as in the car industry. One wonders whether he would not have progressed more rapidly had he used such applications as a field testing method for his engines. In the very early days of the orbital engine, Sarich attempted to sell his technology to James Kirby and Victa-Sunbeam, which produced lawn mowers. It is possible that the problems he encountered with these firms convinced him that he had to go for the top car makers. Eventually, Sarich deviated from this strategy by licensing his OCP technology to outboard marine engine manufacturers. This was too good an opportunity to miss and by that time he was already well advanced in negotiations with GM and Ford.

Once he settled on the bold strategy to focus on the major car makers, he had to ensure that:

(a)   the technology was developed to the point where they would seriously consider it;
(b)   the intellectual property was suitably protected so that users had no option but to pay a suitable royalty; and that
(c)   he had the negotiation skills to ensure an adequate royalty for the technology.

Protecting the Intellectual Property

Several authors have commented on the difficulties of successfully appropriating the profit or economic rent deriving from intellectual property.[1] Patenting is often of questionable benefit to inventors and innovators. Many small companies have found it better to concentrate on getting their products to the market than spend valuable resources on patenting. However, in this case patenting was crucial to the success of the venture. OEC's business revolved around successfully selling its intellectual property. All other activities, such as the manufacture of the engine and related devices, were ancillary to getting the large car makers to adopt the technology in volume and to pay royalties on each engine they produced.

The company did not scrimp on patenting. They sought not only to protect the basic inventions and concepts as thoroughly as they could, but they also built several protective layers of patents around their basic ones in a form of peripheral protection and for early warning signals. Sarich would be alerted at the earliest possible moment about any rivals working in the field and seeking to bypass his patents. By June 30, 1991, OEC had registered a total of 504 patents in 8 different areas of engine technology as shown in Table 1.

TABLE 1

**PATENT AND PATENT APPLICATIONS FOR THE OCP ENGINE
AS OF 30 JUNE 1991**

	Number of Patent and Patent Applications
Fuel Metering	104
Fuel & Air Control Systems	77
Lubrication Systems	7
Engine Construction	57
Engine Management	97
Fuel Injectors	149
Exhaust Systems	42
Air Compressor	15
Total OCP Patents	548

Source: Orbital Engine Corporation, 1991 *Annual Report.*

OEC was also protected to some extent by the fact that its technology was no longer a single invention but had a substantial tacit component. Over the years it had developed a sophisticated combustion process and incorporated this into a complex engine system. The years of experience and accumulated know-how gained in the designing, making, and testing of the engine could not easily be copied or expropriated. Much of this cannot be patented, but can be transmitted over a period of time only by the OEC team working together with the licensee. Through on-going research and development, Sarich is constantly upgrading and maintaining his competitive capabilities. This is good protection in the long run, complementing the patents with their limited legal and even shorter technological shelf life.

Selling the Intellectual Property

Sarich had to establish how much to charge for the intellectual property, and then devise negotiating strategies to persuade the car and other engine manufacturers to agree to his terms and conditions. He considered that between $30 to $40 per engine would be a reasonable royalty, considering that the OCP engine could save car makers between $400 and $500 per car.

It would appear that the motor car industry is not a regular buyer of intellectual property in the form of licenses. When it does happen, royalties tend to be low, seldom more than a dollar per item. Considering that General Motors sells about 7 million cars a year, even small unit royalties can quickly mount up to large sums of money. The car makers had many doubts and displayed great reluctance to consider new engine technology. They were also confronted by what they perceived as outrageous demands from the inventor. They had everything to gain by stalling the bargaining process.

Thus Sarich had to develop very sophisticated negotiating skills to effectively market the intellectual property. A not insignificant part of the process was to hold out against attempts by the motor car manufacturers and also well-meaning friends and advisers to persuade him to dramatically lower the price of the technology, or to provide incentives for early adopters of the engine.

Sarich was under pressure to show results for his investors, and year after year he had to persuade BHP and the skeptical media that his technology was indeed as good as he claimed it to be, and that it would bring substantial gains in the near future. Every year that passed without contracts signed and the engine used eroded the credibility of these claims, and made it easier for the motor car companies to press for better terms.

As time passed, OEC kept improving the technology but the original patents were also getting older year by year and closer to expiration. The company thus had to keep up an expensive program of development and patenting around the original designs to protect its technology and to extend its earning time span.

The initial rounds of agreements were not for large-scale manufacture, but rather to test the engine with an option to enter into longer-term ongoing arrangements. Thus, after the excitement of an initial agreement for a license option, a period of testing and long drawn out negotiations would commence, delaying the process even further. The testing of a new engine takes time. The client would seek to exhaustively verify the operational characteristics provided by OEC, install test engines in cars for extensive driving tests, and if serious about adopting the technology, engage in exercises of car redesign to explore the potential of the new engine. At the same time, the client companies would seek to bypass the patents and find ways of using the technology without having to pay the high royalties OEC demanded. They could take the engines apart to see if they could do reverse R&D to bypass the OEC patents.

OEC charged substantial fees and royalties for their test engines. This bold and somewhat unusual policy must have increased the adoption barriers, but there were also advantages. Apart from providing useful income (revenue up to 1991 exceeded A$110 million) this policy ensured that the testing was taken seriously by top management in the motor car companies. The decision whether to adopt a new engine technology would be taken only at the highest levels of the company, and in Sarich's view there was little point in providing test engines to the backroom R&D staff unless there was firm interest and commitment right at the top.

Several motor car companies preferred to keep their license agreements confidential for competitive and public image reasons. In some cases they modified and extended the OEC technology and exhibited it as their own development. There have even been examples where car executives publicly made disparaging remarks about the OEC engine, which received wide publicity in the media, while dealing confidentially with the company. Whether these comments were genuine views or negotiating ploys will never be known for sure, but when they occurred, Sarich and OEC executives had to once again reassure OEC's partner BHP and its shareholders about the potential and future prospects of the technology.

OEC finally reached agreements with a number of major motor car companies, including Ford and General Motors. By March 1992 the company had signed up 17 license agreements as shown in Table 2, and more were being negotiated.

Technological Innovation Takes Time

Sarich developed his prototype in 1972/73, and it took twenty years before the first production engines would be manufactured in the Michigan plant. While this appears to be a long time, particularly for impatient investors, it is not long for a major technological innovation. The first engine took about eight to ten years to develop to the point where it was treated seriously by the motor car companies. The new OCP 2-stroke engine with direct fuel injection took about three to four years to develop to a similar level, and it was ready for serious testing around 1986/87. Another four to six years for the adoption process is not unreasonable.

Figure 1, from the company's 1990 Annual Report, shows a comparison of the time taken for earlier engine innovations. Even if a certain latitude in the interpretation of the various stages of innovation is allowed for, the OEC engine development has been fast rather than slow.

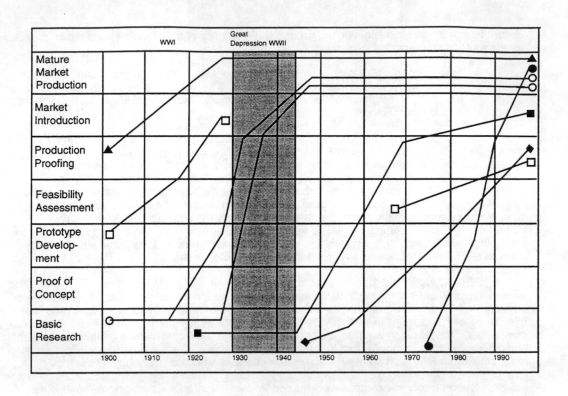

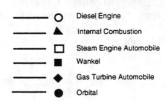

FIGURE 1

**"THE COMMERCIALIZATION OF THE OCP ENGINE HAS BEEN RAPID
IN COMPARISON TO OTHER GENERIC ENGINES"**

Source: Orbital Engine Company, *1990 Annual Report.*

TABLE 2

HISTORY OF LICENSE-RELATED AGREEMENTS
FOR OCP TECHNOLOGY

Date	Company	Type of Agreement
Dec-83	General Motors Corporation	License Option
Apr-84	Outboard Marine Corporation	License Option
Dec-84	Brunswick Corporation	License Option
Jun-86	Outboard Marine Corporation	License
Sep-86	Ford Motor Company	License Option
May-87	Walbro Corporation	License/Mfg & Joint Venture
May-87	Japanese engine manufacturer	License Option & Develop. Agreement
Jun-87	Brunswick Corporation	License
Jun-88	Ford Motor Company	License
May-89	General Motors Corporation	License
Jul-89	Bajaj Auto, India	License
Feb-90	prestige automotive company	Development Agreement
Mar-90	Honda Motor Company	License Option
May-90	motorcycle manufacturer	License
Jan-91	Fiat Auto, Italy	License
Jan-91	Outboard Marine Corporation	Expanded License
Mar-92	large automotive company	License

Source: OEC, *1991 Annual Report* and *Press Release*, March 1992.

SUBSEQUENT EVENTS

The company has continued its R&D activities and has become increasingly successful in selling its intellectual property. However, by September 1992, the time of writing the teaching notes, the technology still had not been adopted for a production car, although several companies were claimed to be very close. For example, Ford was road testing about 60 cars both in the United States and Europe.

By June 30, 1991, the company had 548 patents in 8 areas of engine technology registered, as shown in Table 1. By March 1992, seventeen license agreements had been signed as shown in Table 2. The company was earning around A$28 million a year in license fees, and hopes were high that the engine technology would soon be adopted for production cars. Exhibits I and II give key financial figures for 1990 and 1991.

In May 1992, at the age of 53, Ralph Sarich announced his intention to step down as Chief Executive of the Orbital Engine Company within two years. "I've always been emphatic about having back-ups in any specialized position and the only weakness was in my own position," said Mr. Sarich, "so I set about filling the gap and I believe that if anything happened to me today, the management and the company would not miss a beat." He also stated that he would continue to have a close involvement with the company and remain its Chairman. On July 1, 1992, the company announced that Mr. Kim Schlunke, formerly Executive Director of Engineering, would be the Group's new Managing Director.

---

[1]   The challenge of achieving returns on intellectual property is discussed by David Teece in "Profiting from Technological Innovation: Implications for Integration, Collaboration, Licensing and Public Policy," in *The Competitive Challenge: Strategies for Industrial Innovation and Renewal*, ed. David Teece, New York, Harper & Row, 1985, pp 185-219.

EXHIBIT I
ORBITAL ENGINE CORPORATION
PROFIT & LOSS ACCOUNTS EXTRACTS

	1991 ($000's)	1990 ($000's)
Revenue from trading operations	28,157	26,498
Interest income	2,695	1,302
Other income	828	727
TOTAL REVENUE	31,680	28,527
Operating profit	25,381	23,485
Income tax	6,722	6,847
Profit after tax	18,659	16,638
Acc. profit a. tax (begin. of yr.)	22,491	5,853
Acc. profit a. tax (end of yr.)	41,150	22,491

Source: Orbital Engine Company, *1991 Annual Report.*

EXHIBIT II
ORBITAL ENGINE CORPORATION
BALANCE SHEET EXTRACTS

	1991 (A$000's)	**1990** (A$000's)
Cash	32,089	6,380
Receivables	12,699	16,192
Inventories	879	385
Other	252	11
TOTAL CURRENT ASSETS	45,919	22,968
Receivables	10,856	7,473
Investments	1,402	1,402
Property, plant & equipment	19,139	12,734
Intangibles	272,567	258,321
Other	12,072	8,952
TOTAL NON-CURRENT ASSETS	316,036	288,882
TOTAL ASSETS	361,955	311,850
Creditors & borrowings	6,376	1,422
Provisions	1,427	917
TOTAL CURRENT LIABILITIES	7,803	2,339
		1
Creditors & borrowings	15,000	5,000
Provisions	14,533	8,351
TOTAL NON-CURRENT LIABILITIES	29,533	23,351
TOTAL LIABILITIES	37,336	25,690
NET ASSETS	324,619	286,160
Share Capital	143,755	136,436
Reserves	139,714	127,233
Accumulated Profits	41,150	22,491
TOTAL SHAREHOLDERS EQUITY	324,619	286,160
Shares issued & paid. (50c)	287,509,100	272,871,618

Source: Orbital Engine Company, *1991 Annual Report.*

ANDERSEN CONSULTING (EUROPE): ENTERING THE BUSINESS OF BUSINESS INTEGRATION

Case Description

Andersen Consulting is one of the largest and most successful consulting companies in the world. Focused in the area of information systems consulting, it also enjoys the reputation of being one of the best managed professional service firms in any business. The case describes the historical evolution of Andersen Consulting, and the core management processes that have contributed to the company's rapid growth and consistently high profitability.

In the 1990s, however, the company is facing a major new challenge. The information systems (IS) market is in the midst of dramatic change. Andersen's historical strengths in the systems integration (SI) business are no longer enough to meet the company's growth and profit objectives. Consistent with its tradition of pioneering new applications of IS capabilities, the company is pursuing the concept of "business integration" to help its clients build new sources of competitive advantage through integrated business, information, and people strategies.

To help clients re-engineer their businesses, Andersen must develop a range of new competencies and must integrate these competencies with its existing SI skills and resources to deliver the value proposition inherent in the business integration concept. This task of building and integrating new competencies requires some basic changes in the very management processes that have so far served as the anchors of the company's enormous successes. The case describes these new challenges and the actions Andersen is taking to respond to them.

While these challenges are being faced by the company on a worldwide basis, the case focuses on the specific situations and tasks confronting its operations in Europe.

Teaching Objectives

In spite of the fact that a growing number of MBA and executive program participants come from or seek to join professional service firms (PSFs), relatively little attention is typically paid in strategy, business policy or general management courses to the special problems and challenges of managing such companies. The primary objective of this case is to provide a broad overview of these special aspects of PSF management.

As described by David H. Maister, effective management of professional services firms depends on maintaining the right balance and coherence among four factors.

The case provides a vehicle for exploring each of these four issues as well as the interactions among them that must be managed to ensure effective functioning of such companies. While instructors can either build this framework inductively, by guiding class discussions to cover these issues one by one, or present the framework first and then use the case to illustrate each of the factors and their interactions, the objective in the first part of class discussion is to help students understand the concepts and the framework which, I believe, are particularly useful for anyone working for or with any PSF.

Teaching note copyright © 1992 INSEAD, Fontainebleau, France. This teaching note was written by Sumantra Ghoshal, Associate Professor at INSEAD, to assist instructors in classroom use of the case. It is intended to be used as a basis for class discussion rather than to illustrate either effective or ineffective handling of an administrative situation. Financial support from the INSEAD Alumni Fund European Case Program is gratefully acknowledged.

Once the need for balancing these four factors is understood, students can begin to realize the challenge Andersen Consulting is facing as it tries to broaden its market to "business integration." This broadening of the market for the firm's services changes all the other factors: the company must expand into new markets for professional workforce, it must adjust to the very different economic structure of the business of business integration and must, therefore, adapt its organizational structure to bring the overall system into balance again. Yet, at the same time, it must continue in its traditional businesses. The second part of the class discussion focuses on the tension created by these diverse demands, and the alternative ways the company can deal with these demands. The teaching objective here is to move beyond understanding of concepts to using these concepts to build judgments about administrative choices and their consequences.

For a more specialized audience, such as managers from PSF companies, the case can also be used for detailed discussions on what is perhaps the most critical management issue for such firms: how to hire, train, and develop the highest quality professionals. Andersen has a highly sophisticated system with great strengths but also perhaps some potential weaknesses. Its practices for recruitment, promotion, compensation, evaluation, counseling, training and work assignments provide an excellent backdrop for debating the pros and cons of different people and skill development approaches for PSFs. At the core of this debate lies the more general issue of how to manage learning in knowledge-intensive firms—a topic which is of increasing importance to service and manufacturing companies alike.

Figure 1
Key Issues for Management of PSFs

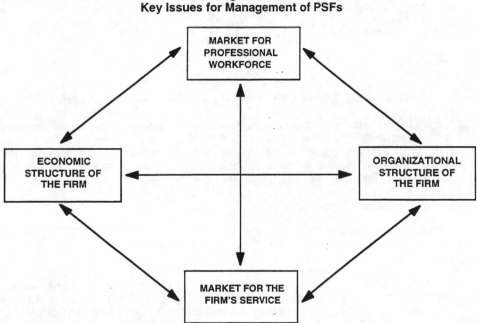

Classroom Use

The case was written for use in the Business Policy course where it is ideally positioned towards the middle of the course to bring in the special issues connected with management of PSFs. It can also be used in a course on organizational behavior (OB) or on human resource (HR) management. In an OB course, the case may be used to illustrate the special organizing challenges for professional bureaucracies and adhocracies. In an HR course, relatively more emphasis can be placed on the people development issues. Finally, the case can also be used in a service management course, to focus on professional service firms as distinct from firms providing other kinds of services.

Assignment Questions

The following questions can be assigned for students to prepare themselves for class discussions:

1. Why has Andersen Consulting been so successful?

2. How should it manage the business integration practice? Should the differences between the approaches of the U.K. and French organizations be allowed to continue?

3. How should the company respond to the stresses being created as it tries to develop its competencies in the areas of strategy and change management?

Supporting Reading

The choice of readings depends on the course in which the case issued. For a business Policy or Service Management course, I recommend David H. Maister, "Balancing the Professional Service Firm," *Sloan Management Review*, Fall 1982. For an organizational Behavior course, I suggest Henry Mintzberg, "Organization Design: Fashion or Fit?" *Harvard Business Review*, January-February 1981. While both readings are somewhat dated, they are classics and students typically enjoy reading both articles.

Teaching Plan

Question 1: Why has Andersen Consulting been so successful?

If the Maister article is assigned as pre-reading, students tend to respond in terms of the four sets of factors in Figure 1 and note how they are all in excellent balance in Andersen. Without the article, they still raised broadly the same set of issues, but without a structure. The instructor can, however, lead to a structure simply by noting the comments on separate boards, or parts of a board. Generally, discussions focus on the following:

1. The economics of Andersen's practice

Students quickly point out that a basic aspect of Andersen's business is the exceptionally high leverage of partner time. It is manifest from Exhibit 1 that, worldwide, Andersen's partner to non-partner ratio has gone up from about 1:20 to 1:30 between 1987 and 1991. Europe has an even steeper ratio; up from about 1:26 in 1987 to about 1:40 in 1991. Exhibit 5 suggests that the average ratio for PSFs is about 1:7. This is where the crux of Andersen's economic success lies: such a high leverage of partner time allows the company to remain competitive in terms of its effective hourly rate, and yet generate high income for partners and also adequate margins for satisfactory compensation to non-partners and investment in human resource and practice development.

2. Organization structure

While the case does not reveal the actual distribution of non-partners between the manager and the consultant/associate consultant levels, some reasonable estimates can be made. Two sets of facts are known: firstly, about 50 percent of professional recruits become managers and only 20 percent of managers become partners; and secondly, it takes about 6 years for a high performing professional to be promoted to the position of project manager and about 4 years for a high-performing manager to be admitted to partnership. Using these two facts and following the logic of computation in Table 5 of Maister's article, one can expect a distribution of 1:6:30 for partners: managers: consultants in Andersen (Europe) in 1991. Comparing these figures with the PSF averages provided in Exhibit 5 of the case shows the relative shape of the Andersen pyramid vis-à-vis that of a typical PSF:

Figure 2
Andersen's pyramid vs. that of a typical PSF

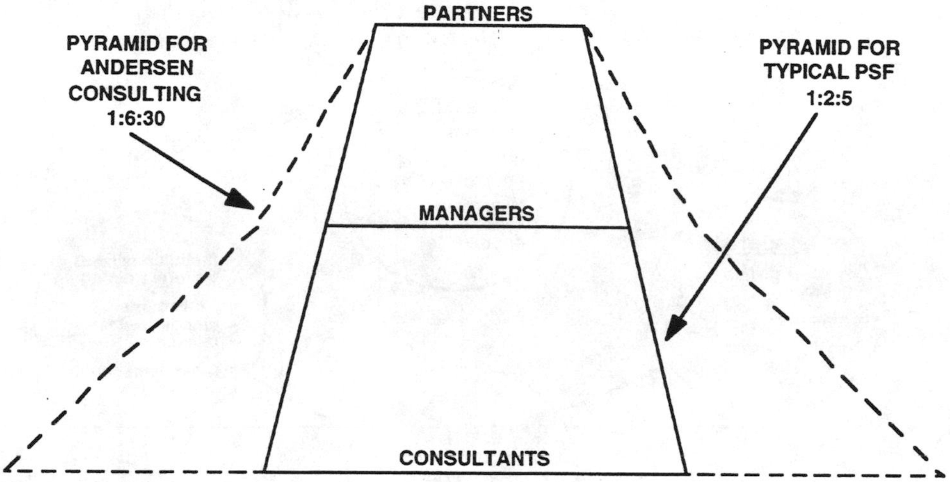

3. The IS market

The economics of Andersen's business and the resulting organization structure of the firm are directly related to the nature of the IS market. Following the "brains," "grey hair," and "procedure" classification of professional service projects described by Maister, Andersen's business is largely in the "procedure" domain. The instructor may take a little time here to elaborate the differences among these types of projects since these differences become crucial at the later stage of class discussions, when systems integration and business integration projects are contrasted. Broadly, the differences can be summarized as below:

Figure 3
Different types of professional service projects

	"BRAINS" Projects	"GREY HAIR" Projects	"PROCEDURE" Projects
1. Nature of client's problem	Unique, extremely complex, and at the forefront of profession-al/technical knowledge	"Customized" output for familiar problems	Well-recognized and familiar problems, client uses PSF for efficiency
2. PSF's requirement for success	Creativity, innovation, pioneering new approaches, concepts, or techniques	Experience with similar projects, resulting in knowledge and judgment	Availability, established systems and procedures, efficiency
3. Selling proposition	"Hire us because we are smart."	"Hire us because we have been through this before."	"Hire us because we know how to do this efficiently."

It is the "procedure" nature of Andersen's classic IS work that allows the high non-partner to partner ratio and lies at the core of the management processes that drive the company. The instructor can spend some time here to elaborate how all of Andersen's systems are tightly oriented to deliver standardized solutions effectively and efficiently to meet generic systems integration needs of its clients.

One can use the 7-S framework to illustrate this fit between Andersen's market needs and its internal organizational attributes:

Figure 4
Internal consistency of Andersen's management approach

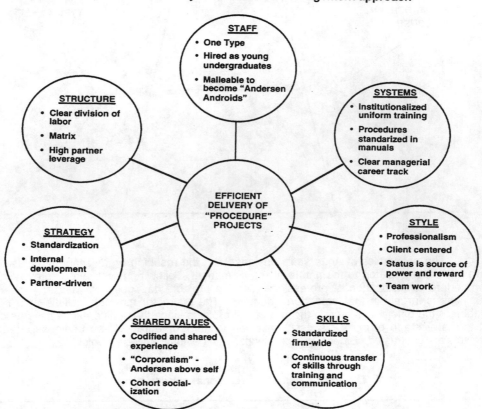

4. Professional capabilities

Finally, as for any professional service firm, Andersen's success has been due to its ability to hire, train, develop, and retain people. Once again, Andersen's HR practices provide a copybook example of a consistent set of policies and administrative systems to develop and deploy professional workers. While students will raise the issues in somewhat of a random manner, the instructor can group them as shown in Figure 5 to provide a coherent picture at the end. This part of the discussion can be expanded and elaborated in greater detail if the case is used in an OB or HR course.

Figure 5
Administrative systems for building and leveraging Andersen's professional workforce

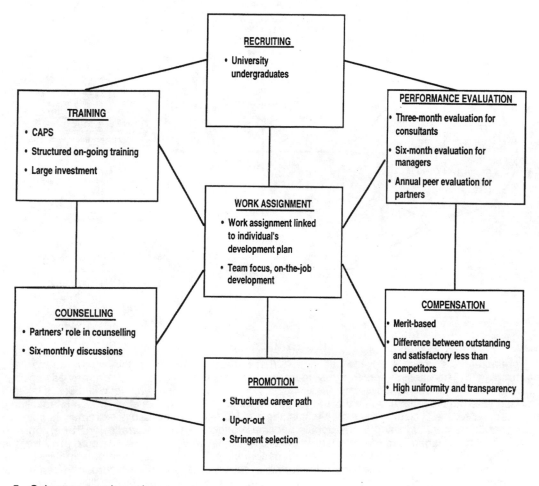

5. Coherence and consistency

Once all the four issues, viz., practice economics, organizational structure, market demands, and professional development have been discussed, the instructor can lead the discussion to the consistency and coherence among all four as a key explanation of Andersen's success (see Figure 6). By the time these four factors and their interactions are summarized, students develop a simple but clear understanding of the basic issues related to management of professional service firms. If the class has discussed other service management cases in earlier sessions, the instructor can bring those examples in for comparison and contrast. I typically compare Andersen with Saatchi and Saatchi and also with McKinsey.

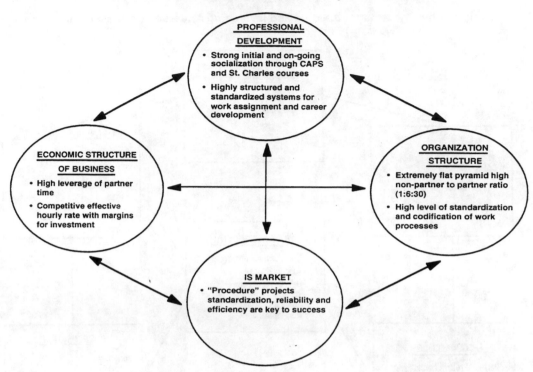

Figure 6
Andersen's success formula: consistency and coherence

Once students fully understand the factors that have undergirded Andersen's phenomenal success, I ask the question, "What is necessary to keep this wonderful machine running?" The question forces the students to think about the conditions that are assumed in Andersen's management systems, the violation of which will make the model collapse. It takes a little time but students ultimately come to the realization that a high level of growth is absolutely essential for the system to function. As it is, the attrition rate of Andersen is extremely high; while about 50 percent of joining professionals become managers (about average for PSFs), only 20 percent of managers become partners (against the PSF average of about 50 percent). Also, the total period of 9-12 years required for a high performing professional to reach partnership level is high by PSF standards. Therefore, any further steepening of the pyramid through even higher attrition rate or longer promotion periods can severely affect the company's ability to attract and retain best talent. If these two parameters are kept at present levels, the only way the system can function is if the company <u>continues to grow at 25-35 percent per year</u>.

As this need for growth becomes clearly understood, the instructor can then raise the question, "Can Andersen expect to achieve this growth over the next five to ten years as it continues to focus on its current practice areas?"

This question leads to a discussion of the IS market. It is clear that competition in Andersen's practice area is becoming more intense—with hardware suppliers like IBM and DEC, custom software specialists like Cap Gemini and traditional SI vendors like Andersen converging on a collision course. At the same time, while the SI market was expected to grow at 30 percent per year in Europe, the share of consulting services in total SI revenues was becoming larger. Increasing visibility and competencies at the front-end consulting requirements, therefore, was becoming essential for protecting the more traditional and relatively standardized SI work.

It is only in this context of the need for continuing high growth in a rapidly changing and increasingly competitive market that Andersen's strategy of focusing on the "business integration" market begins to make sense. One can then move to a more detailed discussion of the implications of this strategy by asking the question:

Question 2: Why can Andersen not continue with its existing proven success formula? What is different about business integration?

Students tend to quite rapidly identify some of the differences between the requirements of the business integration practice vis-à-vis Andersen's traditional bread and butter business. However, while they quickly identify specific areas of difference, it is only when the points are aggregated on the board that they begin to ask if it is not a fundamentally different business.

The distinctions between the two businesses can be captured in the form of the following table:

Figure 7
What is different about business integration

	Andersen's traditional IS practice	The needs and success criteria in the business integration market
1. Nature of projects	• "Procedure" • Customers demand reliability and efficiency	• "Brains" and "Grey Hair" • Customers demand creativity, innovation, and unique expertise
2. Economic structure	• High leverage of partner time • Relatively low effective hourly rate	• Greater partner involvement in projects • Relatively high effective hourly rate
3. Organization structure	• Steep pyramid—high non-partner to partner ratio • High levels of codification and standardization of work procedures	• Relatively lower non-partner to partner ratio • Unique features in each project—relatively more "one off" solutions
4. Professional development	• One type of people and skills • Uniform and standardized training for all • Standardized and single track careers • Uniform compensation systems • "One firm" culture	• Different types of people and skills • Differentiated training and development needs • Dual career tracks may be necessary • Compensation must match external professional benchmarks for different skills • "Pluralist" culture may be necessary

391

To surface all the issues in this table through a normal case discussion process will take a significant amount of time—between 20 and 40 minutes, depending on the group. Should available time permit such a discussion, it can be very rewarding since it is here that the participants get some insights into the different demands for different kinds of professional service practices. However, in a normal single session format, the instructor may simply present these differences in a pre-prepared overhead transparency as one view and invite debate and discussion on this view. While this increases lecture time, it brings the issues out in much less time and the participants may often prefer such an "efficient" process and get almost equal value in terms of developing their understanding about the management of PSFs.

At this stage, the instructor can initiative the next round of discussions by asking the question:

Question 3: What should the company do?

Students tend to be polarized in their views about how Andersen should approach the business integration market. One group advocates a completely separate set-up for building the strategy and change management practices—the French model, but even more extreme. Others believe that to differentiate itself from competitors, Andersen must internally integrate IT with strategy, change management and operations capabilities, even though it would require a fundamental change in the company's management processes and administrative systems. In other words, they support the UK model but claim that it is too diluted and not sufficiently radical.

I prefer to take up the first view first. The arguments of those who recommend a clear split between IT and strategy/change management focus on the following three issues:

1. Andersen's historical success has been built on the concept of teamwork. There are no individual stars, and clients hire Andersen, not any of its individual employees. This internal cooperation and subjugation of individual egos to belong to an institution lies at the core of Andersen's strategy in the IS market. In the foreseeable future, business integration will provide only a small share of the company's revenues, and it must rely on its traditional business for its bread and butter. The company must, therefore, fully protect the norms of homogeneity, equity, and standardization. The only way to do so would be to build the strategy and change management practices completely outside the existing organizational and administrative frameworks.

2. At the same time, given the very different professional norms, skills, and expectations of strategy and change management consultants, Andersen will not be able to attract and retain the best talents in these fields if they make these professionals subject to Andersen's existing norms and practices. In fact, these skill areas need precisely the opposite norms: recruitment at all levels, diversity of skills and career paths, perhaps even a star system and its attending internal competition. So, in the interest of building strengths in these practice areas, Andersen must create a completely different administrative framework.

3. History and experience also support the claim for separation. After all, the partners in Andersen Consulting should draw some lessons from their own history of separating from the company's audit and accounting practice. The separation was inevitable, given the different logics of the two practices, and the advantages of the separation are manifest from the subsequent success of the consulting area. Precisely the same reasoning justifies clear separation of the strategy and change management areas from the existing practice.

As for how to build up the capabilities separately, opinions tend to vary within this group. A few advocate that Andersen should not try to build the new practice areas in-house but should create a strategic alliance with an existing and well-established organization such as McKinsey or BCG. Most participants disagree on the ground that such an alliance would only tie up Andersen with one player, thereby excluding the client groups of other strategy consultants. Besides, it is not clear that any strategy consultant will agree to such a proposal since most of the highly reputable and large firms are themselves building in-house IT consulting capabilities.

A majority of the group advocating separate organizations for IT and strategy/change management practices converge on the French model but suggest the need for even clearer separation between the two specialization areas. They argue for an overall Andersen organization with three key practice areas—audit and accounting, IT consulting, and strategy and change management—under the governance of a common Board of Partners (see Figure 8):

Figure 8
Structuring for clear differentiation

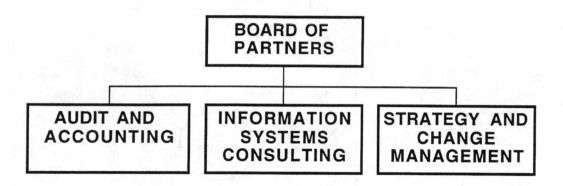

Such a clear separation, the group suggests, might provide an additional benefit. The clear need for cooperation between the IS consulting and strategy and change management practices may also lead to a greater amount of cooperation and integration between these two practices and the company's audit and accounting arm. Basically, the separation of strategy and change management from the IS group, done before there is serious acrimony, will lead to rethinking overall group level governance and coordination issues.

At this point, the instructor can turn to the group that has been advocating a more integrated organization by asking them the question, "Why do you disagree with this analysis and recommendation?"

The primary objection of this group tends to focus on the assumption that Andersen can protect its current IS practice, as is. These students point to the statement of Terry Neil at the very introduction of the case: Andersen's success has been built on its ability to stay ahead of the commoditization envelope. The traditional IS business of Andersen is fast becoming a commodity in which low cost will be the primary success requirement. Also, competitors like IBM, DEC, EDS (who have acquired SD-SCION) and Cap Gemini will attack this business with their expanded and relatively more multi-dimensional skill base. Andersen will be squeezed from low-cost small vendors at the bottom and high capability integrated solution providers at the top. Under this scenario, Andersen will fail to protect the growth and profitability necessary for the "Andersen Way" to function. As a result, efforts to protect and isolate the current practice will lead to a complete unraveling of the system they claim.

In the view of this group, however, the round of change the company is confronting in the early 1990s is qualitatively different from earlier changes. Moving from computerized payroll systems to integrated accounting and payroll systems on to the current practice of System Integration dealt with increasingly more complex projects but did not require a fundamental change in Andersen's business logic, and therefore, in its basic administrative systems and processes. The change in the 1990s, on the other hand, would require the company to respond to a fundamentally different business requirement. Andersen can no longer rely on "procedure" projects; it has to learn to deal simultaneously with "procedure," "brains," and "grey hair" projects.

While this point can be made with different degrees of clarity, the instructor can structure (perhaps with some editorializing) the argument as follows:

Figure 9
Need for building multidimensional capabilities

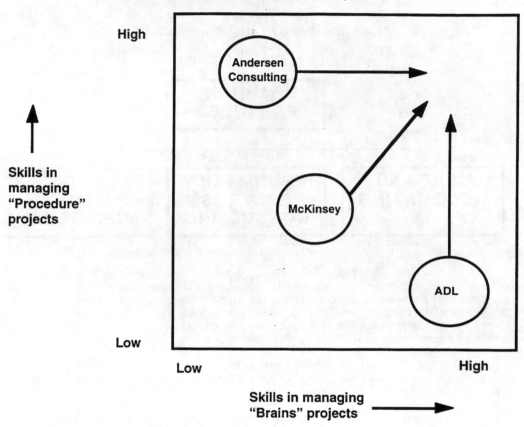

All Andersen's systems support an orderly and efficient process of incremental knowledge building through constant diffusion of new experience through training and formalization procedures. Coupled with uniform and disciplined implementation through the institutionalized project team structures, these systems gave the company unparalleled strengths in managing "procedure" projects. In contrast, other companies (I use the example of ADL, but instructors use the Cray Research case as an example of the same iconoclastic approach) rely on an "adhocracy" structure and more fluid processes to create a unique, one-of-a-kind solution to highly complex and often unprecedented "brains" projects. And some (I suggest McKinsey) specialize in the middle area suitable for "grey hair" assignments. The changing nature of the IS market will require that large size worldwide players like Andersen develop the capability to simultaneously manage all kinds of projects (the top right hand corner in the matrix in Figure 9).

The debate now shifts to whether this top right hand position is a feasible one for any PSF. How can a company protect the coherence and consistency across its various administrative structures and processes if it tries to do "all things for all people?" Would such an effort not lead to a strategy and an organization that are too ambiguous to be efficient for "procedure" projects and simultaneously too complex for the free-wheeling environment necessary to manage "brains" projects?

The instructor can adopt some different courses of actions at this point. He or she can let the debate flow for a while, without trying to reach a consensus or a conclusion, and then bring the discussions to a close with some summary observations. This is entirely appropriate because the main pedagogical objective of familiarizing the students with the special issues and challenges of managing professional service firms has, by now, been accomplished. I, on the other hand, prefer to take a stronger advocacy position in class and lead the discussions to what I see as happening to many PSFs; their transformation to truly network organizations.

In my course, typically the students (at least in the core business policy course in the MBA program) would have already been exposed to the concept of network organizations. In essence I would have argued in these preceding classes in favor of a broad shift in organizational forms from the multidivisional or matrix structures to the network structure (Figure 10):

Figure 10
Organizational transformation in the 1990s

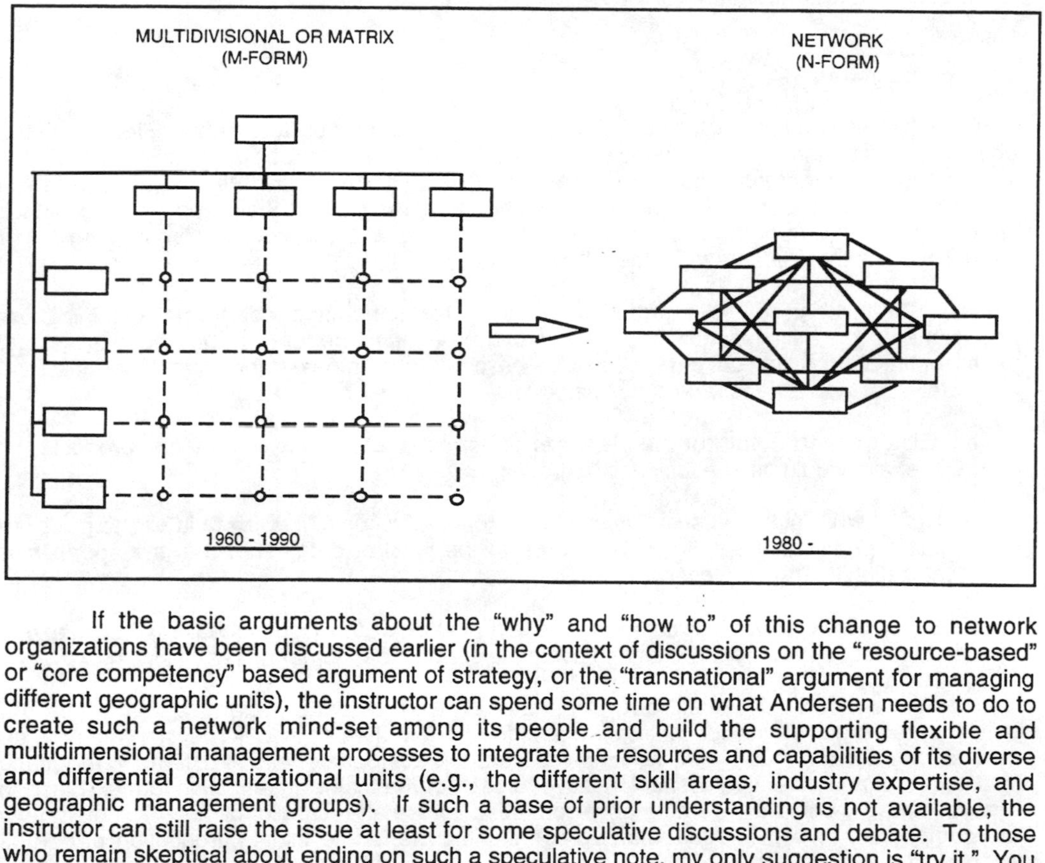

If the basic arguments about the "why" and "how to" of this change to network organizations have been discussed earlier (in the context of discussions on the "resource-based" or "core competency" based argument of strategy, or the "transnational" argument for managing different geographic units), the instructor can spend some time on what Andersen needs to do to create such a network mind-set among its people and build the supporting flexible and multidimensional management processes to integrate the resources and capabilities of its diverse and differential organizational units (e.g., the different skill areas, industry expertise, and geographic management groups). If such a base of prior understanding is not available, the instructor can still raise the issue at least for some speculative discussions and debate. To those who remain skeptical about ending on such a speculative note, my only suggestion is "try it." You may be surprised by the excitement and enthusiasm even a brief and inconclusive discussion will create.

POLAROID CORPORATION TEACHING NOTE

Overview

Polaroid was a highly entrepreneurial company, built by its inventor-founder, Dr. Edwin Land. In the early to mid-1980s, the company was under severe competitive pressures. There was a significant question whether its traditional management style and strategy focus could be maintained. The company had been driven by a strong central entrepreneurial head, had grown through a form of adhocracy, and had been positioned as a well-niched leader in a proprietary technology field. The case focuses on the strategy issues the company now faces, what major thrusts it must undertake to deal with these issues, and the organization and control system changes which will be necessary to make the adaptation. The case is a superb vehicle for investigating alternative primary organization structures, how these fit with strategy, what control and incentive systems should support them, and the problems of making transitions from one strategy focus to another.

The case fits readily with readings on corporate culture, organization/systems, strategy formulation and entrepreneurial or innovative contexts.

Session Structure

The session tends to structure itself readily around four or five themes. First, we usually open by investigating the new strategic issues which Polaroid must face in the early 1980s. Then we investigate what organizational format will be most useful in meeting these needs and why. In this process, we actually have individual students or teams present their proposed organization structures on an overhead viewgraph for critique by the entire class. As preparation for this session we ask the students to do the following.

"Set forth in a clear organization chart form the kinds of formal organizational arrangements you believe would be most appropriate in the future for Polaroid. Draw this chart in pencil or in carbon ink on paper that can be converted into a transparency in class. Or alternately, develop a transparency for class.

a. Give enough detail for the viewer to understand what activities, plants, products, key people, etc. would be in each specific grouping.

b. Define what planning systems, measurements, and controls you would use to guide and evaluate performance in each area down to the level of detail shown in the approximate organization chart in the case.

c. Be prepared to orally discuss the reasoning behind your recommendations. Organization charts must be prepared in neat and complete enough form to hand in at class time."

We consciously seek out a functional organizational chart, a market/product divisionalized organization focus, and a matrix focus. We then attempt to develop the pros and cons about each structure. Finally, we investigate the appropriateness of different performance measurement and incentive systems relative to each of the major organization forms. Since the case is relatively complex, we strongly recommend its use after simpler cases on single product line companies, entrepreneurial start-up companies, and some initial introduction of portfolio techniques.

Teaching note copyright © 1996 by James Brian Quinn. This note prepared by Professor Quinn and Penny C. Paquette, Research Associate.

EARLY '80s STRATEGIC ISSUES

It is helpful to open the case with a discussion of the strategic issues facing Polaroid Corporation in the early 1980s. After many successful years as a patent-protected company, Polaroid is being increasingly pressed by strong competitors both in the United States and from a Japanese base. New technologies, dominantly electronic, are beginning to impact Polaroid's camera positions. Finally, a series of small "copy cats," who ignore patent positions, are beginning to produce look-alike camera systems for the marketplace. These forces create an interesting "competitor analysis" situation. The pressures they cause in the marketplace are already being felt by Polaroid whose ROA has dropped some 50%.

Competitor Positions

The competitor positions in 1982-83 look like this:

1. Eastman Kodak is moving strongly in the United States with its superb brand name, extensive distribution channels, and deep technological capabilities. Since instant photography could impact Kodak's very profitable film processing business heavily, in the early '80s it appeared that Kodak would have to maintain a strong position in this high volume film marketplace.

2. Japanese companies were targeting the Polaroid marketplace in two ways. Fuji Films—as a high volume, low cost producer with a strong international distribution system for its quality, branded products—could be a powerful competitor in the films market. Although the Japanese camera companies had not yet targeted the Polaroid position, they could easily enter with sophisticated products using spin-off technologies from their 35mm camera systems. Thus, Polaroid could face very strongly positioned competitors in both films and cameras.

3. The "copy cats" would enter the marketplace with very low cost camera systems, imitating either Polaroid or Kodak. With very low manufacturing costs due to their "developing country" bases of operation, they could possibly disrupt the cameras portion of the marketplace. But they would probably not be important players in the film market, where both Eastman Kodak and Polaroid made their profits.

4. All electronic camera systems (like the Sony Mavica) were beginning to be discussed. All camera systems were undergoing a very rapid improvement due to electronics. The costs of electronics were dropping so rapidly that Polaroid had to consider precisely what its position would be relative to "electronic cameras" and "all electronic photography."

Major Strategic Issues

World market potentials were growing substantially outside the United States. Although the U.S. marketplace seemed to be stagnating (after the burst of sales stimulated by Eastman Kodak's entry), world markets for instant cameras and films were growing at a very rapid rate. Polaroid's returns on assets were substantial overseas, although this is somewhat obscured by the fact that so much of the company's headquarters, research, and corporate overhead activities occurred in U.S. facilities. Nevertheless, the growth of the European and Far Eastern markets raise serious questions about how much production Polaroid should undertake overseas, both for cost and market-servicing reasons.

Increased size seemed an impending threat for several reasons. As the company moved above the $1 billion sales level, it would be difficult to maintain the small company, flexible, ad hoc, innovative environment it had enjoyed in the past. Key questions were how to maintain the flexibility needed for innovation and market responsiveness, how to replace Dr. Land's extraordinarily innovative capabilities, how to motivate the company to both innovate in response to the growing electronics capabilities of competitors, yet to decrease costs substantially to deal with the potentials of the "copy cats" and the Japanese-based competitors.

Cost controls and efficiency were absolute necessities in the new marketplace. The instant camera field was in a state of serious "shakeout." This meant that the company had to focus heavily on automation, cost cutting, and scale efficiencies to be successful in this maturing environment. A major issue was how Polaroid could obtain needed efficiencies and cost controls, without losing the extraordinarily innovative values which had been the touchstone of the company's prior positions.

Diversification began to look like an extremely attractive alternative for Polaroid. In what directions should it diversify? What skills should it emphasize in this diversification? What product areas were natural adjuncts to its existing lines? Did Polaroid have either the inclination, resources, or management skills to undertake a substantial diversification program? If so, what criteria should be set for diversification? Of great concern in any diversification program would be: (1) the adequacies of Polaroid's financial control systems, (2) the capacity of its functionally-oriented organization to integrate new lines, (3) the willingness or ability of the culture to accept new entrants.

All of the above pose significant organizational issues. Chief among these are the following: How should Polaroid realign its primary organization to obtain a greater focus on markets, profitability, and efficiency? How should the successors for Dr. Land and Mr. McCune be selected? Tested? What should be the relationship between domestic and overseas operations? Should the company be organized on a regional, world product, market/product, functional, or matrix basis? If major changes are to be made away from its (essentially) functional organization, who should manage each important unit? How can the company's primary structure be best matched to its future strategic needs? Can the company make needed moves in ways which enable it to maintain its culture, despite the changes in industry structure, competition and scale it faces? If so, how? What skills should the successor to Dr. Land and Mr. McCune have? If you were to choose a successor from the group of potential candidates, who would it be? Where would the other candidates be positioned in the primary reorganization? What activities should be centralized in the reorganization? Which should be decentralized? Why?

CHANGING THE PRIMARY ORGANIZATION

To obtain depth in the organizational discussion, we ask each student (or individual executive study group) to prepare an organization chart in the format suggested above. We then reproduce their organization charts on an overhead viewgraph-making machine in the classroom. Selected students then present these on a screen and explain and justify their recommendations. This usually turns into a lively debate on the pros and cons of each organization form and individual activity structures within them. To capture this debate, we try to outline on the blackboard the pros favoring each major organization type as the discussion develops. (See later section.) And we try to make sure that each group covers certain key issues in each functional area. These are briefly outlined below.

Marketing: How can marketing research be better tied into product decisions? Where should the market research function be positioned? What does the rest of the organization do to facilitate the introduction of new products? How can the forecasting capabilities of Polaroid be improved? How can the salesmen be organized to maximize their impact, yet eliminate duplication of calls on customers? What are the most important market segmentations? To what extent do camera sales, film sales, industrial sales, and consumer sales need to be cross-coordinated? To what extent do their channels overlap? Should the same sales forces serve more than one of these four market segments? How should international marketing be handled vis-à-vis domestic marketing? Where should product policy, pricing, advertising, image development, and segment targets be determined for the Polaroid line?

Production: How can Polaroid get the maximum benefit of economies of scale in production? Where should purchasing be performed? If production is decentralized within production divisions or left as a functional unit, how should transfer prices be established? Where should production schedules be set? Who should be responsible for finish stock inventories? How can production be organized best to insure development of production technologies in connection with new products? Should Polaroid continue its orientation toward producing in small towns in New England? How much of its production should be done overseas? How should this be coordinated with U.S. production? Should production engineering be coordinated worldwide? If so, should the function be within engineering or production? If the organization stays functionally-oriented, how should production investments be evaluated, coordinated, and integrated into other functional investment patterns? Where should quality control be positioned? Who should set standards for productivity and quality in production?

Engineering/Research: How should R&D be organized to stimulate entrepreneurship? How should the transfer into production and marketing be organized? What motivation systems should be put in place to stimulate this? How should research be planned? Evaluated? Where should production or plant engineering be? Where should fundamental research, new product research, and applied research be positioned relative to engineering? How can engineering be made more marketing oriented?

Centralized Functions: What activities should be centralized in Polaroid? Why? This series of questions allows the professor to bring out the needs to centralize certain functions for strategic reasons, control reasons, specialized skills reasons, coordination reasons, and so on. The company's particular strategy and its intended degree of decentralization, coordination, etc. should determine what particular functions are centrally coordinated. These should vary widely depending on the particular corporate strategy and organization strategy undertaken.

The Functional Organization

As the students explain their particular approach to organizing, we try to bring out the fact that different primary organization forms seem to do certain things better than others. At the end of this discussion, we literally try to have arrayed on the blackboard the major considerations in organizing using each form of primary grouping. A summary of these issues follows in this and the next two sections. A functional organization has special utility under the following circumstances:

A. To leverage special skills (such as those of an outstanding researcher, marketer, production person, etc.).

B. To develop depth in certain specialty skills (i.e., when the company's strategy depends upon depth in technology, marketing, finance, etc. rather than fast moving adaptation to market changes or coordination of marketing, production, finance, technology).

C. To create flexibility to mix changes. When the mix of products, orders, or scale of orders changes rapidly, a functional organization may be desirable—such as in a job shop situation—because people can be easily moved around within the function to make up ad hoc teams.

D. To obtain economies of scale, when production facilities, distribution channels, large research apparatus, etc., are involved. The functional organization avoids duplication of investments that might be required by a market/product division grouping.

E. To bring the full power of the corporation to bear, for example, in acquiring financing, presenting a full product line to customers, or negotiating with governments.

F. To obtain consistency of action, for example, in controllership, legal affairs, public relations, internal personnel policies, and so on.

G. To avoid shared or joint costs when common facilities might be required for two divisions to operate efficiently together through the same distribution channels, production facilities, or research facilities.

H. To obtain a longer-term focus. Since outcomes and their costs are more difficult to isolate in a functional system, this structure tends to be less driven by short-term ROI, ROA, or profit center considerations. Functional organization allows the corporation to isolate long-term research, public relations activities, and so on as "corporate investments" to develop over a longer time period.

I. To coordinate across product lines. Coordination is facilitated because a single marketing, production, or technology group controls its whole interface across product lines.

The Profit Center (Market/Product) Division Organization

A market/product division grouping tends to be useful under other circumstances. Most critical among these are the following:

A. More profit orientation is possible because these units can be set up as "smaller profit centers" where more individuals can see the direct impact of their actions on product line profits.

B. Self control is more feasible because individual managers can more clearly see the impacts of their actions on profits and can self direct toward this goal.

C. Market/product divisions give more individuals general management "profit responsibility" in their careers and the opportunity to exercise control over a totally integrated organization. Consequently, such people are better trained to later assume top management positions.

D. Market/product divisions by being smaller and more profit oriented tend to respond more rapidly to changing marketplace needs than functional groups which tend to become bureaucratic.

E. Market/product groups help control overhead costs because they so clearly impact divisional profits if generated within the division. If generated at the corporate level and passed on to the divisions, the divisions become "devil's advocates" for reducing these overheads.

F. Market/product divisions tend to allow individuals to run their own businesses on a more entrepreneurial basis. Consequently, it is easier to attract entrepreneurially motivated people into such units.

G. Because market/product divisions tend to be smaller in size, people can see more of the total operation, identify more with it, and feel more directly rewarded for their own performance. Consequently, such units can increase morale.

H. Market/product divisions highlight costs or profitability problems by making output and costs easier to measure. In addition, such divisions can respond faster to such problems.

I. Because units tend to be smaller, people can <u>coordinate</u> their activities more easily <u>across the lateral interfaces</u> among functions. However, conversely, coordination among product units tends to become more difficult.

J. <u>Acquisitions, divestitures, or spinouts</u> become easier because entire units can be brought in or disposed of without having to be integrated in detail with ongoing marketing, production, or technical groups.

K. <u>Performance measurements and performance rewards</u> are easier to achieve because of the smaller scale and more direct connections between actions and outcomes.

The Matrix Organization

Matrix organizations are useful for still other purposes. They tend to come into being when complexity makes communications or focus too difficult to achieve through straight functional or product market groupings. Their major advantages are briefly summarized below.

A. <u>Communications among units</u> can be facilitated because all participants in a decision can join in it simultaneously, even though they are in separate organizational (functional or product) units. In addition, typically, Accounting or Management Information Systems are changed to accommodate both lateral and vertical needs in a matrix organization, thus increasing the richness of information available.

B. <u>Training for management</u> is improved because functional specialists have an opportunity to participate in joint decisions and see the impact of their decisions across functional lines.

C. <u>When complexity is great</u>, matrix organizations may be a requisite, especially when several strategic dimensions are pulling in different directions. The matrix organization makes sure that all strategic interests (e.g., regional, product, customer, economy of scale) are served.

D. <u>Safer decisions</u> are likely because matrix decisions tend to be made or heavily influenced by committees. Consequently, a compromise form of decision tends to emerge, and all relevant factors tend to be looked at.

E. Matrix organizations are essential <u>to deal with discontinuity</u>—ad hoc types of situations where small teams must be assembled for a short time for the purpose of exploration, development, new product introduction, debugging, etc. Specialists can maintain their base in their "home operations" while joining together for a short period of time on teams under the coordination of a team leader or using a participatory or consensus form of decision making.

F. <u>Team spirit</u> can be enhanced by matrix organizations within large functional organizations. Smaller teams working on projects with specific goals can tend to develop their own internal esprit de corps, although their parent units may have become somewhat large and bureaucratized.

The Dominant Strategic Thrust

Which primary mode of organization should be chosen depends on the assessment of what one considers to be the critical strategic factors facing Polaroid. If one considers that profit orientation, market response, diversification, and general management development are the most important issues, one would opt for some form of market/product division structure. If one considers that the most crucial factors for success are the development of highly specialized technical skills, economies of scale in production facilities, avoidance of duplicate investments, consistency in product presentation, etc., one would choose a functional organization. If one feels that neither of these two sets of considerations is dominant, but both are important, one might move toward a matrix organization.

The matrix organization also offers some significant advantages as a transition organization—for example when moving from Polaroid's traditional functional organization to a future organization which might be market/product grouped. It always takes several years for people raised in one kind of organization culture to adapt to a new one. Consequently, a matrix organization might be very useful for teaching people how to operate in a more "profit-focused" environment, to develop needed new information systems, and to put into place stronger controls cutting across the individual divisions.

Once the dominant form of organization is decided upon, one can move on to the next question—what the primary focus within that form should be. Should Polaroid organize on the basis of markets (i.e., industrial, consumer, government, etc.)? Should it organize by products, (i.e., films, cameras, batteries, sunglasses, etc.)? Or should its primary focus be regional (U.S., Far Eastern, European, etc.) units? There is some rationale for each of these, given the critical strategic issues Polaroid faces.

Note, however, that a new camera-film system needs to be conceived, developed, and introduced with close coordination between film and camera units. Film improvements for existing cameras do not need as much coordination, nor do new cameras to use existing film systems. A totally new product line like "an all electronic camera" would need an entirely new group of skills which might lie largely outside the capabilities of the current organization.

Distribution channels for cameras and films seem to overlap substantially. However, there are many film stores that do not carry cameras. Polaroid sells to a large number of chain supermarkets, discount stores, and camera chains. These "national accounts" may need special handling. Coordination of image, pricing, and presentation clearly need corporate guidance. The overall development of successive product lines also need such guidance. Note that the innovation of the SX-70 cost several hundred million dollars and that new product lines for Polaroid are likely to involve similar risks.

Any new organization will have to be acceptable to Mr. McCune and Dr. Land. It is important to note that both of these men have managed in a functional organization structure all their lives. They may find it difficult to adapt to a different organization form and management style.

Control and Performance Measurements Systems

As students begin to present their proposed organization charts, it is very interesting to ask certain questions concerning the control systems needed for each organization form. Several of the most important issues to raise are suggested below:

A. How does one measure performance in a functional organization? Who is responsible for profits? Who sets the performance standards for the individual divisions? Note that under a true functional organization, only one person (the president) is responsible for profits in the organization. Note also that production engineers set production standards for their own units, marketing managers set internal standards for their units, and so on. Consequently, a significant loss in efficiency or profit orientation can result. The alternative is to have a central staff group of some sort set standards for the functional groups. This automatically creates certain conflicts.

B. How can staff costs be controlled? How does one measure the performance of centralized staffs and determine a relevant level of costs for them? Getting students to understand the difficulty of measuring outputs for staff units is crucial. Understanding the problems of performance measurement when using a functional organization is most difficult. Both need substantial inquiry.

C. What form of incentive plans should be put in for each organization form? What type of incentive plan is appropriate for a functional organization? What can marketing really be held responsible for? After some probing, it becomes clear that marketing might be held responsible for "margin control" or "gross margins." Production can be held responsible for its costs, provided objective work standards and costs can be established—not an easy task. Then, variance analysis systems can establish variances due to mix changes, volume changes, labor efficiencies, materials utilization, which might be caused by other groups. Pushing the students back to basic cost accounting concepts is very useful here.

D. How should performance be measured in market/product divisions? The usual student answer is to make these "profit centers." One then asks what costs should be included in the divisions' costs? Shouldn't profits be related to assets used? If so, which assets do the students have in mind? This leads into the question of what portion of working capital, corporate overhead, research and development, total corporate assets, etc. should be included in the divisions' measurements? How should the company set a cutoff standard, or "hurdle rate" for each division? Should all of these hurdle rates be the same? Why? Why not?

E. In a market/product division structure, how are major new product programs (like an all-electronic camera) handled? Who is responsible for their costs? Their profits upon introduction? How much influence should the individual divisions have in determining the direction of these major programs?

F. Are ROI, ROA, or "profit" standards sufficient to manage divisions? Shouldn't there be non-dollar goals and non-quantitative goals for technology development, image development, human resources development, and so on? What impacts will a market/product divisional structure have on innovation? How can the deleterious effects of such an organization be decreased?

G. Where should the controllership activity reside? Should it be solely corporate? Should divisions have their own controllers? If so, to what extent should these be responsible to corporate? To their division heads? These questions usually lead to some lively and helpful debate.

H. How should transfer prices be calculated between supplier divisions (e.g., batteries) and user divisions (e.g. cameras)? How should transfer prices be established between production and marketing if a functional organization is used? If a functional organization is used within divisions? What should be the basis of transfer prices between U.S. producing units and foreign selling units? How should currency exchange profits/losses be handled in this relationship?

I. Where should planning activities be lodged in each organization form? What time horizon is appropriate for planning in Polaroid? How should "the plan" be used in Polaroid for stimulating creativity? Controlling direction? Controlling productivity and efficiency?

J. In a decentralized market/product divisional structure, how should the incentive plans be structured to stimulate profitability? Productivity? Innovation? Maintenance of the corporate value system? Development of new technologies? Attention to human resources goals? Attention to other non-quantitative goals? How should innovators of major new product lines (such as an all-electronic camera) be rewarded? How can this be rationalized vis-à-vis the operating divisions?

These are all very important issues and should be brought out in relationship to each of the major organizational forms. Obviously, the case can be run anywhere from 1 1/2 to 3 hours easily. It can form a cornerstone for discussions of organizations, control systems, and other incentive and support systems in manufacturing types of organizations. This case should precede the Royal Bank of Canada cases which bring up similar issues in the context of a services industry.

SUMMARY OF OUTCOMES

The organization structure at Polaroid underwent a two-phased development. First in 1983, Mr. Booth was placed in charge of the Consumer Products line worldwide. Mr. Wensberg was made head of Commercial/Industrial markets, and Mr. Young was made head of Marketing. However, all production facilities continued to report to Mr. Booth who was also COO. Within a relatively short period of time, both Mr. Wensberg and Mr. Young left the company for high level positions elsewhere.

The company was then reorganized into a matrix format. The functionally centralized Research, Engineering, Production, and Marketing divisions each had internal "product group heads" laterally coordinating their activities with the other three functions toward Consumer Markets, Industrial Markets, and Other Markets. A corporate level Product Manager coordinated each of these lateral groups for a single market area. Later, these units were developed as SBUs under the titles of Consumer Photography, Industrial Photography, Magnetics, and New Businesses. The New Businesses area included fiber optics, photovoltaics, specialty chemicals, and optics.

Within this framework, Polaroid also developed several separate "freestanding" divisions for small product lines (such as batteries, chemicals, and other specialties) which it sold directly into other marketplaces. The company started several major development programs— announced in its annual reports—which became the Spectra system of instant photography, its 35mm Instant system, and an Advanced Electronic System for future cameras. These were set up as ad hoc development teams financed directly by corporate.

Manufacturing was coordinated worldwide by a single head. Purchasing was centralized at the corporate level. Marketing was centralized under a single head with two regional units (North America and International). Research and Engineering were centralized as were Finance, Legal Affairs, Personnel, Strategic Planning, and Patent Activities. In 1986, Mr. McCune had become Chairman of the Board, and Mr. Booth had become President and CEO.

While the actual actions taken by the company do not indicate either proper or improper handling of a particular situation, they are helpful to the professor in bringing out different viewpoints in discussions. Following are a few other major thrusts publicly announced by Polaroid Corporation.

Other Key Thrusts

In addition to these organizational changes, Polaroid began several other major strategic changes. By 1986, it had pushed its Technical and Industrial Photography group up to 40% of its total sales. This group's products included professional and commercial photography, visual presentation products, identification systems, and medical and scientific data recording.

Consumer Photography still made up 60% of Polaroid's product sales. Most of these were in instant camera systems and films. In 1986, Polaroid introduced its Spectra camera and film system which gave print quality approximately equal to that of 35mm enlarged prints. Although Polaroid had entered the 35mm instant marketplace, this product was not selling well. Minolta had introduced its Maxxum system in early 1980. This was a 35mm single lens reflex camera with all-electronic focusing, light setting, and timing capabilities. The Maxxum was selling well. In the instant photography field, Spectra had many of the same features as the Maxxum.

Polaroid's Magnetic Media Group was selling video cassettes and floppy disks (at first manufactured in Japan) through Polaroid's established distribution channels. A series of other products were being sold through what became known internally as Polaroid's "bridgeheads" division. Products like LCD materials, sunglasses, medical diagnostics, photovoltaics, roadside flashers, conductive plastic films, and materials for holography (laser photography) were handled by this group.

Although all-electronic photography had yet to catch on, Sony's Mavica specifications (modified) had been adopted by the Japanese industry as its standard for all-electronic cameras. Canon was soon to release an all-electronic camera, making images internally for display on a television screen. Japan's Fuji Photo Film Company had released a box of film that allowed one to make pictures directly using the camera box as a camera and then simply shipping the box of film in for processing. Electronics technology continued to move rapidly.

As a result of the Supreme Court's decision—finding that Eastman Kodak had infringed Polaroid's patents—Polaroid was expecting to receive a very high cash award. After the conclusion of the Polaroid-Kodak suit, Kodak withdrew from the instant camera market and left Polaroid as the sole supplier of instant products in the United States. Polaroid and Fuji entered negotiations wherein Polaroid allowed Fuji to license its patents outside the United States in return for certain technologies to which Polaroid sought access.

Productivity Increases and Poison Pills

President Booth soon announced the end of Polaroid's unique policy which had basically guaranteed lifetime employment to anyone with more than 10 years of experience at Polaroid. In 1985 an expensive severance program was undertaken to shrink the salaried workforce and to stimulate higher productivity in the company. A number of critics of Polaroid claimed that Dr. Land's policies had made Polaroid into "a bloated bureaucracy."

Polaroid was often discussed as a likely takeover candidate. To offset this, the Board adopted a "Shareholder's Protection Plan" to insure that shareholders realized the full value of their investments in the event of a hostile takeover attempt. Investment analysts noted, however, that Polaroid was among the most vulnerable companies to foreign currency weakness, because the company exported from the United States so many of the products it sold abroad. But with sales concentrated in the major European countries and Japan whose currencies had been weak in the early 1980s, Polaroid stood to benefit substantially if the U.S. dollar weakened. By mid-1986, Oppenheimer and Co. estimated Polaroid's asset values to be in excess of $50 a share, despite shares trading in a range of $25-32 for the preceding year. Oppenheimer broke out the asset valuation per share of Polaroid as follows:

Instant photography business	$28.70
Overfunded pensions	6.35
Real estate (excess value)	7.00
Excess working capital	9.58
Total hypothetical value	$51.63

1986-90 Update

Polaroid grew steadily from 1986-1990. The following table summarizes estimated sales volumes by product lines (in $ millions)

	1986	1987	1988	1989	1990
Amateur Cameras	$185	$186	$160	$130	$140
Amateur Film	$691	$758	$795	$790	$812
Industrial Film	$500	$510	$595	$630	$680
Industrial Hardware	$78	$124	$150	$160	$172
Videotape (floppies in '86 and '87)	$125	$133	$110	$120	$130
Conventional Film				$35	$75
Foreign Sunglasses and Polarizers	$25	$28	$28	$25	$26
Other (Copy service, etc.)	$25	$25	$25	$15	$15
Total	$1629	$1764	$1863	$1905	$2050

Source: B.L. Landry, Polaroid-Company Report, February 26, 1990, Morgan Stanley & Co., Inc.

The introduction of the Spectra gave a boost to instant cameras and film sales, but did not stop the overall decline in the instant market. The 600 series camera was not replaced until 1989 (with the less expensive Impulse), and sales growth for the Spectra slowed quite rapidly. The Spectra was important for other reasons though. It was the first product backed by true consumer research and augured a new approach to marketing, product development, and organization. In its 1987 Annual Report, Polaroid reported that "consumer and market research had resulted in a decision to orient its business by markets, as opposed to by distribution channels, customers, industries, or product lines."

By early 1990, this had led to changes toward a market-oriented matrix organization, reflecting a new focus on three identified user segments (family and recreational, business and practical, and industrial and technical), along with a new advertising campaign—"Nothing works like a Polaroid"—which highlighted the practical uses of instant prints. But Polaroid still maintained centralized research and manufacturing facilities—as well as a group of SBUs working on small new product concepts, particularly in the electronics-magnetics realms.

Polaroid had come a long way from the "technology for its own sake" attitudes of its founder. Its current CEO, I. M. ("Mac") Booth, had a high respect for R&D, but more as a means to make money. Polaroid now had a marketing group to target professional photographers, who for a long time had used instant cameras to produce "proofing" prints. To support this thrust, the R&D group developed a special color film that more closely approximated the results photographers achieve in their finished work.

Besides refocusing on selected marketplaces, Polaroid began to overhaul its operations, steadily reducing costs of goods sold as a percentage of sales as well as marketing, research, engineering, and administrative expenses. In 1986, cost of goods sold as a percent of sales was 56.6%; by 1989 it had come down to 50.7%. In 1985, marketing, research, engineering, and administrative expenses were 39% of sales; by 1989 they were only 33.3%. Manufacturing productivity was improved through formal communication programs and the establishment of work teams in several big plants. The company continued to cut its non-manufacturing workforce by encouraging voluntary departures, by giving clear signals to those who were underperforming, and by offering generous severance benefits. It also began developing products using multifunctional teams working in concurrence (rather than sequentially) and focusing research efforts more effectively. The workforce dropped 8% while volume grew 25%.

While doing everything it could to juice up a market in which it held a virtual monopoly, after the court decisions against Eastman-Kodak, Polaroid took steps to look to the future. In 1989 it entered the competitive fray in the conventional 35mm film business in the United States and the Far East. And in mid-1990 it announced that it had reached an agreement under which

Minolta would sell Polaroid-built instant cameras under its own name in the United States and the Far East. Minolta products have a presence in the U.S. specialty retailing segment that Polaroid's do not. Unlike Kodak's sales of instant cameras and film, such sales would help cover plant overheads and expand demand for Polaroid's profitable instant film packs. In recognition of the source of its profits and to combat the growing importance of electronic imaging in many of its markets, Polaroid had developed its own electronic imaging strategy based on its excellent CCD and film technologies. This played to its traditional strengths both in marketing and hard copy imaging. In 1987, the company said:

> "Soft" imaging—seeing an image on a video monitor—will not replace the hard copy print. It will, in fact, create even more opportunities for instant prints. Just as the "paperless" office never emerged in the wake of magnetic storage, screen viewing will fail, on the imaging side, to provide the necessary record keeping, tangibility, portability, and permanence of a hard copy instant image. . . . It seems likely that the instant share of the hard copy imaging market will benefit most from the growth of electronic imaging. This potential makes it desirable for Polaroid to expand its business base and develop multiple instant imaging systems for the future, from advanced versions of silver-halide based camera and film systems to sophisticated electronic camera-printer devices using unique media. The diversity of these electronic imaging applications also makes it desirable to develop different hardware and media combinations, each designed to serve different needs of the marketplace. Our goal, of course, is to make Polaroid hard copy the medium of choice around the globe.

Polaroid's management had little time to devote to the implementation and expansion of this strategy. In mid-1988, Shamrock Holdings, Inc. (a holding company controlled by Roy E. Disney) grabbed 6.8% of Polaroid's shares and approached management about buying the rest. The case suggests why Polaroid was a logical target. It had low earnings, unexploited technologies, a possible multibillion dollar windfall coming from Kodak, and a very inefficient functional organization structure. But Polaroid fought back and through a variety of actions (many of which were challenged in court) managed to hold Shamrock at bay. In July, Polaroid announced a plan to finance a buyback of its shares through a leveraged Employee Stock Option Plan. Every employee who had at least a year at Polaroid—with the exception of the lowest paid people—as of September 1988, took a reduction in take-home pay of 5 percent; officers suffered a 10 percent reduction. The matching monies the company had been putting into its 401K savings plan was also allocated directly to the ESOP.

The ESOP became an entity unto itself. It borrowed money from banks, used these tax-favored debt funds to buy stock, and paid back the banks with funds contributed by the employees and the corporation over the life of the loan. Shamrock sued, claiming Polaroid and its directors failed to act in the investors' best interest. After six months of legal wrangling, a Delaware judge upheld the controversial ESOP. By 1990 employees owned 20% of Polaroid's shares, and 50% were in institutional hands.

Still, Shamrock persisted, raising its tender offer to $45 a share and unveiling plans for a proxy fight. In January 1989, Polaroid indicated that it planned to buy back $1.1 billion of stock, and $300 million of that would be financed by the ESOP. It also lined up a friendly investor, Corporate Partners LP, a $1.6 billion investment fund organized by Lazard Freres. The arrangement involved a $300 million placement of preferred shares and warrants, which if fully converted would amount to more than 10 percent of the company. In recognition of this stake, Corporate Partners received two seats on Polaroid's board of directors. Shamrock sued again, saying the Polaroid's actions were "another indication of management entrenchment at any cost." When the Delaware court disagreed, Shamrock was forced to withdraw.

On October 12, 1990, a federal judge ruled that Eastman Kodak would have to pay $909.5 million to compensate Polaroid Corp. for violating its instant-photography patents—much less than the $13 billion Polaroid demanded after it won the patent infringement suit in 1985, but still equal to 90% of Polaroid's total earnings from 1976 to 1985, the years when Kodak's transgression took place, and amounting to about $600 million after taxes. Management has recently received much advice as to what to do with the cash. It has increasingly found that the Polaroid brand is well recognized and that its distribution system is an asset. It has done quite well with videotapes, floppy disks, medical imaging products, and some specialized batteries. To leverage its competencies overseas, it has increasingly turned to joint ventures with Japanese and European groups (like Minolta and Philips) who have strong production and distribution capabilities in compatible markets.

1995 Update

The attempted takeover was a rude awakening for Polaroid and forced it to finally recognize that with instant photography it had only a 7% stake in the maturing $15 billion photography industry, while the imaging market—photocopying, printing, video, and photography—was a rapidly growing $150 billion global business. As *Business Week* commented in its July 26, 1993 issue, "Polaroid went on an acquisition binge after Sony Corp. startled the world in 1982 with an all-electronic camera. Polaroid acquired a mishmash of fiber optic, ink jet printer, and medical diagnostic operations. Poor results later prompted Booth to fold or sell off every one. . . . Since 1988, Polaroid has reorganized itself three times. The most recent shuffle came last fall, when it rearranged the business into three divisions: film and videotape products, medical and graphics systems, and other electronic products."

In the late 1980s, Polaroid began two major product development projects, one designed to put instant photography on a level with conventional at least in terms of camera price, size, and technical features. Code named Project Joshua, the Captiva was the most researched product in Polaroid's history and helped to end a six-year downturn in camera sales. The Helios digital laser imager, combining digital electronics with dry development chemistry, was supposed to lead Polaroid into the new world of electronic imaging but got off to a poor start and had to be reconfigured to produce larger prints.

Finally in November 1995 Booth stepped down (as Chairman, President, and CEO) and Gary T. DiCamillo for brought in as Chairman and Chief Executive Officer. Much to the surprise of some analysts, who expected Polaroid to recruit a CEO from the electronics field, DiCamillo came to Polaroid from Black & Decker. He quickly moved to restructure the company, financially, operationally, and organizationally. A February severance program and a December restructuring reduced the workforce by about 2,500 positions. More significantly, the decision was made to scale back manufacturing for the Captiva camera, rationalize and consolidate film coating facilities, curtail several major research and engineering programs and while maintaining a strong research focus concentrate on projects closer to commercialization.

In February 1996 Polaroid announced a management reorganization designed to respond more effectively to customers, strengthen product development capability, and enhance growth prospects. In the 1995 Annual Report, DiCamillo stated:

"This new structure is built around three core areas—Consumer, Commercial and New Business. Each group has global operating responsibility for setting strategy, developing productions and marketing those products to its customers. Each will be accountable for its own sales, profits, and asset management.

"The new structure has some distinct advantages. It will allow us to understand more fully customers' imaging needs, regardless of whether they require traditional photographic or digital imaging solutions. In an imaging market where change is occurring at an accelerating pace, product cycles and windows of opportunity for new products and markets are shorter than ever. The new organization will allow us to move more quickly in response to emerging customer requirements and shifting market conditions.

"Another important benefit of the new structure is that it integrates product development responsibility into each business group. I cannot overstate the importance of this shift. This change will provide a much closer link between the imaging customer and our research and development people, enabling us to lever our technological strengths into a greater stream of new products. Finally, the new organization will enable more immediate customer feedback, allowing us to gauge our success in the marketplace in a more timely fashion. These changes in how we deploy resources, taken together with changes in how we recognize and reward our employees, will move Polaroid to a more performance- and results-oriented culture.

"Both the restructuring and the reorganization reflect my conviction that we can grow our core photographic and emerging electronic imaging businesses. I believe we can leverage our considerable brand power, technological expertise, and global distribution reach to create new growth opportunities and revitalize our instant photography business."

Polaroid Corporation
Financial Summary, 1990-95
(in millions of dollars)

	1995	1994	1993	1992	1991	1990
Net Sales						
United States	$1,019.0	$1,160.3	$1,178.8	$1,145.7	$1,113.6	$1,058.3
International	1,217.9	1,152.2	1,066.1	1,006.6	957.0	913.4
Total	2,236.9	2,312.5	2,244.9	2,152.3	2,070.6	1,971.7
Cost of goods sold	1,236.9	1,324.2	1,296.5	1,178.0	1,082.5	1,011.8
Marketing, research, engineering, and administrative expenses	849.1	788.0	763.0	760.5	741.5	675.6
Restructuring and other	247.0	—	44.0	—	—	—
Profit (loss) from operations	(157.8)	200.3	141.4	213.8	246.6	284.3
Net earnings (loss)	(140.2)	117.2	(51.3)	99.0	683.7	151.0
Net additions to property, plant, and equipment	167.9	146.7	165.6	201.5	175.8	120.9
Number of employees	11,662	12,104	12,048	12,359	12,003	11,768

Source: Polaroid Corporation, *1995 Annual Report.*

410

EXXON CORPORATION 1994 TEACHING NOTE

Overview

Exxon Corporation is one of the largest product-producing companies in the world. The case offers an excellent opportunity to investigate the changing nature of multinational companies and their power relationships with different host countries. Exxon provides an unusual overview of the relative merits of product, vs. regional, vs. matrix forms of organization and the support structures they entail. The case raises sophisticated questions concerning corporate governance, the role of a corporation in host countries, how a company can create a competitive edge in a commodity business operating in very different economic and resource environments, and the complexities of conceptualizing and implementing strategy in a large geographically diversified company like Exxon. Although the case itself is very bland to read, it touches on many important global issues and offers a superb vehicle for bringing out the true complexities of multinational strategy. It raises the basic question as to what the true governance over such a company is and how a company can systematically create value for its many stakeholders.

Session Structure

This case can easily take two periods of 1 to 1 and 1/2 hours each. It can be compressed by limiting discussion to the changing portfolio and organization needs of Exxon. The first part of the session is normally dedicated to: (1) understanding the potentials of large multinational companies relative to their host countries, (2) understanding the potential conflicts between multinationals and their host countries, (3) developing a strategy for Exxon in the late 1970s shortage era. If possible, one should reach closure on this strategy to the extent of developing an organization chart appropriate to the strategy. In the second part, one can concentrate on the strategy Exxon should follow in the mid-1980s oil glut era. The changes between the two strategies are marked and provide an excellent vehicle for relating strategy, structure, resource patterning, and changed power relationships between the corporation and its hosts. Finally, one can ask how the events of the mid-1990s should reshape this strategy, as the world again moved into a high economic growth, cost competitive, high pollution era.

Multinational Support for Host Countries

We usually open the first portion of the case by asking the questions, "Why should the oil holding countries allow any multinational company to exploit their oil? What does the multinational offer to the host country. Why doesn't the host country simply develop and exploit its oil without outside help?" Students or executives quickly respond, "Capital, technology, and (perhaps) marketing." We suggest that the professor challenge the statements by inquiring, "Surely, if the country is sitting on tens of billions of barrels of oil, it can borrow money in the international marketplace, can't it? If the country has so much money, can't it simply buy the technology off the shelf? Why can't it simply sell the oil as crude? There is always a market for crude." This begins to force the students to go beyond these simple generalizations. We suggest that the multinational brings the following capabilities to the host country:

A. Technology—Oil companies provide constant updating of technologies, access to highly specialized technologies like those for deep-sea exploration, specialized expertise in exploiting unusual formations (like heavy oil formations), knowledge about what technologies are available. Most unsophisticated host countries do not have the expertise to buy technologies well.

Teaching note copyright © 1996 by James Brian Quinn. This note prepared by Professor Quinn and Penny C. Paquette, Research Associate.

B. Capital—They also provide easier access to world capital markets, lower cost capital because of long-term profitability and stability, risk capital for the host country, and a high return on investment for the host country (since it essentially makes no investment), and conservation of the host country's own capital resources for infrastructure investments. Actually, multinationals try to invest as little direct capital in a country as possible, raising capital within the country for obvious political reasons. Hence, one should challenge the "capital" argument and develop the specific nature of the capital resources the multinationals do bring.

C. Market access—The multinational has a large distribution and sales system to which the host country's product has instant access on a continuing basis. In addition to simply buying oil, which any company could do on the spot market, the relationship with a multinational brings an implied interdependence, hence more stability in sales for the host country. Because the multinational is sophisticated in trading and mixing oils, it can obtain a higher price for the host country's oil, the host country can avoid being whipsawed by having to trade only in the current spot market, etc.

D. Management—Most host countries lack sophisticated general managers for large enterprises such as oil companies. They lack the specialists needed for particular problems. The oil companies can bring in teams of specialists for short periods of time, rather than having the host country have to develop such teams or hire them full time. Multinationals become major trainers of managers for developing economies.

E. Timing—Multinationals can help countries exploit their resources sooner, thus increasing the present value of those resources. They also allow the host countries to "jump the experience curve" and come in with a relatively low cost operating system quickly.

F. Efficiency—Without the multinationals operating there, the host country's own national oil company might be very inefficient. The multinationals provide a check on such bureaucracies and a pressure on them to improve efficiencies. The major oil companies can bring in world scale processes and systems to create initial low costs for the host country.

G. Training people—Many multinationals establish large technical schools and training centers. These are the equivalent of high quality high schools or universities in the host culture. They also train people in skills for which teachers simply would not be available in an underdeveloped host country.

H. Supplier development—Multinationals help develop local suppliers, provide somewhat guaranteed markets for them, train them in modern techniques, make sure that the local supplier network is producing to world standards, and often help suppliers lower their costs to allow competitive world pricing.

I. Building downstream capabilities—Multinationals can help build downstream capabilities such as plastics or chemical plants, plastic forming units, distribution networks, etc. These let the host country obtain higher value added with little direct investment.

J. Infrastructure development—Large multinationals often build entire ports or cities around a resource development. In addition, they may help with the development of transportation facilities, special government communications facilities, etc.

K. A coalition with the United States—If the multinational is a U.S. multinational, there is an implied relationship with the U.S. government. This often leads to further economic aid, defense support, etc.

L. A basis for emulation—Many multinationals bring management practices, trading practices, plant facilities, wages, etc. that enhance the vision of the local population as to what is possible.

This is especially true in the realm of management practices where the multinationals are much more likely to practice honest, open management than local bureaucracies often do.

M.   A buffer in international relationships—Multinationals frequently provide a buffer for the government in dealing with other countries with which they may have special relationship problems. For example, the multinationals allowed the Arab nations to continue shipping oil, even during the embargo, because multinationals could reroute the oil through friendly intermediate points to markets the producing country could not approach directly. And the U.S. interests in Kuwaiti and Saudi Arabian oil prevents their subjugation by Iraq.

Multinationals bring to developing host countries precisely those things the host countries most need for economic development and growth. Despite much rhetoric on this point, most developing countries now understand the benefits that multinationals can bring, and international practices have been established to help ensure that multinationals do perform more in the interests of their hosts than they did in the late 1800s and early 1900s when they were the epitome of economic imperialism.

Areas of Conflict

However, substantial areas of potential conflict do exist between multinationals and host countries. We have found that an interesting way to bring this out is to divide the class up into groups that temporarily role play as "Norway and Nigeria" (smaller countries with oil), "Britain and Indonesia" (larger countries with oil, one rich, one poor), "Japan, Venezuela, and China" (larger sophisticated countries with special problems) and "OPEC." Then, the professor turns to each group and says, "What potential conflicts exist between your country and a company like Exxon?" Within a relatively short period of time a substantial number of potential conflicts emerge. Principle among these are the following:

A. Control over key decisions—Decisions such as where to ship, what to ship, when to ship, and what the rate of development and exploitation will be a major source of conflict. This sense of dependence on the decisions made in a foreign country is a great irritation to host countries.

B. The desire for ownership and equity buildup in the local country—Obviously, to the extent that profits move out of the country, wealth is lost locally.

C. Competition with the host country's own companies—If the host country has oil companies of its own (as Britain does), clearly outside multinationals absorb some local capital and profits which would be otherwise available.

D. Impact on the supplier industries—A very large multinational like Exxon can swamp the local supplier industry with a few orders. If these are sufficiently profitable and long range, this can change long standing relationships with other nations and markets, jeopardizing the country if the multinational changes its practices.

E.   Conflicting values—Some countries wish to protect their local values (like Moslem fundamentalism) or quality of life or quality of the environment. They fear that a large foreign population or influence will erode traditional or local values. They may also want to use oil revenues for military expansionist policies.

F. Influence in politics—Because of the very large size of an Exxon, its investment patterns can influence local political situations enormously. The company can have interests different from the majority political interest in the country and try to change the local viewpoint by a variety of means short of bribes or corruption.

G. Overdependence on one industry—If the multinational grows the local economy too rapidly, this can make the country dependent on one source of revenues. With a cyclical product like oil, this can create great problems.

H. Dependence of the government on oil revenues—The case points out the dangers of a single revenue source for host countries. If the oil market changes, or if the local country's resources are not favored, the government can be bankrupted along with its long-term plans.

I. Conflicts with socialist philosophies—It is very difficult for a government that is preaching socialism to admit that it needs or can benefit from the efforts of a large capitalist company.

J. Regional development—The company in its own interest may want to develop very rapidly the region in which it operates. This could cause the country a considerable economic imbalance and internal migration problems. It also could change the balance of political power in the country, as in Scotland vs. England.

K. Education/Research—The multinational may prefer to do research in its own central facilities and hire away the best brains in the host country. Even if researchers and technologists are put in local laboratories, their productivity may be lost to the host country if they are working on problems of the total corporation. This is the source of the so-called "brain drain."

L. Amplified economic swings—Because the large multinational has a capital base outside the country, it may want to invest at just the wrong time from the viewpoint of the host country. For example, as an economy like Britain's moves upward, the multinational would tend to invest more in Britain thus overdriving the boom; as the economy fell, it would tend to invest less in Britain, thus amplifying the downswing.

M. Effects on exchange rates—Because the multinational has a large flow of local currency at any given moment, its moves to sell or hold such currency in anticipation of exchange rate changes can amplify swings in the exchange rate. In fact, such "position taking" by large multinationals was blamed for the triggering of several currency crises in Europe.

N. Relations with neighbors—The implied coalition with the multinational's parent country can create some relationship problems with political neighbors. For example, Norway wants to maintain control over the exploitation in the far North Sea to avoid potential conflicts with Russia.

O. Control over raw materials supplies—Countries like Japan which are dependent on external energy sources want to control this access themselves, rather than having it in the hands of a multinational.

P. Pricing conflicts—For its own policy reasons, a country may wish to hold energy prices down during a shortage period (as Japan did) or to raise prices during a glut (to decrease energy use). The multinational may want to have just the opposite strategy.

Q. Wage conflicts—Since multinationals tend to pay relatively higher wages, this tends to cause inflation in the local economy around the multinational. It increases the wage costs of other producers in the area. In addition, the well-paid employees of the multinational may increase the discrepancy between rich and poor and tensions within a developing country.

R. Support existing power bases—Because the multinational tends to want stability in local governments, it may tend to support a regime that does not have a wide popular base or may be corrupt.

S. Responsive to U.S. needs—Assuming that the United States is a major customer for the multinational, it may divert oil or refined products from a host country to the United States when this is inconvenient to the host country (see the British experience).

T. Economic imperialism—The oil company may prefer to export the raw material from the host country and upgrade or add value to this material in another country (for example, the parent country) or in a country where taxes are not as high.

U. Downstream investments—Because of the company's own long-term strategies, it may prefer not to invest in downstream facilities in the host country. This can keep the host from developing new skills and value-added potentials.

After developing such a comprehensive listing, executives and students tend to have a better sense of the problems multinationals encounter internationally. Two possible discussion routes open up. One is to ask how the host country can control each of these potential conflict areas and how the multinational can respond to that control. Another approach is to ask whether each host country has the same interests. In the latter case, it is quite clear that each host's interests are very different. One can then query whether a multinational can have a consistent policy across all host countries. If not, how can it appear to be consistent to the host countries? How can it appear to be fair in its dealings with host countries? How does it have to think about policy vis-à-vis host countries? Any of these discussions can go on for a considerable while. However, we usually move on to the next question, "Given both the potential benefits the company can bring and the potential conflict it may have with hosts, how should one design a strategy for Exxon in the crisis era of the 1970s when Exxon was so dependent on the host countries and they were militantly trying to increase their take from their oil resources?"

Late 1970s Strategy

It is then useful to focus on the kind of world Exxon was anticipating in 1978 and the implications for its strategy. The world considered itself in a period of energy shortage. It was common to assert that "the world is running out of oil, gas, or coal, etc." People were anticipating continuing heavy usage of energy, growth rates worldwide of 4-5% in energy use, and rapidly accelerating energy prices. This situation had prevailed since 1973 and appeared to be a continuing scenario for the relatively long-term future. Given this situation, what should Exxon's strategy have been?

An interesting way to open the discussion about the late 1970s strategy is to utilize the numbers given in the case. These indicate an estimated world investment in hydrocarbon energy over the next decade of $1.5 trillion. If Exxon was to maintain its existing share of market (represented by refinery runs), it would have some 9% of this marketplace. If it projected its past sales growth rate, it would grow at 9.1% per year. Given an existing sales level of $63.9 billion, Exxon would grow to a $153 billion company in 10 years at the 9.1% growth rate. If it invested 9% of the $1.5 trillion (or $135 billion) over this period, this would require a sales base of $202 billion to support it, assuming that it takes $1.50 of sales to support each dollar of assets (total investments). In either event, Exxon becomes a huge company with very large investment needs.

If it is to invest $135 billion over 10 years, it must invest at an average rate of $13.5 billion per year. One can calculate Exxon's current cash flows as $4.4 billion (net income of $2.7B and depreciation of $1.7B) in 1978. This means a shortfall of some $9 billion on an average basis over the decade. A similar calculation could be made for 1981, assuming that Exxon would continue to grow at its historical rate or that it would maintain its share of market by investing some 9.75% of the $2 trillion total world investment in energy expected in the 10 years following 1981. A summary of these calculations follows.

Projected Exxon Corp. Sales and Asset Growth Estimates

	Estimates Based on Maintaining Existing Market Share	1978	1981
A.	Estimated World Investment in Fossil Energy	$1.5 Trillion	$2.0 Trillion
B.	Exxon % of Refinery Runs	9.0%	9.75%
C.	New Investment for Exxon to Maintain Share (AxB)	$135 Billion	$195 Billion
D.	Exxon's Ratio Sales ÷ Assets	1.5	1.8
E.	Sales Volume at end of Decade to Justify New Investment (CxD)	$202 Billion	$351 Billion
F.	This Year's Sales	$63.9 Billion	$113 Billion
G.	Estimated Sales Volume 10 yrs. Later if Investment is Made (E+F)	$265.9 Billion	$464 Billion
H.	Assets This Year	$41.5 Billion	$63 Billion
I.	Total Assets (Investment) 10 yrs. Hence (C+H)	$176 Billion	$258 Billion
J.	Ave. New Assets per Year (C÷10)	$13.5 Billion	$19.5 Billion
K.	Cash Flow This Year (Net Income + Depreciation)	$4.4 Billion	$8.5 Billion
L.	Shortfall for Invest. Needs (J-K)	$9.1 Billion	$11.0 Billion
M.	Dividends	$1.3 Billion	$2.8 Billion
N.	Shortfall If Dividends Not Paid	$7.8 Billion	$8.2 Billion
O.	Current Sales Growth Rate	9.1%	14.5%
P.	Sales 10 yrs. hence at this Growth	$153 Billion	$438 Billion
Q.	Assets to Support these Sales (P÷D)	$102 Billion	$243 Billion
R.	Net New Assets Needed (Q-H)	$60.5 Billion	$180 Billion
S.	Ave. New Assets (Invest.) Needed Per Year (R÷10)	$6.0 Billion	$18.0 Billion
T.	Annual Shortfall (S-K)	$1.4 Billion	$9.5 Billion

Without getting into overwhelming detail, one can establish that if Exxon were to grow at rates indicated in these "projected scenarios," it would have to raise very substantial amounts of capital beyond those being generated internally at the beginning of the period. Clearly, the company would become quite large, and its very size would pose some problems both internally and in its relationships to host countries.

Finance Strategy

One can now raise the next set of questions, "Given these enormous capital needs, what should Exxon's financial strategy be? Where can it obtain such large amounts of capital?" Given the projected annual shortfall of $9-11 billion, Exxon clearly could not raise this on the U.S. equity market. Interestingly, the largest single offering ever presented in the United States in 1978 had been $1 billion in a single year. But this was the beginning of larger-scale direct placements of debt, which increased corporate capabilities and corporate risks enormously. Exxon could undoubtedly raise further debt based on its strong balance sheet. However, one can establish that permanent incremental borrowing would be limited to approximately $1-2 billion per year, if Exxon is to maintain a strong balance sheet. This means that the primary source capital for Exxon will have to be current cash flows, or joint ventures with outside parties. Exxon can raise $1.3 billion per year by stopping its dividend payment, but this still falls short of the investments needed to maintain its market share.

One can ask, "Who might these partners be?" Clearly the host countries would be among the primary sources for such joint venturing, since other oil companies will have similar capital problems. Host country cash flows, given high oil prices, could be very large, especially in the Arab OPEC countries. One can then raise, "What implications does such joint project ownership have for the company and for the United States?" A next major question is, "Where does Exxon earn its money in 1978?" Both from the financial statements of the company and from data in the case, it is clear that the major margins in the oil business were at the well head. At that time, there was a $32 per barrel price, with finding and lifting costs in the Middle East varying from 50 cents to $1.50. Because of refining overcapacity and heavy competition at the transportation and distribution levels, margins at those levels were small. The main value added occurred at the well head. Yet, the host countries now owned the well heads. Where will Exxon make its future profits? This can lead directly to a "value chain" analysis. Another interesting question is where should Exxon invest? As a result of its own $135-200 billion investment, Exxon could create new markets of approximately 1.5 times this amount (i.e., $200-$300 billion) per year for its own sales at the end of a decade. In addition, there would presumably be Keynesian multipliers of growth for the host countries. Thus the patterning of Exxon's investments from a resource, economic growth, and marketing viewpoint is important.

Resources Strategy

Once some general sense of the potential scale of Exxon's operation is developed, one can begin asking, "What should Exxon's resources strategy be? Who owns the remaining oil in the ground?" Clearly sovereign nations do. "Should Exxon attempt to break up OPEC in the late 70s when it was considered the bete noir of the West? Are OPEC's interests significantly different from those of Exxon?" Interestingly, Exxon can benefit enormously from price increases in its raw material. In 1978, it still owned some 22 billion barrels of oil. As OPEC increased the price from $10 in 1973 to $20 per barrel in 1978, Exxon benefited by approximately $220 billion in value (minus taxes). In addition, increases in price allow Exxon to use secondary or tertiary processing on its existing reserves, expanding the number of barrels actually available for exploitation. Within reasonable ranges, there is a "natural coalition" between the oil companies and OPEC. Note the very low profitability of the oil companies until OPEC increased prices.

One should now inquire, "What is the U.S. government's interest in increased prices?" From a government viewpoint, increased prices allow increased exploration for U.S. oil and gas resources. This enhances the potential availability of such resources in the United States, with important defense implications. To the extent that these investments are made in the United States there will be regional economic booms. The government will increase its tax income significantly on energy and its related products. In addition, if the government wishes to encourage conservation, the best way to do this is to allow a price increase. This will decrease externalities (like acid rain, carbon dioxide buildup, and other forms of environmental pollution). The main negative feature is a potential slowdown in economic activity and some inflation. The professor may wish to inquire if on balance the national government's and state government's interests don't also favor a price increase for energy (within reason). Given these events, "What should Exxon's strategy be? Should it invest heavily in the United States? In new resources internationally? How can it afford these investments, unless prices increase? How can it stimulate price increases legally and ethically? Should it significantly increase its domestic portfolio of oil and gas resources? If so, why? If not, why not?"

Again, one should note a broad range of commonality of interest between the host countries and Exxon. The professor should also note the relatively weak bargaining power of Exxon in the late 1970s-early 1980s because of the dependence of Exxon on host countries for raw material sources. A final question is, "Should Exxon significantly shift its portfolio from oil toward coal, gas, nuclear, chemicals?"

Portfolio

This leads directly into a portfolio analysis of Exxon's existing and potential product lines. By listing these on one side of the board and their portfolio roles on the other side, one can graphically diagram an interesting portfolio.

Investment Area	Portfolio Role	Hurdle Rate For Investments
Oil	Cash cow	COC + 5-10%
Gas	Near growth vector	COC + 5%
Coal	Intermediate growth	COC + ?
Nuclear Fuels	Perform Research	Planned Loss
Exotics (solar and fusion)	Public Relations and Defensive Posture	Planned Loss
Chemicals	Near growth, added value	COC + 5-7%
Diversification?	Future star	COC + ?

*COC = Cost of Capital

Groups will tend to vary a bit on what role they think each product line should have. Obviously, the professor should inquire as to the group's reasoning, not impose an arbitrary portfolio. However, an interesting next question is, "What should the average rate of return on the portfolio be in order to maintain Exxon's desired growth rate?" Using the classic Boston Consulting Group formula, one can calculate the required average rate of return as follows:

Exxon Corporation 1978

Asset Growth Rate = % Earnings Retained on Debt Fin. + % Retained on Equity Fin.

Sustainable Asset Growth Rate = $\dfrac{Debt}{Equity}$ × $\dfrac{Hurdle\ Interest}{(Rate-Cost)}$ × Percent Retained + Hurdle Rate × Percent Retained

G = $\dfrac{D}{E}$ (H - i) × P + H × P

15.5% = .18 (H - .08) × .5 + H × .5

$$155 \quad = \quad .09H \quad - \quad .0072 \quad + \quad .5H$$

$$162 \quad = \quad .59H$$

$$27.4 \quad = \quad H$$

Assumptions

G = 5.5% = Rate to grow assets from $41.5B to $176B in 10 yrs.

P = 50% average percent of Net Earnings paid out as dividends $1.3B
                                                                         $2.7B

i = 8% after tax cost of interest

H = Hurdle rate for investments to yield desired growth rate

If Exxon is to achieve an average return on its investments of 22-25%, what rates of return must it earn on each element in the portfolio? Because of the heavy weightings given to oil and gas in this portfolio, they will have to achieve rates somewhat above the targeted average. Coal will probably have to earn a present value rate of return somewhat less than the average, because of start-up costs. Nuclear fuels will probably earn an even lower rate, but should exceed break-even costs, including allocated capital costs. Exotics will be undertaken on a "planned cost" basis, not expecting a positive cash flow at this time. Chemicals should earn near the desired rate of return. Note this is a "strategic reallocation portfolio" and probably should deviate from ordinary risk-return considerations in the short run. Finally, there is the question of diversification.

Mission Statement

With the above pieces of analysis in place, students can be asked to lay out a mission statement for Exxon. This usually ends up being something like: "The world's leading low cost reliable energy supplier." However, one should ask why the choice of the term energy? Why not oil? Why not hydrocarbons? Then one should point out that this definition is inadequate in a number of dimensions. If Exxon is to be successful, it must also include in its mission statement what it brings to the host countries on which it is so dependent, i.e., economic development, revenue or tax collection, resource development, and so on.

In addition, one should specify the continuing distinctive competitive edge of Exxon given the fact that host countries will own its raw materials. What should Exxon do that will let it earn higher margins than its competitors? Should Exxon specialize in downstream activities? Marketing and distribution? Host country development? Host and customer country logistic interrelationships? High technology? Financing? What will make Exxon different from its competitors and hence able to have higher margins than they do? Does it have any special economies of scale, or should it develop certain new economies of scale? Can it gain added margins or returns based upon its exceptional economic development skills and potentials? The professor should point out that unless Exxon genuinely meets the demands of its various constituencies in its mission statement, it is unlikely to be successful in the complex political world of the 1980s and 90s. This may be a natural point to ask for specific suggestions concerning policies to deal with the "conflicts" developed in the preceding discussion.

Distinctive Competency/Value Added

Given the fact that host countries now own raw materials and Exxon can no longer capture much of the value added at the well head, where can it add value? Create a distinctive competency? The attached chart suggests where value can be added by Exxon. Probably the highest potential areas are: (1) developing technology for finding, lifting, and distribution of energy, (2) controlling the logistics between producing and using countries, (3) managing the buying, trading and blending of energy products, (4) using Exxon's distribution system to deliver other (retail and financial) products, (5) becoming an indispensable development partner for its host countries. These are the points in the value chain where it should focus. Note they are all intellectual and services activities. For a complete model of the value chain in this circumstance see Exhibit 1. Focusing on what Exxon can do best and developing "best-in-world" capabilities in these core service activities will be the key to Exxon's new strategy. Critical to this is developing a "best-in-world" information and logistics system in the energy field.

Public Image

If Exxon is to achieve the wider margins it needs to make the necessary capital investments to make the changes the 1970s and '80s call for, it will have to manage its public image well. It wants to appear very helpful to host countries. To customers, it must appear to be working to generate "new energy alternatives." While working with OPEC, it must appear to be unsettled by high oil prices. It must therefore consciously engage in a series of public relations activities to make its customers less unhappy with paying high prices for oil. It must genuinely work on environmental concerns, increasing stability and availability of supplies, and watch its rates of profitability carefully enough to avoid government attacks or new taxes which absorb its profits. It obviously did not give enough attention to environmental concerns, and damaged itself unnecessarily and badly at Valdez. This raises the essential need not to just mouth the interests of stakeholders in a company's mission statement, but to follow this up with resource allocations, performance measures, and controls. How to do this creates some very interesting discussions.

Organization

Given the conclusions from the above discussions, how should Exxon organize its primary structure to achieve its strategy? A useful and activating opening for this discussion is to ask students what activities they would centralize and why. They quickly conclude that finance and controllership should be centralized. Legal activities are also likely to appear quickly. Beyond this, one should think about those activities Exxon should centralize for strategic reasons. These probably include: technology used for trading relationships with host countries, logistics control over the interface between supplier and customer nations, public relations to ensure consistency and adequate attention, exploration to develop new resources in regions of the world where Exxon wishes to have a future presence, information systems which are crucial to maintaining its strategic intelligence functions, government relationships (lobbying, etc.), and executive recruitment and placement.

Next, it is fairly easy to get students to decide what should be decentralized. They will quickly say "operations." One can inquire whether this means marketing, local exploration, refining, chemicals, etc.? Then one can bring in any degree of complexity desired concerning issues such as the location of refineries too large for a single market, exploration in new areas for strategic purposes, etc. One can ask who should manage these local entities. Should they have boards of directors made up of local nationals? If so, to whom are these nationals loyal? What issues does this present?

However, the key to the primary organization is the structure that exists between those centralized functions described above and the "operating units" at local levels. Should the company be organized by product line? By regions? In a matrix format? One can pursue the

Exhibit 1

"Integrated" Oil Companies

Finding and Development

| Research for Techniques | Structure Scanning | Seismic Studies | Experimental Drilling | Developmental Drilling | Infrastructure Development | Transport |

Processing and Distribution

| Plant Engr. | Pre Refining | Refining | Trading | Mixing Blending | Transportation Out | Marketing | Distribution | Service |

Specialized Support

| Legal | Real Estate Mgt. | Corporate Intelligence | Logistics Integration | Taxes | Finance | Personnel Training | Govt. Relations | Long-Range Planning | Accounting |

pros and cons of each of these. Given the high dependency of Exxon on host countries for both raw materials and joint venture financing, it is probably more desirable during the late '70s-early '80s to organize "by regions" in order to obtain close relationships with governments and to be responsive to local needs. Some form of matrix organization is probably essential—i.e., if a "regional organization" form is chosen, a centralized matrix of "product expertise" (oil, gas, coal, chemicals, etc.) may be necessary for efficiency and coordination. If the primary organization is by product lines, some method of coordination among nations and groups will be needed. Many interesting questions can be raised in this organization discussion.

The Mid-1980s Cutback Strategy

The type of analysis described above is appropriate for the mid-'80s strategy, if one believes that there will be continuing growth in the energy markets. However, if one believes that there will be a relatively rapid downturn, then perhaps some other strategy is called for. By 1984, it would be clear that a cutback strategy is essential. One can then begin to query, "How should such a strategy be carried out? What should be cut first? What should be the main thrust of a retrenchment strategy? How should Exxon reorganize if it believes that the industry is in for a serious near-term decline? What elements of the late 1970s strategy would have to be modified or reversed? What should the 'new Exxon' look like?" Following are some of the more interesting dimensions of a "cutback strategy."

By the mid 1980s, it was apparent that the oil-energy industry was in for a tightening up. Oil prices had forced conservation measures which lowered the rate of consumption of fossil fuels to the point where there was a developing "oil glut." Exxon, like most oil companies, began to look for ways to cut back. Exxon particularly concentrated on cutting back its overhead groups and leaning down its operating organizations. After a careful analysis, it sold off some 25% of its service stations, maintaining a larger scale, more selective distribution throughout its network. The throughput of the remaining stations went up some 30% on average. As oil movements slowed, Exxon cut back its total controlled ocean fleet by some 40%. Much of this was accomplished by decreasing leased bottoms. It shut down some 14 refineries and concentrated on its more modern refineries designed to produce lighter products with higher value added. It adopted a new technology called Flexicoking, which allowed the company to shift over to the more available, heavier crude feed stocks. The shift to heavy crudes also opened up more possible resources for the company.

At the retail level, Exxon focused on automation and new convenience products salable through its service stations. As it became apparent that certain operations were not essential, these units were sold or auctioned off. Exxon now pulled back from some of its peripheral activities and dedicated itself to its basic business of oil, gas, and coal. By the end of 1985, Exxon had 23% less refining capacity, 25% fewer gas stations, and 17% fewer employees than in 1980.

Supply Sources

Exxon undertook perhaps the most aggressive search for oil and gas resources in the industry. However, unlike most of its competitors, it concentrated on looking internationally, rather than in the United States. Because of the availability of heavier crudes, tar sands, and so on, it focused on finding a portfolio of locations for such sources that would enable it to maintain secure low cost supplies despite varying world and economic conditions. Wherever possible, it sought sources outside the OPEC nations. It sought to acquire reserves in areas where it already operated and thus could leverage its existing presence. Exhibit 2 shows the kind of sourcing-market portfolio Exxon needed to analyze.

As drilling costs declined because of the surplus supplies of drilling equipment and personnel, Exxon's stable dollar expenditures on exploration actually allowed it to up its drilling

EXHIBIT 2

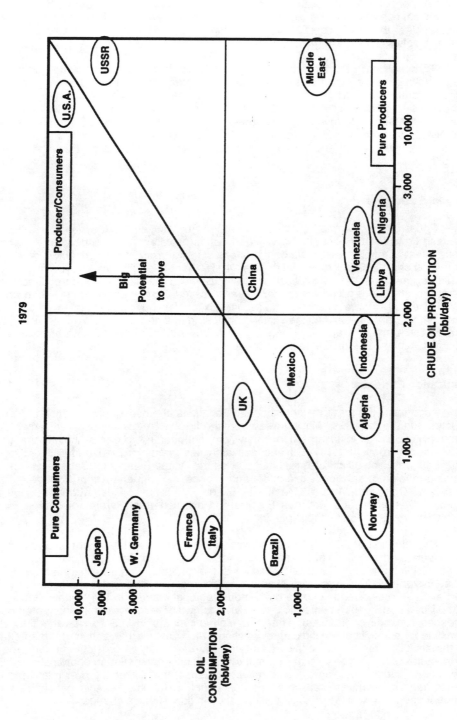

1979

Source: Compiled from data in Energy Information Administration, U.S. Department of Energy, *International Energy Annual 1979.*

423

rates. It maintained a large presence in the North Sea (perhaps the biggest multinational presence), consolidated its relationships with Norway, and it sold its Swedish marketing and petrochemical operations to Statoil. It dropped out of its shale oil relationships with Colony Oil as it became clear that shale costs could not be competitive. It entered into exploration contracts with the People's Republic of China.

Through heavy investments in technology development, its unit finding and lifting costs were the lowest in the industry, giving it a distinctive competitive advantage. In consortia with other companies and host countries (Venezuela and Canada) it pressed heavy oil and tar sand technologies as hard as possible. As distressed properties became available, it began minor purchases of reserves from smaller companies. However, unlike other oil companies, it did not enter into the massive merger movement. Instead, its basic strategy appeared to be to maintain a strong financial position and to be ready to buy out the reserves of distressed companies as they collapsed.

Financial Strategies

Prices broke downward rapidly from 1983 to '86. As it cut back expenditures, Exxon had huge cash flows in 1984 and 1985. While investing heavily in new resources, it managed its balance sheet carefully to avoid big debt burdens. Unlike many of its competitors who had debt percentages of 60-80%, Exxon maintained a 14-17% debt-to-equity ratio. In the mid-'80s Exxon began an aggressive share repurchase program. By 1986 the company had acquired 14% of its stock at a cost of $5.3 billion. Stock repurchases saved Exxon substantial dividend payments, but Wall Street observers noted that, in essence, Exxon was buying back its own reserves at $4-$5 a barrel, which was less than the exploration cost to find new barrels. With its strong balance sheet, Exxon remained optimally positioned to buy out some of the larger, distressed oil companies, if they came on the market. (See Exhibit 3.)

Organization Changes

Accompanying these major cutback reallocations, the overall organization of Exxon was restructured in the mid-'80s. Moving away from the flexible "regionally-oriented" organization of the late 1970s, Exxon installed a dominantly "product-oriented" organization. Major operating units were cut from 14 to 9. Oil and gas activities were grouped under 3 units: Exxon International, to which all affiliates reported outside the United States and Canada; Exxon U.S.A., containing refining, marketing, exploration, and finance; and Imperial Oil of Canada. Other line units were: Coal and Mining, Chemicals, Exxon Enterprises, Research and Engineering, Production Research, and Reliance Electric. In addition, there were, of course, staff and coordinative groups reporting to the president and CEO.

The intention of the reorganization was to eliminate many layers of management, shrink the workforce, and alter lines of command to quicken the pace of decision making. About 90% of Exxon's $8 billion in annual capital spending in the mid-'80s would be handled by only three entities: Exxon U.S.A., Exxon International, and Imperial Oil. The regional offices of the Middle East, Far East, etc. disappeared as did various regional centers in the United States. Exxon U.S.A. divided its 16 departments into three divisions, two of which were fully integrated operating businesses (or mini companies). The third element in Exxon U.S.A. was the financial unit responsible for administration and control functions, etc. This reorganization represented several main thrusts. Clearly, the company was interested in focusing on cost cutting and productivity measures, flexible response to changing market conditions, and optimum coordination of Exxon's sprawling international holdings. It also reflected the fact that Exxon's power relative to its host countries had significantly increased as the host countries got into financial difficulties and were dependent upon oil revenues. Exhibit 4 shows the net flow of these changes.

Exhibit 3

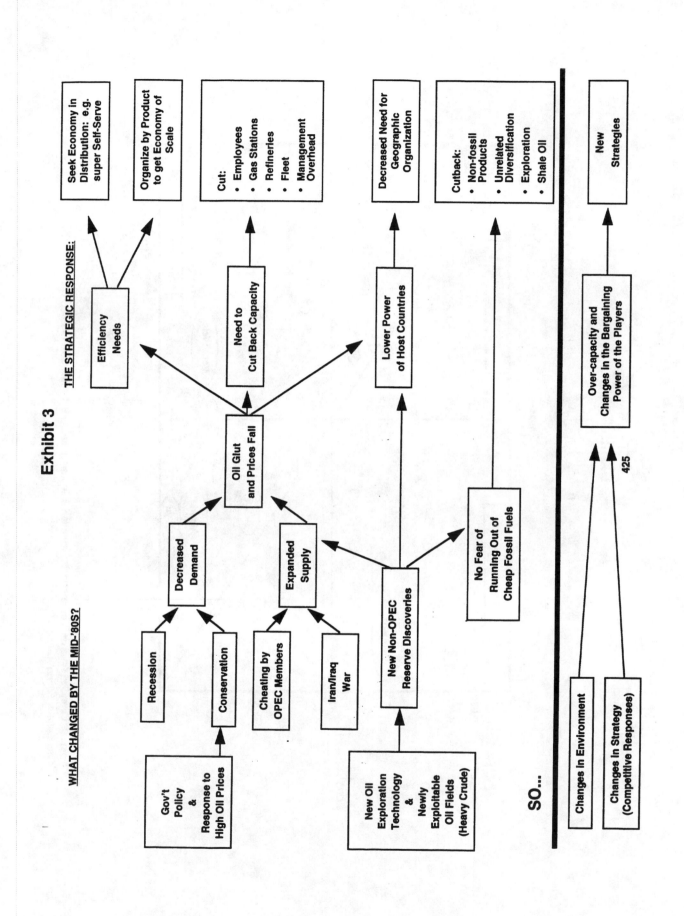

WHAT CHANGED BY THE MID-'80S?

THE STRATEGIC RESPONSE:

Seek Economy in Distribution: e.g. super Self-Serve

Organize by Product to get Economy of Scale

Cut:
- Employees
- Gas Stations
- Refineries
- Fleet
- Management Overhead

Decreased Need for Geographic Organization

Cutback:
- Non-fossil Products
- Unrelated Diversification
- Exploration
- Shale Oil

New Strategies

Efficiency Needs

Need to Cut Back Capacity

Lower Power of Host Countries

Over-capacity and Changes in the Bargaining Power of the Players

Oil Glut and Prices Fall

Decreased Demand

Expanded Supply

New Non-OPEC Reserve Discoveries

No Fear of Running Out of Cheap Fossil Fuels

Recession

Conservation

Cheating by OPEC Members

Iran/Iraq War

Gov't Policy & Response to High Oil Prices

New Oil Exploration Technology & Newly Exploitable Oil Fields (Heavy Crude)

SO...

Changes in Environment

Changes in Strategy (Competitive Responses)

425

EXHIBIT 4

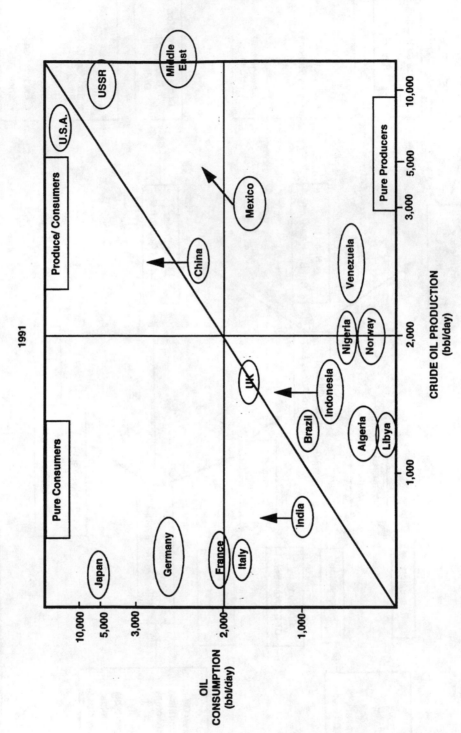

1991

Pure Consumers

Produce/ Consumers

U.S.A.

USSR

Middle East

China

Mexico

Venezuela

Nigeria

Norway

UK

Indonesia

Brazil

Algeria

Libya

India

Japan

Germany

France

Italy

Pure Producers

OIL CONSUMPTION (bbl/day)

10,000
5,000
3,000
2,000
1,000

CRUDE OIL PRODUCTION (bbl/day)

1,000
2,000
3,000
5,000
10,000

Source: Compiled from data in Energy Information Administration, U.S. Department of Energy, *International Energy Annual 1992.*

426

Early 1990s

Despite its continuing strong operational and financial performance, morale at Exxon began to come apart after the Valdez spill of eleven million gallons of crude into Prince William's Sound on Good Friday, 1989. Exxon was widely criticized for its handling of this situation. Before the Valdez incident, Exxon was in sixth place on *Fortune's* list of America's most admired corporations. By 1990 it had slipped to number 110. Despite its high publicity and large cost, the Valdez spill was slowly being assessed by the environmental professionals as much less of a long-term hazard than was at first feared. Yet the cost of cleanup (of some $8,000 per barrel) wiped out all of the profits made by Exxon on its wells, refineries, and service stations in the United States that year. Worse yet the company's handling of the Valdez spill had deeply affected the company and its employees' morale. Criminal trials for its environmental actions could cause Exxon serious long-term problems. This case can be used as a very effective vehicle for arguing that environmental concerns in a major company should be given as much consideration as standard financial and operating parameters. This became very important as global warming, ozone depletion, and local pollution concerns increased in the 1990s.

In the 1990s, world economic growth would force Exxon, once again, to reassess its strategies. One of these was its relative positioning vs. each major supplier and user nation as shown in Exhibit 2-4. Large net producers, such as Indonesia and the Middle East, were becoming consumers as well, while India, China, and Southeast Asia were increasing their demands enormously and would continue to do so in the future. A major shift in oil supplies had occurred as the USSR broke up and its enormous resources became more available to the world. How should Exxon approach this? The trillions of barrels of oil in Canadian tar sands and Venezuelan heavy oils were opened up by technologies jointly developed by the countries and the oil majors. Natural gas supplies seemed extensive enough to last for decades. Each country would require a different strategy as its relative resource and use positions changed. How should Exxon organize to meet this changed portfolio of opportunities and risks? What should it do about the emerging environmental problems fossil energy use caused?

Given the new world marketplace, what should (and must) Exxon's core competencies be? Where in the value chain can it make greater profits than other competitors? What should it outsource? Keep in house? Joint venture? What does all this imply for its organization structure? Power of decentralized units? Planning and control systems? Relations with host countries? The U.S. government? Key suppliers? What policies will give it the combined low costs and high margins it seeks? How can it increase its power relative to its important stakeholders without causing retaliation?

Update 1995

While the actions of a company do not make its decisions right or wrong, the following seem to be the major directions Exxon is taking. The downward slide of oil prices continued during 1993-94, to about $14 a barrel. The entire industry responded with massive layoffs, cutting literally thousands of jobs. Many analysts said that these were jobs unnecessarily added on during the boom of the 1970s and early '80s. While natural gas demand was growing at about 3% annually, oil demand growth had been about 1.8%. Exxon had cut operating costs by 1.6 billion since 1992 and had sold off approximately $1 billion in assets in each of the past three years. The oil industry settled down for a very tight competitive era, as environmental costs increased in European and North American locations.

With sales of $111 billion and profits of $5.3 billion in 1993, Exxon's turnover was equivalent to an economy three times that of Ireland. It produced $1.7 billion of oil per day, only slightly less than Nigeria and marketed almost 5 million barrels per day, enough to meet the needs of both Germany and France. Nevertheless, Exxon had cut one-third of its employees since 1980 and had made higher returns on average than any of its big six competitors until the

Exxon Valdez fiasco. Exxon had a tradition of conservative financial management which had made it tighten up much more rapidly than many of its competitors. Its heavy use of financial management measures allowed it to shift decisions to subsidiaries, which were given greater freedom than in most of its competitors. Exxon had saved over $1 billion in operating costs in America alone during the past two years, cutting half the head office jobs and spending half as much a decade earlier looking for oil and gas, while finding almost as much. Its decentralized, bottom-up culture had served the company well, focusing on profitability and productivity in the downturn, and allowing Exxon greater flexibility than most of its competitors.

By 1994, imports supplied almost 50% of the U.S. domestic market, up from 25% in the mid-1980s. Barred by environmental concerns from drilling in many of the most promising areas of North America, big American companies were investing heavily in China, Russia, Vietnam, Argentina, and offshore areas of Europe. There were two major plays within the U.S. zone though. One of these was near Prudhoe Bay, where a great controversy raged over whether to open the Arctic National Wildlife Reserve for drilling. The other was in the western region of the Gulf of Mexico where huge oil finds were struck in 1993-94 in waters as deep as 3,000 feet. Exxon had lagged in deep water drilling technology. A crucial point was that U.S. finding costs were now about $5 per barrel, vs. about $1.50 for a new barrel in the Persian Gulf area. Perversely, environmental regulations disallowing coastal U.S. and Alaskan exploration forced imports on to tankers which a National Academy of Sciences study said leaked or discharged 30 times as much oil into the sea as offshore production facilities would have. Similarly perversely, foreign governments allow international companies to recoup their capital expenditures quickly, while taking the bulk of their own share later in the projects. Traditionally, the U.S. government has grabbed more up-front, while allowing the companies a larger share of later profits. Oil imports in 1993 came to about $54 billion. Despite dire predictions, technology had allowed the finding cost of oil to decrease steadily, especially when one included the massive reserves of tar sands and heavy oils in Canada and Venezuela (estimated at between 5 and 6 trillion barrels equivalent).

During 1994, Exxon's earnings from chemical operations approached $1 billion, more than double the 1993 results. Its exploration and production earnings grew despite a year-to-year decline of $1.30 per barrel in average crude prices between 1983 and 1994. More importantly, in the last decade, over one-third of the world's land area had become available to private enterprise. This included China and the USSR, as well as offshore Vietnam and Indonesia. Exxon's total resource base of 37 billion oil-equivalent barrels in 1994 was still the largest in the industry. It had a leading position in pipeline-served natural gas for markets in North America, Western Europe, and some Asia Pacific nations. It had lagged in the development of liquefied natural gas (LNG), but was working hard on that problem. Exxon's four base strategies for 1994 were: (1) pursue all attractive exploration opportunities by applying the best available technology and responding quickly; (2) invest in projects that deliver superior returns, even at relatively low energy prices; (3) capitalize on the growing natural gas market, to exploit Exxon's substantial gas resources and to supply profitably developing world markets where it held a leadership position; and (4) maximize profitability of existing oil and gas production, within the context of safe and reliable operations, improvement in operating technologies, and constant cost reductions.

Its exploration activities in 1993-94 had replaced 106% of its production in 1994 overall, and 137% of production in North America. Its aggressive pursuit of exploration technologies had lowered finding costs from about $4.00 per barrel in 1986 to approximately $1.30 per barrel in 1993. However, its downstream earnings, despite substantial efforts to improve them, had dropped about 31% between 1993-94. This was explained as primarily caused by "declining refining margins everywhere." On the downstream side, Exxon expanded its marketing into Eastern Europe substantially, opening approximately 150 new outlets. Domestically, it concentrated on adding or modernizing stations in areas where it had a strong brand position, while cutting back in areas where it was weaker.

Throughout the world, Exxon was committed to being a low cost producer. In its Exxon chemical units, it had reduced costs by 22% since 1990. Exxon Chemical has had a higher return on capital employed than the estimated average returns earned by competitor's chemical operations since the late 1980s. Elsewhere, Exxon was divesting non-strategic assets, strengthening its mining operations to reduce costs, selectively extending mine capacities in the coal and copper industries, and expanding its presence in the Hong Kong electric power business. Its overall operating summary for 1994 is shown in Exhibit 5.

Analysts estimated that Exxon's earnings could grow at approximately 8% annually over the next five years and that its dividends and its 15.3 x P/E multiple made it a continuing attractive investment. Many expected oil prices to ease upward due to heavy worldwide demand. Exxon's natural gas production was expected to grow by a sizable 25% to the year 2000. "Exxon remained a leader in the international downstream business, with a premier refining and marketing network and leading market positions outside the United States in Europe and Asia." Exxon was the third largest chemical company in the United States and the ninth largest in the world. Its active exploration and huge resource base continue to offer downside risk buffers and upside return potentials. Its finances had been kept under strong control; consequently, risks were minimal on the operating side. Uncertainties were primarily in the realm of crude oil price, economic growth, tax issues, environmental costs, and the unknowns of the civil suits behind the Exxon Valdez lawsuits.

New foreign crude oil production in the early years would come largely from the North Sea, while foreign natural gas businesses would fuel future growth. Exxon intended to be an active explorer in Russia, which held huge reserves—estimated at one-fifth of the world's undiscovered hydrocarbon potentials. It also had high potential positions in the Tarim Basin in China and the East China Sea. Exxon had the highest upstream profitability among its major competitors in the preceding five years. Its locations were highly diversified. It had an interest in thirty oil refineries in eighteen countries and a share in nearly 27,000 miles of pipeline, as well as owning or sharing 36,000 service stations worldwide. Exxon was a leader in all of the international markets where it operated and had a number one retail market position in the United Kingdom and an average of a 13% market share in its European operations. It had a well-established presence in the rapidly growing markets of Southeast Asia, particularly Thailand, Singapore, and Malaysia. The company had 22% of refinery capacity and an average 18% market position in these areas.

Exhibit 5
Exxon Corporation
10-Year Operating Summary

	1994	1993	1992	1991	1990	1989	1988	1987	1986	1985	1984
Production of crude oil and natural gal liquids						*(thousands of barrels daily)*					
Net production											
United States	562	553	591	619	640	693	760	756	761	768	778
Canada	251	254	268	278	302	312	249	222	196	145	114
Europe	484	423	396	363	313	351	444	456	473	431	426
Asia-Pacific	325	347	346	342	331	328	345	338	313	337	315
Other Non-U.S.	87	90	104	113	126	120	121	63	53	39	45
Worldwide	1,709	1,667	1,705	1,715	1,712	1,804	1,919	1,835	1,796	1,720	1,678
Natural gas production available for sale						*(thousands of cubic feet daily)*					
Net production											
United States	2,021	1,764	1,607	1,655	1,778	1,827	1,805	1,698	1,919	2,085	2,485
Canada	286	328	326	355	413	417	209	147	142	141	168
Europe	2,842	3,049	3,097	3,010	2,694	2,707	2,787	3,012	2,946	3,114	2,960
Asia-Pacific	827	678	577	411	369	376	332	308	267	250	235
Other Non-U.S.	2	6	54	66	64	58	59	62	55	71	70
Worldwide	5,978	5,825	5,661	5,497	5,318	5,385	5,192	5,227	5,329	5,661	5,918
Refinery crude oil runs						*(thousands of barrels daily)*					
United States	931	841	911	937	868	999	968	1,026	1,080	1,054	1,021
Canada	422	408	391	432	489	487	350	351	332	344	365
Europe	1,425	1,389	1,387	1,401	1,327	1,257	1,200	1,116	1,112	1,003	1,111
Asia-Pacific	521	515	507	464	498	463	430	397	415	399	424
Other Non-U.S.	113	116	107	99	94	93	94	91	93	103	299
Worldwide	3,412	3,269	3,303	3,333	3,276	3,299	3,042	2,981	3,032	2,903	3,220
Petroleum product sales											
United States	1,196	1,152	1,203	1,210	1,109	1,147	1,113	1,057	1,106	1,123	1,149
Canada	520	517	513	527	597	625	433	430	396	404	407
Latin America	426	422	411	391	384	383	386	388	380	377	400
Europe	1,898	1,872	1,847	1,863	1,796	1,718	1,680	1,634	1,636	1,629	1,684
Asia-Pacific and other Eastern Hemisphe	988	962	935	878	869	847	784	619	607	633	635
Worldwide	5,028	4,925	4,909	4,869	4,755	4,720	4,396	4,128	4,125	4,166	4,275
Aviation fuels	403	379	376	372	382	382	344	338	317	326	312
Gasoline, naphthas	1,849	1,818	1,822	1,821	1,742	1,708	1,572	1,488	1,461	1,423	1,404
Heating oils, kerosene, diesel oils	1,644	1,569	1,557	1,561	1,491	1,498	1,424	1,344	1,365	1,367	1,372
Heavey fuels	530	558	546	535	543	507	466	419	463	561	709
Specialty petroleum products	602	601	608	580	597	625	590	539	519	489	478
Worldwide	5,028	4,925	4,909	4,869	4,755	4,720	4,396	4,128	4,125	4,166	4,275
Coal production						*(millions of metric tons)*					
	36	36	37	39	40	36	32	30	27	26	23
Copper production						*(thousands of metric tons)*					
	191	183	133	108	112	119	134	101	79	77	67

Operating statistics include 100 percent of operations of magority-owned subsidiaries; for other companies, gas, cruce productions and petroleum product sales include Exxon's ownership percentage, and crude runs include quantities processed for Exxon. Net production excludes royalties and quantities due others when produced, whether payment is made in kind or cash.

Overview

Sony Corporation: Innovation System provides a clear overview of the innovation process in both a small company environment and later in a large company. Because Sony is a Japanese company, it offers a chance to challenge some of the stereotypes about Japanese management. It allows a thorough discussion of the impact of corporate culture on important management issues like innovation. It also offers an opportunity to evaluate a successful past strategy and to recommend significant changes for the future, as Sony enters a much more competitive, commodity-like stage in its products' life cycles. The development of the video tape recorder is described in some detail so that the professor can bring up various issues that are common to innovations in large organizations. It also offers an opportunity to question why the United States—despite the fact that the video tape recorder was invented by Ampex—did not exploit this remarkable innovation as quickly and as well as the Japanese did. This case makes an excellent vehicle for bringing out issues in the entrepreneurial or innovative context. It also teaches well in sections on organizational adhocracies and corporate culture. It ends with the need to detail a specific program strategy for its latest product, an all-electronic still camera system, called Mavica.

Session Structure

We ordinarily open this case by looking at the start-up stage of the company and comparing it to other start ups in the U.S. culture. Then we look at those factors and practices that make the company innovative as it grows in size. Next, we look at Sony's past strategy and evaluate that. Finally, we develop a future strategy for Sony, given the changes in its products' life cycles and increased competition in the marketplace. The case fits the McKinsey & Co. "Seven S" or "Excellent Company" criteria very well. This can be used as a framework for evaluating the company's past practices, if desired.

Early Success Factors

One can start the discussion with the broad question, "What critical factors led to Sony's successful early formation and initial growth?" The following factors are probably the most important ones to bring out. Again, note how these critical factors relate to the readings on "innovation" and "entrepreneurship."

A. <u>Close to the Need</u>. In the early post-war period, Ibuka produced products and services for which there was a distinct, obvious need. Consequently, he did not need a complex marketing or distribution system for his products. Thus, he was able to generate enough cash flow to keep his operation together and to develop his next generation of products.

B. <u>An Inventor's Outlook</u>. Mr. Ibuka was constantly looking for ways to satisfy a need in a more effective manner: "To do the job better." Consequently, he focused on developing products' whose performance was significantly greater than those currently available. Ibuka intuitively sought a "different way" to accomplish this goal. This lets him avoid entrenched opposition, and offers some potential patent or know-how protection.

C. Developing a Cash Flow. Ibuka's repair services, voltmeters, and radios created a basic cash flow, allowing him to invest in other projects. Almost all new ventures need some method of obtaining early cash flow. Otherwise the long cycle from invention to successful exploitation can kill the company.

D. Missionary Attitudes. Ibuka's charismatic personality and missionary zeal attracted people to the company. His dedication to his people's growth forced him to look for new opportunities, and his commitment to them solidifies their identity with Sony.

E. A Talented Fanatic. Ibuka is both technically skilled and personally determined. These characteristics are essential in the inventor-entrepreneur, who must perceive risks as being lower than others might and who must be willing to put up with the long-term difficulties of starting a company from a new technology base.

F. Clear Concept. Early on, Ibuka develops a clear concept for the company, i.e., "combining mechanical and electrical skills to produce unique products for new applications," which attracts people and gives cohesion to the group's diverse activities.

G. Balanced Team. The technologist Ibuka soon finds a person with similar values, but complementary skills. Mr. Morita handles marketing while Ibuka handles technology and production. As resources permit, Ibuka adds other people with further complementary viewpoints and skills. Typically, no one person has all the skills necessary to a start-up's success.

H. Low Initial Cost. By operating in a bombed-out department store and in old warehouses, Sony keeps its early costs low. This keeps it from building up a difficult financial situation. Ibuka is able to finance the company largely through internal cash flows, his own modest savings, and the investments of a few friends. Ibuka leverages his resources by having suppliers design and produce many items. Because Sony is spending money at a low rate, investors will see it as a lower risk proposition.

I. Flexibility. During this early stage, Ibuka tries many things, only a few of which work. Since innovation is a probabilistic process, it very often requires many false starts before finding a successful solution. In this kind of situation, formal planning is very difficult. Instead, strategy tends to be driven by a few guiding principles and to be highly experimental, opportunistic, and flexible.

J. Young, But Experienced. Ibuka is 37 years old when he starts the company. He is young enough to be extremely vigorous, yet have a substantial degree of experience behind him. These two factors help him raise finances and attract people to the company.

Overall, the professor can note that this start-up entrepreneurship in Japan bears many similarities to such entities in the United States. One can also point out that MITI had nothing to do with this company's development. In fact, MITI was a hindrance rather than a help.

Innovation in a Larger Company

The next set of questions is, "What makes Sony innovative as it grows? What are the characteristics present in an innovative larger company? Why are these things important?" The most important characteristics are probably the following:

A. Small Groups. Sony keeps its innovative teams small. This helps with communication within the team and identity with the team's goals. In the early stages, the teams are led by Mr. Ibuka himself. Later they are led by Dr. Kihara. Small groups can communicate rapidly and effectively to make the maximum number of experiments per unit time. This leads to more rapid technological progress.

B. Fast Turnaround Times. No time is wasted in obtaining decisions or in bureaucratic delays. Small teams and the closeness of these teams to the top of the organization lead to rapid decision making and hence progress.

C. Low Overhead. Even after the company gets somewhat larger, Sony occupies lower cost facilities and does not waste money on overheads. Note that Morita keeps the New York operation in low cost quarters, until its volume is built. This decreases risks and the cost of failed projects.

D. Time Horizon. Ibuka and Morita have extraordinary patience. The VTR project took some 23 years, the Mavica took 28 years. They are not driven by current profitability, but rather goals of innovation and contribution.

E. Overarching Goals. Because of the broader vision that Morita and Ibuka have, they can attract talented people, invest over a longer time cycle if necessary, obtain high motivation from their people, achieve high quality products through a willingness of the people to concentrate on quality.

F. Persistence. All of the above will work only if management itself is determined and persistent in the pursuit of innovation and performance. Mr. Ibuka "never gives up."

G. Hands-On Management. Because Ibuka and Morita visit the laboratories, like to deal with the technologies, and understand their technologies, they perceive lower risks in technological innovation than those less familiar with the process might. They inspire the researchers and keep decision cycle times to a minimum.

H. Little Formal Planning. Because of the essentially chaotic and probabilistic nature of innovation, little formal planning is frequently found in Sony until plants are being built or products are being introduced to the marketplace. Even then, note that formal market research often comes up with wildly wrong answers for radical new products. Many of Sony's new products found first markets that were totally unexpected.

I. Sets Key Targets. Ibuka is able to set a few key and stimulating targets for development. While being heavily involved in the innovation process, he does not set detailed specifications at first. Instead, he sets broad goals and lets others work out more specific goals and solutions. However, to guide the work he sets a few very specific targets which are "strategic," i.e., they will determine the success of the product in the marketplace if achieved.

J. Rewards and Incentives. Sony rewards its inventor-innovators informally, formally, and financially. Sony's management is aware of the fact that technologists work for many goals other than financial rewards. Consequently, it provides high visibility, recognition, and personal support for successful innovators.

K. Acceptance of Failure. Since innovation is a probabilistic process, a certain number of failures are to be expected. Because Morita and Ibuka understand innovation, they set difficult targets and expect some failures. However, they do not tolerate repeated failure from an individual.

L. Multiple Approaches. Sony undertakes several parallel projects toward a new innovation. This helps obtain identity among the project teams, creates several alternatives from which managers can choose, increases the information available for this choice, increases the probability that one of the approaches will in fact work, perhaps shortens cycle times to success because of the competitive atmosphere created, and so on.

M. Planned Transitions. Sony plans the transition from development to manufacturing by having manufacturing people participate on the development team. In addition, it rotates engineers into the marketplace, into production, and into other aspects of operations. This gives the engineers a much broader perspective on what is relevant and what is needed to achieve effective transfer of technology.

N. Hide It and Keep It Simple. Kihara does not have to justify projects in detail during their early phases. Instead, he can work on them long enough to create a model. The model then becomes a concrete basis for arguing against other alternatives. By allowing Dr. Kihara this kind of flexibility, management avoids killing projects prematurely and extends the developmental time horizon.

An Excellent Company?

The above items make a fair catalog of the characteristics of continuously innovative organizations. One can begin to raise some questions as to how to achieve these characteristics in an organization and some of the costs which may be attached to this mode of management. One can compare this to the McKinsey & Co. "Excellent Company" criteria. These are as follows:

A. The company is values driven.
B. The company sticks to its knitting (what it is good at).
C. Management stays close to customers.
D. Management is action-execution oriented; operating in a hands-on mode.
E. The company encourages autonomy and entrepreneurship—it operates in an "experimental mode."
F. The company achieves productivity through people by paying close attention to its people and supporting individuals and groups.
G. The organization is a simple line organization, with lean staff.
H. The company operates in a "loose style" with tight values and management controls on a few key items.
I. The company fosters internal competition (champions) operating in an ad hoc mode.
J. The company's style inculcates trust and loyalty.
K. The company operates with a flexible open style rather than with strict policies and orders.

Sony provides a superb opportunity to use the "7S" structure. Each element of Sony's strategy, structure, systems, shared values, etc. are mutually supportive. Students often find this a useful way to look at strategy in this kind of entrepreneurial context.

One important point should be introduced at this time. The professor should ask the class, "How does Sony's management style match up with the Japanese management style you have so often read about?" One will notice very marked differences between management styles in the Sony, Honda, and Matsushita cases. The differences and appropriateness of these styles should be brought out.

Keys to Past Success

At this point it is helpful to ask, "What have been the keys to Sony's past success in the marketplace?" This can be done as a formal strategic evaluation or just as a way to bring out those aspects of the past strategy which will have to be changed in the future. Among those items which should be brought out in this discussion are the following:

A. New Primary Markets. Each time Sony's profits have surged, it has been because of its entry into a new primary market, i.e., transistor radios, tape recorders, Trinitron televisions, video tape recorders. It has gained high margins by being alone in the marketplace, producing a quality product that people really wanted, limiting production in the early stages, then developing relatively low cost processes to maintain margins. Keys to this strategy are: to be the first innovator, to sell service and confidence as well as the product, to have long-term vision, and to maintain a flexible, fast moving, innovative organization (as suggested in the last section).

B. Distinct Competency. Sony's distinct competency in the past has been in product technology combining state-of-the-art electro-mechanical skills. It has sold stand-alone units which did not have to be tied in to standards developed by others. It has supported this distinct competency with a series of internal policies which give it a unique identity. Among these are the following:

1. Focusing on long-term goals on innovation and quality rather than financial return.

2. Maintaining close contact between top management, the market, and the innovative groups.

3. Developing performance targets which are sufficiently challenging to ensure that the company's product are unique.

4. Focusing on people not positions and titles, operating with a relatively loose structure which is goal driven.

5. Monitoring people with unusual talents and helping them develop through the "godfather" system.

6. Having a reward system matched to goals: rewarding groups for innovation, providing clear recognition for innovators, emphasizing fun or joy in achievement, creating an atmosphere for innovation supported by concepts like "the idea circus."

7. Having clear communications by short circuiting the formal organization, assisting innovators to remove barriers, developing a technological language which is understood by all, top management's walking about and expressing enthusiasm at the operating or bench level, keeping options going as long as possible, etc. (see innovation discussion).

8. Forcing interaction between engineering, production, and marketing by rotating engineers through sales and production, by forcing finance people into the factories, and by avoiding stigma on task forces which were not successful. Sony also avoided the use of committees, developed small "cells" in its factories to solve problems and to motivate individuals, and so on. Sony's policies actively forced interaction.

C. Quality: Lowest Cost to Customer. By focusing on quality in its products, Sony provided the lowest long-term cost to its customers, despite a possibly higher initial price. To accomplish this, it emphasized quality throughout its design process, componentry development, production processes, personnel selection and training, support systems, distributor networks, pricing, and even advertising of product performance (not emphasizing symbols or images but the product itself). Quality was featured in the policies of every functional area.

D. Avoiding Direct Confrontations with Competitors. Until it had a market position established, Sony had been able to avoid direct price or cost competition with those who became its main competitors. As such competition developed, Sony had frequently sold off the product line or dropped it. It has implicitly been willing to take risks and move into areas others could not conceive. Key to this is the intuition of Morita and Ibuka concerning possible market needs and their relationship to available technical solutions.

Critical Strategic Issues for the Early/Mid-1980s

By 1983, Sony was increasingly being forced to compete directly against major market forces like Matsushita, Toshiba, Hitachi, and the private brands groups supplying large distributors like RCA, General Electric, Sears Roebuck, or discount chains. The consumer marketplace had become much more competitive. Competition was on a world level, with major players being in virtually all world marketplaces. The cost of electronics was dropping rapidly and channels of distribution were consolidating, making it difficult to maintain price margins. Componentry had become an important element in all electronics products, and the major component manufacturers were increasingly operating "downstream" in consumer electronics, especially after new products have been established. Product life cycles seemed to be shortening, making it difficult to obtain returns on long-term research investments. Therefore, it is likely that Sony needs to undertake a major review of its strategy. Key considerations are the following:

A. <u>A concept shift to gain initial margins</u>. Should Sony shift more toward industrial markets where performance is often more important than price? Should it engage in more long-term partnerships with powerful mechanical electronics companies in major market areas (such as Europe and the United States)? Should it shift its innovation focus from products to processes, to enable it to defend its products in the marketplace and lengthen its life cycles?

B. <u>Reposition Its Portfolio</u>. Sony's product portfolio contains: television sets, audio equipment, video equipment, and various "other" products. The market for television sets is maturing and highly price competitive, representing a declining percentage of Sony's total sales (from 37% in 1975 to 23% in 1982). Audio equipment (which included stereo components, tapes and tape recorders, radio/cassette recorders, and radios) had represented a fairly stable portion of Sony's sales since the late 1970s (around 25%) despite the fact that individual products had soared and then been replaced by other newer ones like the Walkman. The compact disk player had the potential to boost sales in this product group but might end up simply replacing declining sales in older, more mature audio products. The market for video equipment was exploding, especially in the consumer marketplace, and grew from 23% of Sony's sales in 1980 to almost 43% in 1982. However, the video market was becoming increasingly price competitive and Sony's Beta format was slowly losing market share to the VHS format supported by its major competitors. The "other" category included a variety of products many of which were directed toward industrial/commercial markets.

Geographically, Sony's sales were concentrated in Japan, the United States, and Europe. Since sales in Japan represented a declining percentage of Sony's total sales (32% in 1980 and 26% in 1982) and world markets were growing (29% in United States, 24% in Europe, and 22% elsewhere for 1982), there might be some important opportunities for partnering with major producers or distributors internationally.

Sony's main portfolio problem is to replace declining TV sales with high volumes in other areas. Since consumer electronics and industrial/commercial electronics are rapidly merging in their performance characteristics, Sony should perhaps begin a strong industrial/commercial thrust, both domestically and in selected world markets, working with partners and customers to develop new concepts and then rolling these out through its consumer network. To do this, it needs to amplify its consumer network in the major markets where it competes. This is probably the weak link in Sony's value chain.

C. <u>Innovation Refocus</u>. All of the above suggests that Sony must refocus its innovation on: (1) more industrial electro-mechanical products, (2) process development to maintain quality at low cost, (3) entirely new products capable of opening initial markets in industrial sectors to replace television and to provide adequate growth. In the process, it probably needs to be more selective about new product introduction than it has been in the past and to avoid head-on competition with huge entrenched opposition—especially in areas like personal computers, where others have distinctive marketing leads. Getting this kind of refocus on markets in a highly innovative company like Sony—where the engineers have been kings—poses some fascinating problems.

Possible product areas for development pose no great issue, prioritizing them does. The case notes possible new markets in digital audio devices, video cameras and cassettes, broadcast quality cameras and studio equipment, innovative robotic equipment and accessories, type-recorders, word processors, small portable computers, video games, electro-optics, and so on. It is worthwhile to get the students to array a number of possibilities and then ask for prioritizing criteria. In each area, one should ask what partners Sony might find to do joint research or to provide complementary skills and capabilities in the marketplace.

D. Internal Planning and Controls. To cope with its more competitive marketplace, Sony clearly needs more focus on inventory controls. One can easily calculate that it is having serious troubles at the moment. Sony needs to be sure it can exploit full scale economies in production and in distribution. In the past, it has consciously kept its plant sizes small; can it continue this in the future? It needs much more focus on designs for low cost quality production and flexible automation to achieve maximum throughput in its factories. This may mean some shifts in project targeting, motivation systems; specifically how can this be done? Since Mr. Morita's skills are in consumer marketing, he should certainly be backed by a person with stronger internal control and process skills.

E. Organization. Given the portfolio arrived at above, and the internal needs defined by its new innovation and control strategies, how should Sony reorganize itself? What cultural changes will be necessary? Can it achieve these cultural changes? Should Sony be organized by product lines (as it now is) or by customer class (consumer, industrial, commercial)? Should it have an international product strategy? Be organized dominantly by regions? Why?

Should new product research and development be placed within the major profit divisions? If so, to what extent? If not, how should it be organized? Who should control relationships with Sony's international partners? What kind of technology sharing relationships will be necessary? How can Sony maintain its distinct competency in its new environment? Can it develop a two-cultures system? One culture could be in the manufacturing and marketing of maturing lines and another in the innovation and introduction of newer lines. We would urge the professor to ask the students to draw organization charts of their various proposals and see how things shift depending on which strategy one adopts.

F. Finances. If Sony is to continue its 17% past growth rate, it will double its size in approximately four years. This will call for some $4 billion of assets to support its growth within the next 4 years. How can it generate the needed capital? Its current cash flows are only $382 million per year. Its capital needs approach $1 billion per year (as calculated above). Obviously, an initial surge of capital can be obtained by selling off inventory. But this is not sufficient to carry Sony at its current growth rate.

Because of the Japanese banking structure, Sony can undoubtedly obtain a large portion of its capital needs by increasing its debt structure. However, Sony has not been closely tied to one of the large Japanese banks (as its competitors have). Sony, however, is listed on the New York Stock Exchange and, if its product line is doing well, can expand its equity base and capital access in the United States. Even so, given the large development needs of the future, Sony will undoubtedly have to enter into partnership relationships for longer-term developments.

G. Joining in Marketing Standards? In the past, Sony has attempted to set its own standards as in the Trinitron tube, Beta video tape recorder, and Mavica camera. It has encountered some serious problems later when large companies like Matsushita, RCA, etc. join together to force a different standard into the marketplace. Should Sony now shift its strategy and cause standards to be set before it introduces new products (such as its compact disk [CD] player)? Or should it try to force the market to meets its standard by introducing the product first? This is a very complex strategic issue and affects Sony's capacity to develop a "Distinctive Maintainable Competitive Edge."

H. Strategy for Introducing the Mavica. The Mavica can be used as a single-item example of these new strategic issues. Should Sony obtain an agreed-upon electronic camera standard before introducing the Mavica? Should Mavica be introduced through the industrial market first? How should it be positioned in the industrial and consumer marketplaces? What are the critical performance characteristics it must meet to be successful? Should it be priced for penetration, skimming, experimentation, etc.? Why will people buy an electronic still camera? How will major producers like Canon, Minolta, Fuji, and Kodak respond? What should Sony do about this? Should Sony enter into a co-partnership relationship with any of its major potential competitors? What could it gain? Should the Mavica be introduced as a systems product or a "stand-alone" product? If it is introduced as a systems product (camera, display unit, printer, and electronic enhancing unit), how should these units be tied into the remainder of Sony's product strategy? Where should Sony's emphasis be? How should the Mavica be tied into Sony's organization structure? What would be the most important issues you would anticipate having to deal with in the introduction of Mavica? How would you handle these? This makes a superb discussion vehicle for the specifics underlying Sony's overall strategy.

SUMMARY OF OUTCOMES—OTHER ISSUES

As a result of its product technology leadership, Sony had often not developed sufficient depth in process technologies. To shift the focus to such technologies and a more competitive posture in Sony's maturing product lines, Mr. Ohga became President in late 1982, on the untimely death of Mr. Iwama. Mr. Ohga's career had been largely in production and process innovation. He began to force the company toward a profit-center orientation in early 1983. With this came return on asset (ROA) controls and a much stronger emphasis on inventory controls, production controls, etc. to lean the company down. In 1982-early 1983, the company had a very difficult time, and analysts were very discouraging in their comments. Fortunately, its compact disc player and video tape recorders exploded in their marketplaces and Sony's profitability recovered nicely.

For various reasons, Sony did not bring the Mavica camera to market for several years. It worked towards industry standards and began marketing the Mavigraph printer in early 1986. In addition, various portions of the technology developed for the Mavica system were incorporated in other new products for both consumer and industrial markets. Nevertheless, in the summer of 1986, Canon was the first company to market an all-electronic still camera. At a cost of $10,000 for the whole system, the camera would be marketed mainly to professionals. Analysts predicted that all-electronic photography would not be competitive with conventional photography until the year 2000 but Sony and Hitachi were expected to begin marketing their own all-electronic systems soon.

Sony did begin to establish industry-accepted standards for its entirely new products before putting them in the marketplace. It felt that it had been badly burned by the Beta-VHS conflict. It joined with its most likely competitors in setting standards for the 8 millimeter camcorder and compact disc players. Sony felt everyone had lost as a result of the Beta-VHS conflict and wanted to insure that both customers and Sony did not get hurt in the future.

Sony did shift toward industrial markets. In the process, it developed a series of partnering relationships with both customers and other technology providers. The industrial market both helped absorb early development costs and also added a degree of stability not normally found in consumer products. By working with industrial electronics companies, Sony found it could update its early products in the marketplace and get added technical inputs it could not afford alone. It had joint-ventured with Philips in the development of the compact disc to great advantage, and had entered into an agreement with Advanced Micro Devices to share VLSI technologies and products.

Because of potential tariffs or other trade barriers, Sony had concentrated its non-Japanese production facilities in the United States and Europe. Unlike its competitors who had built plants in less developed countries for cost reasons, Sony felt it would understand the local marketplace better and have a more acceptable name if it produced within its customers' markets.

Sony had many successes in its industrial electronics strategies. It had entered Videotext, made compact disc players for automobiles, was selling video discs to Ford Motor Company, was producing 3 1/2 inch computer disc drives for OEMs, and was working with the groups seeking to make 3 1/2 inch discs standard for new microcomputers, and was selling personal computers in Japan. It had entered high definition television, seeking to penetrate broadcast and industrial markets for this product first. With this product, the company was encountering the "chicken and egg" problem—broadcasters not providing high definition signals because customers did not have high definition sets—and vice versa. Sony had introduced the "Black Trinitron," a CRT with a very high contrast screen. Sony followed up its successful Walkman product with "Watchman," "Discman," "Super Walkman," etc. It also developed a flat display tube used in its flat pocket TVs and computer display terminals and several digital TV systems.

Fluctuating Profits

Sony's profits continued to oscillate as these new product lines were introduced, strong competitors entered the market, and exchange rates fluctuated rapidly. It was hurt badly in the yen revaluation of 1985-86. However, Sony's diversification of production locations helped to offset these problems. And it delayed further declines in its television sales by opening up markets in the People's Republic of China.

One of Sony's main problems was in introducing plant automation. Its culture had demanded rapid responses in production facilities to take advantage of new product innovations. As Sony's video tape recorders and television sales had dropped, it had a large excess workforce which it had to employ. This complicated automating its system. However, Mr. Ohga pressed heavily on automation and by 1986, this problem seemed to be under control.

Sony and Philips had formed a very strong partnership at the components level. Philips was a world leader in compact disc technology, CCD technology, ROM technology, and certain electronics process technologies. The two were jointly developing technical standards for new compact audio-video discs, which might include "talking dictionaries" which could automatically call up stored images or sounds defining a specific word. To accompany this, Sony had developed a small personal computer that contained both Japanese and English dictionaries and Japanese word processing software (a very difficult technical function).

Sony's production strategy paid off as the EEC imposed a 19% duty on CD player imports in the mid-'80s. However, despite excellent publicity and a good product reputation, its 8 millimeter "camcorder" line developed more slowly at first than expected. But by 1990, consumers were adopting this technology so fast that it was rapidly replacing Super 8 moving pictures. Compact discs also did very well. In December 1985 Sony announced that it would produce 4 million units per month in the near future, and it had entered a joint arrangement with CBS for audio discs. Its compact disc plants had been running at full capacity. Some summary highlight of Sony's financial results follow.

	1986	1987	1988	1989
	(¥ billions-except per share)			
Sales-Overseas	¥1.002	¥0.397	¥1.017	¥1.414
Sales-Japan	0.450	0.211	0.538	0.731
Total	1.452	0.608	1.555	2.145
Operating Income	0.042	0.019	0.061	0.160
Income per Share	¥178.400	¥57.300	¥151.000	¥214.700

Note: Data for 1987 are for five months only ending March 31. The others are for twelve months.

Sony hoped to attain a 50/50 breakdown between consumer and non-consumer sales by 1990. When Mr. Ohga took over, its balance was 80-20% in favor of consumer products. Sony invested heavily in semiconductor capability to support its electronics lines. Mr. Ohga changed Sony's strategy so that it would sell its components outside Sony. Without this, it would be impossible to obtain the experience curve and scale economies necessary to have been successful in this business. Sony's market share in video tape recorders shrank steadily, largely because the Beta format was not as heavily supported by rental tapes, mass distribution, and competitor companies as VHS. In April 15, 1985 *Fortune* noted: "The next few years are going to be perilous for Sony. It has a long way to go before it can establish itself in its new businesses. Until then it will continue to be perhaps the world's most exciting consumer electronics company, but living dangerously from magic show to magic show." Mr. Ohga's problem was to maintain that innovative capability while installing the necessary control systems to be more effective in maturing markets. This conflict should be brought out clearly in the discussion.

The sharp rise in value of the yen in 1987 damaged Sony's ability to compete in export markets which still accounted for 70% of its sales. Competition in consumer electronics became even fiercer, and the Betamax debacle emboldened competitors to no longer wait to see whether Sony's latest innovation was a success before jumping into the fray.

To cope, Sony began further expanding manufacturing operations overseas (intending to go from 20% to 35% of manufacturing outside Japan by 1990). While Sony still maintained its high level of R&D expenditures (about 9% of sales) it started sharing technology to force its standards in selected markets. It also began making equipment to be sold by others instead of eschewing the low end of the market. Sony pushed its $32 basic low-end Walkman for sale only in the United States. When it came time to price Sony's portable compact disc player, Morita lowered the price to gain market share and economies of scale in production.

Sony's key thrusts in the later part of the 1980s were towards globalization and diversification. "Global localization" was Morita's word for what he saw as the right type of company for the 1990s. If the yen's rise was the stick that beat Sony toward globalization, the single European market was the carrot that tempted it. "We would like to become a proper European company before 1992," announced Morita. But the acid test of a "local" factory is local content. Here, Sony has gone local more than most. Its European factories average 60% local content and more than 90% in some product areas such as televisions. But overseas manufacturing operations alone do not make a global company. With such a high proportion of production located outside its Japanese home market, Sony thought it wise to decentralize management functions. Sony divided its world into four areas—Europe, America, Asia, and Japan—with the aim of making each virtually self-sufficient. Sony had a policy of giving the top job in foreign operations to a local national. Twenty-three percent of the company was owned by foreigners with the stock being sold on 23 exchanges around the world. In 1989, Sony made corporate history when it became the first Japanese company to have non-Japanese directors—Schulhof from the United States and Schmuckli from Europe—on its main board.

Some of Sony's industrial electronics thrusts were quite successful, such as its launching the 3 1/2 inch floppy disks. Sony soon had 25% of the worldwide market (worth some $900 million in 1989). Telecommunications was its latest emphasis. But this is not what most distinguished the new Sony from the old. It was, rather, the recognition of the importance of software. Norio Ohga, who became Sony's CEO in 1989, was the champion for this project. When Sony developed the compact disk player jointly with Philips in the early 1980s, it found that no record company would issue its material in that format for fear that its own record and cassette sales would be damaged. That—and the experience of video taped movies destroying Betamax—made Sony understand the importance of software.

Ohga wanted to merge Sony's technical wizardry—its torrent of advances in chips, lasers, optics, and consumer products—with the entertainment talents of the West. This led to Sony's $2.2 billion acquisition of CBS Records, then the world's largest record company in January 1988—and the $3.4 billion takeover of Columbia Pictures Entertainment in November 1989. Not since RCA created the National Broadcasting Company in the 1920s—to give people a reason to buy radios—had anyone tried to join the artistic and technological sides of the entertainment business, using each to drive demands for the other.

Sony thought it could control the whole movie and video tape value chain. Its broadcast equipment division manufactured the studio cameras and distributed the tapes and film on which movies were produced. In Columbia Pictures it owned a studio that made movies and decided the formats on which they were distributed. This meant that Sony could ultimately have movies made on high definition film, to be viewed on screens through Sony high definition television systems, and recorded on video in the home on Sony VCRs. It could also re-shoot Columbia's 2,700 film library on 8mm film for playing on its home VCRs or video Walkman.

Sony's 8mm format for video cameras had created another potentially disastrous showdown with Matsushita's production power. However, in May 1990 RCA threw its distribution muscle behind Sony's 8mm format. Industry experts soon expected the two products (8mm and VHS-C) to split the market 50-50. Although the 8mm format held only a 20% share in late 1987, Sony kept up a stream of new features and smaller models, while VHS-C failed to keep up and still only had 30 minute tapes when 8mm's were 2 hours long. This was an interesting reversal of the earlier Sony-Matsushita showdown.

SECTION III: CONTEXTS

Mintzberg, "The Entrepreneurial Organization"

Summary of Reading

THE BASIC STRUCTURE

The structure is simple. It has little or no staff, a loose division of labor, and a small managerial hierarchy. It is not formalized, and makes minimal use of planning or training.

Power focuses on the chief executive, who exercises it personally. It is not uncommon to have everyone report to the chief. Decision-making is flexible, the highly centralized approach allowing for rapid response. Strategy creation is highly intuitive. Strategy tends to reflect the chief executive's implicit vision of the world.

CONDITIONS OF THE ENTREPRENEURIAL ORGANIZATION

External environment is usually simple (understandable by one person) and dynamic (good for flexible structures). Classic case is the entrepreneurial firm, where the leader is the owner. These firms are often young and aggressive, searching for the risky markets that scare off bureaucracies. (Some entrepreneurial organizations are not so aggressive or visionary; many settle down to pursue common strategies in small geographic niches.)

Most new organizations, regardless of sector, seem to adopt this configuration, because they have to rely on personalized leadership to get themselves going. Some older organizations will retain the form as long as their founders are still around. The entrepreneurial organization also tends to arise in any other type of organization that faces severe crisis.

STRATEGY FORMATION IN THE ENTREPRENEURIAL ORGANIZATION

Visionary leadership

One view of visionary leadership is like a hypodermic needle: the active ingredient (vision) is loaded into a syringe (words), which is injected into the employees to stimulate all kinds of energy. Another image is drama, or, more precisely, "repetition," "representation," and "assistance."

Repetition suggests that success comes from deep knowledge of the subject at hand (e.g., Olivier and Iacocca). "The visionary's inspiration stems not from luck . . . but from endless experience in a particular context."

Representation means not just to perform but to make the past live again, giving it immediacy, vitality. Visionary leaders have profound language ability; they see things from new perspectives, but they get others to see them, too.

Assistance means that the audience for drama empowers the actor no less than the actor empowers the audience. Leaders become visionary because they appeal powerfully to specific constituencies at specific periods of time. (Of course, they can then fall precipitously from grace— e.g., Churchill, Jobs, Hitler.)

The entrepreneurial approach to strategy formation in a supermarket chain

This section is a detailed look at how Steinberg's (a Canadian retail chain) fits the concepts of entrepreneurial organization.

445

The "bold stroke" of the entrepreneur is more like "controlled boldness"—the ideas are bold, the execution careful. Central to entrepreneurship is intimate, detailed knowledge of the business or of analogous business situations (the "repetition" discussed above). Clear, imaginative, integrated strategic vision depends on an involvement with detail, an intimate knowledge of specifics.

So long as the business is simple and focused enough to be comprehended in one brain, the entrepreneurial approach is powerful, indeed unexcelled. Nothing else can provide so clear and complete a vision, yet also allow the flexibility to elaborate and rework that vision when necessary. "The conception of a new strategy is an exercise in synthesis, which is typically best carried out in a single, informed brain. That is why the entrepreneurial approach is at the center of the most glorious corporate successes."

But its very strength carries its weakness. Successful entrepreneurship leads to larger organizations, which usually cannot be run as entrepreneurial organizations.

Conceiving a new vision in a garment firm

The genius of an entrepreneur is the ability to pursue one vision for a long time, and then, based on a weak signal, realize the need to shift that vision. "This ability to perceive a sudden shift in an established pattern and then to conceive a new vision to deal with it appears to remain largely in the realm of informed intuition, generally the purview of the wise, experienced, and energetic leader." This section then gives a detailed look at how Canadelle (a Canadian manufacturer of women's undergarments) fits the concepts of entrepreneurial organization.

Lewin's change model of "unfreezing, changing, and refreezing" is used to explain what happened at Canadelle. The first step in unfreezing is to realize that things have changed. The second step is the willingness to step into the void—for the leader to shed his or her conventional notions of how a business is supposed to function.

Change requires a shift in mindset before a new strategy can be conceived. This shift usually occurs in a "eureka"-type flash. After this, the refreezing step requires the blocking out of the situation, so that everything can be made to conform to the new vision. It is here that obsession becomes an effective organizational ingredient. A management that was open and divergent must become closed and convergent.

Leadership taking precedence in the entrepreneurial configuration

In this type of organization, the focus is on the leader. The organization is malleable and responsive to that person's initiatives, while the environment remains benign for the most part.

SOME ISSUES ASSOCIATED WITH THE ENTREPRENEURIAL ORGANIZATION

Centralized decision making roots strategic response in deep knowledge of the operations. It allows flexibility and adaptability. It has a sense of mission.

But the leader does risk getting bogged down in operating details. And it is a risky organization, hinging on the activities of one individual. One heart attack can wipe out the firm's coordinating mechanism. If the leader resists change, adaptability is lessened. Some people find the one-person rule too restrictive.

The entrepreneurial organization might seem anachronistic today, but it remains a prevalent and important configuration. This is because entrepreneurs need organizations; some spheres need small, informal organizations; some large firms need personalized leadership; and ailing organizations of all types need turning around from time to time.

446

Discussion Questions

1. How is the entrepreneurial organization a configuration?

The entrepreneurial organization, which Mintzberg used to call the simple structure, seems like it's too simple to be a configuration. But it does have a collection of organizational attributes that fit together. More precisely, for an integrated set of design parameters, the "needles are set on zero." That is, the entrepreneurial organization has little or no staff, a loose division of labor, and a small managerial hierarchy. It is not formalized, and makes minimal use of planning or training. It *has* a prime coordinating mechanism—direct supervision—carried out by its most important part, the strategic apex, or leader.

2. How does strategy in the entrepreneurial organization relate to the list of strategies given by Mintzberg in his Chapter 1 reading?

The strategy process in the entrepreneurial organization obviously fits with entrepreneurial strategy discussed in Chapter 1. It is based on individual vision. Intentions exist as the personal, unarticulated vision of a single leader, and so are adaptable to new opportunities. The organization is under the personal control of the leader; it is usually located in a protected niche in its environment. In fact, the environment and the organization are both dominated by the leadership.

3. Do entrepreneurial firms seek out simple and dynamic domains, or do simple and dynamic industries require entrepreneurial organizations?

The answer is "both." Most entrepreneurs seek out protected niches in environments which are simple enough for them to understand, and which they *do* understand. The good entrepreneurs like dynamic environments, too, because they like taking advantage of the opportunities that result from change. But environments that are simple and dynamic are well-suited for entrepreneurs. They have the ability to respond quickly to the dynamic changes. And their lean organizations usually out-perform the large stodgy bureaucracies with whom they compete.

4. How does large size fit (or not fit) into the concept of entrepreneurial organization?

Entrepreneurial organizations typically are not large. If the founder of a firm is still around when the firm becomes large, a variant on the entrepreneurial organization will exist in the large firm. The entrepreneurial strategy formation process is often used in large firms. This usually happens when large firms get into trouble. The turnaround typically begins with the appointment of a new leader. That leader's personal vision is the strategy that is followed as the firm begins to turn around.

5. What are the most positive aspects of the entrepreneurial organization? The most negative? Are there any antidotes for the latter?

The entrepreneurial organization's centralized decision making roots strategic response in the leader's deep knowledge of the operations. It also allows for flexibility and adaptability—only one person need act. Another advantage is its sense of mission. Many people enjoy working in a small, intimate organization where the leader—often charismatic—knows where he or she is taking it; the result is often enthusiasm and an organization with which employees can develop a solid identification.

One problem is that the leader may become enmeshed in operating problems and fail to attend to strategic issues. The opposite problem—over-enthusiasm about strategy and neglect

447

of operations—is also common in entrepreneurial organizations. It is also a risky structure, depending on one person for coordination. He or she could become incapacitated, or he or she could become inflexible regarding change. Some people find the entrepreneurial organization too restrictive—only one person calls the shots. The risk of the one-person rule is probably the biggest weakness; this can be partially offset by succession planning.

6. Is there truly such a thing as the "bold stroke" of the entrepreneur? How does this compare with "controlled boldness?"

Students may differ on this question. The author says that the bold stroke of the entrepreneur is more like "controlled boldness." That is, the ideas may be bold, but the entrepreneur executes them carefully. Another pattern of controlled boldness that has emerged from the research is one where the entrepreneur forges ahead for a time, then stops and consolidates.

In another place in the reading, the author says that the entrepreneur must be willing to step into the void. This process is somewhat bold, since it calls on the entrepreneur to shed his or her conventional notions of how a business is supposed to function.

7. The author states that the key to entrepreneurial strategy is intimate, detailed knowledge of the business. What are the implications of this for strategy-making in other types of organizations?

This is closely related to the kinds of hands-on approaches advocated in earlier readings. In his Chapter 2 reading about strategists, "Good Managers Don't Make Policy Decisions," Wrapp mentioned that it is necessary for top managers to be well informed about operations; otherwise their thinking will become too sterile and abstract. Mintzberg's Chapter 5 reading, "Crafting Strategy," compared strategy-making to pottery making—involvement with the materials is crucial in each case. The straightforward implications are that managers in all kinds of organizational configurations need to keep in touch with what is happening below them.

8. In what sense is "the conception of a new strategy an exercise in synthesis?'

In the mainstream model of strategy formulation, strategies come about as the result of *analytical* processes. The organization is intellectually broken down into its components, and a strategy is planned. *Synthesis* is the opposite process—the many things experienced by the strategist are collected, and when some of them seem like they might fit together in an interesting and lucrative way, the strategist puts them together.

Mintzberg's main argument in his "Crafting Strategy" reading in Chapter 5 is that most strategy formation is synthetic, not analytic. The purest example of this point occurs in the entrepreneurial organization. The entrepreneur experiences the reality of the organization, then puts all these pieces together into a coherent, integrated strategy.

9. How can it be that "the entrepreneurial approach is at the center of the most glorious corporate successes?"

Students may argue over this point. Many will say that the most glorious corporate successes have come about as a result of careful planning and analysis. Others will argue, as would the author, that most successful strategies have not formed from these processes. (Quinn makes this point explicitly in his Chapter 5 reading on logical incrementalism.) Planning and analysis are merely ways to operationalize strategies that have formed in other ways. One of the major "other ways" is the vision-driven entrepreneurial strategy process. Iacocca's turnaround of Chrysler and Jobs's foundation of Apple Computer are good examples.

10. *What is your opinion of the statement that "strategic change . . . seems to involve mindset before strategy?"*

Not all students will understand or appreciate this point. As he pointed out in several previous readings (the Chapter 4 reading on generic strategies and the Chapter 5 reading on crafting strategy), a strategy is really a *concept*. Before one can adopt a new concept (i.e., a new strategy), one must change one's mind. Hence the statement that "mindset must change before strategy can change."

11. *The author talks about needing to be open and divergent, followed by needing to be closed and convergent. What do you think of his argument here?*

This is another way of talking about the unfreezing, change, refreezing model. The organization must change by being maximally receptive to new ideas. That is what the author means by "needing to be open and divergent." But once the new concept has formed, it is just as crucial that it be pursued single-mindedly. The "obsessed" organization must go all out to implement the new concept. This is what Mintzberg means when he says "needing to be closed and convergent."

12. *If good strategy-making in a entrepreneurial organization involves intimate knowledge of the industry, how can we tell whether a strategic manager is too involved in operating details, or is learning essentials of the business?*

This is a difficult question. It has no hard-and-fast answer. It may in fact be impossible to tell until after some time has elapsed. If the organization is successful in the long run, then the entrepreneur has probably spent the proper amount of time on strategic and operational concerns. Another barometer would be if the entrepreneur uses the knowledge he/she gains to set up the company in a strategically strong position, or if he/she simply spends a lot of time doing organizational tasks.

Porter, "Competitive Strategy in Emerging Industries"

Summary of Reading

Emerging industries are newly formed or reformed industries that have been created by technological innovations, shifts in cost relationships, emergence of new consumer needs, or other potentially viable business opportunities. "The essential characteristic of an emerging industry from the viewpoint of formulating strategy is that there are no rules of the game."

THE STRUCTURAL ENVIRONMENT

Most structural factors related to either the absence of established bases for competition or the initial small size and newness of the industry.

Common structural characteristics

Technological uncertainty

Strategic uncertainty:

No "right" strategy has been identified

Poor information about competitors, customers, and industry conditions

High initial costs but steep cost reduction

Embryonic companies and spin-offs

> "The emerging phase of the industry is usually accompanied by the presence of the greatest proportion of newly formed companies (to be contrasted with newly formed units of established firms) that the industry will ever experience . . . ."

First-time buyers

Short time horizon

Subsidy

Early mobility barriers

Proprietary technology

Access to distribution channels

Access to raw materials and other inputs of appropriate cost and quality

Risk (raises cost of capital)

"The typical early barriers stem less from the need to command massive resources than from the ability to bear risk, be creative technologically, and make forward-looking decisions to garner input supplies and distribution channels."

Strategic choices

"The emerging phase of an industry's development is probably the period when the strategic degrees of freedom are the greatest and when the leverage from good strategic choices is the highest in determining performance."

Shaping industry structure: many opportunities here

Externalities in industry development: striking a balance between self-interest and industry advocacy (e.g., promoting standardization)

Changing role of suppliers and channels: suppliers and channels may become more willing to play ball as the industry proves itself

Shifting mobility barriers: as industry proves itself, advantage may rest on things other than the original barrier-creators (e.g., may move from technology to mass marketing)

Timing entry

Early entry involves risk, but also lower entry barriers and higher potential return. Early entry is appropriate in four instances:

Pioneer image is important

Get started early on learning curve

Secure the loyalty of early buyers

Cost advantages gained from early commitment

450

Some tactical moves may improve the firm's position:

Early commitment to suppliers may yield favorable treatment in times of shortage

Wall Street may have a "love affair" with the new industry, providing financing ahead of needs and lowering cost of capital

An emerging industry is attractive if its predicted *ultimate* structure promises above-average returns. Firms often enter because of industry growth, profitability of incumbent firms, or predicted large size. "But decision to enter must ultimately depend on a structural analysis . . . ."

Discussion Questions

1. How useful is Porter's idea of "rules of the game?"

"Rules of the game" is an interesting metaphor to describe the structural and dynamic characteristics of an industry. Like most metaphors, it contains some element of truth. The goings-on in a industry *do* resemble a competitive game to some extent, with "opponents" making "moves." But, again, like most metaphors, it draws attention *away* from other interpretations. In this case, the idea of "rules" implies some code of proper behavior that must be followed by every player. But even Porter concedes that in emerging industries, there are no rules. Indeed, one of the most interesting characteristics of emerging industries is that firms may participate in the writing of the rules. Moreover, some of the most successful firms are those which don't follow any kind of rules, or who break the rules, as Cooper, Woo, and Willard discuss in the final reading in this chapter.

2. How well does the author's description of "common structural characteristics" fit with the previous reading's idea that entrepreneurial organizations tend to work best in "simple and dynamic environments?"

The question of dynamism is clear—the description given by Porter has much dynamism: Technology is changing. Strategies are changing. Costs start high but drop. Buyer preferences are in a formative stage. Time horizons are short.

The question of simplicity is more clouded, and could be argued either way. Perhaps if an entrepreneur "got a handle" on *the* significant factor in the environment, he/she could then deepen her/his understanding of it to the point of being a true expert. On the other hand, one could argue that the points discussed by Porter are inherently complex, and there are many of them, so therefore the environment is inherently complex.

3. Porter says the entry barriers in emerging industries center on "the ability to bear risk, be creative technologically, and make forward-looking decisions." He says these are the reasons why "newly created companies"" are observed in these industries. What does he mean? How do these ideas fit with the concepts of entrepreneurial organization from the previous reading?

He means that it is much likelier to find risk-taking, creativity, and forward-looking decisions in an entrepreneurial firm than in an established, bureaucratic firm. For the same reason, the latter kind of firm is unlikely to spin off smaller entrepreneurial firms. So most firms in emerging industries are newly-created, independent ones.

This fits well with the concepts in the previous reading. There, Mintzberg talked about the entrepreneur's willingness to "step into the void." He discussed how entrepreneurs are constantly searching for new opportunities. He mentioned "repetition," a metaphor to represent how the entrepreneur's inspiration stems from "endless experience in a particular context."

4. How well could a skilled entrepreneur, atop an entrepreneurial organization, handle the strategic choices discussed by the author?

At first glance, the strategic choices facing the leader of the firm in an emerging industry seem to be a tall order. But upon further reflection, they seem ideally suited to the kind of person Mintzberg discussed in the previous reading.

One choice is the shaping of industry structure; an opportunistic entrepreneur would welcome the chance to shape things in a way that he/she could understand. Porter also says that the firm must be able to strike a balance between self interest and industry advocacy; this might be easier to accomplish for one person than for a committee in a larger-firm spin-off.

Porter says that firms in this kind of industry must be ready to court suppliers and buyers as the industry changes. A good entrepreneur would probably welcome the opportunity to interact with industry players; he/she would learn more, and would have the chance to mold things to the right shape.

Lastly, Porter says that the firm must be ready to recognize and react to shifting mobility barriers. As Mintzberg pointed out, handling this kind of discontinuity is something at which successful entrepreneurs excel. All in all, Mintzberg's entrepreneurial leader seems well suited to strategic management, as suggested by Porter, in emergent industries.

Bhide, "How Entrepreneurs Craft Strategies That Work"

Summary of Reading

Comprehensive analytical planning doesn't suit start-ups. Entrepreneurs don't have the time and money, and too much analysis can mean that the opportunity is gone before it can be exploited. Studies show that few entrepreneurs do much planning and analysis, and those who do are no more likely to survive their first three years than people who seized opportunities without planning. "Analysis can delay entry until it's too late or kill ideas by identifying numerous problems."

Good entrepreneurs don't get into business without thinking, thought. It's just that they have a quick and cheap method that takes up the middle ground. It has three elements:

1. Screen opportunities quickly to weed out unpromising ventures.
2. Analyze ideas parsimoniously. Focus on a few important ideas.
3. Integrate action and analysis. Don't wait for all the answers, and be ready to change course.

SCREENING OUT LOSERS

Entrepreneurs get lots of ideas and must screen out the bad ones to be able to spend appropriate time on the good ones. This requires not data but judgment and reflection. "New ventures are usually started to solve problems the founders have grappled with personally as customers or employees."

Profitable survival requires an advantage based on either a creative idea, superior execution, or both. Examples of creative ideas: innovative product, innovative process, or unique insight on some external change. But superior execution is necessary, especially if the edge is something that can easily be copied. Examples of superior execution: establishing a brand name, or just doing a mundane thing faster or better than others. "Ventures that obviously lack a creative concept or any special capacity to execute . . . can be discarded without much thought."

Successful start-ups don't need an edge on every front, and capacity varies among entrepreneurs. Nor is there a typical entrepreneurial profile, either on personality or behavior. "In assessing the viability of a potential venture . . . each aspiring entrepreneur should consider three interacting factors:"

1. Objectives of the venture

What is the goal? Large size? Niche? Quick profit? Large size usually requires a revolutionary idea, big money and strong organizations. It requires a balance among the interests of customers, investors, employees, and suppliers, and the organizational skills to build a large organization. A large amount of technical know-how is also often needed.

Niche efforts don't need extraordinary ideas, just solid products. "A niche market will rarely justify the investment required to educate customers and distributors about the benefits of a radically new product," or even radically new production and distribution methods. The key management skill is being able to do more with less.

2. Leverage provided by external change

"Exploiting opportunities in a new or changing industry is generally easier than making waves in a mature industry." It's hard to take away business in a mature industry. There are advantages in new markets:

- Rivals are rough around the edges.
- Customers tolerate inexperienced vendors and imperfect products.
- There are opportunities to profit from shortages.• Things that can go a long way:
  small insights
  marginal innovations
  little skill or expertise
  willingness to act quickly.

Customers may even be hesitant to back radical products, preferring to wait until things settle down. There may be an advantage for the entrepreneur to go with industry standards.

There have been numerous examples of this in computer hardware, software, training, retailing, and systems integration.

3. Basis of competition: Proprietary assets versus hustle

Success in some industries relies on assets—patents, location, or brands. Good management practices are not enough to propel a start-up over structural barriers. By contrast, companies in fragmented industries cannot establish an asset-based advantage, but can achieve high profit through exceptional service. They rely on "hustle." Personal selling skills can be very important, as are institution-building skills such as recruiting stellar performers and reinforcing values.

GAUGING ATTRACTIVENESS

Potential venture should be screened for attractiveness—risks and rewards—compared to other opportunities. One factor is capital requirements. Entrepreneurs should keep these low if they don't have access to capital markets (e.g., sudden cash need because one large customer doesn't make a timely payment). They should favor ventures with low capital intensity that can fund themselves out of cash flows. They should look for a high margin for error—low fixed costs and simple operations can overcome technical delays, cost overruns and slow sales.

Entrepreneurs shouldn't try to undertake more than one project at a time; they should be exclusively committed to their one venture. Costs of shutting down should be low and payback should be quick. The option of cashing in by selling all or part of the equity is desirable. Ventures must fit with values of the entrepreneur.

Small endeavors can be more profitable than large ones. Founders keep a larger share of the profits and there is no dilution of equity through multiple rounds of financing. But entrepreneurs must be willing to dominate in a backwater, which will be profitable but not intellectually stimulating or glamorous. Another thing to avoid: the "land of the living dead," a niche that is not profitable enough to support a business but which cannot be exited because of too much investment.

PARSIMONIOUS PLANNING AND ANALYSIS

Good entrepreneurs minimize their resources spent on researching ideas. They do only as much as seems useful and are not afraid to make subjective judgment calls. There are some uncertainties that no amount of research will resolve. This is especially true for new products or new ideas. Revenues are hard to predict, but insight might be gained by thinking about how customers might buy and use the product or service.

Entrepreneurs must exert themselves to create barriers that avoid their accidentally enriching their competitors. They must also guard against servicing a niche whose costs exceed any potential revenue. If cost disadvantage is significant, then the performance provided must be superior. When addressing a small market, entrepreneurs must make sure that all concerned get a high, quick or sustainable payoff.

"Entrepreneurs who seek to leverage factors such as changing technologies, customer preferences, or regulations should avoid extensive analysis." Research in these circumstances is unreliable, and quick response is undercut by analysis. One exception: "analyzing whether or not the rewards for winning are commensurate with the risks."

INTEGRATING ACTION AND ANALYSIS

Standard operating procedures in large, established businesses often dictate a more deliberate approach to evaluating new ventures. The latter must fit with existing activities. But "entrepreneurs . . . don't have to know all the answers before they act. In fact, they often can't easily separate action and analysis." The benefits of acting before analysis:

- Builds confidence in self
- Builds confidence in others
- More robust, better informed strategies result from use of prototypes (as opposed to market research)

Handling analytical tasks in stages

Good entrepreneurs do only enough research to justify the next action or investment.

Plugging holes quickly

Good entrepreneurs look for solutions as soon as problems begin to occur. Any analysis that is done should be aimed at finding out what to do next, not at what *not* to do (which is the more typical role of analysis).

Evangelical investigation

"Entrepreneurs often blur the line between research and selling." They get prototypes into the hands of customers and potential customers. They seek commitment from just about anyone they meet—commitment to buy, or to invest. This subjective combination of listening and selling does not produce statistically significant market research, but "the deep knowledge and support of a few is often more valuable than broad, impersonal data."

Smart arrogance

Good entrepreneurs' ability to act on sketchy plans and incomplete information is sustained by an almost arrogant self-confidence. But they must have the smarts and flexibility to recognize mistakes, to learn, and to change strategies when necessary. Things don't always evolve as initially conceived. Entrepreneurs must rework concepts when prospects don't buy, and they must sell to people who are interested even if they weren't initially prospects.

"The apparently sketchy planning and haphazard evolution of many successful ventures . . . doesn't mean that entrepreneurs should follow a ready-fire-aim approach. Despite appearances, astute entrepreneurs do analyze and strategize extensively. They realize, however, that business cannot be launched like space shuttles, with every detail of the mission planned in advance. Initial analyses only provide plausible hypotheses, which must be tested and modified. Entrepreneurs should play with and explore ideas, letting their strategies evolve through a seamless process of guesswork, analysis, and action."

Discussion Questions

1. What is your reaction to the author's opening assertion that "a comprehensive analytical approach to planning doesn't suit most start-ups?"

Some students who have been steeped in the "business school religion" of analysis may react negatively to this statement. If they have spent their business school careers learning the value of analysis, why shouldn't an entrepreneur benefit as well? But the author provides the answer. Typical entrepreneurs lack the time and money for a detailed strategic analysis. They also run the risk of missing the opportunity as they carry out the time-consuming analysis. He also cites research showing that entrepreneurs who planned were no more successful than those who didn't. Entrepreneurs *do* think about their ventures ahead of time, but not with detailed analytical planning approaches.

2. Why shouldn't an entrepreneur screen out losers by using more data?

Because what is needed instead is judgment and reflection. Most ventures start to solve problems that the owner grappled with as an employee or customer. He or she already knows what is needed. More data are simply not necessary. What *is* necessary is either a good new idea, a superior ability to execute the venture, or both.

3. "Successful start-ups," says the author, "don't need an edge on every front." What do you think?

At first glance this sounds like heresy. But upon reflection it's not that different from what theorists say about strategy in large firms. You don't need a distinctive competency in *everything*, just in one or two things. The author points out here that the advantage could come from a great new idea, or it could simply come from the brilliant execution of a completely non-original idea. Some students may also be heartened by the author's assertion that successful entrepreneurs vary greatly in personality type. Some are charismatic, many are not. Some are gregarious, some taciturn. Personality doesn't seem to matter.

4. Why are the objectives of the venture a useful mechanism for screening out losing ideas?

The scale and type of idea will point to different requirements for success, thereby helping screen out ideas. For example, a goal of building a large organization quickly typically requires a revolutionary idea. Any big idea typically requires big money and strong organizations. Niche markets don't need big ideas, but may need low costs that can help create a profit even in a small market. A really revolutionary idea may even be a hindrance in a niche market, whose occupant may not be able to afford to educate customers about the radical idea.

5. What are some of the advantages of entering a new market?

The author does a nice job of describing the benefits of new markets. Rivals are rough around the edges, so your company doesn't have to be super-polished. Customers are more tolerant of "inexperienced vendors and imperfect products," mainly because their expectations are lower. Being willing to hustle and do the small things right can go a long way.

6. How does the "basis of competition" help screen out ideas?

If the basis of competition is proprietary assets, you would screen out ideas that require them if you don't have them, or keep them in if you do. Examples would be pharamaceuticals, luxury hotels, and some consumer goods. Similarly, if you have no great idea, but you're willing to hustle, then you would keep ideas that don't need proprietary assets. This would work in many fragmented service industries.

7. How should an entrepreneur gauge the attractiveness of a venture?

He or she should examine the risks and rewards compared to other ventures. A factor to always consider is capital requirements. In general, entrepreneurs should favor ventures that are not capital intensive and whose margins are large enough to support growth through cash flows. Risk is lowered as well in ventures that have simple operations and low fixed costs.

The author makes an interesting point: a venture should be attractive enough to command all of the entrepreneur's time and effort. Otherwise she or he will take on more than one project and they will all suffer from lack of attention. Related to this is the idea that the entrepreneur should be able to shut the venture down "cleanly" if it starts to fail, so as to avoid losses of time, money or reputation. One last attractiveness factor is the potential for selling the equity easily; high liquidity helps the potential entrepreneur escape to another venture.

8. What is your reaction to the author's comments about the uselessness of market research?

The author says that focus groups are no good at predicting demand for products that are truly novel. Focus groups dismissed, for example, the usefulness of copiers. Revenues are also very hard to predict. Understanding how potential customers might use or buy the product can be useful. They might especially help to identify who the buyers would be and then what their needs might be.

9. What are the potential problems with niche markets?

When they finally think about it, students may be surprised to realize that niche markets may simply be too small to sustain themselves. Even a niche must be large enough to support the sales needed to make a profit. If a niche market is too small to support a direct sales force, it may also be too small to support sales representatives. Large companies that decide to invade a niche can often do so with marginal extensions of their lines. A small start up needs to really "wow" the customers in the niche because typically its costs will be higher than its larger competitor's.

10. What is your reaction to the author's assertions about how entrepreneurs must integrate action and analysis?

The author depicts the typical decision-making process in the large firm in unflattering terms. Essentially, the large firm must see how new ventures fit with existing operations. This usually necessitates extensive analysis. Only then will the large firm act.

The entrepreneur, by contrast, has few facts available, so there is really not much to analyze. He or she must act and then assess the consequences of that action. One benefit is that acting builds confidence in oneself and by others. Seeing someone taking on risk can energize others. And even though mistakes can result from action, it can also generate better information than sterile research can.

11. What is your reaction to the author's assertion that entrepreneurial strategies "evolve through a seamless process of guesswork, analysis, and action?"

"Guesswork" may strike some business school students as rather unprofessional. Yet the author's image here is not that different from Mintzberg's in "Crafting Strategy." As he says, launching a new venture is not like launching the space shuttle. You don't have to have all the details worked out ahead of time, and you don't need high precision. You need to have a good idea or the ability to hustle, or both. And you need to be ready to act with intelligence and to learn from the action. Good entrepreneurial strategy is the essence of emergent strategy.

Mintzberg, "The Machine Organization"

<u>Summary of Reading</u>

<u>THE BASIC STRUCTURE</u>

Here are the characteristics of this configuration:

> Highly specialized, routine operating tasks
>
> Very formalized communication throughout the organization
>
> Large-size operating units
>
> Reliance on the functional basis for grouping tasks
>
> Relatively centralized power for decision making
>
> An elaborate administrative structure with a sharp distinction between line and staff

Operating core and administration

Operating core:

> Work flow is highly rationalized.
>
> Tasks are simple.
>
> Skills and training are minimal.
>
> Jobs are narrowly defined.
>
> Emphasis for coordination is on the standardization of work processes.
>
> Workers have little discretion.

Middle line managers have three functions:

> Handle the disturbances that arise in the operating core
>
> Work with staff analysts to incorporate their standards down into the operating units
>
> Support the vertical flows in the organization—action plans down, feedback up

Technostructure: houses the staff analysts who do the standardizing; emerges as the key part of the structure, because the machine organization depends primarily on the standardization of its operating work for coordination; rules and regulations permeate the entire system.

The machine organization is obsessed with control, which has three consequences:

> Attempts are made to eliminate all possible uncertainty.
>
> These are structures ridden with conflict; the control systems are required to contain it.
>
> It keeps as many of its support services in-house as it can.

The strategic apex

Fine-tuning the machine

Finding ever-greater efficiency

Keeping the structure together despite conflict

Frequent intervention in middle line activities, to ensure coordination there

Formal *and* informal power end up in the strategic apex

CONDITIONS OF THE MACHINE ORGANIZATION

Work of machine organization is found in *simple*, *stable* environments:

Work associated with complex environments cannot be rationalized into simple tasks

Work associated with dynamic environments cannot be predicted, made repetitive, and standardized

Machine configuration typically found in mature organizations (large and old)

Also found in organizations that use regulating technical systems (e.g., mass production firms)

The environment may be stable because the organization has acted aggressively to stabilize it (advertising, long-term supply contracts, cartels, vertical integration, etc.)

Configuration is found in many types of enterprises: large and small manufacturing firms, service firms, government agencies, regulatory agencies, etc.

MACHINE ORGANIZATIONS AS INSTRUMENTS AND CLOSED SYSTEMS

Machine organizations are pervasively regulated, so they can be used as *instruments* by outsiders.

But they also try to control their environments, trying to become closed systems, immune to external influence.

Growth is the major goal of machine organizations.

SOME ISSUES ASSOCIATED WITH THE MACHINE ORGANIZATION

Machines may be precise, reliable, easy to control and efficient. But machine organizations include human beings, so the analogy breaks down.

Human problems in the operating core

Taylorism removed humanity from the machine organization, removing the meaning of work.
This has led to absenteeism, turnover, sloppy workmanship, strikes, even sabotage.

Coordination problems in the administrative center

Since the operating core is not designed to handle conflict, the human problems spill out into the administrative structure.

The narrow specialization of the operating core is mirrored in the administrative structure, leading to problems of coordination and communication.

Structure is ill suited to mutual adjustment.

Building of private empires is encouraged.

Adaptation problems in the strategic apex

Coordination problems lead management to use even more standardization, but this only aggravates the coordination problems at the administrative center, since standardization is poorly suited to the nonroutine problems there.

Management responds by using direct supervision in the form of "bumping" problems up the hierarchy.

STRATEGY FORMATION IN THE MACHINE ORGANIZATION

"Strategy in the machine organization is supposed to emanate from the top of the hierarchy, where the perspective is broadest and the power most focused." An integrated strategy is formulated at the top. Implementation follows as the plan is handed down the hierarchy.

This is the theory. The practice (discussed below) is different.

Planning as programming in a supermarket chain

"[Planning] did not formulate a strategy . . . . What planning did was justify, elaborate, and articulate the strategy that already existed in [the CEO's] mind. Planning operationalized his strategic vision, programmed it. It gave order to that vision, imposing form on it to comply with the needs of the organization and its environment. Thus planning followed the strategy-making process, which had been essentially entrepreneurial."

"Is there . . . such a thing as 'strategic planning?' I suspect not. To be more explicit, I do not find that major new strategies are formulated through any formal procedure. Organizations that rely on formal planning procedures to formulate strategies seem to extrapolate existing strategies . . . or else copy the strategies of other organizations."

Planning as an impediment to strategic thinking in an airline

Planning proceeds from the machine perspective, which leads to a fallacy. "Assembly lines and conventional machines produce standardized products, while planning is supposed to produce a novel strategy . . . . Planning is analysis oriented to decomposition, while strategy-making depends on synthesis oriented to integration. That is why the term 'strategic planning' has proved to be an oxymoron."

Roles of planning, plans, planners

If planning does not create strategy, then what role *does* it serve?

Role of planning

Program strategies already present:

codification of given strategy (including clarification and articulation)

elaboration into substrategies

translation into budgets and objectives

460

Role of plans

medium for communication

device for control

Roles of planners

finding strategies

analysts (carrying out ad hoc studies to feed into strategic models)

catalyst (encourage strategic thinking, informal strategy-making)

A planner for each side of the brain: these roles suggest two different orientations for planners:

highly analytic, convergent thinkers who bring order to planning; these are *right-handed planners*

unconventional, creative, divergent thinkers who want to open up planning; these are *left-handed planners*

Strategic change in an automobile firm

If planning is not strategy, then how does the machine organization effect strategic change? This section discusses Volkswagenwerk's painful strategic change. The story suggests the great force of bureaucratic momentum, both physical investments that were difficult to change, and psychological patterns that were difficult to break. Moreover, VW was so tightly integrated that strategic change was impeded. "Change an element of a tightly integrated gestalt and it *dis*integrates. Thus does success eventually breed failure."

Bottleneck at the top

Strategic changes generally have to be achieved in a different configuration, if at all. Problems get "bumped" to the top. As long as the environment is smooth, this works adequately. But when the environment is turbulent, which is when strategic change is most needed, the number of problems increases, and top management becomes overloaded. This leads to either no change or ill-considered change.

The highly departmentalized nature of machine organizations exacerbates this problem. MIS systems don't really help, because strategy-making uses soft information, which is not provided by MISs.

The best way around these problems is to bypass MISs and use networks of informal contacts. Unfortunately, this takes up time and violates the formality premises of the machine organization. Top managers are "thus reduced to acting superficially, with inadequate, abstract information."

The formulation/implementation dichotomy

The basic problem is the separation of formulation and implementation. For this to work, top management needs full and sufficient information, and the environment must remain stable (or at least predictable).

But organizations need new strategies at precisely the times when things have changed unpredictably. And machine organizations *misinform* top management during such times. This all

461

amounts to a need to collapse the formulation/implementation dichotomy in the machine organization during these times. This can be accomplished in two ways:

> The formulator implements: power is concentrated at the top; leader comes up with concept and has the power to personally order others to carry it out; this is the entrepreneurial configuration, at least at the apex

> The implementors formulate: power is concentrated lower down; people in touch with information take individual actions and patterns form; this is the innovative configuration

"We conclude . . . that the machine configuration is ill-suited to change its fundamental strategy, that the organization must in effect change configuration temporarily in order to change strategy . . . . Either it reverts to the entrepreneurial form . . . or else it overlays an innovative form on its conventional structure . . . ."

This is not surprising, since machine organizations are specialized instruments, designed for production, not adaptation. They are performance systems, not problem-solving ones; their forte is efficiency, not innovation.

Strategic revolutions in machine organizations

Overall, machine organizations seems to follow a "quantum theory:" they pursue set strategies for long periods, interrupted by short bursts of change, called "strategic revolutions."

Organization taking precedence in the machine organization

". . . It is organization—with its systems and procedures, its planning and its bureaucratic momentum—that takes precedence over leadership and environment in the machine configuration." The organization typically forces both the environment and its own leadership into modes that support it. This works adequately during stable times. In times of change the organization falters.

". . . The machine organization is a configuration, a species, like the others, suited to its own context but ill-suited to others. But unlike the others, it is the dominant configuration in our specialized societies." As long as there is a need for efficient, mass-producing organizations, this configuration—and its problems—will remain with us.

Discussion Questions

1. What's your reaction to the author's description of the basic structure of the machine organization?

Most students will react negatively to Mintzberg's description of the machine organization. They will not like the highly specialized, routine operating tasks, or the very formalized communication throughout the organization. Even less attractive to them will be how the work flow is highly rationalized, tasks are simple, skills and training are minimal, and jobs are narrowly defined. Perhaps most onerous is the emphasis for coordination on the standardization of work processes. Lastly, freedom-loving students will not like how little discretion workers have.

Nevertheless, students will have to be reminded that machine organizations are responsible for bringing us the low-cost products to which we have become accustomed. Their efficiency is what has made most modern conveniences possible.

2. In the machine organization, why are the units in the operating core large, and why are the middle line units small?

If you have a machine, it makes more sense to create a component with many interchangeable parts that are easily replaced, than it does to create one complex component that must be replaced in its entirety. This is the logic behind the great amount of specialization that exists in machine organizations. And that is why the units ("components") are large.

The large number of rules and the standardized procedures allow the middle managers to oversee the large numbers of people in these units.

3. How is it that "without the standardizers [in the technostructure] . . . the structure simply could not function?"

Machines work best when everything in them is standardized. Likewise, machine organizations only work when everything in them is standardized. That is what the technostructure does. In fact, without the standardizers of the technostructure, there would not be the machine-like quality to the machine organization, and it would be one of the other configurations.

4. Why is the sharp distinction between line and staff seemingly inevitable in the machine organization?

A huge amount of specialization characterizes the machine organization. Everyone in it is reduced to a part in the machine. This specialization extends not only to distinctions among line units, but also to the fundamental distinction between line and staff.

5. What is your opinion of the author's two "central facts" reflecting the "control mentality" in machine organizations?

The first central fact is to "eliminate all possible uncertainty." The second is that machine structures are ridden with conflict. Most students will agree and sympathize with the second. That conflict could exist in such a seemingly repressive structure will not come as a surprise.

But many will be slightly surprised by the first point. "Uncertainty elimination" is not what most students think of when they think of management. Yet it is an obsession in most machine organizations (which are perhaps the dominant organizational form) because uncertainty can gum up the works of the machine.

6. How, and why, is there so much power at the strategic apex of machine organizations?

The strategic apex is the only place where discretion is allowed. Top managers must keep the whole system working. They must resolve conflict. They must fine-tune efficiency. They are the ones who make major decisions. In other words, one consequence of standardizing everything else is that the one non-standardized part, the strategic apex, has much work to do.

7. Why are machine organizations so often found in government? Is this a good thing, as Max Weber thought?

One reason is that the work of many government agencies is routine, e.g., Social Security Administration, Postal Service, IRS. But a more important reason is that government agencies need to be accountable to the public for their actions. Everything they do must be seen to be fair, and so they proliferate rules and regulations.

Despite everything people may dislike about machine organizations (particularly those who work in them), there is little doubt that for providing mass services in a fair manner, this configuration is unexcelled.

8. The author says that machine organizations are found in simple, stable environments. They even try to become closed systems. Why are these things so?

In machine organizations, information is funneled to the top, where decisions are made. Along the way, much of the original information's richness is filtered out. If the environment were complex, a great amount of detail would never reach decision makers, and the organization would fail to adapt. If the environment is simple, then the information processing and decision making tasks are greatly simplified.

It takes a great amount of energy and other resources to set up a machine organization. For example, there are many specialized tasks, which follow standardized procedures, and so on. The organization needs to work in one mode for an extended period of time in order to recoup the expense and maximize the organization's efficiency. If the environment were dynamic, one of two things would happen, neither of them good: (1) the organization would have to change too often, and efficiency would be lost, or (2) the organization would stick with its inappropriate structure and would fail to adapt to the environment.

9. What is your reaction to the section on "human problems in the operating core?" How can it be said that "modern man seems to exist for his systems?"

Most students will agree with the critical tone of this section. The full-blown machine organization is indeed the logical conclusion of Taylorism. The point about "modern man and his systems" is an interesting one. We have invented and implemented the machine organization to help us produce the enormous amount of goods and services needed by our consuming public; there's no escaping our need for such organizations.

Yet many of the people who work in them (even those who themselves purchase the televisions, automobiles, and VCRs produced by machine organizations) don't like working in them. We *hate* them but we *need* them. We set up the systems we must have, but they ultimately enslave us.

10. What is the "irony" of control to which the author refers when discussing coordination problems in the administrative center?

Machine organizations are highly specialized in their operating cores. This means that their middle lines need to be just as specialized. The result is problems of coordination and communication among the middle line managers. The consequence of this is less adaptability and less control, which is indeed ironic.

11. Why does the machine organization end up using so much direct supervision at the top?

Standardization, the dominant characteristic of the MO, is adequate for regulating the day-to-day functioning of the organization, but it is not well suited to the nonroutine problems that are handled by the middle line. Consequently, these are "bumped" up the hierarchy. They are ultimately handled by the strategic apex, which must resort to direct supervision to resolve these issues.

12. How realistic is the author's discussion of how strategy-making in machine organizations is supposed to happen?

464

Students may differ in their assessments of this subsection. Some students will say that this is exactly how strategy is made in machine organizations. It is an analytical process that formulates strategy near the top of the organization, usually articulated in a plan. After this, the plan is handed over to lower-level participants for implementation. Other students, remembering some of the readings from earlier chapters, may be skeptical. For example, the Wrapp reading on "Good Managers Don't Make Policy Decisions" from Chapter 2, and Mintzberg's Chapter 5 reading on "Crafting strategy," and Quinn and Voyer's Chapter 5 reading on "Logical Incrementalism" all point to very different ways for strategy formation to occur in large, complex organizations.

13. In discussing the first Steinberg plan, the author uses words like, "justified, elaborated, articulated, operationalized, and programmed." But he never uses the word "formulated." What is your reaction to this, given the widespread assumption that planning is the way to make strategy?

This is one of the key passages in the reading. Mintzberg wants students to know that planning is *not* the method by which most strategies are formed in machine organizations. It serves a useful purpose, but that purpose has nothing to do with formulating strategy. It has to do with helping to implement strategy, to operationalize it once it has been conceived in some other way. It also has to do with justifying it, which is an often-overlooked function of planning. No doubt students will be surprised by this passage. If not, they *should* be.

14. The author says that he doubts the existence of a planning mode of strategy-making, saying "we do not find major new strategies formulated through any kind of formal procedure." He says that "the term 'strategic planning' has proved to be an oxymoron." What do you think of these statements?

These are strong statements. Mintzberg is known for overstating things to make his points. In this case, he may be stating the point accurately. There is no evidence that planning is a method that leads to new strategies. It is a means to operationalize strategies developed in other ways, hence his characterization of it as an "oxymoron." Some students may accept this, but no doubt many will take issue with Mintzberg on this score.

15. How might formal planning discourage creativity and impede strategic thinking?

Formal planning is a mechanism for patterning the organization so that it runs smoothly, machinelike. The obsession with control that characterizes machine organizations is reinforced by formal planning. Hence, formal planning drives strategy to perpetuate itself. It focuses the organization *away* from new ideas, so it discourages creativity. It tends to drive out entrepreneurial and innovative activities, hence it impedes strategic thinking (in the sense of strategy as something insightful and innovative).

16. What is your opinion of the author's thoughts on the role of planning?

Mintzberg says that the greatest contribution planning can make is to program strategies already present. It does this by (1) codifying the given strategy (including clarification and articulation); (2) elaborating it into substrategies; and (3) translating it into budgets and objectives. Even if students do not accept these as the primary contributions of planning, they will probably recognize them as plausible roles for it to play.

17. What is your opinion of the author's thoughts on the role of plans?

The author says that the primary role of plans are as media for communication and devices for control. As communications media, plans inform people of intended strategy and its consequences. As control devices, they specify what roles departments and individuals must play in helping to realize strategy. They then can be used to compare the patterns realized with the intentions specified. In other words, plans belong under implementation, not formulation, of strategy, even though they are usually classified in exactly the opposite way. Some students will argue for this more traditional view, while others will side with Mintzberg.

18. What is your opinion of the author's thoughts on the role of planners?

Mintzberg says that planners can play three useful roles. First, they may play a role in finding strategies. That is, if strategies truly do emerge in organizations, then one thing planners could contribute would be to help identify these patterns, helping to formalize them and make them deliberate. Second, planners can be analysts, carrying out needed studies. Third, planners can be catalysts, encouraging strategic thinking, supporting informal strategy-making.

Some students will not like this set of roles. They are too much of a come down from the very powerful image of the planner as the formulator of strategy. Other students will be encouraged by this description. Mintzberg describes a very realistic, and useful, set of contributions that can be made by planners. These students will find it more interesting and more challenging to be catalysts and finders of strategy.

19. What is your opinion of the author's thoughts on "planners for each side of the brain?"

Mintzberg says that there are two types of planners. One, the *right-handed planner*, is partial to the rational processes identified with the brain's left hemisphere, and is therefore highly analytic and convergent, dedicated to bringing order to the organization. The right-handed planner programs intended strategies, using plans for communication and control. This planner carries out rigorous studies.

The second type of planner is called the *left-handed planner*. This planner is less conventional, and is a creative, divergent thinker. The left-handed planner is inclined toward the intuitive processes which characterize the right side of the brain, and therefore seeks to open up the strategy-making process. He or she is a soft analyst, tending to conduct quick and dirty studies, finding strategies in strange places, trying to encourage others to think strategically.

Some students may find all of this a bit far-fetched, but there is evidence behind its validity. As Mintzberg points out, some organizations may need to emphasize one type or the other, but most will need a few of each.

20. What does the author mean when he says "success can breed failure?"

As an organization becomes more successful, it grows. To keep itself under control, the larger organization must become more bureaucratic. As it becomes more bureaucratic, it becomes more integrated. As it becomes more integrated, it becomes more efficient. This makes it even more successful, for a time at least. Unfortunately, the integration and efficiency make the organization difficult to change. As the author puts it, "Change an element of a tightly integrated gestalt and it *dis*integrates." The efficiency and integration that create success ultimately make the organization prone to failure.

21. Why does the MIS not solve the machine organization's information needs during a period of environmental turbulence?

The major problem here is the slow transmission speed of most information in management information systems. In a turbulent environment, the top manager cannot afford to wait. MIS also tend to favor lean, hard data, when research has shown that soft, rich information is what top managers use in formulating strategy. In turbulent environments, that kind of information is particularly valuable, but is not provided by the typical MIS.

22. Mintzberg says that strategic change in machine organizations comes about by abandoning that structure and temporarily assuming an overlay of either the entrepreneurial organization or the innovative organization. What is your reaction to this? What are the implications of this?

Students will be surprised by this. Most will have assumed that machine organizations develop strategy using a mechanism, like planning, that is more in tune with the configuration's machine-like elements. Some may even be skeptical of or critical of Mintzberg's views on planning and its use in machine organizations.

Students will have to be reminded that Mintzberg *does* think that planning is useful. It's just not useful for coming up with adaptive strategies at those times when the organization really needs them. It *is* useful for helping machine organizations *carry out* their strategies.

The implications of these views are clear, even if they are rarely acknowledged or followed: Do not dismiss the contributions to strategy development that can be made by entrepreneurial or innovative thoughts and actions. Recognize the limitations of planning. Do not be discouraged or scornful if ideas to lead you out of a strategic morass come from somewhere other than your planning staff. Look for strategies anywhere where you can find them.

23. What is the significance of the subsection that discusses "strategic revolutions in machine organization?"

Machine organizations do not re-set their strategies smoothly. They tend to hold on to a strategy for a long period of time, then go through a relatively brief period of change, then hold on to *that* strategy for a long stable period, then change wrenchingly again, and so on.

This finding has several significant implications. First, managers of machine organizations should not be discouraged if their organizations exhibit this pattern; it is the normal one. To be sure, we might *want* our machine organizations to adapt more smoothly, but the research evidence shows this to be unlikely. Second, top management in machine organizations need to become just as skilled as the good entrepreneurs at noticing the important discontinuities in their environments. It is at those points that the revolutionary change needs to take place. Third, those same managers should realize that these revolutions are unlikely to come about as the result of formal planning processes; the latter tend to prolong the status quo, or else simply copy the industry recipe. Fourth, revolutions are likely to come from the top managers acting entrepreneurially, or champions lower down acting entrepreneurially, or small groups of people lower in the firm acting innovatively.

Abell and Hammond,
"Cost Dynamics: Scale and Experience Effects"

Summary of Reading

Other things being equal, businesses with a large *market share* are more profitable than their smaller-share competitors. An important reason for this is that high-share firms have *lower costs*. These are partly because of economies of scale, and partly because of the experience effect (defined as cumulative number of units produced).

SCALE EFFECT

Large businesses have the potential to operate at lower unit costs. Large-scale manufacturing facilities can be built at lower per-unit costs, and can be operated more efficiently, than smaller ones. The operating economies apply to other cost elements, like promotion, sales, distribution, administration, R&D, and service. Large size doesn't assure scale benefits; it must be supported with appropriate strategies.

EXPERIENCE EFFECT

Applies to all value-added costs—manufacturing, administration, sales, promotion, distribution, purchased components, etc.

SOURCES OF THE EXPERIENCE EFFECT

1. Labor efficiency

2. Work specialization and methods improvements

3. New production processes

4. Getting better performance from production equipment

5. Changes in the resource mix

6. Product standardization

7. Product redesign

This list illustrates that experience-based cost reductions don't occur by chance, but by concerted effort.

There is overlap between scale and experience effects, since increases in size increase experience. The distinction is not too important.

PRICES AND EXPERIENCE

One would expect costs and prices to fall steadily and together. In practice, prices start briefly below cost (development phase), then cost reductions exceed price reductions (price umbrella), until prices suddenly tumble (shakeout); ultimately the price and cost curves parallel (stability).

STRATEGIC IMPLICATIONS

"In industries where a significant portion of total cost can be reduced due to scale or experience, important cost advantages can usually be achieved by pursuing a strategy geared to accumulating experience faster than competitors. (Such a strategy will ultimately require that the firm acquire the largest market share relative to competition.)"

The cost leader has a great advantage. Followers' costs must decrease at the same rate or they will be eliminated from the market. The best time to seize the advantage is at the start, when experience doubles quickly. In fast-growing markets, firms must act aggressively. In slow-growing markets, firms must gain their advantage more carefully.

EFFICIENCY VS. EFFECTIVENESS:
LIMITATIONS TO STRATEGIES BASED ON EXPERIENCE OR SCALE

"The selection of a competitive strategy based on cost reduction due to scale or experience . . . is the selection of cost-price *efficiency* over non cost-price *effectiveness*." Firms must be careful not to sell low-price products that no one wants.

If a firm can answer "yes" to these three questions, then pursuing an efficiency strategy is probably feasible:

1. Are scale or experience advantages available?

2. Are there market segments that will respond to low prices?

3. Does the firm have the resources it needs to achieve cost leadership?

Once having made the decision, "a firm must guard against going so far that it loses effectiveness, primarily through inability to respond to changes . . . . Thus the challenge is to decide when to emphasize efficiency and when to emphasize effectiveness, and further to design efficiency strategies that maintain effectiveness and vice versa . . . ."

Discussion Questions

1. What is the link between market share and profitability? What is your opinion of the authors' explanation for this link?

The authors say that, other things being equal, businesses with a large *market share* are more profitable than their smaller-share competitors. An important reason for this is that high-share firms have *lower costs*. These are partly because of economies of scale, and partly because of the experience effect (defined as cumulative number of units produced). Having a larger share gives these firms the luxury of producing on a larger scale, which is usually cheaper. They also have the opportunity to accumulate more experience, which research has shown tends to reduce costs.

Most students will probably accept this, but it is important to remind them of Pascale's criticism from his "Honda Effect" article. Not all cost reductions are based on scale or experience. At Honda, for example, lower costs were based on better design. This was not a function of experience, as defined by the authors (i.e., a doubling of cumulative output). It was the result of innovation by Mr. Honda.

2. What is "economy of scale?" Does it apply only to manufacturing?

Economy of scale is the production of items at a lower per-unit cost as the size of the facility increases. It certainly applies to manufacturing, but to other things, as well. The authors point to marketing, sales, distribution, administration, R&D, and service. They give an example of advertising for a 30-unit supermarket chain, pointing out that it would need "much less than three times as much advertising as a chain with 10 stores."

3. What is the "experience effect?" Is it relevant in a non-manufacturing business, especially a service business?

The Boston Consulting Group popularized the experience effect or experience curve—each time cumulative volume of a product doubled, total value-added costs fall by a constant and predictable percentage (usually somewhere between 10 and 20 percent).

It is not clear whether the experience effect applies in a non-manufacturing context. The problem is the definition of experience—the doubling of cumulative output. Presumably, if the output of a service business could be measured in units, it would be possible to find out if the cost of providing the service fell by "a constant and predictable percentage." Some of the experience effect sources would still apply—labor efficiency, work specialization and methods improvements, changes in the resource mix, and perhaps even "service standardization."

4. How does the experience curve differ from the learning curve?

The learning curve is usually applied to individuals, and it measures how much additional knowledge about a particular subject is learned as time goes by. It typically starts with a burst of new knowledge gained, followed by some peaks and valleys of learning, and ends with new-knowledge-acquisition tapering off.

The experience curve is completely different. As mentioned above, it is defined as the "constant and predictable percentage" of cost reduction that accompanies each doubling of cumulative output.

5. Why is it not too important to separate scale and experience effects?

This question may stimulate discussion, because not all students will agree with the authors that this is an unimportant distinction. They say this because scale and experience are *intercorrelated*. Experience tends to accumulate faster in those firms that are large; those same firms are the ones who benefit from economies of scale. Trying to keep these intercorrelated things separate is unimportant.

Students who disagree with this will probably have two arguments. First, the authors say that they believe that experience arises from "ingenuity, cleverness, skill, and dexterity." These are valuable and important things that have nothing to do with size, and should be prized on their own merits. Second, firms that have fallen behind in market share cannot hope to compete on size and scale. They probably cannot compete on the basis of experience, either, at least not as it is defined in this reading. But they *may* be able to benefit from "ingenuity, cleverness, skill, and dexterity," and would undoubtedly want to know how to separate those from scale effects.

6. What are the advantages and disadvantages of seeking to be the industry leader? Which way do you fall on this question? How does your answer differ if the industry is growing quickly? If it is not growing?

The advantage is great if leadership is achieved. The industry cost leader is in a position to drive higher-cost competitors (by definition, every other firm) out of the market.

The disadvantage is what happens if a firm tries to achieve cost leadership but fails. The attempt requires enormous outlay of resources, to gain the size and experience necessary. To try and fall short means being saddled with large, expensive facilities that are nevertheless being underpriced by the firm which won the cost leadership contest.

This problem is aggravated in growth markets, which require aggressive strategic actions. Slower-growth markets are problematic in that becoming the leader requires wresting market share from incumbent firms, which they will surely resist, and which is therefore going to be expensive and not very profitable.

7. Examine the authors' discussion of efficiency versus effectiveness. How does this section relate to the earlier reading by Galbraith (Chapter 6)?

Galbraith drew a distinction between upstream and downstream firms. The former tended to focus on production efficiency, the latter on marketing effectiveness, on meeting customer needs. This dichotomy is almost identical to the one drawn by Abell and Hammond in this reading.

Galbraith pointed out that upstream firms tended to be poor diversifiers, because most of the lessons they learned were geared to one area—production. Downstream firms tended to be more successful diversifiers because they focused on customer needs, which tended to be diverse.

Here is the way Abell and Hammond describe the problem faced by firms seeking to use an efficiency strategy:

"A firm [using an efficiency strategy] must guard against going so far that it loses effectiveness, primarily through inability to respond to changes. For instance, experienced-based strategies frequently require a highly specialized work force, facilities and organization, making it difficult to respond to changes in consumer demand, to respond to competitors' innovations, or to initiate them. In addition, large-scale plants are vulnerable to changes in process technology, and the heavy cost of operation below capacity."

This is very close to the kind of criticism articulated by Galbraith.

Mintzberg, "The Professional Organization"

Summary of Reading

THE BASIC STRUCTURE

"An organization can be bureaucratic without being centralized." This happens when work is complex yet stable. Professional skills are perfected by standardized operating programs.

The work of the professional operators

". . . The professional organization relies for coordination on the standardization of skills, which is achieved primarily through formal training." It hires specialists and gives them considerable autonomy.

Professionals work independently of each other because they have learned what to expect from one another. The complexity of skills ensures that discretion remains.

"Training, reinforced by indoctrination, is a complicated affair in the professional organization." Typically, it starts in professional school, followed by on-the-job training, supplemented by indoctrination. The goal is the internalization of the profession's set procedures.

While the machine organization sets its own standards, the standards of the professional organization originate in the self-governing associations to which professionals belong. Other forms of standardization don't work in professional organizations. The work is too complex to be standardized by analysts. Outputs of professionals cannot be easily measured. And direct supervision and mutual adjustment impede professional autonomy.

The pigeonholing process

At the operating level, the professional organization is a set of standard programs—a repertoire of professional skills—applied to known situations, called contingencies. This process is sometimes called pigeonholing. The professional has two tasks—to diagnose the contingency and to execute the program.

The machine organization is a single-purpose structure. The professional organization applies more varied programs, but in a circumscribed way. Fully open-ended diagnosis, with no programming, requires the innovative organization.

The administrative structure

The operating core is the key part of the professional organization. Support staff is also well-developed. The technostructure and middle line are not highly elaborated in the professional organization; they can do little to coordinate professional work.

The administrative structure is elaborated. The democratic nature of the professional organization requires that the professionals control much of the administrative work. There are many committees and task forces. But the support staffs are not organized democratically. In most professional organizations there are "parallel and separate administrative hierarchies, one democratic and bottom-up for the professionals, a second machinelike and top-down for the support staff."

The roles of the administrators of professional work

Compared to managers of machine and entrepreneurial organizations, these managers seem to lack direct power. But they can exercise indirect power.

First, they spend much time handling disturbances in the structure, usually brought about by the imperfections of pigeonholing. These must often be resolved by several administrators negotiating.

Second, administrators "serve in key roles at the boundary of the organization, between the professionals inside and the influencers outside: governments, client associations, benefactors, and so on." They act as buffers, and as seekers of support, from the environment.

The administrators gain power because they are at the locus of uncertainty. The ones who obtain resources for, or buffer, their units are the ones who gain power. But "the professional administrator maintains power only as long as the professionals perceive him or her to be serving their interests effectively."

CONDITIONS OF THE PROFESSIONAL ORGANIZATION

The professional organization is typically found in complex yet stable situations. The technology cannot be highly regulating or automated, or it could be rationalized and the organization made into a machine organization. If the technology were *highly* complex, it might require multidisciplinary teams, and the professional's autonomy and independence would be curtailed.

The professional organization is often found in universities, schools, consulting firms, law and accounting offices, social work agencies, and hospitals. In industry, it might be found in craft businesses, like ceramic products.

STRATEGY FORMATION IN THE PROFESSIONAL ORGANIZATION

The "standard" strategy model is "almost totally at odds with what really happens" in professional organizations. But strategy can also be the creation of patterns in a stream of action over time. The question for professional organizations then becomes "which actions?"

"The key area of strategy-making in most organizations concerns the elaboration of the basic mission . . . . In professional organizations . . . this is significantly controlled by individual professionals." Other important areas of strategy here include the inputs to the system, the means to perform the mission, the structure and forms of governance, and the various means to support the mission. Some of these things come under the direct control of professionals, some under the control of administrators, and yet others require the participation of a variety of people.

Decisions made by professional judgment

Determination of the basic mission is mostly left to the judgment of professionals as individuals. But there is a subtle constraint on their autonomy, namely, what the *profession* considers appropriate. Professionals may be free from administrators and from colleagues in other disciplines, but they are not free from colleagues in their own discipline.

Decisions made by administrative fiat

Certain types of decisions, less related to professional work per se, can be the exclusive prerogative of administrators. The best example is financial decisions. Most support services fall into this category. (The support services central to the professional work tend to fall into collective decision-making.) Central administrators also may play a prominent role in controlling procedures, e.g., committee assignments. And in times of crisis, they are granted more power.

Decisions made by collective choice

Many decisions are handled in interactive processes that combine professionals and administrators. One of the most important of these decisions involves "the definition, creation, design, and discontinuation of the pigeonhole s. . . ." Others are hiring and promotion of professionals, budgeting, and design of the interactive processes.

Models of collective choice

The most common model of collective choice is the *collegial* model, guided by common interest. Another model is the *political* model, where participants seek to serve their self-interest. Neither model dominates all the time; some combination is to be expected.

A third model is the *garbage can* model; participants are guided by a lack of interest. It is characterized by solutions looking for problems, problems looking for solutions, the fluidity of participants, and random occurrences of opportunities to make choices. This model exists, but is not dominant.

A fourth model is *analysis*. It is guided by rationality and calculation. It features prominently in the professional organization because professionals like to be rational.

Strategies in the professional organization

The process of strategy-making may be different, but professional organizations are inundated with strategies (i.e., patterns in actions). Standardization of skills encourages patterning. Collegiality promotes consistency of behavior. Even politics works to resist changes in existing patterns. The garbage can model represents the unexplained variance in the system.

Many people are involved in the strategy-making process, but there are forces that encourage strategic cohesion: the centralized forces of administrative fiat; the broad negotiations of collective action; and the forces of habit, tradition, and ideology.

"Overall, the strategies of the professional organization tend to exhibit a remarkable degree of stability. Major reorientations in strategy . . . are discouraged by the fragmentation of activity and the influence of the individual professionals and their outside associations." But *narrower* changes happen constantly—new contingencies, new programs, new clients, new pigeonholes. "Thus, the professional organization is, paradoxically, extremely stable at the broadest level and in a state of perpetual change at the narrowest one."

SOME ISSUES ASSOCIATED WITH THE PROFESSIONAL ORGANIZATION

The professional organization is unique among the configurations in that it is very democratic and provides operators with extensive autonomy. Professionals tend to emerge as highly motivated individuals who can perfect their skills and still develop personal relationships with clients. But democracy and autonomy contain the seeds of the chief problems of the professional organization.

Problems of coordination

Standardization of skills is a loose coordinating mechanism at best. It works poorly at coordinating the work of professionals with support staffers. The need for coordination *among* professionals is also handled poorly, which often leads to conflict.

Problems of discretion

Complex professional skills require the exercise of considerable judgment. This is fine if the professionals are competent and conscientious. If they are not, it plays havoc. Client needs may be ignored.

The needs of the organization might also be ignored. Professional organizations need loyalty from their members—to support their strategies, to staff their administrative committees, and to see them through conflict with the professional associations.

Problems of innovation

Major innovation depends on cooperation. Existing programs may be perfected by the single individual, but new ones usually cut across established specialties, and so call for collective action. But the reluctance of professionals to coordinate produces a resistance to innovation.

Professionals tend to be *deductive* and to engage in *convergent* thinking; they see specific situations in terms of the general concept. Innovation requires *induction* and *divergent* thinking—the inference of the new general solution from the particular experience.

Public responses to these problems

Outsiders try to control professionals either through direct supervision or by standardizing the work. As discussed earlier, these rarely work. "All these types of controls really do . . . is destroy the effectiveness of the work." Change can only *seep* in through the professional associations, and the methods *they* use to control the quality of professionals.

Discussion Questions

1. How can an organization be bureaucratic yet decentralized?

This seemingly paradoxical condition stems from Mintzberg's definition of what makes an organization bureaucratic. He said in a previous reading that an organization that relies on any of the four methods of standardization was by definition *bureaucratic*. Since the professional organization relies on standardization of skills, it is bureaucratic. But its operating core professionals have extensive power to do their business as they see fit, so the professional organization is a decentralized structure.

2. What is the author's definition of professional work?

He says that it is work that is complex yet stable. Its complexity requires that it be carried out and controlled by people with special training. Its stability ensures that professional skills can be perfected by standardized operating programs.

3. What is the difference between standards as used in machine organizations and professional organizations?

The machine organization sets its own standards; these typically emanate from the technostructure. By contrast, the standards of the professional organization originate outside the organization, in the self-governing associations to which professionals belong.

4. Assess the following statement: "Professional organizations cannot rely extensively on the formalization of professional work or on systems to plan or control it."

Professional work is too complex to be standardized by analysts. Outputs of professionals cannot be easily measured. Direct supervision and mutual adjustment, or for that matter *any* form of outside control, impede professional autonomy. So professional organizations cannot rely on formalization, systems, or direct supervision for control.

5. How can it be that "both direct supervision and mutual adjustment impede the professional's close relationship with his clients?"

Traditionally, professionals are given complete control over how to service a client. No one tells a physician how to treat a patient, no one tells a university professor how to teach a course, and no one tells a CPA how to conduct an audit. If a professional were to submit to direct supervision, her or his control over the servicing of the client would no longer be complete. Similarly, if servicing decisions were made by committee, individual autonomy would obviously be compromised.

6. What is the significance of pigeonholing in professional organizations?

Pigeonholing is *the* key process in professional organizations. Professionals have standardized procedures for any contingency they encounter. Their most important tasks are to figure out which contingency they are facing (called *diagnosis*) and then to apply the correct standardized procedure to that problem. In other words, they must find the right "holes" into which to place the clients with whom they are dealing. For example, if a person has chest pains, the doctor must diagnose whether it is angina or indigestion, and then place the patient on the appropriate treatment.

7. Why is the operating core the key part of the professional organization?

In a professional organization, all the important activity is done by the professionals. They learn the standardized programs. They learn the diagnostic techniques. They exercise total control over the provision of services. They are the ones who belong to the professional organizations who control what is considered appropriate professional conduct. And the professionals are the people who make up the operating core of professional organizations. This is what makes the operating core the key part of this configuration.

8. If standardization of skills is the main coordinating mechanism in the professional organization, why is the use of liaison devices so high?

Professionals may not need to mutually adjust in order to provide services; they have autonomy as far as that goes. But they are the ones responsible for much of the governance of the professional organization, at least those parts clearly not part of administrative fiat. Because of these collective choice decision responsibilities, professionals find themselves involved in many standing committees and task forces.

9. Are the administrators of professional bureaucrats powerful or powerless?

In some respects they are powerless. They can administer only at the pleasure of the professionals in the operating core. And they must make sure not to encroach on the autonomy and discretion of those professionals. But as the author points out, they have some sources of indirect power. They handle disturbances and they serve in crucial boundary roles. "Good" outcomes of conflict handling enhance power. And the acquisition of resources from outside groups can also increase the prestige and power of a professional organization administrator.

10. What happens if members of a professional organization use a sophisticated technical system?

Their autonomy is reduced. A sophisticated technical system could work against the professionals in one of two ways. If the system is very rational, it might be amenable to formalization. This would ultimately convert the organization to a machine form. If the technical system is extremely complex, it may not be standardizable enough to be taught as a set of professional skills. The organization might have to rely on teams of professionals mutually adjusting. The professional organization would ultimately be transformed into an innovative organization.

11. Mintzberg says that the "standard" strategy model is "almost totally at odds with what really happens" in professional organizations. Why?

The standard model says that strategies are formulated before they are implemented, that planning is the central process used in formulation, and that structures must be designed to implement these strategies. In professional organizations, most key organizational services are provided by professionals acting alone, not as the result of formulated strategies. Skills obtained under the auspices of independent professional associations, and not planning, are the basis of strategy. Structures in professional organizations are very loose, really only collections of independent actors; they are not "designed" by centrally-acting strategists.

12. The author says that "the key area of strategy-making in most organizations concerns the elaboration of the basic mission . . . ." What is your opinion of this? What are the implications for professional organizations? Is this reminiscent of anything from previous readings?

Most students will agree with this basic assertion. If strategy is not for the specification of the firm's purpose, then what is it *for*? The implications for professional organizations are straightforward. Since the basic mission of most professional organizations is the provision of the services the professionals have been trained to provide, then the key area of strategy in most professional organizations will be controlled by the individual professionals. Of course, they *will* be constrained by norms of what the *profession* considers appropriate.

This is connected to Mintzberg's discussion in his Chapter 1 reading on the five Ps of strategy. Specifically, this is the kind of strategy he meant when he discussed *disconnected strategy.*

13. What is your reaction to the discussions of "administrative fiat" and "collective choice?"

Many students will have come into the course with the idea that many strategies are developed using what Mintzberg here calls "administrative fiat." Most students will probably be comfortable with this notion as a method for strategy-making with respect to some aspects of professional organizations.

Most students will be unfamiliar with the "collective choice" idea. Unless one has been in a professional organization, the idea of collective choice is foreign. Most will find the distinctions among collegial, political, garbage can, and analytical models to be quite interesting as a result.

It is important for students to be exposed to these ideas, since many students in business schools today will find themselves in a professional context. Many are studying to be public accountants. Some may go on to law school, or even medical school. Many are likely to find themselves managing in hospitals, or perhaps government agencies that have many professionals.

14. The author says that even though the process of strategy-making may be different, "professional organizations are inundated with strategies." What is your reaction to this statement?

Students will have to be reminded that strategies are not only *planned*. They can also be *patterns*. Planned strategies may be rare in professional organizations, except for those areas controlled by administrative fiat. But patterned strategies *are* abundant. In a university, for example, each professor has a different strategy. Each department, exercising collective choice, has a different strategy. The administration has its own strategy for things like building construction and parking. Joint committees that oversee the university library have their own strategy.

15. How serious are the problems of discretion? In particular, how serious is the problem of loyalty?

The problems are serious for clients and host organizations. If incompetent or lazy professionals abuse their discretion, clients will at best receive poor service and at worst may be harmed. Professional organizations whose members are loyal only to themselves or the profession will damage its ability to deliver on its overall strategy, will hinder its efforts to administer itself, and will impair its ability to handle conflicts with professional associations.

16. Why does "the reluctance of the professionals to work cooperatively with each other [translate] into problems of innovation?"

Most sophisticated innovation requires teams of people, usually from different disciplines, mutually adjusting. This runs against the grain of most professionals. They like to work independently, at least on the basic provision of services. (They may work together on governance.) Because they are reluctant to adopt the mutual adjustment so typical of innovation, the professionals in professional organizations inhibit it.

17. What is the difference between convergent and divergent thinking? Why does it matter? How is this distinction related to material from previous chapters?

Convergent thinking tries to fit particular situations into the general framework that has been created by a profession. Professionals try to *converge* on the solution to a problem. Divergent thinking takes a particular situation and tries to see how many ways it can be developed.

It is an important distinction because convergent thinking (which is related to analysis) inhibits innovation. Divergent thinking, by its very nature, induces innovation. This has implications for strategy-making beyond the innovative kind. Earlier readings, particularly Mintzberg's reading on "Crafting Strategy," discussed how strategy-making is less an analytic, convergent process, and more a synthetic, divergent process.

18. Why doesn't standardization of work processes or outputs work in the professional organization?

Standardization of work processes is possible if the skills are fairly simple. Then they can be standardized by analysts in the technostructure. If they are complex, as they typically are in professional organizations, then technocrats cannot hope to formalize them.

It is difficult to standardize the outputs of professional work because it is difficult to measure the outcomes. How can one tell if a person being treated for mental illness is "cured?" How can one say that a university graduate is truly "educated?"

19. What is the author's recommendation for changing and controlling the professional organization, and what's your evaluation of it?

Outsiders try to control professionals either through direct supervision or by standardizing the work. As discussed earlier, these rarely work. "All these types of controls really do . . . is destroy the effectiveness of the work," says Mintzberg. He argues that change can only *seep* in through the professional associations, and the methods *they* use to control the quality of professionals.

Many students will take issue with Mintzberg on this. It seems a weak way of effecting change. And it is useless in a crisis. But he is probably correct. Individuals who have been victimized by professionals can sue them. But control of professionals in a general sense, and for the future, probably *does* depend entirely on how the professions control *themselves*, and the people who join them.

Maister,
"Balancing the Professional Service Firm"

Summary of Reading

Professional service firms (PSF) have emerged in many service industries, such as law, consulting, investment banking, accountancy, architecture, engineering, and universities. Yet the topic of managing them has been neglected. PSFs sell the services of their individuals or teams of individuals, not the whole firm. There tends to be a lot of interaction with clients and a lot of customization. Both these things require individuals with high skill levels. PSFs compete in two markets: the "input" of skilled professionals and the "output" of their services. Balancing these two flows constitutes the special challenge of the PSF.

The framework explored in this article has four interrelated elements: two markets—one for the professional work force and one for the firm's services—and two structures—the firm's economic structure and the firm's organizational structure. Successful PSF management requires a balance among these four elements.

THE ORGANIZATIONAL STRUCTURE OF THE PSF

The archetypal PSF has three organizational levels: junior, manager and senior. In a consulting firm these might be called junior consultant, manager and vice-president, respectively. In a CPA firm the corresponding titles might be staff accountant, manager, and partner. At a university the levels would be assistant professor, associate professor and professor. There is nothing magical about this common number of levels, but it is reminiscent of the medieval guild system of apprentice, journeyman and master, a system which in some ways still exists in modern PSFs.

PROJECT TEAM STRUCTURE

What determines the relative mix of the three levels? The nature of the service provided. Customization leads to a project structure with three major activities: client relations, project management, and performance of detailed professional tasks. Typically, senior people do client relations, managers do project management, and juniors do the project tasks. A vernacular term is that the three levels are "the finders, the minders and the grinders." Things need not be this rigid; juniors might be given "management" tasks and managers might be encouraged to hone their client relations skills.

CAPACITY PLANNING

The mix of these three activities shapes the firm's capacity. Professional staff are like "machines," and a balance must be struck between activities and the machines needed to perform them.

THE ECONOMIES OF THE PSF

Most PSFs are partnerships, some are corporations. Regardless, they tend to have few fixed assets, require capital only to fund accounts receivable and other working capital. The vast majority of revenues are disbursed as salaries, bonuses and partnership profits. It is common to see an even three-way split among salaries, staff support and partnership profits. Sometimes the latter can be as much as half.

Revenues are based on the billing rate—"the hourly charge to clients for the services of individuals at different levels of the hierarchy. The ratio between the lowest and highest rates in some firms can exceed 3 or 4 to 1." Project team structures allow firms to leverage the skills of the seniors with the efforts of the juniors. "The firm can obtain higher rates for the juniors' efforts because they are combined with the expertise and guidance of the seniors."

The billing multiple

The billing multiple is the billing rate per hour divided by the total compensation per hour. "The average multiple for most firms is between 2.5 and 4." The appropriate billing multiple will be influenced by the value added by the firm's services and the demand and supply conditions for those services. If a firm can deliver services with a mix weighted toward juniors, it will get a higher multiple.

"The billing multiple is intimately related to the break-even economics of the firm." If compensation is $Y and overhead is also $Y, then break-even will be a bill of 2$Y. To get to break-even at a 50% utilization rate, the firm would charge 4$Y, which is common in many PSFs.

THE PSF AND THE MARKET FOR PROFESSIONAL LABOR

The common three levels in PSFs lay out a clear career path. The typical person starts at the bottom and the expectation (implicit or explicit) is that she or he will be promoted through the levels at an appropriate pace. Failure to adhere to that pace results in people leaving for greener pastures or being "counseled out." "It is this characteristic, perhaps more than any other, that distinguishes the PSF from other types of organizations."

Promotion policy

While many things attract people to PSFs, career opportunities play a large role. There are two important dimensions: "the normal amount of time spent at each level before being considered for promotion and the 'odds of making it' (the proportion promoted)." These variables are important screening mechanisms. Good recruiting doesn't eliminate the need to move people out. The "risk of not making it" also motivates people to work hard, which is particularly important in light of the great working freedom most professionals have.

Accommodating rapid growth

There are four strategies that can be used to allow faster growth:

1. Improve the hiring process to get a higher proportion of "promotable" juniors.

2. Speed up the "apprenticeship" process with training and development.

3. Use "lateral hires," bringing in experienced people to non-junior levels. This is usually avoided because of the adverse effect on the morale of juniors.

4. Modifying the team structure (discussed further below).

Turnover

Some PSFs have high turnover, i.e., low odds of "making it." This is called a "churning" strategy. Benefits are that seniors can earn the surplus value of juniors' efforts without having to repay them with promotion. The screening built into this approach leaves only the "best" people in the firm. Firms that follow this strategy tend to be very prestigious. Junior people are willing to work there anyway because of the added development they get from doing that. They can often leave for positions in lesser firms than they would not have gotten without the exposure to the churning firm. They also tend to refer later clients to their original firm.

THE MARKET FOR THE FIRM'S SERVICES

". . . One of the most basic linkages in the dynamics of the PSF [is] the direct link between the market for professional labor and the market for the firm's services." The key linking variable is the quality of available and "attractable" professionals. Top professionals will be attracted to firms that provide exciting and challenging projects, or good opportunities for professional development and personal fulfillment. Symmetrically, firms that do these things need to attract top professionals.

Project types

Professional service projects may be characterized into three types:

- "*Brains:*" the client's problem is complex and at the cutting edge of professional knowledge. PSFs will sell the professional craft of its people. Key elements are: creativity, innovation, and pioneering of new approaches, concepts and techniques.

- "*Gray hair:*" highly customized output that is not as innovative or creative as the brains project. Clients seek out firms with experience in their type of problem. The PSF sells its knowledge, experience and judgment.

- "*Procedure:*" involves a well-recognized and familiar type of problem. There is some customization, but mostly the required steps are programmatic. Companies turn to the firm because of efficiency. The PSF is selling its procedures, efficiency and availability.

Project team structure

Project structures vary with the type of project:

- *Brains projects*: extreme job shop, nothing routinized, every project "one-off." Opportunities for leveraging juniors are scant, partly because of the difficulty of figuring out in advance how to deploy them. Ratio of juniors to seniors is low, which affects the organization's shape.

- *Gray Hair projects*: Problems are more familiar, so there is some predictability to how many juniors will be needed. A bit more like a disconnected assembly line than a pure job shop.

- *Procedure projects*: Usually have the highest proportion of juniors. Steps are well established and can therefore be delegated to juniors. Appropriate responses can be "programmed." Looks much more like an assembly line.

The choices made by the PSF in mixing its project types are some of the more important in balancing the firm. They affect project team structures and thereby influence the economic and organizational structures of the firm.

CONCLUSIONS: BALANCING THE PROFESSIONAL SERVICE FIRM

Figure 3 in the reading summarizes the links among the four major elements involved in balancing the PSF. Firms must figure out how to distinguish between "levers" (variables under its control) and "rocks" (variables not under its control).

"Perhaps the most significant management variable is the mix of projects undertaken and the implications this has for the project team structure." It affects the firm's economics and structure and both markets, yet it is rarely monitored by PSF managers. Project team structures commonly change over time. More juniors will lower costs, so pressure from competition will create pressure to add juniors. If there is a life cycle to professional services, a particular type of project will move from brains to gray hair to procedure, increasing the proportion of juniors along the way.

It will be more profitable for firms to do new projects that are similar to recently-completed ones. The savings caused by learning effects can be, for a time, kept by the firm. Over time, clients will want to share in the savings. Thus, firms will do well to "lead the market." Repetition of projects will create a personnel problem, since professionals seeking development and challenge will shy away from repeating projects. One solution is to capture the learning in the efforts of juniors by increasing their proportion.

The proportion of juniors *in a particular practice area* will tend to increase over time. "If this is allowed to proceed without corresponding adjustments in the range of practice areas, the project team structure of the firms will be altered, causing significant impacts on the economics and organization of the firm. The dangers of failing to monitor the project team structure are thus clearly revealed. . . . Successful PSF management is a question of balance."

Discussion Questions

1. What are the two markets in which PSFs compete? What is so important about them?

They compete as buyers in the market for skilled professionals and as suppliers in the market for professional services. The author points out that what PSFs usually supply is the skills of their professionals. They are the intermediary between professionals and those requiring professional services. PSFs will succeed at providing services only if they succeed at attracting qualified professionals.

2. What is your reaction to the typical organizational structure of PSFs?

Most students, except perhaps for accounting students, will be unfamiliar with PSFs. It should be interesting to hear their reactions to what appears to be an ancient form of organizing, dating back to the middle ages and the guild system. Professors, who inhabit one of the more rigid forms of PSF, will be able to enlighten their students about life in the PSF.

3. How are project teams typically structured?

The work on a project is usually a mix of client relations, supervision/coordination, and technical work. Typically, senior people manage client relations, managers supervise and coordinate, and juniors do most of the technical work. In well-managed PSFs, managers get some exposure to client relations and juniors get some "management" work to do. This helps people in each group develop useful skills for promotion and firm development.

4. What is your reaction to "the economics of the PSF?"

It should be interesting to see whether or not students are impressed by the typical disbursement of firm revenues in a PSF. Unless there are lots of sophisticated machines, perhaps in a medical practice, PSFs tend to have relatively few assets. So revenues go mostly toward funding expenses, most of which are salaries. With prudent management of the proportion of juniors and managers, seniors can receive handsome rewards, up to half of revenues in the author's estimation.

5. What is the significance of the billing multiple?

The billing multiple is the ratio of billing rate to compensation rate. The author points out that most firms aim at a billing multiple of 4, meaning that they charge the client four times as much as what it costs the firm to provide the service. The higher the proportion of juniors, the higher the multiple, making project team structure an important aspect of firm profitability.

6. *What is the gist of the relationship between the PSF and the market for professional labor?*

PSFs try to attract the best labor possible, realizing that their judgment will occasionally be wrong. Promotion policy will help make the resulting adjustments, as less-qualified people either leave or are counseled out. This policy also helps motivate juniors, who even as juniors have very flexible work schedules. Firms with very restrictive promotion policies tend to be very prestigious, attracting only the best and keeping only the very best. Juniors see a temporary appointment in such firms as worth the effort, thereby perpetuating the system.

7. *What is the point of the section on "accommodating rapid growth?"*

Because of the finite size of the professional labor market, PSFs have only four strategies available to them if they wish to grow. They can try to hire better people who are likelier to get promoted. They can speed up the juniors' development process. They can hire senior people directly into the firm. And they can manipulate the mix of people assigned to project teams.

8. *What is the nature of the market for a PSF's services?*

Clients tend to want high levels of expertise, but not all their problems are interesting. Top professionals tend to want to work on projects that require high levels of expertise and *are* interesting. The author describes the three major categories of projects needed to serve clients' needs. "Brains" projects are the most interesting and challenging, and will tend to attract the best professionals. "Procedure" projects are completely programmed and routine, and only juniors will want to work on them. "Gray hair" projects are in between. To attract the proper mix of talent, firms will want to achieve a proper balance among these three types of projects.

9. *How is project team structure affected by type of project?*

Brains projects are the most fluid, resembling the innovative organizations discussed in the next chapter. They tend to have a higher proportion of senior people. Procedures projects have a much higher proportion of junior people, and their project teams look more like machine organizations. Gray hair projects are in between, resembling, according to the author, a "disconnected assembly line."

10. *What does the author think is the most crucial management variable in the PSF?*

The mix of projects undertaken. Since team configuration depends on type of project, the mix of teams will be determined by the mix of project types. The mix of teams will collectively determine the overall balance of the firm. If too many projects are selected that need a high proportion of juniors, profits may be high but morale will sink in the junior ranks as they realize that the assumed career path will not materialize in their case. If the mix is slanted toward a higher proportion of seniors, profit will be lower as the big guns are unable to leverage their efforts with those of less-expensive junior people.

The author points out that the proportion of juniors will increase over time *in a particular practice area*. To avoid having too many juniors overall, the firm must keep developing new practice areas. This also helps in another way. Top professionals are loathe to do too many repetitions of particular types of projects, even though doing so is profitable. By constantly developing new areas, PSFs keep their top people challenged and can help avoid a situation where there is too great a proportion of juniors.

Mintzberg, "The Innovative Organization"

<u>Summary of Reading</u>

None of the organizational forms discussed thus far is capable of sophisticated innovation. The entrepreneurial organization can innovate only in simple ways. The machine and professional organizations are performance types, designed to perfect standardized programs. The diversified organization may be a bit more flexible, but its focus on standardized outputs discourages innovation. We need what Toffler called adhocracies.

<u>THE BASIC STRUCTURE</u>

A distinct configuration:

highly organic structure

little formalization

specialized jobs based on expert training

functional grouping for "housekeeping," small project teams for work

mutual adjustment as key coordinating mechanism

considerable decentralization to the teams

Innovation means breaking away from established patterns, so the innovative organization cannot rely on any form of standardization. The innovative organization must avoid the trappings of bureaucracy. Above all, it must remain flexible.

The entrepreneurial configuration can innovate in simple ways, understandable by one person. Sophisticated innovation requires flexibility that can draw together different forms of expertise. Thus the innovative organization empowers experts, but the experts coordinate in ways that allow the combining of their skills and expertise (very different from the professional organization).

Standardization cannot be used, because it drives out innovation. Direct supervision can't be used because the work is complex. So coordination must happen using mutual adjustment, supported by numerous liaison devices. The result is that managers abound in adhocracies, especially project managers.

Adhocracies tend to be decentralized, with power over decisions flowing to those with the information to make them.

Adhocracies take two basic forms: the operating adhocracy and the administrative adhocracy.

The operating adhocracy

This form innovates and solves problems directly on behalf of its clients. "For every operating adhocracy, there is a corresponding professional bureaucracy, one that does similar work but with a narrower orientation." The operating adhocracy creates a novel solution to a problem; the professional organization tries to pigeonhole the problem.

In the operating adhocracy, administrative and operating work tend to blend into a single effort. Examples of this kind of firm are design firms, avant-garde theater companies, and some software development firms.

The administrative adhocracy

The second type of adhocracy undertakes projects to serve itself. The administrative adhocracy makes a clear distinction between its administrative component and its operating core. That core is truncated so that the administrative component that remains can be structured as an adhocracy.

The truncation can occur in three ways:

1. If operations are machinelike, they can be established as an independent organization (Example: pharmaceutical firm that uses R-DNA technology splits off its manufacturing arm)

2. The operating core may be eliminated by contracting out the operating work (Example: NASA during the Apollo project)

3. The operating core may be automated (Example: oil refining)

The administrative component of the adhocracies

In both types of adhocracy, the relationship between the operating core and the administration is unlike that in any other configuration. In the administrative adhocracy, the two are truncated; in the operating adhocracy, the two are blended. Either way, the need for traditional direct supervision is diminished, and managers derive their influence more from expertise and interpersonal skill than from formal position.

Support staff play a key role in adhocracy, because that is where many experts reside, especially in the administrative adhocracy. The staff is not as sharply differentiated as it is in most other configurations. Technostructure plays virtually no role in adhocracies; most analysis comes from experts in the support staff.

The roles of the strategic apex

"The top managers of the strategic apex of this configuration do not spend much time formulating explicit strategies . . . ." They spend much time on handling disturbances, which are frequent in these structures. They also monitor the projects, which are difficult to monitor using MISs.

The most important role is liaison with the external environment. Operating adhocracies tend to live from one project to the next, so top management must work to keep the flow of projects up. "It is a distinguishing characteristic of many an operating adhocracy that the selling function literally takes place at the strategic apex."

Top managers also spend much time reassigning personnel from canceled projects to new projects.

CONDITIONS OF THE INNOVATIVE ORGANIZATION

"This configuration is found in environments that are both dynamic and complex." Environmental dynamism calls for organic structure; complexity calls for decentralization. This is the only configuration that provides both. Firms with this structure usually choose this kind of environment (just as professional organizations tend to seek stable environments).

Adhocracies tend to be young. Operating adhocracies are particularly prone to short lives, since they face risky markets. Other operating adhocracies "die" because they succeed—the organization grows and becomes either a professional organization or a machine organization.

Administrative adhocracies tend to live longer because their industries typically require sophisticated innovation for extended periods. One variant of operating adhocracy that has emerged is the "temporary adhocracy"—it draws together specialists, then disbands them after their task is completed.

Sophisticated technology drives the organization toward administrative adhocracy, because it must find a way to involve the experts in the support staff. Automation also drives them toward administrative adhocracy, because the technostructure loses its influence and the structure becomes more organic and decentralized. Fashion also drives organizations toward adhocracy. The innovative organization is very fashionable these days.

STRATEGY FORMATION IN THE INNOVATIVE ORGANIZATION

"The structure of the innovative organization may seem unconventional, but its strategy-making is even more so, upsetting virtually everything we have been taught to believe about that process." The IO cannot rely on deliberate strategy; its actions must be decided upon individually, according to the needs of the moment. It proceeds incrementally.

"The process is best thought of as strategy formation, because strategy is not formulated consciously in one place so much as formed implicitly by the specific actions taken in many places." That is why these organizations cannot rely upon action planning. "Any process that separates thinking from action . . . would impede the flexibility of the organization to respond creatively to its dynamic environment."

Strategy formation in the operating adhocracy

In the operating adhocracy, "strategy never really stabilizes totally but is responsive to new projects, which themselves involve the activities of a whole host of people . . . . The operating adhocracy's strategy thus evolves continuously as all kinds of decisions [responding to individual proposals] are made, each leaving its imprint on the strategy by creating a precedent or reinforcing an existing one."

Strategy formation in the administrative adhocracy

Strategy-making is similar to the operating adhocracy's, but is "neater" because the administrative adhocracy tends to focus on fewer projects. Administrative adhocracies give more attention to action planning, but of a loose kind, specifying ends but not means.

Strategies nonetheless

"With their activities so disjointed, one might wonder whether adhocracies (of either type) can form strategies (that is, patterns) at all. In fact, they do, at least at certain times." They tend to cycle between periods of convergence on patterns, and divergence, when there are no patterns. In machine organizations, the periods of convergence are long, the periods of divergence ("strategic revolutions") are short. In innovative organizations, the cycles tend to be regular. "The IO . . . seems not only able to function at times without strategic focus, but positively to thrive on it."

The varied strategies of adhocracy

Where do the strategies of adhocracy come from? Some may be imposed deliberately, but most emerge. In some cases, a single ad hoc decision sets a precedent which evokes a pattern. Sometimes a strategy will be pursued in a pocket of an organization, which later becomes more broadly organizational when the organization seizes upon it.

What does management do? "It manages patterns, seeking partial control over strategies but otherwise attempting to influence what happens to those strategies that do emerge lower down." They can do this by managing *process* or through the use of *umbrella strategy*.

A grassroots model of strategy formation

1. Strategies grow initially like weeds in a garden; they are not cultivated like tomatoes in a hothouse. (The strategy process can be overmanaged; it's better to let patterns emerge than to force an artificial consistency.)

2. These strategies can take root in all kinds of places, virtually anywhere people have the capacity to learn and the resources to support that capacity. (Individuals may get an idea by accident; top managers may hit on an idea; or many ideas may converge as the result of mutual adjustment.)

3. Such strategies become organizational when they become collective, that is, when the patterns proliferate to pervade the behavior of the organization at large.

4. The processes of proliferation may be conscious but need not be; likewise they may be managed but need not be. (Initial ideas need not be consciously intended; patterns may spread by collective action. Once the ideas seem good, they may then be managed.)

5. New strategies, which may be emerging continuously, tend to pervade the organization during periods of change, which punctuate periods of more integrated continuity. (In other words, there will be periods of stability punctuated by periods of change. In innovative organizations, these periods cycle regularly; in machine organizations, the stable periods are longer, and the change periods are short and revolutionary.)

6. To manage this process is not to preconceive strategies but to recognize their emergence and intervene when appropriate.

"I call this a 'grassroots' model because the strategies grow up from the base of the organization, rooted in the solid earth of its operations rather than the ethereal abstraction of its administration."

There are really three models of strategy formation: the *learning model* (associated with the innovative organization), the *planning model* (associated with the machine organization), and the *visionary model* (associated with the entrepreneurial organization). "All organizations need to mix these approaches in various ways at different times in their development."

Environment taking precedence in the innovative organization

"In the IO it is the environment that takes precedence. It drives the organization, which responds continuously and eclectically, but does nevertheless achieve convergence during certain periods."

"The strategist of the innovative organization is largely a *pattern recognizer*, seeking to detect emerging patterns within and outside the strategic umbrella."

SOME ISSUES ASSOCIATED WITH THE INNOVATIVE ORGANIZATION

Human reactions to ambiguity

Many people, especially creative ones, dislike structural rigidity and the concentration of power. For these people, the adhocracy is a great place to work. Other people need more structure, and so they prefer the machine organization or the professional organization. Even dedicated members of adhocracies periodically get frustrated by the structure's fluidity, confusion, and ambiguity. Sometimes the innovative form gets overly politicized.

Problems of efficiency

The IO is excellent for devising novel solutions. But it is inefficient. One source is the unbalanced workload. The most important source is the high cost of communication, the mutual adjustment.

The dangers of inappropriate transition

To handle the problems of ambiguity and inefficiency, the firm may elect to change configuration. This is done most easily in the operating adhocracy, which could pick a program at which it is most skilled, and become a professional organization. It could also pick one niche and convert to a machine organization. But these transitions may be inappropriate. Society already has many mass producers—it needs creative organizations.

The administrative adhocracy faces a more serious danger. If it converts to a machine organization, it risks losing its adaptiveness and innovativeness, and so it can eventually destroy itself.

Discussion Questions

1. Why must the innovative organization "avoid all the trappings of bureaucratic structure?"

Bureaucracies are very formalized. Everything is standardized. Jobs are severely circumscribed. These are all things that work to dampen innovation. To innovate, firms must be flexible, unstandardized, multidisciplinary. People can't be allowed to worry about job descriptions, standard operating procedures, or "whose job it is" to do something.

2. What is the distinction between simple and sophisticated innovation, and how valid is it?

Simple innovation involves finding new applications for existing approaches, or finding new niches for existing operations. Entrepreneurs excel at this. Sophisticated innovation consists of discovering new things in the midst of complex fields. This requires extensive training in the complex fields. It also requires groups of people getting their heads together, because complex innovation cannot be done by people acting alone. Obviously, the distinction is valid.

3. Why must mutual adjustment be used to coordinate members of an innovative organization?

Standardization, in any form, cannot be used, because it drives out innovation. Direct supervision can't be used because the work is too complex. So coordination must happen using mutual adjustment, supported by numerous liaison devices. Mutual adjustment has the added benefit of bringing together teams of people who tend to do a better job at sophisticated innovation.

4. What is the distinction between an operating adhocracy and an administrative adhocracy?

The operating adhocracy innovates and solves problems *directly* on behalf of its clients. Examples would be research and development organizations, design firms, and some consulting firms. The administrative adhocracy undertakes projects to *serve itself*. The best examples are the top managements of firms in dynamic and complex environments, whose operating cores get in the way of top management's flexibility. The best example would be an oil refining company, whose operations are very routine, but whose industry is very dynamic and complex.

5. What does the author mean when he says that "for every operating adhocracy, there is a corresponding professional organization?"

Operating adhocracies are multipurpose problem-solvers. Faced with a problem, they will *create* a *new* solution. Mintzberg's point is that many of the problems faced by operating adhocracies have been faced by other organizations in the past. Some of them may have developed a standard solution to the problem, which they will apply to it each time they encounter it. This describes a professional organization—it doesn't come up with anything new, but merely applies the same solution to a problem, over and over. One might say that professional organizations are single-purpose problem-solvers.

6. How can the strategic apex of an organization with a machine bureaucratic operating core ever be truly an adhocracy, as the author suggests is the case in the administrative adhocracy?

At first blush, this *does* seem to be difficult. There is always a risk that the routine part of the administrative adhocracy will "contaminate" the strategic apex, making it less flexible and adaptable. But that is precisely *why* the administrative adhocracy form arises. Managers want to minimize the risk of contamination, so they truncate the organization's operating core. This may not remove all the problems, but it is better than trying to become a machine organization, which will surely drive out innovation and adaptiveness.

7. Why would most of the experts on which adhocracy is dependent be housed in the support staff, thereby making it the key part of this configuration?

In either kind of adhocracy the need for traditional direct supervision is diminished, and managers derive their influence more from *expertise* and *interpersonal skill* than from formal position. Support staff play a key role in adhocracy, because that is where many experts reside, especially in the administrative adhocracy. The support staff contains most of the experts who can help the adhocracy create the novel solutions, the innovations, for which it is known. The staff is not as sharply differentiated as it is in most other configurations. Technostructure plays virtually no role in adhocracies; most analysis comes from experts in the support staff.

8. Which is the more challenging job, top management in a machine organization or top management in an adhocracy?

This question is intended to stimulate discussion. The top management of machine organizations needs to be able to make the organization efficient for long stable periods, and then be able to recognize the need to adopt some different approach after a brief revolution. The different approach is usually based on either entrepreneurial or innovative initiatives.

The top managers of innovative organizations must be able to handle its frequent disturbances, monitor all the projects, but mostly to act as liaison with the outside environment. In particular, they must keep the flow of projects up.

Each type of top management has its own challenges. The management of innovative organizations may seem to be a bit more "exciting," but students will have a range of opinions about this.

9. What does the author mean when he says that a successful operating adhocracy may have a short life?

The life of a successful operating adhocracy is short because success breeds growth, and growth means greater size. As we saw in Chapter 6, increases in size typically lead to greater formalization and standardization. In other words, as organizations succeed and grow, they become machine organizations. So the successful adhocracy becomes, after a time, something other than an adhocracy.

10. What happens when the operating core of a machine organization is automated?

Automation drives the machine organization toward administrative adhocracy. The problem of motivating bored workers disappears, as does the control mentality of the structure. The distinction between line and staff becomes blurred, and the technostructure loses its influence. The administrative structure becomes more organic and decentralized. The operating core can be truncated, and the remaining strategic apex converts to an adhocracy, able to adapt more flexibly to environmental conditions.

11. Mintzberg says that in adhocracies, "strategy is not formulated consciously in one place so much as formed implicitly by the specific actions taken in many places." What is your reaction to this statement?

This question is intended to stimulate discussion. Many students will be puzzled by this statement. In most organizational forms we have examined so far, there is at least *some* "explicitness" to strategy-making. Machine organizations have their revolutions, missionary organizations have their ideologies, entrepreneurial organizations have their leaders' visions, and even professional organizations have the norms of the professions to which their workers belong. Here, we have strategy being formed *implicitly*. As foreign as this may sound, students will have to be reminded that this is indeed what happens in adhocracies. There is too much flux in them for it to be otherwise.

12. How do you react to the statement, "any process that separates conception from action—planning from execution, formulation from implementation—impedes the flexibility of the organization to respond creatively to its dynamic environment?"

This harkens back to Mintzberg's reading on "Crafting Strategy" from Chapter 5. There, he decried the tendency in the strategy literature to recommend that thinking and action ought to be separated, that analysis should happen first, and execution (or implementation) later. In his potter metaphor, the author pointed out that most potters don't spend a few days thinking, and then a few days doing pottery; they *think* and *do* at the same time. This is how they get ideas. Precisely the same dynamic holds for adhocracies.

13. The author says that administrative adhocracies must rely on "action planning . . . of a loose kind." Is this a contradiction in terms?

To some extent, it is. Mintzberg says that the action planning in administrative adhocracies should focus on ends, not means. In that case, it sounds much more like performance control than action planning. What the author probably means by this phrase is that administrative adhocracies might profitably use modified versions of strategic planning, mostly for giving guidance to their truncated operating cores.

14. How might managing an adhocracy be like "trying to drive an automobile without controlling the steering wheel?"

Managers of adhocracies, to use the author's phrase, "can accelerate and brake but cannot determine direction." The solutions created by the people working in adhocracies cannot possibly be envisioned in advance—they are completely new, by definition. Consequently, managers would be wasting their time if they tried to be very directive. In that sense, it *is* like trying to steer without using the steering wheel. Adhocracy managers *do* have some tools to control strategy-making, though. They can control *processes* and they can articulate strategic *umbrellas*.

15. *What's your reaction to the "weeds in the garden" metaphor?*

Many students will find the metaphor a bit weak, since it is difficult to think of a weed that ultimately is worthwhile. (And this is despite the author's comment on dandelions being a salad green in Europe.) Nevertheless, the author makes his point. Not all strategies need be deliberately developed ("hothouse"). Some may just "spring up" ("weeds in a garden").

16. *What are the implications of the idea that "strategies can take root in all kinds of strange places?"*

This is an admonition to managers to keep an open mind about where strategies come from. Not all good strategies will emanate from top management, or from corporate planning staffs. Sometimes, people at relatively low levels of the organization will have good ideas that can be developed into a strategy. As Pascale's reading about the "Honda Effect" in Chapter 5 pointed out, the Japanese are very good at getting their strategic ideas from a variety of places in their organizations.

17. *The author says that the process of grassroots strategy "may be conscious but need not be; likewise, it may be managed, but need not be." How do you react to this?*

This is another one of those admonitions to management. The lesson is to be flexible. Sometimes it makes sense to be very deliberate. Other times it is more sensible to be loose, and to let things emerge. Managers must be able to use either mode, and to recognize the times each is the more appropriate.

18. *Why is the following statement important: "To manage this [grassroots] process is not to preconceive strategies but to recognize their emergence and intervene when appropriate?"*

The answer to this is very similar to the answer to the previous question. Successful grassroots management requires monitoring and *selective* intervention. Some emergent strategies will not be worthwhile, and should be discouraged. The worth of others will be ambiguous. Still others will be clearly valuable. The role of management is to let all of these emerge until they are "judgeable," and *then* to decide on them. Preconception of strategies would be appropriate were a firm pursuing *planned* or other forms of *deliberate* strategy. But that approach would be detrimental to grassroots strategy-making in the innovative organization.

19. *How does the strategy formation process described in this reading relate to the Wrapp reading from Chapter 2?*

Wrapp described the manager as standing in a stream of operating actions and decisions. She or he assesses these operating actions and decisions, keeping some in mind, discarding others. Eventually, she or he puts some of these pieces together, and a strategy forms. This is very similar to the grassroots model discussed in this reading.

20. *Why isn't adhocracy the structure for all organization?*

Not all organizations need to be innovative. Not all organizations need to be set up to solve unique problems. Some organizations are needed efficiently to produce consumer goods. Others are needed effectively to provide high-quality professional services. Still others are needed to fill niches in simple industries. To meet the first need, one should design a machine organization. The second need is best met by a professional organization. And entrepreneurial organizations excel at filling the niches in simple yet dynamic industries.

21. *How well do you think you would tolerate the ambiguity of adhocracy?*

This is purely a discussion question. There may be a more severe split in this question than many instructors would expect. Most students like structure. They like to be told what to do and when to do it. Even though most students like the idea of freedom, they also have a hard time visualizing the lack of structure characteristic of innovative organizations. It is likelier that MBA students, or other more mature students, will better appreciate the freedom available in adhocracies.

22. *What is your reaction to the author's statement that "society has more mass producers than it needs; what it lacks are true problem solvers?"*

This is obviously a value judgment on the author's part. There certainly *are* many mass producers. But it is difficult to say if there are too many. It is a little easier to agree with the author's statement that there is a lack of true problem-solvers. There probably can never be too many innovators.

23. *Why may an administrative adhocracy be threatened with extinction if it transits to machine organization?*

If an administrative adhocracy converts to a machine organization, it is usually because management is tired of the perpetual change which characterizes administrative adhocracies. But the standardization of the machine organization puts the administrative adhocracy at risk of losing its adaptiveness and innovativeness, and so it can eventually destroy itself.

Quinn, "Managing Innovation: Controlled Chaos"

Summary of Reading

Some large enterprises are highly innovative. How do they do it? Effective management of innovation seems to be the same whether a company is large or small.

There are many reasons why small companies *appear* to produce a disproportionate number of innovations. Innovation occurs in a probabilistic setting. Many more innovations fail than succeed. But since they are scattered widely, they receive little notice. A big company that seeks to innovate must absorb all the risks and costs itself. A small company does not risk losing an existing investment base or cannibalizing customer franchises. It does not have to change its culture, negotiate with its unions, or deal with consumer advocates and government regulators. Finally, new companies do not have to face the psychological pain and economic costs of layoffs, plant shutdowns, and displaced supplier relationships. "Such barriers to change in large organizations are real, important, and legitimate."

Nevertheless, society expects large organizations to absorb the risks in ever-more-complex technology. No single enterprise can develop these systems, yet their complexity makes effective communications difficult, and increases the possibility of error. "But proper management can lessen these effects."

OF INVENTORS AND ENTREPRENEURS

Research suggests that the following factors are crucial to the success of innovative small companies.

Need orientation

Entrepreneurs tend to be achievement-oriented. They believe that if they do the job better, rewards will follow. But they are able to adjust and become more customer-oriented as their resources get low.

Experts and fanatics

Company founders tend to be pioneers in their technologies and fanatics when it comes to solving problems. This allows them to perceive success as being likelier than others do, so they persevere.

Long time horizons

Their fanaticism causes inventor-entrepreneurs to underestimate the time needed to succeed. This makes them seem "irrational" from a present-value standpoint.

"For both psychological and practical reasons, inventor-entrepreneurs generally avoid early formal plans, proceed step-by-step, and sustain themselves by other income and the momentum of the small advances they achieve as they go along."

Low early costs

Innovators work at home, in garages, etc. They work nights and weekends. They expend "sweat capital," but little real money. If they fail, few people know, and little is lost. This decreases risk.

Multiple approaches

Technology usually advances through a series of random insights, often triggered by serendipitous interactions between the entrepreneur and the outside world. Only the highly committed can survive, and even enjoy, this chaos.

Of the initial public offerings made in 1962, only 2% survived twenty years later. "Small-scale entrepreneurship looks efficient in part because history only records the survivors."

Flexibility and quickness

Unencumbered by bureaucratic apparatus, inventor-entrepreneurs can act experimentally with little time lost. This may be crucial for "finding early markets where neither innovators, market researchers, nor users can quite visualize a product's real potential."

Incentives

Inventor-entrepreneurs can foresee tangible personal rewards for success, like recognition, power, independence, technical contribution, and money. This diversified set of incentives means that "they do not panic or quit when others with solely monetary goals might."

Availability of capital

America has a rich variety of sources of financing. Financers have a characteristic approach:

1. They evaluate a proposal's conceptual validity.

2. They evaluate the people attached to the proposal.

3. They analyze specific financial estimates in depth.

"Timeliness, aggressiveness, commitment, quality of people, and the flexibility to attach opportunities not at first perceived are crucial. Downside risks are minimized, not by detailed controls, but by spreading the risks among multiple projects, keeping early costs low, and gauging the tenacity, flexibility, and capability of the founders."

LARGE COMPANY BARRIERS TO INNOVATION

Top management isolation

"Many senior executives in big companies have little contact with conditions on the factory floor or with customers who might influence their thinking about technological innovation." Risk perception is inversely related to familiarity and experience.

Intolerance of fanatics

"Big companies often view entrepreneurial fanatics as embarrassments or troublemakers."

Short time horizons

"The perceived corporate need to report a continuous stream of quarterly profits conflicts with the long time spans that major innovations normally require."

Accounting practices

"By assessing all its direct, indirect, overhead, overtime, and service costs against a project, large corporations have much higher development expenses compared with entrepreneurs working in garages."

Excessive rationalism

"Managers in big companies often seek orderly advance through early market research studies or PERT planning." This drives out the things that lead to innovation.

Excessive bureaucracy

Bureaucratic "efficiency" causes delays. Also, interactive feedback is also lost, opportunities are missed, and risk rises.

Inappropriate incentives

"Reward and control systems in most big companies are designed to minimize surprises. Yet innovation, by definition, is full of surprises."

HOW LARGE INNOVATIVE COMPANIES DO IT

Here are the most important patterns that characterize successful large-company innovation.

Atmosphere and vision

"Continuous innovation occurs largely because top executives appreciate innovation and manage their company's value system and atmosphere to support it . . . . Innovative managements . . . project clear long-term visions for their organizations that go beyond simple economic measures . . . . These are not 'management fluff,' but have many practical implications. They attract quality people to the company and give focus to their creative and entrepreneurial drives." They can also channel growth by concentrating attention on profitable actions. They can recognize a realistic time frame for innovation. And they can help attract investors.

494

Orientation to the market

"Innovative companies tie their visions to the practical realities of the marketplace . . . . [They have] a strong market orientation at the very top of the company, and mechanisms to ensure interactions between technical and marketing people at lower levels."

Small, flat organizations

"The most innovative large companies . . . try to keep the total organization flat and project teams, . . . normally . . . only six or seven people . . . . [They] also try to keep their operating divisions and total technical units small—below 400 people." This means that only two management layers are needed.

Multiple approaches

One can't be sure which of several approaches will dominate a field. Technologies tend to advance in "accidents." Innovative enterprises seem to move quickly from paper studies to physical testing, encouraging several prototypes to proceed in parallel.

Developmental shoot-outs

"Many companies structure shoot-outs among competing approaches only after they reach the prototype stage." They find this practice provides more objective information, decreases risk, and helps ensure that winning options move ahead with committed teams.

Skunkworks

Highly innovative companies use "skunkworks," small teams of engineers, technicians, designers, and model makers with no organizational or physical barriers to developing a new product from idea to commercial prototype. This eliminates bureaucracies, speeds communication and experimentation, and instills a high level of group identity and loyalty.

Interactive learning

"Recognizing that the random, chaotic nature of technological change cuts across organizational and even institutional lines, [large innovative] companies tap into multiple outside sources of technology as well as their customers' capabilities." They can form closer relationships with customers, or even with competitors—joint ventures, consortia, and limited partnerships. They can also try to guarantee first markets, fund academic research or venture capital firms, and spin off equity.

"Formal market analyses continue to be useful for extending product lines, but they are often misleading when applied to radical innovations."

A STRATEGY FOR INNOVATION

Here are some of the things managers can do to establish the right culture for innovation.

An opportunity orientation

"Entrepreneurial companies recognize that they have almost unlimited access to capital and they structure their practices accordingly. They let it be known that if their people come up with good ideas, they can find the necessary capital . . . ."

Structuring for innovation

"Managers need to think carefully about how innovation fits into their strategy and structure, their technology, skills, resources, and organizational commitments . . . ."

Complex portfolio planning

"To allocate resources for innovation strategically, managers need to define the broad, long-term actions within and across divisions necessary to achieve their visions." This problem requires a portfolio strategy much more complex than the popular four-box Boston Consulting Group matrix. Managers must protect both short-term gains and long-term prospects.

AN INCREMENTALIST APPROACH

". . . Few, if any, major innovations result from highly structured planning systems [because] the innovative process is inherently incremental." Breakthroughs happen randomly. The outcome of an early approach is unpredictable. It is best to pursue several paths. Open up many networks. Keep many options open.

"Managing innovation is like a stud poker game, where one can play several hands." The player knows the likely ending size of the pot and the general path to winning. He/she buys a card (a project) at a time, to gain information about the pot and the probabilities, folds hands as they become discouraging, and risks more only after knowledge increases.

Chaos within guidelines

"Effective managers of innovation channel and control its main directions. Like venture capitalists, they administer primarily by setting goals, selecting key people, and establishing a few critical limits and decision points for intervention rather than by implementing elaborate planning or control systems."

Early on, many options are pursued; they narrow down as more is learned. Even so, "side bets" are kept.

Special ways are found to reward innovators: percentage of sales from new products; promotions for key innovation managers; simulated stock options; new companies with workers given equity positions. Rewards should be visible and significant, e.g., "playing pinball," which is giving widespread recognition for a job well done and the right to play in the next exciting game.

MATCH MANAGEMENT TO THE PROCESS

"Executives need to understand and accept the tumultuous realities of innovation, learn from the experiences of other companies, and adapt the most relevant features of these others to their own management practices and cultures. Many features of small company innovators are also applicable in big companies."

Discussion Questions

1. How important is it to know that "innovation occurs in a probabilistic setting?"

It is crucially important. Nine out of ten ideas fail as products. This means that to get ten reasonable products, a company needs to start 100 projects! Managers who think that their firms can be innovative with only a smattering of product development efforts are sadly mistaken. They must generate *many* ideas and see where they take the company. A basketball game is a good analogy: if two teams are shooting poorly from the floor, a team can still win if it takes more shots than the other team.

2. What are some of the forces that inhibit innovation in large organizations?

Almost all of the things Mintzberg mentioned in his reading on machine organizations. Top management is isolated. The organization does not tolerate fanatics. Planning cycles encourage short time horizons. The control mentality create accounting practices that frustrate innovators, encourage excessive rationalism, and create excessive bureaucracy. Lastly, incentives are oriented toward minimizing risk and are inappropriate for innovation.

3. How important is it for an innovator to have a long time horizon?

It is very important because many innovations take a very long time to bear fruit. The author cites a range of 3 to 25 years! Most innovations take more than 10 years to become commercializable. Therefore, inventors must be willing to persevere for long periods. Some large companies cannot wait that long.

4. What is your reaction to the notion that innovators face "low early costs?"

Some students will be a little puzzled by this. They will be thinking of the enormous costs large companies have to bear if they want to invest in new business. But that misses Quinn's point—it might cost a lot to *produce* the new products, but *developing* them need not be costly. Many inventors develop prototypes on a shoestring. There is no reason large companies cannot do the same.

5. How is the idea of "multiple approaches" related to Mintzberg's previous reading on adhocracies?

Mintzberg discussed how sophisticated innovation relies on mutual adjustment. People must *interact* to gain the proper insights for complex innovation. And that is one of the points Quinn is making here. Innovators must take multiple approaches, reach out to the "outside," and get good ideas wherever they may be.

6. Is the subsection on "flexibility and quickness" related to the entrepreneurial organization, to adhocracy, or both?

In some sense it is related to both, because either the entrepreneurial or the innovative organization, as described by Mintzberg, has the ability to respond quickly and flexibly. But the discussion here is somewhat more closely related to the innovative organization, since it discusses experimentation. Entrepreneurial organizations are less likely to engage in experimentation.

7. How important is the notion of high availability of capital in the United States?

In some ways it is important, in other ways it is overstated. Any innovative organization will be aided if it has ready access to capital. It is also true that the United States has a well-honed venture capital system for getting financing to people with good ideas. But there are other ways of doing it, as the author readily admits. The best alternative is to have capital available within the large company. This is how most Japanese innovation occurs.

8. Examine the list of large company barriers to innovation. How well have the elite Japanese companies handled these problems?

By using techniques like open communication and an emphasis on work groups, the elite Japanese companies have been very successful as innovators. These companies have been able to generate a long-term perspective. Most of their growth has not come from acquisition, but from internal growth, which provides opportunities for innovators.

Most of all, the elite Japanese companies are characterized by aggressive innovation. Japanese firms are good innovators. They do not segregate R&D, production, and marketing from one another. The innovation process is diffused widely throughout the organization, enlarging the strategic alternatives available to the firm.

9. How does the subsection on "atmosphere and vision" relate to previous readings?

It is closely related to "strategy as perspective" (from the Chapter 1 reading "Five Ps for Strategy") and "Ideology and the Missionary Organization" (from Chapter 7).

10. Are "small, flat organizations" adhocracies? What about skunkworks?

Small, flat organizations *are* adhocracies. The latter tend to be small, to facilitate the mutual adjustment that must go on. They are also flat, meaning that they have few management layers above them. This is because adhocracies tend to be self-regulating. Skunkworks are simply a specific variation of adhocracy, one that is split off from the parent corporation to ensure release from the bonds of bureaucracy.

11. How does the notion of "interactive learning" differ from the "standard" strategy model, like the one presented in Chapter 3?

The "standard" strategy model is very much dominated from the top. Whatever thinking or learning goes on, goes on in the strategic apex. The environment is not "experienced," it is "scanned." Strategy is formulated, articulated in a plan, and then it is implemented.

"Interactive learning" couldn't be more different. Thinking and learning happens everywhere, but especially where there is knowledge that can be brought to bear on problems. This is usually at lower levels. The organization's people interact directly with the environment, which consists of other people involved in similar technological endeavors. And strategy *forms* and *evolves* as information improves, things become clearer, and the appropriate uses for innovations become apparent.

12. In the innovation context, how important is it to have "an opportunity orientation?"

It is decisively important. Almost anything else will tend to lead to a risk-averse bureaucratic approach. Firms will start looking for places to cut, instead of looking at how to fund new ideas. If firms wish to remain in the innovation context, they must realize that *any* good idea is very likely to find funding, from outside the firm, if need be. Just because things are not going well is no excuse for failing to fund a good opportunity. To not fund a good opportunity is to take the first steps out of the innovation context.

13. How does the "complex portfolio planning" discussed by Quinn here differ from the portfolio approach discussed by Henderson in Chapter 11?

The BCG approach is a way of assessing the cash flows of various businesses in a firm, and of reallocating those flows. Quinn argues that innovation requires a different approach. Firms must intelligently assess both their current returns and their future prospects. He offers no short-cuts for doing this, saying only that it is a complex and difficult process.

14. Why is it that "few, if any, major innovations result from highly structured planning systems?"

Planning works poorly in the innovation context because the innovative process is inherently incremental. Breakthroughs happen randomly. The outcome of an early approach is unpredictable. It is best to pursue several paths, to open up many networks, and to keep many options open. This loose approach does not fit well with structured strategic planning. In this context, strategies *form*, they are not formulated.

15. What are the implications of saying that one element in technological innovation is "random breakthroughs interacting across laboratories and borders?"

There are several implications. The random nature of the breakthroughs negates any contribution that might be made by a structured planning approach. Strategies must be allowed to *form*, they cannot be *formulated*. The interaction characteristic means that innovators must be allowed to communicate, to mutually adjust. Lastly, that this process cuts across organizational boundaries means that innovators must constantly be in touch with their colleagues in other organizations. The bit of knowledge needed to push an idea over the top may already exist in another place or in another person's mind.

16. How does the subsection on "chaos within guidelines" relate to Mintzberg's notions of umbrella and process strategies?

Here is what Quinn says at the beginning of this section: "Effective managers of innovation channel and control its main directions. Like venture capitalists, they administer primarily by setting goals, selecting key people, and establishing a few critical limits and decision points for intervention rather than by implementing elaborate planning or control systems." This is a good description of umbrella strategy— channeling main directions; setting goals; establishing critical limits. It is also a good description of process strategy—selecting key people; decision points for intervention.

17. How appropriate are Quinn's references to "poker games" and "side bets?"

Given the probabilistic nature of innovation, these metaphors are highly appropriate. Quinn is not alluding to the macho, competitive nature of poker, but to the successful player's need to know the odds and the size of the pot. Knowledge of both of these things improves if the player plays incrementally. And overall odds of winning money are improved if the player also places side bets, in case the poker game doesn't pan out.

18. What are your feelings about Quinn's comments concerning incentives?

Students may differ on the examples the author gives, but there is little doubt that managers seeking innovation must themselves be innovative in their use of incentives. Mere exhortations that the effort is "like a start-up," in the absence of true start-up-like rewards, will turn people off. Many of the incentives Quinn recommends may seem elaborate (e.g., the separate companies and the accompanying equity positions for employees), but they *do* have the advantage of replicating the atmosphere in innovative start-ups.

Mintzberg, "The Diversified Organization"

<u>Summary of Reading</u>

THE BASIC DIVISIONALIZED STRUCTURE

The diversified organization is set of semi-autonomous units ("divisions") coupled by central administrative structure ("headquarters"). Divisions are created to serve distinct markets and are given control over the operating functions necessary to do so. Each appears to be a self-standing business, but headquarters *does* exist, distinguishing the diversified organization from a set of independent businesses.

Roles of headquarters

Performance control: sets standards in quantitative terms, monitors results (i.e., standardization of outputs is prime coordinating mechanism, with minor supplement from direct supervision).

Development of overall corporate strategy: establishment and maintenance of portfolio of businesses.

Management of funds movement among divisions: taking excess cash from some divisions and investing it in others.

Design and operation of performance control system

Appointment and replacement of division managers

Provision of support services common to all divisions

Structure of the divisions

It has been common to label diversified organizations "decentralized." But decision making power tends to remain with the few managers who run the businesses. It is actually the *centralization* of power within the divisions that is most compatible with the divisionalized form of structure.

"The effect of having a headquarters over the divisions is to drive them toward the machine configuration . . . . The proliferation of the diversified configuration . . . has the effect of driving many suborganizations toward machine bureaucracy, even where that configuration may be inappropriate . . . ."

The key to this is the standardization of outputs, namely, granting divisional autonomy while exercising control over performance. This is based on two assumptions:

1. Each division must be treated as a single integrated system with a single, consistent set of goals.

2. The goals must be operational ones, i.e., amenable to quantitative measurement.

Only the machine organization fits comfortably into the conventional diversified organization, by virtue of its integration and its operational goals. When organizations with other configurations are drawn into a diversified organization, they tend to be forced into machine organization. This is another manifestation of the phenomenon that concentrated external control of an organization (here, by headquarters over divisions) formalizes and centralizes the structure.

Summary: the diversified organization has a small strategic apex, a small technostructure (to design the performance control system), a slightly larger support staff, and divisions composed of machine organizations.

CONDITIONS OF THE DIVERSIFIED ORGANIZATION

Diversity of markets above all else is what drives organizations to adopt the diversified configuration. Three kinds of market diversity:

1. Product and service

2. Client

3. Region

In theory all three may be the basis for divisionalization. But the second and third usually lead to incomplete divisionalization, because the central organization is encouraged to hold on to central control of critical functions. This reduces divisional autonomy, leading to less-than-complete divisionalization. For example, insurance companies keep investment at headquarters, and retailers keep merchandising and purchasing at headquarters. Regionally "divisionalized" firms like bakeries, breweries, cement producers, soft drink bottlers all lack the autonomy normally associated with divisions that produce distinct products or services.

Size in itself does not bring on divisionalization, but most large corporations use divisionalization. One reason is protection—large organizations are risk-averse, and diversification lets them spread the risk. Another reason is that large firms tend to dominate their markets, and need to diversify to find opportunities elsewhere. Also, diversification feeds on itself, creating a cadre of aggressive middle managers.

Age is also associated with diversified organizations. Maturing markets encourage firms to diversify.

Governments divisionalize because the central managers cannot control the agencies directly. They settle for divisionalization supported by standardization of outputs and machine-organization divisions.

STAGES IN THE TRANSITION TO THE DIVERSIFIED ORGANIZATION

1. *Pure functional form:* operating activities form one integrated, unbroken chain from purchasing through production to marketing and sales.

2. *By-product form:* as integrated firm seeks wider markets, a less-risky way to do it is to sell intermediate products.

3. *Related-product form:* sells a variety of end products to markets that have a "common thread"—core skill, core technology, central market theme.

4. *Conglomerate form:* a pure divisionalized form; each division serves its own markets, producing products unrelated to those of the other divisions.

SOME ISSUES ASSOCIATED WITH THE DIVERSIFIED ORGANIZATION

The economic advantages of diversification

It has been argued that the diversified configuration offers four advantages over the machine organization:

1. Encourages the efficient allocation of capital (headquarters can put its money where it chooses)

2. Helps to train general managers (they can run autonomous divisions)

3. Risk is spread across different markets

4. Is strategically responsive (divisions can fine-tune their machine organizations, headquarters can concentrate on the portfolio of businesses)

But is the diversified organization with 397 divisions truly better than 397 independent companies?

1. Williamson says that a diversified organization can allocate money more efficiently than can capital markets. But an investor looking at her own portfolio of, say, ten businesses has more information than an investor in a diversified organization which has ten divisions.

2. The diversified organization *does* provide some management development activities that are hard to find in independent companies, but it could be argued that the president of the fully autonomous company gets more development than the manager of a division that is constrained by headquarters.

3. It may be that independent companies are more vulnerable during economic downturns, but diversified organizations may conceal bankruptcies by holding on to ailing divisions too long. Also, the track record of highly divisionalized companies has been poor.

4. Divisionalization seems to inhibit, not encourage, the taking of strategic initiatives. The performance control system dampens the inclination to innovate. Entrepreneurship does not flourish under diversified organization.

The contribution of headquarters

What does the headquarters of a diversified organization contribute, compared to the board of directors of an independent company?

Neither can be involved in day-to-day management, but each *should* be involved in goal-setting and performance control. Diversified organization headquarters probably do a better job at this, but their larger size, large number of divisions, and widely held ownership negate much of this advantage.

Large diversified organizations tend to be rather closed systems. They control their internal divisions *and* their external environments. But when problems arise in a division, control is difficult, particularly if the diversified organization is very diverse. This is probably why firms characterized by "controlled diversity" outperform those with conglomerate diversity.

The social performance of the performance control system

The quantitative nature of the performance control system in most diversified organizations drives out goals that cannot be measured—product quality, pride in work, customers well served. The economic goals drive out the social ones.

This would not be a problem if economic and social consequences of decisions could be easily separated, but they are not. This drives the diversified organization to act in socially unresponsive, sometimes irresponsible, ways.

The diversified organization in the public sphere

Governments often respond to social problems with agencies in a divisionalized configuration. Ironically, this only aggravates the problems of power concentration and social irresponsibility. The problem is actually worse in government, since most of its goals are social, and so ill-suited to performance control.

There are other problems. Divisions cannot be divested in government. And regulation often precludes the needed autonomy of the division.

In conclusion: A structure on the edge of a cliff

"The pure (conglomerate) diversified configuration emerges as an organization perched symbolically on the edge of the cliff. . . . Ahead, it is one step away from disintegration—breaking up into separate organizations on the rocks below. Behind it is the way back to a more stable integration, in the form of the machine configuration. . . . Hovering above is the eagle, representing the broader social control of the state . . . ."

<u>Discussion Questions</u>

1. Why is the diversified organization driven toward standardization of outputs?

The diverse nature of the divisions means that they must be given autonomy. Headquarters cannot possibly keep track of what needs to be done in each business unit, so it lets the unit managers handle that. But to maintain some control, headquarters mandates that the divisions meet some performance targets. To make these targets meaningful across divisions, the system used to measure them is standardized. Hence, the diversified organization ends up with standardization of outputs, financial performance ones in their case.

2. Why are the divisions of the diversified organization driven toward machine organization?

Headquarters cannot control the divisions *directly*, but it must find a way to control their performance. This is facilitated if two assumptions are met: (1) each division must be treated as a single integrated system with a single, consistent set of goals, and (2) the goals must be operational ones, i.e., amenable to quantitative measurement. The best configuration for meeting these conditions is the machine organization. Also, when organizations are tightly controlled by outside forces (as the divisions would be by headquarters), there is a tendency for them to become machine organizations.

3. How desirable is the divisional autonomy Mintzberg discussed? How possible?

Students may be divided on the first part of this question. Some who are very interested in headquarters' maintaining control would find the idea of divisional autonomy *un*desirable. The counterargument is that in corporations with diverse businesses, headquarters is *incapable* of knowing how to run all the different businesses. The answer is to grant the business unit managers the autonomy to run the businesses, but keep them under some control.

There seems to be a lot of difficulty at achieving divisional autonomy. Headquarters people seem inevitably to want to control things, even at the business level. Of course, this is not *truly* inevitable. In theory, it *should* be possible for divisional autonomy to be achieved.

4. In what sense is the middle line the key part of the diversified organization?

503

Even if the autonomy of divisions is only partial, divisional managers (the middle line in diversified organizations) have a great deal of responsibility for assuring that the business strategy in the division is properly formed. True, headquarters measures their performance *after the fact*, but the only thing controlling them *during* the formation of the strategy is their own ability, their own quality. This makes them the key part of the diversified organization.

5. Is the diversified organization a response to market diversity, or do such firms seek out diverse markets?

The answer is a little bit of each. Firms facing diverse markets will respond better to each segment if they have separate units handling each one. This has been shown for a long time, ever since Dupont first did it in the 1920s. But once an organization has divisionalized, it is relatively easy for it to "plug in" another division to its headquarters. As a result, diversified organizations *do* tend to seek out even-more-diverse markets.

6. Why does growth in size seem ultimately to lead to divisionalization?

Size in itself does not bring on divisionalization, but most large corporations use divisionalization. One reason is protection—large organizations are risk-averse, and diversification lets them spread the risk. Another reason is that large firms tend to dominate their markets, and need to diversify to find opportunities elsewhere. Also, diversification feeds on itself, creating a cadre of aggressive middle managers who want to diversify and divisionalize even more.

7. Which of the variations on the diversified organization—related-product and conglomerate—is more "pure?" Which would you expect would be more effective?

If "pure" is defined as "most autonomous," then unquestionably the conglomerate form is purer. Each division is a.completely different business. Headquarters would be hard pressed to understand each, and therefore to intrude on the affairs of each. In a related-product corporation, headquarters could know more about each division, because each would be connected, in some way, to some well-known aspect of the business. Divisional autonomy would be lower.

But for exactly the same reasons, it would be expected that the related-product form would be more successful. If headquarters seems bent on curtailing divisional autonomy, it is best if they know something about the business level at which the division is operating. This knowledge is much greater in a related-product firm than in a conglomerate.

8. Which of the four advantages of the diversified organization do you find the most compelling?

This question is intended to stimulate discussion. The four advantages are: (1) efficient allocation of capital, (2) training for general managers, (3) spreading of risk, and (4) strategic responsiveness. Students will no doubt differ on which of these is the most compelling. Capital *is* more efficiently allocated in a diversified organization, even though individual investors have power removed from them. Diversified organizations *do* tend to provide lots of management development opportunities, but there is nothing quite like running a business without the safety net of headquarters. Risk *is* spread in diversified organizations, but that does not seem to have improved their performance, overall. And diversified organizations *are* able to add divisions to respond to new strategic thrusts, but they are rarely the initiators of these new thrusts.

9. What is your opinion on the question of which is better—a headquarters, or a board of directors?

This question is designed to stimulate discussion. Neither can be involved in day-to-day management, but each *should* be involved in goal-setting and performance control. A headquarters probably does a better job at this, but the larger size, large number of divisions, and widely held ownership of diversified organizations negate much of this advantage. There is probably a greater possibility of society's exerting some control over a business if it has a board than if it is a division of a large corporation. All in all, this question is a value judgment.

10. What do you think of the author's criticism of the social effects of the performance control system?

Some students may take issue with Mintzberg on this, but in general his criticism is well-taken. Performance control systems focus on quantitative goals, and social goals are not well-suited for them. Yet economic and social consequences of decisions are difficult to separate. As a result, diversified organizations may act unresponsibly, or even irresponsibly, when it comes to social performance.

Mintzberg, "Generic Corporate Strategies"

Summary of Reading

Extending the core business

These strategies involve going beyond the core business:

Chain integration strategies: also called vertical integration; getting into businesses backward or forward in the operating chain

Diversification strategies: encompassing within the organization other, parallel businesses, not in the same chain of operations:

Concentric: related to some distinctive competence or asset

Conglomerate: unrelated to some distinctive competence or asset

Entry and control strategies: chain integration or diversification may be achieved by internal development or acquisition. Both of these involve full ownership and control of the diversified business, but there are other possibilities:

Full ownership and control:

internal development
acquisition

Partial ownership and control:

majority, minority partnership, including:

joint venture
turnkey (temporary control)

Partial control without ownership:

licensing
franchising
long-term contracting

Combined integration-diversification strategies:

　　Byproduct diversification: selling off byproducts in the operating chain

　　Linked diversification: one business leads to another

　　Crystalline diversification: linked diversification pushed to its limit

Withdrawal strategies: cutting back on the businesses that the firm is in by:

　　shrinking

　　liquidating (opposite of internal development)

　　divesting (opposite of acquisition)

Reconceiving the core business

"After a core business has been identified, distinguished, elaborated, and extended, there often follows the need not just to consolidate it but also to redefine it and reconfigure it—in essence, to reconceive it."

Business redefinition strategy: business definitions are concepts that exist in the mind; concepts are redefinable

Business recombination strategies: efforts to recombine different businesses in some way, either tangibly (e.g., selling complementary products) or conceptually (e.g., railroad business is reconceived as transportation business)

Core relocation strategies: getting back to the "center of gravity:"

　　Move along the operating chain (e.g., go from flour milling to providing diversified products to homemaker)

　　Shift between dominant functions (e.g., from manufacturing to marketing)

　　Shift to new business (e.g., from selling paper to selling food)

　　Shift to new core theme (e.g., from soap company to being in the personal care business)

<u>Discussion Questions</u>

1. The author says, "In a sense, all strategies are in some sense niche, characterized as much by what they exclude as by what they include. No organization can be all things to all people. The all-encompassing strategy is no strategy at all." How does this relate to earlier parts of this reading? To earlier readings? What is your opinion of this statement?

These comments are similar to Porter's warning about being "stuck in the middle" which were quoted earlier in the reading: "Being 'all things to all people' is a recipe for strategic mediocrity and below-average performance." They also evoke Quinn's remarks from Chapter 1, where he said that effective strategies "develop around a few key concepts and thrusts." In the Chapter 1 reading on the "Five Ps of Strategy," Mintzberg said that "strategy as position can extend beyond competition. . . . Indeed, what is the meaning of the word 'niche' but a position that is occupied to *avoid* competition." Where some students may part company is in the final sentence. Some will argue that there are some firms which *do* successfully follow an "all-encompassing strategy."

2. The author says that "given the common tendency to proliferate market segments, it makes sense for the healthy organization to rationalize them periodically, to purge the excesses." What do you think of this statement?

This statement is a reflection of the research findings, from many sources, that show that successful firms have a tendency to grow, then consolidate, then grow again, then consolidate again, and so on. In his study of successful entrepreneurial companies, Mintzberg called this the "inchworm" strategy—the worm moves forward by stretching, then pulls itself together, then stretches forward again, and so on. Some students may argue that firms must continue to grow, all the time. The research findings would indicate otherwise.

3. Mintzberg says, "All businesses have popular conceptions. Some are narrow and tangible, . . . others broader and vague. All such definitions, now matter how tangible, are ultimately concepts that exist in the minds of actors and observers." What is your opinion of this statement?

This question is intended to stimulate discussion. Students who are in the "rational" school of thought on strategy will be either puzzled or scornful about this statement. They will argue that strategies are (or should be) precisely written plans that specify in detail what the firm is about. These plans are firm, concrete, not abstract.

Others will agree that, if one conceives of strategy as a perspective, a firm's strategy is indeed a "concept that [exists] in the minds of actors and observers." A statement, or definition, of strategy is nothing more than an attempt efficiently to describe the actions of a large group of people. Even if all those actions are concrete, their definition is an abstraction.

Lasserre, "Managing Large Groups in the East and West"

Summary of Reading

There is no one best method for managing large groups of businesses. Asian Pacific approaches differ markedly from European and North American methods. This article highlights the differences between Europe and Asia.

EUROPEAN CORPORATE ARCHETYPES

Industrial groups: "Characterized by a portfolio of business activities which share a common set of competencies and in which a high degree of synergy is achieved by managing the key interdependencies at corporate level." These could be called "Strategic Planning" groups.

Industrial holdings: "Corporations in which the business units are clustered into subgroups or sectors . . . . Synergies are strong within subgroups and weak between subgroups." Value creation is delegated to subgroup management; the corporate level implements planning and control systems. These could be called "Strategic Control" groups.

Financial conglomerates: "Characterized by a constellation of business units which do not necessarily share any common source of synergies and whose corporate value is . . . created by the imposition of management discipline, financial leverage, and the management of acquisitions and restructuring." These groups rely heavily on financial controls systems and could therefore be called "Financial Control" groups.

ASIAN CORPORATE ARCHETYPES

Entrepreneurial conglomerates: "widely diversified into a large number of unrelated activities ranging from banking, trading, real estate, manufacturing and services. These groups are usually under the leadership of a father figure" who is the key strategic actor. Little attempt is made to manage synergies. Value creation is based on the father figure's ability to leverage financial and human resources, make political connections, make deals, and impose loyalty and discipline on business units. These are common in Southeast Asia, Korea, Taiwan, and Hong Kong.

Keiretsus: These "constitute super groups, or clusters of groups in which businesses are either vertically integrated . . . or horizontally connected. Although some companies in the groups exercise greater 'power' than others, Keiretsus are not hierarchically organized. They are like a club of companies that share common interests." Value is added by informal coordination of key activities, transfer of expertise in personnel rotation, and strengthening of supplier-distributor chains.

National holdings: These "have been formed more recently as an expression of industrial independence . . . to capitalize on domestic markets and public endowment." Value creation stems from "nationality."

GROUP MANAGEMENT: A COMPARISON

Two dimensions can be used to capture the distinctions among these various ways to organize: *organizational setting* and *corporate control*.

Organizational Setting

Federation: The center plays an important role in managing synergies. Integration and coordination are the major sources of advantage. Methods include centralized functions, strategic planning, strong corporate identity and socialization of personnel. Typically found: European industrial groups, some Asian national holdings.

Confederation: Center allocates resources, guards corporate identity, renews strategy. Business units have strategic autonomy under the "corporate umbrella." Has bottom-up planning, negotiated strategies, autonomy, and central financial and human resource mechanisms. Typically found: European industrial holdings, Asian national holdings.

Constellation: Organized as many uncoordinated businesses. Each unit is linked (directly or indirectly) to the center. Role of the center is "hands-on" in Asian entrepreneurial conglomerates and "hands off" in European financial conglomerates. Characterized by "one-to-one contractual agreements" between the center and the business units.

Connexion: Either no center or several centers. Some loose coordination (meetings) and some tight coordination (long-term contracts). Keiretsus are best example.

Corporate Control

"Corporate control describes how groups ensure that business units' performances and behaviors are in line with corporate expectations." Five major methods exist:

Financial controls: Uses financial goals based on financial standards. Most common in European financial conglomerates.

Control by systems: Based on implementation of planning and control mechanisms like strategic planning, capital budgeting, control reviews, etc. Predominates in European industrial holdings and industrial groups.

Control by strategy: Emphasis is on the appreciation of the strategic trajectory of the business units and how they fit into the corporation's strategy. Uses task forces, conferences, informal meetings and so forth. Most common in European industrial groups and, to some extent, Keiretsus.

Personalized control: Exercised by direct interface between group chairman and business unit managers. Is subjective and holistic. This is the nearly exclusive method used in Asian entrepreneurial conglomerates.

Ideological control: Focus is to make sure that managers have internalized the values of the group and are behaving accordingly. What matters most is development of strong beliefs, norms, and values. Most important processes are recruitment, selection, socialization, training, and personnel rotation. Prevails in Asian national holdings and vertical Keiretsus.

COMPARING EUROPEAN AND ASIAN GROUPS

Asian and European groups live in different worlds. Each type of organizational approach tends to differ in how it controls its operations and how it designs its organizational setting.

Asian approaches

Keiretsus emphasize connection through either strategy or ideology.

Entrepreneurial conglomerates favor a constellation setting based on personalized control.

National holdings tend to be confederations that are knit together using ideology—a sense of belonging and a nationalistic stand.

European approaches

Financial conglomerates are constellations driven by numbers.

Industrial holdings tend to be confederations that rely on systems to keep things under control.

Industrial groups are federations that coordinate using structures and regulations.

Western corporate designers tend to use an "engineering" approach. They believe that human behavior can be manipulated by organizational mechanisms. Asian corporate designers think of enterprises as living entities where groups and individuals can gain through cooperation. Organizations are compared to families, seen not as machines but as "'codified' relationships."

DECODING ASIAN FORMS

Western firms often try to emulate Asian firms that are giving them trouble. "This . . . reflects an engineering view of the organizational world: the machine 'works' in Japan, why don't we import the machine? It is as if we asked US society to renounce individualism." It would be better to try to understand how relationships function in Asian organizations, to "decode" rather than "imitate." This requires three attitudes:

Get rid of *a priori* judgments

Western managers too often rely on ready-made explanations for Asian success, e.g., Japan, Inc. This "causal engineering" thinking is too simplistic. They should work first to understand the functionality of social structure, and only second work on causality.

Invest in the study of cultures and societies

"One of the dangers of 'instrumental' thinking is that it bypasses what is not considered of immediate relevance. Cultural and social knowledge are all too frequently considered to be a waste of time. . . ." But organizations and business behavior are part of a society's cultural heritage, and Asian cultural heritage is "very rich, complex, and heterogeneous." Western managers should make the necessary efforts to understand it.

Resist the temptation of "easy translations"

It is all too easy to adopt superficial and naive so-called "Asian" ways of doing things. Deeper understanding is required.

<u>Discussion Questions</u>

1. How do the European types of corporate structure differ from the familiar North American types discussed by Mintzberg in the previous reading?

Not much at all. *Industrial groups* are essentially diversified organizations with strong headquarters. *Industrial holdings* are collections of diversified organizations under a very large corporate umbrella. The groups that form the holdings are really just indicative of an extra layer of hierarchy or management. *Financial conglomerates* are much the same as unrelated conglomerates in North America.

2. How do the Asian types of corporate structure differ from the ones found in North America?

Quite a bit. *Entrepreneurial conglomerates* may superficially resemble "regular" conglomerates, but the key difference is that the former are headed up by a *patriarchal* entrepreneur, literally a family figure. *Keiretsus* are large groups of firms that share a common interest and much interlocking control through informal contacts and interlocking boards. There is no analogue in North America, but there is no reason why there couldn't be. Keiretsus are similar to the spider's web organization mentioned by Quinn, Anderson and Finkelstein in their Chapter 6 reading, "New Ways of Organizing." Lastly, *national holdings* appear to be unique to those countries, seemingly mostly in Asia, that appear to be emerging from developing status and wish to propel themselves along more quickly with nationalized companies that compete globally. There is nothing similar in North America.

3. What are the distinctions among the four organizational settings described by the author?

The differences relate to the role of the center. In *federations*, the center is strong and exerts direct control over the units. In *confederations* the balance of power between the center and the units is more balanced. *Constellations* come in two forms, ones whose centers are "hands on" (as in the entrepreneurial conglomerates) and ones where the centers are "hands off" (as in European financial conglomerates). Either way, the centers in constellations have one-to-one contractual relationships with their units. Lastly, in the *connexion* type of corporation there is either no center or many centers (much as in the spider's web). This form is really a network.

4. How do the different types of corporate control relate to what we have seen earlier in this book?

Financial control is virtually identical to the standardized financial control used by the archetypal diversified form Mintzberg discusses in the previous reading. *Systems control* is also closely related to this, perhaps more so in a diversified form that has matured into a machine form. *Strategy control* is related to Hamel and Prahalad's strategic intent. *Personalized control* typical in entrepreneurial conglomerates is the entrepreneurial organization writ large. Lastly, *ideological control* is closely related to the missionary organization's primary coordinating mechanism.

5. What is your reaction to the author's comments about the different organizational approaches of Europe and Asia?

The author is subtly critical of the Western tendency to see things in a mechanistic, instrumental way. It should be interesting to see how many students see things that way as well. He says that the Asian approach is much more organic, holistic and social. It cannot be adopted like a machine part. It must be *lived*. There are many managers in the West who would understand this. They are the ones who have worked long and hard to create distinctive cultures in their firms. But too many Western managers think that a better culture is available to them in a short time with relatively little effort. Such is not the case.

6. What is your reaction to the author's comments about how many Western managers view cultural and social knowledge being "a waste of time?"

Students may not fully appreciate how, particularly in engineering-oriented organizations, direct consideration of social phenomena is not valued at all. There may even be some students who agree with this view. The author's point is that all people are embedded in a cultural heritage. Many astute Asian business people have made the investment needed to understand Western culture. Western managers must make the same investment or they will be unprepared for doing business in the East.

Porter, "From Competitive Advantage to Corporate Strategy"

Summary of Reading

A diversified company has two levels of strategy: business unit (or competitive) strategy, and corporate (or companywide) strategy.

Competitive strategy concerns how to create competitive advantage in each of the businesses in which a company competes. Corporate strategy concerns two different questions: what businesses the corporation should be in, and how the corporate office should manage the array of business units.

The track record of corporate strategies has been dismal. From 1950 to 1986, the 33 firms studied had divested many more acquisitions than they had kept. "The corporate strategies of most companies have dissipated instead of created shareholder value."

A SOBER PICTURE

Here are some results based on a study of 33 companies:

More than half of acquisitions in new industries were divested

More than 60% of acquisitions in entirely new fields were divested

Fourteen companies left 70% or more of their new-field acquisitions

For *unrelated* acquisitions the divestment rate was a startling 74%!

COMMENT BY AUTHOR: Some scholars advocate using shareholder value to judge performance. But this works only if you compare "shareholder value that is" with "shareholder value that might have been" (without diversification). Since that is virtually impossible, a different measure is used—the number of units retained by the company. This "seems to be as good an indicator as any of the contribution of diversification to corporate performance."

"Only the lawyers, investment bankers, and original sellers have prospered in most of these acquisitions, not the shareholders."

<u>PREMISES OF CORPORATE STRATEGY</u>

Successful corporate strategy builds on a number of premises:

- Competition occurs at the business unit level (it is the business units of corporations that compete; corporate strategy grows out of and reinforces competitive strategy)

- Diversification inevitably adds costs and constraints to business units (these include not only the obvious ones like overhead, but also the time and energy spent explaining things to headquarters and complying with corporate policies)

- Shareholders can readily diversify themselves (people can buy their own portfolios, usually more cheaply than a firm because they do not have to pay acquisition premiums; corporate strategy must therefore add something truly distinctive)

<u>PASSING THE ESSENTIAL TESTS</u>

How attractive is the industry?

The industries chosen for diversification must be structurally attractive or capable of being made attractive. Attractive means that there are high entry barriers, suppliers and buyers have only modest power, substitutes are few, and rivalry is stable. A feeling of "good fit," low entry cost, or early industry growth often seem like good reasons to diversify, but they will not offset fundamentally poor industry structure.

What is the cost of entry?

The cost of entry must not capitalize all the future profits. A company can enter new business by acquisition or start-up. Acquisitions are being tried in an increasingly efficient merger market; multiple bidders are commonplace. In a start-up, entry barriers must be overcome. In general, the more attractive a business, the higher its entry cost.

Will the business be better off?

Either the new unit must gain competitive advantage from its link with the corporation, or vice versa. If the benefit happens only once, the diversified company should divest as soon as possible.

"The better-off test does not imply that diversifying corporate risk creates shareholder value in and of itself. Doing something for shareholders that they can do themselves is not a basis for corporate strategy . . . . Diversification of risk should only be a by-product of corporate strategy, not a prime motivator."

"The whole point of diversifying . . . is to create shareholder value rather than to avoid destroying it."

<u>CONCEPTS OF CORPORATE STRATEGY</u>

The three tests of corporate strategy are so difficult that most diversification fails. Four concepts of corporate strategy have been put into practice; "ignoring any of the concepts is perhaps the quickest road to failure."

Portfolio management

This is the most commonly used concept. Sound businesses are acquired, usually in some bounded way, to limit the expertise needed by top management. The acquired units are autonomous, and their managers are compensated according to unit results. The corporation supplies capital, management skills, and performance review. Resources are transferred from cash generators to cash needers.

The validity of this concept has eroded. Good acquisitions are easy to find. A corporate headquarters is no longer needed to supply capital for a sound strategy. Management skills are more widely available, and, anyway, the feeling is that management is better with industry-specific knowledge.

But the sheer complexity of the management task has ultimately defeated the portfolio managers. As the corporation gets too large, its managers make mistakes. A new team is brought in to pare the company down to manageable size and scope. This approach may still work in developing countries, but not in advanced economies. "Portfolio management is no way to conduct corporate strategy."

Restructuring

"This strategy seeks out undeveloped, sick, or threatened organizations or industries on the threshold of significant change. The parent intervenes, frequently changing the unit management team, shifting strategy, or infusing the company with new technology." It may also make complementary acquisitions. The result is a strengthened company or industry. The stronger units are then sold off, as the parent can no longer add value.

This concept is sound because it passes all three tests of successful diversification. The cost of entry is low, the companies/industries have unrealized potential, and they are better off after being acquired. "Ironically, many of today's restructurers are profiting from yesterday's portfolio management strategies."

"Perhaps the biggest pitfall . . . is that companies find it very hard to dispose of business units once they are structured and performing well . . . ."

Transferring skills

The first two concepts seek to create value through the relationship between headquarters and the units. The last two concepts exploit the interrelationships among the units.

This leads to the often ill-defined concept of "synergy." The *proper* way to approach synergy is through the *value chain*. Each unit in a diversified company has its own value chain. Synergy occurs when units either transfer skills among similar value chains, or share value-chain activities.

Transferring skills leads to competitive advantage only if the similarities among businesses meet three conditions:

1. The activities involved in the businesses are similar enough that sharing expertise is meaningful. Broad similarities are not enough.

2. The transfer of skills involves activities important to competitive advantage. Peripheral skills are not important for this.

3. The skills transferred represent a significant source of competitive advantage for the receiving unit, i.e., they are advanced, proprietary, and beyond the capabilities of competitors.

This approach will meet the three tests of acquisition if the firm truly mobilizes distinctive expertise across units. Firms can lower entry costs, make a difference, and even restructure so-so industries, if they implement this properly. If the company exhausts opportunities to infuse expertise into the unit after the initial post-acquisition period, the unit should ultimately be sold. The approach can be used either through acquisitions or internal development.

513

Sharing activities

This involves sharing activities in the value chains among business units. This can be potent because it enhances competitive advantage by lowering cost or raising differentiation. But it has costs, like increased coordination and compromise of activities' designs so that they can be shared. But developments in technology, deregulation, competition, and information systems have provided many opportunities to create competitive advantage.

This approach requires an organizational context that reinforces inter-unit cooperation. The typical diversified organization, with autonomous divisions, does not fit. The company must use horizontal "mechanisms"—strong sense of corporate identity, clear corporate mission statement emphasizing cooperation among units, a supportive reward system, cross-unit task-forces, and other mechanisms.

This concept meets the three tests. Units are better off because of the tangible advantages they gain from one another. The internal barriers are cheaper to overcome. But the firm must still make sure that the industry is structurally attractive.

CHOOSING A CORPORATE STRATEGY

Both logic and experience "suggest that a company will create shareholder value through diversification to a greater and greater extent as its strategy moves from portfolio management toward sharing activities." The four concepts are not mutually exclusive, and may indeed support one another.

Successful diversifiers have made a disproportionately low percentage of acquisitions where the opportunity to transfer skills or share activities was absent. They operate in fields where each is related to many of the others. They make heavier-than-average use of start-ups and joint ventures. Successful companies have very good records with start-ups, but companies in general nevertheless seem to favor acquisition. Start-ups are often less risky than acquisitions, as Japanese diversification has shown.

". . . None of the concepts of corporate strategy works when industry structure is poor or implementation is bad, no matter how related the industries are."

An action program

A company can choose a corporate strategy by:

1. Identifying the interrelationships among already existing business units.

2. Selecting the core businesses that will be the foundation of the corporate strategy.

3. Creating horizontal organizational mechanisms to facilitate interrelationships among the core businesses and lay the groundwork for future related diversification

4. Pursuing diversification opportunities that allow shared activities.

5. Pursuing diversification through the transfer of skills if opportunities for sharing activities are limited or exhausted.

6. Pursuing a strategy of restructuring if this fits the skills of management or no good opportunities exist for forging corporate interrelationships.

7. Paying dividends so that the shareholders can be the portfolio managers.

Creating a corporate theme

"Defining a corporate theme is a good way to ensure that the corporation will create shareholder value. Having the right theme helps unite the efforts of business units and reinforces the ways they interrelate as well as guides the choice of new businesses to enter." But companies must avoid creating shallow themes.

"The failure of corporate strategy reflects the fact that most diversified companies have failed to think in terms of how they really add value . . . . [They need] a sharper focus on the tests of diversification, and the explicit choice of a clear concept of corporate strategy. . . ."

Discussion Questions

1. The author says, "The corporate strategies of most companies have dissipated instead of created shareholder value." Based on what appears in this reading, what is your reaction to this statement?

Reaction to this assertion depends partly on whether one accepts the author's variable, number of units divested. If one accepts it as a valid measure of diversification success, then he's probably correct. The data quoted in the reading indicate that the vast majority of units were divested, presumably because the corporations no longer felt that they were worth keeping, i.e., they were no longer increasing shareholder wealth.

The author also demonstrates that the most popular technique of corporate strategy, portfolio management, has been a failure. This, too, supports the conclusion that most corporate strategies have not increased shareholder wealth.

2. What is your reaction to Porter's three premises of corporate strategy?

Porter's three premises are (1) that competition occurs at the business unit level, (2) that diversification inevitably adds costs and constraints to business units, and (3) that shareholders can readily diversify themselves.

Some students may take issue with these premises. For example, many people believe that diversification *helps* make a company more profitable, by opening up new opportunities; Porter points to the costs and constraints of diversification. But in general, these premises are right on target. The key question as the business level has always been, "What must I do to compete successfully in this industry?" This is the basis of the first premise. The third premise was raised by Mintzberg in his reading in this chapter—is it truly better to spread risk through corporate diversification, when individual investors can do the job themselves?

3. How useful are Porter's three essential tests of diversification?

Porter's three tests are (1) how attractive is the industry; (2) what is the cost of entry; and (3) will the business be better off? These are extremely useful. Only by passing them does a firm operate under the proper premises. For instance, since competition happens at the industry level, and since corporate strategy builds on competitive strategy, then the nature of industry structure is crucially important. Since diversification adds costs and constraints, firms must take cost of entry into account. And since shareholders can diversify themselves, what is the corporation contributing by taking on the diversification itself?

4. The author says that "ignoring any of the concepts is perhaps the quickest road to failure." What does he mean by this?

The answer to this starts with the observation that if you diversify without having an underlying concept, you will surely fail. There has got to be some theme, some rationale, guiding the firm's diversification. Porter argues that, ideally, firms should be able to look at their corporate strategy through the lenses of all four concepts. But if they fail to use *any*, even the now-discredited portfolio approach, they will surely fail.

5. Porter says, "Portfolio management is no way to conduct corporate strategy." What is your opinion?

This is a provocative statement. The portfolio approach has dominated the literature, and the teaching, of corporate strategy for over twenty years. To baldly assert that it is no way to conduct corporate strategy is extremely controversial. As a result, students will differ in their assessment of it.

But Porter is probably correct. The greater efficiency, and expertise, of having a corporate headquarters allocate capital, relative to individual investors, is simply no longer true. And large-scale diversified organizations are just too difficult and complex to operate with portfolio management. There are too many variables for which the portfolio manager has to keep track.

6. What is your opinion of the restructuring concept?

The premise behind restructuring is for poorly performing units, with potential, to be drastically turned around by coldly objective purchasers who add value by injecting new management, new technology, etc. The approach tends to pass the three tests. The purchase price paid by the restructurer is usually a discount. The industry being entered typically has potential. And the restructurer *does* add something to the unit's operations; once this is no longer true, the restructurer spins off the unit.

Restructurers seem like the right people to whom to sell poorly performing units, if a corporation has a failed portfolio strategy. The problem is, to whom do the restructurers sell once they're through with a business? Implied strongly in most of Porter's discussion is that units may often be better off *independent*. This mirrors one of Mintzberg's arguments from his reading in this chapter.

7. What is your assessment of transfer of skills as a corporate strategy concept?

Porter's three conditions are (1) the activities must be similar enough that sharing expertise is meaningful, (2) the transfer of skills must involve activities important to competitive advantage, and (3) the skills transferred represent a significant source of competitive advantage for the receiving unit. There is little doubt that if the skills to be transferred meet these three conditions, they should be excellent bases for diversification.

8. Why would we expect the sharing of activities to be particularly important for corporate strategy?

The sharing of activities gives the potential for lower cost and higher differentiation. This is despite the coordination problems and the need for various new systems. As the author points out, developments in technology, deregulation, competition, and information systems have provided many opportunities to create competitive advantage.

This concept meets the three tests. Units are better off because of the tangible advantages they gain from one another. The internal barriers are cheaper to overcome. But the firm must still make sure that the industries are structurally attractive.

9. Porter says that both logic and experience "suggest that a company will create shareholder value through diversification to a greater and greater extent as its strategy moves from portfolio management toward sharing activities." What is your opinion of this assertion?

Sharing activities is tangible, based not on insight but on *hard work*. The same is true for transferring skills. The other two concepts rely on special insight on which units should be acquired (restructuring), or questionable assumptions about what analysts can do (portfolio management). That is the logic to which Porter refers. As for the experience he mentions, much of the evidence he cites shows that the more successful firms make sure they have lots of opportunities to share activities or transfer skills.

10. What is your reaction to the author's comment that successful diversifiers tend to use start-ups more than do the average diversified companies?

This is not surprising at all. Throughout this text, mention has been made of the greater success of related diversification. Related diversification tends to be based on similar skills. Most firms diversifying through start-up would tend to base their new businesses on existing skills. This would lower the risk and increase the likelihood of success.

11. Does the section on "creating a corporate theme" link to anything from previous readings?

This section is reminiscent of the missionary organization, with its emphasis on collective vision as the basis of strategy. The basic difference is that most missionary organizations operate at the business level, but Porter is advocating the use of these concepts at the corporate level. The section is also reminiscent of Mintzberg's Chapter 1 discussion of strategy as perspective, the direction of strategy using a worldview.

Yip, "Global Strategy . . . In a World of Nations?"

<u>Summary of Reading</u>

Whether, and how, to globalize have become two of the most burning strategy issues for managers around the world. Globalization is a more integrated international approach than the now-familiar multinational (also called multidomestic) strategy.

Three steps are necessary for developing a worldwide strategy:

1. Developing the core strategy, usually for the home country first.

2. Internationalizing the core strategy through international expansion of activities and through adaptation.

3. Globalizing the international strategy by integrating the strategy across countries.

Multinational companies know the first two steps well, but the third step less well since globalization runs counter to the accepted wisdom of tailoring for the national market.

Strategic managers must understand and cope with *industry globalization drivers*, and must manage *global strategy levers*.

What is global strategy?

Setting strategy for a worldwide business requires making choices for a number of "levers."

Market participation

Countries need to be chosen for their potential contribution to globalization benefits. This may mean entering a locally unattractive market.

Product offering

The ideal is a standardized core product that requires minimal local adaptation. Cost reduction is usually the most important benefit of product standardization.

Location of value-added activities

In a global strategy, costs are reduced by breaking up the value chain so that each activity may be conducted in a different country.

Marketing approach

A uniform marketing approach is applied around the world, although not all elements of the marketing mix need be uniform.

Competitive moves

Need to be integrated across countries. The same type of move is made in different countries at the same time or in a systematic sequence. The best example: counterattack in a competitor's home market as a parry to an attack on one's own home market.

518

Benefits of a global strategy

Cost reduction: Can come from several sources:

Pooling production or other activities for two or more countries

Exploiting lower factor costs by moving activities to low-cost countries

Exploiting the flexibility of having several locations, each with a different cost level at any given time

Enhancing bargaining power

Improved quality of products and programs

Under a global strategy, firms focus on a smaller number of products and programs, which can lead to improved quality

Enhanced customer preference

Global availability, serviceability, and recognition can enhance customer preference through reinforcement

Increased competitive leverage

A global strategy gives more points from which to attack and counterattack competitors

Drawbacks of global strategy

Increased coordination needs

Increased reporting requirements

Added staff

Strategic levers have their own pitfalls:

Market participation can incur an earlier or greater commitment to a market than is warranted.

Product standardization can yield a product that does not entirely satisfy any customers.

Activity concentration distances customers and can result in lower responsiveness and flexibility. It also increases currency risk.

Uniform marketing can reduce adaptation to local customer behavior.

Integrated competitive moves can mean sacrificing revenues, profit, or competitive position in individual countries, particularly if operations in that country are used to attack competitors.

Finding the balance

The most successful worldwide strategies match the company's level of globalization to the company's potential for globalization.

Industry globalization drivers

Market drivers

Homogeneous customer needs: creates opportunities to market standardized product

Global customers: these buy centrally for decentralized use

Global channels: these buy on a global, or maybe regional, basis. Middlemen may buy low in one country and sell high in another country

Transferable marketing: some marketing elements, like brand names and advertising, may require little local adaptation

Cost drivers

Economies of scale and scope: scale at a given location can be increased by participation in multiple markets, combined with standardized products or concentration of activities

Learning and experience: can accelerate the accumulation of learning and experience

Sourcing effectiveness: centralized purchasing can lower costs

Favorable logistics: transportation costs and schedules can be favorably affected

Differences in country costs and skills: firm can concentrate certain activities according to cost and skill factors

Product development costs: it is cheaper to develop a few global products than many national products

Governmental drivers

Favorable trade policies: import tariffs and quotas, nontariff barriers, export subsidies, local content requirements, currency and capital flow restrictions, technology transfer requirements; all of these can affect competitive moves

Compatible technical standards: creates opportunities for product standardization

Common marketing regulations: absence of these creates problems, e.g., certain types of media may be restricted in certain countries

Competitive drivers

Market, cost and governmental drivers are essentially fixed for an industry at any given time. In contrast, competitive drivers are entirely in the realm of competitor choice.

Interdependence of countries: can be created through global strategy, usually through sharing of activities. These will create cost advantages in all countries dependent on them

Globalized competitors: matching or preempting individual competitor moves (e.g., entering markets, introducing products, using uniform marketing) may be necessary.

Changes over time: as the industry globalization drivers evolve over time, so too will the appropriate global strategy

More than one strategy is viable

Industries vary across drivers: No industry is high on every one of the many globalization drivers

Global effects are incremental: Firms can offset "globalization driver disadvantages" by making good strategic lever choices. E.g.: a firm with good technology can use it to offset globalization disadvantages.

Business and parent company position and resources are crucial: The possibility of pursuing, or even the potential for effectiveness of, a global strategy may be compromised by a lack of resources or poor strategic positioning.

Organizations have limitations: Factors such as structure, management processes, people, and culture affect how well a desired global strategy can be implemented.

<u>Discussion Questions</u>

1. In the introduction, the author gives some reasons as to why the idea of globalization has become so popular. What is your opinion about the worthiness of globalization?

This question is designed to stimulate discussion. Sometimes it seems that globalization has become so fashionable that it is recommended to everyone, regardless of its merits. Whether or not globalization makes sense for a firm all depends partly on the situation with the "drivers" the author mentions.

If those point to the efficacy of globalization, there are some benefits: (1) cost reduction (e.g., from pooling production); (2) improved quality of products and programs (based on greater focus); (3) enhanced customer preference (based on reinforcement); and (4) increased competitive leverage (more places from which to launch attacks and counterattacks).

2. Yip says that the market participation "lever" may occasionally require that a firm enter a locally unattractive market. What is your opinion of this idea?

If the author is correct, he is advocating that a firm deliberately create a BCG-style "dog." This is something that the Boston Consulting Group said a firm should *never* do. But it is precisely the kind of thing which exposes the flaws in the BCG model. This shows that it often *does* make sense to have a dog in the portfolio, because it might help the firm to achieve other ends.

3. The author emphasizes the benefits of a standardized core product. What is your opinion about this aspect of globalization?

This is obviously an important element of globalization. Almost by definition, a globalized firm must offer standardized products across the face of the planet. What is interesting about the idea is that it runs against the grain of the concept of ever-more-focused segmentation that seems to be gaining ground in marketing. For example, some soup companies will sell different formulations of a brand in different neighborhoods of a city! Another problem is that product standardization can yield a product that does not entirely satisfy any customers.

4. Which set of industry drivers do you think is the most important?

There are four sets of industry drivers: (1) market drivers, (2) cost drivers, (3) governmental drivers, and (4) competitive drivers. Some students may argue that nothing is possible unless the government allows it, so the government drivers are the most important. Others will argue that governments don't have the resources to regulate everything, so that there is plenty of room for maneuvering. They may argue that the competitive drivers are, as the author points out, always available to firms, so *they* are the most important. Others may assert that cost is always such an important factor, and source of competitive advantage, that the cost drivers are the most important.

It is difficult to say which set is most important. It would depend on the particular circumstances of the industry. Students may nevertheless argue the various positions outlined above.

5. What does the author mean when he says that global effects are incremental?

Yip means that, if a firm makes intelligent strategic choices, it can still succeed even if its strategy is mismatched with industry globalization drivers. He gives the example of a firm with good technology but little else to recommend it for globalization. That firm could gain a little bit now, and perhaps more later. It doesn't all have to come in one bite. Indeed, the resource and skill constraints are so large that it is unlikely that even large firms would be able to globalize quickly. And most of the large firms that are now interested in globalizing have gotten to the point where it is feasible for them only after a long period of corporate evolution.

Bartlett and Ghosal,
"Managing Across Borders: New Organizational Responses"

Summary of Reading

International companies must now simultaneously optimize efficiency, responsiveness and learning. This typically means adding a third dimension—geography—to existing functional and business structures. The problem is exacerbated by units being divided by distance and time and managers being separated by culture and language.

FROM UNIDIMENSIONAL TO MULTIDIMENSIONAL CAPABILITIES

To simplify this difficult management task, managers made some simplifying dichotomous assumptions:

- national responsiveness vs. global operations
- centralization vs. decentralization of key resources and assets
- central control vs. subsidiary autonomy

These unidimensional choices became limiting after a while. Firms need to be strong along three dimensions. "Strong *geographic* management is essential for development of dispersed responsiveness . . . . Effective competitors also need to build strong *business management* with global product responsibility if they are to achieve global efficiency and integration . . . . Finally, a strong, worldwide *functional management* allows an organization to build and transfer core competencies—a capability vital to worldwide learning." To develop this three-part effectiveness requires a multidimensional approach with a balance among the three management groups.

OVERCOMING SIMPLIFYING ASSUMPTIONS

Developing a truly multidimensional approach was difficult because of the pervasiveness of three simplifying assumptions:

- There is an implicit assumption that the roles of different units are uniform and symmetrical, i.e., that different businesses, functions and geographical divisions can all be managed the same way.

- There is an assumption that interunit relationships should be clear and unambiguous, which leads corporations to create relationships on the basis of dependence or independence.

- Management typically assumes that one of its principal tasks is to institutionalize clearly understood mechanisms for decision making and simple control mechanisms.

Firms that were successful at implementing multidimensional organizations were the ones who successfully challenged these assumptions. They *differentiated* tasks and responsibilities. They built and managed *interdependence* among units. They searched for the complex mechanisms needed to *coordinate* and *coopt* the differentiated and interdependent units in sharing vision. These are the central characteristics of the *transnational corporation*.

FROM SYMMETRY TO DIFFERENTIATION

"Just as they saw the need to change symmetrical structures and homogeneous processes imposed on different businesses and functions, most companies we observed eventually recognized the importance of differentiating the management of diverse geographic operations . . . . Many companies are creating different levels of influence for different groups as they perform different activities."

FROM DEPENDENCE TO INTERDEPENDENCE

"The reality of today's worldwide competitive environment demands collaborative information sharing and problem solving, cooperative support and resource sharing, and collective action and implementation." Independent units risk being defeated by organizations that can move in a coordinated fashion across markets and functions. Being centrally dependent has its risks, too, primarily those of being unresponsive to local events and conditions.

Long histories of dependency or independence can be difficult to break and change. Yet some firms have done it. "The most successful did so not by creating new units, but by changing the basis of the relationships among product, functional, and geographic management groups." They made integration and collaboration self-enforcing by making cooperation necessary for the achievement of self-interested goals.

Three important flows seem to be at the center of emerging organizational relationships:

- Flow of parts, components and finished goods. This stems from product interdependence.

- Flow of resources, to counteract the previous independence or total dependence.

- Flow of intelligence, ideas and knowledge.

These interdependencies are different from the more typical ones. Those were "pooled" interdependencies. The newer ones are "reciprocal" interdependencies.

FROM CONTROL TO COORDINATION AND COOPTION

The simplifying assumptions of symmetry and dependence/independence allowed companies to use simple controls—either tight controls for dependent units or loose controls for independent ones. Interdependence requires more complex control methods. Similarly, greater differentiation of units requires greater differentiation of management processes.

The greater flows of parts, resources and information made coordination a central management function. But this comes with a high cost. Better approaches were to increase the use of previously underutilized things like socialization of managers, formal systems and social processes. Management's task becomes one of rationing the use of these new methods and matching them to the proper applications.

Roles of units might vary dramatically, from strategic leader with corporate-wide business management responsibility to mere implementer of strategies developed elsewhere. These roles must be managed in different ways. The strategic leader must have freedom yet support; its controls must be light, but controls over resource and information flows might be quite intense. The implementer unit would have tight operating controls and standardized systems to coordinate flows.

Differentiation can have a fragmenting and demotivating effect. That is why corporations must also use *cooption*: "the process of uniting the organization with a common understanding of, identification with, and commitment to the corporation's objectives, priorities, and values."

"The management process that distinguished transnational organizations from simpler unidimensional forms was one in which control was made less dominant by the increased importance of interunit integration and collaboration. These new processes required corporate management to supplement its control role with the more subtle tasks of coordination and cooption, giving rise to a much more complex and sophisticated management process."

SUSTAINING A DYNAMIC BALANCE: ROLE OF THE "MIND MATRIX"

In a multidimensional organization, the functional, product and geographical units must have different roles for different activities. These roles will evolve and change as conditions change. "[The] ability to manage the multidimensional organization capability in a flexible manner is the hallmark of a transnational company." Good managers used classic tools like organization structure and management systems. They used them to shift things around to prevent atrophy or entrenchment.

But successful transnational companies had an additional element. They focused on *individual* members of the organization. They all tried "to develop multidimensional perspectives and flexible approaches at the level of the individual manager."

The mentality of who constitutes the structure is as vital as the structure itself. Managerial mindset is what holds these diverse tasks together. That is a mindset "that understands the need for multiple strategic capabilities, that is able to view problems from both local and global perspectives, and that accepts the importance of a flexible approach." Managers should resist trying to create a "real" matrix structure, but should instead create one in their minds.

"Our study has led us to conclude that a company's ability to develop transnational organizational capability and management mentality will be the key factor that separates the winners from the mere survivors in the emerging international environment."

Discussion Questions

1. Why does a multinational firm need all three kinds of management?

It needs *geographic* management to ensure responsiveness to national markets. It needs *business* management to achieve global efficiency—through manufacturing rationalization, product standardization and low-cost global sourcing—and integration. *Functional* management allows firms to build their core competencies, which they can then share—the key to learning.

2. What is your reaction to the "simplifying assumptions" identified by the authors?

These assumptions are likely to be shared by many students. The first, that management is the same regardless of business, function or location, is an old one that is still believed by many people. The authors are correct in pointing out that each of these dimensions alone is enough to change the management task. The second simplifying assumption, the idea that interunit relationships should be clear and unambiguous, is widely held, as is the resulting reliance on relationships of clear dependence or clear interdependence. But the authors point out that interdependence and cooperation are superior, albeit more difficult, under the circumstances in which transnational corporations find themselves. Lastly, most students will agree that management is responsible for institutionalizing control mechanisms, and the simpler the better. But this ignores the need for more sophisticated mechanisms, along with the need for cooption—a better common understanding of the organization's goals and values.

3. Why does differentiation make sense?

Differentiation has made sense since Lawrence and Lorsch first thought of it as a concept. Basically, if you are facing a diverse environment, your organization must be more diverse. In the case of a transnational corporation, if it operates many businesses composed of many functions in many countries, it must create as many different management schemes as it needs. It should not assume that one size of management approach will fit all.

4. What are the problems with dependence or independence as multinational approaches?

Independent units will be overwhelmed by transnational companies that have the ability to integrate research, manufacturing, and other scale-efficient operations, and that have the opportunity to cross-subsidize the losses from battles in one national market with funds generated by profitable operations in other markets.

Dependent units will lose local market responsiveness and will also be unable to respond effectively to strong local competitors. They may also fail to sense potentially important local market or technical intelligence.

5. What do the authors say is the best strategy for achieving interdependence?

They suggest moving to interunit relationships based on explicit, genuine interdependence. They suggest making integration and collaboration "self-enforcing" by making it necessary for each unit to cooperate in order to achieve its own interests. All of this involves weaving together three flows: of goods, of resources and of information.

6. What is the significance of moving away from "pooled interdependence" and toward "reciprocal interdependence?"

Pooled interdependence is not a very strong form of interdependence. It is merely the "adding up" of all the activities of the various units. All the units are "collectively responsible" for the company's success in the sense that if enough of them are successful individually, the firm will be successful. Needs of one unit may be met by another unit, but only through either coercion or persuasion.

Reciprocal interdependence is the strongest form of interdependence. Each unit relies for its success on each other unit. This makes them vulnerable, but also motivates them to cooperate. Ultimately, cooperation will make all the units collectively stronger.

7. How do the authors suggest companies go about moving from control to coordination?

They are a bit vague on this point. They decry the use of simplistic control mechanisms, but don't have anything specific to offer in exchange. They tout "socialization of managers" and the use of "formal systems and social processes." But it is not clear what they mean. Whatever it is that firms choose to do should be "robust and flexible." This no doubt is as opposed to simplistic and rigid.

The authors do give some good examples of how to vary the coordination and control tools with the situation. Units with significant strategic responsibility should have loose controls and lots of information. Units whose only responsibility is to implement strategies should have tighter controls, mostly over flows of goods.

8. What is your reaction to the concept of "cooption?"

The word has tended to have different meanings in other contexts than it does here. It usually means something like subtly buying people's allegiance by, for example, putting them in charge of something that they previously opposed. Here it means getting people to buy into the goals and values, the culture, of the company. That is close to the ideological strategy discussed by Mintzberg in a previous chapter.

9. What is the key to successful management of transnational corporations?

The authors think that flexibility is key. They underline this with a point they made in an earlier reading—managers are better off having a "matrix in their minds" than trying to actually create a matrix form. As flexible as those are supposed to be, they are not as flexible as the "virtual matrix" in a manager's mind.

Mintzberg, "Beyond Configuration"

Summary of Reading

FORMS AND FORCES

"Lumpers" are people who categorize, who synthesize. "Splitters" are people who analyze, who see all the nuances. From the standpoint of organization, "both are right and both are wrong. Without categories, it would be impossible to practice management. With only categories, it could not be practiced effectively."

The author was mostly a lumper until a friend asked him if he really wanted to "play LEGO" with his concepts. "This reading is presented in the spirit of playing 'organizational LEGO.' It tries to show how we can use splitting as well as lumping to understand what makes organizations effective as well as what causes many of their fundamental problems."

The configurations are *forms.* Many organizations seem to fit naturally into one of the original five suggested by the author. But some do not fit, to the lumpers' chagrin. To respond to this, five *forces* have been added, each associated with one of the original forms:

> *Direction* in the entrepreneurial form

> *Efficiency* in the machine form

> *Proficiency* in the professional form

> *Concentration* in the diversified form

> *Learning* in the innovative form

Two other forces exist that are not necessarily associated with a particular form:

> *Cooperation*, represented by ideology

> *Competition*, represented by politics

For the lumpers we now have a *portfolio of forms*, and for the splitters we now have a *system of forces.*

Both views are critical for the practice of management.   "One represents the most fundamental forces that act on organizations. All serious organizations experience all seven of them, at one time or another, if not all the time. The other represents the most fundamental forms that organizations can take, which some of them do some of the time. Together . . . these forces and forms appear to constitute a powerful diagnostic framework by which to understand what goes on in organizations and to prescribe effective change in them."

When one force dominates an organization, it is drawn toward the associated *configuration*, but must deal with *contamination*. When no force dominates, the organization is a balanced *combination* of forces, including periods of *conversion* from one form to another; there is a problem of *cleavage*. Contamination and cleavage require the management of *contradiction*, which is where ideology and politics come in.

<u>CONFIGURATION</u>

Dominant forces drive an organization to one of the pure forms. These are not "real," but are abstract models designed to capture some reality. Some organizations *do* match the pure forms closely. If the form fits, the organization should wear it. Configuration helps outsiders understand an organization. The consistency of configuration keeps workers from being confused, and helps the organization be effective and efficient.

Contamination by configuration

The harmony, consistency, and fit that is configuration's greatest strength is also its greatest weakness. The dominant force can become so strong that it drives out everything else. For example, control in machine organizations may contaminate the innovators in research; but the "looseness" in adhocracies may contaminate the accountants.

Configuration out of control

When the need arises for change, the dominating force may act to hold the organization in place. The other forces have atrophied, and so the organization goes out of control. For instance, the machine organization in need of a new strategy may have no entrepreneurs and no innovators left to give it its new direction.

The dominating force may drive the organization out of control directly, by simply becoming too strong, e.g., an obsession with control in the machine organization.

Miller and Kets de Vries have developed five organizational "neuroses" that correspond roughly to the five forms:

Dramatic: the entrepreneur who takes the organization on an ego trip

Compulsive: the completeness of control in machine organizations

Paranoid: the collective tendency in some professional organizations

Depressive: a result of an obsession with the bottom line in diversified organizations

Schizoid: the need to innovate, but to get the commercial benefits from innovation, means a constant oscillation between divergent and convergent thinking

In other words, behaviors that were once functional become dysfunctional when pursued to excess.

Containment of configuration

"Truly effective organizations do not exist in pure form. What keeps a configuration effective is not only the dominance of a single force but also the constraining effects of other forces." This is *containment*. "To manage configuration effectively is to exploit one form but also to reconcile the different forces."

<u>COMBINATION</u>

Configuration is nice if you can have it. But some organizations all of the time and all organizations some of the time cannot have it. They must instead balance competing forces. Organizations like this are called *combinations*. It is probable that roughly half of all organizations are combinations.

Kinds of combinations

When only two of the five forces meet in rough balance, that is a *hybrid*. Some organizations experience *multiple combinations*. In some cases, the forces interact in a steady state. In other cases, the interaction is separable in place and time.

Cleavage in combinations

Sometimes combination encourages *cleavage*. Instead of one force dominating, two or more confront each other to the point of paralyzing the organization. A good example is the innovative drive of R&D against the machine-like drive of production.

Combination of one kind or another is necessary in most organizations, because effective organizations usually balance many forces. Configuration merely means a tilt toward one force; combination is more balanced.

CONVERSION

Few organizations stay one form or combination; they undergo *conversion*. These may result from external changes (innovations, or suddenly unstable markets). Conversions may be temporary, as in the machine organization that becomes an entrepreneurial organization during a crisis.

Cycles of conversion

The forces that may destroy the organization may instead drive it to another, perhaps more viable, configuration. For example, the inherently vulnerable entrepreneurial form may grow and become a machine organization.

The most common life cycle begins with the entrepreneurial form. Growth leads to the machine form. Even greater growth leads to the diversified form.

Another life cycle occurs for firms dependent on expertise. They move from the entrepreneurial form to either the professional form (if they can standardize their services) or the innovative form (if their services are more creative). Another common conversion is when an innovative form settles into a professional form.

Ideology is a more important force in young organizations. Politics is a more important force as an organization ages.

Cleavage in conversion

Some conversions are easy because they are so overdue. Others are more difficult and conflictual. The forces that create the conversion also create the possibility of cleavage.

CONTRADICTION

"Organizations that have to reconcile contradictory forces, especially in dealing with change, often turn to the cooperative force of ideology or the competitive force of politics. Indeed, I believe that these two forces themselves represent a contradiction that must be managed if an organization is not to run out of control."

"While it is true that each can dominate an organization, and so draw it toward a missionary or political form," more commonly they act differently, as *catalysts*.

Cooperation through ideology

"Ideology represents the force for cooperation in an organization, for collegiality and consensus." It encourages members to look inward, to take their lead from the imperatives of the organization's own vision. One important implication is that the infusion of ideology renders any particular config- uration more effective.

Another implication is that ideology helps an organization manage contradiction and so to deal with change. The innovative machine or the tightly controlled innovative organization handles these contradictions by having strong cultures. "Such organizations can more easily reconcile their opposing forces because what matters to their people is the organization itself, not any of its particular parts." This is how Toyota gets efficiency and high quality at the same time.

Limits to cooperation

But ideologies are difficult to build and sustain. And established ideologies can get in the way of organizational effectiveness. It may discourage change by forcing everyone to work within the same set of beliefs.

This has implications for strategy. Change *within* strategic perspective, to a new position, is facilitated by a strong ideology. But change *of* perspective—fundamental change—is discouraged by it.

Competition through politics

"Politics represents the force for competition in an organization, for conflict and confrontation." It can infuse any of the configurations or combinations, aggravating contamination and cleavage. In a configuration, the representatives of the dominant force "lord it" over others. In a combination, representatives of the various forces relish opportunities to do battle with each other.

Politics may be a more "natural" force than ideology. Left to themselves, organizations seem to pull apart rather easily. Keeping them together requires considerable and constant effort.

Benefits of competition

"If pulling together discourages people from addressing fundamental change, then pulling apart may become the only way to ensure that happens." Change requires challenging the status quo. Politics may facilitate this; if there are no entrepreneurial or innovative forces stimulating strategic change, it may be the *only* available force for change.

"Both politics and ideology can promote organizational effectiveness as well as undermine it."

Combining cooperation and competition

Ideology and politics themselves have to be reconciled. Pulling together ideologically infuses life; splitting apart politically challenges the status quo. "Only by encouraging both can an organization sustain its viability. . . . Ideology helps secondary forces to contain a dominant one; politics encourages them to challenge it."

The balance between ideology and politics should be a dynamic equilibrium. Most of the time ideology should be pulling things together, contained by healthy internal competition. When fundamental change becomes necessary, politics should help pull the organization apart.

COMPETENCE

What makes an organization effective? The "Peterian" view is that organizations should be "hands on, value driven." The "Porterian" view says that organizations should use competitive

530

analysis. "To Porter, effectiveness resides in strategy, while to Peters it is the operations that count."

We must "find out what really makes an organization truly effective. We need to understand what takes it to a viable strategy in the first place, what makes it excellent there, and how some organizations are able to sustain viability and excellence in the face of change."

Here are five views of organizational effectiveness:

1. *Convergence*: there is "one best way" to design an organization

2. *Congruence*: the contingency or "it all depends" approach

3. *Configuration*: "getting it all together"; fit the organizational pieces together to create a coherent, harmonious picture

4. *Contradiction*: manage the dynamic tension between contradictory forces

5. *Creation*: "the truly great organization transcends all of the above, while building on it to achieve something more. . . . These organizations invent novel approaches that solve festering problems and so provide all of us with new ways to deal with our world of organizations."

"The most interesting organizations live at the edges, far from the logic of conventional organizations, where as . . . in biology (for example, between the sea and the land, or at the forest's edge), the richest, most varied, and most interesting forms of life can be found."

Discussion Questions

1. How much does the "getting it all together" approach really add to the "it all depends" approach?

It adds quite a bit. The contingency ("it all depends") approach says that you should design your organization to fit environmental contingencies; e.g., if the environment is turbulent, you should have an organic structure. The configuration ("getting it all together") approach says that we know that many design elements actually should go together, i.e., they should not be picked individually.

A decision to build a machine organization is really a decision to put many elements together—narrow (rather than broad) job specialization, action planning (not performance control), centralized (not decentralized) decision making, many small units (instead of a few larger units), functional (as opposed to market-based) grouping. This argument is similar to the one Waterman, Peters and Phillips make in their "7S Framework" reading—everything interrelates and fits (or *should*).

2. What's your assessment of the author's definition of ideology?

Some students will question Mintzberg's definition of ideology. He calls it a "strong culture," encompassing the traditions and beliefs which (1) distinguish an organization from others and (2) infuse life into its "skeleton." Critics will wonder why he feels it necessary to introduce a concept in addition to the already-familiar "culture." If a firm has a strong culture, then it has an ideology. But what if it has a weak culture? Does that mean it has a weak ideology, or *no* ideology?

3. What is your opinion of the idea that the term bureaucratic applies to any structure that relies, for coordination, on any form of standardization?

Students will find this a bit odd. The terms "bureaucracy" and "bureaucratic" have negative connotations, so few people will question the use of the terms with regard to the machine organization. This will probably also be true for diversified organizations, which tend to be large and formalized. But this assertion implies that professional organizations and missionary organizations, which rely on standardization of skills and norms, respectively, are bureaucratic, too. Many students will question this. But it is true that professional standards can be very strict, and organizational norms can be very strict. So those two types of organizations can be as restrictive as organizations burdened by many rules.

4. What is the distinction between training and indoctrination?

Training is aimed at imparting skills or knowledge. It is a key design parameter in professional organizations. It is a substitute for formalization in obtaining standardized behavior. Indoctrination, by contrast, is aimed at standardizing norms. It is a tool for socializing organization members, and is usually more psychologically intense than training. It, too, is a substitute for formalization, in this case the standards being internalized as deeply rooted beliefs.

5. In what sense are function and market the only two real bases for unit grouping?

Functional grouping, based on what is done in the work process, is a familiar basis of unit grouping. It is always available to the organizational designer. So the root of this question is whether or not market grouping is indeed the only other basis. Mintzberg mentions three possible bases—product, client, and geographical area. His argument is that each of these is simply a surrogate for market. Products are targeted for particular markets. Clients, in the aggregate, *are* the market. And geographical areas are markets. So, market *is* the only other basis for grouping.

6. How does action planning differ from performance control?

Action planning specifies the actions of workers *before* they do them. It is an important design parameter in machine organizations. Performance control specifies desired outcomes, and leaves the necessary actions up to the workers. It is an important design parameter in diversified organizations.

7. How do the concepts of liaison positions and integrating managers differ?

Liaison positions are considerably weaker than integrating managers. Liaison positions are jobs created to coordinate the work of two units. Those who serve in them must use their powers of persuasion and negotiation to bring the two sides together. Integrating managers have formal authority over the units they link. They are liaison positions, only with authority.

8. What is the distinction between vertical and horizontal decentralization?

Decentralization means the diffusion of decision-making power. Vertical decentralization means that formal power is diffused by top managers to lower-level managers. Horizontal decentralization is the diffusion of either formal or informal decision-making power to non-managers, such as operators, analysts, and support staffers.

9. What is the distinction between selective and parallel decentralization? How useful is this distinction?

Selective decentralization refers to the dispersal of power over different decisions to different places. An example would be giving the organization's staff attorneys power to make legal decisions, but giving its real estate experts the power to make real estate sale or purchase decisions. Parallel decentralization means the dispersal of power over various decisions to the same place. The best example is the position of division manager in a diversified organization. Each division manager is given the same set of decision making powers—e.g., how much can be invested, how much can be granted in pay increases, the amount of latitude in business planning, etc.

10. What are the implications of the "age and size" hypotheses?

The implications are straightforward—as an organization gets older and larger, it gradually becomes a machine organization. It is characterized by the dominance of standardized work processes (formalized rules) and the prominence of the technostructure (which writes the rules). The rules allow the organization to have larger units. Lastly, the organization is more specialized. All of this adds up to machine organization.

11. What are the implications of the five "environment" hypotheses, taken as a whole?

The more "difficult" is the environment, the more adaptable must be the organization. Adaptability means organic (the opposite of bureaucratic) structure, i.e., coordination is not based on standardization. It also means the dispersal of decision-making power to places closer to where the decision should be made, i.e., decentralization. And it means being "differentiated," i.e., divided up in ways as complex as the environment, including specialized divisions for specialized markets.

The one hypothesis which doesn't fit these implications is the one which says that bad times lead to temporary centralization of an organization's structure. This means that when things go wrong, top management takes the reins a bit more tightly. The quickest responses can come from organizations run by one person, or a small number of people, and this is frequently what is needed in a crisis.

12. How can fashion affect the choice of structure? Is this good or bad?

Organizational structure, like other aspects of management, has its fads and fashions. A few years ago, matrix structure was very fashionable. Many organizations adopted a matrix form, even though it was not appropriate for them. Today, many organization designers denigrate formalization, even though it is widely recognized that rules can be very effective, in the proper circumstances. Most students will agree that this is a bad thing. Organization design should be based on the situational factors of age, size, technical system, and environment, and on how the parameters fit together into a proper configuration.

13. What is your opinion of the "seven pulls on the organization?"

Students will differ on the usefulness of the "pulls" concept. Some will say that it adds little to the seven parts and six coordinating mechanisms discussed earlier in the reading. Others will argue that it is these pulls that lead the organization to finally end up in one configuration or the other. They are the driving forces behind the formation of configurations.

14. How can the operating core of an entrepreneurial organization be organic?

The term "organic" has positive connotations, and is usually reserved for describing organizations whose workers have lots of freedom and decision-making power. These attributes are not typical of entrepreneurial organizations, whose strategic apexes tend to reserve most power to themselves. But Mintzberg uses the term "organic" as the opposite of "bureaucratized." In that sense, the entrepreneurial organization is organic, since it has no standardization. The entrepreneurial organization does not rely on any form of standardization for coordination; its prime coordinating mechanism is direct supervision.

15. In what sense is the diversified organization not a complete structure?

The term "diversified organization" applies to only part of the structure of such firms. It describes only the structure of the overall corporation. It does not describe the structures of the various divisions. In theory, each division could have a unique structure. (In practice, they tend to be machine organizations.)

16. What is your reaction to the distinction between "lumpers" and "splitters?"

This question is intended to stimulate discussion. Many students will find this distinction a bit flippant. Here we are, trying to discuss the serious topic of business strategy, and Mintzberg is using terms like "lumpers" and "splitters." But he is using these colloquial terms to make a point. Management literature has been filled with material of the "splitter" variety for a long time. Splitters are analysts, and as Mintzberg mentioned in his earlier reading on "Crafting Strategy," it is not at all clear that analysis/splitting is the way managers operate. Managers are synthesizers, i.e., they like to put things together, or "lump" them. By using these slightly flippant terms, the author is highlighting this distinction.

17. The author says that "all serious organizations experience all seven" of the fundamental forces. Form groups and have each group analyze, for the seven forces, an organization its members know well.

This is an exercise that will help bring the forces "alive" for students.

18. What's your reaction to the author's notion that none of the configurations "exists at all?"

Some students may respond by saying that if this is correct, then why bother studying them? But Mintzberg's point is that any construct or model, whether it be about strategy or configuration or anything else, is an abstraction. A model is a mental conception of reality, intended to help the person appreciate "reality." It is a tool for understanding. And that is all the author's configurations are. As he says, the model constitutes "a powerful diagnostic framework by which to understand what goes on in organizations and to prescribe effective change in them."

19. How common are the pure configurations? Can you think of some examples?

The author cites research showing that slightly more than half of all organizations are pure configurations. That is just one study. Students may have different opinions about the proportions.

There are some good examples. McDonald's is a good machine organization, at least in its operating core; some might argue that it is an administrative adhocracy—a machine core with an innovative strategic apex. Hewlett-Packard is a good example of an operating adhocracy, as would be any local advertising agency. The college or university at which the students are studying would be a good example of a professional organization. So would any law firm or accounting firm with which students are familiar.

534

20. *What is your reaction to Miller and Kets de Vries's five organizational neuroses?*

This question should stimulate discussion. Miller and Kets de Vries's work may be very solid, but many students will find Mintzberg's attempt to attach each neurosis to a corresponding pure configuration to be a stretch. Nevertheless, there is at least a kernel of plausibility to this. The entrepreneurial organization is thoroughly dominated by its leader, whose vision drives the organization. Machine organizations are typically pervaded by a control mentality. University faculty will not be strangers to the idea that threats to professional autonomy and control are viewed with something resembling paranoia.

The two biggest stretches are associated with the depressive and schizoid neuroses. The standardization of outputs does drive the diversified organization toward machine bureaucracy, but it is not at all clear that "depressive" is the correct metaphor. Lastly, one could argue that "constant oscillation between divergent and convergent thinking" is healthy, not schizoid.

The fundamental point underlying Mintzberg's discussion is valid regardless of any defects in these metaphors—a configuration dominated, perhaps overwhelmed, by one force, will contaminate itself, perhaps pathologically.

21. *What is your reaction to the author's discussion of combinations?*

Most students will react favorably to this discussion. It is difficult to find abundant examples of the pure configurations. It is easy to find elements of each force in any organization. Most students have an easier time characterizing an organization as a hybrid or other combination. In this section, Mintzberg gives them tools that help them do this.

22. *Describe the similarities and differences between the two major patterns of conversion.*

One major pattern of conversion is from the entrepreneurial form to the machine form, and perhaps on to the diversified form. The second starts with the entrepreneurial form and moves to either the professional or innovative form.

The main similarity between the two is their beginning with the entrepreneurial form. Almost everything else is different. The first cycle is driven by growth, which encourages formalization and the adoption of the machine form. The second cycle is driven by expertise. If the expertise can be standardized, the transition is to the professional form. If it cannot be standardized, the organization becomes an adhocracy.

23. *How does ideology augment or diminish an organization?*

Ideology helps in several ways. It is the driving force for cooperation in the firm. It encourages members to look to the organization's vision. Most important is ideology's ability to help members reconcile the many contradictions they will encounter in their organizational lives. As the author says, "Such organizations can more easily reconcile their opposing forces because what matters to their people is the organization itself, not any of its particular parts."

But there are problems. Ideologies are difficult to build and to maintain. And established ideologies can get in the way of effectiveness; they inhibit change by forcing everyone to work within the same set of beliefs. Strategic change within a perspective is aided by a strong ideology; change of perspective—fundamental change—is discouraged by it.

24. *How does politics augment or diminish an organization?*

Politics usually hurts, according to the author, because it is the force for competition, "for conflict and confrontation." If it dominates, it may create a politicized organization. Or the dominant part of a configuration (e.g., the technostructure in a machine organization) may "lord it" over the weaker parts. In a hybrid or combination, politics may incite factional disputes.

But politics can also help. If reactionary forces dominate a firm, it may be politics that gets it to change. It is a force that can be used to challenge the status quo.

25. What is your reaction to the author's discussion of how ideology and politics should work together?

Some students may find it paradoxical that organizations which balance ideology and politics are the most effective. But, then, organizations are filled with paradox.

Most people agree that it's a good thing for scientists to be familiar with practical things, and for marketing people to understand the principles that underlie the products they are selling. It is the tension between the opposing forces that leads to the greatest learning.

The principle is the same for organizations. If an organization is too "set in its ways," it will atrophy. If it is too divided, it will never have the chance to establish a good pattern or strategy. What is needed is a creative tension between the stability of ideology and the challenge of politics.

26. What is your reaction to the author's five views of organizational effectiveness?

This question is intended to stimulate discussion. The first three views capture the evolution of thinking in more-or-less sequential order. It started with the "one best way" approach. The well-known contingency, or "it all depends," approach followed. Mintzberg was one of the chief architects of the configuration approach, which argued that organizational pieces fit together in coherent, internally-consistent, ways.

The fourth and fifth views are new, at least to some extent. The previous answer gave some insight into why contradiction can be a good thing. The "creation hypothesis" is problematic in that it provides no guidelines. Presumably, a management "playing organizational LEGO" would be involved in building new, cutting-edge organizational forms.

27. Which of the following most resembles organization design: solving puzzles or playing with LEGOs?

This question should stimulate discussion. Some students are always looking for "the right answer." For them, organizational design will always be puzzle solving—get the pieces and make sure to put them in the right places. Other students will have a more flexible view; there may be more than one way to organize in a particular situation. For these students, the pieces are not puzzle parts with only one correct location—they are blocks which can be combined in many different, and creative, ways.

Tushman, Newman, and Romanelli, "Convergence and Upheaval: Managing the Unsteady Pace of Organizational Evolution"

Summary of Reading

"A snug fit of external opportunity, company strategy, and internal structure is a hallmark of successful companies." The test is to maintain this alignment in the face of change.

"The most successful firms maintain a workable equilibrium for several years (or decades), but are also able to initiate and carry out sharp, widespread changes (referred to here as reorientations) when their environments shift . . . . Less successful firms . . . get stuck in a particular pattern."

"For long periods most companies make only incremental changes, and . . . they then need to make painful, discontinuous, system-wide shifts . . . . Incremental change is compatible with the existing structure of a company and is reinforced over a period of years. In contrast, frame-breaking change is abrupt, painful to participants, and often resisted by the old guard."

"Our research strongly suggests that the convergence/upheaval pattern occurs within departments, at the business-unit level, and at the corporate level of analysis."

PATTERNS IN ORGANIZATIONAL EVOLUTION: CONVERGENCE AND UPHEAVAL

Building on strength: Periods of convergence

"Successful companies wisely stick to what works well . . . ." Strategy, structure, people and process all fit together, but are changed incrementally. This takes two forms:

Converging change: Fine-tuning. Well-run companies seek ever better ways of exploiting and defending their missions:

Refining policies, methods, and procedures

Creating specialized units and linking mechanisms

Developing personnel

Fostering commitment to mission

Promoting confidence in accepted norms, beliefs, and myths

Clarifying roles, power, status, dependencies, and allocation mechanisms

Converging change: Incremental adjustments to environmental shifts. "Even the most conservative of organizations expect, even welcome, small changes which do not make too many waves. The process is well known:

Wide acceptance of need for change

Openness to possible alternatives

Objective examination of the alternatives

Participation, in the analysis, of those affected by the change

Market tests or pilot operation where appropriate

Time to learn new activities

Established role models

Known rewards for success

Evaluation

Refinement

Role of executives is to reemphasize mission and core values, delegate incremental decisions to middle managers.

"The overall system adapts, but it is not transformed."

Converging change: Some consequences. "For those companies whose strategies fit environmental conditions, convergence brings about better and better effectiveness. . . . Convergent periods are, however, a double-edged sword. As organizations grow and become more successful, they develop internal forces for stability." Examples: organization structure; employee habits; norms related to operations; special skills.

"This organizational momentum is profoundly functional as long as the organization's strategy is appropriate . . . . However, if (and when) strategy must change, this momentum cuts the other way . . . ." Faced with environmental threat, organizations with strong momentum may not register the threat, or may respond by increased conformity to the status quo.

"A paradoxical result of long periods of success may be heightened organizational complacency, decreased organizational flexibility, and a stunted ability to learn . . . . Those very social and technical consistencies which are key sources of success may also be the seeds of failure if environments change." Tendency is strongest in:

most successful firm in a product class

historically regulated organizations

organizations traditionally shielded from competition

On frame-breaking change

Forces leading to frame-breaking change:

Industry discontinuities:

Deregulation

Substitute products

Substitute processes

Major economic changes

Legal shifts

Product-life-cycle shifts:

Emergence phase keys: product innovation and performance

Maturity phase keys: cost, volume, efficiency

Internal company dynamics:

Size growth

Death of key people

Attitude changes among family investors

538

Revised portfolio strategy

Scope of frame-breaking change. "Frame-breaking change is driven by shifts in business strategy . . . . [It] involves discontinuous changes throughout the organization . . . . Frame-breaking changes are revolutionary changes *of* the system as opposed to incremental changes *in* the system."

Here are some of its features:

Reformed mission and core values

Altered power and status

Reorganization (of structure, systems, and procedures)

Revised interaction patterns

New executives usually brought in from outside the organization

Here are some of its advantages:

commitment to new mission

energy to overcome prevailing inertia

freedom from prior obligations

some from "old guard" may remain

overall number of executive changes is small, but "have substantial symbolic and substantive effects on the organization"

Why all at once? Piecemeal approaches get bogged down in politics, resistance, and inertia. "Frame-breaking change requires discontinuous shifts in strategy, structure, people, and processes concurrently—or at least in a short period of time." Reasons for rapid implementation:

Synergy within the new structure can be a powerful aid

Pockets of resistance have a chance to grow if implementation is too slow

Pent-up needs for change release forces favoring changes

Risk and uncertainty are inherent in change, but are kept short if implementation is rapid

Patterns in organizational evolution. In organizational evolution there are long convergent periods punctuated by reorientation. "The most effective firms take advantage of relatively long convergent periods

. . . Frame-breaking change is quite dysfunctional if the organization is successful and the environment is stable. If, however, the organization is performing poorly and/or if the environment changes substantially, frame-breaking change is the only way to realign the organization with its competitive environment."

"Low-performing organizations either do not reorient or reorient all the time as they root around to find an effective alignment with environmental conditions."

EXECUTIVE LEADERSHIP AND ORGANIZATION EVOLUTION

"During convergent periods, the executive team focuses on *maintaining* congruence and fit within the organization . . .. The key role . . . is to reemphasize strategy, mission, and core values and to keep a vigilant eye on external opportunities and/or threats."

"Frame-breaking change, however, requires direct executive involvement in all aspects of the change, . . . [in] specification of strategy, structure, people, and organizational processes *and* in the development of implementation plans."

"The most effective executives . . . foresaw the need for major change . . . . Ideally, by acting before being forced to do so, they had more time to plan their transitions.

"[But] such visionary [executives] are the exceptions. Most frame-breaking change is postponed until a financial crisis forces drastic action."

"Most frame-breaking upheavals are managed by executives brought in from outside the company . . . [and are] coupled with CEO succession in more than 80 percent of the cases . . . ."

Reasons:

different skills

fresh perspective

strong belief in new mission

unfettered by prior commitments

symbolizes need for change

excitement of new challenge

These typical patterns are far from satisfactory for a particular organization. The vital tasks are:

to manage incremental change during convergent periods

to have the vision to initiate and implement frame-breaking change prior to the competition

to mobilize an executive who can initiate and implement both kinds of change

CONCLUSION

Things to remember when environments change sharply:

frame-breaking change cannot be avoided

changes must be made rapidly

direct involvement of (probably new) executive is needed

there are no patterns in the sequence of frame-breaking changes, and not all strategies will be effective

Issues for executive leadership:

need to manage for balance, consistency, or fit during convergent period need to be vigilant for environmental shifts, in order to anticipate need for frame-breaking change

need to effectively manage incremental as well as frame-breaking change

need to build (or rebuild) top team for frame-breaking change

need to develop core values to act as anchor during frame-breaking changes

need to develop organizational history as a way to infuse pride

need to bolster technical, social, and conceptual skills with visionary skills; the latter add energy, direction, and excitement

Discussion Questions

1. The authors say that the convergence/upheaval phenomenon applies to all levels of analysis— department, business, corporation. What are the implications of this?

Students in the policy course often have a problem seeing the relevance of concepts that typically are most applicable for top management only. Most of the concepts in this text will make people more intelligent members of organizations, regardless of level, because they will understand organizations and strategy making better.

The point the authors make here is even more specific in its relevance for all organizational members. They are saying that even if you are not a CEO, you can expect to see this pattern of convergence and upheaval. It seems to be a "fact of life," maybe even an inescapable part of "human nature," organizationally speaking. "This pattern is normal," should be the message to students. "Learn how to deal with it, at whatever level."

2. How does the section on "building on strength" relate to Mintzberg's Chapter 5 reading on "Crafting Strategy?"

In that reading Mintzberg made the point that stability rules most organizations most of the time. Managing strategy becomes an exercise in squeezing the most out of stability. He emphasized how change, if there is too much of it, can actually *inhibit* strategy making. Strategy is a pattern in a stream of action; if there's too much change, there can be no pattern.

He also discussed how change comes in two varieties—constant, incremental and not terribly important, on the one hand, and discontinuous and significant, on the other. The key to effective strategy making is to recognize, in the midst of stability, these significant discontinuities, and change accordingly. These two kinds of change correspond roughly to these authors' constructs of "converging change" and "frame-breaking change."

3. What is your reaction to the section on "Converging change: Some consequences?"

The authors use some interesting language to describe convergence: it "brings about better and better effectiveness" and it "is profoundly functional." It sounds like convergence is mostly a good thing. But "mostly" doesn't mean "entirely."

The authors point out that convergent momentum is a double-edged sword. "As organizations grow and become more successful, they develop internal forces for stability . . . ." Faced with environmental threat, organizations with strong convergent momentum may not register the threat, or may respond by increased conformity to the status quo. "A paradoxical result of long periods of success may be heightened organizational complacency, decreased organizational flexibility, and a stunted ability to learn."

4. What is your reaction to the statement, "Frame-breaking changes are revolutionary changes of the system as opposed to incremental changes in the system?"

This phrase succinctly captures the difference between the two kinds of change. Frame-breaking change alters the *entire* system, hence, it is a change *of* the system. Convergent change keeps the system intact, merely adjusting its elements, i.e., it is change *in* the system. The phrase is intended to highlight the difference between fine-tuning or incremental adaptation, on the one hand, and upheaval, on the other.

An analogy might be helpful. Convergent change is like adjusting the contrast, the antenna, the fine tuning, etc., on an old black-and-white television set. One merely tries to get the most out of the system. Frame-breaking change is like throwing out the old black-and-white and getting a state-of-the-art color television set with cable hookups and a satellite dish. The whole system is changed.

5. What is your reaction to the author's reasons for the need for rapid implementation of frame-breaking changes?

This question is intended to stimulate discussion. Many students will question the effectiveness of making so many changes so quickly. They will have a point—no doubt frame-breaking change is very traumatic. But overly-slow change might get bogged down in politics; pockets of resistance will have time to form.

There are some positive aspects to fast implementation, too. There may be synergy—if all the pieces are new, they will work together better than some old and some new pieces. Upheavals are preceded by long stable periods during which needs for change have been pent up. The change effort will release forces favoring change, and rapid implementation can exploit them. Lastly, the risk and uncertainty which characterize frame-breaking change are kept short if implementation is rapid.

6. What are the implications of the section on "Patterns in organizational evolution?"

This is very similar to the points made in Chapter 5 by Mintzberg. Here is what Tushman, Newman, and Romanelli say: "The most effective firms take advantage of relatively long convergent periods. . . . Frame-breaking change is quite dysfunctional if the organization is successful and the environment is stable. If, however, the organization is performing poorly and/or if the environment changes substantially, frame-breaking change is the only way to realign the organization with its competitive environment." In other words, there is no need to constantly change; that is in fact a bad thing. But you had better change, and change big, when big shifts happen.

7. What is your reaction to the authors' claim that "most frame-breaking change is postponed until a financial crisis forces drastic action?"

Most students are amazed that this phenomenon exists. They assume that sophisticated managers should be capable of avoiding this type of cycle. They must be reminded that this is the norm. And it is the norm not because managers are idiots, but because there are powerful forces acting on most people who populate most organizations, forces that make stability easy and change difficult.

8. *The authors declare that "most frame-breaking upheavals are managed by executives brought in from outside the company." What do you think of this?*

Some students will be surprised at this, but the authors give a host of reasons as to why this might be a good thing. The new managers bring new skills with them. They bring fresh perspectives to old problems that have plagued the company. They have a strong belief in the new mission. They carry no organizational baggage—they are unfettered by prior commitments. They are likely to be excited by the challenge of the new assignment. And, perhaps most importantly, they symbolize the need for change.

Baden-Fuller and Stopford, "The Crescendo Model of Rejuvenation"

Summary of Reading

"Is rejuvenation really possible?" A firm that has been in trouble must first stop the short-term problems. But it then has to create some long-term momentum and build a durable recovery.

THE CRESCENDO MODEL

"We regard building corporate entrepreneurship as the essential ingredient for lasting rejuvenation." The firm must avoid quick fixes like huge capital investments, reengineering, or shallow TQM. These rarely have any sustainable reward. Our suggestion is to follow the four-step crescendo model. "Crescendo is a musical term meaning 'a gradual increase in volume.'"

Galvanize

Often overlooked is the obvious way to begin—create a top team dedicated to renewal. Rejuvenation requires the repair of the entire organization and how the parts interact. This requires effort from everyone, but starts with the top team. Galvanizing the top team requires an agenda beginning with a broad understanding of the issues and moving to a belief in the value of progress through many small steps. It is better to initiate action than to chase after grand schemes.

Simplify

Building something new often requires cutting some of the old, e.g., old control systems. Simplification focuses action more acutely. It also signals to stakeholders that positive steps are being taken. But simplification is merely a temporary measure.

Build

This overlaps simplification, and involves building new advantages. This is where organizational rather than individual entrepreneurship needs to be nurtured. New challenges must in time be added to the solving of old problems. At this step, articulating a vision and a direction for progress is very helpful, as is experimentation. But experiments should be small to reduce risk. Learning also starts slowly but builds until the organization becomes skilled at developing new skills and advantages. It is at this point that teamwork should be introduced.

Leverage

"The final stage is leveraging advantages and maintaining momentum. As the organization grows in competitive strength, it can expand the sphere of its operations into new markets, new products, and new parts of the value chain." Tools to accomplish the leveraging include acquisitions, mergers, strategic alliances, or internal development. The speed of expansion must not be too great that it stifles innovation.

These four steps are not discrete stages. They merge into one another. The process tends to be messy, a characteristic of most complex organizations. It may also have to happen more than once.

Rejuvenation happens in loops of learning. Like the samba, there may be one step back and two steps forward . This is what happens in simplification and building. In the early stages of renewal, cutting may have to be radical. In building, progress happens best in small iterations. Those spread the risk. Steps can get bigger as rejuvenation occurs. Small steps also help to encourage an entrepreneurial culture.

GALVANIZING THE TOP TEAM

Mature organizations may have flashes or pockets of entrepreneurship, but they need commitment from top management to make the needed connections. Initial moves are often made by a new CEO, but building a team ensures continuity if someone leaves. These teams should span all functions to maximize their intuition. This typically also involves the organization's power brokers, who otherwise could slow things down.

An effective top team avoids vacillation, extraneous outsiders and quick fixes. All members of the team must share an understanding of the problem and the need to engage in concerted action to solve it.

Sensing the need to start

It is difficult to sense crisis, and even more difficult to recognize opportunity. Vague signals may evoke nothing more than general concern and tinkering with symptoms. More precise signals may provoke nothing more than this because of a lack of shared will to respond. If the signal does not seem urgent, managers may put it aside to deal with other problems. If it seems too urgent, management may be paralyzed by the needed complexity of response.

Even competitive analysis can lead to complacency. Competitors may be doing better than the firm is on some measures, but not all. Many aspects of poor performance can be excused: "It's not our fault." Competitor benchmarking analyses can even be used to justify the status quo: "If what others are doing were even possible, we'd be doing it too." Mature organizations are often trapped by the illusion of accounting profits. The latter are of necessity based on the past, not the future.

Successful rejuvenators develop measures that create a sense of urgency early. A broader scorecard, balanced between financial and nonfinancial goals, seems likelier to lead to success. It would help anticipate where trouble might start by amplifying signals that warn of danger and dampening signals that tend toward complacency.

Triggers for action

Sensing doom does not seem to be as effective an action trigger as falling profits are. While difficult, it is possible and desirable for a firm to anticipate a crisis before becoming debilitated by it. The earlier the message is understood, the better. Getting the message from inside (e.g., a manager or shareholder) is better than getting it from outside (e.g., customers or suppliers). Anticipating a crisis allows response at much lower cost than responses after the onset of crisis. Actions which appear in retrospect to have been low risk may at the time have seemed very risky.

Empowering management

Another necessary condition for rejuvenation is a top team that believes it has the power and responsibility to do something. The team must take a systemic look and avoid quick fixes. "The top team must also appreciate that it does not have to know all the answers before it can act. Its job is to chart the direction ahead and enlist the aid of others in finding durable solutions." This appreciation typically comes gradually.

Blame is often fastened on outside factors like "the environment, poor demand, overfussy customers, adverse exchange rates, even the weather." Sometimes previous management regimes are blamed. All this blaming misses an important point—only the top team has the responsibility and the ability to get the organization out of its mess.

It is also quite common for management teams to point to particular functions as the problem. This is naive. Organizations are complex systems with many interrelated parts. It is the system that is typically at fault.

CHOOSING EFFECTIVE ACTION

Teams trying to rejuvenate a firm have tried many approaches: lots of data gathering, lots of experimentation, examining how other firms have done it. But false paths and blind alleys can seduce these teams into thinking they've made progress.

"The steps we suggest mark out the most effective path of action are in stark contrast to other actions we observed." Simplification involves cutting to the core. Building creates the foundation for corporate entrepreneurship; it requires an extended time perspective. The approaches discussed below fail to address key issues effectively.

Scrap everything and start afresh

The firm should save what is of value. Only if all else fails should an organization be extinguished.

Seeking outside support

This is not a viable substitute for internal action. Firms have a duty to lobby government, but not to the extent that other actions are paralyzed.

Top-down directives that address symptoms, not causes

This can lead to discouragement of corporate entrepreneurship and unhealthy vacillation between extreme directives issued by top management.

Going for the big hit

Making large-scale investments in state-of-the-art technology and systems at initial stages of the process is rarely effective. It is a kind of quick fix that commits the firm to a long-term course of action that may not be the right one. Adding much new capital equipment without an increase in skill base courts disaster. These *can* pay off once the firm has built its entrepreneurial capabilities.

Culture change programs without corresponding action

This sends a signal that there is no immediate crisis. Culture may need to change, but not at the expense of taking no action. In a crisis, immediate action is a crucial necessity.

The quick fix: TQM or process reengineering

Almost all rejuvenators do TQM, but not in a quick fix way. Instead, they make a considerable investment of time, energy and effort. They make sure to acquire the needed skills. TQM and reengineering require persistence and patience.

THE WAY FORWARD

What is needed is to galvanize a top team committed to action. Critical choices need to be made about strategic scope. Entrepreneurship must be built. North American managers tend to favor top-down approaches with lots of specification. In Europe "those whose job it was to look after a whole portfolio often preferred to work on encouraging managers to embrace the values of creativity, innovation, and challenge to conventions without specifying the actions or processes." Setting challenging targets in these circumstances often leads to more durable change. It is not clear which is the better approach. But "real transformation of a business cannot begin in earnest without the recognition by its top managers that a new direction must be found."

Discussion Questions

1. What is the key point of the "crescendo" metaphor?

The authors believe that too many managers intent on organizational rejuvenation try to do too much too quickly. A crescendo must be reached only after a long, gradual increase in volume. Just as a symphony will reach its climax only after a long introduction, so should an organization bent on rejuvenation go into high gear only after it has built its capacity to do so.

2. Why is it so important to galvanize the top team?

This is so important that the authors devote much of the reading to it. Whether they realize it or not, organizations that need rejuvenation are facing a crisis. It may come soon, or it may come later, but it *will* come. The top team in such an organization must share an understanding of the seriousness of this situation, and must be prepared to *act* on it, not just think about it. Moreover, it must be prepared to act in a way that emphasizes action that will help in the short term but especially help in the long term. A top team that is not galvanized to walk this tightrope will surely fail.

3. What is the point of simplifying?

The top team must quickly identify what are the core areas for organizational action. Once those have been identified, they must be emphasized above all other possible activities. This will strengthen the core in a time of crisis, it will free up resources from extraneous activities to allow greater focus on the core, and it will help all stakeholders, inside and outside the company, get a sense that things are happening. But the authors point out that simplification can be only a temporary thing.

4. What is the significance of building?

Simplifying can be only temporary. *Building* is what will carry the organization into a durably successful future. In addition to solving old problems better, building must be about finding new challenges. It should also be about experimentation, but only at times when the organization has the ability to learn from the inevitable downs that will come with the ups of experimentation. Lastly, it is during this stage that the company should implement teamwork. This is a difficult organizational process to put in place, but successfully done it can lead to enduring success.

5. How does leverage fit into the rejuvenation model?

Leverage is, in a sense, the crescendo. After the building process has created a solid foundation of new advantages, the company must use them to create even more advantages and even more success. It is only after going through the painstaking processes of galvanizing, simplifying and building that the organization is ready to reach a peak and really try to stretch itself.

6. What is the point of the section on "Sensing the need to start?"

The authors catalogue a host of excuses that top managers use to avoid concluding that an urgent situation is at hand. Here is a partial listing: The problem is temporary. We must move slowly to avoid upsetting the existing order. It is someone else's fault that we are in trouble. The problems lie in specific areas of the organization; they are not widespread. The financial figures tell us what is wrong.

Most of these excuses are prescriptions for continued problems. Difficulties may be temporary, but many are likely to become chronic. Action-oriented change must be undertaken since the situation is urgent. Blaming others is unproductive since we are the ones responsible for improving the situation. (It is also often the case that a bad situation is of our own doing.) Urgent, crisis-like situations are rarely caused by the mistakes of a subset of the organization. It is usually the system that is at fault. Lastly, too many firms overrely on financial figures. Those can tell only about the past. A firm in need of rejuvenation needs to look to the future.

7. In this book we have looked at methods for competitive analysis. Yet in this reading the authors say that competitive analysis can be used as an excuse for inaction. How can that be?

In any competitive analysis a firm is likely to find that some competitors are performing better, but also that some are performing worse. While the former situation may cause alarm, the latter may cause a false sense of complacency. Even competitive benchmarking can be problematic. One firm identified a competitor's practice as so unlikely that "if it was so great we'd be doing it too." The lesson is that if a company does competitive analysis, it must take the results to heart and use them to galvanize rejuvenating action.

8. What is at the heart of the authors' criticisms of TQM and reengineering?

The authors do not dismiss the value of these tools out of hand, but point out two caveats. First, firms should not throw away everything they have done, which is often the prescription with TQM and reengineering. Instead, by using simplification, firms should save what is of value. Second, TQM and reengineering are too often seen as quick fixes. Undertaken with patience and persistence, they hold good promise. But undertaken in the wrong spirit, they will undermine the rejuvenation process, a process that requires the firm to build its capabilities methodically, reaching a crescendo slowly, not quickly.

SECTION III CASES

Overview

During the late 1980s and early 1990s, Sony Corporation purchased both CBS Records and Columbia Pictures Entertainment, Inc. The case presents a clear overview as to why Sony made these strategic moves and some of the problems it encountered in implementation. The entertainment industry provides a marvelous vehicle for discussing the management of creative intellect (in the music and movie industry). The case can be developed as an acquisitions strategy case, an organization case, or a case on the complexities of managing creative intellect. All three blend well. The case ends with Sony Entertainment in trouble. Although students may quickly conclude that Sony "never should have bought these entertainment businesses," the question remains, "How could Sony participate in the high margin portions of its businesses?" Its electro-mechanical consumer products have increasingly become highly competitive commodities. It has suffered by not being able to control the distribution of the "value producing software" on its devices. The end of the case leaves open where should Sony go in the future.

Session Structure

We usually open the case by asking what problems Sony was attempting to resolve with these acquisitions. Then we ask whether it paid too much, and how one would evaluate a purchase price under these circumstances? We then ask what should Sony have done differently in trying to manage its movie and records businesses? In that process, we ask what are the critical factors one can control in these two industries? How does one establish control for these elements? How did Sony fail to do so? How should the acquisitions have been organized relative to the old Sony products divisions? What strategic controls should have been put in place and why? How could one have brought about the synergies that Sony sought? If one looks at the numbers carefully, Sony could have made very substantial profit gains on its acquisition. The long-term payoff from the portfolio of software that Sony purchased is yet to be determined. How can financial analysts evaluate the value of such assets? How can one evaluate the potentials of a contract with Michael Jackson or Pink Floyd? Can a large corporation manage such creative endeavors? If not, then how do the film companies (like Warner Brothers or Disney) do so? The case tends to be great fun. It's biggest problem is in getting students beyond "second guessing" and thinking creatively about how Sony "could have" managed this operation to success.

The Acquisitions

We generally start the case by asking, why did Sony make these two acquisitions? What were its basic strategic reasons? Using some data summaries from the Sony Innovation case and the financials of Sony Entertainment, one can discern the following trends. (1) Margins on hardware are decreasing. Hardware items are becoming essentially commodities requiring high R&D support, high risk, and low potential gains. (2) Because of the Sony strategy of continuous innovation, its profits are very volatile, depending primarily upon the recent introduction of a high profile new product. (See Exhibit 1.) (3) Value-added has shifted from hardware to software and Sony wishes to participate in this value creation. (4) Sony was stopped or delayed in making certain significant hardware innovations by lack of a software distribution and support structure. This was notably true for VTRs, CDs, and DAT (digital audio tapes). (5) Sony needed to move its value-producing operations overseas because of the growing strength of the yen and the risk it was exposed to in world marketplaces. It particularly wanted to enhance its position in the United States. because of the high technology, low cost, and "lead market" nature of the U.S. marketplace. All of these are very reasonable strategic considerations and should be placed in front of the students at the beginning of the case.

How could one justify this acquisition on a financial basis? The CBS Records acquisition looks quite reasonable. Even without income enhancement, CBS Records was earning an average of about $135 million per year over the last five years. Assuming a purchase price of $2 billion, this converted to a 14.8 P/E multiple. Successful management of CBS Records could easily make it into a good financial investment. However, one should ask, "How can purchasers analyze the potentials of the unknown and volatile future earnings in this business?" Clearly, most of the value of the acquisition will depend upon its management after purchase.

Was the $3.4 billion for Columbia Pictures Entertainment a reasonable offer? Clearly one has to look beyond the history of profits and cash flow to answer that question. Even a generous five-year averaging of profits (1985-89) would yield only $35 million per year, requiring a 100 X price earnings ratio to justify the purchase. One should question whether this is a valid basis for evaluation. If not, what should be used? How does one place a value on a portfolio of old movies? Certainly, Sony had to recognize that Columbia Pictures did not have a strong stream of new releases to provide profits in the next few years. Consequently, it was likely to be three years before strong profitability could be obtained. Probably the best way to evaluate Columbia Pictures' value would be to run a cash flow analysis on the likely yields from each of the pictures in its portfolio. Then one would have to multiply that profitability by an appropriate P/E ratio. If one looks at the 45 X P/E ratio Viacom had paid in its acquisitions, one would have to expect only $80 million in average annual earnings. Is this a reasonable expectation? Looked at in this fashion, one could easily conclude that the risk of the Sony acquisition was relatively minimal. It could sell off the division later if necessary. The key problem is how to manage the acquisition.

One can then focus again on strategic fit. How could one manage Sony Entertainment to improve stability, grow profits, and capture higher margins than those available on hardware? What will it take for Sony Entertainment to improve hardware margins? Improve Sony's innovation process by closer coordination with the marketplace? Provide software leverage for Sony in new markets? Can it use Sony Entertainment strategically as a sensor of impending changes in the marketplace? To protect profits through copyrighting and the uniqueness of the talent on the copyrighted material? To increase prices more easily as inflation occurs? To decentralize Sony away from its Japanese manufacturing base? Properly developed in these terms, the Sony Entertainment acquisitions could make strategic sense.

Implementation

Hence the real question is implementation. How can a large corporation manage such creative endeavors? Students will tend to say that they cannot. However, one can instantly ask how it is that Disney, Warner Brothers, MGM, ABC, etc., have been able to do so?

How does one think about strategy in this circumstance? How can Sony create unique value? Clearly, it has the potential of deep pockets. This allows it to play statistical games that independent producers cannot. It could potentially lock in directors and artists with long-term contracts. It has the Loews' distribution system which allows some stability in a volatile marketplace. It can leverage any successful movie or record in its other operations. For example, a hit song can be used in movies and the hit song of movies can be published for release. Successful songs can be used in advertising Sony products to obtain double value. The note from the *Economist* on "sunk costs, the hit rule, nobody knows anything, and talent and hunch" suggests that ordinary marketing research is not very useful in this kind of marketplace. Instead, success is dependent on people selection, concept selection, limiting risk, rolling the dice often enough, and leveraging successes. One can ask a series of questions to bring out these points.

1. Where can Sony Corporation add value? What would be the distinct competency of Sony Entertainment in its marketplaces?

2. What kind of concept should it support? Should it emulate the Disney strategy?

3. What are the strategic controls the Corporation should maintain? (Suggestion: concept, culture, people, portfolio selection, and resource limits.)

4. Why is there no written strategy? Should there have been one? How would you use it? How would you keep a written strategy up to date? Is it needed?

5. How does one play a very low probability, unknown payoff game? (Suggestions: produce enough products to average risks, keep production costs low, choose books with high recognition, choose a few known box office draws as actors in each movie, avoid high budget movies like *Water World*, provide profit incentives, select and concentrate on some relatively profitable or stable markets (kids' movies, clean movies for seniors, musicals, or sophisticated comedies.)

6. How can Sony offset some major risks? Copying? Piracy? Big budgets? (Suggestion: a portfolio strategy with a number of small-but-sure pictures coupled with a few high profile (book, actor, director) pictures each year. This can stabilize incomes and allow upside potential. But even hits must be budget controlled.)

7. What can be planned? (Suggestion: atmosphere, number of releases, people selection, communication, incentives, style, portfolio, timing, sequence.)

8. How should Sony Entertainment be organized? Around a few key producers? A star stable? A starburst organization?

9. What type of motivation system should be used? In movies, profits are so hard to determine that shares of gross are normal. Could Sony change this incentive structure? It needs incentives to control costs, to share risks, and to encourage quality and continuing longevity of successes. How can these be instituted?

10. What kind of coordination-communication is needed with headquarters? Why did Ohga and Schulhoff operate the way they did? How would you have changed this? Can a movie business be run on a tight leash from abroad? If not, what should have been done?

The core question is how can one manage in a low probability, highly unpredictable, intellect and talent-oriented marketplace? This is precisely the same question that one runs into in managing a group of venture capitalists, investment bankers, software developers, scientific researchers, etc. The students should not be allowed to avoid the question by simply saying, "Sony did it badly." They have to say exactly what should have been done differently. After all, Sony did pick two very successful high profile producers to head its movie operations. It did choose Mickey Schulhoff who knew the Sony operation yet understood America quite well. Mr. Ohga was a well-known figure in the entertainment world and understood its complexities well. Precisely, what could have been done differently?

Organization

A. There are a host of interesting organizational questions. How did Sony Entertainment fit with the old Sony culture? Should the Sony culture have been transferred to Sony Entertainment? What elements of culture were important? How could they be shared? Managed? What else should Mr. Ohga have done?

B. Why did Sony develop the two headquarters? What were its advantages? Disadvantages? How can one develop new businesses across two such diverse cultures. What should have been done to develop the synergies between products and software? Why did Sony try to avoid contact between its product and software groups in the early stages? How would it have avoided dominance of the old Sony culture if it had not? How could Sony use its software groups to better guide or leverage its hardware groups?

C. What organization form should have been used in Sony Entertainment? Should it have formed around a "studio" concept with a starburst of individual pictures using different directors, actors, external financial leverage, and centralized production, film screening, and risk taking? How should the music group be organized? If the key to this business is a person with a "high probability hunch record" how do you find them, incent them, encourage them to work inside a larger organization like Sony? In the music business, should the organization essentially be inverted? The rock stars or musical talents are the key driving force. Shouldn't they be allowed to dictate almost everything concerning their product? If not, what should Sony control? How would you arrange this balance with the rock stars? How does one control such volatile talent? We often ask, "How do you control Pink Floyd?"

D. How can one use the Loews Theaters to advantage? Could Sony get a significant amount of brand recognition from them? How should it use the chain to differentiate its own movies or stabilize earnings? How would it organize the Loews Theaters? This is a classic situation for an "infinitely flat" organization. Should there be any coordination between the theater chain and the entertainment producing groups?

E. How should Sony organize to take advantage of its multimedia capabilities? Perhaps the most interesting uniqueness of Sony Corporation is that it is the only company in the world with a highly creative mechanical-electronic product group, entertainment producing capabilities, and entertainment distribution capabilities. How can Sony leverage these to advantage? How can it use the software talents in the U.S. to help guide or facilitate multimedia development? It is a cliché in innovation that one should involve users to the maximum extent possible. If this is true, then why wouldn't Sony's ownership of entertainment units be a major advantage for its product innovators? If the stock market is valuing integrated distribution, entertainment, and software producing companies highly as it has in other marketplaces (like telecommunications), then why wouldn't Sony's concept work?

F. What should the overall structure of Sony look like? Assuming that it stays in various aspects of the software business as an essential component of its entry into multimedia, how should the software business be organized? If it does not make its own software, how can it share in the value from that created by others? Should Sony organize on a "product basis worldwide"? Regionally? On an "open network basis"? In a hybrid form? Ask the students to draw a proposed organization chart for Sony. This can be quite interesting.

Strategic Controls

This is a good point to bring out the strategic controls idea. Whenever a company has a very different older core competency and wants to move to a new core competency—or a combined one—how can it both allow desirable decentralization, yet maintain adequate control? The keys lie in the following areas:

1. Values or concept control: The creation of a thoroughly shared vision, which provides a check on concepts of new products before they are released.

2. Goal control: This is obtained by thorough agreement on goals sought and measures of success. There should be multiple goals for growth, profits, risk, stability, integrity, image, innovation, productivity, style, etc. If values and goals are clearly shared and performance measured against them, a high degree of decentralization can be permitted.

3. Clear limits: By setting clear limits on capital, purchase contract, alliance, program expenditure commitments, the corporation can ensure that no smaller unit places the entire corporation at risk. What should these be and how should they be set for Sony Entertainment?

4. Organization structure: Organization structure is itself a control. One can control the size of units, the responsibilities they are allowed, the way they interact, the power of the individuals in each organization over its plans, budgets, and operating commitments. The degree to which the central office overrules unit decisions will determine the actual degree of decentralization.

5. Communications: Close personal and computer communications can allow a high degree of decentralization, if the above structures are in place. Communications are the basis for building trust. Trust is the basis for decentralization. What type of communication system would have been appropriate for Sony Entertainment? Mr. Ogha put a great deal of emphasis on this. What else should he have done?

6. Intelligence systems: The corporation and each of its units needs to have the capacity to sense changing environments, competitive moves, and potential new opportunities and threats. If this is in place at the corporate level it can provide essential information for corporate managers to query their decentralized units, to intervene appropriately, and to maintain control on a timely basis. How should such a structure look for Sony?

7. Motivation systems: People tend to perform against what expectations are set and rewards are received. How should Sony have set up its motivation systems for the entertainment groups? How should these be coordinated with those for the innovation groups in Japan? Should a single entertainer or "hunch manager" be allowed to make more than the CEO of Sony? What kind of balances must one seek among such different units of Sony? How? Why?

8. Selection of key people: This is clearly the most important strategic control in the present setting. How can a Japanese corporate management really do this in a complex American-dominated entertainment world? Was there anything that Sony could have done better? How would one establish a system to select people and monitor their performance? What elements of performance would be important?

These types of strategic controls work very well in dealing with the "unknowable," which is the purpose of strategy in this kind of situation. One cannot predict in this type of a marketplace even a reasonable percentage of the possible events and outcomes. Much depends on culture, people, and motivation systems. Consequently, one must establish a structure of controls that allow high degrees of freedom toward understood goals, and within agreed-upon limits and visions. However, such broad structures are not enough. They must be backed up with very carefully constructed intelligence, feedback, electronic, financial measurement, and personal observation systems. One can ask for each of the kinds of strategic controls outlined above exactly what form of control system is needed to support it.

What Happened

Ultimately, in late 1995, Sony took a $3.2 billion write-off on Sony Entertainment. This was primarily the huge "goodwill" account built up as a result of the purchases, plus a $500 million write-off on films that did not seem likely to cover their costs. Earlier, realizing that Sony Pictures Entertainment had a very desirable asset in its Sony Theaters chain and the potential write-off of its goodwill, Mr. Schulhoff tried to find a partner who needed some tax losses and distribution. Other entertainment-distribution companies were selling at high premiums. However, Mr. Schulhoff was not able to find a buyer as of the time this note is written.

Analysts and critics said that the core problems in Sony Entertainment's development were:

1. Putting Guber and Peters in charge of Sony Pictures Entertainment without adequate controls, and then letting them stay on too long. Guber unfortunately sponsored some very

high cost films, like *Hook* and *Last Action Hero*, which flopped initially. *Hook* may eventually recover its costs in television, tape, and reissue runs.

2. Sony spent too much (over $100 million) on upgrading its physical facilities. In an industry which tends to work on open lots, Mr. Guber's decision to build an expensive art deco production center was a poor investment. Unfortunately, Mr. Guber seemed to have complete control over Sony Pictures Entertainment. Operating very much as Mr. Ohga does—selecting a few key people and then giving them their heads—Schulhoff waited too long to remove Guber and Peters. By then significant damage had been done. Physical facilities' costs and the cost of each individual movie should have been carefully controlled. A portfolio of releases (as suggested above) and a tighter incentive system toward profits could have been helpful.

By 1994, Sony did have some large-scale hits in *Little Women*, *Legends of the Fall*, and *Bad Boys*. Its television programs "Wheel of Fortune," "Days of our Lives," and "Married With Children" were also strong. Nevertheless, Mr. Schulhoff was under extreme pressure to turn the entertainment groups around. Many attributed his slow responses in firing Guber to the practice of giri (or moral obligation) to employees and superiors that was an important portion of Sony's style. Many claim the problem was that Guber was a creative genius, not a manager. Finding someone who understood the picture business, was credible, yet had managerial skills, was the critical problem for Sony. The huge write-off was a major blow to Sony's pride. Plagued by poor health, Mr. Ohga stepped aside in favor of Nobuyuki Idei in mid-1995. Mr. Idei is a marketing person with strong controllership skills.

About this time, Sony's digital video disk was moving to the marketplace. Unfortunately, this time Sony's usual leadership role had been preempted by a coalition of Time Warner and Toshiba which had introduced its own Digital Video Disk player earlier than Sony. Interestingly, digital video disk would have been the ideal collaboration between Sony Pictures Entertainment and the hardware sections of Sony. Sony's version (developed with Philips) could hold 3.7 gigabits of information, enough for 135 minutes of video. Sony said its engineers were devising a way to put a second, semi-transparent layer of data on the same side of the disk which would double its total capacity. Toshiba-Time Warner demonstrated a version that held 5 gigabits on each side. DVD had the potential of revolutionizing the home video industry the same way that CD had revolutionized the home audio market. All of this indicated that Sony had not solved its problems of effective communications between its software divisions and its hardware groups in the design process.

At the end of the case, there is the question, "What should Sony do in the future?" As of this time, no clear lines of strategy or organization have appeared. This leaves the students with a wonderful opportunity for an open-ended strategy development.

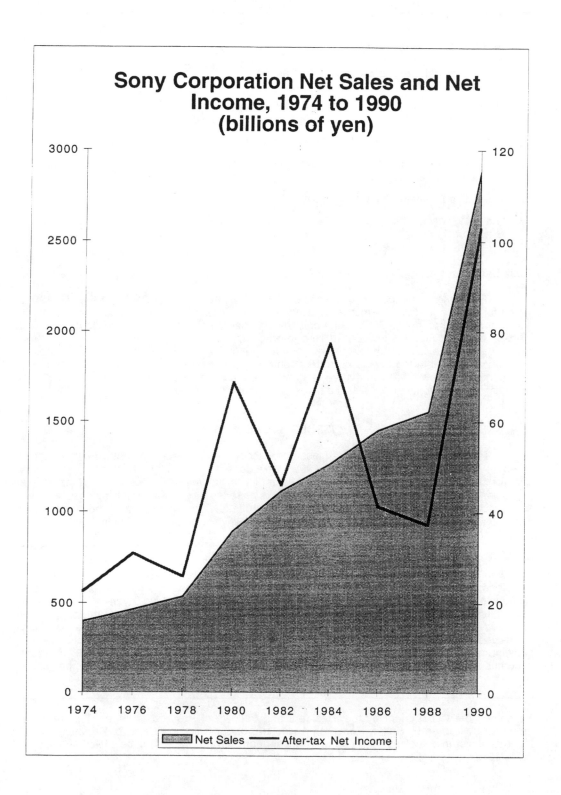

Sony Corporation Net Sales and Net Income, 1974 to 1990 (billions of yen)

Net Sales ▦ After-tax Net Income ▬

THE VANGUARD GROUP, INC. (A) TEACHING NOTE

Assignment Questions

1. Evaluate Vanguard's characteristics as an organization. What are its strengths and vulnerabilities?

2. How is Vanguard like Wal-Mart or Home Depot? How is it different? Do you think Vanguard's market share will continue to grow like Wal-Mart's and Home Depot's or not?

3. How should Fidelity, Dreyfus, T. Rowe Price, and others compete with Vanguard?

4. As Jack Bogle, would you be attempting to develop more in-house Vanguard asset management capability? Or picking outside managers?

5. Would you continue the minimal advertising/promotion strategy?

6. As Jack Bogle, what would you be changing now? What are his biggest risks? His biggest opportunities?

Case Background

The Vanguard Group, Inc. had come a long way since it formed itself in 1974. By 1992, it was a formidable force in the mutual fund industry, noted for its lineup of low cost no-load funds. Vanguard's Chairman and CEO, Jack Bogle, had instilled a tight-fisted culture at the organization, whose non-profit status allowed it to zero in on client returns. Bogle also had emerged as a spokesman for his vision of a "better" mutual fund industry, becoming along the way perhaps the most quoted mutual fund executive in the country, as he argued for more candor on the part of fund companies, lower fees, and more responsible product offerings. Bogle's vision had steadily brought Vanguard to its position as the third largest mutual fund group in the country.

ISSUES ADDRESSED

The case is a useful tool for classroom discussion for three reasons. First, Vanguard faces an interesting set of problems in 1992. How does it continue to advance in the industry? Most of the obvious answers, i.e., raising fees to pay for updating technology, proliferating their products, and developing new distribution networks raise the risk of compromising its ideals. Has the company in fact painted itself into a corner with its low-cost low value-added product line? What steps should Vanguard take to compete with Fidelity and other organizations?

The second important issue raised by the case is how Vanguard will or will not change the landscape of the investment management industry. Money managers charge significant fees based on the premise that they can "beat the market." Most fail to do so, however, but still collect their fees. Not only does Vanguard offer products which help educate the consumer about the real costs of managing money, but Bogle is a willing commentator on a variety of ethical and pricing issues within the money management industry. Thus, Vanguard attracts its core audience—relatively knowledgeable investors who understand pricing and performance claims, but it also threatens to have an impact on mutual fund pricing for other types of clients—less knowledgeable investors more in Merrill Lynch's or Fidelity's sights. As a result, Vanguard becomes an interesting issue for discussion, is this the way the mutual fund industry is heading?

Teaching note © copyright by the President and Fellows of Harvard College. This note was prepared by James E. Sailer, Research Associate, under the supervision of Professor Jay O. Light to assist in the classroom use of The Vanguard Group, Inc. (A) case. [5-294-064 dated 12/10/93]

The third issue to discuss is somewhat related to the second, and it revolves around Vanguard's mission. Bogle, a well-spoken and opinionated man, struggles when explaining Vanguard's mission to the casewriter. Most companies can define their goals in terms of profits for investors or perhaps serving a constituency (the United Way, for example). But what steps to take to serve Vanguard's mission are very unclear. For instance, market share would be used very differently in an organization like Vanguard's; although Bogle's strict dictum is that "Market share is a measure, not a goal. Market share must be earned and not bought," he seems to be of two minds on the issue. At any rate, the questions "How should Vanguard define and fulfill its mission? and Is Vanguard a position force for the money management industry?" are central to understanding the impact Vanguard can and could have.

Placement in Course

The case should be assigned along with "Note on the Mutual Fund Industry: 1992," and may be used in a module with "Merrill Lynch and Company (1986)" and "The Vanguard Group, Inc. (B)." If the instructor intends to use Vanguard (B), the instructor should be careful to keep the (A) case away from particular fund offerings the company should make, instead focusing the discussion around Vanguard's general strategy and business situation.

OUTLINE OF CLASS

The class discussion should focus around getting a complete understanding of Vanguard's current positioning. To do this, the instructor should begin the class by asking a general question, "What are the characteristics of Vanguard?" As students respond, the instructor may utilize the center board for the general characteristics, and utilize side boards for more specific issues. The following are some sample headings and student responses:

The Characteristics of Vanguard (center board)

- pioneers

- drastically alter (ruin?) the industry's pricing structure

- low cost, no load, low fee pricing

- customer service focus, not products or performance

- focus on candor

- technology follower

- little paid advertising or promotion (The case states this, but a follow-up question at some point must be why do they advertise at all? And while they do not advertise as heavily as Fidelity, Dreyfus, or others, they have an ad in *The Wall Street Journal* virtually every day of the year—so clearly advertising is part of their strategy.)
- rely on free press (i.e., *Money* magazine) to promote funds

- plain, vanilla products, which attempt to offer "dependable return"

It is important that the students have a clear understanding of the Vanguard product line. As Exhibit 2 shows, most of Vanguard's business comes from fixed-income instruments, with money market and bond funds together accounting for approximately 63% of total assets under management. The expense ratio for fixed income funds ranged from 21 to 30 basis point, while expense ratios for equity funds ranged from 19 basis points for index funds to 75 basis points for some of the actively managed funds. Similarly, nearly all of the fixed income funds were managed internally (Wellington Management had remained manager of just five taxable bond funds), while Vanguard managed only the index products on the equity side.

In many ways, Vanguard's fixed-income business was different from its equity fund business. Since bond fund yields vary less than equity fund yields, the bond fund business was perhaps more suited to Vanguard's low-cost, low value-added approach. Investors in equity funds, however, tended to seek higher volatility and higher returns. Vanguard's funds, especially its lineup of index funds (which had almost a quarter of equity fund assets) promised decidedly average or "predictable" results compared with some of the more actively managed funds offered by its competitors. Since Vanguard outsourced the advisory capacities for many of its equity funds, it also had less control over expenses, which, for its bond funds, is a primary focus.

Students who do not scrutinize the Vanguard product offerings and/or deeply think through the implications of its low cost strategy many not see the distinctions between the two businesses.

Vulnerabilities in the Future

- competition from others, i.e., Fidelity's Spartan line

- Vanguard has painted itself into a corner, where the only way to improve is by offering lower and lower fee products—but how much more can they be lowered?

- distribution difficulties—will Vanguard pay to become part of an automated teller system, for instance?

- sophisticated niche is their only niche

- management succession—why are his top employees so young? Will the organization be able to keep the same focus when he leaves?

- what if money market fund has a default on one of its payments and the net asset value falls below $1? Vanguard has no capital reserves to cover the fund, as others have done

- given the fact that they certainly do not pay Fidelity scale wages, how will they be able to attract top quality personnel?

- in a down market, will people flee index funds?

- does the fact that they are a technology follower doom them to poorer service and a reputation for being "behind the times?"

- poor relationships with money managers, especially Wellington

Performance

- growing rapidly (Exhibit 5)

- market share also increasing, although equity fell in 1990 (Exhibit 6)

- economies of scale means lower average fees in future

- have cornered the market on the low fee game—huge barriers to entry before someone else could try to compete with them

- customer service ratings are excellent, even though their technology lags

- funds consistently perform well on a long-term basis

- similar to Wal-Mart in that Vanguard was the first low cost provider of broad product line on the block, but Vanguard does not have geographical advantages Wal-Mart possesses—when Wal-Mart moves into a region, no one can compete, but Vanguard has no physical region

Missed Opportunities

- overseas funds

Vanguard's Mission

- serve shareholders (if their mission is to serve existing shareholders, then why do they allow new shareholders when Bogle admits size is such a concern?)

- bring price competition to industry

- Bogle's revenge on industry which fired him (A fact not in the case is that Bogle's firing from Wellington Management came when he was recuperating from one of his heart attacks)

- Bogle as Ralph Nader? Vanguard as Ben and Jerry's?

- beat other companies (a la Horatio Nelson)

- make money for executives by driving expenses down

The Response of the Competition

To set up this discussion, a comparison of funds of essentially equivalent character may be listed on the board. The numbers capture a great deal of the competitive situation among the "big three."

U.S. Government Securities Funds

Fund	Management Fee	Total Annual Expenses	Load
Fidelity	.30+	.70	0
Merrill Lynch	.30-.50	.78	4.0
Vanguard	.008 (at cost)	.26	0

At this point, the instructor should elicit opinions of how Vanguard's competitors have responded and should respond to Vanguard.

Merrill Lynch

<u>Characteristics</u>

- seller of convenience to unknowledgeable investors

- fees and loads are 200% of profits

- high fee, extensive branch network organization

- mostly undistinguished equity products, and some popular fixed income products

<u>Response</u>

- must continue to emphasize customer service staff

- keep playing to its strength

- will probably have to lower fees/loads as price competition eats away at its market share, but milk it until then

- lower fees now to forestall losing business?

Fidelity

<u>Characteristics</u>

- powerful marketing machine

- strategy: have lots of funds, some of them will prosper, and then promote them heavily through print and television advertisements (a stark contrast to Vanguard's promotion—when Health Care fund goes well, Bogle writes to shareholders and tells them to be careful about buying it)

- strong belief in stock picking

- heavily research-oriented, "kick the tires" operation

- funds to meet nearly every conceivable wish of fundholders (except international?)

<u>Response</u>

- introduced Spartan line

- opening retail stores around the country

- leading edge in technology, distribution

- continue to focus on "star" system—portfolio managers with big names (Lynch, Smith, Vinik) to attract clients and highlight differences with indexer Vanguard

- begin to offer more quantitative offerings and continue with specialized product lines

While the comparison of government security funds in enlightening, the students should be reminded that price isn't everything. When only 40% of customers know whether they have a load or a no-load fund there is a substantial argument to be made the price is not the prime, or even the primary, consideration for fundholders. Expense ratios, in fact, rank behind performance, reputation of fund manager, and the number of funds managed by a firm as criteria for individuals' selection of funds. Clearly, Merrill Lynch and Fidelity have been squeezed by Vanguard, and each has had to lower fees or loads, or offer new low fee products, but it is not at all clear that the lowest price will be the sole, or even the most important—differentiator in the future.

Vanguard's Course

At this point, the students should focus on the decision point of the case, and offer strategies for Vanguard to follow going forward. The diversions into Merrill Lynch and Fidelity should have given the class some understanding of the competitive climate Vanguard is facing. The following are possible student suggestions for Vanguard's strategy:

Strategy for Vanguard

- continue to drive down costs and pass the savings along to shareholders

- drive costs down and use the money for advertising and technology

- raise fees by a few basis points and use the money for advertising

- divert some resources toward helping clients make asset allocation decisions

- go after 401(k) market, the last real opportunity for growth

- offer more differentiated product line

EPILOGUE

Not long after the case was published, Vanguard came out with a new product, the so-called "Admiral" line of funds. The four Admiral funds were Treasury funds of differing lengths, with expense ratios of 15 basis points for investors with $50,000 or more. Bogle made clear his intention to drive cost and expenses down, and also emphasized he's content with being a technology follower.

Bogle's initial public statements about the Admiral line came in a closed-door meeting of wealthy Vanguard investors held in Boston, just a few blocks from Fidelity headquarters. News of the meeting, and Bogle's announcement, were leaked to the media, and Vanguard publicly announced the new funds were "a shot across the bow" at rival Fidelity.

Overview

The Battle for Paramount case is very timely. It brings out the convoluted considerations one sees in the current wave of telecommunications mergers. It provides an excellent discussion vehicle for both the processes of takeover and the analytics underlying takeovers. The case presents a lively history of the offers and counter offers made for Paramount Communications, Inc. (PCI) and the interactions of the personalities involved on both sides. It raises many questions about how one can evaluate an acquisition candidate, and how this evaluation might differ for various suitors. It also poses some fundamental questions about the nature of economies of scale in the new information marketplace.

Session Structure

One can open with the question "What is the intrinsic value of Paramount?" This could lead to a discussion of what its likely profit and present value potentials would be if operated under current management. Second, one can ask what is its special value to each of its major suitors? Why does Viacom want it? Why does QVC want it? What could their capabilities add to its value? How do the personalities of Sumner Redstone, Barry Diller, and John Malone affect the situation? Why do they keep upping the ante? What would have been an optimum strategy for each party? How would each have implemented the acquisition, if consummated? Why did the bidders use the various financial instruments described? What should Mr. Diller and Mr. Redstone do at the end of the case? Why? The case is an unusual opportunity to look at various aspects of diversification, power, and strategy in a highly "unknowable" marketplace like entertainment and telecommunications.

Competitive Maneuvers

The best way to open this case is to ask; What is the "intrinsic value" of Paramount Communications? This involves a relatively standard financial analysis of Paramount's past and projected cash flows, an appropriate risk discount, and the application of a reasonable P/E multiple to determine the value of the acquisition to any given party. Once this is done, the class should explore the series of competitive maneuvers, ultimately resolved by the relative attractiveness to each of the bidders. Note this attractiveness varies based on the "intended synergies" that the buyer brings to the merger. It also hinges on the personalities of the key players. By walking through the acquisition sequence step by step and asking at each step, "What was going on here? Why did the parties act this way?" the professor can bring out many intriguing issues about merger and acquisition techniques. This teaching note provides a summary of the sequence of events from which the professor can raise Why? Why not? issues. Next is a profile of each company and its leader which allows an analysis of what the "synergistic values" were to each company and the power issues it posed for its CEO. Finally, there is a summary sheet on what actually happened at the end of the case and a clear statement of "lessons" from the case. By looking at the latter, the professor can target specific questions in the discussion of the sequence of events leading up to the merger (i.e., the whys and why nots suggested above).

VIACOM-PARAMOUNT MERGER
TIMELINE

7/93   A deal for a merger between PCI and Viacom almost closed but collapsed over price

9/9/93   Merger between PCI and Viacom discussed at PCI's board meeting

9/13/93   Viacom acquisition of PCI for $8.2 billion announced. Bid was $69.14 per share ($9.10/share in cash). Other suitors expected (Diller/Malone). For each of 118.5 million shares Viacom to pay 0.1 share of Class A, 0.9 share of B, and $9.10 cash. Offer contained no price protection. Cash raised through $1.5 billion in bank debt.

9/14/93   PCI and Viacom said they would seek investment of major regional telephone company. Spurned offer from Southwestern Bell Corp. (valued its cable systems at $2.4 billion). Diller considered a bid while the value of the deal falls from $8.2 billion to $7.7 billion thanks to the drop in Viacom's share price.

9/21/93   Diller and QVC offered $9.5 billion or $80 per share for PCI. Deal included $30 in cash and 0.893 shares of QVC then trading at $56 per share.

            • Viacom bid had fallen to $63.175 per share from $69.14 originally ($7.5 billion).
            • Financing: QVC had $6 billion in borrowing capacity and PCI had $1 billion in cash. To cover debt service, QVC had free cash flow (EB,I,T, depreciation /amortization) of >$200 million. Also Walt Disney Co. expressed an interest in buying some PCI assets.
            • A possibility existed of teaming with Turner Broadcasting System, Inc. or TBS might make a bid of their own (this was doubtful considering the decision of Comcast and Liberty to back Diller).
            • By allowing PCI to be acquired, Davis had effectively put PCI "in play."
            • Partners: Comcast and Liberty each agreed to purchase $500 million in QVC convertible preferred at $65.45 per share (initial dividend 6.5% and switches to 7.5%). The stock was convertible to QVC common when QVC common reached $100 per share.

9/22/93   Viacom offer was down to $7.2 billion ($60.56 per share); PCI's stock surged by 10% ($7.25); QVC ended the day up 12.5 cents. This could be interpreted two ways:

            • The market thought Diller could add more value to PCI than Redstone.
            • The market did not think QVC could win.

            At this point, of course, Redstone could have taken his $100 million, picked up his option on 20% of PCI, and sold to Diller at $80 per share.

9/23/93   Redstone vowed not to change the value of his bid. Cast doubt about the QVC financing.

9/24/93   Viacom filed an antitrust lawsuit against QVC, Liberty Media, and TCI. Singled out John Malone as causing injury to Viacom and consumers of cable services. Stock market, antitrust lawyers, and QVC were unimpressed. Allegations:

            • Without TCI, programmers cannot gain "critical mass."
            • Refusing to renegotiate with Showtime and Movie Channel in an effort to force Showtime into merger with Encore.

9/29/93   Home Shopping Network put merger with QVC on back burner until PCI bid was clarified.

9/29/93   Viacom said to be far along in talks with Cox Enterprises Inc. and Southwestern Bell Corporation.

- Planned to buy convertible preferred for cash. Viacom needed $2 billion to match QVC offer.
- The lack of voting control could be a stumbling block.
- Cox and SW Bell were partners in phone and cable service in Britain.

9/30/93   Disney agreed to license 350 of coming movies to Encore for more than $1 billion ending its relationship with Showtime. Encore got rights to Touchstone and Hollywood Pictures from 1997-2003. Encore also got 10-year access rights to Miramax Films starting in 1994.

9/30/93   Blockbuster Entertainment Corp. agreed to buy convertible preferred stock at $70 per share (convertible to Viacom class B) for a total investment of $600 million; dividend of 5% and redeemable in 5 years. Although the parties hailed the agreement as a long-term strategic relationship, a provision allowed either party to cut the investment in half if the PCI-Viacom deal did not go through by August 1994. Blockbuster's Chairman, H. Wayne Huizenga, joined the Viacom board.

9/30/93   Chemical bank agreed to supply $800 million to $1 billion for QVC and raise the remaining amount from other lenders. $3 billion total financing effort.

10/5/93   NYNEX agreed to infuse Viacom with $1.2 billion by purchasing convertible preferred at $70 per share. NYNEX would not get a management role but did get 24 months to form a strategic alliance with Viacom in which VIA will not talk to other Baby Bells.

10/6/93   Herbert Allen presented Felix Rohatyn bank commitments for $3 billion in loans to QVC. Speculation: (1) QVC or VIA could boost bid by offering protection to PCI shareholders against stock price drops. (2) Some think QVC might launch tender offer buying majority of shares with cash and the remainder with stock or other securities.

10/8/93   TCI agreed to purchase Liberty for about $3.8 billion in stock after which Malone will control 20% and Magness will control 28%. Reasons:

- New regulations by FCC to limit vertical integration were less than expected.
- It was necessary to retain TCI position as powerful player amid consolidations.
- The move could mask expected losses by Encore of $100 million.

10/11/93   Late on October 10th, BellSouth was described as close to a decision to invest between $500 million and $1.2 billion in QVC.

10/12/93   PCI directors authorized the company to begin "informational discussions" to evaluate QVC's offer.

10/13/93   BellAtlantic Corp. announced plans to acquire TCI for stock valuing TCI at $16 billion (approx. $35 per share). In addition, it would take on TCI's $10.3 billion in debt. Plan was to pursue the interactive video future.

- Co-chairmen: Malone and Raymond Smith (current chair of BellAtlantic).
- Malone would end up with $1 billion of BellAtlantic stock and Magness would own $1.6 billion.
- TCI would get 5 of 15 seats on the board.
- Together they could be worth $33 billion including stock and debt.
- TCI might have to sell off cable systems in the BellAtlantic region due to federal law.

566

10/13/93	BellSouth Corp. was expected to announce acquisition of 22.5% of Prime Management Co., an Austin, TX-based cable operator with 500,000 customers.
10/18/93	Cox Enterprises Inc. and Advance Publications Inc. agreed to invest in QVC on the same terms as Comcast and Liberty Media. Each would do the following:

- Purchase $250M million of QVC common at $60 per share.
- Purchase $250 million of convertible exchangeable preferred stock with 6% stock or cash dividend, convertible at $65.45/common share.

10/21/93	QVC delivered a proposed acquisition agreement to Paramount.
10/22/93	QVC announced a two-tier takeover strategy valued at $9.5 billion boosting the cash portion of its offer to $40 per share:

- Cash tender offer for 51% of PCI stock at $80 per share.
- QVC stock for the remaining 49% valued at $80.71 per share.

10/25/93	Viacom matched QVC's bid with a two-tier offer valued at $9.4 billion (QVC's bid had dropped to $9.4B):

- Cash tender offer for 51% of PCI stock at $80 per share.
- A package of securities valued at $80 per share for the remaining 49%. (0.20408 shares Class A, 1.08317 shares Class B, and 0.20408 share convertible exchangeable preferred).

10/27/93	Paramount and Criss-Craft announced plans to launch Paramount Network in January 1995. Management said the plan would not be affected by a PCI merger. QVC launched its tender offer announced the previous Friday thus Viacom had a two-day headstart. The offers expired on November 24 and 22, respectively.
10/29/93	QVC amended a previous lawsuit filed in Delaware Chancery Court which had asked to delay Viacom's offer until QVC obtained regulatory approvals. The new features requested that the court block the Viacom tender offer because Paramount did not talk to QVC before allowing Viacom to amend its offer. In addition, QVC took issue with the poison-pill anti-takeover defense.
11/2/93	Time Warner and Tribune Television announced plans to launch WB Network in August 1994.
11/2/93	Paramount received October 28 letter from Mr. Diller indicating he was willing to discuss all aspects of the merger if PCI would allow QVC to compete on a "level playing field." QVC received October 29 letter from Donald Oresman, PCI general counsel, saying Paramount was ready to meet.
11/4/93	Viacom received commitments for $4.5 million in financing including a $1 billion bridge loan should regulatory matters delay the $1.2 billion NYNEX investment.
11/6/93	Viacom increased its bid by $5 per share from $78.72 to $83.72 ($85 cash for 51%).
11/10/93	Viacom added Comcast Corp. as a defendant in its antitrust lawsuit against TCI and further alleged that the proposed BellAtlantic acquisition was anticompetitive in nature.
11/10/93	Paramount won the bankruptcy auction for MacMillan with a bid of $552.8 million.
11/11/93	TCI was said to be interested in Matsushita's MCA unit because of antitrust issues surrounding Liberty's stake in QVC.

11/11/93   BellSouth agreed to invest $1.5 billion in QVC for a 14% stake and a place in the three-way partnership that controls QVC while Liberty agreed to divest its stake:

- BellSouth to pay $1 billion for new common stock and replaced the $500 million investment of Liberty.
- Liberty to sell its 14% stake on the open market or to QVC at $60 per share.
- If the bid fails, Liberty to keep its stake and BellSouth to invest $500 million.

11/12/93   QVC increased offer to $90 per share for 51% and common and preferred stock valued at $76.92 for the remainder. Total value was $10.6 billion or $88.51 per share.

11/15/93   Paramount directors rejected QVC bid as too conditional due to legal and financial contingencies.

- Mainly this served as a recommendation to shareholders not to tender to QVC.
- FTC approved recommendation that Liberty divest its QVC holdings.

11/16/93   The Delaware Chancery Court heard arguments from QVC that the Paramount directors illegally agreed to be acquired by Viacom.

11/22/93   Judge Jack Jacobs convinced both bidders to extend the deadline for tender offers for two days. Paramount was removed from the S&P 500 stock index at the close of trading.

11/24/93   Delaware judge Jack Jacobs ruled against Paramount.

- Threw out the lock-up option valued at $428 million.
- Barred PCI from dropping poison pill for Viacom and not QVC.
- Ruled the deal with Viacom was a sale, not a strategic alliance, obliging directors to follow the Revlon duty.

11/26/93   QVC and Viacom agreed to freeze their bids during the appeal of the Chancery Court ruling.

12/7/93   *The New York Times* reported that WMS Industries, Inc., a company 24.9% owned by Redstone, purchased 500,000 shares of Viacom Class B stock accounting for 20% of the trading between the last week of September and mid-October. This fueled speculation that Redstone was trying to boost the price of Viacom stock at the time when QVC's bid had appeared.

12/9/93   The Delaware Supreme Court upheld the decision of the Chancery Court confirming invalidation of the lock-up provision and the no-shop clause. In addition, the judge said he would have invalidated the $100 million breakup fee if QVC had challenged it.

12/14/93   Paramount agreed to put itself up for auction to "all present and prospective bidders" with bids due on December 20.

- Dropped its poison pill for both bidders.
- No special committee of independent directors organized to consider the bids.
- Bidder must leave its offer open for 10 days after gaining enough stock to complete the bid. This provision lasted until February 1.
- Beyond the highest market value, Lazard would analyze protection from price decline and growth prospects.

12/20/93   QVC increased its bid to $92 cash for 51% of Paramount shares with a back end consisting of 1.43 QVC common shares, regular preferred stock with a dividend of

6% (changed from convertible preferred with a dividend of 5%), and warrants for the right to buy QVC shares at $70.34 per share.

12/21/93   Viacom requested time to submit a higher offer while QVC reserved the right to increase its bid further in response.

12/22/93   Paramount agreed to be acquired by QVC, but the offer must remain open until January 7.

- Viacom shares jumped by $4 as traders thought the battle was over and then quickly returned to normal, closing up 87.5 cents.

1/7/94   Viacom agreed to acquire Blockbuster and increased the cash offer for Paramount to $105 per share for 50.1% of the shares but decreased the back end from $69.40 per share to $51.66 per share by removing Class A shares and reducing the amount of Class B shares.

- QVC claimed that this does not meet the auction terms because the total value of the bid has not increased.
- Only 28% of shares had been tendered to QVC and many were withdrawn with the new offer.

1/11/94   Blockbuster shareholders filed suit against the company claiming that the takeover by Viacom benefited top executives at the expense of other shareholders.

1/12/94   Paramount directors rejected the revised Viacom offer stating that QVC's offer "represents the best value available to Paramount shareholders."

1/13/94   Paramount made a statement that the back end of the offers (required by securities laws to be held open for 5 days) could be changed after February 1 to extend the bidding.

1/18/94   Viacom revised its offers to $107 per share for 50.1% of the shares and a combination of four securities for the remaining 49.9% for a total value of $9.7 billion, or $81.22 per share.

- 0.93065 Class B shares, Viacom preferred stock, 3-year warrant to purchase Viacom stock at $60/share, and a contingent value right (CVR) providing compensation to Paramount holders if Viacom B shares fall below $48 a year after the acquisition.

1/20/94   QVC extended its bidding deadline until January 31, matching Viacom.

1/23/94   Paramount directors endorsed the Viacom bid as marginally superior to the QVC bid.

- Even though the market value is lower, the CVR adds value.

Ameritech Corp.

*   Chicago-based

BellAtlantic Corp.

*   Philadelphia-based: serves six mid-Atlantic states (NJ, PA, VA, WV, MD, DE) and DC

*   Only Baby Bell to have won the right in Federal court to offer video services to its own customers which total 11 million. Others must mount legal challenges of their own. In August 1993, the federal court declared unconstitutional, on First Amendment grounds, the provision of the 1984 Cable Act banning phone companies from offering video in their own service areas.

*   Plans to begin delivering programming to 110,000 homes by 1994. (10/8)

BellSouth Corp.

*   Atlanta-based: services in nine Southeastern states and wireless communications worldwide

*   Substantial cellular operation with coverage in United States, Europe and Australia

*   Hadn't made a big push to provide video service to homes.(10/11).

*   Talks with QVC centered around common vs. preferred. They thought common was too risky. (10/12)

Prime Management Company

*   Privately held, Austin, TX-based. With subscribers in Houston, this could compete with Southwestern Bell.

*   Partially owned Community Cable TV in Las Vegas which served the whole city with a fiber loop.

*   Brought interactive TV, PPV, CATV and alternative communications systems as well as knowledge of pricing and distributing entertainment to BellSouth.

NYNEX Corp.

*   New York-based

*   New York and Boston service areas

*   Largest cable provider in UK

Southwestern Bell

*   Had agreed to acquire cable systems owned by Hauser Communications Inc. for $650 million (10/13).

- Served TX, OK, AK, MO, KS

US West

- Owned 25.5% of Time-Warner's Entertainment and Cable Operations.

- Could not as of yet provide HBO and WB movies to customers.

- Time-Warner to spend $1 million of investment on interactive networks.

Options for Content Joint Venturers

- Capital Cities/ABC, Inc.

- Dun & Bradstreet Corp.

- Dow Jones & Co.

History

- Born in 1970 when CBS was forced to spin-off rerun business.

- 1987 bidding war between Redstone and management LBO team.

- Biondi hired by Redstone in 1987. Had methodically paid down debt.

- Had recently has been close to selling cable properties to Southwestern Bell.

Deal Chronology

- 9/27: Felt free to play for time so that QVC stock price would fall and Viacom will not have to raise bid.

- 9/27: Hired private detective agency to investigate QVC.

Holdings

- Cable Networks: MTV, Nickelodeon, Showtime, VH-1, Nick at Nite, Comedy Channel (1/2), Lifetime network (1/3) MTV Networks Group: fastest growing CATV network

- Television Stations

- Produce Syndicated Programming

- Cable systems serving 1.1 million subscribers

Allies

Blockbuster Entertainment Corporation

- Sought to protect home video retailing which is under competition from pay-per-view.

- Wanted to release PCI movies on video before pay-per-view.

- Wanted to cut dependence on home video which represented 85% of operating profits.

- Owned approx. 70% of Spelling Entertainment; might purchase remainder. Bought Republic Pictures through this unit for $100 million earlier in 9/93.

NYNEX Corporation

- Before the battle for PCI began, they identified four companies to pursue and two of them were PCI and Viacom.

- New York and Boston are local service areas facing much competition from alternate local access providers. Learning more about entertainment would give them something more to offer.

- First crack at providing technology to transform Viacom cable into interactive network handling video and voice.

- Would get access to MTV, Showtime, etc., but (1) Viacom must offer it to everyone, (2) at that time NYNEX could not show programming in its territory (see BellAtlantic).

- CFO Jeffrey Rubin saw beaming video to homes as low-profit commodity business in the future.

Financial

- Class A and Class B shares traded on the American Stock Exchange

- Market capitalization of $7.9 billion with $2.7 billion in debt

- Asset value of $68 per share. Analysts said this is good currency for the deal because it saved on tax and has upside potential due to trading at 90% of the aforementioned asset value (9/13)

- Other side of coin: Viacom's stock traded at 16 times cash flow, had doubled in the past year, and the deal offered no downside price protection.

VIACOM-PARAMOUNT MERGER
PROFILES OF PARTICIPANTS—QVC, INC.

History

- Had been courting Home Shopping Network, Inc. for awhile. Proposal to merge in $1.4 billion transaction was put on hold for PCI bid. Stock had fallen 23% since June because of this bid.

- Put $70 per share bid for PCI (with Malone) on hold for the above earlier in the year. This reportedly had more cash than first Viacom bid.

- Since Diller took over, expanded business plan including a second lifestyle network in the works. He had added upscale retailers like Saks Fifth Avenue and Warnaco.

- Next step: let cable subscribers interact with TV sets.

Deal Chronology

- Three reasons for increased stock price after bid: (1) Confidence in Diller by major institutional investors such as Gordon Crawford of the Capital Group (9/24); (2) Depressed price to start with (Home Shopping Network deal); (3) Not a realistic chance of QVC winning

Allies

- John Malone: TCI, Liberty

- Comcast owns part of QVC

Financial

- NASDAQ traded, Market capitalization of $4 billion (9/16).

- Capital Group owns 763,000 QVC shares (9/24).

Synergies with PCI

- Could use PCI programming already in the vault to create new cable channels.

- Might improve movie studio and TV production through better management.

VIACOM-PARAMOUNT MERGER
PROFILES OF PARTICIPANTS—TELECOMMUNICATIONS, INC.

History

- Bob Magness, now 69, started cable industry in 1956; sold off cattle to raise money. 1972: collection of small systems, nearly bankrupt, hired Malone.

- In the 1980s, acquired small systems and CATV groups, spun some off.

- Nation's largest CATV operator (10 million homes out of 60 million). Served one of every 4 cable homes and owns cable systems in 48 states.

- Early September announced plans to launch a hybrid music-video and home shopping channel with Bertelsmann Music Group which would compete with MTV and VH-1.

- Had, with Malone, in the past been accused of anticompetitive behavior. Questions remained as to whether his involvement in this deal is anticompetitive. He must deal with government regularly due to rate issues.

- In 1989, Malone offered $70 per share for Paramount.

- In late 1980s when satellites caused competition for CATV, Malone acquired stake in Netlink USA and purchased Tempo Enterprises. Later, formed Primestar Partners Ltd. to launch Ku-band satellite: 100 channels, 18 inch dish.

- Teamed with US West in UK (10/13).

Holdings

- 23% of Turner: since bailout of CNN, TNT, TBS. Second largest shareholder to Ted Turner.

- With Liberty held a stake in many CATV channels: Discovery Channel, Turner Broadcasting, Black Entertainment Network, Family Channel, American Movie Classics

- Controlled Home Shopping Network

- Invested $180,000 in BET in 1979 (first move into programming).

- Shared ownership: Asia Business News (Singapore) and Pte. Ltd.

- 10.5 million subscribers (out of 60 million market) for CATV.

Options

- Had approached Matsushita and Sony about acquiring their studio holdings.

Financial

- Malone was instrumental in convincing Wall Street to concentrate on cash flows and assets rather than losses.

- Cash flows of $1.1 billion in 1993 off revenue of approx. $4 billion.

Liberty Media Corporation

<u>*History*</u>

- Spun-off from TCI in 1991 to defuse criticism in Washington that TCI was too powerful.

- Failed in past attempts to create a partnership of Encore with Showtime (Viacom)

<u>*Holdings*</u>

- Owned 90% of Encore (launched in 1991 by TCI). Five-year rights to most of the output of MCA's Universal Picture.

- Several other cable channels that supply programs to TCI, Viacom, and Comcast: Family Channel

VIACOM-PARAMOUNT MERGER
PROFILES OF PARTICIPANTS—OTHERS

Time-Warner Communications, Inc.

- Held a 9% stake in QVC.

- Had been looking for a way to unwind this investment for cash. A QVC merger with Paramount might allow a tax-free way to do this by Time-Warner acquiring some of PCI's assets.

- In 1989, a Delaware court ruled that the only exception to the "business judgment" rule is the selling of a company. This did not apply to the Time-Warner deal because it was a stock merger rather than an acquisition such as Viacom-Paramount. Therefore, Davis will be forced to take the highest offer.

Turner Broadcasting System Inc.

History

- Recently purchased Castle Rock Entertainment and New Line Cinema Corp. (August 1993).

- Anti-trust problems if he tried to bid for Paramount because of Time-Warner's 21% ownership of TBS.

- Had $80 million in cash and only $1.7 billion in long-term debt and another $1.5 billion in borrowing power, but Malone backed Diller.

- Deal with PCI would have been an opportunity for Time-Warner to "monetize" its $1.4 billion stake in Turner by (1) acquiring some of PCI's assets (Simon & Schuster) with little tax liability or (2) forced divestiture by FCC giving Time-Warner two years to reinvest proceeds.

Holdings

- Cable Networks: TNT, TBS, CNN, Cartoon Network

Comcast Communications

- President Brian Roberts (age 34), son of founder and Chairman Ralph Roberts

History

- Davis had long been searching for strategic merger/acquisition including a1989 bid to break up Time-Warner, had since talked with TBS, Inc., Capital Cities/ABC, Inc., GE's NBC, TCI, Criss-Craft Industries Inc., Geffen Records (sold to MCA Inc.), Thorn EMI (parent of Capitol Records), Bertelsmann AG (Germany), and Phillips Electronics (Holland). The deals seemed to break down for three reasons: (1) he did not want to overpay for an acquisition; (2) he did not want to accept too little for PCI shareholders; (3) he wanted to retain control.

- Predecessor CEO Charles Bluhdorn died in 1983 after which Davis streamlined the company.

- Earnings had recently been flat and stock price has dipped from 60s to 40s.

- Takeover advances by Carl Icahn and Irwin Jacobs in the 1980s.

- Struggling after cancellation of "Cheers," but also recent success with "The Firm" and "Indecent Proposal." Two management regimes had come and gone at the studio since Diller left and the production was faltering.

Holdings

- Paramount Pictures: movie and TV production studio

- Cable Networks: half-owner of USA Network; Sci-Fi Channel (1/2), Madison Square Garden Network (100%)

- Television Stations

- Produce programming: three new shows, Wings

- Syndicated programming: "Star Trek: The Next Generation," "Deep Space Nine," "Untouchables," "Entertainment Tonight"

- Sports: Owner of Madison Square Garden, Knicks, and Rangers

- Publishing: Simon & Schuster

- Motion picture library

- Sequel franchises: "Star Trek," "Beverly Hills Cop"

Takeover defense

- Poison pill in place

- Agreement with Viacom: Viacom had an option on 17-20% (24 million newly issued shares) of Paramount's common stock at $69.14 triggered by a rival bid. Secondly, in the event of a successful bid PCI must pay Viacom $100 million. Payment would show up as a 7-year subordinated note which would show up on PCI's balance sheet as an asset worth $2.2 million in principal and interest.

- Agreement with Viacom: PCI could not open talks with a rival bidder unless the rival bid isn't "subject to any material contingencies related to financing."

- A number of class action shareholder lawsuits were filed in Delaware regarding the "lock-up" agreement described above.

Why Attractive to Viacom

- Could form fifth broadcast network

- Businesses: Cable and broadcast programming and distribution, filmed entertainment, and publishing

- Market capitalization of $15 million with debt of only $3.5 million

- Total of 12 broadcast stations together

- Paramount ($800 million per year for producing movies and TV shows compared to $100 million for Viacom) would enhance Viacom's ability to develop original programming.

- New cable channels

- Movies of MTV shows ("Beavis & Butthead")

- Interactive formats from video and publishing libraries.

Financial

- Trades on the NYSE, 120 million shares outstanding

- Market value of $6.8 billion

- Asset value of $77 per share.

VIACOM-PARAMOUNT MERGER
POSITIVES AND NEGATIVES BY COMPANY

Viacom

Positive

Receive publishing and production assets

Synergies between existing lines of business

Combination of affiliates allows for network

Redstone/Biondi have a history of squeezing profit out of assets

Negative

Definitely paying a premium for PCI

Debt service may force sale of productive assets

Can management run a motion picture studio?

QVC Network

Could prevent a fifth network

Positive

Diller's proven entertainment management skills

Experience in interactive TV may serve well in future

PCI assets may provide programming for Liberty Media stations

Negative

No real synergies between QVC and PCI

Definitely paying a premium for PCI

Debt service may force sale of productive assets and hinder creativity of management

Paramount Communications

Negative

Control would be lost to Redstone

The back end securities are squirrelly

Positive

Shareholders receive a premium for shares

Finally a productive use for cash

VIACOM-PARAMOUNT MERGER
PERSONALITIES

Sumner Redstone, Chairman of Viacom, Inc.

- Age 70

- Owned 76.3% of Viacom (0.763 x $7.9 billion = $6.03 billion as of 9/10)

- Acquired Viacom in 1987 for $3.4 billion.

- Would have 69.8% of voting stock and 38.5% equity in new company under first deal.

- In 1965, as theater owner, Davis asked him to lead a shareholder committee to protect against tender office. In the late 1980s, however, PCI and Viacom were involved in a lawsuit over movie rights.

- Reputation as shrewd entertainment investor.

- Attorney, taught at Harvard Law occasionally.

- Built family-owned drive-ins into 800-screen chain of theaters, National Amusements, Inc.

- Had a history of using lawsuits in business dealings: several years ago sued Time-Warner's HBO over monopolistic practices hurting Showtime.

Martin Davis, Chairman and CEO of Paramount Communications, Inc.

- Age 66

- Owned no significant stake in Paramount

- Had been a vocal champion of delivering value to shareholders. Known, however, for overbidding in 1989 Time-Warner deal. [After Diller entered the fray, Davis was in the same position that Time was in when Davis upped the bid to $200/share.]

- Sold the financial services unit of Gulf & Western (predecessor of Paramount) for $2 billion in cash. Reputation for cleaning up ugly conglomerates but spent half of proceeds on stock repurchases and small acquisitions such as publishing, broadcasting properties and mid-size theme parks.

- Initial deal had him staying on as CEO but everyone was sure that Redstone would call the shots.

- Had spent entire career at same company.

- Never felt a 4th network would be worth the risk.

Barry Diller, Chairman of QVC

- Early career at ABC network running programming operations.

- Used to head the Paramount studio (through its most successful years) but was ousted by Martin Davis (about 10 years ago). He had supported Davis for the top position after Bluhdorn died.

- Went on to run News Corp.'s Fox studio. He launched the Fox network, the 4th network that most said could not be done. Murdoch refused to give him equity so he left. Then spent 10 months roaming the country with his PowerBook considering his options.

- Recruited by Brian Roberts to head QVC in 1992, made a $25 million investment and has controlling interest along with Comcast and Liberty in that they have agreed to vote their shares together.

- His $25 million investment was then worth $480-500 million including stock options and other arrangements.

- Rock solid relationships (except with Jaffe) and instincts for success were main strengths. Idea-driven and creative. Expected to be able to wring more growth and exciting new businesses out of Paramount than Redstone or Davis.

John Malone, CEO of TCI and Chairman of Liberty Media, Corp.

- Controlled QVC through Liberty with Diller and Comcast Corp.

- Called "King of Cable" for strong-arm tactics with competitors and suppliers.

- Needed software: Paramount

- Shy to the point of awkwardness in social situations. (9/27) Spare time with family, sailboat, antique car collection and horses. Drives RV from Denver to summer home in Maine each year.

- Education: degrees from Yale and Johns Hopkins, Ph.D. in operations research.

- Owned 26.3 million shares of Liberty super-voting class B, 50.4% voting stake worth $671 million. (9/27) Most of personal wealth was in Liberty before TCI's reacquisition.

- Career:

  - Financial expert, AT&T's Bell Labs in '60s. 300-page paper on maximizing profits in regulated industry

  - McKinsey & Co.: brief stay

  - General Instrument Corp.: manufacturer of CATV equipment—met Bob Magness.

  - Hired by Magness as CEO of TCI in 1972.

Frank Biondi, CEO of Viacom

- Age 48

- Seen as logical successor to Davis

- Time, Inc. veteran (ran HBO unit) and oversaw Coca-Cola Co.'s TV operations before being sold to Sony.

Stanley Jaffe, President of Paramount

- Age 52

- Former movie producer at Paramount

- Took current job in 1991. Credited with turning around MSG unit and beefing up production.

Brian Roberts, President of Comcast Corp.

- Age 34, Wharton graduate, son of Chairman Ralph Roberts (the family owns 80% of the voting stock)

- Started selling cable subscriptions during high school for father.

- Recruited Diller when Diller resigned from News Corp. and said that he wanted to become an entrepreneur. They talked about plans to deal for MGM/UA and NBC.

VIACOM-PARAMOUNT MERGER
LEGAL ISSUES

Revlon Rule

- 1986 Delaware Supreme Court decision that once a company puts itself up for sale, it is obligated to open up the bidding process to the highest price.

- PCI-Viacom argument was that the duty did not apply in this case because this was part of a long-term strategy rather than just a maximization of cash. (Shouldn't this be the same at least for the security portion of the deal?) They argued that only Viacom fit the strategy.

- Previous rulings by Delaware courts had ruled that "bust-up" provisions such as the antitakeover defense deal with Viacom illegally impeded the bidding process.

- A number of shareholder suits had been filed seeking to open up to other bidders.

- Paramount lawyers then had to argue the other side of the case from the Time-Warner litigation. They had to argue that PCI had a reason to reject more generous bids as opposed to the Time-Warner argument that Time should take the highest bid.

Texaco, Inc. Settlement

- Mid-1980s: Texaco settled for $3 billion after a Texas jury found that it interfered with an agreement by Pennzoil Co. to buy Getty Oil Co.

- Viacom could conceivably sue, however (1) the agreement with PCI included a provision allowing PCI to ignore the commitments if it is legally bound to consider other offers; (2) PCI could simply wait for a vote of shareholders and then choose another suitor after the offer is rejected.

Regulatory Hurdles

- Malone controlled significant stakes in QVC and TBS.

- Justice Department's new antitrust chief, Anne Bingaman, likely to be more aggressive than Republican predecessors.

- Concern if buyer had significant movie studio interests.

- Concern if program producer acquired television operations.

Matsushita/MCA

- Partners with PCI overseas in video distribution and theatrical exhibition.

- They also owned the other 50% of USA Network (valued at $1 billion). The partnership agreement could force one partner to sell or buy-out in the event of a change in control of the other. Also, PCI could not expand in advertiser-supported cable entertainment network business unless it partnered with MCA. MCA could either force the cheap sale of PCI's share, the premium sale of its share, or participation in deal.

Bells and CATV

- Freed in early 1993 to offer CATV services in their own regions.

Miscellaneous

- Diller could talk to investors, but Redstone was legally unable because proxy materials had not yet been issued to shareholders.

VIACOM-PARAMOUNT MERGER
VALUATION AND TECHNOLOGY ISSUES

Valuation by Jeffrey Logsdon, Seidler Cos. (9/24)

- Cash flows for VIA-PCI would grow 12-16% annually.

- Diller-QVC-PCI faster than 20% and if you add Home Shopping Network, 30% range.

Valuation by Lisbeth Barron, S.G. Warburg, (9/29)

- Computed total market value counting debt and cash on the books after merger with PCI on terms of current offers.

- VIA at 25% premium for expected cash flow growth of combined company. PCI-VIA cash flow of $1.2 billion would grow 12% for 3-5 years.

- QVC at 19% premium for expected cash flow growth of combined company. QVC-PCI cash flow of $817 million would grow at 14% based on (1) Diller's unique ability and (2) QVC growing faster than VIA.

"Diller Sizzle" Valuation

- PCI advisers worried that QVC may be worth only $35/share based on multiples.

Contentions about Valuation

- Redstone purchased 413,600 Class B shares, 15% of trading volume, between July 5 and August 20. QVC camp claims this was an attempt to increase stock price rather than part of stock repurchase plan which occurred at 1/5 the rate of this buying spree.

- Redstone claimed that Malone torpedoed Viacom stock on 9/16 by announcing the joint venture with Bertelsmann. (9/29)

Technology Issues:

Lines—Cable advantages

- Bells would have to spend $200 million combined to upgrade to video-quality lines capable of reaching 94.2 million TV homes.

- Cable already reached 95% of those homes (62% subscribe) and broadband lines can carry heavy load of video, voice and other digital data. But they still needed to transform one-way video to two-way digital.

Lines—Phone Company Advantages

- Cable companies lacked high-speed switching technology and the expertise in management of complex networks.

- Local monopolies provided cheap debt and huge cash flows.

VIACOM-PARAMOUNT MERGER
TACTICAL CONSIDERATIONS

Paramount-Viacom Explicit Synergistic Opportunities

- Broadcast network: The 12 local stations of the merged entity could serve as affiliates for a fifth broadcast network whose programming would be produced at the Paramount Studios.

- Cable channels: These would be made possible by a combination of successful cable programming executives, Paramount's substantial video library and Viacom's 1.1 million cable subscribers.

- Movie production: Viacom expected to produce movies based on the themes of MTV shows such as "Beavis & Butthead."

- Interactive television: Using the video library and the Paramount publishing library, the merged company could produce interactive video formats.

Initial Equity Market Reaction to QVC Bid

The following day, September 21, in trading on the American Stock Exchange (ASE), Viacom's Class A shares fell 4.22%, while in NASDAQ trading, QVC's stock showed a modest increase of 12.5¢. There are three possible interpretations of this result:

1. The market thought Mr. Diller can add more value than Mr. Redstone.

2. The market expected QVC's bid causing a 10.76% decline in value over the previous three trading days.

3. The market did not think Diller has a chance of winning.

Redstone and Davis Tactics

Refusal to raise bid: Redstone's stalling tactic allowed Viacom to do three things: (1) let the QVC bid to be devalued through market trading, (2) line up an investment from a third party to sweeten the Viacom bid, and (3) file a lawsuit against the QVC camp.

Focus on Malone: Lastly, by minimizing the Diller factor, they hoped to negatively affect the price of QVC stock.

TCI

After receiving a Ph.D. in operations research from Johns Hopkins University, Malone worked as a financial expert for AT&T's Bell Labs once writing a 300-page paper on maximizing profits in regulated industries. It was in his employment at General Instrument Corporation, a manufacturer of cable television equipment, that he met Bob Magness, the Chairman of TCI.

Magness, presently 69 years old, started the cable television industry in 1956 selling off cattle to raise money. By 1972, his collection of small cable systems was nearly bankrupt. It was the year that Magness hired Malone as the CEO of the financially-strapped company.

Reasons why the Paramount Communications board would not OK formal negotiations with QVC

Two explanations of the board's decision are (1) material contingencies remained because QVC continued to discuss additional investments with other parties especially and (2) Paramount remained legally bound by the Viacom merger agreement to continue preparing the Viacom transaction.

Other Threats to Viacom

On another front, Viacom was dealt a blow on September 29 when Walt Disney Corporation agreed to license 350 future movies to Encore for more than $1 billion. The agreement, which granted rights to Touchstone and Hollywood Pictures from 1997-2003 and Mixamax from 1994-2003, ended a similar relationship with Viacom's Showtime.

NYNEX Investment in Viacom

It was not clear what the billion dollar investment would bring them. For one thing, NYNEX, unlike BellAtlantic, had not won federal court approval to provide video programming in its home territory. In addition, under FCC guidelines, Viacom had to offer its programming to everyone at competitive rates. Lastly, the lack of a management role and the relatively meager % return on investment did not seem to offer much for $1.2 billion, especially in comparison to U.S. West's purchase of 25.5% of Time-Warner, Inc.'s entertainment and cable operations.[1]

BellAtlantic-TCI Merger

The combination of the largest U.S. cable system operator with the Philadelphia-based Baby Bell would provide benefits to both companies. BellAtlantic was the only one of the seven Baby Bells that had the right to offer video services in its 11 million home region which includes New Jersey, Pennsylvania, Virginia, West Virginia, Maryland, Delaware, and Washington, D.C. Other Bells must launch a legal battle of their own as BellAtlantic did in federal court. TCI's broadband cables would supersede a costly investment by BellAtlantic in video-quality lines. BellAtlantic, however, provided technological benefits such as high-speed switching, expertise in managing networks and send-receive technology. The financial benefits included cheaper debt and high cash flows. Regulatory hurdles remained in front of the completion of this deal as TCI might be expected to divest its cable holdings in the BellAtlantic territory.

Although it would seem to greatly increase the financial backing in the QVC camp, the merger might hurt Diller's bid more than it helped for three reasons: First, Diller had been negotiating an investment by BellSouth of between $500 million and $1.2 billion. The presence of BellAtlantic seemed to have scuttled those discussions for the time being especially after BellSouth concurrently announced its acquisition of Prime Management Company, an Austin-based cable operator with 500,000 customers. Second, the antitrust issues would appear to be mountainous after Liberty's stake in QVC is consolidated into TCI and then BellAtlantic. Third, in order for Diller to remain in control of any merged entity, he was forced put a limit on the level of financial backing from the cable and local telephone behemoths.

---

[1] U.S. West, another Baby Bell, paid $2.5 billion for their Time-Warner stake, but received in return a management role in the entertainment unit and a billion dollar investment by Time-Warner to jointly develop interactive networks.

Other Events

- On September 28, Home Shopping Network announced that it would place the QVC merger on the back burner until the bid for Paramount is clarified.

- Between October 22 and November 3: At this point in the bidding process where both bids were similar, there was additional jostling in the media industry. First, Paramount and Cris-Craft announced plans to launch Paramount Network in January 1995. As if the announcement of a fifth network was not enough, six days later, Time-Warner and Tribune Television announced plans to launch WB Network in August 1994.

- Post Chancery Court rules: The beleaguered Paramount board had much to think about after the ruling. Board members Lester Pollack and Irwin Schloss would now get an opportunity, they were said to have requested prior to the litigation, to evaluate the QVC bid.

November 12 Bid by QVC

Also note that the new offer provided Viacom with a four-day timing advantage because the mandatory 1-day period forced QVC to leave its offer open until November 26.

QVC's November 20th Announcement of Financing

QVC also could have raised the cash portion of its bid again (either by increasing the price per share or the number of shares), but since the bid was already $1.3 billion larger than the Viacom bid, Diller instead opted to remove financing contingencies.

Coercive Nature of Tender Offer

November 22: Paramount shareholders had an incentive to tender for the $85 price because the back-end of the deal was now valued at approximately $71/share.

Paramount for Sale

Barry Diller was wary about the process for two reasons. First, if he raised his bid on Monday, effectively he might be bidding against himself. Second, he was suspicious of the Paramount board's ability to cut off further bids at a point where Viacom may temporarily have the higher offer.

December 20: When Redstone did not make a bid, QVC's stock plummeted. Given that the leader in the bidding war appeared to be the loser in terms of stock returns, perhaps this was part of Redstone's wait and see tactic.

January 13 Bidding Rules

This action forbade the suitors from raising the back end after February 1. In effect, the statement removed the opportunity to increase the back end between February 1 and February 7, and basically gave shareholders until February 14 to tender shares.

Other Diller Issues on February 1

- Would this really be the final round of negotiations?

- What Paramount assets should be disposed of, if any? Where can costs be trimmed?

- Are there further litigation issues involved such as suing Paramount for choosing Viacom's lower market value offer?

- How does the bid affect QVC shareholders? Does it maximize the value of their securities?

Redstone Issues on February 1

- Is the Blockbuster merger more worthwhile than just a cash infusion?

- How can he integrate Paramount's assets?

- What Paramount assets should be disposed of, if any? Where can costs be trimmed?

- How does the bid affect Viacom shareholders? Does it maximize the value of their securities?

VIACOM-PARAMOUNT MERGER
NOTABLE QUOTES

"It's a logical deal with terrific synergies, and one plus one equals two and a half with Viacom and Paramount." (Mario Gabelli of Gabelli Funds which owns large stakes in both companies, *The Wall Street Journal*, September 9, 1993)

"We have put together the No. 1 software company in the world, a monster entertainment company. We've succeeded in changing the faces of our own companies and in changing the face of the media business." (Sumner Redstone, September 13, 1993)

"This is the best possible deal for the shareholders of Paramount. With the strength of our balance sheet we have unlimited opportunities—we're not stopping here." (Davis, September 13, 1993)

"We will be the most powerful software-driven company in the world, and that is not an understatement." "We are indeed staggered by what we have wrought." (Sumner Redstone, September 14, 1993)

"Malone and the Roberts family are putting their own money behind Mr. Diller. . . .That is a pretty powerful combination of business judgment that's weighing against Sumner Redstone at this point." (Larry Haverty, Fund Manager, State Street Research, September 23, 1993)

"Our relationship with Paramount is very important to us in USA and other activities. We have a concern about how it all works out, and we want to make damn sure our interests are fully protected." (Sidney J. Sheinberg, President of MCA, September 22, 1993)

"Our proposal had no emotional aspect, other than the fondness I have for the 10 years I spent at Paramount." (Barry Diller, September 23, 1993, on the relationship between him and Davis)

"This is the wildest one I've ever seen. The added wrinkle is what each guy is saying to get his stock up and the other guy's stock down." (Experienced anonymous trader, September 24, 1993)

"Mr. Redstone has a habit of airing the industry's dirty laundry in public." (Mario Gabelli, September 24, 1993)

The QVC bid. . ."would be but the latest step in a systematic and broad-ranging conspiracy to monopolize the American cable industry." "In the American cable industry, one man has. . . seized monopoly power. Using bullyboy tactics and strong-arming of competitors, suppliers and customers, that man has inflicted antitrust injury on. . .virtually every American consumer of cable services and technologies. That man is John C. Malone." (Viacom lawsuit, September 24, 1993)

"Barry came here to a financially strapped company with very little raw material and built a television programming arm and a network. He's a visionary and a gambler, and he's not afraid to take risks. He just didn't give up." (Lucie Salhany, Chairman of Fox Broadcasting—brought from Paramount to Fox by Diller)

Malone likened to "the ringleader" of "the cable Cosa Nostra." (Al Gore while in Senate)

"The whole media business is driven by the fact that it costs a lot of money to create software. . . but the marginal cost, once you have created it, is very low, and that drives all these media companies toward trying to be very large." (Malone, 1989 Senate Hearings)

"Consistent with our legal obligations we will consider the QVC bid if and when we have satisfactory evidence of financing. . . .If we ever get into QVC discussions, we will have other big concerns that go beyond the issues of financing." (Davis, September 28, 1993)

"This is the guy who only discovered the PowerBook a year ago?" (Viacom executive, September 29, 1993)

". . . the preponderance of their offer is in each case a squirrelly piece of paper. I don't believe this is about price. This is now a game of who can come up with the most cash." (Emanuel Gerard, Chairman of Gerard Klauer Mattison & Co.)

"This press conference isn't about Paramount-Viacom. What you see today and in connection with Blockbuster isn't about money. This is about picking the right strategic partner." (Sumner Redstone, October 5, 1993, about the NYNEX deal)

"Our intent is to have a multimedia broadband interactive network. . . .It is important that we have a relationship with a content provider that helps to fill out the strategic portfolio." (NYNEX chairman, William Ferguson, October 5, 1993)

"The thing that is similar about Barry Diller and Viacom Chairman Sumner Redstone is they are long-term players. They don't want to ruin their companies with exorbitant debt levels. They won't get deal fever. There is only so much that anybody will pay." (Jessica Reif, Media and Entertainment Analyst, Oppenheimer & Co., October 6, 1993)

NYNEX's investment in Viacom. . ."is exactly what it sounds like—just an investment. That doesn't get, in my opinion, to the critical skills needed to establish the competence that will be required to be competitive in this business." (Stuart C. Johnson, Group President at BellAtlantic Corp., October 8, 1993)

"We're trying to participate in as many aspects of the market as we can. The guy who has got the best technology, the best quality, and the best access to entertainment and services is going to win this telecommunications war." (Jeffrey Rubin, FGO, NYNEX, October 8, 1993)

"The future of this industry is going to involve the power of content allied with distribution. With Liberty, we know what the assets are and what they can be." (Brendan Clouston, Chief Operating Office, TCI, October 11, 1993)

"Once they had the financing delivered by QVC, I believe Paramount had a responsibility to declare themselves in an auction mode. I can assure you we will assemble a posse if they continue to forestall putting themselves up for sale." (Guy Wyser-Pratte, takeover stock trader, October 12, 1993)

"The telephone business and the cable business are coming crashing together. Every cable company could end up being owned by a 'telco'." (Gordon Crawford, Capital Research Group, largest institutional holder of TCI, October 14, 1993)

"I'll be a shareholder, hopefully a very happy shareholder. I'll be a director, I think I'll be vice chairman—which is, you know, kind of like being vice president." (Malone on the BellAtlantic deal, October 14, 1993)

"They're doing anything they can to get the focus off the fact they have an inadequate bid for Paramount." (Malone on Viacom's anticompetitive allegations, October 14, 1993)

"This supercharges the timetable on when all this stuff is going to happen. This is the dawn of the information age." (Terence Garnett, Senior VP, Oracle Corp., on TCI-BellAtlantic)

QVC and Paramount are "peripheral to" Bell Atlantic-TCI and the outcome is not "central to or a core part of the BellAtlantic and TCI strategy" (Malone, October 14, 1993)

"Our future doesn't hinge on our owning either a cable company or an entertainment company. We'll continue to be a major supplier of equipment, technology, and network expertise to any and all companies." (Robert E. Allen, AT&T Chairman, after the BellAtlantic-TCI announcement, October 14, 1993)

"Attempts to denigrate QVC's businesses together with the positioning of me and my other partners and colleagues as pawns of anyone are only designed for one thing: to take attention away from the obvious difference in the proposals and allow Viacom to complete its acquisition of Paramount Communications at less than its fair value." QVC "is the company whose vision is appropriate to steer Paramount through this revolution." "We recognize the difficulties Paramount is struggling with as a result of the merger agreement it signed with Viacom. We will, however, oppose the continued raising of straw men whose only purpose is to confuse the issue to the benefit of a few individuals and the detriment of all Paramount shareholders." (Diller, October 18, 1993)

"Paramount has great assets. Even Barry Diller says so! Why are they great assets? Why has Paramount performed so well? Simple: because they were strategically shaped and developed by this management. It was this management that took an unwieldy conglomerate of the '70s and turned it into a great entertainment and publishing company. . .and Mr. Diller knows it. He watched from a distance!" "We have a highly developed strategic vision for our assets, which includes a merger with Viacom, opening new opportunities for the combined company that are dramatic and unlimited. Given this record of the Paramount management, it is clear that Mr. Diller's 'I can do it better' cry is just that, a cry." (Paramount statement, October 20, 1993)

"Barry Diller is a charismatic, compelling leader and one of the stronger creative minds in the business, but Viacom is better at getting the most financially out of its assets." (John Tinker, Furman Selz analyst, October 20, 1993)

"In our meetings we talk about the obvious strategic advantages of putting Paramount together with a global media company like Viacom against the advantage of QVC, which is essentially a shopping channel." (Sumner Redstone, October 20, 1993)

". . .because I believed that the future would go to those who were involved in the architecture of interactivity at the convergence of the telephone, computer, and television set. Those that have visited QVC's headquarters saw the power of the infrastructure that had been built and believed with me that QVC's strategy to lay down interactive distribution tracks in retailing information and education services was a sound one. . . .And that is exactly the underlying argument for why QVC and Paramount should be combined." (Diller, October 20, 1993)

Viacom's strategy "is going to be to wear down the opposition, with questions about regulatory problems and lack of firm financing. I think this thing is going to move at a glacial pace." (Larry Haverty, October 21, 1993)

"The QVC group has just taken a huge bulldozer and leveled the playing field." (Peter Schoenfeld, Vice Chairman, Wertheim Schroder & Co., October 22, 1993)

"The QVC bid is demonstrably superior to the bid that is currently on the table from Viacom—hands down. I'm delighted that stockholders will get a chance to indicate which proposal they find more attractive." (Crawford, Capital Group, October 22, 1993)

"Incredibly, in light of Viacom's refusal to improve its offer, the only actions taken by Paramount management and its board of directors have been designed to demean the value of our company or create potential regulatory obstacles." (Diller, October 22, 1993)

"This does not change anything as far as we're concerned because we have been committed to getting the best deal for shareholders, but we are not going to allow shareholders to be stampeded into something that may not represent the best deal for them." (Person close to Paramount, October 22, 1993)

"We believe that the revised merger with Viacom represents superior long-term value to our stockholders." (Davis, October 25, 1993)

"The issue is not what number the network is, the issue is the idea. My feeling is the world does not need another generic broadcast network, and the ideas my company has been working on deal with developing something that can become a defined, recognizable new brand." (Diller on the Paramount Network, October 27, 1993)

"Paramount has the most synergy, meaning they could afford to fire the most people. If Paramount wins, they'll go through this place like General Sherman through Atlanta." (MacMillan editor, November 9, 1993)

MacMillan acquisition is "a significant step in furthering our strategic objective of creating proprietary intellectual properties that can be distributed through a wide variety of media, from printed pages to computer and video screens." (Davis press release, November 11, 1993)

"Passive investments without control never create value for the shareholders." (Jack Grubman, PaineWebber, November 11, 1993, on the BellSouth investment in QVC)

"We wouldn't have done this if we didn't think Barry Diller was going to win." (Peter Barton on Liberty divesting QVC stake, November 12, 1993)

"If I could figure out a way to control this company from up there or down there, I would." (Quote from Redstone last year referring to his death, November 16, 1993)

"I know you're coming after me." (Davis to Diller at July luncheon)

"We have lifted every obstacle in our path, including regulatory issues and financing issues. The only remaining issues, the poison pill and the lock up, are entirely in their control. And to cite them as issues that make our offer highly conditional is hypocrisy that knows no end." (Diller, November 23, 1993)

"I felt overwhelmingly that we were on the right side of this issue. We had made so many attempts--eight separate attempts--to get Paramount to deal with us. We were pushed away each time." (Diller after Chancery Court decision, November 26, 1993)

"It is commonplace for tender offers to have conditions of some kind. That fact does not render them 'illusory.'" "The board did not even ask QVC on Nov. 15 to produce evidence of its financing. . . .But meeting with QVC was the last thing management wanted to do, and by skillful advocacy, management persuaded the board that no exploration was required." (Judge Jack Jacobs, November 26, 1993)

"In the real world, the board responded in good faith" to the QVC bid. (Barry Ostrager, PCI attorney)

"I think this court is aware of what the real-world realities are." (Justice Moore of the Delaware Supreme Court, December 10, 1993)

"Paramount shareholders now get a fair shake and have the flexibility to vote for the best bid. I think the process is fair now." (Ed Hatch, UBS Securities, December 15, 1993)

"How much are bragging rights worth to the winner of the last of the available Hollywood studios? If you are Barry Diller or Sumner Redstone, perhaps an extra $2 billion, maybe $3 billion dollars." (*The Wall Street Journal*, December 20, 1993)

"The winner will really be the loser in the eyes of the stock market." (Jessica Reif, Oppenheimer & Co., December 20, 1993)

"This is in the late stages of seminuttiness, and the question is, are things just ego-driven for this deal at some point?" (Emanuel Gerard, former entertainment executive, December 20, 1993)

"The question is, how can Barry's talents make up in two to three years what he is overpaying for today?" (*QVC insider*, December 20, 1993)

"Our current bid is totally responsible and not filled with an ounce of ego. We aren't winning at any cost--there is plenty of room to build and grow this company. These assets are irreplaceable and five years from now, Paramount will look cheap at this price." (Diller, December 20, 1993)

Very much like a, you know, Van Gogh painting. It's difficult to say what the market will pay for it at any given point in time because of its scarcity or rarity." (Malone in deposition, December 20, 1993)

"it's hard to see how 900 old movies and 6,000 old TV shows could pull a profit--especially after one subtracts the cost of digitizing these archives for electronic distribution over an interactive TV network." (*Digital Media Newsletter*, December 20, 1993)

"Given the conditions in the entertainment industry--like the high costs of making, marketing, and advertising films--even the greatest genius in the world would be hard-pressed to significantly increase the profits of the Paramount studio in the short term." (Hal Vogel, Merrill Lynch analyst, author of *Entertainment Industry Economics*, December 20, 1993)

"Both parties are legally drunk, and they are about to have one more drink." (Larry Haverty, December 20, 1993)

"I can only assume that the telephone users of New York will be subsidizing NYNEX's investment in Hollywood." "It is logical to conclude that the telephone rates in New York are too high if NYNEX has enough excess cash to invest in business ventures which will not immediately subtract costs from the consumer's bill." (Senator Franz S. Leichter in letter to NY Public Service Commission, December 29, 1993)

"They created a merger of two companies to make an inferior bid." (Crawford, Capital Group, on Viacom-Blockbuster merger, January 10, 1994)

"This is a crazy bidding procedure. Nobody's making their best bid, and the process never ends." (*Trader*, January 10, 1994)

"This is an insurance policy against Blockbuster going extinct." (Haverty, January 10, 1994, on the Viacom-Blockbuster merger)

"No one in the Viacom-Blockbuster-Paramount mix knows how to run a movie studio, which is still the crown jewel of Paramount, the way Barry Diller does." (Institutional holder of PCI, January 19, 1994)

"QVC's bid is higher, but Viacom's is more secure." (Lisbeth Barron, media analyst, S.G. Warburg, February 2, 1994)

"I'm comfortable with both Viacom and QVC, but my sense is that Barry can probably run it better." (Mario Gabelli, February 9, 1994)

Anyone who doesn't tender to Viacom because of vague promises by QVC is crazy." (Dickstein on the BellSouth purchase plan, February 9, 1994)

"This was an economic contest, not a popularity contest." (Wall Street executive, February 15, 1994)

VIACOM-PARAMOUNT MERGER
WHAT HAPPENED AFTER THE DEAL CLOSED

Sequence of Events Leading to Final Resolution of the Battle

2/01/94	QVC raised the cash portion of its offer to $104/share for 50.1%, but reduced the amount of the back end after selling $500 million in additional stock to BellSouth.
2/01/94	Viacom increased the value of its back end by offering a security that will be debt paying 8% interest if Blockbuster deal occurs or preferred stock with 5% dividend if the deal is not completed by January 1, 1995.
2/04/94	Paramount directors endorsed Viacom bid.
2/13/94	QVC issued a statement ruling out any changes in its bid.
2/14/94	Viacom attracted more than 60% of the Paramount shares thus winning the bidding contest.

Viacom-Paramount

- Sold MSG Network, Rangers, and Knicks to ITT and Cabletron for more than $1 billion.

- How do you value entertainment properties when they have highly variable and uncertain cash flows and bidders have huge egos willing to overpay?

- Replaced Simon & Schuster CEO Richard Snyder with Jon Newcomb

- Paramount Studios languished during the battle—market share 2nd-to-last at time deal closed

- Blockbuster board reaffirmed merger on August 24, 1994.

QVC

- Barry Diller attempted to acquire CBS in a merger with QVC

- QVC's major shareholder, Brian Roberts of Comcast, didn't want QVC to become affiliated with a broadcast network since Comcast was in cable.

- Offer made to acquire QVC with Liberty Media, which was accepted.

- Diller's stake in QVC was worth $100 million shortly after the Viacom-Paramount deal closed.

Further Reading

Those interested in deal-making in entertainment business can read the following:

- *Fortune*, November 20, 1989, pages 164-210, discusses the battle for Time-Warner.

- *Vanity Fair,* February 1994, pages 66-138, offers an inside story of several Paramount deals.

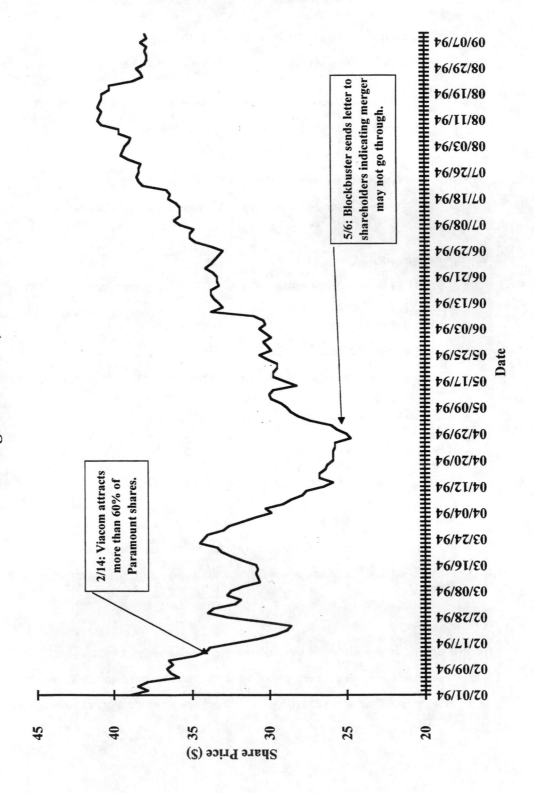

Viacom Closing Share Price, 2/1/94-9/9/94

2/14: Viacom attracts more than 60% of Paramount shares.

5/6: Blockbuster sends letter to shareholders indicating merger may not go through.

Share Price ($)

Date

09/07/94
08/29/94
08/19/94
08/11/94
08/03/94
07/26/94
07/18/94
07/08/94
06/29/94
06/21/94
06/13/94
06/03/94
05/25/94
05/17/94
05/09/94
04/29/94
04/20/94
04/12/94
04/04/94
03/24/94
03/16/94
03/08/94
02/28/94
02/17/94
02/09/94
02/01/94

45
40
35
30
25
20

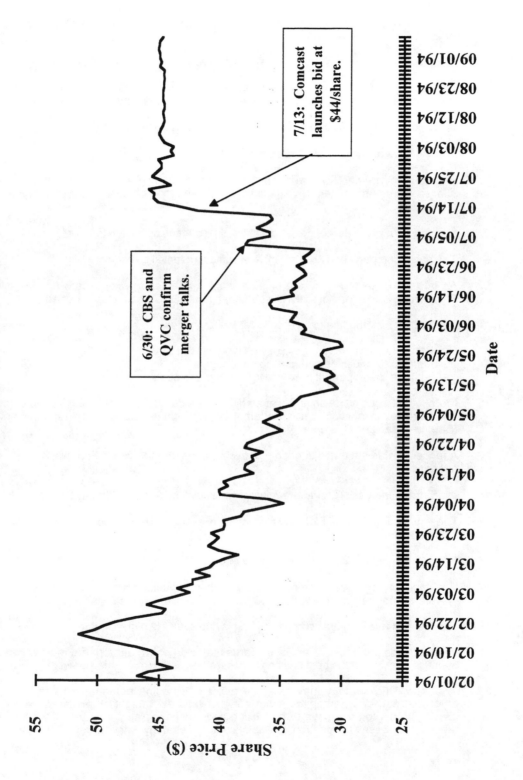

QVC Closing Share Price, 2/1/94-9/9/94

6/30: CBS and QVC confirm merger talks.

7/13: Comcast launches bid at $44/share.

Share Price ($)

Date

VIACOM-PARAMOUNT MERGER
LESSONS FROM THE DEAL

1. Boards of directors do not always fulfill their fiduciary responsibility to look after shareholder interests.

2. Target companies—Paramount—may get caught up in emotions during the deal.

3. Lock-up agreements generally do not protect target shareholder interests. However, they may send a signal that other bids will need to be very high to succeed.

4. High bidders often see their stock go down—Winner's Curse—Hubris.

5. Bidding wars are very costly to bidders.

6. PR can be an effective weapon during the deal by using the media to convince shareholders of the potential value of your offer, and the potential drawbacks to your rival's offer.

7. Litigation is a basic part of deal-making anytime there is conflict in the deal.

8. The same company can be a potential ally and a potential adversary (TCI).

9. As in a poker game, there are times to hold, and times to play a card (stonewalling by Paramount; Redstone not making a better offer until QVC does a tender offer).

10. The ability to line up financing is critical in making a deal.

11. Financing can come from many sources beyond Wall Street.
    - Strategic alliances can be used to raise capital.
    - But there are important risks associated with this strategy.

12. From the perspective of an ally, a strategic alliance during a deal is equivalent to organizing a fund-raiser in politics--it is an attempt to garner influence with the presumed winner (Barbara Streisand Strategy).

13. A tender offer is a method to get a prospective partner to the dance floor when they'd rather not dance.

14. It is virtually impossible for a target firm to insulate itself from a bidder indefinitely.

15. The entry of a rival bidder ends up costing everyone more money, except the target shareholders.

16. Offers that include stock may be highly variable.

17. It is generally in players' interests to signal their commitment to a deal. However, other players cannot be certain whether a signal is a commitment or a bluff.

18. The "Revlon rule" requires companies "in play" to seek the highest price possible.

19. The business judgment rule allows boards to decide on an appropriate merger candidate because they are in the best position to assess how "strategic" a merger is.

20. A stonewalling strategy may have the effect of enraging potential bidders, stirring the emotional pot, and perhaps leading to higher bids than might otherwise have been the case. By this logic, it pays to be kicking and screaming all the way to the altar. Major reason this doesn't happen more: The price of this strategy is the target CEO's job.

Overview

This case takes the Honda Motor Company through a full life cycle transition from its initial entrepreneurial start, through its growth and diversification into automobiles, to its mature competition phase as the number three auto producer in Japan and number four in the United States in 1994. The case focuses first on Mr. Soichiro Honda's early entrepreneurial years, contrasting his actions with those typically envisioned as "Japanese management style." This portion of the case also brings into question the degree to which "Japan, Inc." was responsible for Japan's success in foreign markets. Honda is constantly in conflict with Japanese authorities, regulations, and MITI directives. After describing some of the transitional events leading to Honda's international posture, the case profiles Honda's position in the U.S. and world markets and raises questions about what Honda's strategy should be in the 1990s, particularly in Europe after 1992.

The case goes well with readings on strategy formation, the entrepreneurial context, the innovation context, the mature context, and configuration. It allows an interesting discussion of the strengths and limitations of Japanese planning at the national level. If this case is used along with the Pascale article on "The Honda Effect," one should use that experience primarily as backdrop for developing Honda's strengths and styles in discussing its overall 1994 strategy, and the organizational implications of this style.

Session Structure

Discussion of the Honda Motor Company naturally breaks down into three segments: (1) the entrepreneurial period, (2) Honda's move into the United States, (3) Honda's future strategy in the multinational markets of the mid-1990s. An excursion into Japan's national strategy for development of its industry and Honda's relationship to that can be undertaken at any of several points. If the Pascale article is used, one may wish to bypass this aspect of the case discussion. This case runs well in a tight 75 minute-90 minute class period. It can be used early in the course as a "strategy formulation" case or later as a mature or entrepreneurial "context" case. Students are fascinated by Mr. Honda's story, the Honda line of motorcycles and automobiles, and the myths and facts about the company's development. Honda provides an excellent example of ignoring the conventional wisdom about a maturing industry, reassessing all the rules about participation in such an industry, changing those rules to create a distinctive new marketplace. It also provides an excellent vehicle for discussing global strategies, particularly entry into Europe and a mid-1990s European and multinational strategy.

"Japan, Inc." and "Japanese Management Style"

One can open the discussion by asking the students to describe their perceptions of how "Japan Incorporated" operates and what their perceptions are of the "Japanese management style." The former question quickly evokes responses of:

1. Coordinated research and development supported by the government.
2. Targeted investment with coordinated action by government groups.
3. An emphasis on high technology in emerging markets.
4. Serving a base demand in Japan first, then moving to international markets.

Teaching note copyright © 1996 by James Brian Quinn. This note prepared by Professor Quinn and Penny C. Paquette, Research Associate.

5. Using a capital intensive strategy, with access to Japan's lower cost of capital sources.
6. Coordinated efforts through Japan's large vertically integrated supplier, producer, banking, trading company groups.
7. Strong trade preferences given to exporting companies.
8. National coordination of investments in supplier industries to support the exporting group.
9. Emphasis on non-energy intensive industries.
10. Emphasis on industries with low transportation costs and high value added.
11. Priorities given to manufacturing sectors not requiring controlled distribution networks abroad.
12. Capital support to companies attempting to establish themselves abroad, and so on.

It is interesting to compare Honda's history with these presumptions. Honda breaks almost everyone of these stereotypical rules about what U.S. executives believe the "Japanese advantage" to be based on.

Another interesting opening for this case is to ask, "When you think of the Japanese management style, what does this style connote to you?" In response to this, one would typically obtain responses emphasizing:

1. High degrees of cooperation between labor and management.
2. Group or consensus decisions.
3. Copy cat or replicative design.
4. Relatively slow decisions made with great consensus and certainty.
5. An ultra-courteous working atmosphere.
6. High emphasis on quality circles and worker cooperation in decisions.
7. Company songs and slogans.
8. A strongly managed company identity and culture.
9. A long-term low-risk outlook, and so on.

Again, it is interesting to contrast the early years of Honda Motor Company's actual history against these stereotypes. Honda breaks virtually every one of them. This allows one to ask, "Is there really a single Japanese management style? If not, how did we obtain the perceptions we have of *the* Japanese management style?" Most of the early papers written on the Japanese management style dealt with relatively limited observations within some of the very large, more stable, integrated companies.

Only fairly recently have scholars begun to realize that there are at least three tiers of Japanese companies: (1) the "inner group" of large, well capitalized, high volume manufacturing companies associated with international trading companies and large Japanese banks in Keiretsu structures; (2) a second tier of supplier companies to this "inner group" which are substantially assisted and financed by the "inner group;" (3) a very large number of small "third tier" companies which operate very much like the U.S. or European "fringe companies" in sparse facilities, with little automation, with sweat shop conditions, and with little evidence of the job guarantees, high fringe benefits, and sociable work conditions generally found in the "inner group." This latter group is not as efficient as the overall Japanese average, nor probably as efficient as the small suppliers to U.S. industry. However, Japanese people do work extraordinarily hard, they are well educated, and they do tend to identify with their employers because of the relatively limited social security and union protections available to them. ABC made an excellent program on this topic called, "The Other Japan." Videotapes may be available. William Davidson in his book, *The Amazing Race*, brings out some of the important questions this three tier structure raises for Japan.

The Entrepreneurial Period

The entrepreneurial period of Honda Motor Company's development enjoys many parallels to similar start ups in the United States. One can open this section of the discussion by asking, "What were the critical factors for success in the early (motorcycle) stages of Honda's growth? What made Honda successful in its early stages?" Several factors seem most important. These include, among other things, the following:

A. Honda's personal expertise - The company was initially heavily dependent upon the individual mechanical expertise of Mr. Honda in repairing automobiles, inventing new processes, and producing quality parts.

B. Doing things differently - Because of his unique personality, Mr. Honda tried to find new ways to do things better, and differently. This allowed him to establish small niches, based upon inventions, which were protected from his larger competitors.

C. Determination/fanaticism - Honda becomes a "working hermit." Expends all his savings, sells his wife's jewelry, etc. He studies his products in such detail that he knows them better than anyone else could. Despite frustrations caused by suppliers, the government, and his own technologies, Honda persists.

D. An early cash flow - Soon through his repairs and his sale of automobile wheel spokes, Honda creates the cash flow that allows him further experimentation.

E. Timing - Honda begins at a time when there was a great flux in the Japanese society. His eccentricities are ignored if his product works. He sells off his old business just in time to retain some assets at the end of the war.

F. A genuine need - Honda matches a genuine need for low cost transportation, low cost and available fuels, and food gathering from the countryside. He does not have to build a market. It exists.

G. Doing something unique - Honda does not copy existing solutions, but seeks new solutions which give him a distinctive competitive advantage. His motors were always smaller, more efficient, and more powerful for their weight.

H. Venture financing - Mr. Fujisawa financed the company uniquely, using its own customers as a capital base.

I. A balanced team - Mr. Honda and Mr. Fujisawa were completely complementary in personality, outlook, and management skills. This amplifies the impact of each of their personalities.

J. Innovation in all areas - Honda Motor Company did not just innovate in technology. It innovates in marketing/distribution, financing, and the very target market it chose (a substitute for the bicycle).

K. Sweat capital - Honda and Fujisawa leveraged their limited capital by "staying at work each day as long as it took to keep the plant going." This both lowers investment costs and increases the knowledge of the two key players.

L. Maintaining flexibility - Honda avoids coalitions with its large competitors or the government, either of which could have constrained its actions significantly. This allowed the company to move rapidly and responsively in the marketplace.

M. A dream - Honda had "an overriding vision"—which went beyond merely making money—the pursuit of technology, "a grandiose dream."

N. A distinctive superiority - Honda's products were demonstrably superior in performance characteristics, particularly the engines they contained. This gave Honda a true intellectual core competency that it could leverage against multiple products for many years.

O. Distribution channels - From the beginning, Fujisawa built the strongest distribution channels for Honda both in Japan and in the United States. Again, this leveraged Honda's limited capital resources by a large margin.

P. Risk taking - Both Honda and Fujisawa were willing to risk more capital than they owned (a million dollars for tools when they had $165,000). Yet they limited their risks elsewhere by substantial outsourcing.

Q. Close to the market - Mr. Honda and Mr. Fujisawa stayed close to the market, modifying their product and entering new niches as technological capabilities or market demands changed. Honda constantly tried to expand the primary market rather than simply build share in a selected marketplace. This strategy eased his problems of increasing his volume. While his competitors continued to "milk" a single model, Honda adapted quickly to its changing marketplace.

R. Obtaining scale quickly - By building a full-scale plant, investing heavily in its unique manufacturing equipment, outsourcing non-unique parts, and designing the motorcycle for simplicity of assembly, Honda lowered its costs enormously.

S. Lowest total cost - By concentrating on intellectual economies of scale, simple design in noncritical items, high quality, and a strong distribution network, Honda lowers the "system cost" for its product. These factors also limited warranty costs, allowed more inexpensive distribution, and lowered long-term manufacturing costs.

In these early years, Honda created a classic niche or "focus" strategy. It focused all of its attention on high performance motorcycles, and worked on all elements of the "value chain" to lower its cost and create maximum value for its customer. One should inquire what the "distinctive competency" of the Honda Motor Company is. What is the common thread upon which the company builds its future? Interestingly, if one pursues this subject sufficiently, one finds that Honda's distinctive competency was its enormous depth in motor design and building capabilities. Once Honda realized that it had this distinct competency, it was easy to roll it out into automobiles, then outboard motors, lawn tools, and so on.

By his early experimental work in understanding gaseous flows and combustion in engines, by designing extremely lightweight high powered engines for racing motorcycles, and by searching for unusual solutions like the overhead cam engine, Honda built up a distinctive knowledge competency which could be maintained for an extensive period of time against even its largest rivals. Its traditions of manufacturing motorcycles in this low cost, cost conscious, quality observant market led Honda to build low cost management skills that would serve it well in other mass markets.

This is a good point in the case at which to pursue this question of "a maintainable distinctive competitive edge." Many believe that the two factors that distinguish Honda are: (1) its depth of knowledge concerning internal combustion engines, and (2) its low cost production techniques derived from competing in the small motorcycle field, and (3) its strong distribution network and its concentration of quality presentation and service to customers.

Honda's Entry to the United States

At its "Decision Point," the case asks, "How should Honda develop its U.S. presence? What should its advertising, pricing, distribution, inventory, product, and service policies be in the United States? Why? If the Pascale article is used, this discussion should be kept very short or eliminated entirely. How should these be related to its Japanese prices, production facilities, development activities, and the continuing restrictions by the Ministry of Finance on exports of

Japanese yen?" These questions provide an interesting transition from Honda's early development as an entrepreneurial Japanese company and its later positioning as a worldwide producer of motorized devices.

Honda's entry to the U.S. motorcycle market is a clear example of an "emergent strategy." It was not clearly thought out in advance. It occurred as a series of fast responses to unexpected market conditions. In Japan, Honda's motorcycles had been basic transportation. In the United States, they entered an entirely different marketplace. They became a combination of a "second car for the smart set" and a "recreational vehicle." Neither the motorcycle companies nor the U.S. consumer would have recognized this as a marketplace until Honda's actual offering appeared. Market research prior to entry probably could not have identified this niche. Distribution channels, advertising approaches, product concepts, and lifestyle features all had to be invented interactively. In essence, Honda became the "off the road vehicle for city traffic." Honda's total approach had to be invented as it went along, and it had to be very different.

Honda Motor chose the U.S. market to attack first, believing that if Honda could be successful there, it could roll out that success to other parts of the world. At first Honda tried to sell its products through the traditional motorcycle distributorships and dealers. However, when Mr. Fujisawa saw his dealers at a motorcycle show wearing soiled overalls and dirty grease-covered hats, he began to question this channel of distribution. The Honda "step-through" design was hardly what that marketplace wanted. Yet Honda wanted to maintain its access to the profitable "black leather jacket set." Consequently, it decided to set up a parallel distribution channel. It marketed its "step-through" designs through sporting goods stores and hobby shops. With the assistance of Grey Advertising Inc., Honda changed the image of motorcycle riding. It introduced a classic campaign based upon the theme, "You Meet the Nicest People on a Honda." These advertisements were run in the influential magazines of that day: *Life, Look, Saturday Evening Post*, etc. The Super Cub was positioned as a vehicle, not for delinquents, but as a smart means of transportation for the general public.

From the beginning, American Honda Motor Company had few Japanese in its ranks. Honda began its distribution on the West Coast for two reasons: California was the closest point of entry to the United States and California tended to lead the country in new living styles. Honda's approach—selling motorcycles to the general public—was so unusual, that *Time, Life*, and *Look* at first refused to accept its ads (which stated Honda was the largest motorcycle manufacturer in the world) because they didn't believe this statement. The magazines had never carried motorcycle ads. However, Honda had to back up the success of its ad campaign with a totally different approach to distribution. The "middle class" customers of Honda Cubs and Super Cubs could not maintain their own "bikes" like the traditional motorcyclist did. Consequently, Honda had to support its distribution channels with an extensive parts supply, training system, and point of sale merchandising.

The professor should point out that Honda had created a primary market which was expanding rapidly. Consequently, it was not up against the same competitive pressures it would have been in trying to wrest a higher "share of the market" from established competitors. Honda's entry to the U.S. market coincided with a substantial saturation of the U.S. automobile market. People were looking for new extensions of their love affair with motor vehicles, and the "off the road" vehicle was a natural extension.

In addition to its magazine ads, Honda also advertised on national network television using a unique "humorous but classy" style. These ads focused on an upscale, 16-24 year age group. Honda has continued its humorous approach to motorcycle advertising to date. Honda insisted that his franchised dealers have a genuine repair shop available. He developed high quality jigs and fixtures especially for Honda motorcycle repair. The engine was designed to be split horizontally for easier, less messy repair. Honda rejected the assumption that motorcycles had to be leaky and noisy, designing its vehicles to be slim, clean, and quiet.

The Honda motorcycle introduction campaign in the United States is an interesting example of expanding a very limited market (the black leather jacket set), by repositioning a product to access a majority population. Honda put together a complete "niching" strategy with design, pricing, distribution, advertising, and after service tailored to its particular marketplace. Because of MITI's opposition and the freezing of Honda's access to the yen, the American company financed itself by borrowing from U.S. banks against its inventories. American Honda's capacity to build capital and grow in the United States was greatly influenced by its transfer prices from Japan. As the value of the yen rose against the dollar, it expanded its sourcing in the United States.

ENTRY INTO AUTOMOBILES

A major portion of the discussion can begin with the question, "Why was Honda's automobile entry successful in the U.S. market? Was this due to support or targeting by MITI? Why was Honda able to pick up market share so quickly in an industry which was so capital intensive, mature, and completely dominated by U.S. manufacturers?" These questions will lead to a number of responses, many of which depend upon the students' perceptions of Honda in the U.S. market. Some of these perceptions are based on fact; others on the "image" Honda carefully built up with its motorcycles and around its existing automobile line. Perhaps the most important factors leading to Honda's success are the following:

A. No U.S. competition existed in the subcompact area at the time of Honda's entry. U.S. automobile companies had systematically ignored this marketplace as being "not profitable." They had not considered in their strategies the possibility that well managed companies could use this small car base to obtain the distribution, reputation, and experience curve advantages to take market share away from their larger cars.

B. The oil crisis in the early 1970s gave all Japanese auto companies a lift. U.S. buyers needed small cars quickly. No U.S. capacity was available to produce them. Distributors and dealers of U.S. cars could not sell the large U.S. cars and rapidly agreed to take on the lines of small car producers from Japan. The CAFE standards of the mid '70s mandated a market for the size of cars then most sold in the Japanese market, giving Japanese car makers instant advantages over their U.S. rivals. Honda's superbly efficient motors gave it a special competitive advantage.

C. Distribution availability was crucial to Honda's success. Had quality U.S. car distributors been satisfied with their lines, it would have been difficult for Honda (or any other Japanese producer) to obtain the distribution that was absolutely essential to success. U.S. dealerships had been managed in an adversarial mode by Detroit, rather than as a partnership between producers and sellers. Consequently, dealers were happy to have another automobile with which they could bargain against Detroit.

D. High quality, low cost, and imaginative engineering distinguished Honda's cars from the outset. Honda used interior space well, paid attention to detailed "features," which would add value to the car in customers' eyes, yet not cost Honda anything extra in production. Honda produced very few variations on its basic models. Because of built-in quality, it did not have a significant "after market" warranty cost. This simplified its distribution and follow up problems in the U.S. market. Because the company's production traditions were based on the cost and quality sensitive motorcycle racing business, Honda did not build up large overheads or add "frills" to its cars which had high cost and offered little value added for the customer.

E. Non-dependence on the Japanese market helped Honda. Other Japanese producers had a large dedicated market in Japan. Consequently, they could not initially focus full attention on the United States. Not having such a positioning, Honda could give relatively more focus to its U.S. sales. Honda was the first of the Japanese companies to produce in the United States on a significant scale, identifying itself with this marketplace and "leaping over" the quota barriers which came into existence in 1981. Its timing in this respect was outstanding.

F. A Quality reputation had accrued to Honda through its earlier motorcycle and scooter products. Its clever advertising had positioned these products in the cost conscious, market leader, slightly upscale marketplace which was the identical market it chose for its early cars. People who had used Honda Cubs as motorcycles quickly began to look at Honda's small cars as possible second cars. Again, Honda's clever, humorous, quality advertising campaign hit its market very well. Honda carefully dodged direct competition with the large U.S. producers.

G. A distinctive competency for Honda existed in its motor design. By taking its experiences with lightweight, efficient, motorcycle engines, and applying this know-how to automobiles, Honda was able to come up with a clean, lightweight, efficient engine which could meet all EPA standards from the outset. This high quality engine gave Honda cars their reputation for low maintenance and satisfactory performance over the long term.

H. Honda's culture influenced all of these events. The dominance of engineering over marketing gave focus to the quality design of the car. Its attention to cost controls and details (dictated by successful competition in motorcycles) caused the design of the CVCC "fuel efficient" engines, which by internal agreement had been designed to be "externally efficient" as well. This meant they had few effluents per unit of fuel, and used little fuel in the first place. Honda's production culture focused on low cost manufacture, participation by employees, close linkages between engineers and manufacturing employees, and an integrated concept of marketing, production, and design.

I. Innovative design was featured in Honda cars, particularly in the front wheel drive, CVCC motor, and gear train mechanisms. Focusing on these features gave the cars a stability and traction not available in U.S. cars, where manufacturers stuck doggedly with the rear wheel drive. In addition, the front wheel drive gave added room inside the cabin of the car, which created a sense of comfort and spaciousness along with vastly improved engine and technical performance. From the beginning, Honda's cars tested in the "top quality" rankings and "best engineered" rankings of all cars in the world.

J. Organizational innovation also supported the strategy. Mr. Fujisawa's flat or "paper weight" organization meant that engineering was close to the top of the organization, people worked in small teams which could communicate with each other, bureaucracies were not built up at the corporate level, and engineers could be rewarded for technical work, not just administrative positioning. Workers were expected to participate in design improvements. Marketing and sales people were intimately tied into the design process. Engineers were "encouraged to think like customers," and their technical projects were constantly reviewed by sales, financial, and production staffs.

Honda stayed close to the marketplace by shortening its design cycle to 2-3 years as opposed to the 4-6 years commonly used in the U.S. This meant that its automobile designs could be more "up to date" in the eyes of customers. Workers moved laterally through the organization so that they did not have a myopic view, nor was their personal development squelched. Honda had relative labor peace, because it allowed the workers to analyze their own jobs and set reasonable work standards. Nevertheless, the work pace in Honda factories was very efficient relative to U.S. labor union controlled work paces.

Strategy Issues for the Mid 1990s

The final set of questions in the case has to do with Honda's mid 1990s posture and future strategies. Opening questions might be, "What are the critical elements in Honda's current posture?" Because of its history and the interests of its top managers, Honda has developed a rather unique posture in the automobile industry. It is considered the finest designer and manufacturer of small efficient internal combustion engines in the world. Because it lacked capital in the early stages of its development, Honda had to outsource a very high proportion of its components. Consequently, it developed a very efficient purchasing and logistics system which is applicable to its world operations. Similarly, because of its capital shortages and the cost cutting necessities of the motorcycle industry, Honda developed small-medium scale assembly techniques that are unparalleled in the industry. Honda's plants are much smaller than its competitors' plants, its design cycles are shorter, and it constantly updates its plants by incremental improvements rather than waiting (as the Americans do) to realign an entire plant for a new automotive line. Its plant and design policies have made Honda's overhead structures lower than its competitors, it has higher mobility, and it can focus on quality in a unique fashion. Its advanced technology culture allows it to take risks on plant and auto design innovations and thus to push such features as four-wheel steering which other competitors found more difficult to introduce.

In the mid 1990s, what important issues does Honda face? What should its future strategies be? There are, of course, many possible responses. In general, these may be clustered around 5 or 6 important categories. Some suggestions follow:

A. Positioning the U.S. Honda line. Honda's automobile line needs to be positioned uniquely vis-à-vis the U.S. car lines, European cars, and other Japanese producers. By doing a "competitor analysis," one can see that the most likely future positioning for U.S. cars is toward the "large car, family, and special purpose vehicle markets." These include the broad "center lines" of Ford, Chrysler, and General Motors and the "large car" lines which only American manufacturers produce. Producers in newly industrialized countries like Korea are likely to go after the "price conscious" marketplace, with emphasis on smaller cars, standardized designs, adequate quality, and high volume. Although these cars lack widespread distribution, U.S. distribution channels for automobiles are so varied and available that LDC producers can now find some suitable modes of distribution—including the "automobile supermarkets" which carry virtually any line.

Why should Honda try to expand in the United States? Honda is not as strong as Toyota or Nissan in Japan. Thus, it needs the U.S. market more—to drive down its costs and achieve the quality benefits of the experience curve—than those two competitors. Further, exchange rates are making the cost of production in Japan very high. Because it was a late, import entry to the United States, Honda was stuck with very low quotas under the "voluntary quota system." Consequently, it needed to expand production in the United States to gain on its major competitors. Because of its mode of entry to the U.S. market, Honda had an excellent quality reputation to work from. Distribution channels were available to Honda, if it positioned itself as a high value-added, slightly upscale (but slightly smaller than European or American cars) producer focusing on the "smart" buyer who sought quality and value, not luxury. Its position had to be a quality-high image position, yet with costs below U.S. companies or the Europeans and with the flexibility to keep the line up to date.

In order to produce in this "non-generic"—middle market—position, Honda had to do certain things extremely well. It had to keep its plant costs low ($250 million vs. $600 million investment for other Japanese producers), remain non-union (a $9 per hour advantage vs. others), focus its car lines to achieve volume and experience curve benefits on a limited segment of the market, keep its plants producing to capacity for full overhead absorption, and obtain very efficient, fast response distribution in the United States. All of these fit well with Honda's culture and past practice. In the early 1990s it enjoyed a $1500 per car advantage over competing U.S. car lines. It was able to ship cars back to Japan at a profit as exchange rates moved against the yen.

One should question how U.S. automakers might go after Honda in its markets. The initial response from students will be advertising directly against the Accord using comparative features and ads. However, some more sophisticated counterpositionings might be very interesting. Honda was able to take away a large portion of American manufacturers' markets (like the VW Beetle had earlier) because it represented a symbolic lifestyle shift for children away from their parents' big car, solid, past. As Honda becomes the accepted car of the U.S. middle class, a new market will emerge for the "next generation" of automobile buyer. U.S. companies can target the "progeny of Honda owners" by setting up Honda in their ads as the "stodgy middle class car of the past." At a minimum, this will force Honda to make model changes more rapidly.

If the U.S. auto industry can recognize new emerging lifestyles and position niched cars for the children of Honda owners, it may be able to grow for itself the next generation of automobile owners in the United States. Similarly, in Japan, there is a growing market for those with lifestyles not attuned to the uniformities of the past. By presenting the same "young lifestyle cars" in Japan, U.S. manufacturers may be able to create a market there for the next generation of U.S. cars. Such "lifestyle shift symbol" products are becoming increasingly popular for Japanese youths asserting their independence. However, of course, any such entry will have to have a very clear quality capability associated with it. There are some major psycho-demographic opportunities in these two positionings.

B. Positioning the Honda line in Europe. European producers seem to be emphasizing high priced, uniquely styled, upscale, small volume marketplaces. Thus, the most likely opening for Honda would be a "well styled, quality, less specialized, slightly smaller, automobile for the U.S. and world markets." It would be niching "below" the Europeans and the large U.S. car manufacturers in price—and above smaller U.S. and LDC autos in quality and price. This is a very delicate positioning to pull off. It requires very careful maintenance of quality, image, and costs. It also requires meeting the demands of the increasingly individualized U.S. and European marketplaces with a large number of choices in features, yet maintaining a high value/price ratio. Again this is clearly not a "generic strategy."

In the European market, Honda has the potential of achieving scale, cost, and/or quality advantages over most individual car lines there. The exhibits show that each major European market is dominated by one or two domestic manufacturers. Yet each of those manufacturers has a significant vulnerability (in terms of total volume, costs of its domestic location, or quality). As a result, virtually all countries have left open the "high quality/high value niche, for the smart buyer" that is Honda's forte. The European market generally splits itself into high-end specialty cars with macho or "sex appeal," vs. a low-end market which is fuel/cost efficient. The niche in between is the segment Honda is best qualified to attack.

Honda's main problem in Europe will be to avoid a coordinated government-company coalition providing a subsidized or policy-supported counteraction in each country. Because of the employment security arrangements in Europe, there could be significant pressures on individual automakers if Japanese cars displace workers and jobs. Some of the markets themselves are already "controlled markets." There is a question as to how much these will be opened as the EEC develops. Spain, Italy and France are the main problem areas in this respect. Some of these countries have resisted British-Japanese cars, even when they contain 80% European content. Consequently, Honda's strategy has to emphasize what it can bring to each European country (in job and investment terms) to offset that country's potential displacements. This will mean a careful structuring of purchase arrangements in different countries as well as a location strategy for assembly plants.

Perhaps Honda can use its motorcycle divisions to help in this job offset. During the early transition of Eastern Europe to a more capitalistic form, motorcycle markets should boom, especially in East Germany. Honda's product line is ideally positioned to take advantage of this transitional shift. Thus, Honda may be able to demonstrate job growth for its host countries, even as it displaces some auto manufacturing there. However, each country will make sure that its dominating producer does not disappear. Honda's real strategy has to be the placement of component and feeder plants in its motorcycle and auto divisions to take advantage of Eastern Europe and EEC expansions. It must at all costs avoid being considered a "foreign" automobile company. This can lead to some very interesting discussions.

In this discussion, one can ask, "What countries are likely to lose share in the expanding European marketplace?" These would be ideal targets for Honda. Another question is, "Why did Honda enter a coalition with Leland in Britain?" The probable answer is that Britain was a large market, with no national dominance, with high labor costs, lower productivity, and generally lower quality. This could be a demonstration of Honda's capacity to provide jobs, increase productivity, and become a national asset. Honda might feature its presence as being a defensive strategy for countries to avoid losing position in the new European marketplace. It could consider locating its three major lines in different portions of the European marketplace: high quality/price Acura (Britain), mid-market Accords (France or Belgium), low end Civic or Citi (Italy or Spain), motorcycles (Germany). This is a good point at which to introduce concepts of strategic groups around product, market, and cost considerations in coordination.

C. Multinational production. Honda must choose a manufacturing strategy which optimizes its positions around developing new marketplaces, exchange rate shifts, market responsiveness, and lowest cost production. In the United States, Honda has some significant maintainable advantages. Its early move to producing in the United States gave it overhead advantages vs. its slower moving Japanese competitors. Honda is well established in the U.S. marketplace with a non-unionized workforce. This gives it important cost advantages vs. U.S. manufacturers. Because of its plant technologies, Honda's cost structure in Japan appears sufficiently lower than its competitors that it can both take share from those competitors and make more money per vehicle than they. Honda probably needs to continue emphasizing an increased volume strategy in Japan to obtain further experience curve benefits and to capture the knowledge and further experience its U.S. factories can offer. However, Honda needs a more significant presence in Europe. Should this presence be obtained by building a plant "from the ground up" or should Honda go into a joint venture with a European company? The latter approach is much more likely to get Honda around the restrictive entry problems in the European market. It must choose its partner well. Since it wants to differentiate itself from the luxury German cars, its best joint venture would probably be with a British, French, or Italian manufacturer, currently in trouble, but wishing to upscale its line. Several candidates suggest themselves.

Honda has also positioned itself well relative to the problems created by the strengthening Japanese yen. Its U.S. manufacturing capabilities give it significant protection from exchange rate shifts. However, Honda suffers compared to other Japanese producers using a Canadian base. Perhaps, Honda should move production of its new Acura line into Canada in order to gain both the concessions Canada will offer and the exchange rate differences there. An interesting question exists as to whether Honda should introduce its new mini-car, the Citi, into the United States. This would tend to put it into direct competition with LDC producers, and might trade down its image. The European marketplace, with its high priced cars, would tend to offer Honda an interesting quality-price niche, if it could produce there.

In the near future, Honda's biggest multinational competitive issue will be meeting Toyota's large volume, low cost, positionings in the U.S. and Japanese marketplaces. Potentially, Toyota has the capacity to beat Honda on a quality-price basis worldwide. Honda therefore needs to position itself "slightly upscale" from Toyota and obtain a slight premium price for its products through more sophisticated product positioning, quality design, engineering, and performance. Its biggest competitive advantage in the U.S. market is its already established relatively low cost and non-unionized production facility. The biggest question for Honda is how Nissan, with its much larger financial capacities, may respond. Clearly, Honda needs to have a "triad" strategy. It needs strong positionings in Japan-South East Asia, Europe, and North America. One should note that Honda to date is almost alone in not developing strong coalitions in non-Japanese marketplaces. (See K. Ohmae, *Triad Power*, p. 134, Exhibit 9-1.) It probably needs such coalitions in Europe, chosen with an eye toward their potential to move Honda upscale—without government interference—into the luxury/specialty market should it choose to go that direction.

Another interesting question is whether Honda should begin to make lower priced cars in NIC or developing country areas. In time, these locations might provide some interesting subsystem supply potentials, especially in South East Asia. Such a supply strategy should probably be phased into Honda's strategy.

D. Diversification. In what directions should Honda attempt diversification? How will this affect its other activities? From what strengths should Honda attempt to diversify, if it does? These questions can open up several interesting avenues of discussion. In the past, Honda's core competency has been in engine design and manufacture. Each one of its products was premised upon a superior engine design. This is an area where Honda has extreme depth. Consequently, diversification should probably be based on this special competency. In fact, Honda centralizes all of its engine R&D in Japan and concentrates its sourcing and manufacture of key engine components there. By concentrating on this "core competency," Honda can leverage its capabilities worldwide. It might even use other small motor products to gain market recognition in countries where it is currently unable to have a significant automobile manufacturing capability.

In specialized situations, this immediately suggests other leisure products, like snowmobiles, outboard motors, and "all terrain vehicles." It also suggests the possibility of creating major markets in outdoor lawn and gardening equipment which requires efficient, light gasoline engines. In the U.S., Briggs and Stratton has a virtual monopoly over small 2-cycle engines used for household equipment. Honda is one of the few companies in the world which could take over this market from Briggs and Stratton. Should it sell its motors on an OEM basis? Should Honda diversify its distribution of leisure end products or feature them through its Honda automobile dealerships? How can it obtain mass distribution in this already competitive field? How can Honda develop a "family line" resemblance which plays off of its past quality successes in automobiles and motorcycles? These questions will open up an interesting set of issues for discussion. As is suggested in the "Summary of Outcomes" section, Honda has pursued some such diversifications.

E. Honda image. What image should Honda attempt to present? Probably, it should begin to present its distinctive competency (advanced, lightweight motor design) more in its advertising. Honda's customers tend to be quite similar to those for European cars—upscale, educated, sophisticated, and slightly older (30s and 40s) than low cost car buyers. Its positioning should probably be among the sophisticated, sporty, young executive set. The company should anticipate that some form of quotas are likely to be continued, offering it a chance to move slightly upscale in its U.S. product positioning.

F. National policy considerations. As Honda builds its presence in Europe, the United States and Japan, this creates an interesting issue. Is Honda really a Japanese company? For example, shouldn't Honda U.S.A be considered an American company? It will certainly be exporting from its U.S. base to Japan and Europe. Should we therefore consider Honda U.S.A. as a U.S. company and support its exports to Europe? If we do, are we not supporting a Japanese company against the (U.S.) GM and Ford companies operating in Europe?

As Japanese companies become further based in the United States will they act as U.S. companies? If so how will they affect U.S "competitiveness?" Will they improve levels of U.S. competitiveness outside of their own operations? How does this correlate with our fear of Japanese investment in the United States? One should compare the present tendencies of the Japanese to invest in the United States to the benefits obtained from European investment here in earlier years. Our U.S. production infrastructure was essentially built by European capital and technology. Not only does this help us with productivity but lowers demands on our own U.S. capital sources, and lowers average U.S. capital costs. One should begin to ask whether in ownership terms the Japanese companies are any different from American companies anymore? Their pension funds and our pension funds own both sets of companies. As there is increasing investment across borders in this fashion, which group of companies should U.S. policy support? One might even suggest that if exchange rates were allowed to float freely, and companies were not subsidized by government policy, "competitiveness" would take care of itself.

How should U.S. companies respond to the entry of Japanese auto manufacturers? Obviously, they should attempt to meet the quality, response time, and cost potentials of these manufacturers. Conversely, they should perhaps consider forming coalitions with lower cost country automobile companies (like Daewoo) and invading the Japanese market, where small price cuts could severely hurt the cash flows of major Japanese companies. A strong coalition entry in Japan (especially using an established Japanese manufacturer there) could potentially hurt Japanese manufacturers far more than countering their production in the United States.

A final note to develop is that with such coalitions, the automobile industry is developing as a new "global oligopoly." Instead of national markets dominated by oligopolists, global competition is governed by the network of coalitions built up among competing groups. In the long run, there is a question as to whether companies can develop a distinctive competency in this kind of marketplace. National markets and national competitiveness issues may become moot. As technologies transfer across borders, can the companies which produce in LDC or NIC positions force wages and profits down to unacceptable levels in the developed countries? Will automobiles become such commodities that they will be treated just like minerals or agricultural products are today? Is it essential that nations maintain a transportation producing capacity for reasons other than market competition? If so, how should countries structure and compensate for such values received?

From a national strategy viewpoint, it is probably desirable for countries not to resist the entry of manufacturing companies like Honda. If domestic manufacturers cannot beat them, it is better to assimilate such companies into the economy and gain the benefits of their economies of scale, design techniques, management techniques, and product cost and quality features. Although the Europeans are currently trying to do so, it is probably best not to differentiate between "domestic" companies and truly international companies producing domestically. In the long run, consumers, labor, and the domestic economy will benefit.

SUMMARY OF OUTCOMES

While a company's actions do not necessarily represent correct or incorrect responses to changing strategic issues, they may be helpful to the professor in bringing out different aspects of the discussion.

After Honda brought out its new Acura line, repositioning itself slightly upscale in the U.S. marketplace (but not as pricey as the Europeans), it established a separate marketing division and dealer franchises for the Acura cars. It extended its model options substantially, allowing some 30,000 combinations of features—as opposed to only 3,000 a few years before. It was able to use the Japanese market as a test market, since Japanese tastes increasingly moved towards slightly larger cars with highly individualized features.

Honda had introduced its mini-car (Citi and Today) products in Japan. But it had been reluctant to introduce these products into overseas markets where quotas applied. Its market share in Japan expanded with the Today and Acura "Legend" products. It expanded its number of models extensively in Japan, feeding the individualizing of automobile designs there. Its Acura line, with the Integra and Legend models, pushed Honda increasingly toward direct competition with European cars.

Like all Japanese manufacturers, Honda had exploited the price umbrellas created by the "voluntary quotas" agreed to between United States and Japan. By selling higher priced cars in the United States, Japanese producers had created a pricing umbrella permitting Korean companies like Daewoo and Hyundai to move in with low cost, small car strategies. It liked to price its cars in the United States at 60-70% above the "current exchange price" in Japan. As consumer resistance developed to higher priced Japanese cars in the United States Honda's flexible production facilities, however, would allow it to expand its production in the United States if the yen remained too strong. Honda had attacked this problem by installing highly flexible manufacturing systems, welding was 90% automated, while final assembly was only 5% automated. This allowed the company to move quickly to expand volume, if necessary, as well as to individualize its cars. A recent *Time* article pointed out that Honda's changeover from one model year to the next was accomplished in a few minutes while in U.S.-owned plants, it might take days or even weeks of costly downtime.

To maintain its distinctive competency, Honda very carefully controlled engine manufacture and quality of all operations. Its U.S. operations often "slavishly" followed its Japanese ones. Before turning out the new Accord in the United States it flew 200 workers to its Japanese plants where they worked until they could teach their co-workers in the U.S. to produce in a similar fashion. It gave workers the same kind of group responsibilities in the United States as it did in Japan and had only two job classifications compared with as many as 100 in some unionized U.S. plants. Parking spaces were not allocated to executives, and executives were expected to eat in the plant with workers. While Honda had not been able to find U.S. suppliers willing to meet its quality and delivery standards in the mid 1970s, it worked with suppliers in the United States to achieve over 90% "domestic content" in the early 1990s.

Mid-1990s Developments

In 1995 Honda reached 30 million cumulated autos produced throughout the world, one-third of that coming in the last five years. It produced in 19 facilities in 14 countries. Its global structure represented Honda's long-time corporate philosophy of manufacturing in the markets where products were sold. Five million of Honda's cars had been manufactured in North America, 24 million in Japan, and 1 million elsewhere. Civic and Accord models accounted for 19 million units or 63% of all the cars it had produced.

Honda's all new re-engineered 1996 Civic was classified as a domestic car in the United States. It expected to export 40,000 North American built Civics to more than 50 countries. American Honda led all U.S. manufacturers in automobile exports to overseas markets. In 1993 Honda became the top automobile exporter to Japan, capturing more than 20% of Japan's import car market. The Civic local content was now 92%, while Honda had exported over 300,000 cars since its first manufacture in the United States. Honda had a total U.S. employment of over 15,000 "associates" and had invested more than $3.8 billion in the United States since 1982. It also produced nearly 870,000 motorcycles, 1.1 million lawn mowers and 860,000 engines in the United States. It had developed an engine plant in Anna, Ohio, performing the same functions as seven different plants in Japan. The plant produced approximately 587,000 automobile and motorcycle engines in 1995. Its combined UK and U.S. auto production units increased sales in Western Europe by 8.9% in 1995, the only Japanese automobile line to increase European sales in face of a strong yen. Continuing its decentralization of production, Honda opened operations in Vietnam and was constructing an auto plant near New Delhi in India. The latter (Honda Siel India Ltd.) would be 60% owned by Honda and would begin production in 1997.

In July 1995, Honda announced an engine that would improve engine power and reduce fuel consumption. The new three-stage VTEC engine achieved improvements of 20% in fuel economy and 40% in power output, while reducing emissions. Honda's multi-matic transmission was the first continuously variable automatic transmission system designed for high output engines to be mass produced. The 1995 Honda Accord ranked first among the 20 models in its class for customer satisfaction while its new four-wheel drive auto designed with Rover opened up new markets for Honda in the United States. R.L. Poke & Company's annual study of automobile owner loyalty had found Honda number one in owner loyalty among all makes for three consecutive years and number one in import owner loyalty for sixteen straight years. In a J.D. Power and Associates' 1993 study of vehicle dependability, Acura had ranked second only to Mercedes in a study of 30 name plates and 154 models. Its new 1995-96 Civic and Accord lines achieved great acclaim from the rating institutions, who said "these cars carried two great designs to new heights."

The most ominous threat to Honda was the switch of Japanese buyers away from premium features and toward price. Ford and Chrysler had exploited this to enter the Japanese market.

Honda Passenger Car Sales in the United States
Year-to-date Comparisons as of 10/95

	1995	1994	95/94	95 Mix
Honda division total sales	556,486	556,492	0.0	87.5
Civic	240,648	228,716	5.2	36.4
Accord	283,368	313,851	2.8	42.8
Odyssey	21,275	0		
Passport	22,821	20,078	3.4	3.4
Prelude	11,195	13,925	-19.6	1.7
Acura division total sales	82,474	99,056	-16.7	12.5
Legend	16,720	31,878	-47.6	2.5
Integra	52,383	58,878	-10.8	7.9
NSX	621	451	37.7	0.1
Vigor	250	8,024	-96.9	0.1
TL	12,500	0		
Honda's total U.S sales	638,960	655,548	-2.5	
Industry sales total	7,363,915	7,629,006	-3.8	
Honda market share	8.7%	8.6%		
Honda division import sales	145,533	164,466	-11.5	
Civic	66,179	58,980	12.2	
Accord	46,884	91,561	-48.8	
Acura division import sales	82,474	99,056	-16.7	
Honda's total import sales	228,007	263,522	-13.5	
Honda U.S. domestic sales	410,953	392,026	4.8	
Domestic to total sales	64.3%	59.8%		

Source: Honda Motor Company.

Retail Sales in Japan by Manufacturer
Year-to-date Comparisons as of 10/95

	1995	1994	95/94	95 Mix
All vehicles				
Honda	506,955	452,488	12.0	8.8
Toyota	1,695,194	1,710,275	-0.9	29.4
Nissan	933,148	857,758	8.8	16.2
Mazda	309,354	335,683	-7.8	5.4
Mitsubishi	696,001	626,814	11.0	12.1
Fuji	288,530	290,413	-0.6	5.0
Isuzu	125,334	117,458	6.7	2.2
Daihatsu	341,104	332, 024	2.7	5.9
Suzuki	513,421	481,169	6.7	8.9
Imports	274,710	203,193	35.2	4.8
Total	5,757,830	5,469,778	5.3	
Passenger cars				
Honda	352,171	295,818	19.0	11.8
Toyota	1,147,818	1,198,195	-4.2	38.6
Nissan	708,979	642,687	10.3	23.8
Mazda	149,884	191,058	-21.6	5.0
Mitsubishi	212,314	201,054	5.6	7.1
Fuji	111,678	102,078	9.4	3.8
Imports	253,325	181,493	39.6	8.5
Total	2,973,893	2,853,220	4.2	

Notes: Imported Accords, Civics, and Crossroads are included in Honda sales instead of Imports.
Passenger car figures do not include mini-vehicles.

Source: Honda Motor Company.

THE PILLSBURY COMPANY TEACHING NOTE

Overview

This case lends itself to a variety of positionings in the course. It is a very strong case on the formation of a strategy, on the politics of decision making, on diversification strategies, and on acquisitions strategies. The case focuses on the turnaround at Pillsbury engineered by Mr. William Spoor in the late 1970s. The processes through which Mr. Spoor brought about this change are fascinating in themselves. But the case ends with a decision point at which the new CEO, Mr. Stafford, needs to reassess his portfolio and determine the future growth vectors of the company. We usually position the case along with several other diversifying companies, i.e., Continental Group, General Mills, and Gallo Winery.

Session Structure

We normally open the case by looking at the sequence of steps Mr. Spoor undertook as he began the turnaround at Pillsbury. These can be broken up into several steps: (1) the way the strategy itself was first developed, (2) the way goals were handled during the turnaround, (3) the early organization moves Mr. Spoor made and why, (4) the actions surrounding the divestiture of the "chickens business." These steps combine a series of analytical moves with a series of powerful political or "process" steps.

The next stage of discussion focuses on the redeployment of assets during the central portion of the turnaround. This involves a focus on the consumer foods and restaurant businesses. Finally, the last portion of the discussion focuses on the current portfolio, its needs, a new strategy for Pillsbury, and the specific steps Mr. Stafford might take in developing a strategy for the future. Depending on the skills of the professor, a 1 1/2 hour class session can be about equally divided between the analysis of past moves and the analysis of future strategy needs. The case provides an especially powerful vehicle for looking at the practical politics of change and the structure of an acquisitions strategy.

Developing Spoor's Strategy

We normally open this portion of the case by asking, "What do you think of the way in which Mr. Spoor developed his strategy at the beginning of the case? What were the most crucial process steps? Why were they undertaken?" Perhaps most crucial among these were:

A. Involving the general managers so that they would identify with and implement the strategy effectively.

B. Going to outside authorities, consultants, and so on to obtain credibility for analyses and objectivity of information.

C. Involving the Board for two reasons: (1) to obtain their input and identification with the new strategy, (2) understanding what opposition might exist to a major strategy change.

D. Doing a thorough competitor analysis which both gave Pillsbury some specific targets and also helped executives understand exactly what their competitors' strategies were.

Teaching note copyright © 1991 by James Brian Quinn. This note prepared by Professor Quinn and Penny C. Paquette, Research Associate.

E. <u>Developing a broad vision</u> for the company which focused on longer term potentials. This focus avoided implicitly or explicitly criticizing the previous management, yet gave a new challenge for the organization. Since so many of the prior management were still in place, it was essential not to create a strong coalition among them against the new strategy.

F. Performing a careful <u>strengths and weaknesses analysis</u> which helped to focus on the real strengths of the company and to identify weaknesses which had to be corrected relatively quickly.

The Way Spoor Handled Goals

The goal structures set forth in the case provide fascinating examples of managing goal formulation and implementation. There are three different statements of goals in the case: (1) those which Mr. Spoor presented to the Board of Directors prior to his appointment, (2) those which were presented to the outside security analysts, (3) those which were later developed and used for internal control purposes. One can start this section off with the general question, "What do you think of the way in which Mr. Spoor developed new goals for Pillsbury?" Most audiences will then note the "very explicit goals" which Spoor used. The professor can then ask "but were they so explicit? Let's look at those that went to the Board prior to his appointment. Why were these goals expressed so generally?" The discussion then breaks down into three levels.

<u>Goals to the Board</u>: Prior to Spoor's appointment, the goals presented were fairly broad—statements of principle, or carefully phrased positions concerning management style, people needs, etc. While offering direction, these goals were unlikely to create opposition because they appealed to the values of the Board members and to most members of general management. Again, these goals avoided being critical of the prior management in any real sense. It was essential that the new management not alienate those it would have to rely on to support and implement its new strategy.

<u>Goals to the security analysts</u>: When the new management presented its goals to the security analysts, some were quite explicit, some were rather general, and some simply stated that "options are open." The new management team wanted to signal to the security analysts and the company itself that a new regime had begun. Those goals which were made explicit were ones which everyone strongly believed could be accomplished. Others were left more general or vague in order (1) to avoid tipping opponents' hands to the new Pillsbury strategy or (2) to avoid making commitments which, because of factors beyond the management's control, could not be met. The professor can ask, "Why did Mr. Spoor want to go to the security analysts?" There are probably two reasons: (1) the desire to send a clear signal to the security analysts and the organization, and (2) a desire to further commit the Board to these more aggressive goals. In a process sense, Mr. Spoor created a powerful symbol for the entire organization to see and follow.

<u>Internal Goals</u>: These goals were very explicit and numerical. At this time, the new management had begun to consolidate its power base, wanted to obtain clear internal commitment to the goals, and wanted the goals to be used as criteria for evaluating performance and perhaps evaluating future divestitures or acquisitions. Therefore, goals must be as clear and explicit as possible. However, they must also appear reasonable and attainable to those inside the company. The earlier process steps taken to involve Pillsbury management helped in all of these considerations.

Early Organization Changes

To implement the strategy, Mr. Spoor undertakes several important early organization changes. Probably most critical among these are the following:

A. <u>The Selection of Key People</u>: Mr. Spoor selects a new finance officer, personnel officer, acquisitions officer, and R&D officer to report directly to him. These individuals give Spoor access to a new objective body of data concerning the company in its most critical strategic areas. If Spoor is to accomplish the turnaround, he must have clear evaluations of: its financial capabilities and performance, its personnel capabilities, its technological capabilities and its true acquisition potentials.

B. <u>Concentration of Information</u>: Mr. Spoor quickly has all operating managers report directly to him. This does two things: (1) it gives Spoor more direct power over operations, (2) it eliminates all filters to information between the line and Spoor and ensures that his information base is vastly improved. It also leverages Spoor's own personality and individualized management style to obtain implementation quickly.

C. <u>Restructuring the Management Board</u>: Spoor's restructuring of the Management Board again concentrates power at the top. It bypasses the power bases of people who have been in strong positions before. By reducing the number of board members from 15 to 7, Spoor also increases the ratio of his own personal appointments to the number of those who might represent opinions of the past. The board now numbers 4-3 with new managers or appointments dominating the board.

D. <u>Isolation of Petersen</u>: Audiences are likely to comment on the way in which Mr. Petersen was handled. This is a most complex discussion. Mr. Petersen was a very much admired and able person. By putting him in charge of the Consumer Foods Division, the top management group created what could have been a "no lose" situation for itself. If Mr. Petersen gets along well with Mr. Spoor and performs well, Consumer Foods will do well for Pillsbury. Mr. Spoor will obtain credit for this performance, as will Mr. Petersen. On the other hand, should Petersen not do well, Mr. Spoor can still "win" in this situation. Audiences like to speculate on various possibilities here.

The Chickens Divestiture

The professor can ask, "Why did the implementation process start with the divestiture sequence? Why did Mr. Spoor choose 'chickens first'? What do you think of the way in which he handled the divestiture process?" Following are several critical factors one may wish to bring out in this discussion.

A. <u>Chickens First</u>: Why did Mr. Spoor choose to divest of chickens first? This was a large scale, complicated divestiture. If it could be carried out, it would send a clear signal to the rest of the organization that performance was to be the main criterion for continued support. The divestiture would have high impact on the variability of profits, and it would accomplish several other purposes simultaneously.

B. <u>From a Financial Viewpoint</u>: The divestiture process by cutting losses, increases returns at the same time that it decreases investment. Consequently, the management gets a "double dip" of benefit on its R/I ratio. When a divestiture is sold, cash is freed up for redeployment elsewhere. This strengthens other operations and strengthens the power base of the new management in those areas. It also "cleans up the balance sheet," making access to capital for further investments more feasible.

C. <u>The Honeymoon Period</u>: If a major controversial move is to be undertaken, it is probably wise to take it during the early stages when the Board feels a commitment to let the new CEO demonstrate his capabilities. This is often called the "honeymoon" period.

D. <u>Before "Foods"</u>: It is essential to get rid of the chickens business before one can define the company's goal as being in the "foods business." At this point in time, the "chickens" business can be attacked strictly on performance criteria. Later, the definition of being in the "foods business" might complicate things.

E. Freeing up Management Time: By divesting chickens and other "side shows," management can focus more attention on the remaining strong aspects of the Pillsbury portfolio. This gives more focus to the strategy and helps improve performance.

F. The White Paper Process: The professor can ask, "Why does Spoor undertake this elaborate process to divest of chickens? Why are the white papers used?" The chickens divestiture attacks some very strong power centers, it has important cultural implications, and it is a first difficult step that Spoor is asking the Board to take. Consequently, it takes time to build up: concern over the issue, awareness of the extent of the issue, new information about the issue, and a willingness to make a hard decision. The white papers provide a stronger information base for the decision. From a political viewpoint, they also let the new management know exactly where its opposition stands, and to develop arguments on crucial issues. Some audiences will also comment that the process helped isolate a major potential opponent, Mr. Hannald.

G. Random Events: One can ask, "What influenced the timing of the divestiture?" Clearly the finding of a suitable buyer, the opportunity to sell in an up cycle, and a bit of pure luck were involved. In divestitures as in many other aspects of management, opportunism is important. How it affects divestiture decisions and the need for flexibility and opportunism should be noted.

At the end of this discussion, the professor can point out that divestitures have to be handled with great care. A management cannot announce a clear goal for specific divestitures, for fear of losing key people and driving the value of the divestiture down before it is sold. Other divestitures made by Pillsbury suggest that Mr. Spoor was willing to "give the managements a chance" to put their operations in order. If they did not, they very often came to Spoor and told him that they thought he should sell off their divisions. This suggests the power of specific goals, well formulated to obtain consensus.

Change Processes

As the discussion of the case develops, we normally keep a section of the blackboard under the caption "processes" to catalog the process steps undertaken during the case. Although not complete, the following list suggests some of the important "process management" concepts which are brought out by the case:

A.   Developing a dream or vision attractive to many.
B.   Knowing one's goals, but perhaps announcing only a few at a time.
C.   Using broad or general goals at first to obtain cohesion.
D.   Moving through "corridors of indifference."
E.   Building awareness among critical players.
F.   Legitimizing options.
G.   Building credibility for ideas and the management team.
H.   Selecting key people.
I.   Building one's information base.
J.   Using symbols to communicate widely in an organization.
K.   Changing the flux step by step.
L.   Managing the sequence of events.
M.   Allowing time for change (planned waiting).
N.   Crystallizing consensus.
O.   Obtaining commitment and identity.
P.   Managing coalition (team) development.
Q.   Shifting the focus to broad issues (a great company).
R.   Making macro organization changes.
S.   Changing the culture.

In this case, to accomplish what he needed to do, Mr. Spoor had to change the strong ongoing culture of Pillsbury. This could not be done overnight. It required a series of managed changes. Each of the above process steps can provide a basis for discussion among students or executives as to how well they were handled and how they contributed to the ultimate strategy change. Note that strategy formulation and implementation are largely interactive, simultaneous, or overlapping events.

The Politics of Change

This case brings out some interesting aspects about "the politics of change." One can first point out that politics are a portion of any realistic change process. Politics need not be used in a pejorative sense. Politics includes the processes of obtaining power, dealing with power, and creating sufficient consensus to move—"the art of the practical." The case allows one to bring out some commonly used methodologies in organizational politics. Some of the most important ones are outlined briefly below.

A. Isolating opponents or bypassing their power bases.
B. Discovering opponents' positions.
C. Creating no-lose situations.
D. Building an independent power base.
E. Avoiding countercoalitions.
F. Sequencing targets to reuse resources.
G. Using broad goals to obtain cohesion.
H. Using specific goals to force action.
I. Redeploying resources to reinforce a power base.
J. Forcing competition to increase motivation or to isolate opponents.
K. Managing coalitions.
L. Planning politics along with analytical moves.

Spoor's Style

The professor can ask what aspects of Mr. Spoor's style seem appropriate to this situation. Which aspects are most helpful? Are there some aspects of his style which you do not like? As a change agent, Mr. Spoor seems to use certain very common techniques:

A. Operating as a "challenger and questioner," rather than an order giver, helps create commitment in those actually carrying out the change.
B. Keeping "options open" allows flexibility and opportunism.
C. "Not announcing a full program" allows one to use information developed later.
D. Staying ahead of the organization allows him to "manage the process" as well as the informational aspects of decision making.
E. Spoor's energy, directness, and analytical ability, allow him to dominate analytical situations.
F. Spoor's "scorecard" technique gives him protection from a Board attack. Similarly, those who meet performance criteria also feel secure in the organization.

However, there are clearly some issues and problems with Mr. Spoor's style. Chief among these would appear to be the following: the fear he sometimes creates in individuals causing them to be less than candid; his inconsistent handling of Mr. Good's strategy in Consumer Products; his commitment to several people that the "route to the top" was clear; perhaps an excessive dominance of his personality; the tendency of a strong personality like Spoor to create a dependency among the next line of management; his sometimes precipitous actions which may have lost some good key people; the potential that overuse of numbers can drive the organization in peculiar directions. However, there is little evidence that the latter problem occurred at Pillsbury. Mr. Spoor seemed to have kept a good balance between "people-oriented" and "performance-oriented" goals.

The Redeployment Strategy

As resources become available from the divestitures and improved profitability, how should they be redeployed? The audience will usually respond, "To Burger King." One should develop why this is a useful strategy. Obviously, there is a growing market there. However, Burger King offers some other interesting characteristics. First, one can grow the company three ways: by efficiency or margin changes, by product mix changes, and geographically. Second, the Burger King restaurants can largely be self financing, thus leveraging the resources of Pillsbury. Third, the restaurants are relatively low risk because the concept has been proved, and each new restaurant represents a manageable risk. Fourth, Burger King can provide a "throttle" on growth, allowing the new management a steadily controlled growth pattern—one of their major goals. Finally, the combination of the above meant that Burger King could achieve a very high return on invested capital for Pillsbury and thus was a natural "star" for the early strategy.

Other restaurant concepts also offered opportunities. However, one should note that a number of experiments were necessary to achieve a relatively few steadily growing restaurant lines. Restaurant concepts are notably difficult to create from scratch and maintain. And the randomness by which such concepts can be acquired is well represented by the way in which "Steak and Ale comes in over the transom" to Pillsbury. Often, such opportunities—because of external factors—only become available at a particular moment.

Redeployment to the agricultural division in the early stages of the strategy was modest. Agriproducts was growing relatively slowly. It was providing cash for the rest of the company. It was at the historical and value roots of the company. Consequently, it was reasonable to support it as a "cash cow" during this period and not to consider divestiture too seriously.

Consumer Foods was the most complex area for redeployment. This group was in its maturity phase. While it should have been providing heavy cash flows for the company, it required heavy investments in marketing, distribution, and product development to maintain its competitiveness. Because this was a portion of the slower moving "old Pillsbury" culture, it was more difficult to obtain efficiency changes and cost cutting measures to make the division more effective. Margins were slim, and payoffs from marketing investments tended to be long term. Finally, in the early years, Mr. Petersen was heading this division. All of these factors made it a less desirable target for redeployment.

Acquisitions in New Areas

Because the "eating away from home" trend was growing so rapidly, a number of new restaurant concepts were tried. As noted above, the probability of any one of these succeeding was relatively low. Consequently, it was natural that Pillsbury undertake a number of different trials to succeed in a relatively few new restaurant concepts. Acquisition opportunities also tend to appear somewhat randomly, hence the timing and direction of acquisition strategies are not as controllable as internally generated growth. How an acquisition strategy should be developed to be both well planned and opportunistic will be taken up in later sections of this note.

1985 CRITICAL STRATEGIC FACTORS

In 1985, Mr. Stafford faces some very interesting strategic questions. Most important among these is how he can maintain the very powerful growth surge that Mr. Spoor has brought the company. In Mr. Spoor's last presentation to security analysts, the company seems to have been committed to a 12-15% earnings per share growth, 18% return on equity, and 25% return on investment targets. One should ask whether and where such growth rates are possible. What does the current product portfolio look like? What are the main portfolio needs? From the data in Exhibit 3, one can establish that in 1984 Consumer Foods created a net cash flow of +$50 million, Restaurants absorbed capital at a rate of -$44 million, Agriproducts provided a cash flow of +$17 million. The return on assets in Consumer Foods was 17.4%; in Restaurants it was 15.7%; and

Agriproducts it was 6.7%. Note that the above cash flows are after-tax cash flows while the profits are before tax earnings on assets. Taxes have to be approximated. However, even on a pre-tax basis, the earnings goals will be difficult to achieve. What issues does this pose for Pillsbury's future portfolio?

Agriproducts' profitability would appear to be less than desired. This suggests the sell off of many of its assets to generate cash for redeployment. Probably, Pillsbury should keep only that portion of Agri's assets which directly support other elements of the business, like flour mills supporting consumer food lines.

Consumer Foods needs an internal redeployment strategy emphasizing those product lines which are both growing and able to generate substantial margins. In 1985, these would appear to be frozen products, refrigerated products, and specialties like pizzas. The product line needs to be adapted to developing consumer tastes in dining. A major trend is toward products prepared elsewhere but eaten in the home, such as: pizzas, delicatessen products, snacks, etc. The area needs to be targeted line by line, but developed as a cash generator to support the growth aspects of Pillsbury's total portfolio.

Restaurants. Burger King may be approaching saturation levels in its potential penetration. However, in 1985 it would appear that there were 3-5 years more of growth for this particular concept. It should be developed both as a "near growth" vector and to "generate cash" for the company. As a cash absorber in the past, this will be a difficult potential turnaround. However, many of the chain's assets are highly leveragable. This could be done by sale and lease back arrangements or by limited partnership arrangements essentially selling Burger King's real estate assets to limited partners and then renting them back. Finally, there needs to be a continuing pressure to maintain Burger King's margins by innovative menu changes, forceful cost cutting, etc. However, by 1990, the restaurant business will need a new "growth force." What should it be?

Overall, the company at first appears to be in reasonably good shape with some strong cash flow divisions and near growth potentials. Its most apparent problem would appear to be a "future growth" star or "Super Box." If the company continued its current asset growth at 13.5% per year as projected, it would double its size in 4.6 years requiring an increment of $2.6 billion in assets. By 1990, it would be approximately $8.4 billion in sales with an increment of about $4.2 billion in assets having to be developed. Given these growth needs a major question is, "What should be the criteria for the development of a major growth factor, or "Super Box"?

However, upon more careful investigation, a rather insidious problem is clearly developing. Although the company is profitable and growing, it appears to be paying dividends of about $49 million. This can be calculated as follows: $139 million of After-Tax Earnings convert to only $90 million in stockholder equity increase ($1046 million - $956 million = $90 million). The company is clearly borrowing to pay its dividends. It is borrowing from its suppliers for this purpose, since it has paid down its debt by almost $69 million in 1984. The company appears to be "managing" its balance sheet and shareholder policies to appeal to the stock market, rather than building investments for the future. Bringing out this point can lead to some interesting discussion.

Criteria for Acquisitions

Some of this growth will obviously be provided by internal mechanisms, but some must come from acquisitions. An acquisitions strategy should start—as we have above—by establishing overall corporate goals and the specific purposes of the acquisitions strategy within those goals. In this case the purpose is to obtain a "future star" or Super Box. Next, one needs to define the criteria for acquisitions. For Super Box to be significant in the company's 1990 posture, it will clearly have to have sales of $2 billion or more. What other criteria should one assess for Super Box? Several of the most important are suggested below:

A. A sales growth rate in excess of 25% per year.
B. A current size of more than $500 million in sales (to achieve $2 billion by 1990).
C. A competent existing management.
D. Being able to generate a cash flow fairly soon.
E. Being number one or number two in its market place.
F. Having certain controllable growth characteristics.
G. The merged company being controlled by Pillsbury.
H. Preferably being a friendly takeover to maintain management in place.

Possible Candidates

Next, the professor can ask the class for some possible candidates that might fill this role. In short order the students quickly suggest some new restaurant concepts like a Chinese restaurant, a Mexican restaurant, a health food chain restaurant, etc. They may also suggest the possibility of acquiring convenience food stores, overseas distribution, hotels, motels, or spas. They may suggest entirely new product lines with major potential like the soft drink industry or beers. They frequently suggest specialty foods concepts that match trends to convenience eating in the home—branded meats, foreign delicacies, etc. Depending on the imagination of the group, a wide variety can quickly appear.

The professor should now ask, "What special competency are we building on? What kind of company do we want to be?" This causes some amount of refocusing among the candidates. However, a number of candidate industries are likely to remain. At this point one can ask, "What criteria should be used in placing priorities among the candidates?" Finally, however, most groups will suggest pursuing several options, "Because we don't know which ones will really work out." By pursuing several simultaneously, Pillsbury can increase the probability of eventual success. Perhaps Super Box is not a single product or chain concept, but several linked together.

An Overall Acquisition Strategy

We usually end this particular session by pointing out the components of a major acquisition strategy as exemplified in the case. The following items are those most commonly and usefully developed by companies:

A. A clear definition of corporate strategy, product market scope, distinct competency.

B. The specific goals for the acquisition criteria (i.e., diversification, rapid growth, future growth, etc.).

C. Criteria for acquisition screening:
   1. Industry classes,
   2. Specific candidate companies,
   3. Possible priorities among industries and companies (sequences).

D. Developing planned flexibility in terms of:
   1. Easier, more low cost capital access,
   2. Slack management capacity,
   3. A decentralized organization,
   4. An empowered champion/activist,
   5. Financial controls to manage the acquisition.

E. Establishing a grapevine or network to develop candidates.

F. Involving top management to obtain key people's support.

G. Empowering an activist whose future with the company depends on successful acquisitions.

H.   Investigating the physical, fiscal, and organizational aspects of each candidate.

I.   Implementing and following up the acquisition as it is merged into the company.

SUMMARY OF OUTCOMES

Although the data in the case covers up to May 1985, a few major events have already taken place when the first edition of the book was published. Overall, in the first year under Mr. Stafford, the company continued its strong growth patterns and its sales volume surpassed that of its arch rival, General Mills.

As soon as Mr. Stafford became CEO, the Consumer Foods group was reorganized into two groups: (1) U.S. Foods, headed by Mr. McBurney, and (2) International Foods and Ice Cream, headed by Mr. Morrison. Then, the group's domestic divisions (Dry, Refrigerated, and Frozen) were regrouped around such concepts as Meals and Snacks, Vegetables and Side Dishes, Breads and Baking Products, and Ice Cream. Domestically and internationally Pillsbury made quite a number of acquisitions in the Consumer Foods area including Jeno's (whose pizzas complemented Totino's presence in that marketplace), Joan of Arc (whose line of specialty canned vegetables the company had previously tried to acquire), and RT French's potato business.

The major event in the Restaurants area was the acquisition of Diversifoods, Inc. for $390 million in cash and the assumption of $80 million in debt. The addition of Diversifoods' more than 350 Burger King franchisees allowed the company to reach its goal of owning about 20% of all the Burger King outlets. Of Diversifoods' 1,000 other restaurant units Pillsbury retained only the Godfather's Pizza 850 unit chain. It planned to use its restaurant management expertise and pizza technology to turn the chain around. Pillsbury also acquired the Quik Wok Chinese fast food concept which had the potential to yield a high ROA with a low capital investment and per store sales of $600,000. Both of these concepts allowed Pillsbury to enter the rapidly growing home delivery market. The Restaurant group was broken down into two sections, Burger King (which included the Quik Wok and Godfather's Pizza chains) and S&A Restaurant Corp. (which included the two main chains, Steak and Ale and Bennigan's, and other full-service concepts like Bay Street which featured seafood).

To help finance its growth in the restaurant field, Pillsbury developed an innovative investment vehicle, the Burger King Investors Master Limited Partnership, which traded on the New York Stock Exchange. The Partnership acquired the real estate from restaurant properties owned or leased by Burger King and operated by franchisees. Rental income, based generally on a percentage of the restaurant's gross sales, now flows directly to the Partnership. Pillsbury was thus able to redeploy funds invested in properties Burger King did not operate and use the $69 million proceeds to pay down debt assumed in the Diversifoods acquisition.

The Commodity Marketing group was placed under the Chief Financial Officer, signaling a possible sell off of that unit. In fact, the company sold its edible dry bean and rice milling businesses which made up some 40% of the group's sales, reduced its storage capacity significantly, and is continuing its efforts to reduce its exposure to the troubled agricultural markets.

The Late 1980s

Mr. Stafford "went back to basics" trying to improve the operations of Pillsbury, he put strong emphasis on customer relations and strengthening the consumer food lines and their national distribution. While the consumer food lines did well between 1985 and 1988, the restaurant group peaked in 1985 and lost ground to its powerful competitors, mainly McDonald's. Despite Stafford's efforts, including $91 million in write-offs in 1987 to slim down the restaurant group, it lacked the lean operating philosophy of McDonald's—and reportedly had built up "operational sloppiness." Pillsbury's Board became nervous and asked Mr. Spoor to return to an active role overseeing the company, helping to slim it down, and perhaps get it ready for a breakup. In keeping with the late 1980 philosophy, Wall Street analysts were calling for Pillsbury to split up its two businesses, and let the restaurants operate as an independent company. Both Stafford and Spoor publicly stated they did not want to do this.

The situation with Mr. Spoor looking over his shoulder became intolerable for Stafford. In August 1988 the Board brought in Phillip L. Smith, formerly the head of General Foods Corporation (now a division of Philip Morris). By then, virtually all of Pillsbury's divisions were hurting. *Business Week*, August 8, 1988 summarized as follows: (1) Burger King was hurting from flat sales, sloppy operations; (2) Steak and Ale was trying to sell beef to a cholesterol wary public; (3) Bennigan's struggling to move from a purveyor of liquor to singles to an eatery for baby boom families; (4) Distron's Burger King franchisees were fleeing from the distributor; (5) baking mixes had too high a cost in a fierce market, with few new hit products; (6) frozen pizza's too fast price increases nearly killed Totino's; (7) frozen fish was encountering intense competition and squeezed margins. In September 1988, Grand Metropolitan PLC of Britain offered $5.2 billion or $60 a share for Pillsbury. Seventy-four percent of the stock was offered in response to the tender, despite poison pills in place at Pillsbury. The purchase was completed at $5.6 billion in January 1989.

Grand Metropolitan had grown extensively by acquisition. Its CEO, Allan Sheppard, was aggressively moving to make Grand Met "a powerful global player" in the three sectors it knew well: alcoholic beverages, food, and restaurants. Grand Met's combination of $2.2 billion in food products, $3.0 billion in restaurants, and $4.6 billion in alcoholic beverages (mainly acquired with Hueblein's) made a good match for Pillsbury's $3.6 billion food products and $1.1 billion of remaining restaurants. Grand Met moved in quickly, but not ruthlessly, installing better control systems and slimming down Pillsbury's corporate overheads. Under Burger King chief executive officer Barry J. Gibbon, a dozen new product lines were introduced, and Burger King began recapturing share. Gibbon became a "turnaround hero." He streamlined Burger King's management, moved decisions to the front line, gave more bonuses for performance, introduced a raft of new products (including pizzas and salads), upgraded operations with automated kitchens and an 800 complaint number, and so on. *Business Week* noted: "Have it your way" came back with a new meaning for both staff and management. The customers now have everything their way. Between 1988 and 1989, Grand Met's sales jumped from $6.0 billion to $9.2 billion. Its profits jumped from $575 million to $732 million. No member of the Pillsbury Company was on the Board of Grand Metropolitan in 1989.

Case Objectives and Use

Cadbury Schweppes, P.L.C. is an international food conglomerate headquartered in the United Kingdom. As it entered the 1990s, the firm faced twin pressures associated with intensifying global competition in its markets and changing competitive conditions within the European community. The case illustrates and raises key concerns of multinational corporate strategy, including product diversification and geographic expansion issues, and thus it is an excellent vehicle for stimulating discussion in these areas.

Case Synopsis

Founded in 1831 as a processor of cocoa and chocolate, Cadbury's first major diversification followed an 1847 innovation enabling a cocoa butter byproduct to be used in edible candies. Other early diversification efforts led to a variety of chocolate beverages and beverage mixes by the early 1900s. By the first world war, Cadbury offered a wide range of confectionary and beverage products, and enjoyed large market shares in England and most Commonwealth countries.

During World War II, the firm was forced to reduce its product lines by more than 85%, but with decentralized production of 29 confectionary brands, Cadbury still maintained wider lines than most of its U.S. rivals. However, maturing industry conditions made new product introduction very difficult, costly, and risky. Faced with limited growth prospects in its traditional markets as well as threatened takeover, Cadbury merged with Schweppes, a worldwide producer of soft drinks and mixers, in 1969. Throughout the next two decades, the firm pursued worldwide expansion in the confectionary and soft drink markets. By the 1990s, however, it was still smaller than many competitors (e.g., Mars in confectioneries; Coca Cola in soft drinks). With increasing competitive pressures, questions arose as to whether Cadbury could compete head-to-head with the larger firms who tended to possess greater sales, marketing, and distribution capabilities.

Analysis

Strengths:

- Major brands: The future of Cadbury depends largely on the name recognition and quality reputation of its brands. Currently, several of them (e.g., CDM, Mounds, Canada Dry, Schweppes) dominate their market segments.

- Management experience: Top management has been relatively stable for several decades. In fact, the CEO is 50-year-old Dominic Cadbury, a member of the founding family. Several individuals are well-respected for their knowledge and understanding of market conditions.

- U.K. market share: For the time being, Cadbury's dominant U.K. position seems secure. Therefore, the company can focus resources on growth in areas outside the United Kingdom.

- Debt leverage: Currently, the firm is highly leveraged. This is favorable when one considers that current conditions make hostile takeovers likely throughout the industry. Cadbury's high debt levels make it a less desirable takeover target.

- Segmentation: Many of Cadbury's products (e.g., Schweppes, Roses, Canada Dry, Mounds, York Peppermint Patty) are positioned in distinct market niches, and this offers some protection against predatory behavior by large competitors.

Weaknesses:

- Financial position: Cadbury operates on thin margins, has very limited working capital, and is heavily leveraged. Thus, there is little capital available for acquisition, product development, or other aggressive expansion efforts.

- Firm size: Although many food and beverage firms operate on thin margins (like Cadbury does), large competitors enjoy greater absolute profit levels due to their higher sales volumes.

Opportunities:

- European markets: Within the European community, the confectionary market is dominated by many small, family-owned firms. Most of these firms face the same expansion pressures as Cadbury, and suffer from similar resource limitations. As a mid-sized firm, however, Cadbury's problems are less severe than those of smaller firms. Thus, there are opportunities for Cadbury to acquire or merge with some smaller firms having favorable market positions.

- Third-World markets: Cadbury has gained footholds in some Third World markets (e.g., Indonesia, Malaysia), but its presence is still weak. In some of these countries (i.e., those with developing economies), confectionary markets are likely to enjoy greater growth than Cadbury's European and U.S. markets.

- Global ties: Just as Cadbury licensed its U.S. production to Hershey, it is possible to form joint ventures, licensing arrangements, or even to orchestrate a friendly merger with larger, stronger partners. Then, the financial muscle of those partners can be used to sell, market, and distribute Cadbury products.

Threats:

- Competitive environment: With intensifying competition, larger rivals may choose to confront Cadbury directly, in its key markets. Because of its resource limitations, Cadbury may have considerable difficulty surviving such frontal assaults.

- EC barriers: As the European Community becomes unified, some continued consolidation is likely at the retail levels. By virtue of their size and amounts purchased, the larger retailers would have greater bargaining power over Cadbury and other suppliers.

- House brands: The larger retailers also would have more resources that could be used to integrate backward, developing house brands of some products currently sold by Cadbury. The effect would be a squeezing of Cadbury's margins and/or reduction in the shelf space available to its products.

Key Issue:

- The preceding discussion of strengths, weaknesses, opportunities, and threats suggests a single key issue that Cadbury must address: growth. It is clear that a no-growth strategy is not viable within the industry. Thus, growth is essential if Cadbury is to remain competitive in a world full of corporate giants.

<u>Recommendations</u>:

- <u>Concentration</u>: Cadbury should protect current markets with creative, yet familiar promotional themes. Since new product development seems to yield little return, R&D should focus on process technologies to reduce distribution and manufacturing costs.

- <u>Acquisition</u>: Cadbury should enter new markets by acquiring small-but-growing firms throughout Europe. Products offered by these firms should differ from Cadbury's current products, yet they should still fit within or complement the existing product line.

- <u>Joint venture</u>: For more saturated markets, and geographic areas/regions where Cadbury does not enjoy a significant presence, the firm should seek joint venture partners with strong distribution and promotion capabilities. Ideally, the partners' and Cadbury's product lines should be complementary rather than competing.

Discussion Questions

1. Define Cadbury's primary product categories. How does the firm match up against competitors in each market segment?

2. What, if anything, is Cadbury's competitive advantage? What are the key threats to future expansion in the EC? How can Cadbury's competitive advantage be used to overcome those threats?

3. How should Cadbury be organized? What organization structure would best facilitate future geographic and product line expansion? Keep in mind that the firm's tight margins suggest that efficiency is a major concern. How might Cadbury organize to gain (a) the flexibility needed for expansion and (b) the efficiency needed to compete within each local product market?

SCANDINAVIAN AIRLINES SYSTEMS (SAS) IN 1988 AND THE EUROPEAN AIRLINE INDUSTRY TEACHING NOTE

Case Description

In 1981, when Jan Carlzon assumed the presidency of SAS, the company was at a state of near bankruptcy having lost 63 million SEK in 1979-80 and another 51 million SEK in 1980-81. It was losing market share, even in its home territory, had a poor reputation for punctuality and service, and its aging fleet mix and limited route network did not meet market needs. From this position of near collapse, Carlzon managed a dramatic turn-around operation that led the company to a record profit of 443 million SEK in 1986 and to the winner's stand in the "Airline of the Year" award from the Air Transport World magazine in 1984. The case describes the strategic, organizational, and behavioral revolution initiated and managed by Carlzon that led to such dramatic performance improvement, in such a short time period.

By 1988, however, the company was still confronting a number of challenges that threaten its long term viability. Its costs were too high and its fleet needed urgent replacement demanding a level of investment the company seemed unable to muster. Organizational energy was also ebbing, soothed by the rewards of international acclaim and operating profitability. To deal with the situation, Carlzon launched a "second wave" of change, involving a further round of major strategic and organizational redirection. Was the new direction appropriate? Could the new strategy be implemented? How could he reinvigorate the organization to run the next leg of the revitalization marathon? These are some questions that Carlzon and SAS had to effectively respond to if the company was to emerge as one of the survivors in the rapidly consolidating global airlines business.

Teaching Objectives

The case aims to raise the following issues for class discussion:

1. Strategy and Management in Service Businesses. Many of the key concepts and tools of strategic analysis have been developed in the context of manufacturing businesses. Most of the popular cases of competitive strategy and general management also tend to focus on manufacturing companies. This case provides an opportunity to discuss some of the general concepts such as the issue of generic strategies, core competence, and diversification strategy in the context of a service business and allows the participants to examine if those concepts and analytical techniques still remain appropriate and useful.

2. Management of Strategic Change. Between 1981 and 1984, SAS went through what is perhaps one of the most celebrated and well-known cases of dramatic turnarounds. Analysis of the strategic, organizational, and cultural changes made by the company provides a rich basis for a more general understanding of the management of dramatic transformation in large world-wide companies.

Further, a key challenge in managing strategic change is the inevitable slackening after a battle is won while the overall outcome of the war is still uncertain. Change needs to be managed in phases, and ultimately as an ongoing activity, and the transition from one phase to the next is often the point where many companies and managers falter. The second wave of change in SAS post-1986 raises this important issue of managing phased revitalization and can provide some insights into the timing and process of changing gears as a company moves from the stage of turnaround to the stage of building the competencies necessary for long-term viability and self-renewal capability.

Teaching Note copyright © 1988 by Sumantra Ghoshal. This note was written by Professor Sumantra Ghoshal of INSEAD.

3.   Role of the General Manager. While a number of recent articles and cases describe the very different strategic needs and organizational demands large corporations are facing in an environment of global competition, deregulation, and turbulent change, relatively little attention has been paid to the management implications of all these changes. Without effective managers in place, sophisticated strategies and subtle organizations fail and the great risk of many large corporations is that they are trying to implement third generation strategies with second generation organizations and first generation managers.

While the dramatic changes in strategic approaches (either from generic strategies to layering multiple sources of competitive advantage or from a pure product-market focus in strategy formulation to simultaneous attention to building resources and core competencies) and organizational forms (from the vertical hierarchy to the horizontal network) have profound implications for the roles and tasks of managers at all levels of the organization, nowhere are the new management challenges as extreme as at the very top of the company. The CEO must provide leadership in the process of corporate transformation and must create and sustain the energy, enthusiasm, and commitment throughout the organization necessary for the revitalization process to succeed. The case focuses on the role played by Jan Carlzon, SAS's CEO since 1981, in initiating and managing the transformation process within the company and provides the basis for a debate on the roles and tasks of the general manager in large worldwide companies in the 1990s.

Classroom Utilization

The case was developed for use in MBA courses and Executive Programs on Strategic Management, Business Policy, or General Management. It has also been used in organizational behavior courses (in sessions on leadership of change), in service management courses (Strategic Change in Service Companies) and in courses focused on the strategic, organizational, and management issues in multinational companies.

Given the issues dealt with in the case, it is ideally positioned toward the end of the course by which time students would have covered the basics for most of the issues that are addressed. The HBS video on SAS featuring a question-answer session with Jan Carlzon can be effectively used at the end of the class. Any one or more of the following articles can also be assigned as readings for the class:

- Noel Tichy and Ram Charan, "Speed, Simplicity and Self Confidence: An Interview with Jack Welch," *The Harvard Business Review.*
- John Kotter, "*What Leaders Really Do,*" The Harvard Business Review.

Preparation Questions

The following questions can be assigned for the students to prepare themselves for class discussions:

1.   Between 1981 and 1986. SAS went through one of the most dramatic and visible processes of strategic change. How was this turnaround achieved? Why did it succeed? What can we learn from the process?

2.   Why was the "second wave" necessary? How do you feel about the direction SAS was following in 1988? Will this second round of change work? What might Carlzon do to make it work?

3.   How do you evaluate the role played by Carlzon since his taking over the presidency of the company in 1981? What has he done well? With the benefit of hindsight, what might he have done differently? What lessons do you draw from the case about the roles and tasks of general managers in large worldwide companies?

Teaching Plan

I typically start the classroom discussions by suggesting that the Business Policy Course (where I teach the case) in any case has the reputation of making students pompous and arrogant by asking them to evaluate CEOs and debating what the students would have done if they were CEOs. Given the bad reputation, we might as well indulge in the pleasure and begin the session by evaluating Carlzon's effectiveness as the CEO of SAS. The specific questions I propose are:

Question 1 - *On a scale of 1 to 10, evaluate Carlzon's effectiveness as the CEO of SAS between 1981 and 1989.*

I draw up the scale on the board and ask students to vote by raising their hands if they have given a 1, a 2, and so on till 10. Typically between 70 to 90 percent of students rate Carlzon between 8 and 10. But, almost without exception, a small minority give him a score below 4. A quick discussion (no more than 7 to 10 minutes) yields the following reasons for the evaluation:

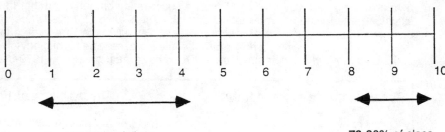

10-30% of class	70-90% of class
1. Creating a short-term revival but destroying, in the process, any chances for long-term survival of the company as a viable airline.	1. Successful turn-around: restoring profitability and dramatic improvement in performance
2. Not paying attention to the key issues of cost and sustainable growth.	2. Establishing a specific and sustainable niche for the company: effective differentiation strategy.
3. Personal aggrandizement: Carlzon is more important than SAS.	3. Restoring company identity: creating a new vision and building company-wide commitment.
4. Destroying middle management morale and commitment.	4. Reviving employee pride and morale.

While this start-up is a bit melodramatic, it does capture the students' attention and raises energy levels. Both sides in the obviously polarized group strongly disagree with each others assessment and are, in fact, a bit surprised at the very significant differences in their evaluation. (The polarization is rarely so clear in a class of senior executives, who tend to be more balanced and comprehensive in their evaluation, or in a class dominated by Anglo-Saxon MBA students most of whom tend to be very positive toward Carlzon. It is typically the Japanese, German, French, and Scandinavian students who tend to be on the negative side.)

Having set up the debate in this manner (and thereby also identifying the positions of all the students - a great help in deciding on whom to call for each point in the following discussions), the instructor can promise to come back to the evaluation in the concluding part of the class and proceed to the assigned questions.

Question 2 - *Between 1981 and 1986, SAS went through one of the most dramatic and visible processes of strategic change. How was the turn-around achieved? Why did it succeed? What can we learn from the process?*

While there are a flood of comments at this point, students invariably list the same set of issues—creating an effective strategy, resource allocation decisions that fully supported the strategy, giving meaning to the strategy by creating a simple and energizing vision to which people even at the lowest levels could personally commit to, supporting the vision through an elaborate and well implemented culture change process, and the visible, personalized drive of the leader—even though the order in which the issues are listed vary from class to class. I ensure that each issue is discussed and elaborated, but overall I try to manage the discussions so that the following points are made.

a. The Failure Of Success Is Widespread But Not Inevitable. I try to begin the discussion by highlighting that historically SAS was a successful company and that the 1979-1981 situation represented a somewhat sudden fall. The reasons for this failure, however, are embedded in the processes of past successes. Taking a little time to elicit the causes of the company's historical success clearly identify the asset and technology-driven strategy of the company, which were precisely the sources of the problems in 1979-81.

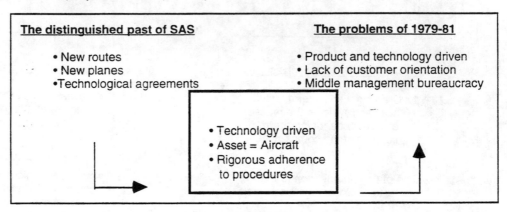

The distinguished past of SAS	**The problems of 1979-81**
• New routes	• Product and technology driven
• New planes	• Lack of customer orientation
•Technological agreements	• Middle management bureaucracy

• Technology driven
• Asset = Aircraft
• Rigorous adherence to procedures

I take a little time to emphasize the generality of this process of past success formulae becoming ossified into entrenched norms which often become the major source of future problems for companies: the rule of "failure of success." To highlight this point, I often use a chart derived from Richard Pascale's *Managing on the Edge* (see Exhibit 1) which shows the performance in 1988 for all the 43 "excellent" companies listed in Tom Peters and Bob Waterman's best-seller, *In Search of Excellence.* All but 13 of these companies had slipped in their performance and some were indeed facing bankruptcy or takeover threats. Two points can be made from this table: first, failure of success is widespread and, second, while widespread, it is not inevitable since some companies manage to successfully adapt their approaches and remain on the winner's stand decade after decade. Making this point at this stage helps set up the later discussion on the role of the general manager in creating a process of renewal within the company.

b. The Turnaround Dish Is Sweet And Sour. A successful turnaround process needs actions for both restructuring and revitalization. Restructuring involves some "hard" actions: changing formal structure, changing top management, portfolio choices often involving decommitment or divestment of certain businesses and segments and focus including fresh investments in other businesses and segments, headcount reduction, delayer, etc. Revitalization focuses on the "soft" issues of creating a vision, building employee morale and commitment to the vision, developing a coherent and well-functioning top management team, etc.

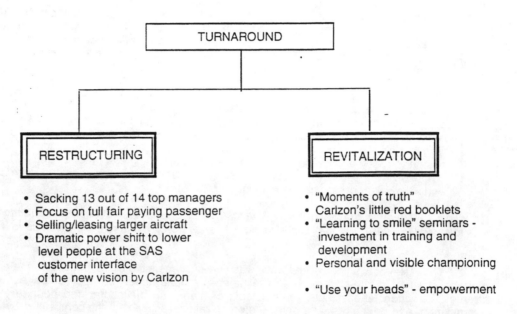

```
                        ┌──────────────────┐
                        │   TURNAROUND     │
                        └──────────────────┘
                    ┌───────────┴───────────┐
        ┌───────────────────┐      ┌───────────────────┐
        │  RESTRUCTURING    │      │  REVITALIZATION   │
        └───────────────────┘      └───────────────────┘
```

- Sacking 13 out of 14 top managers
- Focus on full fair paying passenger
- Selling/leasing larger aircraft
- Dramatic power shift to lower
  level people at the SAS
  customer interface
  of the new vision by Carlzon

- "Moments of truth"
- Carlzon's little red booklets
- "Learning to smile" seminars -
  investment in training and
  development
- Personal and visible championing

- "Use your heads" - empowerment

Many companies try to manage a turn-around focusing on restructuring alone: often they get into an ever-narrowing spiral where each restructuring temporarily improves financials but, in the absence of actions to deal with more fundamental problems, get the company into worse trouble again needing another restructuring, and so on (see Exhibit 2). Other companies focus only on revitalization—spending endless executive hours debating vision and long-term "strategic intent" (see Gary Hamel and C.K. Prahalad, "Strategic Intent," the *Harvard Business Review,* May/June 1989) but, in the absence of the "hard" restructuring actions, the debate becomes entirely futile. Even if a vision statement is produced at the end, it has no effect on the organization except perhaps to serve as a new source for cynicism. Effective turnaround processes require *simultaneous* actions on both fronts, so that one reinforces the other. Restructuring is a "sour" dish, causing pain, confusion, and conflict. People need revitalization action - the sweet dish - to feel reassured that at the end of the tunnel lies an attractive company that is worth belonging to. This enticement is necessary for people to suffer through the agony of divestment, headcount cuts, and other unpleasant restructuring actions. Similarly, the pain itself gives teeth and meaning to the revitalization process. Effective turnaround, thus, is a sweet and sour dish, neither just sweet nor just sour. Once again, this is a point I return to in the last part of the discussion on the roles and tasks of the general manager—the ability to cook a sweet and sour dish, to be simultaneously the nurse and the surgeon—is a key requirement for the job.

c. Personal Commitment Is Key. Effective turnaround requires analysis to identify and commit to a new strategy but, more than that, it requires the unleasing of organization energy to single-mindedly pursue the new direction. Without such energy, turn-around of a large company is almost impossible to achieve since it requires new behaviors at all levels of the company. Each employee must personally commit to the new direction for without such commitment, the energy is hard to muster. This requires courage on the part of the CEO to personally embody that commitment, and a coherent top management team to prevent inconsistent or mixed messages. It also requires an embedding process to communicate the new direction throughout the company and to help institutionalize the new behavioral norms. Sending a vision or strategy statement by mail rarely creates this

631

energy and commitment since they require not only intellectual understanding of why the changes are necessary but also an emotional experience of confronting reality (crisis or underperformance) and recognizing the costs of not changing.

Carlzon's actions illustrate some of the tools and tasks necessary for building such organization-wide commitment to a turnaround: the catchy yet meaningful and energizing slogans, his personal leadership of the process, the massive educational intervention through which the emotional appeal could be carried to the lowest levels in the company, and so on.

The instructor may, in the course of these discussions, bring in other company experiences such as those of GE and Jack Welch or Motorola under Bob Galvin. Such a broadening may be particularly useful if the case is being used in programs for senior executives. In such cases, the Tichy and Charan article ("Speed, Simplicity, and Self-Confidence: An interview with Jack Welch," see list of recommended readings) may be assigned together with the case for class preparation. These other examples both re-emphasize the general points but also suggest subtle variations in how the restructuring and renewal processes can be managed.

Question 3 - Why was the "second wave" necessary? How do you feel about the direction SAS was following in 1988? Will the second round of change work? What might Carlzon do to make it work?

The issue of why the second wave was necessary gets the class to focus on the need to manage change in bite-size pieces. The other questions about the appropriateness of the strategic direction leads to the general topic of managing the scope and boundary of an organization, and on the task of aligning the organizational scope with the competitive dynamics of the industry and the core competencies of the company.

a. <u>Managing Change in Bite-Size Pieces</u>. A company in crisis often faces a long hard climb to restore its competitive viability. Exposing the total task at one time or attempting to deal simultaneously with all the actions necessary can overwhelm the company. The SAS Carlzon inherited in 1981 had some pressing short-term problems due to poor financials and deteriorating operating performance and employee morale. At the same time, the company faced a set of longer time viability issues: size problems vis-à-vis global giants like British Airways and Air France from Europe, the assault from American mega-carriers, the problems of low population base and high cost inherent in its Scandinavian roots, and many others. To deal with the short-term turnaround and the long term competitive viability issues simultaneously could potentially have led to lack of focus, at least, and to confusion and paralysis, at worst. Renewal is often a marathon, but it requires running in short 400 meter bursts if nothing else, because of the cognitive limits of people.

The first wave of change at SAS focused on the short-term turnaround issues. At the end of the turnaround, SAS achieves immediate financial viability, but is far from establishing a long term sustainable competitive position. The second wave begins to deal with this second challenge.

One issue I spend some time on is the task of managing the transition between the phases within a process of strategic transformation. While breaking down the marathon into shorter distances is useful and perhaps necessary to create hope, focus and energy, it also creates a difficult problem of shifting gears and of declaring a new battle when the troops want to relax, having just won a difficult fight. Creating short-term mileposts, as Carlzon did with the first wave, is essential to energize the process, but it also creates the problem of contentment and return to "business as usual" once the milepost is reached, even though the actual journey is far from complete.

The reasons for the "second wave" need to be understood in this context of the need to break down the transformation process into bite-size pieces. The challenge for initiating the next step in the journey is to leverage the energy created by the "win" in the earlier round. This requires upping the ante, creating a more powerful dream to justify the next round of change. Here incremental improvements may not be sufficient for they may appear to the organization as pretexts for deferring well-deserved rewards and rest. The need for further changes and their benefits must be clearly established, and the objectives themselves must be ambitious enough to be deserving of another round of commitment.

b. The Scope of the Company. While the "SAS Service Chain" concept may have been justified from this perspective of serving as the next phase of corporate ambition, questions are inevitably raised by students about the appropriateness and realizability of this strategy. Given the repeated emphasis on "sticking to your knitting" and on "refocussing" in the recent business press and the well-known failure stories of "service supermarkets" both in the airline industry in the U.S. and in other service businesses (e.g., Saatchi and Saatchi), a large cross-section of students raise questions about the service chain concept which they view essentially as unrelated diversification. Those who started the class with a low rating of Carlzon tend to be particularly vocal at this state: why should SAS expect to be successful in credit cards, road transportation, or hotel management, they ask?

Given the strong normative environment against diversification at least in the West, most students tend to be skeptical about the service chain strategy. A few (often the Japanese) raise a question however: over the last decade companies like Honda, Yamaha, Hitachi, Toshiba, Mitsubishi, and others have entered a wide range of businesses and have, indeed, significantly widened their product and business portfolio. Typically, these companies tend to be highly admired in the West. How then can the service chain concept be ruled out of hand as unfeasible? Is the challenge indeed one of implementation? (If no one asks this question, I introduce it myself.)

This issue inevitably leads to a controversy but the debate, at least initially, tends to be based on ideology, assertion, and anecdote rather than on facts of the case or on concepts. I allow the debate to continue for a while and then intervene with the question, "How do we make sense of this mess? How can we think about this more systematically?"

I follow this question up by introducing the concept of core competencies (see C.K. Prahalad and Gary Hamel, "Core Competency and the Corporation," The *Harvard Business Review*, May/June 1990). Typically, the students have already been exposed to the issue of diversification, typically with concepts and data drawn from the work of Richard Rumell, Michael Porter, Cynthia Montgomery, etc. Much of this work focuses on the notion of relatedness from a product-market point of view. Increasingly, as the resource based view of the firm is gaining ground, they tend to have been exposed to the concept of core competency also in earlier classes. I draw on those earlier discussions to raise a question, "What is SAS's core competency?" If students have not been exposed to the notion of core competency, it may be useful to spend a little time explaining the concept. One way to do so quickly and effectively is to ask the question (following C.K. Prahalad and Gary Hamel's work), "How do you put six Hondas in a two-car garage?" If the instructor is a little patient, the question leads to some funny answers such as "putting them on top of each other," "buying very small Hondas and a big two-car garage," etc. Then the instructor can show the picture in Exhibit 3 and explain that Honda sees designing and building the world's best engines as its core competency, and leverages this competency in a diverse range of businesses from motorcycles and cars to powerpacks and lawn mowers. Even though, from an external product market point of view, these businesses may appear to be unrelated, from the perspective of the company's core competency, each of the businesses leverage the same competency and provides Honda with the basis for building competitive strength in a wide variety of activities.

As the discussion shifts to SAS's core competency, at least a small group of students begin to argue that managing the customer interface in delivering a service is indeed the capability that the company has begun to excel in. On this basis, this group of students argues in favor of the "second wave" strategy since SAS's competency in managing the customer interface in service delivery is crucial to each element within the service chain. Others question if SAS indeed has any unique capability in managing "moments of truth" and also SAS's ability to succeed in the other businesses even if it did have such a competency. While the debate typically remains inconclusive, the points raised by both sides help clarify the concept of core competencies and also raise the question of how to determine the appropriateness of a strategy premised on such a capability-focused view of the firm.

c. Strategy for a Small Company with Global Ambition. It is at this stage that the discussion can be broadened to a review of the structure of the industry and how SAS can develop a sustainable competitive position in the business. A quick review leads to the following lists of key industry characteristics and SAS's major strengths and weaknesses.

INDUSTRY TRENDS	SAS'S STRENGTHS & WEAKNESSES
• Deregulation • Competition from regional feeders • Relative growth of charter and seat only • Growing dominance of mega carriers • Crucial importance of CRS • Stagnation of business segment • Increasing competitive pressure from non-European carriers	**Strengths** • Service orientation • Image • Strong culture and employee commitment • Kastrup hub (?) **Weaknesses** • High cost • Aging fleet • Small size • No presence outside Europe • Small home base • Losing momentum • Middle management not fully on board • Resource constrained

Once this analysis is in place, the instructor can ask the question, "What are the strategic options for SAS?"

A number of alternative approaches tend to be proposed. Some suggest that the company may try to create a sustainable niche while remaining as a regional (European) airline. Others challenge whether SAS can do so, given the trends of globalization and deregulation: why would customers choose SAS if they are forced to change airlines and planes? Given the increasing polarization of the market between global mega-carriers and small regional feeders, was SAS too small to ever become one of the first kind and too large to become one of the second? Generally, the class tends to find this alternative unfeasible, if nothing else because of Carlzon's ambition and personality, the expectations of employees and shareholders (the three governments) and the difficulties of downsizing to the extent that might be necessary to survive economically as a regional feeder.

A second alternative is to "go global." Given the resource constraints, the only route to a truly global position is through strategic alliances or mergers. Participants note the difficulties SAS has faced in building such alliances or mergers and many remain skeptical about whether alliances can really work in the service-intensive airline business. It is clear, however, that this is the approach the company is taking through most participants tend to be skeptical about whether the strategy can succeed.

It is in the context of this debate that the instructor can return to the issue of the service chain (generally, I have found that some students invariably raise the issue, facilitating the transition). If no student has made the argument, the instructor can pose it himself or herself: is the service chain concept not an attempt on the part of SAS to change the rules of the game in the airline industry, and to create a new set of rules within which the company might have a better chance of achieving its ambition? SAS is trying to combine its underlying core competency, with the underlying functionality requirement of the business traveler to create a new set of customer expectations and, thereby, its unique source of competitive advantage, schematically:

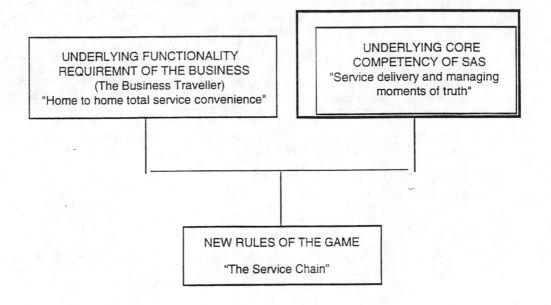

Once again, the objective of this discussion is not to obtain substantive convergence of views on the appropriateness of SAS's strategy but to help the students recognize the distinction between a strategy that attempts to enhance a company's competitive advantage within the existing structure and functions of an industry and a strategy that attempts to change that structure by creating new functionality or meeting existing functionality through completely new means.

Question 4 - How do you evaluate the role played by Carlzon since his taking over the presidency of the company in 1981? What has he done well? With the benefit of hindsight, what might he have done differently? What lessons do you draw from the case about the roles and tasks of general managers in large worldwide companies?

The first part of the discussion on evaluation of Carlzon's role and performance really serves as a basis to re-emphasize, pull together, and consolidate some of the issues raised in response to the earlier questions. Most students remain fully supportive of the actions Carlzon took between 1981 and 1985: the differentiation strategy focused on the theme of the "businessman's airline" (though I have had some female students complain that they never fly SAS because of that slogan), the investment philosophy of using expenses as a resource to support the chosen strategy, and the dramatic culture change initiative. Differences of opinion on Carlzon's performance focuses on his actions post 1984-1985. While a number of students support the service chain concept, others remain skeptical. But the criticism of Carlzon becomes particularly harsh on three scores: he failed to create an effective middle management structure, he failed to build a balanced top management team, and he made the airline too dependent on him personally.

While most students agree on the unfortunate need to by-pass the middle management in the crisis-driven change environment of 1981-1983, some believe that Carlzon missed the opportunity of rebuilding the bridge in the 1984-1988 period when the immediate financial situation had become less threatening. Similarly, while sacking the entire top management team may have served as a powerful if inhumane signal to the organization in 1981, he had the opportunity to attract the best talent to SAS in the middle of the decade and thus build up a cohesive and powerful top management team by 1988. Some trace Carlzon's failure in building such a management structure to his ego: he was the banyan tree under which other trees could not grow. This dominance of a highly self-confident individual (the tape reinforces this image of Carlzon) may have been a reason why the company failed in its efforts to build strategic alliances, they claim. Each of these assertions, often based on information and analysis not in the case, is hotly debated, however, by the "supporters" of Carlzon in the class.

The concluding part of the case discussion focuses on the general lessons that can be drawn about the roles and tasks of the general manager. While the students return to a number of issues raised earlier (e.g., the need to be both the surgeon and the nurse), I try to ensure that the following points are adequately discussed. Often, if I am teaching the case in a single session, this last part becomes more a lecture than a discussion.

a. Providing direction and purpose. In an organization built around the need for distributed initiative and entrepreneurial freedom at operating levels, there is an enormous need for a common vision for the future and a shared set of values to serve as a corporate lightning rod that can capture the otherwise diffuse energy and channel it towards powering a single company engine. A shared set of vision and values is vital for establishing a long term direction and purpose to a company, and providing them or creating a process for developing and embedding them throughout the company is one aspect of the general manager's job the case highlights.

Carlzon's ability to provide such a direction and purpose to SAS also illustrates the three characteristics that distinguish an energizing and effective strategic vision from a catchy but ineffective public relations slogan. First, his vision incorporated a strategic focus that provided a simple and clear business direction. The vision was widely publicized, both internally and externally, and all tasks and functions within the organization were examined for consistency with the chosen corporate direction.

Second, he modified the company's portfolio of assets, activities, and business so as to create a strategic infrastructure and an organizational scope that was consistent with the business vision. For example, the aircraft fleet mix was modified to replace a high fixed cost, high capacity fleet by a lower fixed cost, high frequency fleet that was necessary to meet the needs of the business travelers.

Ultimately, however, changing the fleetmix was not enough to support the new business direction. Carlzon believed that to attract the business traveler, SAS had to offer a total package that could meet the clients' needs—from the time they ordered their tickets to the time they got back home after the trip. To meet this need, Carlzon had to radically alter the organizational boundary and scope of SAS. The SAS service chain concept expanded the company's portfolio of businesses to include a hotel network, surface transportation, reservation system, credit card operations, and a revamped catering business.

But establishing a strategic vision and adjusting the corporate portfolio are not enough to embed a new direction and purpose within a company: it is also necessary to establish a new set of supportive cultural and behavioral norms. Carlzon followed through with the extensive investment in the culture change process - taking his message to every employee in the company - without which the new norms could not have been institutionalized.

b. Leveraging Corporate Performance. While aligning the company's resources, capabilities and commitments to achieve common long-term objectives is vital, top management must also achieve results in the short-term to remain viable among its competitors and credible with its stakeholders. Thus, the second key task of the general manager is to provide the controls, support and coordination necessary to leverage resources and capabilities to their highest levels of performance.

While the jury is still out on whether Carlzon will ultimately succeed in making SAS one of the survivors in the airline industry, his success in improving the company's short term performance is well-established. In evaluating his personal role in achieving the shortterm performance improvement, I try to highlight three aspects of his contributions.

First, he forced an external orientation into the internally focused SAS. By directing attention to customers ("moment of truth") and competitors ("best airline in Europe"), he directed attention to the realities of SAS's performance deficiencies and created explicit benchmarks which are essential for performance improvements.

Second, he established highly stretched targets: for example, starting from one of the industry's lowest levels of on-time performance, he set the goal to be the best in Europe within two years. Instead of incremental "realistic" targets, he set ambitious goals and extremely demanding performance standards which are a second key requirement for dramatic performance enhancement.

Finally, having set ambitious goals and demanding standards, he replaced the old model of top-down interference by one driven by local autonomy and responsibility and corporate level support. He resisted the temptation of sending headquarters storm troopers to take charge at the first sign of difficulty, trusting the local managers instead to meet the challenge he had laid down. He delegated clear responsibilities to his managers for achieving these goals, supporting them with resources and expertise. At the same time, he traveled extensively, keeping in contact with all levels of the organization and using these personal contacts to create and maintain a bottom-up momentum for accomplishing his ambitious objectives.

c. Ensuring Continuous Renewal. Despite their enormous value, either of the first two roles, if pursued to the extreme, can result in a company's demise in the long term. A fixation on an outmoded mission can be just as dangerous as a total pre-occupation with shortterm performance. Even together, they can lead to a company falling victim to the phenomenon of failure of success as successful strategies get elevated to the status of unquestionable wisdom and effective organizational processes become institutionalized as unshakable routines. As strategies and processes ossify, management loses its flexibility, and eventually the organization sees its role as protecting its past heritage—the state that SAS found itself in before Carlzon took over the presidency in 1981.

The third key role of the general manager is to prevent this from occurring and there are several important ways in which he or she can ensure that the organization continues to renew itself, rather than just re-inventing its past. Once again, Carlzon's actions in SAS illustrate how a general manager can execute this vital responsibility.

First, throughout his decade-long stewardship of SAS, Carlzon has continuously reinterpreted and expanded the company's ambitions within the scope of the broad vision he articulated at the beginning. The first wave, the second wave, and the further broadening of ambition to become a global player (by 1988 he indeed seemed to be into a process that may well be described as a third wave) represents a continuous evolution of the organization's goals and tasks, while at the same time protecting the continuity and integrity of its broader vision and mission. Carlzon builds "Change into Continuity," as described by Prof. Paul Evans (see "The Dualistic Organization" in P. Evans, Y.L. Doz, and A. Laurent (eds.) *Global Human Resource Management*, Macmillan, London, 1990) - a key requirement for continuous renewal.

Second, the process of renewal also requires a "dynamic imbalance" - an environment of constant questioning, challenging, stirring up, and changing things in a way that forces adaptation and learning. The dramatic decentralization of both authority and responsibility and the empowerment inherent in the assertion "use your head instead" is a powerful engine for creating such an imbalance. The shift from a bureaucratic vertical hierarchy to a "network of entrepreneurs" is a key tool for general managers to create and legitimize dissent and personal initiative which are the greatest defense an organization can have from ossification.

Finally, developing a strong external orientation is a third safeguard against inertia. It is a key task of general managers to constantly orient the company to its customers and benchmark it against its competitors to counteract the internal focus that is often a large company's price of success. "Moments of Truth" was a powerful slogan to push customer-orientation into the company and "being the best in Europe" institutionalized competitive benchmarking as a key management system in SAS.

I tend to conclude the class by returning to the student ratings of Carlzon. "How do you feel about your ratings, now that we have had some time to discuss the various actions?" Very few high raters feel any need to change their scores. Not infrequently, however, some of those who had given Carlzon a very low score tend to revise their opinion—to the cheer of Carlzon's "supporters" in class.

Exhibit 1

FAILURE OF SUCCESS IS WIDESPREAD

STATUS OF 43 "EXCELLENT" COMPANIES, FIVE YEARS LATER

EXCELLENT	SOLID BUT LOSS OF LEADERSHIP	WEAKENED POSITION	TROUBLED
1. ALLEN-BRADLEY (ROCKWELL)	1. BRISTOL-MYERS	1. AMDAHL	1. ATARI
2. DISNEY	2. DEC	2. BECHTEL	2. CHEESEBOROUGH POND'S
3. BOEING	3. DELTA	3. CATERPILLAR	3. AVON
4. EMERSON	4. DOW	4. DANA	4. DATA GENERAL
5. FRITO-LAY	5. DUPONG	5. HEWLETT-PACKARD	5. FLUOR
6. IBM	6. HUGHES (GM)	6. KODAK	6. KMART
7. INTEL	7. LEVI STRAUSS	7. RAYCHEM	7. NATIONAL SEMI CONDUCTOR
8. JOHNSON & JOHNSON	8. MARRIOTT	8. SCHLUMBERGER	8. REVLON
9. MARS	9. STANDARD OIL AMOCO	9. TI	9. WANG
10. MAYTAG	10. 3M	10. TUPPERWARE (DART)	
11. MACDONALD'S			
12. MERCK			
13. PROCTER & GAMBLE			
14. WAL-MART			

Exhibit 2

THE VICIOUS CYCLE

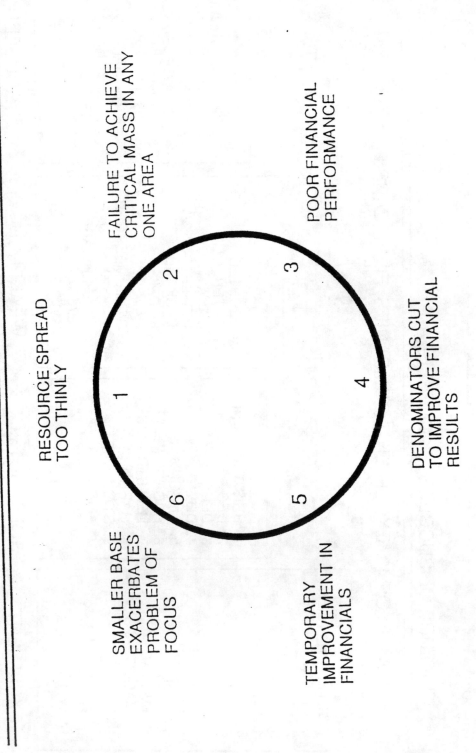

RESOURCE SPREAD
TOO THINLY

FAILURE TO ACHIEVE
CRITICAL MASS IN ANY
ONE AREA

POOR FINANCIAL
PERFORMANCE

DENOMINATORS CUT
TO IMPROVE FINANCIAL
RESULTS

TEMPORARY
IMPROVEMENT IN
FINANCIALS

SMALLER BASE
EXACERBATES
PROBLEM OF
FOCUS

Exhibit 3

AN ALTERNATIVE CONCEPT OF THE COMPANY

HOW DO YOU PUT FOUR HONDAS IN A TWO-CAR GARAGE?

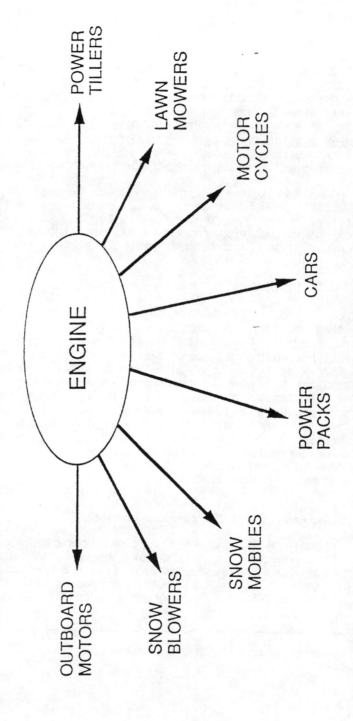

ESCAPING THE TYRANNY OF BUSINESS UNITS

Overview

The Peet, Russ, Anderson and Detroit (PRA&D) case provides an excellent discussion vehicle for many of the most pressing organizational issues in modern professional firms. Although the case deals with an "accounting" company, its issues are equally applicable to professional consulting, financial services, real estate, brokerage, and similar professional services. Its main focal points are: (1) <u>organizing a professional concern</u> which involves a need for highly trained specialists, localized strategy, international coordination for large client services, <u>ad hoc</u> cross-functional coordination on specific projects, targeted activities toward particular customer segments, and the cross-selling of services among different activity groups, (2) <u>obtaining strategic focus in a professional services organization</u> by customer class, by product, and/or by differentiating services, (3) <u>developing a management information and control system</u> which allows sensible decisions in strategic planning, overhead allocation, investment for new client development, investments in technologies, and cost allocations for billing purposes, (4) <u>the needed support structures for a management information system</u> to obtain maximum flexibility, lowest cost, a differentiable service base, barriers to entry for competition, and support for recruiting and maintenance of high-quality professional personnel.

This case ties in particularly well with the Quinn, Doorley, Paquette and Quinn and Paquette articles. It also fits well with the professional context chapter. The focal point of the case is on how one of the Big Eight (or Big Six) accounting concerns should rearrange its organization structures, incentives, and information systems for maximum competitiveness in the 1990s. The case has both national and global dimensions.

Session Structure

The case is so complex that it is desirable to <u>first</u> lay out and group the issues that any solution must deal with. <u>Second,</u> we suggest that the class set forth the several major strategic positionings that PRA&D might take. <u>Third,</u> we suggest having the class present organization structures which would support each of the major strategic options. In order for this to be effective, we strongly urge that the class be asked to work in teams to draw up a complete organization chart showing the relationship between the seven types of organizational units and partners defined in the case section entitled, "Organization and Incentive Issues." <u>Fourth,</u> we suggest defining the specific control systems and incentive systems needed to go with each "macro strategy" or "macro organization." <u>Fifth,</u> we suggest a specific discussion of how the information system can best be structured to help PRA&D develop new business opportunities and target strategic opportunities for the company. This portion of the discussion can be combined with a discussion of how strategic planning itself can be organized within a highly decentralized services company.

Issues Posed by the Changing Environment

We find it useful to first list the issues posed by the changing external environment in professional accounting, and then look at the more specific issues encountered within PRA&D. One can then cluster these as issues to be dealt with by specific strategic thrusts, particularly the new organization structure and PRA&D's information/control systems. We usually start by asking the question, "What are the major pressures from the <u>external</u> environment that PRA&D must

---

respond to?" Then we develop a separate set of issues around the question, "What specific internal challenges does PRA&D face?"

Major environmentally stimulated problems include the following:

A.   FTC actions are increasing competition and price pressures.

B.   Trends toward diversification into specialized services and consulting create pressures on quality and objectivity.

C.   Decreases in growth rate create pressures on the accounting portion of PRA&D's business.

D.   Diminishing ratios of staff to partners create problems in maintaining accounting partners' incomes.

E.   Increased competition demands higher overhead ratios for practice development, recruiting, etc.

F.   Mergers have forced PRA&D to compete increasingly against a few very large competitors, each with a broad line of services worldwide. These large firms will increasingly encounter antitrust pressures nationally and internationally. If PRA&D hopes to merge, it will have to move quickly.

G.   The scale and broad range of services of all the Big Eight firms make it increasingly difficult to niche or to differentiate a single firm's services within the industry. PRA&D has to decide what its particular strategic advantage can be in the 1990s.

H.   All Big Eight firms are moving to a global posture. PRA&D has not been strong in this respect in the past, yet this seems to be a major strategic thrust for it. (See exhibits in the case.) It needs to decide how it can obtain competitive advantage relative to its somewhat larger Big Eight rivals.

I.   Management consulting services seem to be increasing in scale and profitability. PRA&D needs to consider exactly how it should position its own consulting activities in the consulting industry and relative to its audit activities.

J.   Growing consulting's market share; although larger clients seem to be purchasing tax and consulting services "well in excess of what they spend on audits," the accounting industry does not seem to be participating as well as it could in this growth. How should PRA&D position relative to this opportunity?

K.   The accounting profession's diversification into management advisory and consulting services has created some inherent conflicts. Since other management consulting firms are being hurt by these services, they are likely to pursue antitrust remedies, if possible. They can also cast considerable doubt on the objectivity of accounting firms providing such services. This could severely damage the core business of PRA&D.

L.   The fact of a consulting practice creates major issues of relative pay for the two groups within PRA&D. It also creates a two-cultures problem. PRA&D needs to decide on policies to resolve these potential "conflicts of interest" with the "objectivity" needed for its audits. This creates particular conflicts at the top of the concern, where most partners are from the audit branch. Only professionally certified accountants can officially approve an audit. Consequently, some method of approval must be found by which the full firm certifies the audit, yet those not qualified to certify can be held responsible, although they may be bypassed in the decision.

M. The tendencies of FTC to push for further "deregulation" and competition in the public accounting industry need to be addressed. How far should PRA&D diversify, what priorities should it give in diversification? What limits should it set on such diversification? How can it avoid potentially devastating malpractice lawsuits?

Internal Challenges

While the internal challenges cannot be strictly separated from those created by the environment, some do have their roots in PRA&D's past history, structure, and practices. Focusing on these separately helps to lengthen the time horizon (future) of the discussion, to give some sense of urgency and sequencing, and to fill out the issues more completely before moving on to a discussion of solutions, which tend to be fragmented and partial, unless the full range of issues is in front of the students. We generally develop several columns of issues on the blackboard before proceeding to cluster these around "Key Strategic Issues" for solution. Some key internal issues follow:

A. The differences in style and pay of PRA&D's consultants vs. its auditors creates a host of pay and cultural issues. How can income be appropriately shared between different partners? Should opening salaries be normalized? Is there any way to set cross-divisional standards which are fair to both sets of parties?

B. How should income and investments be shared among the different divisions? The extremes range from equal sharing for all partners to highly differentiated sharing by lines of business, location, specialties, personal profit contributions, etc.

C. How should the top-level structure reflect the increasing importance of consulting? Should the number of Executive Committee members be apportioned between the two main branches of the business? If new businesses are to be grown should they be apportioned at the Executive Committee level? Since the audit group has held all power in the past, how can it be persuaded to give up some of the powers of resource allocation it has? Which particular powers should be given up? Shared? Held at all costs? If the above power relationships are to be sought, how must the election of partners be changed? How can this be implemented?

D. How can PRA&D maintain quality control? PRA&D's reputation has been built on its quality performance in the past, how can it maintain quality control now? What activities should it centralize? How can it ensure quality over service activities like auditing, tax, financial analyses for mergers, consulting activities, etc.?

E. PRA&D's emphasis on autonomous professional partners has in the past led to extreme fragmentation and underdeveloped future partners. How can PRA&D maintain its desired decentralization and autonomy, yet obtain the coordination it needs?

F. How can PRA&D set priorities? Given all of the local, regional, specialist, accounting, consulting, international, multinational, sectoral, etc. opportunities it faces, how can PRA&D organize to attack new markets? What incentive structures are needed for this?

G. There is a growing gap in size between PRA&D and its largest competitors. If this is not addressed quickly, PRA&D may be relegated to either a secondary role in a merger or to becoming a second-tier company. What are the advantages and disadvantages of a merger for PRA&D? What kind of partner should it seek? Do any potential merger partners seem more logical than others? What criteria should PRA&D use in this search?

H. The case says, "PRA&D had often placed more emphasis on current profitability than long-term investments in the many growing areas of accounting and consulting." It also seems to be underinvesting in technology, despite its very capable information consulting group. What

644

changes are needed to get partners to invest longer term? Are any control or structural changes needed to bring this about?

I. There seems to be a shortage of partners to cover all of the existing locations and activities within PRA&D. Since each added partner means a dilution in profitability for other partners (as does investment in longer-term programs), how can such activities be stimulated? (Note: PRA&D was already suffering from lower billing rates and profitability in some key growth areas, especially in specialized industries.) Clearly, its past structures were not handling this problem.

J. Can PRA&D segment its markets so that it can grow the distinctive specializations needed for each marketplace? Must it compete in all major markets in order to maintain its position in the Big Eight? If not, what priorities should be set for focus, avoidance, etc.?

K. What primary structures should PRA&D use for its organization? Should it maintain the separation of accounting and consulting as its primary structure? Within accounting should it organize around specialized practice units? Industry units? Regional-practice office activities?

L. Communication and coordination among operation units is a crucial issue. How can PRA&D obtain desired synergies between different activities? How can it improve its transfer of specialized knowledge within its accounting or management consulting groups?

M. How should PRA&D's bottom-up planning system be revised? How should it change its overhead control practices? In whatever structure it uses, how can partners outside the particular specialty participate in partner evaluation?

N. How can incentives be shifted appropriately within any proposed organization structure— especially to share information, cooperate on projects, or invest in personnel or market development for the future? How can incentives be provided to move key people from one location to another? How can local offices be stimulated to participate in audits or projects which are not solely (or primarily) within their control? How can they be encouraged to provide first-rate people for such projects?

O. How can PRA&D encourage its partners to invest in technologies which cut across all organization units? If PRA&D is to use its capabilities to the fullest, it needs to be able to call forth solutions from anywhere in the organization and to query anyone in the organization who might have specific knowledge about the problem. Further, it needs to be able to know how to assemble the best possible team for any particular project. Its information system must give it the most advanced possible information about each client, that client's history, any specialized knowledge the company has on the client's industry or situation, relevant competitive information about the client's industry (without abrogating confidentiality requirements), information on the cost of past similar services for the purposes of bidding, and information on PRA&D's own competitors in order to position a bid properly.

P. PRA&D's overhead cost control system is a major issue. With its costs shifting toward overhead costs (of technology development and maintenance, client development, personnel development, etc.) and away from client-billable costs, how can PRA&D make sure that it bills for and recovers the costs of these overheads? How can it control the actual overhead costs? How can it estimate the value-added to its client? Can it bill on a "value-added" basis as opposed to a fee-for-time-expended basis? If so, how can it maintain comparability between billings to various clients? If not, how does it avoid either legal problems or ill will?

Macro-Strategies and Organizations

The preceding array of issues is clearly quite formidable. A first step in resolving the strategy problem is to ask, "What major strategy alternatives exist for PRA&D?" Perhaps key among these are the following:

1. Merger with a firm (or firms) having complementary skills. For example, merging with a large consulting company (like Booz, Allen, Hamilton) or a major European accounting firm poses one set of opportunities and problems.

2. Specializing solely in accounting (non-consulting) activities could give PRA&D an unassailable ethical and "objectivity" position.

3. Specializing by size of client (*Fortune 500* or Multinational 500 companies) or specializing by industry group (manufacturing, financial services, health care systems, etc.) could perhaps offer PRA&D higher leveragability, greater depth from the clients' viewpoint, and less complex control problems.

4. A highly autonomous, localized, regional strategy could be developed focusing on large firms with dominantly local or regional activities where local or regional offices could assemble virtually all the resources necessary for an accounting relationship.

5. Acquiring a large number of relatively small localized accounting and consulting firms and integrating these into a large national or global network. This is a strategy successfully followed by other well-known accounting and consulting firms. PRA&D would essentially become a unifying policy source and holding company for its own existing divisions and the newly acquired smaller activities, perhaps merging them into local and regional office networks over a long period of time.

6. For each of these potential strategies, one should ask, "What distinctive competencies must the firm have to compete on this basis?" How does it organize to get economies of scale and scope? Within the structure selected, how does it target new markets? Obtain desired and essential synergies? Handle the compensation and incentive problems raised above?

Potential Organization Structures

At this point, one can begin asking the students to present the organization structures they drew up as a portion of their assignment. For this purpose, we ask students to: "Draw a formal organization chart setting forth clearly the relationships among (1) the accounting and management consulting groups, (2) specialized practice units, (3) industry specialist units, (4) regional offices (if any), (5) practice offices, (6) activity partners (responsible for tax, systems, bankruptcy, merger and acquisition, etc. services), (7) audit or practice partners (coordinating large audits or consulting projects nationally or internationally), and (8) managing partners and the Executive Committee."

We generally ask members of each student "study group" or "team" to outline the main features of their proposed organization and to explain how it copes with the major strategic issues presented. Without dwelling on the details of each organization form, this tends to bring out the complexities involved. It also assures that the students will have thought concretely (rather than vaguely) about the issues the case raises. The usual issues of centralized vs. decentralized organizations, matrix potentials, cooperative vs. formal authority relationships, and measurement and reward systems will quickly emerge. If possible during this discussion, it is desirable to have the student team presentations on an overhead viewgraph projected onto a screen, while the professor and the remaining students raise questions around specific policy issues and the professor tracks responses to these issues on the chalkboard or whiteboard. This is where it is helpful to have earlier clustered the "External Issues" and "Internal Challenges" and developed a few certain "key factor" or "key policy issue" headings. Although a variety of such headings are possible, one such clustering is suggested below:

1. Distinctive Competency—PRA&D's past distinctive competency seems to have been servicing large national or multinational clients with a full range of audit and accounting services. This is a feasible positioning for PRA&D in the future, if PRA&D concentrates its resources on this goal. This would tend to imply the buildup of offices in major cities in all three areas of the trade "triad" areas (Japan, Europe, and North America). PRA&D might therefore seek out an alliance with a similar prestigious European firm (or groups of firms in individual countries) and in Japan. Or it could concentrate on U.S. multinationals with a "major cities" strategy. This could allow PRA&D to build a series of "centers of excellence" in a few selected U.S. cities, obtaining enough specialists in each of these locations to have a critical mass. It could consciously build up its specialists in new market areas, like health care systems, services operations, high technology management, taxes, pension management, mergers and acquisitions, and bankruptcies. In these few areas, it could concentrate its management consulting services as well, to seek potential added synergies. By concentrating on these few areas, PRA&D could obtain both depth and scope within a selected sector.

2. Meeting Cost Competition—requires that PRA&D automate its audit and consulting processes as much as possible. Along with other key strategic moves, this will demand a significant long-term investment in information technologies to capture data from client systems, run all the required audit checks, develop sophisticated packages for identifying potential problem areas, and keep auditors and field staffers up to date with current IRS, SEC, FASB, and court rulings. Leveraging partners' incomes will probably require recruiting fewer people for routine audit functions, but requiring that they have higher computer and analytic skills. It will undoubtedly be necessary for PRA&D to undergo cutbacks in the audit staff as the automated systems come on line. The automated systems must provide some methodology for capturing solutions to complex problems found in one area and displaying these solutions for PRA&D use throughout the firm. While such procedures will probably cut down on the volume of audit fees—and perhaps other routine activity fees—they should increase margins. Total PRA&D margins can be increased by an enhanced focus on other special services (tax, bankruptcy, pension, international exchange rate, MIS, etc. services) and the higher technical fees that PRA&D can charge there.

3. Servicing Large National and International Clients—Along with the above organization and information shifts must come a clear primacy in allocations toward servicing these large clients. Once a client is designated as a National or International Account, appointed audit or practice partners should be understood to have line authority over the firm's relationship with that client. They should be allowed to designate which individuals they want from any local office to work on such clients' activities, provided they are willing to "pay the price" for that individual. Thus, different billing rates might be appropriate for individuals in similar technical skill and experience categories (with different team skills or located in different offices). And audit partners could approve overtime or special premium time arrangements to obtain these people. A complex computer schedule of each person's available time could be kept constantly updated at each local office, with the local practice office partner being essentially the coordinator of that schedule, just as a production planning manager would coordinate the demands of several product managers through a physical factory facility. A similar schedule could automatically be generated for all personnel at headquarters.

All of this would imply a sophisticated macro-scheduling capability at the headquarters' offices, where practice partners could do their initial scheduling across the entire system. These macro-schedules would be approved by the Executive Committee as soon as possible after the audit was contracted. With dual scheduling facilities at both local and national levels, a more equitable bargaining structure could be established, also allowing more efficient use of personnel across the entire system. A similar system could serve the management consulting practice. This requires a sophisticated firm-wide approach to information systems and the long-term support this calls for.

4. The Dual Culture Problem—The potential conflicts of background, style, pay, and culture between the accounting and management consulting groups need to be resolved—as does the potential "conflict of interest issue" of having PRA&D accountants auditing the results of solutions recommended by its consultants. At a minimum, this calls for a clear demarcation between the two functions. Most accounting firms carry this all the way up to the top level. Although the Executive Committee may contain representatives from both groups, lower hierarchies tend to be quite distinct.

Some accounting firms give special incentives for "cross-selling" between the two groups. Others prefer not to offer specific incentives, raises for "cooperation" other than as informal encouragement. Still others have separated their consulting activities completely, even allowing the consulting groups to have separate names (a la Braxton Associates within Touche Ross). The handling of this particular issue can be the subject for considerable classroom debate. The more the two groups are separated, the lower the risk of disastrous lawsuits. The closer the association, the greater the probability of synergy. Perhaps the best methodology for handling this is to have multiple informal lines of communications, seminars, presentations, etc. in which each of the two groups informs the other about its current activities, problem solutions, client lists, etc. But many other solutions are clearly possible.

5. Controlling Quality—The issue of controlling quality in a professional service operation is very complex. Clearly, the firm needs a set of audit rules that are constantly updated and enforced by Practice Partners and Practice Office Partners as well as specialists at the headquarters' level who become arbiters of policy on quality issues. Most firms have one or a few individuals who are known as "the granddaddy of tax authority," "the firm's auditing czar," "the king of bankruptcies," etc. All major final reports in these specialties are discussed with and approved by these coordinating officers before they may be released to clients. However, much of the discipline of audit and tax work can now be built into the management information system. It is very important to emphasize the potential power of MIS systems in maintaining basic quality control in services.

6. Partner Compensation—This is one of the most complex issues the case poses. The solution clearly depends upon the kind of strategic positioning and organization structure that PRA&D chooses. One of the most important issues is to separate out long-term investments in technology, personnel, and practice development. Total sums for these activities should probably be controlled at the top level. In a partnership enterprise, this becomes very complicated. It is hard to get 100 or so partners to agree on overall budgets which are likely to injure their personal incomes.

Consequently, it is probably necessary to have the partnership agree that an Executive Committee make proposals for such sums, subject to overall partnership approval. Once the firm-wide sum is agreed upon, the Executive Committee would be empowered to make allocations to various offices and activity groups. Probably, these longer-term budget items should not be considered in any given partner's profit and loss statement, if such statements are used for compensation purposes. However, if one does not include them, there is the tendency of each unit to spend its allocated monies in a less controlled fashion. The tradeoffs of responsibility controls vs. needs for strategic investment provide an interesting area for discussion.

More basic is the question of how to compensate partners in a structure which requires significant cross-selling, solution sharing, cooperation on projects, and maintenance of quality and image. Firms vary widely in their approaches to this issue. Some use elaborate formulas or negotiation practices for "sharing" the benefits of cross-selling and cooperation. Others use simple formulas like 50-50 percent sharing on all joint project margins in a given office, and do not worry about the "double accounting" that this requires. Others use negotiated sharing agreements. Still others merely adjust the participating (or uncooperative) partners' salaries for "cooperativeness" on a subjective evaluation basis, using peer review techniques. These companies then simply share partnership income "across the board" or on a relatively simple formula that allocates partnership income to different levels of the partnership (with those inside each "level" having an equal partnership share); such "levels" might include junior, full, senior, and managing partners. Others adjust partnership income "shares" in a complicated negotiation process once a year. Again. the pros and cons of these methodologies provide an interesting basis for discussion. However, more and more firms are finding that to obtain the degree of cooperation, long-term outlook. and cross-selling they want, they must move toward much more equalized partnership compensation which rewards total firm profitability rather than individual unit or personal activity profitability.

7. Potential Radical Organization Structures—This case provides an ideal opportunity to pursue some of the new radical organization structures outlined in the Quinn and Paquette article. PRA&D could be restructured in an "infinitely flat" or "spiders web" mode. There is no reason to believe that in a highly professional organization such as PRA&D, it is necessary to have traditional spans of control of 5-10 people reporting to a single authority. Audit teams can clearly be constructed on an ad hoc—or "self-directed team"—basis, as can management consulting teams. For years, Arthur D. Little operated with only two levels of organization—Vice Presidents and Associates. A similar structure could work for PRA&D's Consulting Group. In the same manner, a relatively simple three-level structure of Accountant, Specialist, or Partner could work in the Accounting Group. Within the partnership structure itself, it is possible to operate with a single level of "partner." Such structures essentially create a pool of talent which can be assembled ad hoc for particular task forces, audit teams, or consulting teams. The lack of a formal reporting structure facilitates such approaches.

If the "infinitely flat" mode is used, one needs to ask questions about compensation. Individuals obviously must be paid enough of a base wage to attract them to PRA&D. Beyond that, their base compensation can be increased each year as suggested by a carefully designed "peer and partner review program." A performance review at the end of each task, as well as a performance review emphasizing skill development, energy level, cooperation, and account development factors important to the whole partnership can be used to evaluate individuals, whether they be Partners or Associates. While incentive arrangements can be made around the profitability of individual task or team activities, many companies find that a simpler structure of personal evaluation—accompanied by annual increases and annual bonuses—contributes much more to the cooperation, skill development, and client development such companies need. It is interesting to pursue how such an evaluation plan would vary among the seven different types of Partner activities defined in the case. It is also important to discuss how needed equity can be maintained between the groups.

It might be interesting to note that Arthur Andersen operates with a very simple "equal sharing of profits" compensation system for its partnership across the entire globe. AA&Co. finds that this compensation structure makes partners more willing to perform client building, personnel development, investment, and cross-sharing activities. Other accounting firms have extremely elaborate methods for calculating "partner shares" at the end of each year. Either system will depend upon the development of a culture attuned to that particular compensation system.

One could also consider a "spiders web" configuration for PRA&D. Each office could be established as a separate entity linked only to the rest of the firm by an information system, an evaluation system, and a set of policies for quality standards and compensation. There is no essential need for an elaborate multilevel partnership structure or professional hierarchy, if the information system and the policies described previously are in place. The "spiders web" operates as a group of independent nodes each responsible for the practice in its particular defined areas, but also responsible for responding immediately and effectively to other elements in the web, upon request. This can be done only if a properly designed information system is in place.

Under either the "infinitely flat" or "spiders web" system, there are some interesting problems in trying to define methods by which the internal firm and outside parties can recognize superior performers. Obviously compensation is one route. However, many people need the psychological lift that a title change (or implied power shift) gives them from time to time. Under these two systems, retitling schemes are very difficult to apply. Still, there are many examples of institutions and firms which have operated without elaborate hierarchical title shifts. Such title structures came into effect largely through the use of the Hay Associates' Point System which classified people by job titles and set ranges for a pay scale around those job titles. These structures were brought into being largely to compensate for the rigidities introduced by production line procedures—large bureaucratic functional and specialist organizations—when these were the dominating forms of enterprises. This case provides an ideal opportunity to discuss other modes of organization and compensation.

8. A Strategic Information System - Critical to any of the major strategies, organization structures, or solutions to PRA&D's situation is a well-designed information system. Such an information system must concentrate on the minimum-sized repeatable units—"smallest replicable units"—of information the system requires. (See Quinn and Paquette, "Technology in Services: Creating Organizational Revolutions," *Sloan Management Review*, Winter 1990.) The Arthur Andersen & Co. approach provides an interesting basis for comparison.

Arthur Andersen has developed its own integrated communication network (AANET) linked by fiber optics to (virtually) all of its 243 offices in 54 countries worldwide. In the near future, it hopes to have all of the offices interconnected on this system. This means that information can be transmitted in a secure fashion among its many offices worldwide.

In its Chicago headquarters, Arthur Andersen collects all of the information released by SEC, IRS, FASB, etc. and places these on a CD ROM (Audit Reference Resource) disk monthly or bi-monthly. In addition, anyone who finds a unique solution to a problem they believe will prove applicable in another area is invited to place that solution in a Subject File and classify the problem under captions dictated by an Information Retrieval Code. These solutions (in paragraph form) are also placed on the CD ROM, as are general policy statements, procedural shifts, etc. agreed upon by the partnership. Copies of the CD ROM disks are then distributed to all of AA&Co.'s offices worldwide. Individual auditors or consultants can go into the field carrying their current CD ROM (and earlier ones if so desired) with their small portable CD ROM player. As a result, each auditor or consultant has in his/her hands an updated library with a power almost equal to the central libraries of any other accounting company.

In addition to the above, Arthur Andersen is progressing towards instituting an "electronic bulletin board" system, which allows a person anywhere in the system to query whether anyone else has encountered a special problem they are confronting—or has a solution to it. This query is broadcast throughout the entire electronic bulletin board system. Each person on the network checks his/her bulletin board daily and notifies the sender, if they have a solution or further information on the problem presented. Thus, Arthur Andersen can link together its (approximately) 250 offices worldwide, giving each office access to the full information power of the firm. This system is not posed as a "ultimate solution." However, it does provide a significant challenge to students and a benchmark for the professor to consider in discussing this critical issue.

9. Market Orientation—The above organizational, incentive, and information systems in combination offer the opportunity for PRA&D to market-orient its overall practice. By having measures at each local office which are market-oriented, it can collect information about the number of promotional calls, repeat calls, follow-ups, new clients developed, promotional activities undertaken, etc. by customer class. In addition, the information system can break down the entire firm's work to see whether adequate attention is being given to the various classes of customers most sought by the firm. This is most important for targeting and developing new clients in specialized fields like health care, pensions, financial services, high technology, etc. If compensation systems are also linked to such market-oriented activities, this will go a long way toward resolving some of the concerns Mr. Johnson has about strategic focus in the company.

However, such information will be useful only if it is linked to a strategic planning system which targets these markets carefully. Because each office's potential clients and interests may be very different, the planning system cannot be entirely "bottom up." Instead, guidelines for priority markets, activities, skill development, information system development, etc. must be developed by the Executive Committee or a similar senior management group. Each local group can then be asked to make proposals—and be measured—as to how it will fulfill these targets over the next 3-5 years. In a negotiated planning session, these can be converted into tracking points to make sure that each office does have both a plan to fulfill and a basis for evaluating future activities.

SUMMARY OF OUTCOMES

Because this is a disguised company, specific outcomes and actions cannot be set forth here. The company is still working on the problems indicated in the case. However, it did attempt a very complicated multiple matrix organization centered around Regional Practice Partners with planning and coordinative responsibilities, Practice Partners with individual company audit responsibilities, Local Office Partners with day-to-day deployment and local business responsibilities, and Specialists groups developed at 4-6 "centers of excellence" around the world. This structure and the elaborate incentive and performance measurement plans that went with it later became too burdensome. The firm is now experimenting with a much simpler structure.

In order to increase its international presence, PRA&D sought a major merger partner. However, after considerable investigation PRA&D's partnerships found the merger partner's culture was too different from its own. After long negotiations, both partners backed away. PRA&D is now seeking major European and Japanese alliances. However, it delayed the development of its information system so long because of its "autonomous partner" and "profit-oriented" incentive systems that it is having a difficult time maintaining the preeminence it once had in its marketplaces.

Overview

Nintendo of America is a superb organization and control system case dealing with the role and relationships of a foreign subsidiary inside a large multinational concern. Nintendo of America is by far the largest portion of Nintendo Inc. The North American marketplace provides the leading edge market for video games. Mr. Yamauchi, CEO of Nintendo Corporation Limited (NCL), allows his son-in-law, Mr. Arakawa, to develop the U.S. marketplace in a relatively decentralized fashion. Nevertheless, game development (the crucial element of strategy) is closely controlled in Tokyo. There are various levels of strategy in the case: the international strategy of NCL, the North American strategy of Nintendo of America (NOA), and the strategy dynamics of how Nintendo must adapt to both changing software competitors and the technologies which allow totally new game capabilities. After years of Nintendo's being the leading game producer, Sega suddenly poses a serious threat to Nintendo's 80% dominance. The market has become so large that it is clear Nintendo can no longer be as dominant as it had been in the past. The question is "How can Nintendo respond to all the competitive forces which surround it?"

However, even more interesting are the organization and control system issues. What controls does NCL need? Why? If NCL is to be the software center, what do you think of its innovation structure? Why has Arakawa used such "loose" management controls (i.e. no strategic plans or budgets)? The case provides a superb vehicle for discussion of very flat, service-oriented, and networked team organizations. Embedded in the case are potentials for very interesting discussions on "How can one attract and nurture software developers?" How one controls a highly creative enterprise from abroad? How one thinks about strategy when the total output of the company is really intellect and software?

Session Structure

One should dive right into the issue of What NOA's role should be within Nintendo as a whole. Should it remain just a marketing arm? Should it enter production? If so, of what? Software? Hardware? Both? Should it primarily adapt Japanese-created products to U.S. markets? What should its role be vs. the European divisions? From these discussions one can proceed to the more specific issues of managing software, customer service, fast response marketing (etc.) activities and the structures needed for implementation.

To develop these concepts one needs to focus first on the nature of the opportunities and threats present in the marketplace, and particularly in the U.S. marketplace. What should NCL's overall strategy be? How can it be unique in the future? How can and should it guide software development? How should it organize for this? What kinds of guidelines and limits should it set for NOA? What should the role of NOA be in the new marketplace? Should it develop software? Why? Why not? What activities should be centralized in Japan? Decentralized into various geographical areas? What geographical areas should NOA control? Should there be parallel structures and emphasis in Europe? Southeast Asia? If so, how do all these relate to NCL and NOA? To support this, what types of strategic controls should NCL maintain over NOA? What kinds of controls and motivation systems are important within NOA? What kind of organization forms should it use for its program acquisition and development activities? Distribution activities? Telephone answering and servicing activities? What kinds of organization charts are pertinent for each of these? How can these units be coordinated laterally? How can performance be measured in each area? What sorts of performance evaluation and reward systems are appropriate in each area?

Teaching note copyright © 1996 by James Brian Quinn. This note was prepared by Professor Quinn and Penny C. Paquette, Research Associate.

Overall Strategy

To set the framework for the rest of the case, one should pursue these questions. What should Nintendo Corporation's overall strategy be? How can it be unique in the future? How can and should it guide software development? What are Nintendo's unique strengths? What are its major vulnerabilities?

Strengths: Nintendo's primary strength currently is its distribution system, combined with a well recognized brand name. It has been very successful financially. It is still the leading electronic game publisher in the world, and most of the profits in the games industry have gone to "publishers," not the software writers. It is completely dominant in the Japanese games industry. In North America it has leveraged its brand and distribution capabilities remarkably well with its *Nintendo Power* publication and its elaborate "help service." Within this, it has a huge installed base of machines which will naturally call for further software. Its "Game Boy" and "Gateway" concepts for mobile games are extremely strong. It also has a few "genius" game designers and hardware creators like Yokoi and Miyamoto. With its distribution power, it should be able to enter strategic alliances to acquire specialized technology like that needed to improve graphics presentations, to obtain network or theater chain distribution, or to attract independent game software developers.

Vulnerabilities: Its vulnerabilities are its haughty style, its tendencies toward ruthlessness, and the wide variety of new competition in the field. Perhaps most important among the latter is the possibility of large distribution companies (like Wal-Mart or Toys "R" Us) providing distribution access for new game designs directly to game innovators. This is, of course, what happened in the PC field, where assembly companies like Dell could gain immediate access to the marketplace through mail order and large-scale wholesale-retail distribution chains. The "publishers" role depends upon distribution and its capacity to attract new games from independent parties. If SEGA achieves sufficient distribution and is willing to aggressively pursue independent designers through allowing them higher margins, Nintendo's sourcing could be in trouble. Further, Nintendo's great game designers are aging. One wonders whether their tastes can continue to fit the younger marketplace or indeed the world market. The possibility for game designers to achieve direct distribution through Internet (allowing interactive development, widespread customer testing, and extensive word-of-mouth promotion for their products) is an important new development. Although Nintendo has a direct broadcast capability in Japan, it has nothing to match the SEGANET being developed in coalition with U.S. broadcasters. Although Mr. Yamauchi's moralistic views on the appropriateness of certain types of game content have had very positive effects in the past, there is a question whether his views match those of the modern marketplace. Are they appropriate criteria for North America, Europe, or the emerging countries? If Yamauchi abandons these standards, how can he differentiate Nintendo's products from all others? Should he segment the marketplace as Disney has done and produce only clean, family style games? If so, will this allow Nintendo to continue its successes in the arcade and entertainment park marketplaces?

Uniqueness: After outlining these kinds of strengths and vulnerabilities, one can hammer on the question, what will make Nintendo unique in the future? What policies should it adopt to achieve this? How does it handle the technology development issue? To date, it has continued to utilize semiconductor—rather than CD-ROM—technologies. This would appear a highly defensible strategy through the end of the 1990s, when it looks like semiconductor technologies will reach the limit of their compression potentials. Should Nintendo produce games on CDs as well and make them available for PCs? Should Nintendo form alliances with extremely competent information compression groups like AT&T or semiconductor groups like Toshiba or Intel? Is it possible for Nintendo to achieve a competitive edge through hardware technology? Can it really compete against the innovativeness of Sony, Intel, Silicon Graphics, and all the other potential hardware producers in the world? Since it does not make its money on hardware, should it not just regard this as a "razors" business, make its money on the "blades" (software), and use its huge bargaining power to force down the prices of potential hardware suppliers? The equipment portion of the business will certainly be a commodity with significant overcapacity for all suppliers in the future. Clearly, Nintendo should continue its own internal software development, which has been so successful in the past. Should it expand this significantly? If so, how can it offset the risks of the very substantial development costs now necessary to create a game?

Software: One generally concludes that the key to Nintendo's future success will be its access to independent game designers. How should it change its policies relative to these parties? Should it still insist on "up front money" from them? Should it insist on exclusivity? How can it attract non-Japanese designers? Should its internal game development continue to be centralized in Japan? Won't this tend to miss the emerging game markets in other areas of the world? Should it allow its decentralized regional divisions to develop software? If it does, what kinds of strategic focus and controls will be necessary? Should it continue all "production" only in Japan? Why? Why not? If it decentralizes production, what kinds of controls will it need? Can it maintain the quality it wants? Perhaps the key to this whole area of inquiry is the conception and maintenance of quality in games. What is the source of such quality? What controls are essential in achieving it, pre-production. post-production? Post-marketing? Can quality—in the production sense—continue to be a competitive edge for anyone in the games business? If not, doesn't quality come down to the quality of intellect, software, and entertainment in the games? How does one stimulate differentiation in this dimension? Control it?

Geographical Strategy: NOA's Role

How should Nintendo approach its world markets? To be successful in a market, must it be dominant there? Can it just use the world as a marketplace for Japanese-developed games? How important are cultural factors in games (other than word translation)? Will Nintendo miss major opportunities if it doesn't tap worldwide game creation capabilities. What elements of games should it standardize? Leave for local variation? How should it control prices? Presentation? Post-sale service? Personnel policies? Image?

The above questions will help to define the desirable role of NOA within Nintendo Corporation, Ltd. (NCL). Assuming that NCL does allow some expanded role for its regional groups in terms of software design and production, what strategic controls should be maintained in Japan? How can and should NCL control decentralized operations in its geographic regions? Unquestionably, the most important strategic controls are: (1) selection of key people, (2) concept control over games released. (3) quality controls over game content and production, (4) image control, (5) commitment controls over capital expenditures and major program commitments, (6) control over distribution channels and pricing policies, (7) control over contract commitments to game developers, (8) Investment controls, (9) incentive systems. One might enter this discussion by asking, "What are the critical factors for Nintendo's future international success?" What are the major variables it absolutely must control? With these questions, one should obtain the above array of suggestions, plus or minus a few. This leads naturally to the question, what should be decentralized? Performed solely in Japan? Decentralized to the divisions, but controlled from Japan? Decentralized to the divisions and controlled there? Within this structure, what should NOA's role be as a decentralized division? Should it control all of North America? Should it control all English-speaking countries? Should it be given the primary or "lead role" in ferreting out new game concepts for North America? Should it be dominantly a marketing organization for NCL? Is it sufficient to just set up NOA as a wholly owned subsidiary with profit responsibility? What else should it provide to NCL? Ask the students to draw organization charts for the various possibilities they propose and to define specific controls for each possibility.

Software Development

In any strategy, software development will be a critical skill. Ask the students, "What do you think of Yamauchi's style in encouraging software development?" While his centrist style undoubtedly would discourage many American software designers, it seemed to work well in Japan. Perhaps the key skills in managing software for this purpose are creating incentives to attract developers, developing a sense of trust so they can work independently, and having the "intuitive sense" to choose games correctly. Clearly Yamauchi has demonstrated the latter. However, will he be able to do so in the future as he ages? If not, how does one clone this critical skill? Is the breakdown of R&D activity described on page 923 a proper organization for R&D? If not, how should it be changed? Essentially what Yamauchi has done is to create several competing software design groups for game development and a third software-hardware design group focusing on information compression and other technologies which extend the capability of games. To date, these small (30-40 person) teams have been able to out-design the world. Can Nintendo discipline the software development process through software built into its platform? Can it provide design "macros" to insure quality in decentralized designs? Is there any substitute for personal observation?

Will it be possible to operate in the past mode as the market expands in future years? If profitability depends upon one or two "true hits" each year, couldn't this system continue? At what point in the development process should management intervene? Note that the heaviest costs occur after the product moves into distribution. Is there any way to extend the kind of beta site and "game bug" evaluations that NOA uses? Most critical is the issue, "Can Nintendo continue to attract superstars like Miyamoto as independent software designers become millionaires by forming coalitions with Nintendo?" How can Nintendo deal with this dichotomy? Will the traditional Japanese method of sharing profits through bonuses be sufficient? How can NCL link its game designers better with the market information from its decentralized geographical units? Can it hope to develop products suited to the wide variety of world marketplaces it will encounter in the future, without decentralizing software design? If it does decentralize design, what critical controls must it maintain? At what point in the software development process? From what location should these controls be exercised? In Japan? In the regional divisions?

The NOA Organization

The unique organization and style of NOA should provide some lively discussion. Why did Mr. Arakawa set up NOA in this fashion? Why does he not use budgets? Will budgets be necessary in the future? Are the controls (action memos and authority charts) adequate without using formal budgeting? Is a strategic plan possible? If so, what should be the relative roles of the regional divisions vs. NCL? What is the effect of approving all expenditures above $50,000? Can this be continued? Note that the division describes the latter control as a matter of keeping management informed. It is also describes the action memos as primarily communications devices. Clearly these have been effective for Mr. Arakawa and Mr. Lincoln during the early development of NOA. They are at the heart of maintaining an extremely flat organization, with its advantages of fast response. Arakawa has tried hard to avoid bureaucracies, having seen these destroy other game competitors in the United States. Typically, the students want to put into place all of the usual financial controls of operating companies. Let them do so, then ask whether or not this is a company that can tolerate this form of rigidity. If they say it cannot, then ask them to define the precise sets of controls that are needed and how they can be implemented.

Consumer Service: One of the most interesting focal points for this discussion is the Consumer Service group. These are people who must interact with customers on a continuing basis all day long. They sit at a single telephone in a small, but comfortable booth. This is a crucial element in quality control; it provides market feedback. How can NOA control this? Obviously personnel selection is important. Beyond this, NOA keeps track of the mechanical details of timing of response, length of conversation, etc. However, it also uses a "listening in" switch whereby supervisors can—unknown to the operator—tune in to a customer-service person's conversations to see that the style, content, etc., are proper. Nintendo says it uses this information primarily to train and upgrade its people. However, it should also use the information for promotion and compensation purposes. How would you suggest this be done? One cannot emphasize too much that the detailed knowledge these service people have of the various games and of NOA's policies are extremely important factors in competition. Yet they have little or no opportunity for upward movement. How does one manage in such circumstances? This parallels the need to manage people in a customer response capability in many other industries (such as banks, airlines, insurance companies, customer service activities, etc.) where there are few vertical hierarchies for advancement. This is a classic example of an "infinitely flat" organization referenced in the Quinn, Anderson, and Finkelstein article.

Information Systems: Another critical element of management is the information system connected to Nintendo's distribution outlets. In this kind of business, rapid responses to market changes are essential. Breaking down customers into segments by age, usage, geography, and social-economic levels is critical. Nintendo—with its larger·size—should be able to break down information into greater detail than any of its competitors. With this, it should be able to target its development and promotional activities to a much greater extent than anyone else. It can use its *Nintendo Power* and Consumer Service groups to expand this data base. Staying at the forefront of information technology use is crucial. This is a wonderful place to use object-oriented software, which allows breakdown of information into different formats and the mixing and matching of this information in an infinite variety of ways.

Product Development: Another fascinating set of organizational issues surrounds product development. Note that it is virtually impossible to predict in advance whether a game will be successful or not. Although seemingly simple, games can no longer be developed by a single person. They require a team. Each member of the team is a specialist: programmers, statistical analysts, designer creators, artists, musicians, etc. This is a true ad hoc team situation. Ask the students, "What problems would you expect to run into with this type of organization? Who should manage each group? How do you connect the groups to market needs. How do you enforce time schedules? Are time schedules as important as quality of product? How do you determine quality of product? How can you control costs in development?" Note all of these are issues common to the entire entertainment world, as well as accounting or law firms, advertising agencies, fashion design, research laboratories, etc. Since market research is not useful in this type of situation, how does one judge the adequacy of a game's quality? Even ranking systems like Nintendo's do not seem to work precisely. However, they may work well as a "triage" possibility; those that achieve very low scores can be tossed out, those that achieve very high scores can go ahead, but must be carefully monitored. As in Sony Entertainment's movie business, this is essentially a low probability, high payoff statistical game where one must be willing to take high early stage (lower cost) risks, recognize successes (or failures) rapidly, and then push them to the hilt (or kill them) quickly. This is hard to do from abroad. NOA and NCL (Japan) are in a unique position to do this because of their size. As the largest marketing element in Nintendo, NOA might be able to provide early signals for the entire (non-Japanese) organization.

Changing Relationships

To date, Nintendo's great strength in Japan has offset the importance of NOA. How should NOA's role change as its size increases relative to Japan? Will Mr. Arakawa's knowledge of the U.S. marketplace turn out to be a critical advantage for Nintendo? As Europe and Southeast Asia develop, must Nintendo arrive at policies for encouraging local management, new software, and strong information sources in those areas? Given the short cycle time it has to do this, how should it best proceed? Perhaps the most difficult thing to overcome is Mr. Yamauchi's tendency to discount the new forms of competition. A key question in the case is, "When should Mr. Arakawa go to NCL?" Will he be able to take over from Mr. Yamauchi as the older gentleman ages? Yamauchi's style has been highly centrist. He may find it extremely difficult to let go. And Arakawa's long tenure in America may make a transition difficult as well.

As the case indicates, action must be taken rapidly on the new technology front. Nintendo did enter a strategic alliance with Silicon Graphics and move rapidly toward 32-bit technology. However, as it makes moves of this sort, Nintendo inevitably begins to lose the "shifting cost" competitive advantages of its installed base. Should it make its old stand-by games compatible with the new system? Offer low cost updates? Can it design a software platform that will enable it to move up into even faster (64-bit architectures) if these occur? What does it take to do this?

The Nintendo of America case provides a superb basis for a full discussion of all levels of corporate and international strategy in one of the most rapidly evolving industries in the world. Students can identify with the product. There is much data in the case to indicate that the market could be segmented by age, income, education, geography, style preferences, etc. Nintendo needs to decide "what markets it can dominate" and then focus its endeavors on these. The key question is how?

SUMMARY OF OUTCOMES

While fiscal year 1995 (ending March 31, 1995) saw Nintendo Co., Ltd., slide further in net sales and net income from its 1993 highs, gross margins improved slightly with a higher percentage of software sales. Overseas sales decreased by 24%, reflecting the stronger yen, poor economic conditions in Europe, and increased product and price competition especially in the United States.

Exclusive technology developments were introduced that included Virtual Boy with true three-dimensional, moving images and the Nintendo Ultra 64 game system which the company claims "is superior in terms of speed and performance, in texturing and shading pictures, in rendering real time characters and environments, and finally in the ability to rewrite the rules of video game play." And the impact of Advanced Computer Modeling, which created the most successful new title in home video game history (Donkey Kong Country) with sales of 7.5 million units in only five months, is adding years of life to 16-bit Super NES and Game Boy technology which some believed had lost its relevance. In a reaffirmation of its commitment to meet the never-ending demand for a better game-playing experience, Nintendo invested in Rare, Ltd., the U.K. game developer who created the Donkey Kong Country and other best selling titles.

Mr. Yamauchi states in the June 1995 letter to shareholders that "we are committed to the sole mission of delivering interactive entertainment to the home. We realize that potential markets exist for related forms of software; and for delivering them in locations outside the home. But we believe actively pursuing those businesses necessarily limits the ability of any company to fully focus itself on the needs and wishes of its primary game-playing customers."

Overview

Usually we use the Mountbatten case as the last case in the course. It summarizes many aspects of strategy formulation, strategy formation, organization. and implementation. It is an exciting case that plays on a world scale. Students and executives tend to identify with the players and the historic events depicted. The case involves a negotiation strategy in which Mountbatten is the facilitator as well as one of the key players. Mountbatten is given "plenipotentiary" powers by the prime minister of England to negotiate the release of India from the British empire. The case is a summary of the strategic events and interactions which ultimately lead to that goal. Through the movie "Gandhi," students have a vague sense of the events surrounding these decisions. But the movie did not bring out Mountbatten's role or any of the crucial interactions involved. An excellent documentary by PBS, the Public Broadcasting System, did go into these events somewhat more. However, since this was a very long series, few participants will really know the history.

Session Structure

The overall structure of the session involves first understanding some of the political and power interplays that preceded Mountbatten's departure for India. Second, one can look at the strategy itself and analyze how one can design a "win-win" strategy for Mountbatten and England in this complex environment. Next, one can look at the various steps in the management of this negotiation process. It is helpful to break the process down into three stages: (1) the actions Mountbatten undertakes soon after coming to India, (2) his actions in dealing with the four principal negotiators, (3) his management of the overall process and the understanding one can draw from his methodologies for other situations. Then, it is helpful to evaluate the process and its outcomes from the viewpoint of all the major parties. Usually, students and executives praise Mountbatten elaborately.

About 25 minutes before the class is over, one can hand out Mountbatten and India (Part II) contained in this note. We allow about 5 minutes to read this very quickly. Then we ask "What do you think of Mountbatten and his negotiation process, now?" The Part II note sets forth the horrors that occurred as India fell apart after its partition. Usually, there are some comments which mildly change the evaluation of the management process derived above. Then, as a final shocker, we hand out Mountbatten and India (Part III), also contained in this teaching note. The students are then put in an active mode and asked, "OK. What do you do now if you are Mountbatten?" Having critiqued his actions and found them brilliant, or somewhat wanting, the students are asked to take action themselves. Now, one can move on to a direct strategy involving action of major forces in a complex and unknown situation. This note will cover the handling of all three parts of the case.

PART I

This session opens by asking, "What should Mountbatten have done before he left England? Why did he do the things he did?" This brings out some very interesting political points. Chief among these are the following:

A. Why does Mountbatten accept? It is clear he is risking both his life and his reputation. However, his values and his sense of noblesse oblige require that he take on the challenge. There is no greater challenge for his career than this. If successful, it will be an even greater capstone than his World War II successes.

Teaching note copyright © 1987 by James Brian Quinn. This note prepared by Professor Quinn and Penny C. Paquette, Research Associate.

B. Why does Attley select Mountbatten? Students usually respond, "Because of his knowledge, because of his sympathy with the movements in Southeast Asia, because he is very able and could handle this difficult process, etc." All of this is true. But, Attley is also setting up a win-win situation for the Labour Party. If Mountbatten is successful, Attley wins. If Mountbatten fails, Mountbatten (not the Labour Party) fails. Attley can say, "If Mountbatten couldn't do it, no one could have." This is a common methodology used by political figures. They select a person of high rank from the opposing party to represent the country on its most complex negotiations, thus insuring the party's own security.

C. Why does Mountbatten make these particular demands? Many of them are simply symbolic. He wants to establish a relatively higher profile so that he can increase his bargaining leverage with both Attley and the Indians. The establishment of a precise date for the break is a very powerful symbol that England will, in fact, act this time. Discussions have been going on for a long time, and there is much distrust on the part of the colonial leaders. To have any hope of success, Mountbatten had to signal a clear break with the past. Several of his moves were designed with this in mind.

D. Why does he ask for plenipotentiary powers? Students will usually respond, "To have the authority he needs to negotiate." One can then ask, "Does the government give up anything in this process? Does it actually gain by this delegation?" Students tend to be perplexed at first. Then they slowly realize that the government can keep enough controls over Mountbatten to protect its own interests. Both Mountbatten and the government gain by the plenipotentiary powers. Mountbatten gains flexibility in negotiations. He gains apparent power in the negotiations. Yet, he still must refer back to London for final approval. This "double approval" process is useful in most negotiations to add leverage to the powers of the negotiating party.

E. What strategic controls does the government need? What strategic controls does it have? The most important controls it has are "goal controls." By making sure that Mountbatten understands and identifies with the goals it wishes to achieve, the government has its strongest control over the process. If Mountbatten does not share these goals sincerely, he will unconsciously undermine the government's position and perhaps destroy its very purposes in the negotiation. Whenever one has a representative negotiating at a long distance, the goal identity of that person should be carefully assured. Selection of the person to represent England is the second strategic control the government has. By selecting a person of stature, skill, understanding, and values appropriate to its goals, the government has the greatest possible insurance that its own purposes will be well served.

Approval control is another important level of strategic control. Although Mountbatten has "plenipotentiary powers," he cannot actually commit England. The government has the ultimate control by approving any treaty that he may come up with. Organizational control is another powerful strategic control. The government controls the appointments Mountbatten may make to his team. It also has the right to remove Mountbatten from his post. These two powers also insure that Mountbatten cannot make commitments that the government would not wish to honor. Open communications are an important strategic control. The government must make sure that it has a way of understanding what Mountbatten is doing in time to use its other controls. This portion of the control system is not specified in the case write-up. However, the Prime Minister would insist on periodic communications and, if wise, have independent channels of communications to check on what Mountbatten's team might be saying.

Coalition power is another form of control. By having the capacity to offer or withhold Commonwealth status, presumably a large bargaining chip, the government can control to a large extent whether a coalition takes place and the terms of that coalition.

Commitment controls are another major strategic control. Mountbatten cannot call on military resources, fiscal resources, or other implied resources of the government, without its own vote or approval. Again, these implicit constraints bound the realm in which Mountbatten can really negotiate or cause the British government to move in directions it may not desire. One should note that these tie in very well with the concepts of "grand strategy" developed early in the course.

Corporate level or grand strategies tend to involve setting major goals, setting controls on operations, establishing communications systems, motivations systems, overall organization structures, key appointments, etc.

Strategic Analysis and Strategy Formulation

Before Mountbatten leaves for India, what kinds of strategic analysis should he have undertaken? How does one determine strategy in this kind of situation? This is a good point at which to introduce some ideas about world-scale strategic analysis. In this type of situation, one first looks at the <u>major forces</u> and <u>movements</u> in the world with a view to aligning strategy in congruence with these forces and movements. If a nation (or large corporation) does not align itself with such forces, it will either surely lose, or have to use such inordinate amounts of resources to resist these forces that it will become exhausted. It is interesting to ask the students, "What were the most important forces at play in the world at that time?" Clearly, the following are among the most important: anti-colonialism, the revival of religious movements, nationalism, socialism, restructuring of the less developed world, emergence of the "Third World" as a political force, Britain's decline as a military and industrial power, the emergence of the East-West conflict, the Cold War confrontation between the United States and Russia, the emergence of China (a next-door neighbor) as a communist state, the attempt by Russia to subvert the governments of neighboring nations and convert them to Stalinist communism. Britain must recognize these great forces and position itself in a way that it can "win" in the long run. The forces are too powerful for Britain alone to resist.

Next, one analyzes the major <u>interests</u> representing some of these forces in this particular negotiation. In this case, the most powerful interests involved are: (1) those of the Congress Party, (2) those of the Maharajas, (3) those of the major religious movements (Hindu, Moslem, Sikh), (4) those of the extreme left political activists looking to destabilize India, and (5) those of the professional civil service and Army in India. Each of these interests represents a power base that Mountbatten must deal with. He must analyze the nature of that power base and how important it is to his most important goals. He must assess the possibility of coalitions and countercoalitions among these interests.

The next factor he must analyze is the <u>actors</u> who will lead these "interests." Key among them are of course Nehru, Gandhi, Patel, and Jinnah. Not only must he analyze the interests they represent, but their own peculiar relationship to these power bases. Such a multi-level analysis of forces, interests, and actors is essential in any world-scale negotiation.

Finally, Mountbatten must analyze any potential <u>constraints</u> to reaching his goals. These may be provided by the powers described above, or they may come from other forces within his own establishment. He must find a workable coalition among forces, interests, and actors both within his own power base and those of opposing parties. This requires an assessment of his own options and those of the opponents. By keeping his opponents separated in the early stages of the negotiation, he can increase the leverage of his own coalitions and help prevent coalitions from forming among his opponents.

As a portion of the strategic analysis, Mountbatten must determine what <u>goals</u> provide a feasible focal point around which the needed joint coalition can form. The key elements in this appear to be: (1) establishing a British Commonwealth of multi-racial nations with India in it, (2) maintaining the influence of Britain in world affairs, (3) avoiding bloodshed if possible, (4) moving as rapidly as possible to avoid undue risk and expenditure of resources, (5) making sure that the world feels that the Indians are responsible for whatever outcome occurs, (6) obtaining a broad-based Indian agreement which gives legitimacy to whatever outcome does occur. In such a complex situation, Mountbatten must know that the ultimate outcome is "unknowable." Consequently, he has to establish a flexible posture relative to each individual goal to ensure that Britain wins regardless of how forces may combine to produce extraordinary later outcomes.

Managing the Early Process

At this point, the professor can begin to build whatever process management model he or she prefers. However, certain aspects of Mountbatten's management of the early stages of his process seem clear. These are briefly outlined below:

A. Understanding what goals are feasible. This is one of the purposes of Mountbatten's early inquiries with his own staff and the power centers in India and Britain.

B. Understanding the system constraints. Again, Mountbatten uses multiple information points to help him understand the constraints of timing, key personalities, and powerful interests.

C. Building personal credibility. Mountbatten's early actions in India in meeting with Indian leaders, being more visible, making a speech at the coronation, etc. build his personal credibility and help him bypass the power base of others.

D. Changing the flux of the decision process. Mountbatten has to send signals that something has changed radically, and that he is the focal point of that change. This causes diffuse powers to focus on him and increases his leverage.

E. The use of symbols. Mere words will not make this point. Consequently, Mountbatten changes a number of symbols, painting the austere offices of his palace, riding through the park, inviting Indians to his table, having Indian aides de camp, etc.

F. Building his information base. Through Ismay, Abell, the provincial governors, his own intelligence services, the police, etc. Mountbatten quickly builds his information base by using multiple channels of information.

G. Building a power base. Crucial to any movement in the negotiations is the perceived power base of Mountbatten. He improves this first by obtaining "plenipotentiary" powers, and forming tacit coalitions with Nehru, Gandhi, and Patel. He extends his power base by bypassing those of the key players and obtaining identity with the Indian people. All of these elements help him gain flexibility and bargaining leverage.

H. Forming coalitions. By forming coalitions both in Britain and in India, Mountbatten helps to define the zone within which decisions can be made and to predispose various parties to these decisions.

I. Controlling the sequence of events. By controlling the sequence in which he sees the key players, reveals his intentions to the Indians and English, allows interactions among key players, and deals with critical issues, Mountbatten can control the process and possibly its outcome.

J. Splitting opponents. By keeping his opponents separated, Mountbatten avoids countercoalitions or the building of their information base to a level that is higher than his own. He tries to use whatever small differences exist to leverage his own positions.

K. Isolating key issues. Mountbatten quickly isolates those issues which are under his control and those which are not. He then concentrates on those which he can possibly control—i.e., the issues of timing, partitioning, and joining the Commonwealth.

L. Moving through zones of indifference. By finding those areas where there are common interests or his opponents are not overly concerned, Mountbatten can build a more powerful apparent coalition than may really exist. He holds off on those issues which are most likely to split his coalition, until after the coalition is heavily committed.

M. Setting few targets. Mountbatten does not lay out a complete program or try to deal with all of the issues faced by the major parties. Instead, he focuses on the few strategic goals described above. This keeps Mountbatten and his opponents from diffusing their efforts and helps to achieve a higher result in the end.

N. <u>Maintains multiple channels of information</u>. To avoid becoming isolated—and to have more information than anyone else in the negotiations—Mountbatten purposely keeps multiple channels of information open to his governors, staff, police, intelligence units, etc. Nehru himself becomes a crucial element in providing Mountbatten with information which is useful in managing the process. His "private conversations" with key players ensure that he increases his information base without necessarily sharing it with all players.

O. <u>Choosing a few crucial action points</u>. Mountbatten is a master at using bluff, threat, cajolery, etc. to achieve a series of partial movements forward. He does not waste effort on things he knows he cannot deal with or control.

P. <u>Obtaining incremental agreement</u>. Through the steps above, Mountbatten first obtains agreement "in principle" from most of the key players. He then tests the limits of these "principles" by raising specific issues as they come up. He does not try to get detailed agreement until the very last moment. In fact, he withholds the details of the plan until the famous scene in which he slaps the plan down on the table in front of the group.

Q. <u>Controlling timing</u>. Crucial to the entire process is controlling the timing at which the various key elements must be decided or when key players come together. After understanding the nature of the partial coalition he can create between Nehru, Gandhi, and Patel, he moves to try to bring Jinnah into this as far as he can. In doing this, he realizes the ultimate constraint of Jinnah's position. He uses the partial agreements already made to force detailed agreement. He does this by controlling deadlines and the possibility of public embarrassment of key players.

R. <u>Maintaining flexibility</u>. Since he cannot know either the sequence of events in detail or the outcomes which may be possible, Mountbatten maintains his own personal flexibility and the flexibility of his positions as long as possible. Even at the last moment, he is willing to rewrite a thoroughly drafted proposal in order to accommodate what he perceives as a disastrous level of opposition from Nehru. He does not dwell on defeats, but works on those elements over which he can maintain some control.

S. <u>Focusing on programs</u>. When Mountbatten cannot get full agreement on the <u>goals</u> of releasing India from the Empire, he shifts over and concentrates on the <u>program itself</u>. He can get the key players to agree on release of India, although they would violently disagree on the specific goals (i.e., a separatist Moslem state, etc.).

T. <u>Forming strategy dynamically</u>. Although the broad outlines of Mountbatten's strategy are clear at the beginning of his trip to India, the ultimate nature of the strategy cannot be worked out in advance. It must be <u>created interactively</u> as events and powerful forces interplay with each other. Note that the ultimate strategy which is adopted was not one which Mountbatten would have accepted at the beginning of the processes analyzed above.

U. <u>Being lucky</u>. One should also note all of the results achieved were not acts of intellect. Mountbatten was clearly lucky on a number of occasions when events turned in his direction. He could easily have been killed at a number of different points in the process.

Evaluating Mountbatten's Actions

At this stage it is interesting to ask whether Mountbatten "was a good manager." Generally, everyone thinks he did a superb job. One can then ask, "Why is he a good manager? What makes Mountbatten a good manager?" Typically, the answers come back in terms of Mountbatten's personal style—i.e., he is said to be:

A. Confident.
B. Charming and charismatic.
C. Persuasive.
D. Flexible, not hung up by mistakes.
E. Courageous, optimistic, dramatic.
F. Patient, a workhorse, a leader.
G. He is an organizer, he chooses people well, uses them well, relates to individuals.
H. He is decisive, accepts reality, and deals with what he can affect.
I. He understands politics and deals with the politics of the situation.
J. He gives credit to others rather than seeking it for himself (i.e., the Gandhi plan).

At this point one can raise a series of other questions. For example, one can ask, "Was there clear planning at all stages? Was everyone well served by the solution? What about the Sikhs? Did Mountbatten really understand the situation? Was his Balkanization plan realistic? Did he deal with the politics more than the real facts of the situation? Was he overwhelmed by the personal information received on his visits? Did he use his power to go directly to the people? Should he have done something about Jinnah? Eliminate him? Destroy Jinnah's credibility? Bypass his power base? Why had he not selected a date for freedom in advance? Did he do the kind of detailed planning that would have helped with the transition? Did he really involve the new leaders in such planning so that they would know what they were getting into?"

One should not overdo these criticisms. However, raising a few of them leads well into the next section.

MOUNTBATTEN AND INDIA (PART II)

At this stage, one can hand out copies of the Mountbatten and India Part II case contained in this note. This should not be handed out in advance. Otherwise, the students will second guess the entire process. It undercuts the drama of the presentation. The professor should allow about 5 minutes to read this short "case."

Usually the students are a bit stunned and confused. They may be a little defensive because of their effusive praise of Mountbatten. Consequently, the professor should ease them into the next discussion by saying, "The book, *Freedom at Midnight*, continues with 150 pages of such atrocities. What should Mountbatten have done? How could the process have helped prevent some of this? Was the process itself at fault?"

Usually the students add a few items to their earlier critique. Some better transitional planning could have taken place. Some more involvement of the leaders in detailed planning would have helped. Reorganizing the armies to help in the transition might have facilitated matters. Perhaps the process of dividing his opponents also kept Mountbatten from creating the unity they needed to make the result succeed. And so forth.

However, usually the students then conclude that there was very little—given the strong antagonisms held by the different interest groups—that Mountbatten could have done. This kind of result seems to have occurred in numerous other areas when local nationalist groups took over upon the withdrawal of colonial power. The antagonisms were so great that atrocities continue even today.

MOUNTBATTEN AND INDIA (PART III)

Leaving about 10-15 minutes for discussion, the professor should now hand out the Mountbatten and India Part III case.

This little "one-page case" poses the student with still another dilemma. What should (can) Mountbatten do now? Why does Mountbatten say, "OK, I'll do it." What are the critical factors he must deal with and how can he handle them? By promising the support of Britain and the Commonwealth when needed, Mountbatten had no choice but to accept this particular task, no matter how difficult it may seem. The more relevant question is, "Strategically what should he do? Can he really have any effect?" The following steps summarize—very briefly—what is needed and what happened. Mountbatten must:

A. Create a power base—Mountbatten first asks the three Congress Party leaders Patel, Nehru, and Gandhi to create an Emergency Council. Jinnah is not available for this purpose.

B. Avoid betrayal of leaders—Mountbatten immediately warns the leaders that their supporters "will never forgive them" if he (Mountbatten) is found to have been put back in power after Independence. Consequently, all of the parties agree that none of them will talk about what happens in this meeting until the last of them is alive. By a quirk in history, Mountbatten is that person. To keep the formalities of power in place, he recommends that the Council ask him to be its advisor. He then says, "As your advisor I suggest to the Council...." And he very strongly acts to keep the Council making the formal decisions while he merely is an advisor.

C. Build an information base—Since the situation is in great confusion, Mountbatten immediately establishes a command center into which all information can flow. This helps him and the leaders understand the situation in the best manner possible.

D. Avoid British exposure—In order to avoid subverting the carefully laid position that "the Indians must be responsible for whatever happens." Mountbatten does not want to commit any British forces. He can commit British aircraft without substantial exposure, as long as they do not engage in significant military actions. Otherwise, British troops must be used as little as possible.

E. Identify resources—Mountbatten begins to look for whatever forces are available. A few of the military units are still moderately intact. Some local police forces still have some control. Most of the bureaucracy, however, is beginning to collapse. Fortunately, some of the Maharajas have their own local fighting forces or armies. Can the new government strike a deal with the Maharajas to stabilize the situation without risking their takeover of the country?

F. Concentrate at key points—Even with the limited forces at hand, Mountbatten must concentrate these forces in a few crucial places. What are they? Students usually conclude: Delhi, Calcutta, the border area, and the trains. Mountbatten tries to concentrate his forces in these positions and uses his aircraft to provide the appearance of protection above the trains moving people north and south toward or from Pakistan. He tries to provide an armed force on the trains, where the worst atrocities have often occurred.

G. Build an organization—As quickly as possible, the Emergency Council tries to reform police forces in each of the critical areas. However, this occurs relatively randomly.

H. Use the leaders' power—Gandhi volunteers to go to Calcutta to try to calm that crucial city. He gets a leading Moslem to agree to live in the same house with him. Gandhi says that he will make his life forfeit if the Hindus kill Moslems. He asks that the Moslem leader agree to give up his great wealth if Moslems kill Hindus. The two men stand together—despite great skepticism—and slowly calm the Calcutta area. Gandhi begins one of his great fasts to attract attention to the need for people to stop their slaughter. Slowly, Calcutta calms down as people move out of Calcutta into Bangladesh and from Bangladesh into India.

Once Gandhi feels that Calcutta is secure, he moves to Delhi to try to work the same miracle. Again, he undertakes a fast, saying it will be a fast unto death unless the country stops its madness. A few days into his fast, he is assassinated in his garden after saying his prayers. The people around Gandhi immediately call Mountbatten and begin to say that "it was the Moslems who killed Gandhi."

Final Conclusions

   Mountbatten rushes to the garden where Gandhi has been assassinated. He immediately calls out, "Stop, you fools! Don't you know it was a Hindu?" At that moment Mountbatten does not know that in fact Gandhi was gunned down by an extremist Hindu sect. However, this is a gamble, which once again pays off for Mountbatten. While the police and security forces look for the assassins, Mountbatten and the Indian leaders use Gandhi's death to mesmerize the nation and tranquilize it. Throughout the country there is mourning for the funeral. Throughout the country Gandhi's death and funeral preparations are covered in detail by radio and cinema. In the meantime, the trains carrying people north across the Pakistan border and bringing them south into India and those moving people into and out of Bangladesh continue the giant exodus. The great leaders from all nations come to India to honor Gandhi. The relative calm that the funeral creates assists greatly in the massive movement of millions of people from their homes to new abodes. Despite many more horrible incidents, Gandhi's death pushes the transition steadily toward its conclusion.

   Telling this part of the story makes a dramatic ending to the case and puts the students in an action mode, rather than merely critiquing the actions of another person. We strongly urge that the professor collect all copies of Parts II and III of the case so that they do not get into the "fraternity file system." The drama of these two additions makes the case lively and relevant year after year.

MOUNTBATTEN AND INDIA

Part II

It would be unique, a cataclysm without precedent, unforeseen in magnitude, unordered in pattern, unreasoned in savagery. For six terrible weeks, like the mysterious ravages of a medieval plague, a mania for murder would sweep across the face of northern India. There would be no sanctuary from its scourge, no corner free from the contagion of its terrible virus.... Everywhere the many and the strong assaulted the weak and the few.... Communities that had lived side by side for generations fell upon one another in an orgy of hate. It was not a war; it was not a civil war; it was not a guerrilla campaign. It was a convulsion, the sudden shattering collapse of a society. One act provoked another, one horror fed another, each slaughter begot its successor, each rumor its imitator, each atrocity its counterpart, until, like the slow-motion images of a building disintegrating under the impact of an explosion, the walls of society crumbled in upon each other.

The Punjab, August-September 1947

The disaster was easily explained. [The partition] line had left five million Sikhs and Hindus in Pakistan's half of the Punjab, over five million Moslems in India's half. Prodded by the demagoguery of Jinnah and the leaders of the Moslem League, the Punjab's exploited Moslems had convinced themselves that somehow, in Pakistan, the Land of the Pure, Hindu moneylenders, shopkeepers and amindars (aggressive Sikh landlords) would disappear. Yet, there they were in the aftermath of independence, still ready to collect their rents, still occupying their shops and farms. Inevitably, a simple thought swept the Moslem masses: if Pakistan is ours, so too are shops, farms, houses and factories of the Hindus and Sikhs. Across the border, the militant Sikhs prepared to drive the Moslems from their midst so that they could gather onto their abandoned lands their brothers whom [the partition's] scalpel had left in Pakistan.

And so, in a bewildering frenzy, Hindus, Sikhs, and Moslems turned on one another. India was ever a land of extravagant dimensions, and the horror of the Punjab's killings, the abundance of human anguish and suffering that they would produce would not fail that ancient tradition. Europe's people had slaughtered one another with V-bombs, howitzers, and the calculated horrors of the gas chambers; the people of the Punjab set out to destroy themselves with bamboo staves, field-hockey sticks, ice picks, knives, clubs, swords, hammers, bricks and clawing fingers. Theirs was a spontaneous, irrational, unpredictable slaughter. Appalled at the emotions that they had inadvertently unleashed, their desperate leaders tried to call them back to reason. It was a hopeless cry. There was no reason in that brief and cruel season when India went mad. . . . The gutters of Lahore ran [literally] red with blood. The beautiful Paris of the Orient was a vista of desolation and destruction. Whole streets of Hindu homes were ablaze while Moslem police and troops stood by watching. At night, the sounds of looters ransacking those homes seemed like the crunch of termites boring into logs. At his headquarters at Braganza's Hotel, the Gurkhas' top officer had been besieged by a horde of pathetic, half-hysterical Hindu businessmen ready to offer him anything, twenty-five, thirty, fifty thousand rupees, their daughters, their wives' jewelry, if only he would let them flee in his jeep the hell Lahore had become. In nearby Amritsar, broad sections of the city, its Moslem sections, were nothing but heaps of brick and debris, twisting curls of smoke drifting above them into the sky, vultures keeping their vigil on their shattered walls, the pungent aroma of decomposing corpses permeating the ruins. [340-342]

For hundreds of thousands of Punjabis, the first instinctive reflex action in the cataclysm shaking their province was to rush toward the little brick-and-tile buildings that offered in each important town a reassuring symbol of organization and order—the railroad station. The names of the trains that, for generations, had rumbled past their concrete platforms were elements of the Indian legend and measures, as well, of one of Britain's most substantial achievements on the subcontinent. . . . Now, in late summer 1947, those trains would become for hundreds of thousands of Indians the best hope of fleeing the nightmares surrounding them. For tens of thousands of others, they would become rolling coffins. During those terrible days the appearance of a locomotive in scores of Punjabi stations provoked the same frenzied scenes. . . . In a concert of tears and shrieks, the crowd would throw itself on the doors and windows of the cars. They jammed their bodies and the few belongings they carried into each compartment until the train's flanks seemed to expand from the pressure of the humans inside. Dozens more fought for a handhold at each door, on the steps, on the couplings until a dense cluster of humans enfolded each car like a horde of flies swarming over a sugar cube. When there were no handholds left, hundreds more scrambled onto their rounded roofs, clinging precariously to their hot metal until each roof was lined by its dense covering of refugees. . . .

[For untold thousands, the refugee trains became horror chambers]. . . . After waiting for six hours for their train to leave the station of the little Pakistani town in which he had taught for twenty years, Nihal and his family finally heard the shriek of the locomotive's whistle. The only departure it heralded, however, was that of the engine. As it disappeared, a howling horde of Moslems swept down on the station brandishing clubs, homemade spears and hatchets. Screaming "Allah Akhbar" ("God is great"), they charged into the train, lashing at every Hindu in sight. Some threw the helpless passengers out of their compartment windows to the platform, where their colleagues waited like butchers to slaughter them. A few Hindus tried to run, but the green-shirted Moslems pursued them, killed them and hurled them, the dead and the dying, into a well in front of the station. The schoolteacher, his wife and six children clung to each other in terror in their compartment. The Moslems battered their way inside and began to shoot. . . . [354-355]

The Moslems, September 1947

India's machinations were not the real threat to Pakistan. The new nation, like its Indian neighbor, was about to be engulfed by the most massive migration in human history. The violence racking the Punjab was producing its inevitable result, the result sought by the desperate men behind it on both sides of the border. From one end of the Punjab to the other, taking whatever possessions they could carry, by car, bicycle, train, muleback, bullock car and on foot, terrified people were fleeing their homes, rushing in headlong flight toward any promise of safety. They would produce an exchange of populations, an outpouring of humanity on a scale and of an intensity never before recorded. By the time the movement reached flood tide in late September, five million human beings would clog the roads and fields of the Punjab. Ten and a half million people—enough to form, if they joined hands, a column of miserable humans stretching from Calcutta to New York—would be uprooted, most of them in the brief span of three months. Their unprecedented exodus would create ten times the number of refugees the creation of Israel would produce in the Middle East, three or four times the number of Displaced Persons who had fled Eastern Europe after the war.

For the Moslems of the Indian town of Karnal, north of Delhi, the word was announced by a drummer marching through their neighborhoods, thumping his drum, proclaiming in Urdu: "For the protection of the Moslem population, trains have arrived to carry them to Pakistan." Twenty thousand people left their homes within an hour, marching off to the railroad station to the beat of that drummer. A town crier informed the two thousand Moslems of the Indian town of Kasauli that they had twenty-four hours to leave. When they were assembled at dawn the following morning on a parade ground, all their belongings, except one blanket apiece and the clothes they wore, were taken from them. Then, a pathetic gaggle of people, they started to walk toward their Promised Land. . . .

No one was immune. The Moslem patients at the Lady Linlithgow Tuberculosis Sanitarium in Kasauli were ordered out of the clinic by their Hindu doctors. Some of them had only one lung; others were recovering from surgery, but they were taken to the sanitarium's gates and told to start walking to Pakistan. In Pakistan the twenty-five sadhus of the Baba Lal ashram were driven out of the buildings where they had devoted their lives to prayer, meditation, yoga and Hindu study. Wrapped in their orange robes, their saint, Swami Sundar, on the ashram's miraculous white horse at their head, they marched off chanting mantras, while behind them a mob set their ashram ablaze. . . . [350-351]

Each day at dawn as reconnaissance pilots took off to pick the columns up again, refugees emerged from under the mantle of night to crawl a few more miles toward safety. The sight spread out below their wings on those September mornings was a spectacle such as no human eyes had ever beheld. One pilot, Flight Lieutenant Patwant Singh, would always remember "whole antlike herds of human beings walking over open country spread out like cattle in the cattle drives of the Westerns I'd seen, slipping in droves past the fires of the villages burning all around them." Another remembered flying for over fifteen breathtaking moments at 200 miles per hour, without reaching the end of one column. Sometimes, slowed by some inexplicable bottleneck, it bulged into a thick cluster of humans and carts, then became a thin trickle a few miles on, only to coagulate once more into a bundle of people at the next roadblock.

By day, pale clouds of dust churned by the hoofs of thousands of buffaloes and bullocks hung above each column, stains along the horizon plotting the refugees' advance. At night, collapsing by the side of the road, the refugees built thousands of little fires to cook their scraps of food. From a distance, the light of their fires diffused by the dust settling above the columns merged into one dull red glow. . . .

It was not just a brief trip to another village those helpless Indians and Pakistanis were making. Theirs was the trek of the uprooted, a journey with no return across hundreds of miles, each mile menaced with exhaustion, starvation, cholera, attacks against which there was often no defense. Hindu, Moslem and Sikh, those refugees were the innocent and the unarmed, illiterate peasants whose only life had been the fields they worked, most of whom did not know what a viceroy was, who were indifferent to the Congress Party and the Moslem League, who had never bothered with issues like partition or boundary lines or even the freedom in whose name they had been plunged into misery. [376-377]

Delhi Riots

In Delhi, capital city of India, it began with the slaughter of a dozen Moslem porters at the railroad station. A few minutes later, a French journalist, Max Olivier-Lecamp, emerged into Connaught Circus, the commercial heart of New Delhi, to discover a Hindu mob looting its Moslem shops and butchering their owners. Above their heads, he saw a familiar figure in a white Congress cap whirling a lathi, beating the rioters, showering them with curses, trying by his actions to arouse the dozen indifferent policemen behind him. It was Jawaharlal Nehru, the prime minister.

Those attacks were the signal for commandos of Akali Sikhs in their electric-blue turbans and the R.S.S.S. with white handkerchiefs around their foreheads to unleash similar attacks all across the city. Old Delhi's Green Market with its thousands of Moslem fruit and vegetable peddlers was set ablaze. In New Delhi's Lodi Colony near the marble-domed mausoleum of the Emperor Humayun and the red-sandstone tomb of Akbar's greatest general, Sikh bands burst into the bungalows of Moslem civil servants, slaughtering anyone they found home. By noon, the bodies of their victims were scattered about the green expanses ringing the buildings from which England had imposed her Pax Britannica over the subcontinent.

The riots sweeping Delhi, however, threatened more than just another city. They threatened all India. A collapse of order in Delhi could menace the entire subcontinent. And that was exactly what had happened. The City's Moslem policemen, over half its force, had deserted.

There were only nine hundred troops on hand. The administration, already reeling under the impact of events in the Punjab, was grinding to a halt.

Early in the evening of September 4, with more than a thousand people already dead in Delhi, V.P. Menon, the man who had prepared a final draft of Mountbatten's partition plan, called a secret meeting of a handful of key Indian Civil Servants. Their conclusion was unanimous: there was no effective administration in Delhi. The capital and the country were on the verge of collapse. [368-369]

MOUNTBATTEN AND INDIA

Part III

On that historic September 4th [after independence], the caller to [Governor General] Mountbatten's cool Himalayan mountain retreat in Simla was V.P. Menon. There was no one in India for whose advice and counsel Mountbatten had more respect. "Your Excellency," Menon said, "you must return to Delhi." "But, V.P.," Mountbatten protested, "I've just come away. If my Cabinet wishes me to countersign something, just send it up here and I'll countersign it."

That was not it at all, Menon said. "The situation has gone very badly since Your Excellency left. Trouble has broken out here in Delhi. We just don't know how far it's going to go. The Prime Minister and the Deputy Prime Minister are both very worried. They think it's essential for Your Excellency to come back. They need more than your advice now," Menon said; "they need your help."

"V.P.," Mountbatten said, "I don't think that's what they want at all. They've just gotten their independence. The last thing they want is their former chief of state coming back and putting his fingers in their pie. I'm not coming. Tell them."

"Very well," replied Menon, "I will. But there's no sense in changing your mind later. If Your Excellency doesn't come down in twenty-four hours, don't bother to come at all. It will be too late. We'll have lost India."

There was a long, stunned silence at the other end of the phone. Then Mountbatten said, very calmly: "All right, V.P., you old swine, you win. I'll come down." [370]

The Return of Power

Three people were present at the meeting in Delhi: Mountbatten, Nehru, and Patel.... "You must grip [handle] it," said Mountbatten to those who had called him.

"How can we grip it?" Nehru replied. "We have no experience. We've spent the best years of our lives in your British jails. Our experience is in the art of agitation, not administration. We can barely manage to run a well-organized government in normal circumstances. We're just not up to facing an absolute collapse of law and order. . . . We're in an emergency and we need help. Will you run the country?. . . We'll pledge ourselves to do whatever you say. . . ." "Yes," seconded Patel at Nehru's side, "he's right. You've got to take it."

Mountbatten was aghast. "My God," he said, "I've just gotten through giving you the country, and here you two are asking me to take it back!" Mountbatten thought a moment. He loved a challenge and this was a formidable one. His personal esteem for Nehru, his affection for India, his sense of responsibility left him no out. "All right," he said, "I'll do it, I can pull the thing together.". . . [370-371]
